Ending the French Revolution

# Ending the French Revolution

## VIOLENCE, JUSTICE, AND REPRESSION

### FROM THE TERROR TO NAPOLEON

Howard G. Brown

University of Virginia Press · Charlottesville and London

© 2006 by the Rector and Visitors of the University of Virginia
All rights reserved
Printed in the United States of America on acid-free paper
*First published 2006*

9 8 7 6 5 4 3 2 1

Library of Congress Cataloging-in-Publication Data

Brown, Howard G.
  Ending the French Revolution : violence, justice, and repression from the terror to
Napoleon / Howard G. Brown.
      p.      cm.
  "Winner of the Walker Cowen Memorial Prize."
  Includes bibliographical references and index.
  ISBN 0-8139-2546-0 (cloth : alk. paper)
  1. France—History—First Republic, 1792–1804. 2. Violence—France—History.
3. Justice, Administration of—France—History. I. Title.
DC192.B76 2006
944.04—dc22

                                                                2005031095

# Contents

# Preface

THE FRONT DE LIBÉRATION du Québec (FLQ) carried out two hundred bombings around Montreal from 1963 to 1970. The targets ranged from street-corner mailboxes to the stock exchange; the victims numbered five dead and scores injured. Separatist terrorism reached a crescendo in October 1970, when the FLQ kidnapped James Cross, the British trade commissioner, and Pierre Laporte, Quebec's minister of labor. The FLQ threatened to kill their hostages unless the government paid a half-million dollars and released sixteen FLQ members from prison. In a shocking show of solidarity, radical politicians and union leaders staged public rallies in support of the terrorists. In response, the House of Commons invoked the War Measures Act for the first and only time in Canadian history. This suspended civil liberties and led to an overnight roundup of hundreds of Quebec separatists. Armored personnel carriers and military helicopters clattered through the streets and between the skyscrapers of Montreal. Two days later, Pierre Laporte was found strangled to death in the trunk of a car. The rallies ended, and the repression intensified.

This all happened when I was ten years old, growing up in Saskatoon, almost 3,000 kilometers away. The Canadian Broadcasting Corporation covered the October Crisis almost without interruption, and my teachers, aware of my fascination with these events, let me spend all day watching them on the school television. Although minor by almost any yardstick of political violence in world history, these events loom large in the history of Canada. The half-dozen people killed by the FLQ constitute a fair share of all Canadians killed by civil unrest in the last 150 years. Such a low incidence of political violence has made Canada a model of the rule of law, and Pierre Trudeau's recourse to the War Measures Act became the most famous political act of his fifteen years as prime minister. Of course, I did not understand the full significance of the October Crisis at the time—the privilege I was accorded by my teachers no doubt made a greater impression me than the events themselves—but the issues these events raised about political violence and the state's response to it have only risen in my consciousness ever since.

This is a historical study, but the questions that it seeks to answer have largely emerged from the post–Cold War era. Although glibly considered a golden age for democracy, the 1990s proved difficult, even harrowing, years for many nascent democracies, Russia's experience being only the most strikingly similar to that of France in the 1790s. Fighting the remnants of communism and suppressing the Chechen revolt could be both as chimerical and as dangerous to democracy in Russia as fighting royalism and ending *chouannerie* was under the late First Republic. And yet, almost everywhere, from Mexico to Algeria, from Sri Lanka to Indonesia, fragile and only partially democratic regimes have been struggling to respond to armed resistance movements or endemic lawlessness in ways that preserve government legitimacy and credibility. Finding methods to end cycles of violence, whether in Bosnia or Burundi, Afghanistan or Iraq, depends on particular local circumstances. Nonetheless, studying the French experience of coping with the aftermath of the Terror and Thermidorian Reaction offers insight into the nature of the difficulties and the likely results of certain attempted solutions, especially the recourse to military forms of repression and authoritarian rule. For two centuries, the ideas and practices elaborated in France from 1789 to 1794 have inspired countless democratic movements around the world; shifting attention to violence, justice, and repression from 1795 to 1802 offers a salutary reminder that regardless of their high ideals, transitional regimes always confront the daunting challenge of balancing individual liberty and public security. For that matter, so too do countries with established democratic traditions, as the recent experiences of the United States and Great Britain notably demonstrate. Democracy needs the rule of law, and in both cases, the devil is in the details. As historians teach, general themes become clear only after each case has been understood in its particularity. This book attempts to do that for the French First Republic.

We cannot understand the difficulty revolutionaries had in founding a civic order based on individual rights, representative democracy, and the rule of law without paying special attention to the years between the Terror and the Empire. The apparent lack of idealism or grandeur in these years has left them the subject of far less analysis than the regimes that came before or after. And yet the struggles of the Directory (1795–99) and Consulate (1799–1804) determined the Revolution's outcome. These years are largely known for two characteristics: continual warfare between the revolutionary republic and the monarchies of Europe and a series of coups d'état that shredded parliamentary democracy. As important as these aspects of the period were for shaping the authoritarian outcome, they are insufficient to explain it. We must also understand the full impact of prolonged violence and pervasive fear on the fledgling institutions of liberal democracy.

This book combines extensive archival research, including considerable material only recently catalogued, with pervasive but discrete use of conceptual and historical work from outside the period—scholarship that ranges across such fields as political theory, legal philosophy, and cultural anthropology—to offer a fuller understanding of the failure of liberal democracy in the French Revolution. It also uses a wide variety of historical methods—from the narrative to the statistical, from the institutional to the cultural—to grasp this disappointing outcome. This variety of approaches makes it possible to combine comparative regional data and local case studies with broader national trends and political trajectories. The results significantly alter our vision of the revolutionary period and call for much greater emphasis on the period after the Terror of 1793–94 than it has hitherto received. Furthermore, they illustrate the importance of these later years for understanding the struggles of liberal democracy in our own age, and especially the role of violence and fear in distorting democracy and generating illiberal politics. Despite the ringing slogans of 1789, liberal democracy was not the most important outcome of the French Revolution. Rather, after a decade of disorder, ordinary citizens made a Faustian pact with enhanced instruments of repression. By doing so, they fostered the emergence of a modern "security state," one founded on the legitimacy that came from at last providing public order. Hobbes triumphed over Rousseau.

# Acknowledgments

THE PUBLICATION OF this book affords me the great pleasure of acknowledging the extensive support that made it possible. This includes an American Philosophical Society Research Grant; a National Endowment for the Humanities Summer Stipend as well as an Annual Faculty Fellowship; faculty research grants and research leave from Binghamton University, SUNY; conference support from the Florence Gould Foundation and Emory University; and a publication subsidy associated with the Walker Cowen Prize in Eighteenth-Century Studies. Invitations to present my research, and thus benefit from the collective learning and insight of academic colleagues too numerous to name, came—in order of appearance—from Brock University; the University of Saskatchewan; Trinity College, Dublin; the Institute for Historical Research, London; Cornell University; the Old Regime Group of Washington, D.C.; the University of Maryland; York University; the Toronto Area French History Seminar; the University of York (U.K.); and Keele University.

At one time or another over the past decade, a variety of fellow travelers in history have generously provided comments on written work related to this project or suffered long conversations about it. These include Rob Alexander, Philippe Bourdin, Cyndy Bouton, Mike Broers, Jim Collins, Malcolm Crook, Suzanne Desan, Gordon Desbrisay, Alan Forrest, Clive Emsley, Steven Englund, Bernard Gainot, Jean-Pierre Jessenne, Annie Jourdan, Peter Jones, Wulf Kansteiner, Steve Kaplan, Peter Holquist, Tim Le Goff, Jim Livesey, Colin Lucas, Ted Margadant, Arno Mayer, Jane McLeod, John Merriman, Judith Miller, Jennifer Pierce, Xavier Rousseaux, Michael Sibalis, Don Sutherland, Charles Tilly, Liana Vardi, and Isser Woloch. Steven Englund, Michael Sibalis, and Don Sutherland are especially to be thanked, the first two for so generously providing accommodations in Paris at crucial times, and the last for the sheer pleasure he takes in discussing the problems of violence and justice after the Terror. Despite being at a distinct disadvantage, members of my graduate seminar "Views of the French Revolution" in 2001, 2003, and 2005 also provided helpful responses to the growing manuscript that eventually became this book.

In addition to receiving remarkable institutional and collegial support, this project could not have been conceived let alone executed without the professional expertise so willingly deployed by dozens of librarians and archivists. Among these, special mention must be made of two staff members at the Service Historique de l'Armée de Terre at Vincennes; first, M. Frankhauser, who responded to my pointed queries by first identifying and then having catalogued almost five hundred boxes of previously unused military justice records from 1795 to 1815 (now series J2), and second, Mme. Tsao-Bernard, whose personal kindness and professional assistance ensured that my many research trips to the Château de Vincennes, no matter how hurried, always produced satisfying results regardless of prevailing conditions.

Commercial and professional considerations have come to dictate that a project with the scope and duration of this one simply can not be encompassed in a single volume. Naturally, therefore, this book draws on a number of previously published articles. None of these appears as a chapter, but supporting evidence and some extended passages have appeared in the *Journal of Modern History* 8 (1997), © University of Chicago; the *Historical Journal* 8 (1999), © Cambridge University Press; *Annales historiques de la Révolution française* (2000); and *Historical Reflections/Réflexions historiques* (2003). I am grateful for permission from the editors of these journals to reproduce this material here.

At the center of this project lies a lineage. In terms of this book, at least, I am the intellectual grandson of Richard Cobb, whose last series of lectures on the French Revolution I was privileged to attend at Oxford University, but who would surely have found my work too influenced by the "Huns of social science," as well as the intellectual son of Colin Lucas, my doctoral supervisor, who, though he has never said it, would no doubt have preferred this project over my actual D.Phil. thesis. At least in this incarnation, all faults, whether factual or interpretive, rest solely with me.

Finally, the research and writing of this book has been, for better and for worse, woven into my relationship with Diane Butler. From our first trip to Paris together in 1994, through our marriage at Avignon, the bat in my writer's aerie in Ithaca, and our juxtaposed studies in Binghamton, she has shown great tolerance for the demands made on our life together by *Ending the French Revolution*. Never once has she asked for it to end, but must be relieved that it finally has. This book is dedicated to her as fellow scholar and beloved companion.

Ending the French Revolution

# Introduction

> It was necessary for us to be revolutionaries in order to establish the Revolution, but in order to preserve it, it is necessary to stop being so.
> —Deputy J. Grenier, July 1799

EACH TIME POLITICAL leaders implemented a new constitution, that is, in 1791, 1795, and 1799, they announced the end of the French Revolution. Although the mix kept changing, they repeatedly hoped that a new combination of political liberalism and representative democracy would end the cycle of violence and consolidate a new order.[1] But neither a constitution nor a pronouncement could end the French Revolution. Such a feat required a sustained effort to quell civil violence in its myriad forms, whether as popular resistance, counter-revolution, radical agitation, or common crime. This book examines these efforts and the responses they provoked. More specifically, it explores the deep contradictions and ultimate failure of the attempt to create liberal democracy in the aftermath of the Terror. It does this by focusing on chronic violence, ambivalent forms of justice, and repeated recourse to heavy-handed repression.

The descent into dictatorship that ended the French Revolution was neither simple nor inevitable. The inherent difficulty of founding a liberal democratic regime in the face of intransigent and often violent resistance had been the central problem in the early years of the Revolution. The passage from the Estates General to the Committee of Public Safety was a long march of accepting and encouraging the use of violence to overcome opposition. The reasons for this recourse to increasingly bloody coercion has been the subject of an intense debate, but one which ends with the Terror. Yet the issues remained fundamentally the same for another six years, only now the legacy of the year II made solutions even harder to find. Any use of exceptional measures or armed force to defend the republic smacked of Jacobin-style terrorism; any resistance, popular or otherwise, to the impositions of the new regime was ascribed to factionalism or counter-revolution. As a result, the political culture of the constitutional republic was congenitally deformed, an illiberal democracy unable to transcend its situational ethics.[2] Furthermore, historians' teleological insouciance about the dictatorial denouement tends to detach the period from 1795 to 1802 from the history of the French Revolution. And yet it was during these years, more than during the *fuite en avant* of 1789 to 1794, that Frenchmen confronted the full challenges of establishing both the rule of law and representative democracy on the ruins of a corporative order.

## Periodization

"The Revolution is over," asserted François Furet in his famous assault on scholars who analyzed the Revolution in terms of the revolutionaries' own ideological claims, political categories, and historical periodization. Rather than encouraging a diversification of scholarship on the French Revolution, however, Furet's polemic helped to breathe new life into old issues, namely the origins of the Revolution and the causes of the Terror. The relationship between 1789 and 1793 (and by implication between 1793 and 1917) became the revolutionary terrain on which neoliberals waged their ideological campaign.[3] This served to reify the already prevailing notion that the most important issues raised by the Revolution largely disappeared after 1794. Historians of a socialist bent had presented the overthrow of Robespierre on 9 thermidor II (27 July 1794) as the decisive defeat of egalitarian ideals and the definitive triumph of the revolutionary bourgeoisie. Many revisionists challenged socioeconomic explanations and focused instead on discourse as the *summa summarum* of revolutionary politics; yet, they too agreed that Thermidor marked the moment at which the Revolution exhausted itself. Even postrevisionist accounts make Thermidor a revolutionary terminus, a pivotal moment for the twin pathologies of French democracy: on one side lie the totalitarian tendencies of using popular sovereignty to create a unified political will; and on the other side lies an oligarchic liberalism based on notions of a limited capacity to exercise the opportunities of citizenship.[4]

Histories of the French Revolution that focus on democracy usually end in 1794, when the expansion of democratic ideology was halted and reversed, or in 1799, when the exercise of democratic practices was halted and reversed. But the French Revolution entailed a great deal more social and political upheaval than can be ascribed to democracy. The abolition of seigneurialism and redefinition of property, the realignment of church and state, the remaking of gender roles and family structures, the placing of limits on the exercise of political power, all of these extended beyond democratic impulses and belong to the rationalizing and liberal aspects of the French Revolution. It is rather misleading, therefore, to define the Revolution primarily in terms of the trajectory of democracy.

That the Revolution did not end in 1794 or even 1799 is further confirmed by the persistence of endemic violence. Most studies of violence during the French Revolution neglect the period after 1795, when Paris ceased to be convulsed by popular revolt. This ignores the dynamic of revolutionary violence after the flood had crested and the most compelling justifications had worn thin.[5] And yet, too much violence came after the Terror for it to be excised from the rest of the Revolution. Historians concerned with body counts for the Terror accept tallies for the civil war in the Vendée based on the period 1793–96 because a shorter period simply does not make sense. Furthermore, any effort to understand revolutionary violence in the Midi has to include anti-Jacobin *égorgeurs* as well as revolutionary *terroristes* and, therefore, necessarily extends to the reaction of years III to V and ought to include the insurgencies of years VII and VIII, as well as the repression of year IX. Likewise the history of the guerrilla struggle in western France known as *chouannerie* runs from 1792 to at least 1801, if not to the trial of Georges Cadoudal in 1804. Across the country generally, massive and homicidal persecution of priests certainly did not end until 1800. That same year resistance to conscription and the killing of gendarmes both reached their peak nationally. Brigandage, a confusing mélange of traditional banditry and persistent counter-revolution, was another scourge lacerating the social body throughout the First Republic. If brigandage changed significantly before 1802, it was more in official vocabulary than roadside praxis. Thus, the varieties of violence and their distinctive chronologies make it impossible to accept either the Paris-centered or democracy-based periodization of the French Revolution. Any effort to understand the violence unleashed for and against the Revolution cannot end with Robespierre but must follow France's tortuous journey from a bloody reign of virtue to an even bloodier reign of military prowess.

Rather than take turning points in democracy as the end of the French Revolution, it is more analytically useful to adopt a periodization based on the conditions that generally mark the end of revolutions. A truly post-revolutionary regime must be at least structurally secure; that is, the new regime must no longer face a serious domestic threat of being replaced. This condition is usually achieved when: (1) the form of government is accepted by the great majority of the political elite; (2) the ways in which the political elite is constituted (that is, the principal means of turning social power into political power) have become fixed and stable; and (3) the new regime is able to deploy enough coercive power to overcome whatever opposition has not been dissipated by a growing sense of the new regime's legitimacy in the eyes of the populace. By these criteria, the French Revolution ended in 1802. That year brought a remarkable confluence of critical events: silencing parliamentary opposition by purging the Tribunate and Legislative Body; creating a modus vivendi between secular state and religious populace with the Concordat and Organic Articles; achieving peace with victory through the Treaty of Amiens; rallying members of the former elite through an amnesty for émigrés; fusing old and new elites in the lists of notables; re-creating a martial caste with the Legion of Honor; and, not least, fixing the future of the state executive through the Consulate for Life. Each of these developments was a decisive step in resolving issues that had wracked France since 1789. Only then was the Revolution over.

The need to extend the periodization of the French Revolution to include 1795–1802 gains further support from trends outside of France in the past generation. In recent times, the basic tenets of liberal democracy have spread to a remarkable number of countries. Around the world, new democratic and market-oriented regimes struggle to hold free elections, uphold the rule of law, encourage economic growth, and preserve social order, all at the same time. These fledgling regimes face excruciating dilemmas about the need to manage the economy, curtail free speech, manipulate elections, violate their constitutions, and use armed repression in order to survive and attain their exalted goals. All of these issues were inherent in ending the French Revolution. Even in established democracies, efforts to assure the security of individuals and institutions threaten to compromise many of the freedoms so loudly proclaimed. Thus contemporary events challenge historians of the French Revolution to explore beyond the roots and fruits of Jacobinism. In order to understand the difficulty revolutionaries had in consolidating a civic order based on individual rights, representative democracy, constitutionalism, and the rule of law, we must pay special attention to the neglected years between the Terror and Empire. Although the failure to secure liberal democracy in France at the time has left these years the subject of far less analysis than the regimes that came before or after, it is these years that most anticipate the problems facing fledgling liberal democratic regimes today.

## Scholarly Inheritance

Despite a general lack of attention to the years after 1795, historians have not been wholly indifferent to the failure of liberal democracy in France at the time. Existing analyses fall into several broad analytical perspectives. From the Marxist viewpoint, the years between the Terror and the Empire constituted the "bourgeois republic" as an embodiment of political conservatism and social reaction.[6] This interpretation contrasts the egalitarian aspirations of 1793–94 with the socially elitist expressions of 1795. The unimplemented Jacobin constitution of 1793 had put equality ahead of liberty, promised universal manhood suffrage, and proclaimed the right to work, subsistence, and even insurrection. In contrast, the Thermidorians wanted to ensure that France would be governed by "the best," that is, "those who, owning a piece of property, are devoted to the country that contains it, to the laws that protect it, to the tranquility that maintains it."[7] Those without property, therefore, were denied full participation in politics. Historians who stress the social exclusions of the "bourgeois republic" believe that it failed due to a lack of popular support. The unequal distribution of property that resulted from the sale of "nationalized properties" further increased social antagonisms to the point that they could not be overcome by the moral and institutional means available to a nascent liberal democracy.[8] Thus, excluding the mass of peasants and artisans from a greater share of wealth and power deprived moderate republicans of the broad base of support they needed to be able to parry challenges from political rivals without resorting to armed force.

Another important cluster of historians has provided explanations that reflect the approach of Vilfredo Pareto. These historians stress that it was largely the Thermidorian elite's inability to manage postrevolutionary politics that led to Brumaire, portrayed as the substitution of political will for political skill. In these accounts, the leading figures of the Directory appear as something akin to a faction composed of second-rate revolutionaries insufficiently talented to govern the tumultuous republic but determined to cling to power even when it meant subverting the constitution.[9] Such men repeatedly rejected opportunities to broaden the regime's political base, whether among conservatives or democrats, in favor of a series of coups d'état and exceptional measures that eviscerated the regime's liberal principles. A prominent strain in this interpretation highlights the Directory's hostility toward republicans on its left, the so-called "neo-Jacobins," which is interpreted as a suicidal rejection of modern pluralist politics. In this version, narrow conceptions of political purity rendered would-be liberals incapable of consolidating a democratic republic.[10]

The Directory's failure to establish stability on the basis of consent has also been treated according to the tenets of Emile Durkheim. The revolutionaries' construction and exploitation of patriotism as an antidote to the alienation bred by the demolition of France's traditional corporative order marks the French Revolution as a founding event of modernity. The later historical evolution of patriotism into nationalism, however, highlights the weakness of purely political values as the basis for societal bonding. The political and ideological basis for overcoming internal conflict almost inevitably expanded to include affective cultural factors such as language and religion. However, the study of revolutionary festivals, for example, exposes the difficulty of using cultural practices to ameliorate the social anomie created by revolutionary upheaval. The ten annual festivals created on the eve of the Directory were designed to emphasize "only what could enhance national reconciliation and the sense of revolutionary closure."[11] Such cultural events strove to immerse individual liberty in a collective unity. The incarnation of this societal unity was the secular but sacralized *patrie.* Despite much progress in this direction, the pacific project of cultural bonding proved no match for endemic conflict. Lynn Hunt has claimed that democratic republicanism—which she astutely treats not as an ideology but as a mix of rhetorical assumptions, symbolic innovations, and collective political practices—"was the most important outcome of the Revolution." And yet it did not take root. In 1799, "republicanism crumbled from within," she writes, without further explanation.[12]

This variety of interpretations invites some clarification of post-Thermidorian republicanism. First, the political class hurt the later First Republic more by its political exclusiveness than its social exclusiveness. It is true that their identity was "bourgeois" insofar as it was predominantly urban, biased against the caste of former nobles, and determined to preserve the revolutionary property settlement from which they and their ilk had almost all benefited personally; however, their origins were too diverse to make them representatives of a coherent social class. Not until after 1802, when notability was defined on the basis of property ownership and state service, did a coherent sociopolitical elite begin to emerge. In the meantime, Thermidorians-cum-Brumairians, and their supporters around the country, became a "syndicate of revolutionary politicians"[13] whose response to events amounted to trying to form a "party of institutionalized revolution" a century before it emerged in Mexico. Thus, it was political— rather than social—exiguity that undercut the regime's ability to stabilize and consolidate the republic. Second, this intolerance of political opposition led to repeated violations of the Constitution of Year III. Neither personal incompetence nor political cynicism adequately explains this pattern. Rather, a legacy of political strife untrammeled by clear limits to political contestation made it difficult to separate differences of opinion from efforts to subvert the regime. Third, the ambiguity of political opposition arose from the gap between the goals of the political elite and the social realities of 1795. Despite its intensity, the Terror did not complete the revolutionary transformation of France—far from it—and republicans were determined to finish the work. Their profound anticlericalism, their hostility to former nobles, and their commitment to an ideology of individual rights all served to alienate the mass of rural Frenchmen. Fulfilling the Thermidorian vision of the postrevolution, therefore, required a sustained *Kulturkampf* against many of the traditional values that shaped French life. A plethora of revolutionary festivals, a panoply of sacred republican symbols, a cult of the *patrie,* and a culture of jingoism could not create sufficient loyalty to the new order to overcome prevailing support for village autonomy and traditional religion. Given the level of latent resistance in the land, efforts to ensconce the republic meant continued recourse to revolutionary expedients that contradicted the constitution.

As we saw with the problem of periodization, as insightful as previous analyses have been, their rather narrow focus on the defining features of liberal democracy overlooks the violence that persisted as long as the practices of modern politics came before the construction of a modern polity. Since many opponents' loyalty to the constitutional order was suspect, elections became referenda on the very nature of the polity rather than contests over who would lead it. In the absence of even minimal consensus over political norms, the Directors and their friends interpreted all challenges to their leadership as mortal threats to the regime. Although certain forms of political violence have been the subject of specialized studies,[14] their focus has remained firmly fixed on the perpetrators with little attempt to examine the state's response and the effect this had on public support for the regime. This study does not ignore the actions and motives of the men, women, and sometimes children who openly challenged the republic's vision of order.

Rather, it restores them to a context in which their recourse to violence as well as that of the state competed vigorously for social acceptance and hence legitimacy. It is in this light that it becomes easier to see that the Thermidorians' combination of liberalism and democracy failed mainly because the Directorial regime took office without the institutional capacity to restore order. As long as the regime could not ensure the security of persons and property, it could not generate the legitimacy it needed to place effective limits on factional struggles for power. Regardless of whether the coup d'état of 18 brumaire VIII (8 November 1799) was considered assassination or euthanasia, few Frenchmen mourned the death of the Directory. The crisis of 1799 seemed to confirm a widespread belief that the regime was too flawed to provide public order and domestic tranquility. And yet, as we shall see, the regime had long decided to put security before democracy. It was its methods of doing so, however, that prevented the Directory from earning the legitimacy it needed to survive its final summer of discontent.

## Conceptual Clarifications

Shifting the focus from democracy to disorder suggests the value of a more Hobbesian approach. Since Hobbes's time,[15] no regime had experienced the level of institutional breakdown, social chaos, and pervasive violence that confronted the French First Republic. Hobbes's answer to civil strife and the fear it engenders, of course, was the coercive power of a sovereign (whether incarnated in an individual or an assembly) that was conceptualized as indivisible, inviolable, relatively autonomous, and essential to converting a mass of individuals into a unified society.[16] In contrast to Machiavelli, Hobbes drew attention to the essential legitimacy that the sovereign earned from subjects by quelling civil strife and assuring social stability. Ending the war of all against all, or anything like it, induces "Awe" in the people, argued Hobbes, and the people in turn support the sovereign because its rules make life more commodious and predictable.[17] Thus, Thomas Hobbes's Leviathan has a certain kinship to Max Weber's definition of the state as "that agency in society which has a monopoly of legitimate force."[18] But what is legitimate force and what illegitimate violence? Who decides? On what basis do they decide? Weber never attempted to answer these questions. He did not describe the practice of repression, nor did he analyze the ways in which a state's use of force could enhance its authority and thereby increase the legitimacy of its coercive power.

Most people accept Hobbes's assertion that force is necessary to preserve the social order but reject his claim that the sovereign should have unrestricted use of force. If the methods of repression are generally deemed excessive, then it becomes a discredited use of force, or what could be called "domestic state violence." The difference between legitimate use of force and domestic state violence is easily missed. Violence and the legitimate use of force are not interchangeable concepts; they are intrinsically opposites, even if extrinsically indistinguishable. Despite appearances, the difference between force and violence is not like beauty, in the eye of the beholder, nor is it merely a matter of semantics. Hannah Arendt's statement, "Violence can be justifiable, but it never will be legitimate,"[19] captures an essential aspect of violence; it is a quasi-moral concept generally linked to assessing means in terms of ends. Therefore, to describe the use of force as violence is to question its legitimacy in terms of social harmony and public order. Nonetheless, even if described as violence, the use of force could still be justified by the norms it seeks to establish. This was the attitude of French revolutionaries, especially after the overthrow of the monarchy in 1792. They did not deny acting violently—in other words, disrupting existing social relationships through the use of force—but they justified their violence as an indispensable means to build a more just social order, one based on abstract concepts such as liberty, equality, and fraternity. By 1793, however, both those who revolted against the Jacobin-dominated National Convention (Vendéans and Federalists) and those who built the apparatus of the Terror on the basis of repressing these revolts (Jacobins and *sansculottes*) sought to justify their use of force as counterviolence necessary to secure a greater level of social justice. Such a pattern is not unique to the French Revolution and always presents a problem of subjective perspective. Differences of opinion about the justness of a particular social order compared to a potential alternative become the basis for assessing the use of coercion. It is deemed illegitimate, and therefore takes on the appearance of violence, only in the eye of the beholder. Under these conditions, describing a particular use of force as violence essentially condemns it on moral grounds. States frequently deploy force against their own people in ways that are widely judged to be unacceptable and thus immoral. Hence, there is a need to distinguish between legitimate force and domestic state violence, something neither Hobbes nor Weber did. This distinction should not be made exclusively on the morally subjective terrain of assessing whether the end justifies the means.

In other words, historical debates about the merits of the constitutional republic as a political project undertaken in the aftermath of the Terror need to be distinguished from assessing the ways in which force was used and the responses these generated. Taking a Hobbesian approach to understanding the First Republic does not mean being sympathetic to the concentration of coercion that ended the French Revolution: on the contrary, this book highlights the fear that any form of violence, including state-sponsored violence, generated in the populace. My purpose is to understand the context in which the constitutional republic deployed force, the precise nature of its various forms of coercive force, and the ways in which it sought to have them accepted as legitimate force rather than viewed as domestic state violence. Separating an assessment based on means and ends from one based on methods and responses requires conceptual clarity about the state's use of force.

Sergio Cotta, an Italian legal philosopher who wrote in response to the Red Brigade of the 1970s, developed a theory of violence that distinguishes between force and violence on the basis of their structural characteristics.[20] Both have a physical dimension and disturb existing relationships, but violence is distinguished from other forms of force by being sudden, unpredictable, discontinuous, and disproportionate. Nature offers a good example of this contrast. Although a lengthy drought may damage crops more than a hailstorm, only the storm is violent. In human affairs, Cotta argues, an act of force does not become violence as long as it displays measure along three axes: internal, external, and purposive. *Internal measure* means using force with regularity and precision in order to increase its effectiveness and decrease collateral damage. *External measure* means using force in accordance with a broadly accepted social, moral, or legal norm. *Purposive measure* means using force to defend or establish a specific form of polity. An act of force may conform to one or even two of these forms of measure and yet still be extremely violent; only the presence of all three modalities prevents an act of force from becoming violence and thereby losing legitimacy.[21] These three forms of measure are named according to their relationship to the act, not to the government that orders it or the agents who carry it out. It must be stressed that "purposive measure" is not related to an abstract end such as liberty or equality (or even racial purity or social justice) but only to the specific form of polity deemed capable of realizing such an end.[22]

Cotta's theory of violence helps us to analyze the use of coercive force by the constitutional republic (that is, once the republic was a clearly defined polity) with a greater awareness of the moralistic tint that any judgment about its ends would inevitably cast on an assessment of its means. At the same time, we must remain alert to the moral judgments and discursive strategies of those people who actually witnessed resistance and repression during the period. This will help to reveal how the constitutional republic's deployment of force could either erode or enhance its authority. Such an exercise will involve evaluating such tangible matters as the sharp increase in death penalty cases, the use of military justice to try civilians, and the army's role in replacing community policing with policing communities. Rather than merely disparaging such illiberal tendencies, it is important to investigate the extent to which contemporaries viewed them as necessary and even legitimate, especially considering that our own standard of mea-surement—the rule of law—was only in its infancy.

Concentrating attention on the methods and modalities of repression raises two interwoven issues that are fundamental to understanding the broader significance of the role of violence, justice, and repression in ending the French Revolution: the search for both stability and legitimacy through adopting the rule of law and the centrality of exceptional measures that violated the rule of law in order to defend and impose the republic. Periods of rapid sociopolitical realignment often provoke popular resistance and open revolt, which in turn almost invariably causes the state's use of force to deteriorate into a morally tainted domestic state violence. To overcome the social alienation that results from excessive repression then requires the political elite to develop new means of restricting its own use of force while still protecting the new sociopolitical order. This cycle was repeated often in French history, but the years from 1797 to 1802 were especially important because this is when so many methods of repression developed in the period from early absolutism to the Terror were redeployed, only now wrapped in the restraints of a fully modern notion of the rule of law or defined explicitly as inherently dangerous exceptions to it.[23]

By developing the rule of law not only to promote liberty and equality but as a means to prevent the state's use of force from degenerating into dis-credited forms of domestic state violence, the French revolutionaries went well beyond Hobbes's theory, which was limited to the idea of rule by law. The revolutionaries shared his opposition to customary law, his support for the unbridled power of the sovereign to make law, and his belief that the sovereign was constituted on the basis of consent. Despite sharing some of Hobbes's basic assumptions, however, the revolutionaries' emphasis on civil rights and representative democracy transformed his "rule by law" into what we understand as the "rule of law." The basic difference is between a government that operates *through* the law in the name of serving the com-mon weal—the basis of enlightened absolutism—and a government that operates *under* the law in the sense that a constitution places limits or constraints on its action, usually in the name of individual liberty. Like peace or freedom, the rule of law is essentially an absence more than a presence. It signifies "an attitude of restraint, an absence of arbitrary coercion"[24] by the government, its agents, or other powerful members of society. In addition, the rule of law upholds certain basic tenets of criminal justice. These include protection from retroactive legislation, a presumption of innocence, access to legal counsel, and the assurance of a prompt and public trial before independent and impartial magistrates.

The Thermidorians enunciated all the basic principles that define the rule of law in the autumn of 1795 when they implemented the Constitution of Year III and the *Code des délits et des peines.* Despite this founding moment, scholars have done little to investigate the actual operation of criminal justice (as opposed to revolutionary justice) during the period.[25] The study of such practices undertaken in the next few chapters reveals that, although the republic made significant progress toward effective criminal justice, as far as the actual rule of law was concerned, it remained a wolf in sheep's clothing. Subversion of the rule of law by opponents and supporters alike simply increased the government's recourse to unconstitutional methods of coercion. Even in less tumultuous parts of the country, the republic was so shallowly rooted that using force to defend it was inseparable from continuing the revolutionary transformation of French society.

As just noted, the legitimate use of force usually means preserving or restoring order. It is far harder to have the deployment of force accepted as legitimate if it is being used to transform society. The problem became all the more acute when "exceptional measures" that violated the constitution and the rule of law were invoked in the name of defending the republic and yet manifestly functioned as socially transformative violence. Theorists as different in their political perspectives as Carl Schmitt and Giorgio Agamben share a concern with the intrinsic need of liberal democracies to use exceptional measures to preserve themselves.[26] Both thinkers highlight the profound tensions between legal norms and sovereign authority that result from recourse to exceptional measures. Schmitt preferred to see these tensions resolved in favor of sovereignty exercised by a state executive; Agamben wants them resolved by refusing to accept the state of exception as either legal or necessary but as the antithesis of politics. The relevance of Schmitt's assessment of the juridical relationship between democracy and dictatorship can best be appreciated only after the historical details of 1795–1802 have been covered; that analysis has therefore been left for the epilogue to this book. In contrast, Agamben's response illuminates from the outset the significance of turning to exceptional measures to end the French Revolution.

Agamben has traced the power of temporary, legally defined exceptionalism over the past two centuries in more philosophical terms than Schmitt, but his conclusions are equally political. Recent infringements of civil liberties, infractions against international law, and violations of widely accepted definitions of human rights, all in the name of a "war on terror," have led Agamben to state, with a certain polemical intent, that the state of exception has today reached its fullest deployment around the world. As a result, he argues, it is pointless to try to restore the primacy of norms and rights by bringing the state of exception back within its spatially and temporally defined boundaries. Instead, we must recognize that the state of exception has become the norm and can be reversed only by restoring the vitality of popular politics. Agamben's theoretical position, if reversed historically, reveals the significance of the role of exceptionalism in ending the French Revolution. As we shall see, from 1797 to 1801, the political elite reacted to the alienation and loss of legitimacy created by exceptional measures that violated the rule of law not by abandoning them but by more closely regulating them. Furthermore, the normalization of various forms of exceptionalism as part of the Napoleonic apparatus of rule, all in the name of security and all with broad public support, helped to replace the messy political contestation inherent in representative democracy with a security state designed to generate consensus and willing to use coercion to do it. The "state of exception," despite being packaged as a necessary addendum to the rule *of* law, became the basis for a massive extension of a Hobbesian rule *by* law. Thus, examining the fate of France in the early nineteenth century, on one hand, and confronting Agamben's concern that the "state of exception" has itself become the norm in the early twenty-first century, on the other, are mutually illuminating exercises. How does liberal democracy survive the state of exception invoked to save it?

## Overview

The Constitution of 1795 created the Directorial regime whose primary purpose was to consolidate revolutionary achievements within the framework of a liberal democratic republic. But six years of revolutionary calamity had rent the very fabric of the polity and left the new regime with little power to stitch it together again. Extremist factions on the Jacobin left and the royalist right fought one another in towns and villages throughout France. Economic chaos, foreign war, Catholic hostility, and widespread banditry exacerbated the pervasive political strife. At first the Directory tried to end the revolutionary cycle of violence by applying an amnesty for all revolutionary crimes and implementing impartial justice and strict obedience to the law. This high-minded attempt to instill the rule of law failed. Not only did the amnesty have a partisan bias, it also deprived the new regime of the moral authority it would have acquired through punishing some of the most heinous crimes of the Terror. Furthermore, efforts to apply the rule of law depended heavily on a new system of criminal justice given great independence from the government. Elected judges with considerable legal expertise but a history of partisan politics, together with a remarkably liberal set of protections for the accused, greatly limited the Directory's ability to stabilize the republic through the judiciary.

Under these conditions, measures designed to promote liberty thwarted efforts to provide security. The collective violence of the early Revolution degenerated into increasingly solipsistic violence. Every day the government received a litany of reports containing lurid details of intercepted couriers, stagecoach holdups, assaults on government officials, and the intimidation of witnesses, too many of which went unpunished due to lamentable policing, ramshackle prisons, and a fledgling judiciary. Despite meting out far more repression than historians have realized, the new jury-based justice system defended village mores at the expense of the republican concept of order. By the summer of 1797, it was clear to the government that the justice system had yet to master the epidemic of banditry and political crime. When so many communities refused to cooperate with a regime based on the rule of law, the regime sought alternatives by ignoring the constitution and resorting to force, even though this seriously eroded its political legitimacy.

Exasperated by the threat posed to the regime's survival by popular disaffection and resurgent royalism, the Directory abandoned a strict adherence to the rule of law in favor of increasingly authoritarian means of restoring order. This major shift began with the coup d'état of 18 fructidor V (4 September 1797), which annulled many of the recent elections and purged crypto-royalists throughout the country. Although it hesitated to abandon constitutional legalism altogether, the so-called Second Directory believed it had to increase its use of military means to end the epidemic of violent crime. Because the local ties and general ineptitude of the other "forces of order"—the National Guard and the gendarmerie—often made them politically suspect, the government used the army to protect law and order and to shore up the new regime. Local officials requisitioned soldiers to execute the mandates of government, disperse illegal gatherings, seize malefactors, make routine patrols, seek out deserters and draft dodgers, and fight brigandage, a dangerous amalgam of banditry and resistance to the republican regime. This wide range of tasks frequently brought army officers into conflict with civilian authorities, themselves torn between defending the local community against state intrusion and regulating internal instability. Three areas of civilian-military relations generated special tension: requisitioning national guardsmen to form "mobile columns" supported by regular troops for the pursuit of brigands; putting towns under a state of siege (a form of martial law); and using military courts to judge highway robbers and extortionists as well as rebels captured with arms in hand. Each of these instruments of repression shifted power from elected civilian and judicial authorities to appointed military commanders, thereby eroding the republican ideal of a political culture based on active citizenship and representative democracy. The Directory had come to believe that military force would have to be used to restore order before the judiciary could be trusted to maintain it. But the use of force had partisan purposes as well.

The Fructidor coup highlighted the inherent weaknesses of liberal rule. Rampant disorder in the summer of 1797 allowed the narrative of republican self-defense (first developed to explain and justify the Terror) to rise to the level of a paradigmatic myth. In doing so, it provided both a tendentious explanation for the sources of instability and radical solutions to it. A sharp increase in executive power in the wake of the Fructidor coup made it possible to contain counter-revolution, republicanize the judiciary, and professionalize the gendarmerie. All the same, the Directorial regime's revolutionary proclivities made it unable to prevent exceptional measures needed to defend the young republic from becoming domestic state violence used to persecute former elites and transform society. The resulting exploitation of ostensibly defensive measures for offensive purposes punched great holes in the regime's already dented credibility. The Second Directory's repeated recourse to authoritarian methods left the would-be liberal and democratic republic in ruins. The Brumaire coup d'état did not resolve these issues and is a highly misleading shorthand for the tortuous transition from democracy to dictatorship.

Efforts to establish a liberal democracy failed, and the French Revolution came to an end only after prolonged violence, perpetrated both by and against republicans, provoked widespread support for novel forms of controlled repression. The escalating judicial and military repression that resulted was far greater than previously known and provides the central continuity between the Directory and Consulate. Furthermore, the crackdown that occurred from 1797 to 1801 was a pivotal moment in the history of repression in France, not as bloody as the Terror but more fruitful in generating the pattern of "liberal authoritarianism" that confronted every uprising of the nineteenth century. The Faustian pact that ordinary citizens made with the so-called forces of order enabled the creation of a modern "security state" based on administrative surveillance, coercive policing, and the legitimacy that came with restoring and maintaining order. The emergence of this security state ended the French Revolution. Only the apparatus of the security state made it possible to allow émigrés to return, priests to take up their ministries, and citizens to respect the authority of the republic. It also provided Napoleon Bonaparte with the basis for his personal dictatorship, which may have been predictable but was certainly not inevitable.

## Representative Regions

The level of violence and instability in the late republic depended greatly on the interaction between local, regional, and national experiences. Therefore, efforts to understand how the late republic sought to reduce civil strife and the consequences this had for liberal democracy in France require a national study that pays careful attention to local circumstances. In an effort to achieve this balance, four regions have been chosen for special emphasis. The choice of regions was determined by their range of experiences during the Revolution and the availability of comparable sources, especially court records. Given the importance of military aspects of repression in the period, these regions were defined on the basis of military jurisdictions. During the years 1795–1802, France was divided into twenty-six military districts, each of which covered an average of four departments. These military districts reflected the influence of both physical and political geography. In a few cases, they came close to replicating provinces of the *ancien régime*. This study concentrates on four of these military districts. Furthermore, in order to understand the importance of truly local factors, one department in each district (see figure 1) has been the subject of even closer

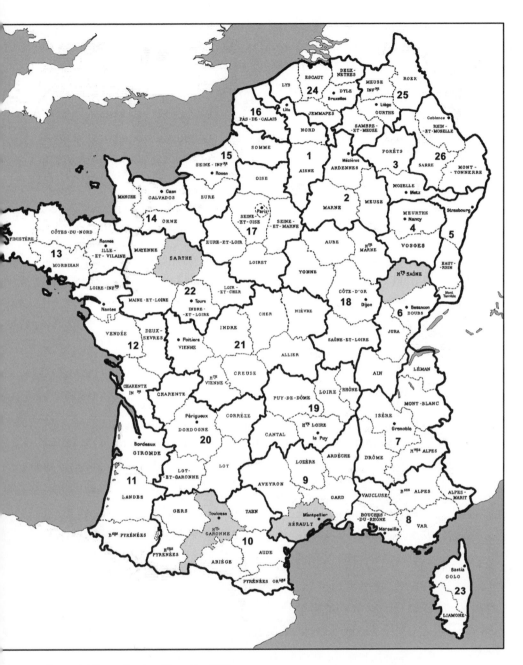

Fig. 1. Military districts (fructidor VII) 1799.

scrutiny. The four districts on which this study is mainly based were selected to represent a wide variety of social, economic, cultural, and political differences across France. The Tenth Military District included areas of remote mountain villages (the central Pyrenees), a large Jacobin-dominated city (Toulouse), and a localized peasant rebellion (that of 1799 in the Garonne valley). The Sixth Military District contained the former Franche-Comté, a region where serfdom helped to provoke widespread antiseigneurial rioting in 1789. This area also generated a large number of refractory priests (about two-thirds refused to take the oath to the Civil Constitutional of the Clergy) and had a porous frontier close to émigré centers in Switzerland. In western France, the Twenty-second Military District took in regions hit hard by civil war and *chouannerie,* as well as quiescent parts of the Paris basin where open-field farming and vagabondage thrived side by side. Finally, high political mobilization, both for and against the Revolution, intense sectarian violence, and endemic banditry characterized the Ninth Military District, which engulfed large parts of the southern Massif Central and Mediterranean coast. None of these districts lay in anomalous parts of France at the time, such as the recently annexed territories of Belgium, Luxembourg, the Rhineland, and the county of Nice, or in the former provinces of Brittany and Provence, all of which faced distinctive problems of integration or were dominated by the most extreme forms of political violence. Furthermore, none of the four districts emphasized in this study lay in the most thoroughly integrated regions of the country, such as the Ile de France, dominated as it was by the capital, or Champagne, a region of good communications, high literacy, and easy conscription. Picking regions characterized by extreme disorder would be unrepresentative; choosing areas of substantial tranquility would be uninformative.

Whereas the study does not focus on provinces dominated by extremes of either civil strife or general quiescence, these four districts did include both these features. Extreme disorder is well represented by both the western side of the Rhône valley and the eastern part of the *Vendée militaire.* High levels of stability and tranquility are represented by encompassing some of the Paris basin (Beauce and Orléanais) as well as a significant portion of the eastern uplands (Vosges Mountains). The four departments to be studied most closely—the Sarthe, Haute-Garonne, Hérault, and Haute-Saône—were chosen because they best typified their respective military districts and in themselves constitute a broad spectrum of revolutionary experience. They also reflect a variety of political trajectories during the

First Republic. These varied from remaining solidly republican through-out the period (Haute-Garonne) to swinging wildly from one extreme to another (Hérault). Moving down to the departmental level also made it possible to carry out one of the most important aspects of this study, a comparative assessment of the work of regular criminal courts.

# PART I
## The Directory and the Problem of Order

ENDING THE FRENCH REVOLUTION by consolidating the republic on the basis of representative democracy and the rule of law would have been a remarkable and heroic achievement. The conditions were certainly not propitious. When the Directory took office in late 1795, it was faced with overcoming the legacy of not one, but two illiberal regimes. It had to consolidate the defeat of monarchical absolutism as well as to overcome the civil strife and political animosities bred by the Jacobin dictatorship. The full magnitude of this dual challenge emerged during the fifteen months between the overthrow of Robespierre on 9 thermidor II (27 July 1794) and the amnesty of 4 brumaire IV (26 October 1795). These months saw the Convention struggle to exit the Terror before it could even imagine an end to the French Revolution. In the process, deputies came to realize that the future of the republic depended on replacing the moral quagmire of revolutionary expediency with the rule of law. Even then, it took the Germinal and Prairial riots in the spring of 1795 before they finally began to discuss a new constitution.

The Constitution of Year III was simultaneously both a strategy to rally the nation behind a new regime—and thereby consolidate revolutionary achievements—and a goal in its own right: the embodiment of key principles of the early Revolution in a modern republic. The Thermidorians based their efforts to rehabilitate the republic on the political premise of 1789: representative democracy would shape the law; the law would control the exercise of coercive force; and political liberty would be assured. But with their eyes on liberty, the Thermidorians neglected security. Their hope that the rule of law would end domestic strife and build legitimacy for the republic foundered on both the unprecedented social and economic chaos of the mid-1790s and the republic's persistently revolutionary character. Much had yet to be done, especially in carrying republicanism to the countryside, where the vast majority of Frenchmen lived. The Thermidorians deplored the demagogic and populist excesses of 1792–94, but this was not enough to endear them to the stolid men of property who dominated French society. As a result, efforts to adopt more scrupulous means severely limited the Directory's ability to put a swift end to endemic violence and widespread resistance.

The chapters in part 1 focus on the Directory's central dilemma of whether to adhere to constitutionalism and the rule of law despite stubborn resistance and widespread disorder or to use political exclusion and armed force to impose a republican concept of order. These chapters explore key issues in this dilemma ranging from the Convention's political amnesty of the eleventh hour to the effects of jury nullification in blunting political repression. What emerges is a stew of contradictions and incompatibilities. The Directory implemented an astonishingly liberal set of procedures to protect the rights of the accused at the very moment that the republic faced a novel economy of violence in which the restraining rituals of collective violence had largely collapsed and rampant lawlessness was made even more lurid by multiplying fears of political and criminal conspiracy. Likewise, the fledgling system of criminal justice proved its ability to mete out massive amounts of repression while also proving unable to overcome traditional village mores that condoned interpersonal violence and resistance to authority. A careful assessment of the Directory's problem of order in its early years helps to clarify the crisis of 1797 and the decision to alter dramatically the mix between liberal constitutionalism and revolutionary exceptionalism.

# 1 The Crisis of Republican Legitimacy

During times of parties and revolutions, it is difficult for words such as order, security, and public tranquility to have as clear a meaning as during times of calm and political reason. Each faction thinks that public order is disturbed, that the security of the State is compromised, if their party does not triumph.

—Minister of Police Lenoir-Laroche, *Le Moniteur universel,* 18 germinal IV (7 April 1796)

THE SITUATION CONFRONTING the Directory has since become familiar to all fledgling democracies facing a legacy of social upheaval and widespread violence. As a regime based on a liberal democratic constitution, the Directory's legitimacy depended heavily on its willingness to respect constitutional limits and uphold due process. This meant that the regime's policies would be judged on procedural characteristics as well as on results. Nevertheless, the Thermidorians repeatedly fudged or even openly ignored procedural norms for the sake of political expediency. The tension between constitutionalism and expediency became particularly acute after all the revolutionary rhetoric about the oppression of the *ancien régime* and after the republic itself had been badly discredited by the arbitrary excesses of year II. This dual legacy required republicans to make a shift from emphasizing ends to emphasizing means. In a pamphlet about ending the Revolution published in the summer of 1795, Representative Audouin admonished his colleagues that in the future they were to be "energetic, but less in the revolutionary sense than in the constitutional sense."[1] In fact, over the next four years, constitutionalism replaced popular sovereignty as the concept most frequently invoked in political debate. As the interminable wrangling of the period makes clear, the focus on liberal ideals during the Directory far exceeded the importance of similar rhetoric in the Legislative Assembly when forms of democratic representation dominated political debate. After 1795, no matter where men stood on the political spectrum, from avowed royalists to unrepentant terrorists, they found themselves turning to the discourse of constitutionality to voice their criticism or defend their actions, even if only to gain partisan advantage. The near hegemony of constitutional discourse meant that flagrantly unconstitutional behavior always eroded political legitimacy.[2]

The difficulties inherent in the constitutionalist approach were manifest from the start. The Thermidorian deputies who sought to establish the republic on the rule of law were the same ones who boldly violated their new constitution both in letter and spirit.[3] The two-thirds law imposed on elections to the Councils by the Convention subverted the concept of representative democracy, supposedly the bedrock of republicanism. In addition, barring relatives of émigrés from holding elected office clearly contravened the newly adopted constitution, a point that supporters of the idea soon conceded.[4] Doing so *after* the elections added to the travesty of democracy. Much could be said and was said to justify these measures, but they still smacked of opportunism. In this atmosphere of uncertain legitimacy, only monumental naiveté and an exaggerated belief in the power of republican rhetoric[5] could explain why the government imagined that the judges and local officials elected in October 1795 would dedicate themselves to the rule of law. After all, these men were chosen by the very voters the Convention did not trust to choose republicans as national deputies. What would compel the newly elected justices of the peace, judges, and public prosecutors to uphold the highest principles of jurisprudence when the authors of the constitution found it acceptable to adopt such a heavy-handed expedient as the law of 3 brumaire IV (25 October 1795), an omnibus bill of political exclusion?[6] Nullifying the recent election of émigré relatives to various local offices could hardly have encouraged their remaining colleagues to forego expedients of their own. Although the Directory's inaugural proclamation announced to the French people that henceforth the fundamental principle of government would be "an inflexible justice and the strictest observance of the laws," the same proclamation included a promise "to wage an active war on royalism, revive patriotism, and repress with a firm hand all factions."[7] The example set by the regime's founding fathers suggested that it was the second statement that carried the most meaning.

Thus, the Directorial regime did not develop a crisis of legitimacy; it began with one. The Directory's formal institutional arrangements were a bold attempt to create modern liberal democracy, and yet the parlous state of France in the mid-1790s bred deep contempt for republican politics. The exalted spirit of liberty and equality had degenerated into a smeary uncertainty. Frenchmen simply could not reconcile the liberal ideals of 1789 with the squalid politics of 1795. Though liberty was still under conceptual construction, it was obvious that a political order in which violence played a major role had not assured freedom. A free society does not experience fear as a salient feature of public life. To succeed, therefore, the republic needed more than a liberal constitution and legal protections for civil liberties; it needed more than a plethora of elections, an air of equality, or a veneer of democracy; the republic needed to provide peace and security. As long as the Directory could not separate political strife from basic issues of personal security, it could not generate enough legitimacy to survive. The design of the Directory embodied liberal ideals of freedom, but it proved a short-lived regime because it failed to provide freedom from fear.

Uncertain legitimacy and widespread trepidation made citizens reluctant to participate in the new polity, whether this meant holding public office, serving as jurors, or simply voting. In the first six months of the regime, to cite but one example, twenty-nine men either resigned from or refused places on Montpellier's eight-man municipal council. Criminal courts had to impose stiff fines to get jurors to do their duty because the loss of voting privileges proved insufficiently coercive. Across the republic, even the most important elections, those for town councillors, rarely brought out more than 20 percent of the electorate.[8] Such a debilitating withdrawal from the opportunities of citizenship was not a rejection of the republic per se. Most Frenchmen did not desire a return to the *ancien régime*, nor, by 1795, did they believe it was possible. And yet, citizens were deeply alienated by the economic crisis, continued warfare, and religious persecution associated with the republic. A government that had to "liquidate a crushing past and march, denuded of everything, toward an utterly uncertain future"[9] could hardly attract collaborators at the local level. In this climate, refusing to take part in political life also had much to do with self-preservation and future standing in local communities. The constant turnover in political personnel since 1789 as a result of collective violence and executive purges amply demonstrated the risks of political involvement. Where the Revolution had been especially tumultuous, however, it remained more dangerous to cede power to opponents than to take the risks of political engagement. Better to be an oppressor than oppressed. Thus, with deep reluctance to hold office except in areas of extremism and without a national consensus on either the limits of politics or the basis of social order, fear remained a key feature of local politics. No matter the number of military victories, the extent of annexations, the permanency of land sales, or the stability of currency, the Directory could win lasting legitimacy only by making it both honorable and safe to participate in public life. This it did not do.

## Transitional Justice and the Amnesty of 1795

The crisis of legitimacy at the start of the Directory and the persistent tension over constitutionalism and expediency owed much to the Thermidorians' failure to establish an effective form of retributive justice in the wake of the Terror. The obvious problem at the time was that any attempt to apply an impartial legal standard as the basis for a retributive justice that held "terrorists" accountable for their excesses would have deprived the republic of many of its most ardent supporters. Thus, the Convention's final failure was its inability to create what has come to be called "transitional justice," that is, a compromise between politics and law designed to broaden the regime's base of support. Political scientists have concluded that it is not the sheer number of convictions nor even the percentage of convictions that makes retributive justice effective after a change of regime; rather, it is far more important to have a clearly articulated policy of retributive justice in order to establish the new regime's credibility in moral terms.[10] The Thermidorians failed to develop such a policy due both to the desperate politics of personal survival and the unstable concept of justice generated during the Convention.[11]

Late in the evening of 4 brumaire IV (26 October 1795), the Convention passed its last decree: an amnesty for "acts purely related to the revolution." According to the rhetoric of the moment, only pulling a veil over the past could put an end to political hatred, factional struggles, and the interminable cycle of violence these generated. This momentous—but largely neglected—decree was presented to the Convention as necessary to "erase the memory of errors and mistakes that had been committed during the Revolution." More important, this act of amnesia was described as "the only means of ending the Revolution."[12] But the heated political climate following the elections and the Vendémiaire insurrection gave the amnesty a strong bias in favor of republicans. Coming the day after the laws of 3 brumaire IV, the amnesty explicitly did not apply to *vendémiaristes,* émigrés, and priests. Nor did it apply to rebels still locked in armed struggle with the republic in western France. Although the amnesty did not cover all political crimes equally, no deputy objected. The law favored radical revolutionaries, those who had committed crimes due to "an excessive zeal and blind rage for liberty,"[13] while explicitly upholding renewed persecution of refractory priests and official émigrés.[14] Even a proposal to extend the ban on office holding to participants in the *sans-culottes* uprising of May 1795 failed.

The amnesty followed months of harassment, beatings, mob assaults, arbitrary arrests, and prison massacres directed against Jacobins and functionaries of the Revolutionary Government throughout the country. Viewed in the light of this "White Terror," as well as the royalist uprising of 13–14 vendémiaire IV (5–6 October 1795), the amnesty appears as a not unreasonable attempt on the part of beleaguered republicans to protect fellow travelers. The Conventionnels who voted for the measure included many who had worked closely with deputies now under arrest for their part in the Terror. Of course, there were also the many other leading officials appointed to high-level posts by the Convention and now in prison awaiting trial, notably those who had turned the Commune and War Ministry into *sans-culottes* fiefdoms. Equally, departmental prisons contained hundreds of men whose "terrorist" activities had relied on the support of deputies on mission who themselves had survived the purges of year III and continued to sit in the National Convention. Moreover, deputies knew that the elections had created a moderate if not reactionary magistracy inclined to ignore or exonerate violence directed at Jacobins. Various trials around the country on the eve of the amnesty, however, suggest that the Conventionnels' fear of overt judicial persecution was overblown. In other words, the amnesty was not necessary to preserve thousands of "terrorists" from the scaffold or even the *bagne.* Supporters of the amnesty more plausibly believed that giving radical republicans absolution would help to end internecine strife between various strands of prorevolutionary sentiment and thereby unite them all behind the nascent constitutional regime. According to the judges on the Criminal Court of the Haute-Saône, the amnesty was both a veil and a pardon "that we expect to result in a sincere forgetfulness of the past, a perfect union of all French republicans, and an unalterable accord for the strengthening and prosperity of the Republic."[15] And yet the amnesty undercut the Directory's ability to appeal to moderate revolutionaries who had suffered during the Terror. Too many felt legally emasculated by the amnesty and resented the rogue republicans who benefited from it.

Although the amnesty favored Jacobins, it also protected many of the thugs and vigilantes of the Thermidorian Reaction. Thus, it left both factions intact and fostered a climate of continued political violence. Furthermore, many magistrates appreciated the freedom not to prosecute acts of anti-Jacobin violence and even excused political murders as a form of justice.[16] Under these conditions, the Directory found it difficult to persuade members of either party that the regime could and would exact atonement for injury. Local politics made it clear that a strategy of relying on the rule of law could not bring the Revolution to a close unless it included some form of punishment for criminal abuses of power during the Terror. By preventing anyone from being punished for "acts purely related to the Revolution," the amnesty beautifully avoided defining the difference between what had been politically necessary and what had been criminally gratuitous. Protecting rogue deputies, *sans-culottes* militants, and village terrorists further sullied the republic in the eyes of potential supporters. The presence of all those *amnistiés* in society, men who had been imprisoned, indicted, and sometimes even sentenced for their activities during the Terror, did not incline their neighbors to forget the crimes perpetrated in the name of public safety. In sum, the amnesty adopted in 1795 eliminated any effective form of transitional justice; thus, rather than helping to heal the wounds of Revolution, it encouraged them to fester.

In lieu of transitional justice, the first year of the Directory saw repeated efforts to ameliorate the amnesty. Like so many of the circumstantial laws adopted in the revolutionary decade, the law of 4 brumaire IV was badly written and yielded widely variable results. The difference between "acts related purely to the Revolution" and crimes punishable by the Penal Code of 1791 was less than obvious. Moreover, the law lacked provisions for appeal, made no mention of soldiers, and did not deal with compensatory damages. The Directory asked legislators to fix these flaws,[17] but conservative deputies in the Council of Five Hundred insisted on linking the amnesty to the exclusionary law of 3 brumaire IV. The entire spirit of amnesty soon disappeared amidst tumultuous debate and sinister cries of "To the Abbaye!"[18] The parliamentary fracas eventually led to a badly compromised bill on 15 frimaire V (5 December 1796). Although deputies generally agreed that excluding the relatives of émigrés from voting or holding elected office was unconstitutional, a majority casuistically defended the measure by arguing "that an apparent breech can sometimes conform to its spirit and be necessary for its defense,"[19] and so only agreed to reduce the exclusion to émigrés and their relatives. In exchange, the bill broadened the amnesty to participants in the Vendémiaire uprising, as well as *chouans* now that civil war in the west had officially ended. The extension of the amnesty to crimes of revolutionary resistance was the only logical response to Deputy

Thibaudeau's mordant critique. "An amnesty must be complete," he argued, "because if it is partial, it is partisan; it is no longer a great act of national clemency, but impunity granted by the strongest party to itself."[20] As further compromise, the exclusionary law of 3 brumaire IV was extended to all those who had formally been amnestied, which mostly meant former "terrorists."[21] The result of this sporadic yearlong debate, therefore, was to increase the scope of national clemency by including certain right-wing opponents of the republic while at the same time decreasing the pool of potential candidates for political office by excluding all those formally granted an amnesty. This became a characteristic feature of the Directorial regime: seeking the *juste milieu* at the expense of a broad political base.

The Thermidorians' hope that an amnesty would rally republicans of all stripes, whatever their excesses or whatever their grievances, is understandable; but they were not prepared to live with the consequences. Within a year, the Directory began harassing amnestied revolutionaries. This was not based on new crimes they had committed. In fact, the government's problem in dealing with challengers to its left was their ability to stir up discontent while remaining largely within legal bounds.[22] Whereas the Directorial regime could have begun with a form of retributive justice limited and controlled by the new legal structures, the flawed amnesty forced it to use police harassment to distance itself from political pariahs within republican ranks. Such tactics did nothing to restore the dignity of victims of revolutionary violence and simply took the regime down the path of arbitrariness and exceptional justice. Thus, left largely unmodified, the amnesty wreaked havoc for the constitutional regime and its effort to instill the rule of law. Rather than inaugurating a period of national reconciliation, the amnesty eliminated the possibility of a limited retributive justice that would have appealed to the sort of "men of '89" that the regime most needed to win over. This enabled both extremes to preserve a dangerous purchase on national politics. The resulting *politique de bascule* contributed mightily to prolonging the French Revolution.

## The Directory as a Revolutionary Regime

The problems surrounding the amnesty of 1795 reveal how difficult it was for the Directory to become a postrevolutionary regime. The Directory had to do more than protect the republic; it had to make France republican. Although constitutionalism was central to its legitimacy, the Directory's survival also depended on its ability to complete other tasks at the heart of the republican project. Foremost among these were establishing the primacy of the secular state-nation over the church-centered local community and establishing France's expansion to her "natural frontiers." Each of these tasks provoked enormous domestic opposition and made it all the more difficult for the Directory to adhere to representative democracy and the rule of law. Being in thrall to bellicose patriotism and angry anticlericalism thus made the Directory as much a revolutionary republic as a constitutional one, inclined to prefer coercion to compromise and force to favor.

If there was a single policy issue on which the survival of a liberal democracy in France depended in 1795, it was the attitude the republic would take toward Catholicism. Order could not be restored and the French Revolution ended until the religious issue had been resolved. The Concordat as the ultimate resolution to the problem was an unlikely as well as unsatisfactory outcome. It took a decade of republican intolerance and ineptitude to make the Concordat possible in the first place and attractive in the last. Although the Thermidorians had dressed up their separation of church and state as freedom of worship, the new clothing came with strict sumptuary laws: religion was to be kept quiet, dull, and indoors. The reopening of churches in the summer of 1795 allowed over ten thousand priests to resume their ministries, including thousands recently released from prison or returned from exile.[23] Despite the survival of the constitutional church, the religious revival of 1795 proved to be largely refractory and royalist. Hence the expiring Convention's maniacal idea that previously refusing to take an oath of loyalty to the 1791 Civil Constitution of the Clergy, even though it was now a dead letter, made a priest a counter-revolutionary rebel with little hope of republican redemption. When the new officials of the Directory took office, therefore, they had the unpopular task of enforcing the essentially terrorist law of 3 brumaire IV, which banished (under penalty of death) all refractory priests from the republic.

This renewed anticlericalism was more than a matter of faith: republicans were intent on dissolving the religious glue that held villages together in defiance of the nation. Various displays of piety had long functioned as essential enactments of community. By outlawing such practices as the bells of Angelus, calvary stations, penitent parades, and funeral processions, the Convention knowingly and deliberately subverted the rituals of public life that helped to give villages and neighborhoods their sense of collective identity. And yet most elected officials were inclined to turn a blind eye to acts of public piety. The harshness of laws against refractory priests made such officials even more reluctant to cooperate with the government. Although republican departments arrested a considerable number of refractory priests in the course of year IV—twenty-nine in the Haute-Garonne; almost forty in the Sarthe—these men were generally old and infirm and, therefore, subject to internment rather than deportation or death.[24] From time to time, however, magistrates did apply the law in all its terrible rigor. On 25 nivôse IV (13 January 1796), the Criminal Court of the Haute-Saône condemned to death Pierre-Joseph Cornibert, an aging Capucin monk better known as Père Grégoire. His crimes: spurning all revolutionary oaths, carrying on clandestine services in the woods around Meurcourt, and, above all, possessing a damning parody of the Marseillaise that included the refrain, "Aux armes, vrais chrétiens, catholiques romains, marchons, mourons, que notre sang abreuve nos sillons." Père Grégoire's condemnation and execution at Vesoul was the first political use of the guillotine in the Haute-Saône. It sent a shock of horror throughout the region and provoked such opprobrium that, although the Criminal Court sentenced more than a dozen priests to prison or exile, it never sent another to the scaffold.[25]

The republic's renewed anticlericalism sparked innumerable outbursts of violence, as lawmakers surely knew it would. The success of collective action in getting churches reopened and constitutional priests replaced by refractories in year III emboldened citizens to meet force with force when local officials tried to apply the harsher policies of year IV. Every department experienced this religious violence. Often the number of protestors simply overwhelmed the police and municipal officials. Such clashes exposed the provocative impotence of law enforcement. In a typical incident, over three hundred people came together to rescue a refractory priest from the hands of gendarmes in the isolated Confracourt Wood (Haute-Saône) on 18 prairial IV (6 June 1796). Even putting priests in prison did not secure them. At Béziers, several hundred citizens stormed the local jail, beat up the jailor, and freed what he called "that monster of Jesus Christ," the *abbé* Joseph Mailhac.[26] Such incidents revealed that renewed religious persecution was badly discrediting the lawful exercise of authority. That the struggle was between the predominance of a secular republic over religion-centered communities is made obvious by the regime's rude handling of the constitutional church. Here was an institutional opportunity for the republic to make real inroads into peasant communities. But too many directorialists considered constitutional priests only half-hearted republicans inclined to fanatical and retrograde ideas. The fact that any priest, whether refractory or constitutional, tended to respond more to local pressures than to the demands of the state made them all unreliable. The unofficial slogan of the constitutional church—"priests submissive to the laws"—did little to improve matters. Their legal status made them all the more dangerous when agitating for true freedom of public worship. Even in a department as divided as the Sarthe, central administrators proved hostile to the constitutional clergy: "the priests are again redistributing their daggers and their poison with the audacity of crime and the impudence of success," they complained.[27]

Republican officials who refused to temporize with religious resistance often responded with a heavy dose of armed force. Following a pattern established in 1792–93, they commonly sent several brigades of gendarmes, a column of national guardsmen, or a company of regular soldiers to deal with relatively minor disturbances. This could lead to real embarrassment. Sending a hundred grenadiers to St-Nicolas-de-la-Grave a week after women had occupied the local church did nothing to help arrest the leading agitators—who successfully hid behind a wall of silence—but a great deal to exasperate the local population.[28] Unfortunately for the regime's credibility, this was far from the only case in which local officials let a crowd of women demanding Catholic rituals goad them into over-reacting.[29] There was no doubt that every time the republic made a concession to Catholicism, numerous priests took advantage of the opportunity by flouting the law, inciting trouble, and even preaching rebellion. But these priests were not a majority; most priests simply wanted to be allowed to engage in traditional religious practices in relative peace. Republicans' unwillingness to tolerate these practices and their use of heavy-handed coercion to stamp them out ensured that resistance to other state demands often fused with religious resistance to produce yet more violence.

The Directory soon realized the damage that misdirected coercion was doing to its authority. Witness the often overlooked *Pastoralis sollicitudo* of July 1796.[30] Pius VI's draft circular described disobedience to the Directory as "a crime which would be severely punished not only by earthly powers, but worse, by God himself, who threatens with eternal damnation those who resist government." A papal statement of this sort exhorting priests to prove their submission to the regime would have preempted the Concordat. When the Directory realized what had been at stake in the failed negotiations, it published the draft document, only to have it greeted with skepticism from refractories and embarrassment from republicans. A great opportunity had been missed, and nothing like it recurred again before 1801. Witness also the government's own policies following Portalis's famous speech to the Council of Elders in which he boldly stated: "Force and violence have never succeeded in religious matters. Must we agitate spirits at the end of a revolution, at a time when they wish only for calm?"[31] By the autumn of 1796, the minister of police, Cochon de Lapparent, was instructing officials not to disturb peaceful priests by demanding oaths from them. A few weeks later, lawmakers abrogated part of the law of 3 brumaire IV, reinvigorating the anticlerical laws of 1792–93. Residual doubt about so-called "deported" priests led some departments to practice a policy of no arrests, no releases; others boldly freed all their clerical prisoners.[32] Here, finally, was at least a de facto policy that could assist in placating the countryside. But it was typical of the Directory that it came a year late and was not actually adopted de jure. This ensured that anticlerical officials could continue legally to harass and even persecute priests. The sustained uncertainty also ensured that committed Catholics attached maximum opprobrium to the regime. In short, the policy was odious and ineffective. The most active refractory priests remained at large, busily subverting the regime by flouting its laws.[33] And so continued a veil of tears for refractory priests and a fount of resistance to the republic.

If the regime's hard line on refractory priests and public worship threatened the coherence of village life, then violent reaction from villages threatened the coherence of the republic. The protracted debates that followed the right-wing elections in the spring of 1797 led local officials to expect genuine freedom of religion balanced by severe penalties for political agitation.[34] Had the Thermidorians been willing to adopt such a stance earlier, it would have eviscerated much of the political reaction that gathered between 1795 and 1797. As it was, by the summer of 1797, the quasi-totality of parishes had resumed some form of Catholic worship, most of it led by refractory priests. Even though still illegal, public processions and church bells—the visual and aural symbols of traditional community—could once again be seen and heard throughout the country. Rather than trying to dissociate popular demand for Catholicism from the more elitist opposition to the republic that fed royalism, Directorial republicans stubbornly clung to policies that helped to fuse Catholicism and royalism into a more comprehensive rejection of the regime.

The Directory's war policy was as integral to its quality as a revolutionary regime as its religious policies and generated a similar groundswell of opposition and violence. By 1795, the patriotic national defense that had done so much to revolutionize the Revolution had become an essential source of political legitimacy. The Thermidorians needed the moral authority that bellicose patriotism gave the republic and happily used the country's new military might to wage a war of expansion. Defense of the Revolution came to mean securing France's "natural frontiers" and became a war aim synonymous with republicanism. Settling for anything less was equated with capitulating to the forces of royalism, both French and Anglo-Austrian. And yet only an aggressive war effort could force the republic's enemies to accept France's expansion to its "natural frontiers." If French armies occupied the lands bordering the Rhine and the Alps, but the enemy refused to accept their annexation to France, yet more territories beyond the Rhine and the Alps would be conquered. These could then be used as bargaining counters in order to obtain peace on republican terms.

Continued aggression abroad spelled continued coercion at home. The Directors assumed office at a time of severe military reverses along the Rhine, stalemate along the Alps, and renewed civil war in the west. At the same time, financial and economic crises brought a near-total collapse of military supply services.[35] The Directory responded with revolutionary expedients: another forced loan, this time of 600 million francs (equivalent to two-thirds of the specie in France!), and another levy of horses, in this case one in every thirty in the country, as well as continued use of military requisitions.[36] All of these measures provoked enormous hostility and often violent resistance. The departments that showed any real success in collecting the forced loan had to resort to billeting troops on recalcitrant proprietors, an odious practice reminiscent of the seventeenth-century drive to absolutism. And still the final sum raised was less than one-quarter of what the law demanded. The levy of horses likewise yielded only half the expected total. In both cases, the resources wrung from an exhausted economy were of real assistance in the war effort. Nonetheless, the level of obduracy they aroused compared to the diminishing returns they produced led to both measures being wound up early in 1797.[37]

Military impressment provoked even greater conflict and coercion than collecting cash or requisitioning supplies. The deplorable conditions of army service together with a galloping war-weariness inspired massive desertion. In December 1795, the Directory moved to reverse this trend. In the spirit of earlier revolutionary emergencies, Minister of War Aubert-Dubayet appointed two dozen special *agents militaires* to fan out across the country and press local authorities and the gendarmerie to round up draft dodgers and deserters. He chose a mix of Jacobin generals and former Conventionnels—all hard-headed and hard-hearted men known for their terrorist past. Some of these men acted like representatives on mission, ordering troop movements, making officer appointments, forming national guardsmen into mobile columns, and seizing the parents of draft dodgers as hostages. The energetic efforts of *agents militaires* helped to swell republican armies by a net fifty thousand soldiers in a few months. At the same time, however, some of the agents became so odious that their collective mission was canceled in the spring of 1796.[38] The concerted effort to replenish the shrinking armies required extensive use of force. This recourse to revolutionary men and methods in order to carry on the war effort clearly eroded the early Directory's efforts at constitutionalism.

As was so often the case around the country, opposition to military service and resistance to the Directory's uncompromising religious policies combined to pose a formidable challenge to the republic's authority. Draft dodgers and deserters became insurgents in waiting. Regions without a tradition of military service, such as the southwest, often rebelled openly. When soldiers appeared in the countryside west of L'Isle-Jourdain (Gers) in 1796 in search of refractory priests, several villages rang the tocsin in a call to arms. More than a thousand men and women turned out and easily disarmed the small detachments. A few weeks later, another large crowd composed of individuals from as many as forty communes and led by Dasolles, justice of the peace at Monferran, marched on L'Isle-Jourdain, where they broke into the prison and freed two of Dasolles' sons, one a priest and the other a deserter. The crowd then smashed its way into a warehouse in order to recover church bells confiscated in year II. Although the department authorities at Auch initially resisted the army's offer of assistance, the second incident won them over, and they promptly issued orders to assemble "an imposing force." The authorities supplied the names of four refractory priests and several leading deserters. The republican column was charged with rounding up deserters and again confiscating church bells. They began with a house-to-house search at L'Isle-Jourdain. A fifty-man detachment then marched into the countryside, where an ambush by three hundred men led to a veritable pitched battle. Only the sustained use of regular troops over several weeks finally subdued the region. Although deserters began to flow into the staging depot in Toulouse, the regime paid a high price for this local triumph. The district of L'Isle-Jourdain contributed heartily to the royalist uprising that erupted around Toulouse in 1799.[39]

It was axiomatic to the regime that resistance to the republic was support for monarchy. Opposition to religious restrictions and military service certainly provided fertile soil for royalist agitation. Regardless of republican rhetoric, however, not every form of opposition was a manifestation of royalism. Many refractory priests refused to cooperate in counter-revolutionary conspiracies. These included some of the most influential bishops outside of France as well as many opponents of the new religious order inside the country.[40] Deserters and draft dodgers were even less political and rarely held to royalism as a matter of conviction. And yet being condemned to a marginal existence in the republic made them prime candidates to join the royalist cause. For those who actively assisted counter-revolution, the difference between fighting for the republic and fighting for the king was a matter of choosing between serving the nation and serving their own communities. As outlaws, refractories—whether secular or religious—relied heavily on the support of fellow villagers and the insularity of the village community for protection from dutiful officials and the local police. For this reason, *insoumis* became individual avatars of community resistance to the demands of the republican state. Naturally, wherever royalists were busy organizing counter-revolution, they could count on a few priests for moral support and on reluctant draftees for local muscle.[41]

Counter-revolutionary royalism went beyond mere resistance and involved at least some willingness to take risks and make sacrifices in order to bring back the monarchy. The few thousand émigrés who joined Condé's army or landed at Quiberon were among the most dedicated opponents of the Revolution. This served as the pretext for including an article in the Constitution of Year III banning in perpetuity the return of all individuals on the official list of émigrés (estimated by the Directory to be 120,000 persons). Such a ban was about property as well as politics. It ensured that land seized from émigrés remained in the hands of its new owners, whether peasant proprietors, urban *rentiers,* or the republic itself. The ban also treated émigrés as irreconcilable enemies of the republic, that is, as diehard royalists one and all. Factional rivalries had a hand in this. Official lists of émigrés had grown substantially in 1793–94, especially in the Midi following the Federalist Revolts, and Jacobins wanted to keep their erstwhile victims out of office under the Directory. Furthermore, republicans' fear that if relatives of émigrés gained office they would serve as a fifth column for a royalist counter-revolution easily trumped any impulse toward political inclusion and so squelched the possibility of a property-based *rassemblement pour la république.* Only the right-wing majority in the Councils was willing to end the blatantly unconstitutional ostracism of émigrés' relatives from the body politic. That this discrimination was revived after Fructidor underscores just how thoroughly exclusionary politics were woven into the fabric of Directorial republicanism.

The Directory's exclusionary policies helped to ensure that it got what it feared. Those émigrés who returned to France—they numbered in the tens of thousands—but could not get their names removed from the official list of émigrés, whether legally or not, could only hope for the regime's demise. Many actually worked for it. Thus, wherever royalism took a militant form, émigrés played leading roles. Émigré activists generally belonged to the camp of *les royalistes purs et durs* and took the lead in organizing violence against the regime. The success of their operations depended on their ability to exploit the various sources of opposition. Advocates of constitutional monarchy and proponents of absolute monarchy both tapped into the wellsprings of popular resistance. However, they found it difficult to cooperate amongst themselves, so bitter was the resentment against the perceived perfidies of the early Revolution. This has led some to suggest that the Directory should have been less paranoid and followed Carnot's lead by inviting moderate royalists to participate in the regime.[42] Yet such a suggestion presumes that the government could tell the difference between opportunists and purists, all while coping with conspiracies that spawned regional violence or used elections to subvert the regime.

## Party Politics

Here lay another central aspect of the choice between republican constitutionalism and revolutionary expediency. The Directory failed to adhere to the democratic aspects of the Constitution of Year III largely because it could not distinguish life threats to the regime from challenges to its authority and purpose. Neither the royalist right nor the democratic left could be easily parsed. Both had their conspiratorial elements, both used elections as a stalking horse to transform the regime, and both trailed off into factional politics at the local level.

The Directory continued to exclude émigrés and their relatives from full citizenship because it was primarily through them that the Count of Provence and his court in exile at Blankenbourg; the Count of Artois at Edinburgh, then the royalist Agency in Paris; the Count of Puisaye in Brittany; and the British secret service operative William Wickham at Berne were all able to organize and fund counter-revolutionary violence in the French interior. Though the machinations of these leaders are generally known, the full extent of their campaign on the ground is still poorly understood. It certainly ranged far beyond the obvious efforts in western France.[43] In

Languedoc, for example, rebel units wearing royalist insignia appeared in five distinct regions ranging from the Haute-Loire to the Gers. This inspired major exercises in military repression involving hundreds of regular troops and thousands of national guardsmen.[44] The defeat or dispersal of these minor insurgencies took place at the same time as the Vendée and *chouannerie* were being pacified. In fact, rebels in the Aveyron managed to procure an amnesty for themselves modeled on the one offered by General Hoche in the west. In a fit of naive optimism, however, the department commander required the insurgents only to swear "to return to their native region and to forget all resentment"; he did not even demand that they turn in their guns.[45] But for a while at least, violence subsided.

As obtuse and disorganized as the "pure" royalists often were, even they could see that by the summer of 1796 isolated acts of counter-revolutionary violence generated more fright than fight and so hurt the royalist cause. Therefore they abandoned their plans to overthrow the regime through simultaneous uprisings, or even to sap its credibility through sporadic attacks, and accepted the new "Grand Plan" as a largely legal means to restore the monarchy. This required absolutists to cooperate with constitutionalists in an effort to gain control of the republic by winning elections in the spring of 1797.[46] Such a strategy meant turning off the financial spigot for para-military "companies" and instructing royalist commanders to stop all violent activity.[47] Rather than making it easier for the Directory to ensconce the republic, however, the reduction in violence and shift to an electoral strategy made it harder for the government to know where the real perils to its future lay. This is made most evident by the emergence of the secret "Philanthropic Institute," with its independent branches in various departments but with no overt connection to a national organization. These cells avoided public mention of the monarchy while supporting unavowed royalists as candidates for local and national office. All the same, an inner circle known as the "Coterie of Legitimate Sons" swore allegiance to the Pretender and continued to plan special operations, including cooperating with the Paris Agency in setting up a military coup against the regime, preferably led by the traitorous General Jean-Charles Pichegru once he had been elected to the Councils. The electoral triumph in the spring of 1797 helped the Institute spread to as many as seventy departments, where it busily influenced public opinion, co-opted local officials, and meddled in the National Guard. Only then did the directors Barras, Reubell, and La Révellière-Lépaux discover the Institute's true nature and precipitate the coup d'état of 18 fructidor V.[48]

The Triumvirate chose not to publish their evidence about the Institute as justification for the coup. Perhaps this was because they knew more about the Institute's modus operandi than about the individuals involved, or perhaps it was because the Institute's main purpose was to substitute a coordinated electoral strategy for the politics of violence. As far as the Institute was concerned, the decidedly reactionary drift of public opinion augured well for the elections of 1798. So promising was the political climate in the summer of 1797 that General Pichegru, now president of the Council of Elders, put off leading a royalist coup and committed himself to constitutional methods. Although antirepublican violence had risen sharply on the eve of the elections and spiked again around the anniversary of 9 Thermidor, there is little evidence that this was either coordinated or part of a royalist conspiracy.[49] Rather, it was quite clearly the fruit of spontaneous agitation based on ridding the country of Jacobins once and for all. Given the paucity of available evidence on a nationwide conspiracy based on counter-revolutionary violence, it was the Triumvirate's good fortune that the Baron de Saint-Christol and Dominique Allier launched their assault on the citadel at Pont-Saint-Esprit (Gard) before hearing news of the coup. Even better, by calling themselves the "The Army of the Two Councils," the paramilitaries gave the government just what it needed, prima facie evidence to support its claim that Fructidor had been a necessary preemptive strike against a royalist plot that centered on the Councils and radiated throughout the country.[50] The failed attack on Pont-Saint-Esprit ironically confirmed the premise of the "Grand Plan," that is to say, that as far as organized royalism was concerned, piecemeal violence and isolated acts of insurgency only played into the regime's hands. In this sense, overtly counter-revolutionary violence went a long way toward legitimizing the Directory's use of force and disregard for its own constitution.

Much of the success of the royalists depended on mobilizing fears of Jacobinism. Here too the regime had difficulty distinguishing various strands of opposition, of knowing when differences of emphasis and strategy slipped into subversion of the regime, either overtly or covertly. Just as republican officials seemed to find royalists behind every bush, many ordinary citizens relentlessly denounced the threat posed by Jacobins. It is difficult for a modern democrat to appreciate this near-hysteria, especially given the egalitarian language often employed by republican critics of the Directory. Many republicans had an admirable desire to expand the franchise, but it is worth recalling that a lot of republicans also had blood on their hands. Most Jacobins refused to disavow the violence that had brought them to power and kept them there, and they never abandoned their hope of returning to power by force—hence the sympathy for Babeuf expressed by such newspapers as the *Journal des hommes libres* and *La Chronique de la Sarthe.* Furthermore, Jacobins' continuing penchant for the language of violence, such as was expressed in the Pantheon Club at Paris, could not be dismissed as mere rhetorical excess, not after Marat, Hébert, and Robespierre. If Jacobin politics had really changed, why did Antonelle, a prolific writer on social egalitarianism and representative democracy, publish an article in December 1795 in which he said, "I want to kill, to wipe out the nobility"?[51] How were his fellow Frenchmen to judge such language? Finally, Jacobins showed no more scruples about the mechanics of democracy or the limits of the constitution than those who heartily opposed the republic. The Jacobins of Marseille and Nîmes pioneered the use of subpoenas to take political opponents into custody on the eve of elections. Elsewhere, Jacobin army commanders used troops to gain control of electoral assemblies and determine the outcome.[52] When contemporaries brought these various elements of Jacobinism together they saw genuine "terrorists," that is, men who had adopted ardent patriotism as moral cover for local tyranny.

The contribution made by republican extremism to the Directory's dilemma needs to be viewed from two angles: that of the ordinary citizen and that of the government. Officials who enforced the latest laws against priests and émigrés were "terrorists" in the eyes of most of the population. Not so for republicans. According to the *Journal de Toulouse,* "the strict execution of laws may be called terrorism" by royalists and religious fanatics, but, when the constitution is followed, "terror" becomes a "chimera which can only find room in a madman's head or a villain's heart."[53] The law was the crux of the matter. For most Frenchmen, "terrorists" were republican officials, past or present, who committed gross violations of the traditional "laws" of the community as anthropologists would define them.[54] For the government, on the other hand, Jacobins became "terrorists" when they violated the actual laws of the republic, especially the Constitution of Year III or the *Code des délits et des peines,* in order to persecute their opponents or subvert the regime. These conflicting definitions left plenty of room for subjective judgment, as the dizzying number of appointments, dismissals, and reappointments during the period attests.

At first the Directorial government appointed hundreds of Jacobin-style republicans as departmental, cantonal, and court commissioners. The number multiplied when the Councils authorized the Directory to fill vacancies in elected offices of local administration and the judiciary.[55] In the meantime, the government began to reap the hatred and turmoil these appointments provoked. It was the Jacobin extremists' penchant for abusing state power that earned the regime such animosity. Take for example the actions of Sébastien Seguin, a former department administrator of the Haute-Saône whom the Directory appointed as its first cantonal commissioner at Faverney. Seguin assembled a column of thirty dragoons and thirty national guardsmen for a midnight descent on Provenchères, where a refractory priest had recently held services. Not only were the domiciliary searches conducted at an unconstitutional hour, the armed force got carried away, locked up the mayor, and ransacked several houses. Jean-Nicholas Bourgeois, a captain in the National Guard and commander of the expedition, behaved especially badly and was later charged with having "publicly assaulted the good morals of *citoyenne* Cheviron," the mayor's wife. All the same, in a letter to the minister of the interior, commissioner Seguin claimed that he had violated the constitution in good faith, having been "wandering due to an accusation of terrorism" at the time it was adopted and published. As bizarre as this sounds, the minister actually shielded Seguin from prosecution. Had he known more about the commissioner, he would have been less indulgent. Seguin was a bourgeois with aristocratic pretensions who had used his position as department administrator from 1792 to 1794 to become president of the department's *comité de surveillance générale* as well as inspector of horse procurement. In both posts he had shown a penchant for arbitrariness and graft. And now in the year IV, Seguin was the incarnation of the republic in the northern Haute-Saône. The minister's decision to protect him could only have outraged fellow citizens.[56] There had been no guillotine, no incidental killing, and no forced exile, and yet it was precisely this sort of "terrorism" that people around France had come to fear from their local Jacobins.

Like royalism, Jacobinism had its conspiratorial element aimed at toppling the regime. As with royalism, the connection between local sources of violence and grand plots was extremely tenuous. Despite the later fame of Gracchus Babeuf's protocommunist ideology, most of his coconspirators were primarily dedicated to executing a counter-Thermidor, a Robespierrist coup d'état in order to return to the Terror. The coup was planned as a day of slaughter, including all deputies and Directors, to be followed by a collective dictatorship.[57] To this end, the conspirators first tried to corrupt the Paris Police Legion and then the army units at the Grenelle military camp. The fact that decisive action from the government thwarted both efforts has obscured the alarming extent to which "terrorism" had infected the security forces around the capital. The Directors had good reason to respond harshly, but their efforts to conjure a gigantic nationwide conspiracy out of a Paris-based plot alienated a great many republicans. Rather than destroying Jacobinism as a political force, the large police dragnet gave it a rallying point. At the same time, the government's strategy fed provincial fears about the danger posed by local Jacobins and so helped to stimulate the reaction expressed in the elections of year V.[58] Despite these drawbacks, disposing of the Babouvists ended any serious Jacobin conspiracy to overthrow the regime.

## Partisan Politics and Discursive Signifiers

The appearance of modern politics during the First Republic was just that, largely an appearance disguising traditional sources of strife. The interaction between revolutionary forces and social sources of violence is not easy for historians to discern, trammeled as we are by the partisan language of the time. The constant invocation of "Jacobins" and "royalists," "patriots" and "fanatics," the innumerable warnings of "a second Vendée" or a return to "the tyranny of robespierrists," and the political cross-dressing of "royalistes à bonnet rouge" and "terroristes à talon rouge" all serve to obscure other aspects of social and cultural conflict. Some of these are more easily identified than others. Sectarian hatred between Catholics and Protestants in Languedoc; institutional and commercial rivalries between towns in Provence; and class conflict between tenant farmers and landed proprietors in Brittany all fueled revolutionary factionalism. A fine-grained analysis of village politics in the Massif Central, where the sources of fissures were especially obscure, led Peter Jones to conclude that the Revolution was "disciplined to the needs of the rural community and not vice versa."[59] And yet the prevalence of particular factional epithets across France despite its many regional differences suggests a more common, if more amorphous source of civil strife, one fueled by the uncertain legitimacy of the new social order emerging from the Revolution. Although ubiquitous in the period, the terms "Jacobin" and "royalist" are too exclusively political to capture the sense of social and cultural antagonism that infused local politics around the country. Two other widely popular epithets better expressed contemporaries' competing visions of a legitimate social order: *anarchistes* and *honnêtes gens.*

The epithet "anarchiste" had a longer revolutionary heritage than Thermidorian neologisms such as "terroriste," "vandalisme," "buveur de sang," and "anthropophage," and so gained pride of place following the uprisings of Germinal and Prairial III. The word "anarchiste" carried criminal connotations, being associated with the destruction of community through thievery, pillage, and murder. Its association with *sans-culottisme* gave it broader implications of social marginality based on a refusal of social deference, a rejection of property as essential to social standing, and a disparagement of those with wealth and power.[60] This set of conceptual resonances brought together social and cultural understandings of the basis for order in society. Anarchy was obviously the antithesis of order, and so radical republicans were tarred as the opponents of domestic peace, civic morality, and constitutional government.[61] In the lexicon of political ostracism, "anarchists" were juxtaposed to true republicans committed to defending constitutionalism and the rule of law. As such it gained official status in the oath of "hatred for royalism and anarchy" required by the laws of 19 ventôse IV (9 March 1796) and 19 fructidor V (5 September 1797).

Radical republicans responded to being called anarchists by sarcastically labeling their opponents "honnêtes gens," or "respectable folk." The concept of "honnêteté" went beyond morality to include the social respectability acquired through refined manners and graceful sociability. The underlying assumption was that probity, civility, and self-restraint derived from education and social responsibilities. The mass of people were too close to subsistence living to curtail their struggle for survival through carefully calibrated expressions of politeness and mutual respect. Only several generations of property holding could confer the cultural traits of respectability. In this sense, "honnêtes gens" implied the social snobbery that came from unquestioned economic independence. The essential wrong committed by many of those subjected to litigation in the *ancien régime* was to have lacked civility, been unduly intransigent, or resorted to imbecilic violence when greater subtlety and self-control were expected.[62] Such crude actions came to be widely associated with the behavior of revolutionary radicals. They in turn vehemently repudiated such criticism and responded by mocking its cultural foundations. Appropriating the term "honnêtes gens" for the purpose of derision, therefore, was a repudiation of the social hierarchy and attendant values that dominated society before 1789. It also had the merit of putting in doubt any intrinsic association between property and virtue, especially civic virtue. Self-proclaimed "patriots" defined their own social worth in terms of commitment to revolutionary institutions while casting aspersions on "honnêtes gens" as egotistical and reactionary. Here the epithet of choice connotes opposition to egalitarian ideals of democracy, an opposition based on excluding the mass of Frenchmen from social respectability. In the eyes of self-proclaimed "patriots," "honnêtes gens" threatened the republic by refusing its new value system and insisting on the social and cultural markers of the *ancien régime.* It thereby became a derogatory term and shaded easily into charges of being "counter-revolutionary."

The epithets "anarchists" and "respectable folk" were widely used terms of partisan abuse because they expressed a more profound clash of social and cultural values than notions of either class conflict or political ideology alone connoted. Apart from whatever personal advantages were at stake, a great many of the men who were willing to enter the political fray sincerely believed that their opponents' vision of society threatened either personal freedom or social stability, or both. Such beliefs did not create class solidarity, nor did they amount to a coherent political ideology. Nonetheless, they deeply affected the willingness to use violence either to oppose or impose the new order. This relationship between epithets derived from alternative visions of social order, and the politics of factional rivalry is well conveyed by a primitive placard posted in the village of La Salvetat in the western Hérault in August 1799. This notice and (apparently) three others like it were made by painstakingly burning letters into heavy paper (see figure 2).

This text is a mix of apparent contradictions that all seek to legitimize armed rebellion against republican officials. Despite its phonetic spelling and bad grammar, the placard's block-print format and statement of "four copies" were clearly intended to capture some of the authority of official posters. The author does not mention either Jacobins or royalists, yet his text is saturated with the language of factionalism. Everything is couched in a sententious vocabulary designed to sway third-party opinion. The denunciation of blackguards who desire only blood and pillage, brigands whose families know neither virtue nor religion, is coded language for republican extremists. This is confirmed by the brave assertion: "we do not fear the Terror." All the same, the author implicitly denies being a royalist or counter-revolutionary by saying, "we love the republic whenever respectable citizens are in charge." It is almost ironic to see someone with such rudimentary writing skills advocate rule by "citoyens honnêtes," a phrase associated with education and the social elite. This is clearly a sign that popular opposition was not to the republic per se but to the perceived usurpations of power it permitted. The placard accuses the local ruling faction of calling on "rich egoists" to unite, in other words, of trying to constitute a property-based regime devoid of the community obligations formerly assumed by the local elite. The author compounds the denunciation by adding that these men fail to understand that virtue (civic commitment and respectability) is incompatible with crime (dishonest wealth gained through the purchase of "national properties"). In order to set the social order right, the author announces a credit boycott by the artisans and workers of the village (ironically, the supposed social base of *sans-culottisme,* but here the opponents of the republican faction). This reversal of social stereotypes associated with revolutionary rivalries is offset by charges that local leaders have pursued the wealthy (presumably the former elite) in order to cover their own debts. Furthermore, members of the dominant faction are denounced for favoritism, graft, and violence when imposing the exactions of the republic. Local officials are described as villains and their followers as robbers, smugglers, terrorists, and even animals with a herd mentality. In sum, they are all criminal threats to social order. Therefore, their opponents are justified in responding to threats of terror with arms and a readiness to

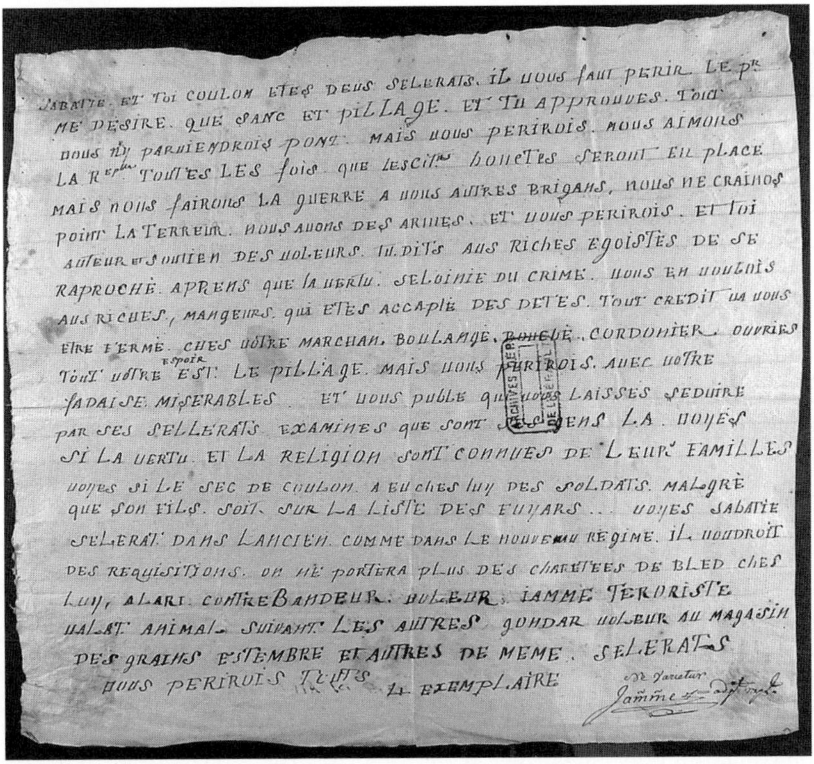

Fig. 2. Handmade placard posted in La Salvetat (Hérault) in August 1799. ADH L 970. (Courtesy of the Archives départementales de l'Hérault)

kill. The author insists that these villains must, shall, and will perish (three references).

Nowhere is there a hint of modern politics. Yet this convoluted and opaque placard captures the essence of local struggles for power and their ubiquitous expression in moral terms. Too often historians simply decode this discourse to find "political" alignments without reflecting on the moral challenges posed by the republic's politics. But we do not need to identify Sabatie, Coulon, Alari, Valat, Gondar, or Estembre, nor do we need to investigate their supposed misdeeds, in order to understand that their legitimacy, and hence the legitimacy of the national cause they chose to support, was cast by ordinary folk in the simple terms of virtue and crime. Thus, the discursive elements of factional conflict at both the national and village level reveal the profound social and cultural conflicts that made the Directory a revolutionary regime and fueled its crisis of legitimacy well after 1795.

The full impact of Catholicism, war, royalism, and Jacobinism on the Directory's crisis of legitimacy was the product of a complex interaction between the inevitable resistance provoked by continuing to push for profound changes in the social, legal, and cultural norms found at the local level and the polarizing political forces at the national level. The Directory's prolonged crisis lay partly in its inability to discern the difference between conflict bred by competition to control the levers of power and pervasive discontent bred by sweeping changes in the institutions and practices that had traditionally given structure and stability to the social order. This is not a facile condemnation of the regime's leaders. These were cruelly difficult matters to separate. The country had little basis for consensus in 1795. The politicians who dominated the Directorial regime were challenged by opponents, on the right and on the left, who strove to control the new institutions of the republic while simultaneously contesting their very nature. For this reason, the syndicate of Thermidorian politicians interpreted any challenge to its rule as a life threat to the republic itself. Equally, Thermidorians tended to interpret ordinary forms of resistance to the exercise of state power, such as reclaiming churches and avoiding conscription, as expressions of royalism and sometimes even as attempts to bring down the regime. This confusion between opposition to the regime's leaders based on rivalry for political power, on one hand, and traditional obstacles to ensconcing republican institutions and values, on the other, encouraged revolutionary responses and an economy of violence.

# 2. The Economy of Violence

> ... the time wherein men live without other security than what their own
> strength and their own invention shall furnish them withall. In such condi-
> tion there is ... worst of all, continual fear.
> —Thomas Hobbes, *Leviathan* (1651)

A VAST INTERPLAY of economic collapse, widespread crime, and political
strife imperiled the Directorial regime from the outset. Each problem was
linked with others. Death due to dearth was the worst it had been since
1709. The helpless begged in aggressive packs, and the hopeless committed
suicide in record numbers. Cities declined in population by 10 percent or
more. The *assignat* experienced such Weimarian inflation that the government had to pay employees' salaries in measures of grain. The grain market,
however, was so disrupted by short harvests, rural hoarding, and wartime
expropriation that grain convoys needed military escorts to protect them
from pillaging.[1] But even soldiers were falling into short supply. By the time
the Directors took office, the army had shrunk 40 percent since its peak a
year earlier. This meant tens of thousands of deserters tromping along bro-
ken-down roads and through hollowed-out woods on their way home. Back
in their villages they found much sympathy for their plight and little for that
of the new government. As official outlaws, deserters provided much of the
manpower for the brigand bands that attacked farmsteads, held up stagecoaches, and assaulted travelers.[2] So prodigious was this criminality that it
later spawned a subgenre of literature. These works reflected a scourge
that stretched across the entire country, from the chouans of Balzac in the
west, to the legendary Schinderhannes in the east, from the *chauffeurs* of
Vidocq in the north, to the *Compagnons de Jéhu* in the south. It is almost
impossible to grasp the extent of social collapse and criminal turpitude
in the mid 1790s—especially since the Directory made no effort to collect

statistical data on crime—but there is no doubt that the regime suffered "France's worst crime wave in modern times."[3] Not since the Fronde had France fallen into such a Hobbesian state of civil disorder.

## Ambiguity and Fear

The near-anarchy of 1795 reflected a profound change in the economy of violence. A society's economy of violence is as important as its class structure or its political organization. Just as the various processes of acquiring and exchanging material goods are basic to the quiddity of any society, the forms and frequency of violence, its place in definitions of honor or justice, its acceptance in politics or private life, are all fundamental to a society's nature. However, the inherently moral aspects of violence make it difficult to delimit for any period, and the destabilizing effects of revolution exponentially multiply the problem. As a result, the economy of violence in the early Directory was highly confused and highly confusing. By infusing elite rivalries and deeper social struggles with modern political ideology, the revolutionary cataclysm altered both the form and meaning of various types of violence. It is the task of historians to find patterns and reveal structures, and yet this often tears off the integument of ambiguity that confronted contemporaries. Persons closest to the context of violence best understood its meaning, whereas any physical or temporal distance from individual acts of violence quickly increased their ambiguity.

The difficulty of interpreting violence (both for contemporaries and historians) was further exacerbated by the conventions of officialdom. Not only were officials trapped in the wooden language of factionalism, but they tended to take violence out of its larger social context, thereby eliminating important cultural signifiers. It is striking that none of the thousands of contemporary descriptions of violent acts read during research for this project—whether administrative reports, personal memoirs, trial records, criminal interrogations, or witness depositions—describes weeping. Shock, horror, revulsion, fright, panic, trauma, terror—all these were commonly described responses to violence. But the tears and sobs of victims, witnesses, friends, and relatives go unmentioned. For some reason, official discourse dissociated acts of violence from expressions of grief.[4] Furthermore, standardized political rhetoric worked to simplify and obscure the polysemy inherent in many acts of violence. The discursive aspects of revolution and counter-revolution provided a convenient, ideologically elevated language for the expression of personal or religious hatreds, clan or communal rivalries, and economic or class conflicts. What is missing, of course, is how revolutionary struggle both exacerbated and disguised these other sources of violence.

We are not dependent on official discourse alone, however. Popular violence generates its own discourse through the forms it takes. Early in the Revolution, the brutal and spectacular nature of crowd violence, in which the victims' heads were severed, corpses dismembered, and body parts mounted on pikes for public display, mimicked the *ancien régime*'s brutal methods of execution—breaking on the wheel, display of body parts on *patibulaires,* etcetera—and thereby gave the violence its meaning as popular justice. Both the limited targets and traditional forms of this violence suggest righteous behavior committed on behalf of the people in order to punish those who had perpetrated injustices against it. It has been claimed that the massacres of September 1792 also mimicked official justice, in this case through the formation of impromptu tribunals that "acquitted" some prisoners; even the discreteness of the killing—behind prison walls and without public display of body parts—acted out the novel, and more modern, way in which the law as an expression of popular sovereignty served to constitute society and deal with antisociety at the same time. The difficulty of accepting this interpretation is that a lot of those killed were neither counter-revolutionaries nor serious criminals—many were nuns and pickpockets. In such a case, imitating the forms of justice may have been an attempt to secure legitimacy for killing in defense of the Revolution, but it was widely understood as nothing more than a mask for criminal slaughter. The problem for observers, therefore, was whether to accept or reject the legitimating discourse propagated by the perpetrators through the forms of violence itself.

Matters deteriorated further after Thermidor. The prison massacres of 1795 involved neither impromptu tribunals nor public rituals. That is, the perpetrators made no attempt to legitimize their actions by mimicking forms of justice. Many of the revenge killings of year III were isolated events, ambushes carried out by murder gangs that superficially resembled traditional youth groups, but whose actions went well beyond mocking, dancing, and "rough music." "Elements of personal vengeance, social rivalry and political struggle mixed with themes of traditional disapproval and community self-regulation" in an attempt to capture the increasing ambiguity of Thermidorian violence. Ritual elements did not disappear: disposing of bodies by throwing them in the Rhône was a frequent practice and

served to purge the community of its human impurities.[5] By the time of
the Directory, popular violence had become so common and served such
diverse purposes that it no longer required the same level of symbolic justification.[6] This development was itself a sign, one indicating the growing
triumph of collective criminality over crowd violence. Acts of violence increasingly shed the patterns and forms that had once constituted a widely
understood discourse of legitimacy.

Thus, the economy of violence after 1795 had a distinctive feature: violence had become less ritualized and more individualistic than it had been
before 1789. The Revolution dismantled social structures and effected rapid
changes in values and systems of representation. These ran the gamut from
the self as citizen to France as nation. In the process, the Revolution not
only destroyed the institutional constraints on popular violence, it eroded
many of the cultural ones as well. This included the diminished role of the
clergy in community life, the decline in deference accorded social status,
the disruption in patronage patterns, and the reduced primacy of the local
community. Though murder gangs may have continued to dress up their
killings in the rituals of retribution or to solicit popular support through
public displays, these did not make them accepted extensions of traditional
society.

In broader conceptual terms, what had once been communicative violence had increasingly deteriorated into solipsistic violence. Violence is
more than a use of force; it is a use of force that is morally dubious because
it harms individuals or relationships in society. And yet, even as a morally
tainted use of force, violence can range from being a mode of communication designed to reshape social relations to being an absolute rupture
in social relations. On one hand, violence makes the clearest statement
about acceptable social relations when it has form and consistency, when
perpetrators ensure that it is regularized, ritualistic, or predictable. Under
these conditions, violence becomes a strategic instrument and an object of
management. In other words, it becomes a deliberate means to a known
end. It may challenge and disrupt existing social relations, but it is not fundamentally antisocial. On the other hand, when violence is essentially an
outburst of unregulated passion, a sudden anger unleashed, or a categorical
refusal of the "other," it achieves little more than a unilateral affirmation of
the individual or group. Such an act of violence is essentially solipsistic.
Furthermore, such violence is antisocial, an expression of a world without
rules, unstable and uncertain. These two aspects—violence as a tool for
changing social relations and violence as a solipsistic destruction of social

relations—are not mutually exclusive; they are polar extremes on a single continuum.[7] The shift along this continuum away from communicative violence toward solipsistic violence that took place in the 1790s has yet to be properly mapped.

The sheer incidence of violence during the late 1790s was enough to frighten most people, but the extent to which it was often ambiguous in motive and meaning made matters all the more alarming. Both highly structured "social" or "communicative" violence and seemingly irrational "antisocial" or "solipsistic" violence generate fear. This fear increases in intensity and spreads to other groups when an act of violence is ambiguous and difficult to interpret. Thus, we need to register more than the increase in crime and violence; we need to note its ambiguity. Consider, for example, how popular broadsheets helped to exacerbate the fear of violent crime both through their widespread dissemination and their tendency toward confusion. In figure 3, the lively image at the center of the broadsheet bears little relationship to the events recounted in the lyrics printed around it (two villains as opposed to one; rescue by a gendarme as opposed to being sabered, trampled by a horse, and left to die alone).

Violence that was not easily interpreted aroused yet greater concerns about prolonged social breakdown. Both the prevalence and the multivalence of violence posed a challenge to the Directory. The combination increased doubts about the republic's viability. No matter their initial inspiration or actual form, subsistence riots, smuggling, highway robbery, housebreaking, arson, and murder all became threats to the constitutional republic. They either embodied an overt rejection of the regime, or they highlighted its inability to provide security.

## Subsistence Crisis

The weakening of the traditional constraints on collective, communicative violence in the course of the French Revolution, which made it both more ambiguous and more solipsistic, and hence more threatening, is clearly illustrated by the forms of violence arising out of grain shortages and high prices. The subsistence crisis of 1795–96 inspired thousands of violent incidents across the country. Many of these were traditional food riots in which crowds provoked confrontations with merchants and officials, thereby bringing the collective solidarity of communities to bear on the problem of prices. Such a riot took place at Montpellier on 19–20 pluviôse

IV (7–8 February 1796), when a large crowd from the *faubourg* Boutonnet imposed price fixing and the municipality cut the price of bread almost in half.[8] Still not satisfied, the demonstrators roughed up municipal leaders, invaded the town hall, and forced the assembly to set the price of bread at a derisory 5 *sous* a pound. The agitation continued the following day as people plundered fish stalls, vegetable stands, butcher shops, and bakeries.

Fig. 3. Complainte véritable sur la mort de Perrine Dugué. Handbill (colored woodcut) produced chez Letourmy at Orléans, 1796. (Courtesy of the Département de l'Arsenal, Bibliothèque nationale de France)

Local commanders arrived at the head of national guardsmen, uniformed students from the School of Health, and a battery of cannons. This show of force dispersed the crowd without bloodshed. Later, following instructions from the minister of justice, a handful of "principal agitators" were tried by the Criminal Court and received harsh punishment, while the rest were exonerated as "misled."[9] Incidents like this had been part of the repertoire of violence in times of dearth for generations. Though a riot could easily get out of hand, time-honored rules of the game established its meaning and controlled its trajectory. These helped to contain the riot and provided officials with a standard set of temporary measures that diffused the immediate crisis and limited judicial retribution.[10]

However, many people did not believe that the Montpellier riot was really about the dearness of food staples. The public prosecutor emphasized that the troubles had been launched in the name of "patriots," which he considered a mask for *sans-culottes*. He also charged the leaders with being part of a "plot intended to trouble the state with civil war by arming citizens against one another and against the exercise of legitimate authority, calls to sedition, provocations to pillage property, acts of violence against persons, revolt against legal authorities and seditious assembly, both armed and unarmed." Though couched in the phrasing of the criminal code, this strongly suggested that the popular quarter had been stirred to riot by political extremists interested more in orchestrating an overthrow of the conservative authorities of Montpellier than in the price of bread. Propagating the idea of such machinations made the riot more ambiguous than it initially appeared. Was it the result of working-class desperation or the return of the "henchmen of terror"? Such questions only heightened public fears, especially after the *sans-culottes* uprisings of Germinal and Prairial in Paris the previous spring.

The subsistence crisis of 1795–96 also led to hundreds of incidents that deviated from the time-honored script for food riots. This eroded any larger social message they may have communicated and gave them the appearance of increasingly solipsistic, antisocial violence. Rather than mobilizing large crowds in marketplace settings or along main arteries of supply, townsfolk began to gather in small groups to make sorties into the countryside. These forays were significantly less organized than the regional incidents of "taxation populaire" that took place in the autumn of 1792. The earlier events generally began with the forced setting of prices in town before proceeding to the countryside. Furthermore, participants distinguished themselves with some sort of rallying symbol, such as a twig in the hat, and were accompanied into the countryside by national guards-men flying a flag or beating a drum.[11] Unlike traditional food riots or even the excursions of 1792, the events of 1795–96 were more clandestine, more predominantly male, and more likely to involve the use of deadly weapons: most of the participants carried muskets, pistols, swords, or pikes. These armed groups raided isolated farms and plundered wagons caught alone on the road. This breakdown of popular protest into a host of sporadic attacks made it harder to distinguish from simple criminal assault, especially when carried out at night. Though such incidents were not unprecedented,[12] their predominance in year IV marked a deviation from the collective action that characterized most popular violence. Leaving so many *assignats* for each *boisseau* of stolen grain may have preserved some of the "moral economy" associated with "taxation populaire," but everyone knew the *assignats* were worthless, especially those *à face royale*, which made this common gesture merely an insult to the republic. Furthermore, the focus on isolated farm-ers and individual wagon drivers, rather than market stalls and municipal officials, removed the possibility of receiving moral legitimation from an approving crowd. That the Thermidorians had replaced the *sans-culottes'* discourse on subsistence with the language of a free market also challenged the justification for such violence on moral grounds. Merchants and farm-ers who might have been hauled before the courts as "speculators" and "hoarders" in 1793–94 were now treated as "respectable folk" victimized by "bands of brigands."[13] Finally, differences of opinion on how to punish these crimes highlighted their ambiguity. The president of the Criminal Court of the Sarthe tended to view them as acts of desperation provoked by the refusal of producers to bring grain to town markets or sell it at an afford-able price.[14] On the other hand, Minister of Justice Merlin de Douai wanted the law applied in all its rigor as the best means to protect property hold-ers. Similar differences of opinion among jurors led to schizophrenic ver-dicts. Most people charged with forcibly obtaining grain at a "vil prix" were acquitted on the grounds of intention; nonetheless, a carpenter received twenty-four years in irons.[15] Perhaps it was his participation in several in-cidents, or the level of "mistreatment" he dealt out, that made the differ-ence. No matter: when townsfolk made clandestine raids into the country-side to obtain grain, whether their actions were morally justified mattered less than the fear they generated. Such actions inevitably made it harder to supply towns, the preeminent locus of republicanism, and threatened a complete breakdown in town-country relations. This in turn threatened the viability of the regime.

Thus the fear and uncertainty spawned by the sheer proliferation of violence in the mid-1790s was compounded by its multiple motives and ambiguous meaning. Moreover, the shift from communicative violence, with its discourse expressed in crowd action, to solipsistic violence, with its furtiveness and lack of disguise, indicated a severe weakening of traditional restraints on violence, and the correspondingly greater burden placed on republican officials to combat crime.

## Brigandage

Even the most cursory treatment of the economy of violence in the 1790s requires addressing the problem of brigandage. No form of violence better reflects the decomposition of society and the ongoing revolutionary struggle over defining its recomposition. Brigandage was a cancer, an ill-defined malignancy, universally feared, hard to treat, and often fatal. Here too the fear and uncertainty spawned by the sheer proliferation of violence was compounded by multiple motives and ambiguous meaning. Eighteenth-century society, especially in those regions that remained marginal to the market and the state, suffered from an endemic petty banditry that swelled at times of dearth or war. This was a banditry of vagabonds and the deracinated, of seasonal laborers and the wandering poor, a barely organized activity characterized by constant thievery, occasional marauding, and incidental extortion, usually based on threats of a late-night fire or a poisoned well. Another, more organized form also existed, one that was familiar to the *ancien régime* but that reached an unprecedented level under the late republic. This was an opportunistic banditry. It took advantage of collapsed structures of authority to establish, with gun in hand and loot in mind, the power of violence over the more prosperous around them. In addition to these traditional forms, there arose structured forms of social and political resistance, often spearheaded by local leaders who organized bands of deserters and counter-revolutionaries into secret militias. It was inevitable that traditional banditry would mix with popular resistance and organized counter-revolution to blur the boundaries of both ordinary crime and righteous rebellion. As far as the republic was concerned, however, it was all politically dangerous, either deliberately or incidentally.

Although brigandage meant robbery by an armed band, contemporaries used the term to cover a gamut of radically different events. Two examples from among the thousands available illustrate how brigandage could range from opportunistic robberies to paramilitary assaults. First, pure crime. On the evening of 6 messidor IV (24 June 1796), just outside the gates of Montpellier on the road to Toulouse, four armed men successively attacked and robbed a farm laborer returning home from the fields, a basket peddler on his way back from Balaru, another farm laborer, two merchants coming from Perpignan, a shoemaker with his ten-year-old son, and a cloth cutter from Montpellier. The total amount stolen came to almost 3,000 livres, mostly in specie—a sizable sum for two hours' work. Though none of these people was seriously injured, they had all been traumatized by having a pistol shoved in their faces.[16] The use of firearms, the proximity to the city, the range of victims, and the failure to identify or catch the bandits gave anyone traveling to or from Montpellier good reason to be afraid. That this was not an isolated case, either for this location or for the region, further justified their fears.[17] This purely criminal brigandage—the classic masked-face, two-pistols-in-the-belt, "Your-purse-or-your-life!" highway robbery—thrived in the social and administrative chaos of the mid-1790s. The perpetrators were antisocial bandits whose solipsistic violence threatened anyone and everyone.

Second, pure politics. Avowedly political banditry also thrived in these conditions. *Chouannerie* is the most famous form, though, as we shall see later, it too had its ambiguities. In extremis, political brigandage took the form of military-style incursions launched by counter-revolutionary activists against southern or western towns. In the south, these went back to 1792 and continued sporadically through to 1802. They took place anywhere from the Basses-Alpes to the Aveyron but were most common in the former Vivarais and Comtat Venaissin. One such attack occurred at Barjac in the northern Gard on 28 germinal IV (17 April 1796). Here at least two hundred men led by a typically motley group of notables—in this case, the inveterate conspirator Dominique Allier, his sadistic lieutenant Guillaume Fontanieu (alias *Jambe-de-bois*, or Peg-Leg), the brigand-priest Béranger, and the barrister Jacques Perrochon—stormed the bourg, overwhelmed and disarmed the garrison of eighty soldiers, and, in order to terrorize republicans throughout the region, shot to death its captain and lieutenant. Now unopposed, the bandits seized the town coffers, looted a number of houses, and took various officials prisoner. The large band then headed into the Ardèche loaded down with booty, service muskets, and a cannon. Along the way, they cut down liberty trees and broke into patriots' houses. When the band tried to enter Bannes, however, a detachment of troops from nearby Les Vans, with the surprising support of local national guardsmen, drove them back and even captured a dozen bandits in the process. In their panic, the rebels abandoned their provisions, their prisoners, and the cannon. Even though much was stolen, everything about this attack points to counter-revolution. Barjac was seized in the name of Louis XVIII. The men wore white cockades, and the leaders sported white belts and white plumes, clear signs that they belonged to the Catholic and royalist "companies" organized across the Midi.[18] The ranks were filled mostly by deserters and marginals recruited with the help of British funds. They acted as the shock troops of an émigré-directed conspiracy to bring down the Directory and restore the Bourbon monarchy. The incident at Barjac was planned as a show of force and as a means to procure cash and weapons for "the cause." It has often been assumed that such attacks were armed expressions of traditionalism that drew their strength from deep-seated Catholic and royalist antipathies to the secular republic.[19] Certainly the leaders believed they were engaged in a form of communicative violence, fighting for a just and proper social order. However, the fact that the citizens of Les Vans and Bannes, ordinarily hostile to the republic, actually helped to repulse the band speaks eloquently of how unsympathetic these violent extremists really were. Royalism of this sort won few converts. Rather, it was a form of intimidation designed to be every bit as frightful as the republic's own use of armed force.

If brigands were isolated highwaymen as well as royalist paramilitaries, they were also everything in between. Obviously, brigandage covered a confusing variety of incidents that were neither clearly organized crime nor plainly violent counter-revolution. It has rarely been noted, however, that this imbrication of criminal and political forms of brigandage greatly increased fears about all forms of organized crime. These heightened fears arose from the matrix of official perceptions as well as the matter of criminal practices. The relationship between these perceptions and practices hinged on the elements of ambiguity that characterized many acts of brigandage. Such ambiguities served to reify certain interpretative frameworks. Two of these are of special importance. On the criminal side, officials labored under a "banditry psychosis." On the political side, they suffered from a "plot mentality." These mental proclivities are understandable given the prevailing economy of violence, but they actually made the situation worse by heightening public anxieties about rampant brigandage throughout the country.

Officials afflicted with "banditry psychosis" tended to make dubious connections between different crimes and attribute them all to a single criminal organization. Supposed connections could be based on any number of factors, such as form, regional density, or proximity in time. Thus, jury directors or public prosecutors would attribute several break-ins that occurred within the same vicinity over several months or even years to a single band. This happened even when the crimes took place under substantially different conditions each time. Where a band did exist and some of its members were arrested, officials frequently added other unsolved crimes in the area to the list of charges. Many of these crimes had nothing in common. The "banditry psychosis" also led officials to lump together individuals who had little, if anything, to do with one another. The official image of a brigand band was that of a slightly inchoate group, "a criminal nebula, where numerous occasional delinquents gravitated around a few especially intrepid malefactors."[20] With this image in mind, officials would inflate an already dangerous band into a virtual army of villains. The most famous example is the "bande d'Orgères." This was a sordid amalgam of 118 men and women, more than a quarter of whom died in prison before their trial by the Criminal Court of the Eure. The eighty individuals who did appear in court were charged with a total of ninety-three crimes, including seventy-five murders. Officials considered this only part of the band: "It must rise to four or five hundred," stated the indictment. That "they had their own signs of recognition and spoke a language of their own" was proof, according to the prosecutor, of a tightly knit criminal organization. However, the trial itself revealed only a very loose agglomeration of criminals with a variety of different leaders. The "bande d'Orgères," the most infamous band of the entire period, was, in fact, more a congeries of criminals thrown together in prison than an organized crime network.[21]

In addition to leading officials to link disparate crimes and assorted individuals with certain bands, the "banditry psychosis" fostered suspicions about grander criminal networks operating across a whole province and beyond. Professional criminals could be extraordinarily mobile, it is true. Richard Cobb has written evocatively of the "route du Nord" connecting Paris to the banditry around Lille, Tournai, and Brussels. Though he finds Dinah Jacob's account, the basis of the official version of the so-called "bande juive" and its extensive operations, too appealing to reject completely, he rightly remains skeptical. His own evidence makes it clear that this was likely five separate groups operating in close proximity and often willing to travel some distance to fence their stolen goods more safely.[22] In western France, the use of criminal slang, like the use of Yiddish in the northeast, certainly led police officials to suspect a vast clandestine

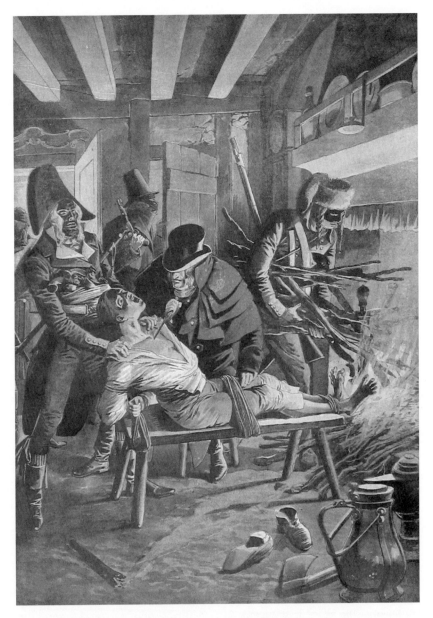

Fig. 4. The brutality of "chauffeurs" in the 1790s, epitomized here by the infamous "bandits of Orgères," remained notorious in the twentieth century. *Supplément illustré du Petit Journal,* no. 939, 5 November 1908. (Author's collection)

criminal organization. This was at the heart of the "bande noire," a sprawling criminal network imagined by the Ministry of Police with the help of two important prison informants, as was so often the case.

It all began with the revelations of Jacques Descantes after he had been condemned to death by the Criminal Court of the Dordogne on 18 brumaire V (8 November 1796).[23] Convinced that his life would be spared if he provided plenty of information about criminal activity, Descantes began by solving a brutal murder he had learned about while in prison at Limoges. As he told it, the crime had been committed by fourteen men, all well-dressed, riding horses, and sporting pocket watches, pistols, and sabers. The leaders were a young innkeeper named Gallifer from Châtellerault (Indre-et-Loire), who had personally crushed the victim's skull with a club, and Luçon, an even younger calico merchant from Saumur. Their accomplices, all named, came from scattered western towns—Tours, Saumur, Angoulème, Périgueux, Rochefort—places visited regularly by "Le Grand Blondin," a dapper Gascon who rode a "fine steed." Descantes told the police "that the watchword between them is to refer to the innkeepers and tavernowners who lodged them as 'gens francs'; . . . that Dallifer [*sic*] and Luçon are the ones who determine the meeting places and write the notices; that in every commune where they meet, they have correspondents who provide the information needed to commit a crime, and that they call that 'distributing the work.'" Descantes embellished his tale over the course of four interviews. The number of crimes multiplied, the list of accomplices grew longer, and the range of activities grew wider: "a large number of these villains came down from Lyon and its environs and settled at Bordeaux and its environs," such as at La Rochelle, Bergerac, and Coutras, he explained. A few weeks went by, and more revelations came out. Soon the minister of police was sending letters to officials throughout the southeast, in the Gard, the Rhône, the Basses-Alpes, the Vaucluse, the Bouches-du-Rhône, etc. When the minister of justice refused to commute Descantes' sentence, he escaped from prison, undoubtedly thanks to the government commissioner of the Dordogne whose sympathy he had won. By then the "bande noire" had been born. At the least, it covered a half-dozen departments in the west; at the most, it was a gigantic organization that extended from the Loire valley to Bordeaux and from there across the entire south to Lyon and Marseille. Here was "banditry psychosis" at its most inflated.

The only reality behind the "bande noire" was a common criminal slang. This was revealed a few months later by another informant, André Pillet, a stonecutter from Tours. It was after being sentenced to death by the

Criminal Court of the Sarthe for a murderous *chauffage* near Tours that he became a prison informant, having been led to believe, like Descantes before him, that his loose tongue would preserve his short neck. Pillet's importance lay in his knowledge of the "argo outré" and "signes particuliers" used by criminals in the Touraine. (On the most basic level, they referred to each other as "garçon," "bon garçon", "franc garçon," and "garçon distingué" in a kind of hierarchy of villainy.) Using this metonymic passport to the criminal underworld, where he had his own enviable record, Pillet revealed the names of thirty-four murderers and robbers and linked individuals among them to a half-dozen of the most brutal attacks in the region. The names included Gallifer ("a bit hunchbacked, branded and probably living on the rue St. Séverin in Paris") and Tailleur ("dit Le Grand Blond . . . se-disant marchand"), both at the heart of the supposed "bande noire." The Ministry of Police made the connection.[24] The principal problem, however, was that Pillet named a different group of perpetrators for almost every crime. Any overlap seems to have been an accident of temporary cooperation, not of any organizational structure. In fact, the infamous "bande noire" of the police's imagination was nothing more or less than the tenuous acquaintance between any number of thieves, murderers, cutthroats, cutpurses, highwaymen, fences, lookouts, and front men who operated in small groups of dynamic composition. Pillet's promise to reveal the names of four hundred criminals and his boast that three hours in a "tapie" (slang for tavern) in any urban center from Blois to Angers would be sufficient for him to penetrate the local underworld make it clear that a shared argot and a common criminal ethos were all there was to the "bande noire." It was frightening enough that Pillet was one of ten men responsible for burning a farmer's feet so badly that months later he still had to be carried into the courtroom to testify.[25] To think that this and dozens of similar atrocities could be traced back to a single criminal organization, even one with a strictly regional scope, could only have induced cold panic in the good citizens and property holders of the region. Brigand bands did exist; in fact, they proliferated. This provided the basis for "banditry psychosis" by establishing its proverbial kernel of truth. However, while the brigands of the late 1790s may have been as cruel and predatory as Visigoths, they did not form hordes or maintain national networks.

Just as local officials tended to invest coincidental connections between small criminal bands with exaggerated significance, the Directory presented the proliferation of bandits as a vast conspiracy deliberately constructed to destroy society. It would be hard to find a more complete statement of the "banditry psychosis" than a message the Directory sent to the Council of Five Hundred on 11 frimaire V (1 December 1796). It focused on robbers who "spread across various departments and desolate town and country."

> These are not isolated malefactors armed against the peaceful citizen by an instinct for crime or a thirst for pillage: these are brigands gathered in bands, organized under leaders, marching according to instructions, forming, in fact, in the midst of society a sort of confederation armed to destroy it piecemeal. Sometimes they penetrate private homes, seizing those who live there and subjecting them to all the forms of violence that the most refined ferocity can invent in order to force them to turn over what is most precious to them; sometimes they take to the roads, attack public carriages and mail coaches, rob them and present travelers with scenes of horror which make them fear even the shortest trips. We cannot pretend that these disasters have the characteristics of ordinary brigandage; for a long time, the enemies, not exactly of French liberty, but of France, have felt that their last resource is this wellspring of crimes which they feed in the heart of the republic.[26]

As this last line suggests, the Directory not only portrayed small groups of robbers as part of a great confederation bent on destroying society but once again blamed Anglo-royalism as the ultimate culprit.[27] Though it is tempting to dismiss this as mere propaganda, it seems to have worked rather well. Local officials were quick to take any signs of royalism brigands may have manifested as evidence that they were part of a coordinated effort to overthrow the republic.

In fact, criminal banditry did often take on a political flavor, even if it was not overtly royalist. Rapine and revenge bore no inherent contradiction, and republican officials, especially those who had served during the Terror, became prime targets. The attack on Citizen Monduteguy and his family at Ustarits (Basses-Pyrénées) in October 1796 is a case in point. Here was a typical *chauffage,* including beatings, roasting of feet, murder of the paterfamilias, and extensive theft. These heinous acts followed a long string of robberies and assaults in the canton over the previous year, but it was this attack in particular that spurred magistrates to act. The prosecutor indicted a total of forty-four individuals and charged them with thirty separate crimes. Monduteguy, a former justice of the peace, was an infamous local terrorist. He had sent seven people to the guillotine during his brief presidency of the *Commission extraordinaire* at Bayonne in year II. He also took the lead in carrying out the orders of representatives on mission to exile or imprison all Basques in the area, a notorious precursor to ethnic cleansing. It is not surprising, therefore, that twelve of those indicted as band members were Basques *miquelets* away from their units.[28] Rather prosaic banditry had turned political, and the authorities took note. It confirmed their suspicions and inspired their actions.

This mix of banditry and counterterror was especially prevalent in Provence, where it blurred into paid assassination. Here rather than robbing or looting their victims, local murder gangs received their rewards from men of substance who wished to remain in the background—Richard Cobb suggests a reception at the local chateau replete with cash, drink, and sex with the servants.[29] Donald Sutherland needs no imagination, just diligent research, to connect the murderous "bande d'Aubagne" in the Bouches-du-Rhône to a set of discrete patrons among the town's traditional elite.[30] But killing could also result from internal band rivalries or as revenge for double-dealing. This is Gwynne Lewis's explanation for why twelve members of the Malbos family all had their throats slashed on their farmstead at Laudun (Gard) in brumaire V.[31] Colin Lucas has also parsed the finer points of political murder in Provence. Though killers frequently knew their victims personally—"'Je viens de venger la mort de mon père' was the commonest of all counter-jacobin phrases after a murder, much more so than 'Vive le roi'"[32]—such relationships were rarely known beyond the locality. Though each of these historians has done impressive work in discerning the motives and mechanisms behind such collective violence, such work risks eliding the opacity of this violence to anyone not in immediate proximity to it. How could outsiders tell what the motives were? When was an attack on a purchaser of national property politically motivated and when was it simply intelligent banditry? Contrary to some accounts, royalist motives cannot be inferred from the victim's status as a purchaser of national property.[33] It simply made sense to pick someone who had plenty to steal, someone resented by his neighbors for being more prosperous or more courageous when property was put up for auction. Rivalry and resentment could ensure a free hand during the robbery and a tendency to keep quiet later. And yet, if republicans believed that bandits singled out purchasers of national property because this was a sign of "patriotism," and they usually did, then such attacks became politicized by perception, if not by original motive.

As with "banditry psychosis," official fears that brigandage was part of a larger royalist conspiracy had some basis in fact; there was, after all, a real royalist conspiracy to destroy the republic from the inside, and it did involve recruiting royalist "companies." This made it harder to tell the difference between brigands who wore the mask of royalism for tactical reasons and those who had a larger strategic purpose in mind. Furthermore, local officials had little incentive to discern the difference. Throughout the Revolution, the "plot mentality" had provided effective justification for using harsh measures against opponents. And yet, royalist brigandage was far more a matter of combining atavistic criminality with antirepublican sentiment than it was of any coordinated campaign to destroy the Directory.

Despite the delusional elements at work in both the "banditry psychosis" and the "plot mentality," it is important to reiterate that, even if they were not linked to grander criminal organizations or offshoots of a great royalist conspiracy, the sheer proliferation of brigand bands directly challenged the viability of the regime. Neither the king's highways nor remote rural areas had been very safe in the eighteenth century, and yet bands of robbers had never really threatened the social order. Under the late republic, however, the sheer frequency and manifold sources of brigandage together made it a grave challenge to the regime's political credibility in the most basic terms. Brigandage under the republic was not primarily a matter of spectacular criminality or even "social banditry," as it had been under the *ancien régime,* when the salt smuggler Mandrin and the robber Cartouche became brigand archetypes as well as popular heroes. The brigand bands that burst forth in the chaos of 1795 offered a more profound challenge precisely because they combined crime and politics, social resistance and counter-revolution.[34] This mélange of motives made it ambiguous violence of the most fearsome sort. Viewed from this perspective, officials' fears about the nature and scope of bandit activity make greater sense.

Brigandage took on an especially threatening demeanor because it challenged the regime's ability to ensure public order within the framework of its new liberal institutions. The Directory openly acknowledged this central aspect of the problem. It minced no words in its message to lawmakers on 13 frimaire VI (3 December 1797), "this bloody anarchy . . . will discredit the republic, will heap opprobrium on its government, will emphasize the weakness of its laws, and will lead the French people to counter-revolutionary regrets and odious comparisons."[35] The proposed solution, of course, was harsher laws and a greater use of force to restore order in the fledgling republic. However, years of revolutionary upheaval had created an indeterminate legitimacy for any and all uses of force and violence for political ends. The mutation of communicative violence into solipsistic violence and the imbrication of crime and counter-revolution increased multivalence and ambiguity. Furthermore, the dubious justifications and competing social visions that accompanied so much of the violence made matters all the more alarming. Thus, any form of violence could generate fear in the populace due to the competing and contested sources of legitimacy working to justify it. This included using force to uphold the law or ensconce the republic. Circumstances such as these often made legality of dubious utility in defining acceptable uses of force.

# 3 Criminal Courts and Concepts of Order

Without the love of laws, no more order, no more government, no more society. What is needed to end the Revolution and allow us finally to enjoy the happiness that the conquest of liberty should provide? Few laws, but good ones, clear, precise and above all well executed: no compromise on this last item.
—*Journal de Toulouse*, 18 vendémiaire V (9 October 1796)

IN ORDER TO understand the role of the courts in confronting the Directory's problem of order, we need to distinguish, as best we can, the cultural obstacles to maintaining law and order using a fledgling judicial system from the instability caused by national political issues. This cultural dimension to the republic's problem of order resulted from two overlapping, but clearly distinct concepts of order, one based on the community and inclined to accept idiosyncratic accommodations between authorities and transgressive subjects, and one based on the state and insistent that subjects conform to legally defined codes of conduct.[1] The extent to which authority was contested openly, even violently, or simply mined and sapped by obstructionism and foot-dragging, depended on its combination of accepted legitimacy and coercive power. By the autumn of 1795, republican institutions had precious little of either. Traditional values and local autonomies reasserted themselves in a renewed clash of cultures at the village level.

## Justice from Organic Society to Revolution

Changes in the judicial system lay at the very heart of the revolutionary project. The Declaration of the Rights of Man and Citizen promised Frenchmen equality before the law as well as protection from arbitrary arrest and unnecessary detention. The early revolutionaries sought to balance individual rights with defense of the polity. Both individual liberty and public security required a powerful state based on the rule of law.[2] The paradox of increasing both individual rights and state power defined the new concept of order. It also constituted a massive assault on the organic society of the *ancien régime.*

Before 1789, order had generally been maintained by largely autonomous communities that called upon the state's machinery of repression only when their own methods had manifestly failed. Order as conceived in the context of the direct and daily interactions between villagers was largely an absence of disruptive conflict rather than an aspiration toward a preconceived standard of disciplined behavior. The essence of maintaining order lay less in enforcing impersonal regulations than in restraining conflict among individuals well known in their community context. In the organic society of eighteenth-century France, therefore, stability and public tranquility depended on a wide variety of institutions that were not extensions of the monarchical state: family, parish, corporation, seigneurie, and religion all exercised social discipline. These enduring sources of nonstate authority made public order inherently paradoxical; simply breaking the law, even violently, did not constitute a breach of public order unless it seriously threatened the village or openly challenged royal authority. The royal courts served more to protect communities from external threats than to suppress internal conflict. Thus, the ability of village communities to regulate themselves was crucial to village cohesiveness and fostered a general mistrust of external authority.[3]

The concept of order embedded in the enduring social structures and attitudes of village communities differed significantly from the concept of order developed during the Revolution. The deputies elected to different revolutionary assemblies, an overwhelming number of them legal practitioners, made a fetish of the law. They gave birth to the liberal fallacy that the law, by starting with a constitution and filling in the gaps, could create a set of institutional arrangements that would liberate individuals to satisfy all of their needs. The National Assembly considered the justice system of the *ancien régime* arbitrary, capricious, and cruel mainly because it had been designed to preserve a social hierarchy based on legal privileges. The lawmakers' alternative, therefore, was a cult of equality and consistency. This meant establishing mandatory sentencing for all felonies. Penalties were chosen to fit the crime; for better and for worse, they could not be tailored to fit the criminal. This contrasted sharply with practices in England at the time, where flexibility in sentencing was reaching its apogee.[4]

The Penal Code of 1791 replaced a variety of penalties, such as banishment, mutilation, branding, whipping, and the stocks, with simple imprisonment or hard labor. The former punishments had always been associated with elaborate shaming rituals carried out in cooperation with village communities; eliminating them saw the work of disciplining offenders pass increasingly from the hands of the populace to those of the state. The revolutionary reforms also removed affiliations between the judicial establishment and the Catholic Church. After 1790, the legal system was no longer imbued with the spiritual value that had turned afflictive punishments into a theater of expiation. Moreover, priests were no longer called upon to read *monitoires* threatening excommunication for anyone who had vital knowledge about a crime but refused to inform the authorities. Finally, the requirement of making an abject apology to God, king, and justice was also eliminated because convicted criminals were no longer treated as sinners. Eliminating both the communal and religious elements from the punishment of crime shifted enormous responsibility to the state's wholly secular judicial apparatus.

This transfer was further enhanced by the separation of criminal punishment from compensatory damages paid to the victim or the victim's family. The prerevolutionary linkages between private judicial initiative, royal prosecution, and personal damage awards gave the former system of criminal justice a pronounced retributive character. When the reforms of 1790 separated criminal and civil justice and transferred all of the costs of prosecution to the state, they not only stripped out most of the retributive elements from the prosecution of crime, they also removed the systemic features that discouraged individuals from turning to royal courts. After 1790, once the victim had reported a crime, it was prosecuted on its merits as a threat to society, not on the basis of the victim's zeal or his purse. Henceforth, the state's standardized and inflexible concept of order was supposed to prevail. The inevitable consequence was an erosion of the mechanisms of internal equilibrium that had sustained communities for generations.

At the same time as revolutionaries imposed a concept of order that contrasted starkly with the organic society of rural France, they adopted laws that struck directly at the institutions that gave rural communities their moral unity. True, the notion of community never actually fit the reality of community. Any agglomeration of peasants, artisans, and larger landholders was bound to be riven by conflicts of authority, family rivalries, and personal hatreds. Whatever the pressures generated by village sociability, they were never strong enough to generate complete consensus.[5] Church, crown, and seigneurie exercised authority by involving peasants in the process of their own domination. And there were always some members of the village ready to reap advantage from cooperating with such authority. Equally, there were always others who profited from invoking the notion of community to challenge rivals as intruders or oppressors. The Revolution cast all of these contests into a new light. The multistage destruction of seigneurialism that began on the night of 4 August 1789, the frontal assault on the Catholic Church embodied in the Civil Constitution of the Clergy of 1790, and the declaration of the "patrie en danger" in 1792 with the massive mobilization that followed utterly recast the tensions between the notion of community and the reality of conflict. Resistance to the Revolution in defense of the community served to infuse this notion with greater meaning. Donald Sutherland has argued that the truly popular movement was counter-revolutionary. But what was counter-revolution? If its royalist elements are set aside and it is treated as a popular movement, then counter-revolution was fundamentally a violent defense of the *idea* of a self-regulating community and thus an idealized version of the prerevolutionary reality.[6] In this sense, the community as an idea and its power to legitimize action was strengthened, at least in the short term, by the revolutionary process.

The ravages of revolution meant that the Directory confronted rural communities that were in important ways both stronger and more autarkic than before. Peter Jones has described a "revalorisation of the 'village'" in the late *ancien régime* but dates an even more profound shift to the Convention's decision in 1793 to replace the traditional term "community of inhabitants" with the more egalitarian "commune." The administrative chaos of the ensuing years, especially after the Terror, helped to make this rhetorical shift a social reality.[7] The elections of 1795 confirmed the trend. The Thermidorian perpetuals whose years in the Convention imbued them with the state-based rule of law were deeply at odds with the mass of officials elected to staff departments, courts, and cantons. The notables elected in the provinces had a natural impulse to reassert local independence. Constitutional efforts to minimize this dichotomy proved clumsy at best. The cantons instituted as part of the Directorial regime were designed to overcome the autonomy of individual villages by grouping six to twelve communes into a single administrative unit. These rural cantons proved extremely difficult to establish and operate. They did not correspond to social realities, engulfing rival communities as they did, and were overwhelmingly burdened with executing state mandates such as requisitions or tax collection rather than providing services. Thus, the new "municipal administrations" proved both too intrusive and not sufficiently representative to acquire popular support or local legitimacy.[8] This made it all the harder to develop a modus vivendi, however precarious, between a republican rule of law and local customary practice. Reports on the state of the country in early 1796 were unrelentingly negative about "public opinion," a euphemism for commitment to the republic.[9] Therefore, one of the greatest difficulties facing the Directory was the even greater gulf the Revolution had opened between the two concepts of order.

## Criminal Justice under the Directory

The difficulties inherent in installing a new legal system and instilling a new concept of order are easily obscured by the sheer chaos facing the Directory in the winter of 1795–96. This would seem to make the mechanics of justice a rather minor matter. And yet, these problems could not be redressed without effective law enforcement. The structure of the courts and the magistrates who manned them would prove crucial to the character and longevity of the new regime.

There is much to be admired in the judicial system of 1795. The Constitution of Year III did not change the principles introduced early in the Revolution and made only modest changes to judicial institutions. The basic structure for dealing with delicts remained in place. Justices of the peace and their assistants, as well as urban police commissioners, rural municipal officers, and their deputies, continued to deal with infractions punishable by a maximum of three days in jail or three days' wages. These were not deemed "offenses against public order." A handful of district-level correctional courts handled misdemeanors (*délits correctionnels*) punishable by up to two years in prison. A single departmental criminal court dealt with felony cases (*délits criminels*) as well as appeals from the correctional courts. At the national level, the Court of Cassation served as an appeals court for procedural issues only; in contrast to many "supreme courts," it did not deal with the substance of cases. The simple hierarchy, national uniformity, and clearly demarcated jurisdictions of the new courts could hardly have contrasted more sharply with the former system, a hodgepodge of overlapping jurisdictions extending from the patchwork of seigneurial justice to the differential privileges of provincial parlements. The republican system of justice epitomized the new concept of order, one based on a uniform code of conduct brought close enough to ordinary people to shape their social interactions.

This study focuses on serious threats to public order and therefore will largely ignore judicial mechanisms used to repress petty offenses. However, controlling minor infractions—graffiti and jaywalking in the modern city, sheep grazing along paths in the revolutionary countryside—tends to reduce the number of major crimes, and so it is worth glancing at justices of the peace. JPs stood at the very nexus of competing concepts of order. Considered by one historian to be "the National Assembly's most inspired creation,"[10] elected JPs bore a heavy responsibility to keep the peace in their villages and neighborhoods. The duties of JPs fell into three categories. Above all, they handled minor civil disputes not involving property and limited to 100 *livres* in value. This was done with small fees, little paperwork, and no lawyers. In this respect, JPs brought a vast improvement over the spotty, sometimes costly, and often corrupt services provided by seigneurial justice. JPs also served as gatekeepers for civil justice. Parties who felt the need to resolve a dispute in court were obliged first to take it before a JP. Here again lawyers were barred. The revolutionaries' aim was to avoid actual lawsuits by requiring the parties to participate in semiprofessional but nonbinding arbitration. In this sense, the office of JP standardized the common practice of using notaries or clerics to help secure infrajudicial settlements. Thus, the JP's role in civil justice was a service provided by the state free of any code to regulate behavior or outcomes. Solutions depended solely on what the parties were willing to accept. Finally, the reforms of early year IV made JPs into police magistrates. In cities and towns, JPs had the assistance of police commissioners, whereas the rural JP remained largely on his own as the main officer of law enforcement for a half-dozen villages or more. Bailiffs, gendarmes, and national guardsmen merely provided coercive force when necessary. All criminal investigations began with the JP. He personally judged petty offenses involving small fines or a few days in jail. His verdict was final. He also exercised considerable de facto discretion in the prosecution of more serious crime.[11] Combining all of these functions in one individual made his personality and his politics crucial in determining the role official justice would play in shaping community relations. By having a role in both civil and criminal justice, either settling small matters definitively or overseeing the preliminary stage of more important affairs, the revolutionary justice of the peace helped to preserve a measure of local autonomy while also providing an instrument for greater state control. No other official so completely embodied the tension between two concepts of order; he was the instrument of both plebeian justice and republican law.

Above JPs stood the formal machinery of criminal justice. The Thermidorians trusted the judiciary more than the Constituent Assembly, which had been forced to compromise with royal authority, or the National Convention, which had allowed the government to co-opt the courts for executive purposes. Thus, the judiciary emerged in 1795 as a substantially independent force. The Constitution of Year III gave judges greater protection from executive authority and brought them together in greater concentrations of judicial power. First, judges were elected by the same electoral assembly that chose national legislators and department administrators. This made them a critical part of the national political elite. Second, department judges served five-year terms and could only be dismissed following impeachment on criminal charges. Third, the twenty or so judges (plus five standing replacements) chosen by a department electoral assembly constituted a single pool of judges. Together, they staffed the department's civil, criminal, and correctional courts on a rotating basis.[12] This system fostered collegiality and gave judges an unrivaled exposure to the tensions and hot spots across their departments.

Besides choosing twenty or so regular judges, each department assembly elected a court president, a public prosecutor, and a chief clerk. The court president was essentially the trial manager. He handled the random drawing of jurors called to duty, convoked them at the appropriate time, took their oaths, instructed them, and summarized the case for them. He also maintained decorum during proceedings and freely deployed whatever ruses or confrontations he thought would elicit the truth.[13] As for the public prosecutor, he took charge of investigating and prosecuting a case only after a grand jury had voted to indict. In the case of rebels captured either alone or unarmed, he was authorized to bypass a grand jury and present the case directly to the criminal court. As the supervisor of all *officiers de police* in the department, however, he had considerable investigative reach—provided these men were willing and able to assist him.[14]

Judges had their greatest discretionary power when presiding over correctional courts. A correctional court president, assisted by two justices of the peace from the local town, made all judgments in misdemeanor cases and could sentence a culprit to as much as two years in prison. If the president of a correctional court believed that an offense constituted a felony, however, he assumed a second role, that of jury director. In this capacity, he drafted and presented formal felony charges to an eight-member grand jury convened at the seat of the correctional court. The six-month stints judges served as jury directors often meant that just when one magistrate was getting to the bottom of a case, he had to pass it on to a successor. All sorts of considerations ranging from laxity or lethargy to factionalism and fear helped to determine whether a jury director rushed to present a bill of indictment before he returned to the civil bench or delayed long enough to leave it on a colleague's agenda. A sense of collegiality could mitigate such tendencies, but frequent illness or recusal posed greater problems. The rotational system also created economic hardship that destabilized the magistracy. In the early years of the Directory, when judicial pay was in arrears and merchants refused paper money, judges regularly resigned their positions simply because they lacked sufficient means to live away from home, in one district *chef-lieu* or another.[15]

The Constitution of Year III provided only limited executive restraint on judicial authority. This came in the form of appointed government commissioners (*commissaires du Directoire exécutif*) attached to each criminal and correctional court. Their functions were largely confined to invoking the law, providing regulatory oversight, and seeing that sentences were executed.[16] A commissioner's greatest legal power lay in appealing a case to the Court of Cassation on the grounds of procedural irregularity. And yet a commissioner's importance was not as limited as it might at first appear. His reports to the minister of justice revealed a great deal about the general conduct of the judges and public prosecutor. This made him a political as well as judicial overseer.

### Due Process of Law

The courts' principal guide to judicial procedure was the *Code des délits et des peines,* adopted without discussion by the Convention in October 1795. The *Code* was both a landmark elaboration of the rule of law and a glaring example of Thermidorian contradictions. It was written almost single-handed by Merlin de Douai, famous as the author of the "law of suspects," and yet it included many provisions designed to prevent the sort of police practices his earlier terrorist legislation had encouraged. Furthermore, the *Code* was adopted on 3 brumaire IV (25 October 1795), the same day the National Convention codified the continued persecution of priests and émigrés. Finally, the *Code* was poorly named. Most of its 646 articles pertained to procedural aspects of criminal justice, whereas its treatment of crimes and punishments made only a few amendments to the Penal Code of 1791.[17]

As a code of judicial and police conduct, the brumaire *Code* was of major significance for the state-based concept of order and the rule of law. In fact, the *Code* helped to define these quintessentially modern concepts. Above all, the notion of public order was given clear definition by the *Code*'s conceptual distinction between criminal and civil justice. Plaintiffs continued to initiate indictments, but now the pursuit of compensatory damages could flow only from a criminal conviction. This meant that the state took sole responsibility for preserving public order and that criminal justice was not intended to provide victims with retributive justice. Here was an enormous change of principles to which historians have paid little attention. This was the revolutionaries' attempt to put an end to the ancillary role that criminal justice had played in sustaining agonistic social practices rooted in notions of personal honor and normative hierarchy that were as old as Western civilization itself.[18]

Despite some overlap in investigative and prosecutorial functions, a perennial source of concern in societies based on the rule of law,[19] the *Code* laid out impressive protections for those accused of crime. "We know that this *chef-d'oeuvre* of theory proved highly defective in practice," wrote an eminent legal historian, without elaborating on its functional flaws.[20] Had he done so, he would have been forced to conclude, somewhat embarrassingly, that its most liberal provisions were what proved least workable. Both investigation and prosecution were remarkably constrained for the period. The *Code* specified elaborate paper trails for summons, interrogations, court appearances, arrest warrants, jail bookings, and posting bail. Any procedural irregularity in investigation or prosecution could result in the later nullification of everything else in the case from that point forward. Particularly noteworthy are the protections from arbitrary arrest and detention. Fully aware of the myriad abuses of police power during the Terror, the Thermidorians sought to ensure greater protection for personal liberty. Merlin's *Code* complemented important provisions of the Constitution of Year III, which specified that a citizen's house was "an inviolable asylum." Domiciliary visits by the police or officials could take place only during the daytime. They had to be based on an official order specifying the purpose of the visit. Furthermore, the *Code* prescribed a penalty of six years in chains (that is, solitary confinement) for anyone who issued, signed, or executed arrest orders without proper authority, detained an accused anywhere but in an official jail, or imprisoned someone without a legal order. Even legal detentions had some strict limits. A citizen's complaint needed corroborating evidence before an arrest could be made. When an accused appeared before a JP, voluntarily or not, he had to be either freed after questioning or remanded in custody to the nearest jury director within twenty-four hours. Once transferred to the district jail, the jailor was obliged to send copies of the arrest warrant to the local municipality and the home of the accused in order to inform his family and friends. After appearing before a jury director, those charged only with misdemeanors could obtain automatic release by posting a bail bond of 3,000 francs.

The *Code* also defined an elaborate system of judicial protections for the accused. These began the moment he was arrested. If witnesses had already given depositions, the JP had to read these to the accused before interrogating him. Any depositions taken after his arrest had to be taken in his presence. This extraordinarily generous provision both kept the defendant informed and discouraged malicious denunciations. Once the affair passed into the hands of the jury director, however, any further depositions could be gathered "secretly," as the *Code* put it—that is, without the accused being present. And yet, obtaining a grand jury indictment required more than "simple suspicion, a simple prejudice"; it required "strong presumption, a beginning of decisive proofs" (art. 237). Since any witness testimony crucial to reaching this level of assurance had to be presented orally and in person, the defendant knew the main evidence against him even before being indicted. Thereafter, once he had been transferred to the criminal court and interrogated by the court president, he received free copies of all police reports, expert statements, and witness depositions pertaining to his case. This enabled him and his lawyer to point out irregularities and to plan an overall defense strategy. At this point the government commissioner verified that every aspect of the arrest and prosecution had been handled correctly. If not, the criminal court met to consider his demand for annulment. This could mean setting aside a grand jury indictment, invalidating the original arrest warrant and starting the whole prosecution over again, or even abandoning the case entirely. Once procedural regularity had been assured, by retracing several steps if necessary, the case went to trial.

The trial, too, included many safeguards for the accused. These went well beyond the elimination of written evidence so often emphasized. If the accused did not have a lawyer, the court was required to appoint one for him. The defense team could then recuse up to twenty jurors without explanation, and more thereafter if the judges considered the motives valid. It is impossible to tell whether this led to attempts to shape the composition of juries along lines of age, occupation, or geographic origin, but if so, they were very rare. On the other hand, it would have taken an extraordinary insouciance for defendants and their lawyers to neglect their right to stage-manage the appearance of defense witnesses. These could be called without giving advance notice to the prosecution, could be recalled at any time, and could be heard either in isolation from one another or in each others' presence, all depending on the defendant's strategy.[21] In contrast, the defendant was entitled to receive a list of prosecution witnesses and the order in which they would appear. Of course, the defense had the right to cross-examine witnesses and always had the last word.

Most important of all, trials were open to the public. Thus, the fundamentally oral nature of the process ensured that anyone who attended the trial would be exposed to all of the evidence made available to the jury to decide guilt or innocence. Pretrial depositions could not be read aloud in court even when a crucial witness failed to appear at trial. The use of such depositions was limited to exposing major inconsistencies in the testimony given by the witness in court. Finally, a jury verdict could be reconsidered only when the five presiding judges unanimously agreed that the jurors had ignored fundamental facts in the case in order to produce a conviction. This led to a new jury vote including three supplemental jurors who had been present throughout the trial. Jury verdicts were based on a majority of ten of twelve in the first instance, or of twelve of fifteen in the second. In contrast, judges could not have an acquittal reconsidered, no matter how blatantly it contradicted material evidence or testimony in court. As the reader will have no doubt concluded, all of this amounted to an astonishingly liberal set of protections for the accused. They conformed fully to the idea of a fair trial or due process as it has been defined by twentieth-century jurists.[22]

All of these safeguards were added to a system of criminal justice that had been in place for only three years—years that had been especially hard on judicial norms. A new legal culture was being created under the Directory, and it took more than promulgating a code of conduct to bring it into being. New safeguards were meaningful only when assured by judicial oversight. Although the archives of the Court of Cassation were destroyed in the fires of the Paris Commune,[23] evidence scattered throughout the records of departmental courts indicates that the high court played an important role in educating lower courts on correct procedures. Even basic matters such as failure to pose the famous question of criminal intent (*question intentionnelle*) or convictions on charges not contained in the indictment were not uncommon. Certain cases are instructive about the punctiliousness demanded by the high court. It was fine for magistrates to reject Claire Maffre's request not to have the prosecutor read out in court the contradictory explanations she had given about her involvement in an armed robbery—after all, this was about the only written evidence allowed in a jury trial—but when the top magistrates in the land discovered that this decision had not been explained to her, they quashed the verdict and sent the case to another court.[24] Similarly, the high court found grounds to annul François Tenton's conviction (for singing royalist songs in public) simply because the prosecution had been unable to supply him with the complete names and occupations of a few of the many witnesses against him a full twenty-four hours before these persons testified in court.[25] And yet, despite the procedural rigor of such decisions, the proportion of verdicts annulled by the Court of Cassation remained relatively small. In seven years, the court overturned only twenty-three verdicts from the Hérault and only sixteen from the Haute-Saône. These are representative numbers for the republic as a whole.[26]

In fact, enforcement of the more stringent regulations on arrest and prosecution came further down in the judicial hierarchy. The detailed procedural safeguards established by the *Code*, together with a general lack of expertise at the lowest levels of the system, led to many more annulments by criminal courts themselves. In the years IV through X, the Criminal Court of the Sarthe nullified 50 indictments (pertaining to 64 defendants) and that of the Haute-Garonne annulled 68 indictments (pertaining to 116 defendants).[27] Cases built on legal sand were either sent to different jury directors for renewed prosecution or downgraded to misdemeanors and sent before correctional courts. In contrast, trumped-up charges could lead to cases being dismissed and defendants freed.[28] All told, the number of nullifications on procedural grounds (*cassation*) at different levels suggests that magistrates were generally able to meet the high standards set by the *Code des délits et des peines*.

The rule of law would have been nothing more than a set of high ideals unless judges had substantial legal expertise and a strong vocational ethos. Though not required to be trained in the law, judges elected in 1795 were almost all men with considerable legal experience. In most instances, this had been acquired both before and during the Revolution. The most prominent positions in the criminal justice system, that of court president and public prosecutor, invariably went to men with long legal careers behind them. In the Hérault, for example, the electors chose as court president Rouch, a former law professor at Montpellier, and as public prosecutor François

Thourel, previously an attorney attached to the presidial court at Béziers, then a judge on the district court there.[29] Their counterparts elected in year IV in the Sarthe were also highly considered by their contemporaries. The court president, an attorney from Le Mans named Ysambart, was described as "educated, . . . sensitive, just and courageous" and the public prosecutor, Juteau-Duhoux, had showed "irreproachable conduct during twenty-five years of work in the judicial system [being] gifted with rare judgment and an uncommon natural intelligence."[30] The importance of such men in the new scheme of things often led to their election to the national legislature. In contrast, many ordinary judges were cut from less substantial cloth. Some had been simple notaries, even bailiffs; others had spent more time as mayors and syndics than as judges. Regardless, they all belonged to the cadres of the Revolution, men who had emerged in 1789–90 to lead the charge against the entrenched interests of the prevailing order. They were also almost all men of substantial property and could be expected to administer justice with a certain class bias. Their status as notables and their experience of revolution, frequently including a period of exclusion during year II, provided a basis for solidarity with their peers.

## The Politics of Justice

The magistrates of year IV came from the upper echelons of revolutionary activists. "Patriots of 1789" and "federalists of 1793" abounded. Although not generally royalist or even antirepublican, most of the judges elected in 1795 tended to hate Jacobins and to mistrust the new government.[31] Whereas political moderates took up judgeships across most of France, open reactionaries triumphed in the Midi. Although the last representatives on mission in the area replaced numerous local officials, the protections of the constitution allowed avowedly antirepublican judges to remain in place. This facilitated a judicial reaction against the new government. Reactionary judges did the most harm simply by failing to enforce the law. Above all, they consistently refused to apply the laws against émigrés and refractory priests. Ministerial correspondence with local authorities and commissioners was painfully repetitive on this point. Such a policy of negligence easily extended to a host of attacks on former terrorists, even if they were appointed officials of the new regime. In one case in the Vaucluse, the local JP did nothing to investigate the collective murder of the government commissioner at Valréas because his brutality as former head of the revolutionary committee there gave the community a right to commit "legitimate homicide," a right the judiciary was obliged to respect! Moreover, even if the minister of justice refused to believe in conspiracies of silence and other such excuses, there was little his agent the court commissioner could do. As long as the government respected the constitution, the rule of law was largely what local judges wanted to make it. In the southeast at least, the Directory's strategy of relying on the integrity of the judiciary to restore public order and political peace manifestly failed; judges sapped the regime with its own tools.[32]

Evidence of this sort makes it tempting to blame reactionary magistrates for politicizing the judiciary. This may be accurate as far as it goes, but such a stance obscures an important paradox at work in the legal establishment of the Directory. Many magistrates had played key roles in earlier phases of the Revolution. Such men understandably found it difficult to administer justice without being plunged back into partisan battles. Periods of wrenching fear, if not serious loss of property or kin, left them bitter and wary. Some could not resist using their positions to persecute their opponents, often justifying it as preemptive self-defense. Yet others worked simply to shield their political allies from prosecution. In either case, the legality of their actions inevitably became a public concern. This ensured that wherever factionalism continued to thrive, so too did a lively debate on the technicalities of police and judicial procedure. In this way, the corrupting influence of local and national politics under the Directory actually became an education in the rule of law.

This important paradox deserves a closer look. Take the experience of Jean-Joseph Janole, elected public prosecutor for the Haute-Garonne in October 1795. A brilliant young lawyer at the Parlement of Toulouse before the Revolution, he became a member of the local district court in 1792 and an activist in municipal politics.[33] In the spring of 1793, he took the lead in opposing the excesses of the representative on mission François Chabot, protector of the local Jacobins.[34] This got Janole sacked as a federalist and forced him to spend the next eighteen months in hiding. In the meantime, he was added to the list of émigrés, his widowed mother was locked up for six months, and he was condemned to death in absentia by the Revolutionary Tribunal at Paris. His friends and allies were even less fortunate: six perished on the scaffold. After the Terror subsided, Janole emerged from hiding and recovered his property, minus what had been pillaged in his absence. Given his experiences during the Terror, it is hardly surprising that Janole became part of the Thermidorian Reaction. He regained his old post on the district court of Toulouse in June 1795 and quickly became associated with the *Anti-Terroriste,* the local organ of former federalists. Janole's subsequent election as public prosecutor in October 1795 soon pitted him against the Jacobin officials of Toulouse.

The discovery of the Babeuvist "conspiracy of equals" put Janole at the heart of a prolonged controversy over due process. On 10 floréal IV (29 April 1796), the Directory ordered all *Conventionnels* without official posts to quit Paris and return to their native departments. This included Marc Vadier, a prominent member of the Committee of General Security during the Terror, who had fallen into such poverty that he was forced to walk almost the length of France to return to the Ariège. While en route, the Directory exposed the "conspiracy of equals" and added him to its list of suspects. When Vadier arrived at Toulouse, Janole promptly had him arrested and, a few days later, sent by coach (!) back to Paris for the trial at Vendôme.[35] The prosecutor of the Haute-Garonne followed up his triumph by having the deputy's son, Jacques Vadier, seized in a "terrorist" café by a throng of gendarmes. The Jacobin municipality cried foul, claiming that the public prosecutor had violated the constitution by not first obtaining an arrest warrant from the local jury director. The government responded by issuing a subpoena to have Janole himself appear before the jury director. Fearing partisan persecution for his arrest of Vadier père, the public prosecutor once again fled Toulouse. Local Jacobins made the most of a sententious magistrate seeking refuge from the law. In the meantime, he and two officers of the gendarmerie were indicted by a grand jury. They opted to be tried by the more favorable Criminal Court of the Ariège. The newspapers at Toulouse turned Janole's trial into a regional cause célèbre. Numerous articles expounded the various legal aspects of the case, while never forgetting their partisan explanation for the course of events. Naturally, the *Anti-Terroriste* saw Janole's eventual acquittal as a vindication of the rule of law, whereas the *Journal de Toulouse* blamed it on a politicized court and stacked jury.[36]

Once back in office, Janole became drawn into the political tensions that mounted in the run up to the elections of 1797. Several rounds of bloody street fighting between *sans-culottes* thugs and royalist dandies helped to prevent the national tide of antirepublicanism from sweeping the elections at Toulouse. Janole zealously prosecuted agitators from the Faubourg St-Cyprien, but thanks to sympathetic jurors they were all acquitted.[37] With his party defeated at the polls, his efforts to prosecute Jacobin violence thwarted by "the jurors' partiality," and his most supportive minister, the conservative Cochon de Lapparent, replaced by the Jacobin sympathizer Sotin, Janole became increasingly isolated in his office. His stature sank further when he refused to prosecute a group of armed townsfolk who had obstructed a search for émigrés at Beaumont and instead tried to prosecute the local JP for conducting an illegal search, which in fact had not taken place. Furthermore, he was soon forced to recuse himself from the prosecution of a leading royalist from Beaumont whom the Criminal Court of the Haute-Garonne sentenced to deportation for advocating resistance to republican laws and a return to monarchy and aristocratic rule. Janole's incessant partisan manipulation of the law so infuriated officials in the Ministry of Justice that they recommended he be impeached under the Penal Code.[38] Tempers were running high in Toulouse as well. The public prosecutor's appearance at the Festival of the Republic on 1 vendémiaire VI (22 September 1797) prompted the large crowd to begin chanting, "Down with Janole! Out with Janole!" and he needed a police escort to make it home safely. Dismayed by this event, he tried to blacken the regime's reputation by giving jury directors instructions to apply the law of 19 fructidor V (5 September 1797) to refractory priests in an even more draconian manner than the law required. The municipality and local press again erupted in denunciations.[39] And yet, even when given the opportunity, the Directory did not replace Janole. He continued to serve until the eve of the elections of 1798, when his term was artificially ended along with all prosecutors elected in 1795.[40] One might have expected Janole to receive a judicial appointment under the Consulate, but he did not. He had plainly used his office for factional ends and so, despite Prefect Richard's strong anti-Jacobinism, could not be trusted with a judgeship. And yet, from a broader perspective, Janole's controversial role had fueled extensive public debate about the rule of law he was supposed to enforce. In this way, his misdeeds, most of them relatively minor compared to the appalling practices of year II, provided an unexpected education in the new standards of due process.

It was not only the machinations of local magistrates that heightened public awareness of the importance of strict legality. The government itself frequently let political concerns infect the rule of law. Several high-profile controversies exposed the cynical way in which the Directory manipulated justice to suit its political purposes. No less a figure than Merlin de Douai, minister of justice in years IV and V, is said to have justified this legal legerdemain with the remark, "C'est la raison d'État qui dicte la jurisprudence."[41] Well-publicized clashes with the Councils and especially the Court of Cassation undermined the Directory's claim to be putting the rule of law above political expediency. Matters would have been worse had effective government propaganda not helped to mask some of its manipulations of exceptional justice.

The government's discovery and exposure of the "conspiracy of equals" in the spring of 1796 gave it a rich opportunity to curry favor with conservatives and the propertied classes in general. On the other hand, Babeuf's arrest incensed radical republicans. Several months later, a bloody skirmish on the night of 23–24 fructidor IV (9–10 September 1796) at the Grenelle military camp, almost certainly set off by government *agents provocateurs,* led to the arrest of 144 men, including a bunch of Parisian militants and die-hard Montagnards. The Directory asked lawmakers to send the whole affair before a military court, arguing that this was a case of armed rebels captured in combat, even though a dozen of the accused had been arrested on the basis of house searches conducted days after the event. Fears that a long criminal trial would stir the embers of *sans-culottisme* prompted the Councils to endorse the use of military justice.[42] The recourse to military justice, the manifestly political nature of the trials, and the speed and harshness of sentences reeked of a return to exceptional justice. In two weeks, the *conseil militaire* (tellingly called a "commission militaire" by the press, thereby echoing the Terror) tried 147 men and convicted 86 of them. Thirty-one of these were quickly shot. The Court of Cassation confirmed the impression of arbitrary and exceptional justice by later annulling the sentences imposed on the rest, all condemned to deportation or hard labor, and ordering that they be retried by a regular criminal court. Although the high judges upheld the government's use of the law of 30 prairial III (18 June 1795), they noted that this law required rebels arrested unarmed and outside the field of combat to be tried by a regular criminal court. This was the case not only for those who appealed their sentences but for some of those who were executed. The supreme magistrates thus rendered a stinging rejection of the Directory's use of military justice in the Grenelle affair.[43] As had often been the case in year III, the Thermidorian elite had once again proved its antiterrorist credentials using terrorist tactics.

The Directory's reputation for judicial honesty took additional blows from the Court of Cassation for its handling of political trials in year V. The first episode came in the "Brottier affair," a royalist plot to overthrow the regime organized by the "Agence de Paris." Although clearly a conspiracy against domestic security and therefore covered by the regular Penal Code, the Directory ordered the conspirators prosecuted on the charge of recruiting soldiers for the enemy, a crime covered by the code of military justice.

When the Court of Cassation agreed to hear an appeal from the defendants regarding the proper jurisdiction for the case, the Directory caused a scandal by blocking the transfer of documents. This set off several days of tempestuous debate in the Council of Five Hundred, where both the Directory and the Court of Cassation were accused of grossly exceeding their powers. In the end, the Council refused to accept the high court's claim to regulate military justice despite an explicit law to this effect (21 fructidor IV [7 September 1796]) because doing so would have been a disavowal of the government and the start of a constitutional crisis. Nevertheless, the controversy seems to have intimidated the army officers who composed the military court, and on 19 germinal V (8 April 1797), they convicted the four principal conspirators, then essentially commuted their sentences from death to modest terms of imprisonment. They also acquitted all seventeen persons accused as accomplices. The audience greeted these verdicts with peals of applause. Not ones to be thwarted by this humiliating verdict, however, the Directors quickly ordered the main defendants prosecuted before a civilian court on charges of conspiracy to overthrow the regime. Here was conclusive proof that the initial charge of recruiting for the enemy had only been a ploy to get the case into a military court. The Directory may ultimately have outmaneuvered the Court of Cassation, but the press and public opinion judged the government's turn to military justice both cynical and unscrupulous. In the end, the accused did not get another trial. The coup of 18 fructidor V arrived first, and so they were simply deported to Cayenne.[44]

The discovery of the "conspiracy of equals" and the arrest of Babeuf and a dozen coconspirators in May 1796 presented the Directory with its greatest judicial dilemma. The chance to trumpet the danger of "anarchists" could not be missed. This called for a great show trial. Prosecuting a conspiracy with ramifications throughout the country made good propaganda for the government, but it also threatened to overwhelm the standards of due process. Those on the left correctly viewed the trial as the basis for a national witch hunt. The addition of a large number of suspects for political reasons, rather than on the basis of evidence, forced the prosecution to exaggerate its claims and seek to convict on guilt by association alone. The dubious inclusion of the deputy Drouet among the defendants provided the basis for sending all the defendants before a High Court of Justice convened at Vendôme. Babeuf and many of his codefendants refused to accept the authority of the court, and when the trial finally began in February 1797, they called it a "Punch and Judy show." Others skillfully deployed an array of legal tactics that exposed the bias of the court against the defendants.[45]

As with most famous trials, the alleged crimes captured public attention, but the judicial duel sustained it. Massive press coverage of the lengthy trial focused far more on judicial procedure than on political conspiracy. The government made available an unprecedented stenographic record, published as the trial unfolded. This official version competed with a melodramatic account published daily by the Babeuf sympathizer P.-N. Hésine and often excerpted in Jacobin papers such as the *Ami du peuple* and *Journal des hommes libres*. The extraordinary level of publicity given the three-month trial became a spotlight turned on the perils of politicized justice. Unfortunately for the government, this extensive coverage greatly aided the defense. As the trial unfolded, it became increasingly clear that the government's claim that it was providing defendants with the fullest guarantees of due process was at best overstated. First, it came out that handwriting experts had been coached by the prosecution; then a key witness admitted that Director Carnot had talked him into adding names to his original deposition; and finally, two other crucial witnesses strode into the courtroom and recanted their pretrial depositions, claiming that they had been coerced by the government. All of these troubles forced prosecutors to abandon the case against most of the accused. Furthermore, the jury voted that the main charge—conspiracy to overthrow the government—had not been proved. The Directory's credibility would have been completely shot had jurors not convicted seven defendants under the exceptional legislation of 27 germinal IV (16 April 1796) against calling for the Jacobin Constitution of 1793. Two were condemned to death (Babeuf and Darthé) and seven to deportation.

Though it appeared a modest victory at the time, these nine convictions proved the worst possible outcome for the Directory. What had been presented as a vast and terrifying conspiracy to overthrow the regime and return France to the anarchy of year II had been reduced in the course of the trial to a handful of isolated radicals condemned for their publications alone. The trial revelations and final verdicts convinced many republicans that there had been no conspiracy at all and that it had been wholly fabricated by the government (in the Ministries of Police and Justice no less) in order to ostracize and persecute Jacobins. A regime supposedly based on law and liberty had engineered the execution of a few utopian dreamers. Carnot, Cochon de Lapparent, and Merlin de Douai had clearly overplayed their hand. Having alienated moderates with their blanket amnesty in brumaire IV, the Thermidorians tried to make amends by using the "conspiracy of equals" (which was real enough, as Buonarotti revealed thirty years later) to draw a clear distinction between themselves and unrepentant terrorists or *sans-culottes* militants. This earned the government undying enmity from the republican left. Babeuf and Darthé became "martyrs for democracy," and the trial at Vendôme a rallying point for democratic opposition to the Directory.[46]

The irony of it all is that much of the adverse reaction created by the trial came from the unusually liberal conditions under which it unfolded. There is no doubt that the government and prosecution had at times been over-eager and high-handed. But this had been exposed by a free press and the government's unwillingness to commit really major travesties of justice. This trial avoided the political tautologies that led to Louis XVI's execution and the muzzling of the defense that sent Danton to the guillotine. The protections afforded the accused by an elaborate jury trial and the unprecedented publicity of the proceedings are precisely what made it a fiasco for the regime. The mistakes spawned by an excess of prosecutorial zeal were easily overlooked by those with a visceral fear of Jacobinism. Unfortunately, even moderate republicans considered it all badly handled and badly timed, giving aid and comfort to resurgent royalism. The disastrous elections of year V proved that the government's fudged liberalism had been the worst of both worlds.

The First Directory had hoped to consolidate the revolutionary settlement by applying the rule of law, but this strategy was often thwarted by partisan judges, especially in the polarized atmosphere of the Midi. However, the Directorial government itself, including the minister of justice who decried such practices, could not resist politicizing the judicial process in manifestly unconstitutional ways. Contemporaries understandably expressed their moral indignation at such practices, but historians are better placed to notice that the attention paid to these travesties was inspired by political rivalry more than a high-minded dedication to principles. Nevertheless, this lively tension between justice and politics served to raise awareness of the rule of law as a source of legitimacy.

## Judicial Repression

Did the intrusion of politics into the operations of justice render the criminal courts ineffectual? Historians have routinely condemned the system without much knowledge of how it worked. Correspondence between public prosecutors and the Ministry of Justice provides plenty of evidence to argue that the regular system of criminal justice failed to uphold the rule of law under the early Directory.[47] But these are invariably the voices of officials dedicated to stamping the authority of the law on French society. One could find a similar array of condemnations for almost any other period of French history. Even today, despite a vastly larger, more efficient, and more professional system of criminal justice, it would be easy to gather an impressive range of examples illustrating the failure of France's current system of criminal justice to meet its fundamental goals. The problem then becomes finding appropriate standards by which to judge the successes and failures of any particular system. Naturally, these standards are historically contingent.

How well did the criminal courts operate given the circumstances of the First Republic? Were the new procedures too beautiful to last, as one legal historian recently remarked?[48] Disparaging comments by contemporaries, as well as the republic's later turn toward military justice, give the impression that the criminal justice system of 1795, with all of its protections for the accused, was not tough enough to cope with the proliferation of crime and violence in the late 1790s. And yet a comparison with the criminal courts of the *ancien régime* clearly shows that the criminal justice system at work under the Directory had markedly increased rates of repression, whether measured in terms of judicial activity or amount of punishment.

It is not possible to make any sort of direct comparison between the level of judicial repression before the Revolution and that experienced during the late First Republic. The *ancien régime*'s variety of courts and thicket of overlapping jurisdictions pose an insurmountable problem for extensive statistical comparisons. That seigneurial courts could handle felonies as well as misdemeanors, that provostial and presidial courts issued summary judgments, that courts of first instance had their judgments appealed to *parlements*, and that salt and tobacco smuggling was handled by separate customs courts all combine to render any effort at uniform calculations foolhardy. Not only does this rule out any usable study of comparative crime rates, it even makes repression rates incalculable. Nonetheless, a few basic comparisons reveal that the criminal courts of the First Republic were impressively busy as well as shockingly repressive.

Despite sporadic efforts to gather more systematic data, the Ministry of Justice never succeeded in getting departmental courts to provide annual statistics, and a national data set did not emerge until 1825. In order to get a reliable basis for general statements, and in order to undertake some regional comparisons based on uniform methods, I have gathered data on four criminal courts, two in the north (Haute-Saône and Sarthe) and two in the south (Haute-Garonne and Hérault).[49] The combined data from these four courts reveal that from 1795 to 1802, departmental criminal courts averaged 74 cases a year, not including misdemeanor cases heard on appeal. The actual totals varied widely from year to year and department to department. The Sarthe averaged only 52 trials per annum, whereas the Hérault, despite having a much smaller population, averaged 95 trials per annum.[50] In comparison, the *sénéchaussée* courts (the backbone of the criminal justice system) in the Guyenne in the last two decades of the *ancien régime* handled only between 20 and 25 cases a year.[51] Thus, despite having to rely on twelve jurors (plus three replacements) and conducting trials entirely on the basis of oral proceedings, the new criminal courts processed two to four times as many cases in a year than the old ones. How much this was due to the consolidation of all trials of felony offenses into a single court, how much to an increase in crime, and how much to increased policing is impossible to say. No doubt all three factors played a part. Whatever the causes, there is no denying that the criminal courts of the Directory handled a heavy caseload.

The sheer number of criminal trials is also a measure of judicial repression. Putting people on trial, even if they were acquitted, involved arrests, time in jail, and tarnished reputations; it could also mean police brutality, lawyers' fees, and lost income. All of these were coercive deterrents and constituted repression. From this perspective, it is worth making regional comparisons about rates of repression generated by regular criminal justice during the late republic. Here we see marked discrepancies between our northern and southern departments. Most important, southern courts practiced a considerably higher rate of judicial repression. This emerges from an assessment of trial frequency, number of defendants, and conviction rates. The southern courts of the Hérault and Haute-Garonne averaged 41 percent more trials per year than the northern courts of the Sarthe and Haute-Saône (86 versus 61). The average number of defendants per case was also higher in the south than in the north (1.53 versus 1.34).

Overall repression rates (defendants per capita per annum) are somewhat less easy to assess, however, and depend a great deal on how one accounts for persons judged in absentia. If the tabulations include all defendants whether or not they were present at trial, we find that the southern courts had an average repression rate 50 percent higher than the northern courts (see appendix A.1). The extent of actual repression involved in trying a defendant still at large is clearly less than trying someone who has already spent time in custody, and yet prosecuting absent defenders did constitute a form of repression. Their property was sequestered and the income it generated passed to the state until such time as they presented themselves for trial. This makes data based on including absent defendants at least partially valid. However, it also tends to skew overall rates of repression. The disparity between southern and northern departments drops sharply when those absent at trial are excluded. Nonetheless, even when making calculations solely on the basis of defendants actually at trial, southern courts still produced 22 percent more repression per capita.[52]

This draws attention to one particularly distinctive aspect of southern judicial culture: the propensity to prosecute defendants who were not in custody, and hence not in court to defend themselves. One out of every three verdicts rendered in southern courts pertained to defendants who had eluded the clutches of the police; in northern courts this figure was only one out of nine.[53] One could speculate at length about the sources of this pronounced difference. Were northern police more adept at catching criminals? (Certainly the gendarmerie was the subject of fewer complaints.) Were southern defendants more afraid of the judicial apparatus? If so, was this due to real or perceived bias within it? Perhaps southerners experienced greater shame and dishonor simply by submitting to the machinery of justice, whether innocent or guilty. Or perhaps southern courts were considered especially harsh. After all, they tended to have somewhat higher felony conviction rates and lower acquittal rates. The felony conviction rate for defendants present at trial was 50 percent in the south versus 43 percent in the north. The acquittal rates were 40 percent versus 45 percent. The differences were made up by misdemeanor verdicts, which averaged 10 percent in the south and 12 percent in the north. (Chapter 8 will assess conviction rates more closely.) But southern criminals could hardly have calculated their chances on a statistical basis. A more credible explanation is that prosecutors were more inclined to seek convictions in absentia as a coercive alternative to lengthy police manhunts. A contumacious conviction often helped to force fleeing suspects to appear in court in an effort to clear their names. Where trying absent defendants was more common, however, the willingness to convict them was less so.[54] Apparently, therefore, southern juries were less inclined to interpret a defendant's flight as prima facie evidence of guilt. Whatever the reason for three times as many people being tried in absentia in the south as in the north—and undoubtedly the cultural legacy of Roman law played a part—this crucial difference should be kept in mind when comparing regional rates of repression.

Whereas the number of trials and overall conviction rates give a sense of *judicial repression,* the frequency of harsh sentences is a measure of *penal repression.* Here, too, the Directory's regular criminal courts had surprising bite. Although the multiplicity of courts and the spotty nature of existing scholarship make it impossible to obtain accurate statistics for penal repression in the *ancien régime*, a reasonable calculation is possible. Extrapolations based on figures from four *parlements* (Toulouse, Rennes, Dijon, and Paris), the cumulative totals for all of the provostial and presidial courts of the kingdom, and the records of those sentenced to the *bagne*, which have the benefit of including those sentenced by the *cours des aides* for salt and tobacco smuggling, enable us to make the following calculations.[55] During the first half of the 1780s, a period of relatively high judicial activity, courts of last resort sentenced to death approximately 190 to 225 people a year throughout France. Another 900 to 1,000 men and women were condemned to hard labor either in the *bagne* or a *maison de force*. About one-fifth of these people were given life sentences. In comparison, under the Directory, regular criminal courts imposed an average of over 550 death sentences a year, about 475 sentences of twenty or more years of hard labor, and 2,400 sentences of four to eighteen years of hard labor.[56] The evidence is clear: the regular criminal courts of the Directory produced roughly two and one-half times the level of penal repression experienced during the peak years of the *ancien régime*.[57]

Such figures belie any hasty judgments about the inadequacy of criminal justice at the time. And yet, even this remarkable level of repression was too little and too late. Though the criminal justice system showed plenty of repressive capacity, it did not fulfill what Thermidorians saw as its primary function—defending the republican order. The judicial regime suffered from the same basic defect as the political regime: citizens were supposed to elect judges and lawmakers alike, but Thermidorians did not trust either to preserve the republic. The elected nature of the judiciary gave it great independence from the executive. The constitution entrusted civil liberty to the integrity of magistrates, but the government soon rued this idealistic arrangement. The government commissioner attached to each criminal court served to monitor the performance of prosecutors and judges but gave the government little coercive authority over them. These were not favorable circumstances for the regime. Judicial independence, the authority that came with legal expertise, and the influence of factional politics all combined to make the magistracy a serious obstacle to the Directory's plan to end the Revolution through a careful application of the rule of law. Was the revolutionaries' beloved jury also to blame? Was it a Trojan horse in which a community-based concept of order snuck inside the walls of criminal justice where they overcame defenders of the republican concept of order? Only a close look at the new trial by jury will tell.

# 4 Trial by Jury

La Sûreté publique
Liberté, Egalité, Justice
L'indulgence pour le crime est une conspiration contre la vertu.
—Letterhead of Fossé, public prosecutor of the Tarn

DESPITE A RENEWED focus on the creation of democratic politics during the French Revolution,[1] scholars have paid little attention to the democratizing effects of the new jury-based system of criminal justice. This is especially odd given the general tendency to emphasize positive aspects of what was by any standard of measurement an extraordinarily messy and often deeply flawed set of experiments in political democracy. If one wants to find citizens playing an effective and often determinant role in the construction of a newly democratic polity, however, one need only investigate the performance of juries. Historians' neglect notwithstanding, the new judicial system played a vital role in drawing citizens into the new apparatus of rule. Revolutionary reformers insisted on making jury duty a key attribute of active citizenship. In so doing, they ensured that jurors, at least as much as justices of the peace and judges, controlled the boundary between community concepts of order and those of the republican state. Citizens decided the fate of the Revolution at least as much when voting for judges and serving as jurors as they did when electing deputies and administrators.

## Juries

Revolutionary reforms in criminal justice were a central component of the democratic project. After the great systemic reforms of criminal justice in September 1791, justices of the peace, correctional court judges, criminal court presidents, and public prosecutors were all elected. The infusion of democracy into the judicial system went beyond elected officials to include English-style juries: an eight-member grand jury for indictments and a twelve-member trial jury for final verdicts. The Constitution of Year III required all jurors to meet the qualifications of an elector, which were considerably higher than those of an ordinary voter. To be eligible to be chosen as electors (that is, to be elected to departmental electoral colleges) men needed to own or lease property that generated income worth one hundred to two hundred days' wages a year, depending on the size of the community in which they lived. This meant that somewhat fewer than a million men were eligible for jury duty.[2] Jurors certainly had greater wealth and influence than most of the defendants who appeared before them, but they were in no way an isolated plutocracy. In fact, jurors came from a wider range of social and economic circumstances than the limited numbers might suggest. Regional variations in the distribution of wealth meant that a considerable number of prosperous craftsmen and better-off peasants qualified, including many leaseholders. Jurors came from the literate "respectable folk," whether urban or rural, who constituted a social penumbra around the notables of the eighteenth century.

Towns were disproportionately represented on juries, but the vast majority of the populace still lived in the countryside, and it would be a mistake to assume that differences in wealth outweighed village notions of justice. The class bias in the criminal justice system stemmed at least as much from the Penal Code of 1791, with its extremely harsh penalties for theft, counterfeiting, and infanticide. Occasionally magistrates complained that the law did not adequately punish theft of grain or threats of arson, but in general jurors tended to temper the full force of the criminal code. Once they had been called for jury duty, however, jurors became implicated in a system tilted in favor of those with property, and even if they were inclined to ameliorate it, they could not always do so. This became both the education and burden of citizenship.

Like the other people in their communities, most men who qualified to serve as jurors preferred to have nothing to do with the apparatus of criminal justice. Taxpayers who wanted to be eligible for election either as electors or as local officials, however, were obliged to register for jury duty at the district correctional court. Four times a year the president and vice president of each department used these eligibility lists to compile lists of two hundred potential jurors for the coming three months. Although broadly representative of electors, these lists could be skewed. Not only was eligibility frequently contested, but choosing specific individuals rather than drawing names at random allowed department administrators to manipulate the composition of jury lists with an eye to political advantage. This became most evident following the Fructidor coup d'état. After the political pendulum swung sharply to the left, many departments discarded the jury lists prepared for the first three months of year VI by department administrators who had just been purged. Their appointed or co-opted successors then prepared entirely new lists. As the minister of justice pointed out, public prosecutors should no longer be concerned about administrators habitually choosing jurors opposed to the social order and the republican government, "now that the Directory has renewed all the administrators suspect of lacking civic spirit and hating the republic."[3] The law of 19 fructidor V (5 September 1797) also responded to widespread concern among magistrates and legislators that it took only three corrupt or unpatriotic jurors on any jury to thwart a conviction; henceforth, any verdicts reached in less than twenty-four hours required unanimity. Though designed to coerce consensus, this apparently made little difference to actual verdicts.[4]

The Constitution of Year III balanced a statement of citizens' rights with a statement of their duties. This was more than a constitutional preamble. It embodied the notion that, as Cambacérès put it, "La République précède le citoyen, et le citoyen précède l'homme." The innovation over the declarations of 1789 and 1793 was to make the fulfillment of duties the path to the enjoyment of rights. Merlin de Douai, author of the Declaration of the Rights and Duties of Man and Citizen of 1795, intended it to "extract the people from the state of disorder in which they find themselves."[5] This logic fit both the immediate concern to end the French Revolution and the metalanguage of a republican civilizing mission. This twofold significance was especially appropriate in the realm of jury duty. If a man wished to participate fully in the rights of citizenship, he was obliged to serve as a juror. By serving as a juror, he would become complicit in defending the new social order, as expressed by the Penal Code, and—theoretically at least—would become instrumental in making the new political order function effectively.

Once department administrators had put an *éligible* on a quarterly jury list, he could be chosen at random to provide jury duty for a monthly session of the criminal court. Just like cantonal administrators, jurors had to serve without compensation for their time or expenses. Anyone who refused to perform jury duty was to be fined 30 francs and deprived of his voting rights for two years. This did not prevent a fairly high rate of dereliction since absentees could usually escape punishment if they produced a certificate of ill health. In an age when men suffered some nagging physical ailment most of the time, ranging from assorted bad humors and chronic respiratory ailments to deadly fevers and excruciating dental decay, reluctant jurors had little difficulty persuading a medical officer to certify their physical indisposition. All too obvious good health could always be overcome by a cash gratuity. Absentee jurors probably resorted to such false certificates of illness less to avoid a fine or loss of voting privileges than to avoid the time commitment and expense of doing their duty. Absenteeism was highest among the better-off bourgeois who lived in the same town as the criminal court. They generally considered their time especially precious, had become accustomed to having less influence on local affairs than their rural counterparts, and were more likely to have the ready money needed to acquire a certified medical excuse. In contrast, country dwellers were more likely to find that jury duty offered opportunities. It permitted them to experience the workings of the larger society, and a stint in the *chef-lieu* could be combined with the sale of wine, the purchase of new boots, or an inquiry into the latest laws on divorce.

## Jury Verdicts

The revolutionaries took exceptional pride in having added juries to their system of criminal justice. Juries were to become the "palladium of liberty" in the new democracy. As a bulwark against the supposed arbitrariness of judges under the *ancien régime,* revolutionaries insisted that jurors deliberate in complete isolation from presiding judges. This permitted jurors to discuss reasons for their verdict without interference or manipulation.[6] It also left them largely devoid of legal guidance. Thus, jurors assumed a large measure of the discretionary powers formerly possessed by judges. In order to prevent judges from substantially altering jury verdicts through punishment alternatives—an essential component of the English judge's ascendancy over juries by the late eighteenth century—revolutionary reformers imposed mandatory sentencing. This still left trial juries with two means to ameliorate the harsh punishments specified by the Penal Code of 1791. The simplest means lay in a jury's ability to convict the culprit of a misdemeanor (*délit correctionnel*) rather than of the felony charge (*délit criminel*) contained in the indictment. In this way, attempted murder could be reduced to physical abuse, thus sparing the life of a defendant and substituting a few months in prison. The jury gained additional control over sentencing by being required to vote on attenuating or aggravating circumstances. Had the thief been a regular guest in the home where she stole the silver cross? Did the neighbors' religious epithets make a shoemaker's violent outburst a misdemeanor rather than a felony? Such a system made jurors a fundamental feature of the new democratic order. The people, that vaunted repository of sovereignty, made laws through their deputies and dispensed criminal justice through their juries.

Despite the importance of the judiciary in the revolutionary project of democracy, the behavior of juries has not been included in recent studies of revolutionary political culture. What little has been said is generally unfavorable.[7] Isser Woloch's engaging and insightful account draws attention to the many charges of indulgence and laxity leveled at juries by judges, public prosecutors, and government officials. But these men were all employed in the business of repression, and their assessments naturally reflected this. Jurors did not have to explain their thinking, leaving only verdicts to speak for them. This calls for statistical analysis. Woloch seems to side with critics of revolutionary juries and cites the few studies that have compiled tabulations. These indicate that acquittal rates hovered around 45 percent. My own research, as well as the impressive recent work of Robert Allen, confirms this. Combining data obtained for four departments (Hérault, Haute-Garonne, Sarthe, Haute-Saône) reveals that an average of 45 percent of verdicts were acquittals, 45 percent were felony convictions, and 10 percent were misdemeanor convictions on felony charges.[8] A closer look, however, reveals that this is not straightforward evidence of a general failure of juries to uphold the rule of law.

Judging the work of juries during the Directory requires a comparative treatment. This can be done several ways. First, comparisons should be made over time. Doing so immediately reveals that the rate of acquittal was not particularly high during the early Directory, when the constitutional republic was still a novelty. In fact, during the First Directory the acquittal rate was somewhat lower (43 percent) than during the early Consulate (46 percent) (see appendix A.1). A similar trend is apparent for the rate of felony convictions, which declined from the First Directory (50 percent) to the early Consulate (43 percent). This was only partially compensated by a modest increase in the rate of misdemeanor convictions on felony charges (7 percent to 11 percent). These trends indicate that juries were generally tougher during the early Directory than they were during the early Consulate. Such a finding contradicts prevailing assumptions about the period.

Even more contradictory is that the lowest rate of acquittal (38 percent) came during the last two years of the Directory. This would suggest that jurors were more reliable in the years before the great judicial reforms of year VIII than after. Such a novel conclusion deserves closer attention (see chapters 8 and 11).

A second comparison confirms that juries generally performed effectively during the constitutional republic. The pattern of jury verdicts in the late republic did not differ dramatically from that experienced a quarter century later (see appendix A.2). In the ten-year period 1826–35, felony conviction rates stood at 45 percent, acquittals at 33 percent, and misdemeanor convictions at 22 percent. The only difference in results, therefore, is the shift of one-quarter of the acquittals to misdemeanor penalties handed out to those initially arraigned on felony charges. Although this may appear to be evidence of improved jury reliability as an instrument of state repression, several changed circumstances should be noted. Both policing and prosecution had been significantly strengthened in the first quarter of the nineteenth century, thus enabling the government to present stronger cases against those it accused. The stronger the case against a defendant, the harder it was for juries to reach verdicts based mainly on traditional mores. Also, restrictions on who could serve as a juror increased a generation later, making them both wealthier and better educated and, therefore, presumably less sympathetic to their social inferiors in the dock. Furthermore, increased flexibility in punishment reduced the likelihood of acquittal due simply to the severity of the Penal Code. Given these considerations, juries during the Directory do not appear to have been especially lenient.

A third basis for comparison is the work of the "special criminal tribunals" set up in 1801 in twenty-seven departments of the west and Midi. Special tribunals tried those crimes considered most threatening to the social order: counterfeiting, vagabondage, prison breaking, arson, and especially armed robbery committed in the countryside. Verdicts were handed down without appeal by a panel of three army officers and five civilian judges. Thus, special tribunals lacked juries and in fact were paradoxically justified as a means of preserving the institution of the jury for cases involving less-threatening crimes (see chapter 12). During their first eighteen months in operation, the special tribunals of the Drôme, Hérault, Haute-Garonne, and Sarthe had a felony conviction rate of 48 percent, a misdemeanor conviction rate of 7 percent, and an acquittal rate of 45 percent. Therefore, the actual results of special tribunals—Bonaparte's version of the monarchy's provostial courts—differed surprisingly little from jury trials under the Directory.

A fourth basis for comparison, regular military courts charged with trying civilians, again confirms that acquittal rates for juries during the late republic were not exceptional. Military courts tried civilians either under the law of 30 prairial III (18 June 1795) pertaining to rebels or the law of 29 nivôse VI (18 January 1798) covering brigands. During two and one-half years (April 1798–September 1800), the six military courts of the Eighth, Tenth, and Twenty-second Military Districts (headquarters at Marseille, Toulouse, and Tours, respectively)—that is, courts operating either in the midst of southern brigandage, western *chouannerie,* or the aftermath of a large peasant insurrection—judged a total of 327 civilians. Only 40 percent were convicted; another 21 percent received misdemeanor penalties, and 38 percent were acquitted. Although the type of crimes involved meant numerous executions, the actual distribution of verdicts is less severe than in the case of jury trials.[9]

Finally, the comparison of rates of penal repression in the early 1780s and the late 1790s undertaken in the previous chapter provides further confirmation that the Directory's regular criminal courts did not lack repressive capacity despite relying on juries. The fact that jury verdicts under the Directory produced roughly two and one-half times the level of penal repression experienced during peak years of the late *ancien régime* may not have been enough to restore order quickly, but it belies any notion of simply failing to cope with crime.

## Jury Nullification

All of this puts criticisms of the trial jury into some perspective; it does not, however, obviate the need to address them. In fact, juries did frequently acquit defendants and often to the great frustration of public prosecutors, trial judges, and the government in Paris. The problem is really whether juries acquitted against the evidence. In other words, it is worth exploring the extent to which juries during the First Republic practiced what modern jurists call "jury nullification." A survey of jury verdicts that pays particular attention to jury nullification will provide a way to assess the influence of traditional notions of public order on judicial repression at a time when republican institutions remained highly malleable.

Understanding the decisions and motives of jurors is not easy in any system. It is particularly difficult for the revolutionary period due to the nature of the remaining evidence. Prior to the Revolution, professional magistrates relied heavily on written depositions and deliberated in camera. Enlightenment publicists roundly condemned this emphasis on written evidence and private judgment as the essential ingredients for judicial arbitrariness. In response, revolutionary reformers went to the opposite extreme. After 1791, trials relied exclusively on oral testimony presented in public. Only by seeing and hearing witnesses and defendants in person, looking them in the eye, so to speak, and observing the cut and thrust of cross-examination could jurors arrive at the personal belief (*conviction intime*) that revolutionary reformers considered essential to a just verdict. In order to prevent any substitution of a written record for this oral drama, the revolutionaries prohibited keeping a modern form of trial transcript. Therefore, extant records deliberately and systematically contain nothing about the verbal performances that lay at the heart of every criminal trial. After all, a theatrical performance cannot be judged by the script alone. Besides, the revolutionaries were determined to prevent trial transcripts from providing the basis to impugn a jury's judgment. They wanted *conviction intime* to be just that, a personal belief based solely on being present at court throughout the trial. Here was the very epistemology of democracy applied to justice.[10]

This has not left historians entirely bereft of evidence. Prior to any courtroom drama, the criminal justice system generated a variety of documents about the events in question. These documents include the original police report or victim's complaint, witness depositions, interrogations of the accused, and the final indictment. Each criminal court also kept a set of registers to record basic information about the outcome of each trial. Although there was no nationally standardized way of recording most of this information, the law required every departmental criminal court to write out in full the questions posed to the jury and their respective answers. These questions needed to address four issues in logical sequence: Did the alleged crime actually take place? If so, did the accused commit the crime? If so, did he or she commit it willfully and with malicious or criminal intent? And finally, did the crime include aggravating or attenuating circumstances? Although jurors were undoubtedly inclined to provide shaded answers to some of these questions, they were required to respond separately to each question by depositing either a black marble for "no" or a white marble for "yes" in a balloting container. The recorded answers to these questions provides an excellent, though still imperfect, basis for a study of acquittal rates and jury nullification under the revolutionary system of criminal justice. In fact, despite the dearth of scholarship on the French jury in this period, in contrast to extensive work on English juries, the questions posed to jurors after 1795 make it possible to draw more definitive conclusions about jury nullification in France at this time than is possible in other times and places. Historians of English jury trials in the eighteenth century speculate intelligently about jury nullification but are unable to assess it with nearly the same precision.[11]

Jury nullification could occur in any sort of trial, but a systematic study of court registers reveals that it clustered around particular sorts of crimes. Figure 5 shows criminal court verdicts for four departments over seven years with crimes divided into ten categories.[12] The findings in this chart conform to expectations in a number of respects. It is not surprising that robbery cases generated the highest rate of conviction: more than three-quarters of defendants. A good share of the acquittals went to individuals included in the trial of others on charges of having received stolen goods from the perpetrators. Being able to dispose of "hot" property both safely and profitably obviously formed a vital part of professionalized robbery. Many robbers could be identified only by first finding some of their ill-gotten gain in the possession of others. Even if a person was caught with stolen goods,

**Fig. 5  Criminal court verdicts by categories of crime**
Defendants present

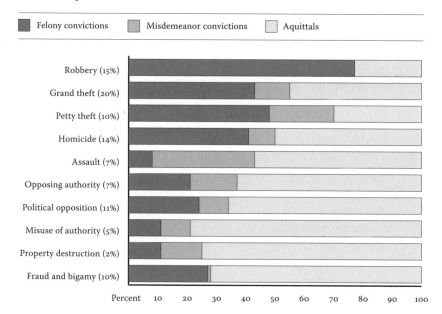

however, it was hard to prove that he had known their provenance when he acquired them. This frequently led to acquittal on the basis of criminal intent. The remaining acquittals on charges of robbery stemmed from lack of convincing evidence tying the accused to the crime. The threshold of what constituted convincing evidence in robbery cases was especially easy to attain. When someone was charged with actual robbery, and not just possessing stolen goods from it, the questions of motive or mitigating circumstances rarely arose to temper conviction. Hence trials for robbery produced a higher conviction rate than any other type of crime. The fact that robbery was a rational, calculated, and imitable crime made it both easy to understand and especially dangerous. Furthermore, acts of robbery sent a frisson of fear up the backs of well-heeled jurors and eliminated their qualms about condemning robbers to many years of disfiguring labor in the *bagne*. Even in the Haute-Saône, where aggravated theft rarely appeared in the court docket, jurors had no difficulty condemning a man and two women to sixteen years of hard labor regardless of the absence of violence in their spate of night break-ins at churches around Porentruy and Lure.[13] Jurors in the Hérault, where robbery was more common, proved at least as merciless. After a wave of arrests and four months of further investigation, sixteen people went on trial in connection with a series of holdups near the Valène woods north of Montpellier. Although the jury acquitted three men and five women of knowingly receiving stolen goods, it also found nine men guilty, all of whom had taken the well-trodden path of hardship from the hills of the Cévennes down to Montpellier. Their difficult life experiences did not soften the hearts of jurors, who condemned five of these men to death and four to twenty-four years of hard labor.[14] This contrasting mix of failing to prove criminal intent against fences and utter certainty leading to the ultimate penalty against robbers represents the most repressive attitude magistrates could expect from jurors. Thus, the conviction rate for robbery serves as something of a maximum against which conviction rates for other crimes can be measured. In other words, it should be expected that no matter the category of crime, at least one-quarter of defendants would be acquitted, usually on the basis of insufficient evidence.

Verdicts in cases of grand theft further illustrate the potential severity of juries and the range of reliable acquittals. Given jurors' powerful impulse to protect personal property, an attitude shared by their poorer countrymen, there is no reason to cast doubt on most acquittals for grand theft. Relying on a juror's personal belief (*conviction intime*) often made it easier to convict a culprit than would have been the case using the *ancien régime*'s system of unequally weighted legal proofs. Under these conditions, prejudices against the most impoverished members of society, especially vagabonds and beggars, probably inspired more mistaken convictions than acquittals. Most acquittals on charges of theft were related to receiving stolen goods or taking property for reasons other than criminal appropriation, such as just compensation for work performed, lack of a clear owner, or simple mischief. The extreme punishments inflicted for theft under the Penal Code of 1791 might have led to more jury nullifications based on simple humanity. After all, stealing a linen handkerchief, a sack of potatoes, or an iron bar could bring eight or more years of hard labor. The possibility of reducing the crime to a misdemeanor helped to ameliorate that problem. Reducing felonies to misdemeanors quickly became an oft-preferred option in cases of petty theft: almost one-quarter of felony indictments led to misdemeanor convictions. The circumstances of the theft did more to inspire misdemeanor convictions than the value of the stolen goods. People worried about planned thievery, especially if the theft involved more than one person. Pilfering objects, whether from an employer or a neighbor, and especially from taverns, public markets, gardens, or fields, produced the largest number of misdemeanor penalties handed out by criminal courts. The circumstances of the culprit also helped to determine the jury's severity. Jean Valjean may have been punished to the fullest extent of the law, but occasionally juries took pity on destitute thieves. When Pierre Lafon, a wool-carder from Carcassonne, stole a national guardsmen's vest at Pézenas and sold it for 20 francs, the jury did not convict him of stealing public property because that would have brought a mandatory sentence of four years in irons. Instead, the jury noted that "misery and hunger" had compelled him to take it, and his misdemeanor conviction led to a brief fifteen days in prison.[15] Here criminal intent had been made flexible enough to cover criminal desperation.

Theft, especially robbery, was not the sort of crime that raised many questions of criminal intention, however. If we want to understand the importance of jury nullification, therefore, it is better to turn to verdicts in cases of homicide as a basis for comparison. Murder is abhorred as much as robbery, but unlike holdups and break-ins, the motive for killing someone is not always criminal. Death could be accidental or the result of self-defense. In this respect, homicide is like many other categories of crime—motives mattered and had to be determined at trial. As much as society condemned killing, half of those tried for it were acquitted, and another 8 percent were convicted only of imprudence. What led to these acquittals or misdemeanor convictions? As with a quarter of all robbery indictments, jurors sitting on murder cases often decided that there was insufficient evidence to prove that the accused had committed the crime in question. However, in a large number of cases, jurors also found that the killer had acted either in self-defense or under attenuating circumstances. Thus homicide offers a more suitable category than robbery for comparing the willingness of juries to acquit perpetrators or reduce their sentences on the basis of motive.

As figure 5 shows, the category of homicide closely conforms to the over-all profile of jury verdicts. Only the three categories of theft brought higher conviction rates than cases of homicide. The large number of cases of theft and the generally high conviction rates associated with them, however, are offset by the smaller number of cases in other categories of crime and the much lower conviction rates they produced. Looking at verdicts in other categories of crime besides theft and homicide draws immediate attention to the high acquittal rates for any type of counter-revolutionary offense or resistance to public authority. In both cases, almost three-quarters of defendants went free. The reasons for this high acquittal rate emerge clearly from jury responses to the *question intentionnelle*.[16]

If we use our data to isolate acquittals on the basis of the *question intentionnelle* from acquittals on the basis of a lack of convincing evidence, it becomes obvious that the *question intentionnelle* was the basis for the bulk of acquittals that amounted to jury nullifications. This was so because using the first two questions to the jury—Is the crime proved? If so, did the defendant do it?—as the basis for an acquittal against the evidence would have made jury nullification all the more blatant. Jurors did occasionally assert that a crime had not been committed despite overwhelming evidence to the contrary. On occasion, one jury might find the evidence of a crime utterly persuasive, whereas a later jury charged with trying others accused of participating in the same crime would conclude, for whatever reason, that they lacked adequate proof of the crime itself and use this as the basis for an acquittal.[17] However, both the prosecution's preparation of a criminal case and the need to obtain indictments from a grand jury strongly militated against this outcome. As a result, only a modest share of acquittals were the result of a trial jury concluding that the alleged crime had not been sufficiently proved.[18]

These same reasons also tended to reduce the number of acquittals based on insufficient evidence against the accused. Nonetheless, this remained an area of potential jury nullification. Should a jury have concluded that a defendant had indeed perpetrated the crime, using the question of criminal intent to prevent conviction might save him from legal punishment and yet still stigmatize him for the criminal act. This judicial stigma began with the initial charges and arrest warrant, gained color when a grand jury found grounds for indictment, and became most visible after a grand jury confirmed that the accused had committed the crime. Furthermore, an acquittal could only partially purge the stigma created by arrest and indictment. Even if an acquittal on the basis of who did it, rather than whether it was done with criminal intent, were manifestly against the evidence—that is, even if it were a matter of jury nullification—such an acquittal could shape the defendant's reintegration into his community. Family members, friends, neighbors, and especially rivals and enemies might well respond with more animosity to a defendant returning to his village if a jury had publicly found him responsible for a crime, even if that same jury had also used the *question intentionnelle* to acquit him. Defendants and their supporters who sought more than mere jury nullification on the basis of criminal intent sometimes intimidated jurors into acquitting them of perpetrating the crime. For example, a violent feud between the Rouch and Teisserenc families over access to a water supply in Lodève led to a trial of the Rouch sons on charges of attempting to murder Barthélemy Teisserenc on the road from Montpellier. The jurors' fear of endorsing reprisals by Teisserenc's kin led to an odd form of acquittal. The jury decided that Jean Rouch had tried to shoot Teisserenc but did not deem it attempted murder, and, since he had missed and therefore the plaintiff had sustained no injuries, the perpetrator could not be convicted of any other crime. Thus, if there was no crime, his brother Pierre Rouch could be acquitted on the basis of a crime not being proved.[19] Had the jury acquitted on the basis of criminal intent, they would have confirmed the crime itself and thereby added legitimacy to the Teisserenc family's desire for revenge.

In other words, exceptional circumstances could produce clear jury nullification on the basis of the first two questions posed to jurors rather than confining nullification to the *question intentionnelle*. And yet, it was easier for a jury bent on acquittal simply to accept the evidence for an alleged crime, as well as the evidence of the accused's role in the crime, and then to nullify the charges through a negative response to the *question intentionnelle*. This reduced friction with magistrates. It also provided the weakest basis for criticism of the jurors' decision. With this option available, juries had little incentive to acquit against the evidence using one of the first two questions. Men who served as jurors found themselves in a liminal position: culturally shaped by village mores but called upon to support the prosecution's sense of social order. By accepting the facts of guilt, jurors could avoid directly affronting the authority of judicial officials, but by using the *question intentionnelle* to acquit, they could avoid offending widespread notions of more appropriate ways to control behavior.

Having established that jury nullification had a far greater likelihood of occurring on the question of criminal intent than on other questions does not mean that all acquittals on this basis represent jury perversity. Many potential crimes really did result from involuntary or unwitting behavior. That is why the legislators included the question of criminal intent in the first place. How then can we distinguish between an acquittal based on the evidence and one that ran contrary to it? It is best to start with a number of assumptions.

First, we can safely assume the validity of acquittals in cases of homicide or other violent crimes when the justification was self-defense, lack of mature discernment, or insanity. All of these justifications for acquittal would have been gratuitous falsehoods if they were not genuine, even though each type of defense offered its own peculiarities. Juries tended to rather strict interpretations of self-defense. Serious injuries inflicted during a brawl, for instance, even if the accused had not been the aggressor, usually led to misdemeanor convictions, not acquittals. Perhaps the greatest leniency of interpretation in cases of self-defense occurred in a case involving a quarrel between two gendarmes over how to handle a draft dodger. This led to an impromptu duel and the subsequent acquittal of Joseph Bolle, the victor and sole survivor, on the less than obvious but fully credible grounds of self-defense.[20] Thus, homicide committed in self-defense, whether with rock or club, knife or sword, pistol or musket, led to a steady but modest number of acquittals.

Juries also had to use their discretion in acquittals attributed to a lack of mature discernment, there being no fixed age at which it became possible to act with malice aforethought. The Penal Code specified that if a defendant were under sixteen years of age, juries would have to answer an additional question: "Did the perpetrator commit the crime with or without discernment?" Although a defendant's age prompted the question, his youthfulness alone did not answer it. For example, a jury in the Sarthe deemed a youth aged fifteen to have acted without discernment when he joined a small band of chouans who disarmed the commune of Courceboeuf and gave him a share of the loot they stole from one of the houses. Apparently the jury held the adults in the band responsible for his presence. In contrast, a jury in the Hérault convicted a homeless and obviously prepubescent street urchin—he was aged thirteen and stood only 1.3 meters (3 feet, 7 inches) tall—of robbing a woman of her gold cross and chain at Montpellier. He was then sentenced to twenty-two years in a workhouse. All the same, the jury acquitted his junior partner in crime, an eleven-year-old, as below the age of discernment.[21] Clearly jury decisions on discernment lacked the nuances of Lawrence Kohlberg's theory of moral development. In fact, they gave considerably more weight to nonpsychological factors such as social independence.

A lack of discernment could also apply to individuals whose mental faculties never met the low grade of village standards. Jurors decided that only an almost lethal dose of feeblemindedness could explain why Claire Vincent repeatedly set her father's house on fire by casually bringing flaming materials into it.[22] Detecting the difference between simple stupidity and genuine imbecility surely presented its problems. Very few people had Joseph Naudet's tragic advantage of not only being moronic but also being deaf and mute, thereby thwarting efforts to determine his level of discernment and earning him an acquittal for using his shoemaker's knife to perforate a local farmer.[23] Jurors also needed to be careful when acquitting people on the grounds of insanity. In an age happily devoid of psychologists, one could expect jurors to be highly skeptical of any claims made by an obviously lucid defendant that the crime had been committed during a temporary period of dementia. Unfortunately, the sheer horror caused by the murder of her five-year-old nephew saved Anne-Claire Martin from the guillotine. Only a spell of madness ("un esprit aliéné à l'époque") made sense of her generously serving him lunch at her house and then hacking him to death with a pruning knife. The trial revealed no cause for hostility toward him or his parents but did reveal that she had attempted to commit suicide several times. If she had briefly hoped that the "sword of justice" would end her days, she received no help from the jury.[24]

Concluding that death or injury had been caused involuntarily, either through an unfortunate accident or some irresponsible behavior, also appears perfectly reliable considering the frequency of misdemeanor convictions for brawls, knife fights, and provoked assaults. Each of these cases appeared before criminal courts either because a jury director wanted to seek the maximum penalty against the accused or because he did not want to decide the issue of guilt or innocence in the correctional court over which he presided. These institutional factors dramatically increased the number of assault cases tried in criminal courts as attempted murder. This common practice placed the onus on juries to weigh the explanations given by the accused as well as those of his accusers before settling on both an appropriate charge and an appropriate verdict. In one-third of assault cases, juries chose to reduce felony charges to misdemeanor convictions. No other type of crime led to such a reduction rate, which merits explanation.

The Penal Code made it easy for juries to reduce an assault charge to a misdemeanor offense. In order to qualify as a felony assault, the victim needed to have suffered the loss of an eye, a broken limb, or bodily injuries serious enough to prevent him from performing manual labor for forty days. These conditions required verification by a medical officer. This official could easily become complicit in bending the judicial process to fit community norms on interpersonal violence. In a number of cases, medical officers insisted that it would take a particular victim up to thirty-nine days, but not forty, to recover adequately from a serious beating in order to return to work. In numerous other cases, juries did the work of making the crime fit the punishment. The room for maneuver was considerable. On the extreme end of severity, a jury in the Sarthe convicted the middle-aged farmhand Gilles Moreau of attempted murder for several assaults he committed during a drunken rage. Although he had threatened to kill one person with a knife and bashed another on the head with a cudgel, he had killed no one. Nonetheless, he himself perished on the scaffold. The jury's harsh attitude surely stemmed from Moreau's history as a vicious bully (and possible chouan) known as Brise-Ville, or Town-Wrecker.[25] At the other end of the spectrum, where extreme leniency prevailed, lay the case of the *maître valet* François Tournier. Although he had struck his victim on the head three times with an axe, the jury bizarrely found that these blows neither had been delivered with criminal intent nor were the proven cause of death. This amounted to double coverage for what the jury obviously considered a justifiable homicide. Appalled at "the alarm spread by such grave excesses" but prevented from handing down any felony punishments, the judges could only use the jury's misdemeanor conviction to sentence Tournier to a year in prison and a fine of 500 francs.[26] These examples of the jury system's potential for extremes of severity and leniency within the broad category of convictions help to highlight their motives. Moreau's execution for drunken assault and Tournier's modest prison sentence for an axe murder suggest that neither a fear of excessive punishment prescribed by the Penal Code nor a lack of convincing evidence account for many of the misdemeanor convictions in cases of felonious assault. Only the jurors' greater tolerance of violence explains their reluctance to see many offenders sentenced to the *bagne.* Such tolerance becomes all the more obvious in cases of acquittal on the basis of criminal intent.

Considering that it was easy for juries to avoid harsh punishments for assault simply by resorting to misdemeanor convictions, why did they completely acquit so many defendants on the basis of criminal intent? Was this largely jury nullification stemming a fortiori from a high tolerance for interpersonal violence? Undoubtedly yes, but not in all cases. The diversity of jury responses to domestic violence highlights the dangers of overgeneralizing about such matters.

The Penal Code specifically prescribed the death penalty for parricide and twenty years in irons for mutilating one's parent, but it made no mention of other forms of familial violence. The sex-based nature of citizenship ensured that all jurors were men; almost all were husbands and fathers too. It is not surprising, therefore, that juries showed leniency toward husbands who battered their wives. Take the case of Guillaume Micouleau (alias Garrabuste), who was charged with attempting to murder his wife. He had whacked her on the head with a heavy stick while she was doing laundry in their *lavoir* and, when she struggled to climb out, pushed her back in and tried to drown her. She survived and therefore so too did he. The jury merely convicted him of a misdemeanor that brought three months in prison and 200 francs in fines.[27] Clearly the jury showed sympathy for Garrabuste's motives, whatever they were. Such was not generally the case when women fought back. For example, Marie Lavigne had cried out to her husband, "There's a scorpion on your neck!" and when he whisked off his hat and pulled back his collar, she repeatedly slashed his neck and head with a pruning knife. He would have died under the assault had a neighbor not burst in and stopped the blows. The history of wife battering that preceded her attack did not soften jurors' hearts. They considered this a crime of passion and, therefore, not premeditated and thus spared Marie Lavigne's life. Nevertheless, she still had to spend twenty years doing hard labor in a *maison de force.* Here are two cases of attempted murder, both in the context of domestic abuse, and it is the female victim of such violence, who, when she responded violently, was punished most severely. Not all juries refused to appreciate the predicament of women who suffered spousal abuse, however. Alexandre Ragot's wife and child took refuge at her parents' house at Moitron (Sarthe) to escape his torments. Despite a clear warning from his in-laws, Ragot appeared at their house five days later. His wife, her parents, and her sister overpowered him and promptly castrated him using a knife and scissors. He survived the ordeal only to see his genitals dug up from the yard of the Prodhomme house and presented in court. This persuasive evidence led to three death sentences. All the same, the jury acquitted the battered wife, Anne Prodhomme, on the ground of lacking criminal intent. The local paper rightly questioned the logic of this verdict, but it did not doubt the justness of it.[28] Furthermore, this case reveals that despite a strong male bias in cases of domestic violence, jurors did not always seek to punish the female victim for perpetrating violence herself.

Such a pattern of jury responses could well stand for the whole category of assault cases. Jurors tended toward leniency when violence took place between individuals who knew each other and had a history of interaction. Nevertheless, there were clear limits. Lying in wait and unleashing a surprise assault on a passerby, whether known or unknown, provoked especially harsh responses. Whereas the Penal Code specified penalties ranging from two years in prison to six years in irons depending on the extent of the victim's injuries, it prescribed the death penalty for any felonious assault committed with obvious premeditation or as an ambush. Traditional codes of honor encouraged violent confrontations in public places. The publicity of the encounter ensured a rough sense of fairness and could powerfully enhance the message of courage or willingness to extract vengeance intended by the assailant. Such public incidents of violence implicated the community and, therefore, could be monitored if not fully controlled by it. Surprise assaults at night or in obscure places were designed to evade this communal involvement. In these circumstances, the state's concept of how best to maintain social order, as expressed by the Penal Code, converged with traditional village ideas about the role of punishment in preserving order. Jury verdicts in assault cases demonstrate the conditions of convergence.

On the other hand, these two concepts of order diverged widely in matters of folk beliefs. Juries tended to show much greater acceptance of popular superstition than magistrates found acceptable. This is best illustrated by the shocking cruelties perpetrated at La Chapelle Gaugain in the eastern Sarthe and the remarkably light sentences that followed. Marie Souriau, the *femme* Foussard, had suffered a long illness and sought the advice of Louis Foucault, a veterinarian from Couture with a regional reputation for divination. He persuaded her that her neighbor, Marie Dubray (better known as the *femme* Besnard), had cast a spell on her and that she would not lift it until her feet had felt the pain of fire. Souriau's husband and two sons, carrying a gun and fire in a clog, went to procure the remedy from Besnard, but her husband managed to drive them off. The *femme* Foussard continued to suffer for another six months. Having grown desperate for a cure, her sons and two companions kidnapped the *femme* Besnard, brought her back to Foussard home, and began applying red-hot irons to her feet in order to force her to reverse the spell. Distraught by the excruciating torture his sons were inflicting on the *femme* Besnard, Pierre Foussard fled his own house. When he returned, he found her feet and legs so badly burned that they bled and "the sole and heel of the left foot hung in shreds." Magistrates quickly prosecuted the Foussards and their friends for this atrocity. When the case came to trial, however, the jury convicted them only of misdemeanor offenses that led to between one and two months in prison. The *femme* Foussard was excused because her long illness and its effects on her moral faculties had led her to believe the bad advice she received; Pierre Foussard was held responsible only for failing to stop the cruelties; the Foussard sons, aged nineteen and sixteen, were deemed to lack mature judgment; and their companions simply believed that the *femme* Besnard was a witch. A male divine, Louis Foucault, had been paid for his advice and so was later tried as an accomplice. His subsequent conviction and sentence of three months in prison and a small fine was the heaviest in the whole case. Such light sentences were the result of attenuating circumstances, to wit: "the ease with which country folk allow themselves to be persuaded about supernatural things, and how they are still imbued with the ancient and absurd belief that witches and divines exist and battle among themselves over the effects of their supposed evil spells."[29] The court's expression of the jury's deliberations artfully blamed the peasants for their credulity. And yet the verdict suggests that jurors shared similar attitudes. They were too representative of the populace for the belief in black magic not to have some purchase on them. Such attitudes continued to have an influence on juries longer than one might imagine. As late as 1830, jurors in the Oise acquitted a man of murdering his brother-in-law by treating it as self-defense against sorcery.[30] This sort of jury nullification provided just the evidence the French state needed to justify its civilizing mission in the countryside.

Blinded by their own sense of superiority, government officials failed to see the injustices that a uniform system of criminal justice could generate. Paradoxically, by being highly sensitive to local issues and individual circumstances, jurors could make the system more just by technically subverting it. Magistrates could hardly defend a breech of judicial procedures as the best means to a just end; therefore, such explanations are not to be found in their correspondence with the Ministry of Justice. All the same, at times juries obviously used their power of nullification to prevent the judicial system from being exploited by malcontents as a weapon against their enemies. Jurors in the Haute-Saône probably had a difficult time deciding who was more malicious, the woodcutter Garnier, who chopped down a cherry tree with his fellow woodcutter Gérard still in it, or Gérard, who insisted on prosecuting him for attempted murder more than two years later. In this case, the jury acquitted Garnier on the basis of criminal intent rather than convict him of causing injury by imprudence—a misdemeanor. This decision appears designed to avoid rewarding Gérard's prosecutorial zeal but nullified the evidence in the process—after all, Garnier chopped down the tree precisely because Gérard was in it.[31] Ironically, nullification based on a commonsense notion of fairness worked to preserve the integrity of the judicial system as society's ultimate mechanism for the regulation of conflict.

Other jury nullifications on the basis of criminal intent reflected jurors' opposition to politically motivated prosecutions—another nefarious by-product of the state's civilizing mission. Despite the ostensible separation of executive and judicial powers, the government found ways to interfere directly in the work of criminal courts. Nonetheless, the jury remained a repository of alternative values the government could not easily penetrate and where apolitical justice could still be done. Early one fine morning, four men from Marnay (Haute-Saône) snuck up on Demolombre, secretary of the local municipality, who lay sleeping in a rye field. They fired a single shot and killed him on the spot. After a preliminary investigation, the jury director from Gray concluded that this was an accident, a prank gone horribly wrong, and so decided simply to have the men judged by the correctional tribunal over which he presided. However, when the government learned that Demolombre was a veteran recently returned from the war and that he had replaced a man sacked for his opposition to the Revolution, it appealed the jury director's ruling to the Court of Cassation. This being the Second Directory, the high court naturally followed the government's lead and transferred the case to another jury director for full prosecution. Despite such efforts, the jury at Vesoul used the *question intentionnelle* essentially to acquit the men, which allowed them to get off with a modest fine.[32] Thus, the government's political paranoia had led to a rigorous prosecution that the jury thwarted in the belief that several months in prison awaiting trial was punishment enough. Of course, juries were not always so apolitical as the Demolombre case suggests. Still, the political motives most likely to influence jury verdicts were those of opposition to the republican regime.

Juries generally sympathized with people on trial for opposing political authority. Like the mass of villagers they represented, most jurors disliked the extended reach of the revolutionary state no matter which regime was in power. When they were not serving as jurors, they were as likely as not to be involved in resisting the new forms of public authority themselves. Men of property did not support the republic just because it was constitutionally designed to favor them. The political struggles inherent in ensconcing the republic created peculiar forms of opposition. For this reason, the broader category of resistance to authority should be subdivided into three types of crime: resistance to public authority per se, disobedience of particular republican laws, and politically motivated violence against the regime. Almost one-fifth of all criminal court defendants actually present at trial were charged with these three types of crime. Their trials produced some of the highest acquittal rates. Taken together, therefore, jury verdicts in these sorts of cases significantly increased the overall acquittal rate during the period. Furthermore, high acquittal rates for crimes of resisting officials or republican laws gave the regime understandable anxiety about its ability to take root throughout the country. The differences between these types of crimes are as important as their similarities, and each needs to be examined separately.

Resistance to public authority occurs under all regimes; it is the scale and scope of this resistance that determines any particular regime's viability. An extremely complicated set of social, economic, cultural, and political factors worked to animate as well as to obviate resistance to public authority. Jurors embodied many of these tensions because as jurors they assumed a position at the precise point where two concepts of order met. On one hand, they were drawn from towns and villages where they formed the broad elite of their communities. As substantial taxpayers, they had a major stake in social stability. They shared the norms and attitudes that had governed their communities for generations and usually subscribed to traditional, community-based notions of how best to preserve that stability. On the other hand, as jurors they were called upon to enforce an alternative concept of order, that generated by national legislators and the state machinery of policing and criminal justice. This made them responsible for upholding the authority of an innovative and alien apparatus of power in which they had little or no personal stake. No wonder they so frequently failed to side with the official instruments of order.

Juries proved especially sympathetic to those who openly resisted public authority. Three times as many people were acquitted (63 percent) as were convicted of felony offenses (21 percent). Equally remarkable, half of these acquittals were based on jurors concluding that the defendants before them had acted without criminal intent. In other words, proven overt resistance to clearly acknowledged officers of the law acting in their official capacity often went unpunished because jurors chose to accept a variety of dubious justifications for illegal behavior as the equivalent of acting without criminal intent. It seemed perfectly natural to excuse a woman's frenzied assault on the gendarmes who had just arrested her husband. And would not most people physically oppose a bailiff removing their furniture? The occasional contretemps with an officious *garde forestier* or passing from a heated verbal exchange to a physical altercation with a pompous and pushy *adjoint municipal* could hardly be avoided by men socialized to defend their honor as much as their property. Nor could jurors convict in good conscience destitute peasants who, in the catastrophic winter of year IV, seized grain and distributed it at an affordable price.[33] Only a jury's sympathy with the defendants could explain how three men who had violently resisted arrest on charges of failing to pay their *patente* tax at Montpellier could be acquitted on the grounds that they had not "willingly" resisted the gendarmes.[34] In all of these cases, to understand really was to forgive.

The bulk of acquittals in cases of resisting authority came when citizens opposed the gendarmerie or National Guard for executing the republic's laws against draft dodgers, refractory priests, and the free exercise of religion. Some of the most blatant jury nullification occurred in such cases. The penalties for resisting authority were relatively light (unless it involved a mob of more than fifteen people—legally termed an *attroupement séditieux*), so it was less a fear of harsh penalties than an implied sympathy with resisters that motivated jurors to negate evidence by acquitting defendants. Many of these acquittals were based on a lack of criminal intent even though handed out to defendants in their absence. But, one might reasonably ask, how could jurors discern defendants' motives when their arrest and interrogation had yet to take place? Projected excuses could be the only explanation. A jury in the Haute-Garonne found that force and violence had been used to free a prisoner from the gendarmerie at St-Nicolas-de-la-Grave, and yet they acquitted the four absent men claiming that they had not acted "wickedly or with criminal intent." Such a verdict said more about the jurors' motives than those of the defendants.[35] In other circumstances, the motives for violence and for jury nullification were equally obvious and, in fact, the same. A pack of villagers clashed with the municipal authorities at Caraman (Haute-Garonne), first storming the town hall to reclaim the rope for the church bells and then breaking into the barricaded church to ring the bells. Jurors sympathized with this act of religious reclamation, however, and duly acquitted the ringleaders.[36] Jurors were all too familiar with the social cohesion the rituals and routines of Catholicism gave to rural communities and had little incentive to punish those who sought to restore them. When confronted by such a manifest clash of two concepts of order, jurors clearly preferred the parish over the state.

As this case illustrates, the categories of resisting public authority and engaging in illegal antirepublican activity tended to merge. Nonetheless, cases involving indictments for crimes not contained in the Penal Code of 1791 constitute a distinct category of politically motivated opposition. Republican governments called it counter-revolution. This term had sufficient elasticity to include "royalistes à la bonnet rouge," that is, republicans of an "extremist" stripe.[37] Rather than distinguish crimes committed by radical republicans from those committed by reactionaries, it is better to separate violent forms of political opposition from nonviolent ones. This latter category included being an émigré or refractory priest returned from exile, harboring such a person, making counter-revolutionary statements in print or in public, and attacking republican symbols, most notably liberty trees. Juries acquitted three-quarters of the people put on trial for such crimes. This courtroom evidence perfectly summarizes the distaste the vast majority of Frenchmen felt for these laws. After all, by the late 1790s only deeply committed republicans invested liberty trees with sacred symbolic value or fostered the belief that epistolary exchanges with exiles was treasonous. It is not surprising, therefore, that acquittal on the basis of criminal intent occurred more often in this category of crime than in any other. Did an old widow sending money to her former priest living in Italy constitute a security threat to the republic? No, concluded one jury. Another went so far as to acquit the municipal agent and another leading citizen of Provenchère (Haute-Saône) of sheltering deported priests despite having clearly welcomed them back from exile, shown them great hospitality, and participated in a variety of their services. The municipal agent was even acquitted of failing to enforce the laws against refractory priests and public worship.[38] This does not mean that all such crimes went unpunished. When felony convictions did occur, sentences were severe, including several executions and more than a score of deportations. However, jury nullification and a lack of convincing evidence combined to acquit most defendants accused of political offenses.

Especially common was the acquittal of people who made statements against the republic. Some of these were simply silly: "Le Directoire est un pouvoir destructif pas exécutif," or "J'emmerde la République et tous ceux qui sont à son service, même les soldats et généraux des armées," or putting a liberty cap on a dog and saying to it, "Allez, citoyen!"[39] Actually prosecuting such verbal frippery reflected an excessive political zeal that jurors gladly thwarted. For example, juries convicted only three of the fifteen people charged with chopping down liberty trees; one received six months in prison, whereas two others were sent to prison for four years.[40] The harsh penalties prescribed for such crimes also encouraged acquittal. The hastily adopted law of 27 germinal IV (16 April 1796) tried to make all political speech run along republican rails. Any public statement, whether made in speech or in print, provoking the dissolution of the legislature or the executive or calling for any constitution other than that of the year III became a "crime against the internal security of the Republic and against the individual security of citizens" and therefore a capital offense. The death sentence could be commuted to deportation if jurors decided that attenuating circumstances accompanied the offending statement. Only after the insurrection of 1799 around Toulouse was anyone sent to the scaffold for verbally inciting a return to royalty. Of course, the context of widespread rebellion proved critical to the conviction.[41] On the other hand, deportations were not so rare. More often, however, when jurors convicted someone of antirepublican speech, they preferred misdemeanor sentences of a year or two in prison. These distinctions could be extremely fine, but some juries felt confident enough to make them. Thus, one Nicolas-Joseph Vacheret was sentenced to two years in prison for crying, "Vive le roi, vive Condé, merde pour la République" in an *auberge* at Vuillemot, whereas a month later Nicolas Pauthier was sentenced to deportation for saying much the same thing ("Vive le roi, merde pour la République") to a clutch of people behind a café at Luxeuil.[42] If there was any real difference between the two offenses, one had to be there to appreciate it.

Almost all such condemnations for nonviolent political crimes occurred in years VI and VII, when Jacobins took advantage of their return to power to stack juries and persecute opponents of the republic. The rest of the time, juries overwhelmingly refused to convict in cases of this sort. This was especially apparent in year V, when the rising tide of antirepublicanism flooded courtrooms across the country. That year there were fifteen people tried for nonviolent counter-revolutionary crimes in the four criminal courts studied here, but none were convicted. Although such crimes continued to be prosecuted under the Consulate, convictions again became extremely rare. A jury in the Hérault even refused to convict in absentia a café owner from Frontignan for some very incendiary remarks about First Consul Bonaparte: "They missed that villain, that usurper, that tyrant at Paris. If I'd been there, the attempt would not have failed, because I would have made it work. Ten like me could go to Paris to kill him, but before long some gutsy republican will spare us from it."[43] In this case, jurors boldly asserted that the evidence of these remarks was insufficient to convict. Thus, jury nullification based on lack of criminal intent, the most common form of acquittal for this type of crime, was stretched to the point of simply denying that a crime had taken place.

Not all trials for political crimes were for such apparently innocuous offenses. Plenty of opponents of the regime went beyond threats of violence to practice the real thing. Despite the seriousness of their supposed offenses, however, individuals charged with violent counter-revolution had only slightly more likelihood of being acquitted than those tried for crimes of nonviolent counter-revolution. Only one in five received felony convictions, whereas two-thirds were released back into society. Perhaps the most striking evidence of juries refusing to see matters from a repressive perspective comes from the Sarthe, where civil war and *chouannerie* had destroyed all semblance of political normalcy in the western half of the department, criminal justice being no exception. Witnesses could not travel from Sablé to Le Mans, for example, for fear of being attacked by chouans along the way. This state of affairs either genuinely delayed putting the Guibert sisters on trial for aiding and abetting rebels or gave magistrates a credible excuse to keep them in prison for over nine months awaiting more propitious circumstances.[44] The trials of others accused of *chouannerie* certainly gave magistrates just cause for concern. Of twenty-three such men tried by the Criminal Court of the Sarthe in year IV, none was convicted of a felony, seven received misdemeanor sentences of between five days and four months in prison, and sixteen were fully exonerated. This could hardly encourage local republicans or officials in Paris. Here, in the midst of a long guerrilla insurgency, jurors repeatedly allowed rebels to return to their villages.

Jury verdicts in cases of violent counter-revolution were generally no more heartening elsewhere. Most of these trials resulted from local factional struggles that had boiled over into violence. The prosecutions all took place after republicans gained control of the machinery of justice. However, even in the Hérault—where jury lists were revised after the Fructidor coup in order to favor republicans—jurors found fault on both sides and frequently used nullification to acquit. In a series of trials, different juries repeatedly confirmed that a conspiracy against the republic had existed in the strife-torn towns of Frontignan, Pignan, and Béziers between the elections of year V and the Fructidor coup six months later. Nevertheless, the various juries acquitted almost everyone charged with these conspiracies, usually on the grounds of lacking criminal intent.[45] This had its internal contradictions, of course. By its very nature, conspiracy is a crime defined by the shared motive of those involved; jurors who voted to affirm a conspiracy and then voted to acquit on the basis of lacking criminal intent had a broader vision of the issues at stake than the government desired. Jurors' propensity to stretch the *question intentionnelle* to cover various justifications for resisting authority, and especially for politically motivated opposition, drew acerbic remarks from Minister of Justice Merlin de Douai. He repeatedly denounced such distortions, referring to the "question de l'excuse" when it was clear that even participating in certain crimes confirmed criminal intent.

> To ask if, in taking part in an act that is criminal by its nature, someone did it with criminal intent, is in itself to pose a ridiculous question that ill-meaning jurors will not fail to resolve in the negative. . . . Under this system, Babeuf would likewise be acquitted because jurors could claim that he honestly believed that the current constitution contravened the people's rights and that all means of overthrowing it were justified.[46]

In contrast to Merlin's sarcasm, however, jurors hardly needed to work out a sophisticated rationale to excuse opposition to the regime based on sincere ideological differences. Instead, jury nullification in cases of conspiracy or violent political opposition may have arisen from unabashed sympathy for the regime's opponents. More commonly, such acquittals reflected both great antipathy to continued political strife and an unwillingness to take sides. In theses cases, jurors declined to serve as instruments of factional oppression.

The greatest exception to the general pattern of acquittals in cases of violent political opposition came in the case of ninety-two people charged with conspiracy against the republic in the Tarn. Of the seventeen people actually present at the trial (which was held at Toulouse to escape the overheated political climate at Castres and Albi), four were condemned to death (including two former department administrators), six to deportation, and five to a year in prison each. The Court of Cassation later annulled the jury director's original bill of indictment on technical grounds, and the entire affair ended with a grand jury at Carcassonne (Aude) refusing to indict anyone.[47] As exceptional as this case was—and it alone significantly inflected the statistics on verdicts in its category—the final outcome did not differ much from the great majority of similar cases. When it came to prosecuting resistance to authority or overt political opposition, the regime found trial juries utterly unreliable.

## The Weaknesses of Juries

Inquiring into jury nullification naturally leads to an investigation of grand juries. Any quantitative analysis of one department's grand jury decisions would require many times the archival effort required to study those of the trial jury. Though the lack of such work is understandable, it is truly regrettable, for the importance of jury nullification at the level of grand juries may well have exceeded that of the trial jury. As the case from the Tarn suggests, grand juries could be equally unsympathetic to prosecuting opposition to political authority.

Several factors combined to make grand juries an especially critical point at which the state legal apparatus had to lean on men imbued with different notions about the role of punishment in maintaining public order. Grand jurors were chosen at random from the same lists of *éligibles* as trial jurors and, therefore, reflected a similar mix of concerns about partisanship. However, it took less time for a citizen to perform the duty of a grand juror. He only had to travel to the seat of the local correctional court, not to the departmental *chef-lieu*, and heard only the prosecution's side of the case. The jury director read out his bill of indictment and called a select number of witnesses to testify, including the plaintiff. Everything was done orally, in camera, and in the absence of the accused. A majority vote from the grand jurors would then decide if the evidence warranted proceeding with an indictment and trial. The oral testimony gave the hearing some semblance of a trial itself, and magistrates frequently criticized jurors for not deciding on the quality of the evidence against the accused but voting instead on his guilt or innocence.[48]

Although travel and procedural considerations lessened the burden of being a grand juror, deliberating at the local correctional court left them more exposed to extraneous influences. Grand jurors were far more likely to know details of the case before the actual hearing. Cases of regional renown generated plenty of background information as a myriad of rumors circulated in taverns and markets. One or two jurors may have been acquainted with family members or friends of the accused, or of the victim, for that matter. Even if no direct personal connection existed prior to the hearing, the proximity of the correctional court made it easy for one side or the other to try to influence jurors through bribery or intimidation. One court commissioner complained that ignorance, cowardice, and factionalism had inspired grand juries to vote against indictment in thirty cases in four months even though they were "perfectly proved." He later supported his complaints with a recent example. A fight between a hussard and a couple of national guardsmen at Lavaur (Tarn) turned into a general mêlée in which several people were injured and one killed. The jury director assembled a grand jury to hear charges against five individuals. "Before and during the hearing, every sort of intrigue was attempted in order to have the accused acquitted; during the session the courtyard and garden of the court were filled with people; intimidated witnesses suppressed part of the truth, and four of the five accused were acquitted. Some jurors were so frightened that they tried to get the jury director to relieve them of their duty to serve in this case."[49] Few cases garnered this level of public attention, but those that did made jury duty an onerous burden for citizens to bear.

## The Politics of Acquittals

This overview of jury verdicts has paid particular attention to acquittal rates and especially acquittals on the basis of criminal intent because this was the easiest means for trial jurors to nullify evidence. As figure 6 indicates, acquittals using the *question intentionnelle* clustered around crimes of opposition to political authority. In fact, 44 percent of all acquittals took place for such crimes, even though these were relatively infrequent cases. In general, jurors did not support the regime's political goals. It is little wonder that after a couple of years the government sought alternative judicial and administrative means of repressing political opposition.

**Fig. 6  Criminal court verdicts by in three broad categories of crime**
Defendants present

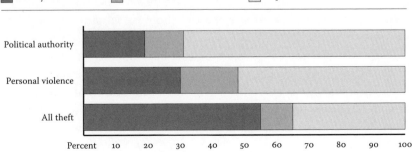

The range of acquittals on the basis of criminal intent in cases of apolitical violence highlights another struggle between the regime and its supposed base of support among would-be electors, the long-term trend of replacing a village-based concept of order with a more uniform, statist concept of the rule of law. The fact that patterns of interpersonal violence changed remarkably slowly between 1550 and 1850 indicates how enduring this struggle remained.[50] Though it is impossible to generate appropriately comparable data across this stretch of time, there is no doubt that the First Republic's system of criminal justice marked a major step toward the ultimate triumph of the state-based order rooted in the rule of law. The explanation for such a large portion of felony assault cases being reduced to misdemeanors or acquittals clearly lay with the jury's role as an intermediary between legislators' notions of justice and the greater acceptance of violence in many regional cultures. Local mores further encouraged juries to take these options. This obviously reflected traditional hostility to the intrusion of the state into village life, especially when exacerbated by the exigencies of war and the Directory's rabid anticlericalism.

Politically motivated violence posed serious problems for most jurors. Undoubtedly some juries sympathized with vigilante attacks on former terrorists or their collaborators. Such was most often the case in Provence but is easily exaggerated. In fact, most political bias in the criminal justice system was more the work of elected officials than of juries. Public prosecutors had fewer powers than under later regimes and therefore relied heavily on jury directors. When public prosecutors and jury directors held similar political attitudes, they could easily determine the whole tenor of a department's caseload. The Hérault provides a perfect example. A turnover in judicial personnel following the coup d'état of 18 fructidor V massively increased the number of cases brought before the criminal court there. Redrafted jury lists then helped to ensure a record number of convictions, even though half of them were against people still on the run.

This raises other critical factors: woefully inadequate policing and risible prison security. Not only was it hard to capture and hold on to perpetrators, their ability to elude capture or escape from jail seriously discouraged witnesses from testifying against them. Without adequate testimony, even willing juries were forced to acquit. Thus, it becomes increasingly evident that the Directory's difficulty in relying on the regular criminal justice system to restore order lay at least as much with the machinery of government as with unreliable juries. No matter the precise share of responsibilities, greater executive control of repression proved an irresistible response.

# PART II
## The Militarization of Repression

THE ARMY WAS the sine qua non of the First Republic, both on the frontiers and domestically. Histories of the Convention, Directory, and Consulate brim with military matters: swelling armies, renowned generals, decisive battles, and landmark treaties. These same histories fail to note, however, that the army's role in defending the republic domestically was equally important to the revolutionary outcome. Not since the early decades of Louis XIV's reign had the army been so important in establishing the state's authority. The influence generals had on national politics has not gone unnoticed, but generalizations about the political importance of the army in the period are invariably based on its intervention at moments of domestic political crisis (Prairial III, Vendémiaire IV, Fructidor V, Brumaire VIII).[1] And yet, it was not at these moments of crisis but between them that the army became a pervasive force in the provinces. A steady militarization of politics resulted from the inability of the regular institutions of the republic to cope with the challenges of ending the French Revolution. This included the judiciary, where most jurors proved unwilling to conduct political repression, the hierarchy of elected and appointed officials who were often factionalized and rarely in place for long, and the broader culture of republicanism, which was at once offensively anticlerical and inspiringly jingoistic. Under these circumstances, the army became an increasingly critical supplement to the regular forms of governance. The army offered expedited justice for use in dealing with political crimes; it furnished the government with less partisan reports on local conditions; it gave courage to weak administrators; and it provided the most important focal point for national pride, whether in the Festival of Victories or in grandiose funerals for fallen heroes such as Generals Marceau, Hoche, and Joubert.

Given that the Directory's legitimacy depended heavily on restoring order and providing security, the role of the army in these matters deserves close study. At first, the army's role during the Directory strongly resembled its role under late absolutism, when it was known as "l'autorité" in domestic matters. This contrasted sharply with the early Revolution, when the army provided little domestic security. By the late 1790s, however, the republic came to rely far more heavily on the army than had ever been the case under the monarchy. This made the character and political leanings of interior commanders of real importance. The more reliable the army became as an instrument of government policy, the more the regime extended its role in public life. Not only did it frequently perform the duties of an overstretched gendarmerie, it wholly replaced the National Guard as the preferred instrument for applying martial law. Military justice too came to play an increasingly important role in imposing the republic.

The coup d'état of 18 fructidor V (4 September 1797) marked the decisive turning point in this process. Excessive attention to the ideological aspects of post-Fructidorian repression has taken it out of the broader context of restoring law and order on republican terms. This context included enhancing the repressive character of the criminal justice system, making the gendarmerie into a distinctly modern and substantially more professional police force, and expanding military justice to include common-law criminals as well as royalist rebels. Despite political opposition to the Directory's increasing authoritarianism, the regime's steady erosion of civil liberties in the interests of greater security responded to the public mood. In a country wracked by fears of crime and sedition, the restoration of order would earn the republic far greater credibility than careful adherence to a liberal democratic constitution. In this respect, the rupture of Fructidor proved as decisive in defining the authoritarian character of the postrevolutionary order as did Brumaire.

# 5 The Army and Domestic Security

> The armed forces that abroad perform the glorious duty of assuring respect for the independence and integrity of the Republic, are called upon in the interior to perform a duty, possibly less brilliant but no less useful: that of assuring execution of the laws and, along with other citizens, of honoring the repositories of civil authority.
> —Minister of War Berthier to district commanders, 5 messidor X (20 July 1802)

THE ARMY PLAYED an unprecedented role in domestic security during the years 1795 to 1802. Well before "citadel practice" emerged in Prussia in the 1830s,[1] the French First Republic saw an almost paranoid defense of the political regime combine with powerful demands for social order to increase greatly the army's integration into the routines of domestic rule. The highly contested nature of the First Republic, however, made its use of armed force for policing and internal repression fraught with questions of legitimacy. The revolutionary trajectory from popular violence to state-sponsored terror in the years 1789 to 1794 greatly complicated the use of force to restore order and thereby end the French Revolution.

As the introduction indicated, although scholars often speak of the state as the monopoly of violence in society, such a statement corrupts Max Weber's original idea by eliding the notion of legitimacy. If methods of repression used in particular circumstances are widely considered excessive, they become discredited and turn into what I have termed domestic state violence. Attempting to analyze various forms of repression without taking an a priori moral stance toward them—that is, without condoning or condemning them—can be facilitated by reducing the assessment of coercive force in terms of whether the ends justified the means and instead assessing coercive force in terms of methods and modalities. According to Sergio

Cotta, legitimate force distinguishes itself from illegitimate violence by being specific and precise in its targets, by being governed by clearly defined
limits, and by being exercised in defense of a defined polity. None of these
was assured in the late First Republic. Though this chapter will not belabor
Cotta's terminology of internal, external, and purposive measure, his theory
helps to refine its treatment of the following questions. To what extent did
generals and officers commanding in the interior share a common vision
of the polity? How constrained were they in the deployment of force? What
was the army's role in policing? Did its various domestic duties provide
security or provoke hostility? Was the application of force in the interior
well regulated? Did the use of military justice conform to the legal norms
of the period?

As noted earlier, taking a Hobbesian perspective on the First Republic
draws attention to its potential to acquire legitimacy simply through assuring social order. Although a wide variety of sources of instability and
insecurity have already been considered, the fear inspired by the regime
itself has largely been ignored. The Directory was the offspring of bloody
revolution. Almost inevitably, therefore, its use of force went beyond efforts
to restore and maintain order. As the progeny of the Convention, the Directorial regime continued the revolutionary aim of transforming French society. For this reason, a great many people believed that the regime was not
essential to preserve order but was itself the source of disorder. The political thinker Benjamin Constant tried repeatedly to reverse this perception
in 1796 and 1797. His important pamphlets sought to win support for the
Directory by developing several intellectual strategies. He lauded the basic
principles of republican government; he tried to dissociate the republic's
early years from the arbitrariness of the Terror; and he sought to win acceptance of the new regime by claiming that a return to the past would cause
greater upheaval than staying the republican course. The election results of
1797 largely repudiated the republic and showed just how hollow Constant's
arguments appeared to his contemporaries.[2] In fact, the regime's persistent
revolutionary character helped to perpetuate the climate of fear that enveloped France in the 1790s. For this reason, the state, whose usual raison
d'être is to provide order, continued to be the fount of much disorder.

To understand better how the Directory struggled to manage and even
legitimize the force it deployed, where this failed, and when it succeeded,
we need to appreciate the role the army played in the economy of violence.
This points at the Directory's problem of establishing its legitimacy through
the use of force, and not just through patriotic ardor or the ideals of liberal

democracy. To be familiar with the appalling state of France in the autumn of 1795 and the widespread loathing republicans had generated, especially in the countryside, is to know that ensconcing a democratic republic without recourse to some harsh measures would have been impossible. Simply applying republican constitutionalism and the rule of law to the continuing civil war in the west and the cycles of violence in the southeast was bound to fail.[3] These regions first needed to be pacified by force. Once he had looked into the sources of strife in the Midi, even Antoine Thibaudeau, that paragon of constitutional self-righteousness, advocated suspending the constitution and appointing a military dictator for the region,[4] which is precisely what the Directory did in western France. Because the Directory was inconsistent, being constitutionalist in principle but often revolutionary in practice, the regime found it agonizingly difficult to have its use of force accepted as legitimate.

## The Army as an Instrument of Repression

One key to public acceptance of the army as a legitimate partner in domestic governance was the extent to which it was accepted as a normal feature of the political landscape. In this respect, the Directory inherited a mixed legacy. On one hand, the long-standing practices of the *ancien régime* served to legitimize military policing so long as it was balanced by other mechanisms of rule. On the other hand, the unrestrained use of military force to impose the Jacobin republic had made the army a discredited instrument of partisan politics. An understanding of this mixed legacy provides an essential basis to assess the nature of the army's domestic role during the constitutional republic.

The army had been an integral part of absolutist rule in eighteenth-century France. Though nominally subordinate to provincial governors, the military commanders appointed for each province had considerable scope for independent action. Because they were free to dispose of the only significant armed force available, provincial commanders constituted an alternative source of authority to *intendants* and *parlements*. Local communities frequently requested detachments of troops to undertake various security functions. Unless a community agreed to bear the entire cost of the mission, however, provincial commanders rarely sent troops. Despite pushy officials who wanted the army to take responsibility for public order, or influential seigneurs irritated by the "insolence" of their tenants, provincial commanders resisted using troops to carry out mundane police functions. The army handled certain matters of prevention (standing guard at annual fairs or public executions) and detention (delivering *lettres de cachet* or arresting public agitators), but its ultimate policing function was to deal with collective violence such as quelling a tax revolt or dispersing grain rioters. But soldiers could be unpredictable in the face of a crowd, reacting with excessive rigor on one occasion and fraternizing on another. As a result, the late *ancien régime* used regular troops as little as possible in the interior. In fact, the number of refusals to use the army for repressive purposes far outstripped the few times it actually cracked heads. Even the military response to the "Flour War" of May 1775 was less aggressive than often claimed and certainly not decisive.[5]

This eighteenth-century reluctance to use the army to crush the crowd made the French Revolution possible. Though there were moments of bloody repression during the "prerevolution," most notably the Reveillon Riots in Paris in April 1789, officers often showed great unwillingness to put down political disturbances, such as at Rennes and Grenoble in 1788. Matters were little different in the hundreds of food riots provoked by the subsistence crisis of 1788–89. Sending small detachments here and there to cope with local disturbances exposed the overall shortage of troops and widespread lack of will to use force against the populace. Not even the presence of whole regiments prevented serious outbreaks of violence in such towns as Cambrai and Rennes. The ultimate failure of nerve came in July 1789, of course, when senior officers told the king that the twenty thousand regular troops stationed around Paris were too unreliable to assert royal power in the capital. Thereafter, military authority largely collapsed across the country. Where incidents of serious repression did take place, they were more often the work of the *milice bourgeoise* or the newly formed National Guard.[6] Thus, after the summer of 1789, the royal army, with its officers demoralized by years of contradictory reforms and its soldiers politicized by revolutionary ferment, no longer had a central part to play in maintaining order. This hastened the success of the municipal revolution and allowed waves of rebellion to sweep the country for years to come. According to John Markoff, almost 4,700 insurrectionary events took place between June 1788 and June 1793,[7] which illustrates the reluctance of even moderate revolutionaries to use the army to restore order and defend the new regime.

All the same, the army continued to perform certain police functions after 1789. As had always been the case, the mere presence of troops helped to discourage disorder, and so they were often assigned to stand guard in markets or outside town halls, provide escorts for grain, or reinforce patrols in the countryside. Civilian officials frequently requested the presence of line units and detachments where there were signs of impending trouble. A timely appearance usually prevented actual violence from breaking out. But the army's role in repressing riots and large-scale revolts was decidedly mixed. Effective and well-disciplined in its response to the sectarian strife at Montauban in May and Nîmes in June 1790, the army proved insubordinate in the face of popular violence at Aix, Marseille, and Lyon in 1791 and into 1792. Revolutionary politics were the bane of military discipline, so much so that four-fifths of incidents of insubordination while performing police functions arose as a result of local conflicts between opposing political groups.[8] Thus, France experienced a lot of violence in the early Revolution, but little of it in the form of repression.

The men who had filled the vacuum of power created by armed insurrection, and whose legitimacy rested on novel concepts of popular sovereignty, simply could not define the difference between acceptable and unacceptable forms of popular violence. This left them bereft of a theory of justice that could have effectively legitimated their own use of coercive force to defend the new regime.[9] Without such a theory, but bent on radical social change and determined to preserve the fledgling republic, national leaders drifted into accepting and even condoning essentially unjustifiable forms of violence. On what basis could order be established in revolutionary France when Parisian Jacobins fêted the mutinous soldiers from Nancy, excused the cold-blooded "Glacière massacre" at Avignon, and protected *septembriseurs* from prosecution?

Whereas in the early Revolution, the royal army was deemed unsuitable for political repression, after 1792, it was unavailable for it. The outbreak of war increased demand for domestic coercion while removing its main supply. With the army and national guardsmen needed on the frontiers, the National Convention encouraged surveillance committees, exceptional tribunals, and *armées révolutionnaires* to proliferate across the country. This became repression administered "on a putting-out basis."[10] The "reign of terror" then became a prolonged struggle to bring these instruments of state-sanctioned violence under control while continuing to wage a life-or-death struggle with counter-revolutionaries and foreign enemies alike. The Terror also involved making the army into an instrument of the new order. The massive purge of senior officers, the intense political surveillance of executive agents and deputies on mission, and the concentration of control in the Committee of Public Safety created an army more responsive to government than had ever been the case during the *ancien régime*. The rank and file was equally transformed. Royal army veterans were submerged in a sea of national guardsmen, volunteers, and fresh recruits. In order to ensure their political loyalty, the new citizen-soldiers were inculcated with republican ideas using a host of radical newspapers and revolutionary marching songs.[11]

Under these conditions, the army gradually became an instrument of government repression once again. But the transformation was slow and uneven. The tide turned against the Vendée rebellion only following the arrival in September 1793 of ten thousand troops released from the siege of Mainz. Likewise, it took the fall of Valenciennes to furnish the core of regular troops used to defeat the Federalist Revolts at Lyon. But the troops of year II were notoriously unruly, an especially dangerous trait in matters of repression. Turreau's "infernal columns" of early 1794 replicated the brutality and self-defeating slaughter perpetrated on the Camisards in the Cévennes ninety years before. Such rampant destruction and uncontrolled killing could only provoke greater determination to resist the republic. Thus, eight months after the final crushing defeat of the "Catholic and Royal Army" near Nantes, the Convention still needed 150,000 soldiers to assert its authority over western France.[12] So numerous, varied, and ad hoc were the many types of armed force assembled during the Terror, however, that it is impossible to isolate the role of the army per se in this unprecedented build-up of state coercion. Suffice it to say that suppression of the Vendée and Federalist Revolts, including the 3,000 people who perished in the sinister drownings at Nantes or the mass shootings at Lyon, the condemnation and execution of 16,500 victims by over seventy military commissions and revolutionary tribunals, and the imprisonment of over 100,000 people as "suspects" never put on trial, would not have been possible without extensive use of military force against the citizens of France.

Not only was the domestic state violence of 1793–94 often terrifyingly arbitrary and counterproductive, but Jacobin ideologues failed clearly to define its purpose. The excesses of the Terror were not inevitable by-products of defending the nascent republic in the midst of a staggering war crisis, as the ruthless pursuit of such varied victims as Girondin deputies and former Farmers General attests. Furthermore, the reign of virtue did not constitute a clearly defined sociopolitical order. In fact, the famous speech Robespierre made on 17 pluviôse II (5 February 1794) to justify the Terror was merely a revolutionary radicalization of Domat and Pascal in which virtue and terror stood in for justice, authority, and force in an embarrassing attempt to put a metaphysical fig leaf over the domestic state violence of the moment.[13] But Robespierre too understood the logic of an excessive use of force. Even while he supported the law of 22 prairial II (10 June 1794) emancipating the Revolutionary Tribunal from all jurisprudence, he started a campaign to recall those representatives on mission whose excesses were discrediting the regime. Such an ominous contradiction led directly to his overthrow.

The outcome of 9 thermidor II did not depend on who controlled the army or how it would deal with urban insurgency; it was simply one more violent *journée* in which the absence of line troops left the government at the mercy of the Paris sections, only this time the most committed sections sided with the Convention. Not until 1795 did the line army finally begin to emerge as a force able to prevent further revolutionary upheaval. The shift began with the rioting of 12–13 germinal III (1–2 April 1795), when the Convention proclaimed Paris under a "state of siege" and briefly placed all available forces under General Jean-Charles Pichegru. Six weeks later, the insurrection of 1–2 prairial III (20–21 June 1795) brought the line army back to the capital for good. What the monarchy had not dared to do in July 1789 or June 1792, the Convention now did in 1795. It deployed a massive contingent of troops against the citizens of Paris. Twenty-five thousand line troops and national guardsmen isolated the Faubourg Saint-Antoine from the rest of the capital, occupied its three sections, and proceeded to round up hundreds of resident "terrorists." At the same time, the army was serving the Thermidorian cause in similar fashion in the Midi. A contingent of several hundred cavalry under General Michel-Marie Pacthod, commander of Marseille, trounced a large expeditionary force of *sans-culottes* from Toulon. Soon thereafter, ten thousand troops arrived from the Army of Italy to put an end to any further revolutionary agitation.[14]

Despite the growing availability of troops for domestic repression, pusillanimous if not outright reactionary legislators failed to prevent the revenge killings in the summer of 1795. Once the Thermidorians let the politics of vengeance take over, they too lacked any theoretical means to distinguish between the legitimate use of force to preserve the polity and the vigilante violence that destroyed it. Moreover, when the Thermidorian Convention excluded all those active in the Terror from local office, it nearly handed the republic over to royalists. Having dismantled the institutions that provided the basis for revolutionary government in 1793, the Convention needed the army more than ever for domestic coercion. That the army could be used to repress reactionaries as well as *sans-culottes* was made clear when it took over the policing of Lyon in June 1795, thereby sidelining the dubious National Guard, and above all by its part in crushing the insurrection of 13–14 vendémiaire IV (5–6 October 1795), when the use of cannons to demolish barricades and slaughter insurgents inaugurated a long tradition of military repression in Paris. Thus, by the time the Directory took office, nobody could doubt that the army was ready to play the sort of role in maintaining order that it had been unwilling to play in 1789, unable to play in the early Revolution, and unfit to play during the Terror. Whether it would be a bulwark of liberal democracy, an instrument of partisan violence, or the basis of military dictatorship remained an open question.

## The Directory and the Politics of Army Policing

A regime as weak as the Directory depended on the army almost as much at home as it did abroad. Though not the sole source of coercive force in late 1795—the gendarmerie and the National Guard continued to operate—the army had clearly become the most responsive instrument available. Military service and repeated purges had rendered the gendarmerie nearly as worthless as *assignats.* The National Guard had fallen either into the hands of reactionaries or into utter desuetude due to economic dislocation and political apathy. Even the policing of Paris, always of paramount importance, had been handed over to the army. The strongly hierarchical nature of army command and the abundance of available senior officers gave the Directory more control over generals assigned to interior commands than over other, civilian institutions of governance. This did not, however, make the army a facile instrument for the government to wield against all forms of domestic disorder or internal opposition. Finding the appropriate level of authority and independence to confer on interior commanders as well as deciding just how much to use the army for policing remained a work in progress throughout the period. The republic's task was complicated by a host of factors: the institutional framework of policing, the constraints of the constitution, the shortage of troops in wartime, the eclectic careers and opinions of officers, and the instability of the government's politics.

In order for the army to contribute effectively to domestic security, for the use of armed force for domestic repression to have "external measure," it needed to be responsive to government control. This required both a framework for command and supply and a set of generals dedicated to upholding the regime. The institutional basis of the army's intervention in local affairs was the military district.[15] The National Assembly had divided France into twenty-two military districts that consisted of three to six departments each. Extending the system to Corsica, Belgium, and the Rhineland brought the total to twenty-six military districts, each with its own general staff and commissary supply service. When the Directory took office, it found more generals on its hands than were needed or expected.[16] Therefore, with a surfeit of generals and obvious difficulty restoring order in the interior, the Directory decided that each military district would be staffed by a division general, two brigade generals, and an adjutant general.[17] Symmetry of this sort among districts was impractical and never realized—there were too many demands in the west and south and insufficient need in the center and east—nonetheless, it served as a basic template determining officer assignments throughout the period. As a result, an average of seventy generals, or one-quarter of those on active duty, were commanding in the interior at any one time, not including generals assigned to command key fortress garrisons throughout the country.[18] Such a concentration of generals in domestic postings underscores the importance of the army in establishing the authority of the republic at home.

Military districts had originally been an extension of national defense and naturally continued to serve the same function under the Directory. Being on guard against potential invasion along the frontiers and coasts obliged many district commanders to keep the bulk of their troops on the country's perimeter even when domestic strife called for more attention inland. The active role of military districts in the war effort meant that when the Directors first took office, about half of the military districts were directly subordinated to frontier armies. This was a legacy of year II, when the entire country was divided between fourteen armies.[19] These dozen districts were gradually emancipated from frontier armies between the summer of 1796 and the peace of Campo Formio in the autumn of 1797. The war crisis in the summer of 1799 later reversed the process, and the independence of many interior districts was restored only in the spring of 1801 following the peace of Lunéville. Generals who commanded military districts attached to regular armies came under the authority of army commanders-in-chief. Unlike generals who commanded combat divisions, however, generals who headed interior districts also corresponded directly with the government. This inevitably created tensions between field commanders, who focused on foreign enemies, and district commanders, who dealt mainly with domestic disorder. Army commanders usually won these disputes, though the struggle could be prolonged when interior commanders had the ear of legislators or ministers concerned about domestic politics. The tension focused above all on the allocation of resources, especially of regular troops. In preparation for the campaign of 1796, for example, the Directory ordered all available troops transferred out of southern France to the Army of Italy; only those necessary for maintaining order were to remain.[20] To General Châteauneuf-Randon, this meant keeping half of the eight thousand men stationed in the thirteen departments under his command (Ninth and Tenth Military Districts). Although the War Ministry supported his claim, the Directory allowed him to keep less than half this number.[21] Such a drastic cut in his regular troops made it impossible to preserve the peace and thus forced every department in the district to mobilize elements of the National Guard. This proved an expensive and largely ineffective solution and confirmed what was becoming painfully obvious: only line troops commanded by regular officers could fully meet the challenges of domestic disorder under the Directory.

The Revolution separated civilian and military functions and gave elected officials the upper hand. A decree of 10 August 1789 fixed the future revolutionary doctrine on using armed force to maintain order by placing the decision to deploy armed force against rioters exclusively in the hands of civilian officials. Henceforth, all army officers were required to swear "never to employ those under their orders against the citizenry except if requisitioned by civilian municipal officials and always to read such requisitions to their assembled troops" before sending them into action. Though hotly debated in terms of defining emergency circumstances, preserving executive authority, and holding local officials accountable for life and property, the new revolutionary doctrine of total civilian control at the local level was repeatedly affirmed.[22] The Constitution of Year III further ensconced this attitude toward domestic security. In marked contrast to the *ancien régime*, army officers could no longer employ troops to guard a market, patrol a town, or quell a riot unless they first received a written order from civilian officials (art. 291). Yet generals did exercise the freedom to station troops where they saw fit.[23] In fact, the Directory initially extended the authority of generals to call up and deploy national guardsmen beyond the borders of their home departments without waiting for approval from civilian officials on the grounds that article 292 of the constitution limited these authorities' requisitions to their own jurisdictions. But the National Guard was highly parochial and not inclined to perform dangerous duties away from home. Relying on it as the main armed force was likely to cost the regime credibility, either with the men who were ordered to serve or with the communities they were supposed to protect. Therefore, after some notorious abuses and plenty of wasteful spending,[24] the Directory concentrated this power in its own hands. In early year V, the Directory began to require generals to obtain prior approval from Paris before mobilizing and deploying national guardsmen in neighboring departments. When the government granted such authority, it always stipulated that army officers and department officials jointly determine the number of men and term of service.[25] This gave department officials a practical veto and thereby preserved the principle of civilian control at the local level. The Directory relinquished its own control somewhat in late 1798 by authorizing generals and departmental officials in thirty-one departments to requisition national guardsmen to assist in the hunt for brigands in neighboring departments.[26] All the same, except in areas where the constitution had been officially suspended, generals never gained full authority over the National Guard, even in emergencies. Those who crossed the line faced a court-martial. In other words, interior commanders were crucial to preserving the regime, but at no time did the republic risk slipping into a Cromwellian rule of major-generals.[27]

Not only did generals not acquire great independence in the interior, they never formed a distinct political constituency. There was never a "party of generals" or a sense that the military was pitted against civilians across the republic, as later became the case in Latin America, for example. Rather, army commanders were well-integrated into the overall machinery of governance. They had their distinctive roles, to be sure, but this aided the government rather than undermined it. Interior commanders were a valuable alternative source of information, one that was usually, though certainly not always, less compromised by local politics than other sources. Often a general's perspective was more helpful than the partisan versions presented by local administrators, legislative deputies, or even the government's appointed commissioners. Early in the regime, Minister of War Annibal Aubert-Dubayet told his colleague, Minister of the Interior Pierre Bénézech, not to bother passing along so much information from the departments: "correspondence with generals informs me infinitely better than local authorities inform you."[28] Ministerial arrogance aside, a little-used series in the French military archives amply demonstrates that the correspondence between interior commanders and the War Ministry contained an abundance of information about politics and the problems of domestic disorder.[29] Minister of Police Marie Sotin was convinced of it as well, believing that generals provided more reliable information on troubled regions than any other source.[30] After all, they were more inclined than local officials to see things from a state perspective. And yet officials in Paris never forgot that the quality of information they received depended on the qualities of the generals who sent it.

In order to make the army an effective instrument of domestic policing, the generals who commanded in the interior needed broadly to share the government's vision of the polity; otherwise, their use of armed force would both contradict and discredit the regime. However, the Directorial government, divided as it was between five Directors and six ministers, showed frequent signs of internal tension not dissimilar to the ministerial politics of the *ancien régime*. Furthermore, the staggering turnover in members of the government meant that they rarely had a full appreciation of the individual qualities and political opinions of the many generals employed in the interior. Certainly a few were personally known to one or more Directors or ministers. Information on those not familiar in government circles often came from trusted deputies, many of whom had been representatives on mission to the armies during the Convention. All the same, annual elections and constant shifts in the political wind made such reports susceptible to varying interpretations. These biased and often contradictory assessments, together with the Directory's own political inconstancy, produced huge instability in domestic appointments. Prior to 1789, provincial commanders usually spent many years in a single post; during the First Republic, generals rarely stayed more than a year in any one place (see appendix C).

The road to stability among interior commanders was long and rough with politics. The generals commanding military districts during the early months of the Directory came from across the political and professional spectrum. There were political figures past and future, men such as A.-P. Guérin du Tournel, marquis de Joyeuse, comte de Châteauneuf-Randon, who had been a representative of the nobility in the National Assembly and a Montagnard deputy in the National Convention, as well as J.-F.-A. Moulin, a civil engineer in 1789 and elected a Director in 1799 while commanding the Army of the West. There were also high functionaries like L.-A. Pille, whose frequent, detailed, and well-organized reports reflected his eighteen months as head of the Commission for Armies and Troop Movements in 1793–94. The first cohort of generals also included a wide range of political attitudes and military aptitudes. There were royalist veterans such as E.-G. Picot de Bazus, a former member of Louis XV's Garde du Corps du Roi, who had twice been cashiered during the Revolution, as well as inexperienced Jacobins like François Bessières, whose army career extended no further back than 1792, but who was nonetheless reactivated and reappointed to an interior command in the wake of the Vendémiaire uprising.[31]

This wide range of professional experience and political opinions made it difficult for the fledgling regime to present a coherent image of its policies. The diversity among interior commanders also made it difficult for them to deploy armed force with "purposive measure," in other words, in consistent defense of a moderate constitutional republic.

It was a full year into the Directory before the group of generals commanding in the interior began to acquire political consistency. The Directory had first to remove outright traitors. Three generals in particular were sacked for their overtly royalist machinations: Montchoisy, Lajolais, and Ferrand.[32] The government carried on removing extremists of one stripe or another, including Picot de Bazus and Bessières. The Directory's military man, Lazare Carnot, and the new minister of war, Claude Pétiet, steadily replaced dubious commanders with more reliable men. The turnover was remarkable. Only four district commanders in place on 1 ventôse IV (20 February 1796) held these same posts on 1 fructidor V (18 August 1797). During the same eighteen months, a half-dozen military districts had at least three different commanders each. Under the influence of moderates in the Councils, Carnot and Pétiet installed numerous tepidly republican generals in sensitive posts. These new appointees were men who owed much of their career success to the Revolution, but who found the Jacobin republic anathema to law and order and favored "anarchist" as an epithet. The most famous of these was General Amédée Willot, a former commander in the Vendée appointed to the sulphurous Eighth Military District (headquarters at Marseille). There is no evidence that he actively pursued a royalist strategy there, but his virulent anti-Jacobinism and strong-arm tactics made him one of the best friends royalists had in Provence.[33] Similar tendencies developed elsewhere. In the Twenty-second Military District (headquarters at Angers), Jean Guiot du Repaire found local Jacobins a greater threat to stability than chouan sympathizers among the traditional elite. In the Eleventh District (headquarters at Bordeaux), B.-A.-J. de Moncey joined a clumsy opposition to local democrats. Commanders of his ilk had a clear influence on the elections of 1797. Not only was it a right-wing landslide, but interior commanders such as the reactionary Willot and the royalist Ferrand were themselves elected as deputies.

After the coup d'état of 18 fructidor V, the Directory purged the corps of generals. This brought the dismissal of at least thirty-eight generals deemed to be royalist sympathizers. Well over half of these men held interior military commands.[34] Clearly the victors in the coup believed that generals commanding in the interior had not done enough to prevent the drift toward royalism and the concomitant collapse in public authority. The government lacked material proof that these men conspired against the regime but acted on any evidence of reactionary tendencies.[35] Endless denunciations, investigations, and recriminations made truth a rare commodity for the government; almost anyone, no matter how unfaithful to the regime or corrupt in their activities, could find a few deputies to support their petitions.[36] Because the government needed support in the Councils to pass laws, but could rarely count on more than a minority of faithful deputies, it needed to earn added support by accepting recommendations from deputies it hoped to win over. If the political climate changed, however, generals appointed on this basis lost their jobs. The result was endemic turnover. The Directory's shift from fearing royalists to fearing Jacobins produced still more instability. In the twelve months between February 1798—that is, just before the government turned against the left—and February 1799, when it was gearing up for another round of elections, forty of the eighty-two generals assigned to interior military districts were moved or sacked.[37] Not all of these changes had political motives, but a high proportion certainly did. Political considerations had the greatest impact in military districts where factionalism had the greatest influence.[38] The influence interior military commanders could have on elections produced constant change as the government attempted to "prepare" elections from one year to the next. Some commanders candidly described their involvement: "the troops . . . have been placed in such a manner as to protect patriots," wrote Adjutant-General Noguès, commander of Ariège, when discussing the upcoming elections.[39] The mixing of political and military influence became almost total when deputies owed their seats to the local military commander or generals were themselves elected—as happened to eight generals in 1798.[40]

In addition to short stints in any one place, generals were unlikely to be assigned to command in their native regions, especially in their home departments. As a result, interior commanders usually lacked intimate knowledge of the areas assigned to them. This limited the subtlety of their responses and made their recourse to force more common than it needed to be. Short stays in any one post and unfamiliarity with an area, however, both helped to keep interior commanders from developing the sort of local attachments that undermined their independence. Being fully aware that his career depended more on the government's opinion of his work than on that of the local populace encouraged a district commander to impose the regime's authority rather than let sympathy temper his response to collective resistance or open violence. Failure to understand this basic rule cost a number of generals their posts. General Joseph Servan's brief tenure as commander of the Twentieth Military District (headquarters at Périgueux) in 1800 provides a glaring example of the discrepancy between function and performance. Despite being appointed with "extraordinary powers to repress brigandage," Servan, famous as the Brissotin minister of war in 1792, betrayed his hard-earned hostility to Jacobins by openly favoring their bitterest opponents, which included protecting the royalist dandies known locally as "jeunes gens du bouton." Even his friend Carnot, himself now minister of war, took offense: "I am distressed to see that far from fulfilling the mission given you by the government, you have only increased the disorder, inflamed the wounds, and reignited the furies of factionalism. . . . Your liaisons and your choices have all been marked by the same tendency. . . . You have ignored the brigands and gone to war with peaceful citizens. It is impossible for me, my dear general, whatever effort my friendship may make, to justify your conduct."[41] Servan had targeted a local faction, not criminals, and that was one definition of domestic state violence. The Consulate promptly rescinded his appointment and recalled him to Paris.

An officer's social conduct while assigned to the interior also shaped perceptions about how well he served the cause of domestic order. Dubious personal behavior alone could bring a quick change of venue. In October 1796, General Antoine Morlot lost his command once the government learned of his violence, arbitrariness, and notorious involvement in gambling and prostitution at Aix-la-Chapelle. All the same, this did not ruin Morlot's career. He was soon put in charge of the Tenth Military District, whose headquarters were then at Perpignan, a fortress about as far removed as possible, both geographically and culturally, from his sources of trouble.[42] But conduct unbecoming an officer could also mean conduct unbecoming a gentleman, and thereby also lead to an embarrassing transfer. The Directory did not hesitate to relocate the talented and politically well-connected "Achille" Duvigneau from command of the Tenth Military District once it learned of his social standing at Toulouse. Indulging his wife's unseemly behavior had "plunged him into an abyss of pressing debt which caused him to compromise the dignity of an army general"; as a result, continued Augereau, his predecessor and erstwhile supporter, "he can no longer handle his assignment effectively, being scorned by everybody, having lost all credit and above all the confidence of his subordinates."[43] Adding to the regime's small supply of credibility thus depended on not ignoring questions of social conduct. But charges of misconduct were also the stock-in-trade of political enemies; therefore, the government could afford to take such charges seriously only when they came from reliable sources. Despite claims from local Jacobins that the very young François Watrin, commander of the Sarthe in early 1796, was socializing with the aristocracy of Le Mans, assurances about his political independence sent by the estimable General Hoche convinced the Directory to leave him in place.[44] Such was the delicacy of assignments to the interior, always balanced between issues of personal character and professional competence. And above both stood political considerations, which came to the fore with every swing of the political pendulum.

The instability of the First Republic increased the importance of generals in local affairs. Whichever faction could count on the local commander had a distinct advantage. This extended beyond the mere application of armed force in partisan ways. Brigade General Cambray made a national reputation for himself by leading the "ambulatory constitutional circle" in the Sarthe. Almost every *décadaire* in the run up to the elections of year VI, Cambray and Rigomier Bazin, the Jacobin editor of the *Chronique de la Sarthe*, led members of the constitutional circle of Le Mans out to another town to establish a local constitutional circle there. Cambray often gave the keynote speech in a day of feasting and oath-taking. The innovative effort paid off with an easy Jacobin victory in the department. Their combined success got Cambray sent to the eastern front and Bazin's newspaper banned.[45] This relationship between newspaper editors and generals significantly affected the credibility of another local commander. Brigade General Pierre Sol, who commanded at Toulouse from September 1795 to March 1798, took special pains to refute the portrait painted of him by the *Journal de Toulouse.* Eventually he earned grudging respect, which helped him to tame the National Guard and preserve his command despite being inclined to protect the "honnêtes gens" of the old judicial capital.[46] Local reputation and involvement in politics thus became key aspects of a general's successful deployment of force in defense of the republic. If generals, unit commanders, and even junior officers did not share the Directory's vision of the republic, they would not fulfill their mandate as guardians of the polity. In such cases, use of the army in domestic policing was perceived as nothing more than personal ambition or factional politics. It then lacked "purposive measure," lost all credibility as legitimate force, and became delegitimizing violence.

Since their most sensitive function was the preservation of order, generals with strong political biases routinely masked them with the language of law and order. It was not so easy, however, to disguise the working relationship between the army and local officials. Any real tension quickly became public, and the government paid close attention to such rivalries. Military esprit de corps and disdain for civilian authorities provoked much of the trouble. Officers had a natural tendency to take the side of soldiers against civilians. Generals would claim that, at the very least, blame was shared, even when their officers were already in prison.[47] Too often this amounted to a cover-up, and unless units were reassigned, troubles would recur. Furthermore, units often had to be moved after developing political prejudices detrimental to their mission. The elitist traditions of the cavalry generally inclined them toward antirepublican politics, whereas artillery units usually had more egalitarian and hence prorepublican sympathies. The attitude of officers set the tone, as did a unit's service record. Being stationed in hotbeds of factionalism rarely left a unit unscathed. Sooner or later, it took sides.[48] Equally, discipline suffered when units were kept in the interior for long stretches at a time. Most assignments to the interior involved dividing demi-brigades, battalions, and squadrons into smaller detachments. Scattering them around several departments in this way eroded the authority of senior officers and gave NCOs more independence than was good for military discipline. This is when local attachments or antagonisms became especially dangerous. Political activism of any sort eroded a unit's reliability. It was worrisome enough when rogue elements savaged the local populace, as happened when three cavalrymen "cut a peaceable farmer to pieces" on the road to Lons-le-Saulnier; it was worse when a whole unit entered into battle with the local townsfolk, as the Ninth Dragoons did at Lyon. City officials had good reason to complain: this was the unit that had sabered to death initial survivors of the *mitraillades* (mass shootings) in 1793 and was still stationed there four years later![49]

The greatest difficulty with establishing the army as an acceptable instrument for domestic policing lay in the Directory's determination to use it for tasks that most Frenchmen opposed. The economy of violence in the period derived significantly from the regime's aggression against rural communities. This had a profound impact on the credibility of the army as a police force. The central problem is illustrated by an incident in the department of the Rhône in early 1798. A detachment of twelve grenadiers, six cavalrymen, and four gendarmes was charged with escorting five refractory priests condemned to deportation. On their way from Lyon to Rochefort, as they crossed the mountains of the Lyonnais in a thick February fog, they were ambushed by hundreds of local residents. A volley of musket fire killed a grenadier and a cavalryman, badly wounded six others, and left the detachment commander with three gunshot wounds. Those soldiers not hit in the initial discharge turned their guns on the wagon full of priests, killing one and wounding another. Riding to the sound of muskets, eight officers of dragoons appeared in time to drive off the attackers. Nonetheless, the villagers managed to make off with the four living clerics, one bleeding profusely. The whole operation had been carefully planned, apparently by a priest from the aptly named village of Chapelle-des-Sauvages, and so invited massive military repression directed from Lyon.[50] This deadly skirmish in the heart of France was certainly not the sort of danger grenadiers and dragoons expected when they joined the army, whether willingly or not. Whatever glory they could earn serving the republic, it would not come from escorting priests, no matter how heroically the soldiers performed on Mount Tarare. And how many villagers in the Lyonnais could separate the army's triumph over foreign powers at Lodi in 1796 from the siege of Lyon in 1793, the effort to kill a wagonload of priests, or insouciant brutality in house-to-house searches? The same ambiguity, if it existed at all, was evoked by the equally loathsome and dangerous tasks of arresting émigrés and rounding up draft dodgers. As long as the regime pitted the army against the village, the officer against the notable, the soldier against the farmer, it would be the source of violence and disorder. Of course, historians who revel in the glories of the French army during the Revolution and Empire have nothing to say about its tragic and sordid role in these tasks.

The army performed other police functions of dubious legitimacy in the eyes of many. The difference between the need to use force to impose the demands of the state and the manner in which it was used had a major impact on popular attitudes. As we know, the First Republic made exorbitant demands for money, men, and materials in order to wage war. Most of these had to be extracted from the populace. When reluctance turned to refusal, the republic turned to billeting. The ancient practice of billeting troops in ordinary homes produced major results, both in increasing the desired yield and in alienating the population. The use of *garnisaires* was neither a uniform practice nor an uncommon experience and could cover a range of possibilities. The law of 17 brumaire V (7 November 1796) authorized imposing soldiers on villages that failed to pay their taxes. The parents of refractory conscripts and the families of outlaws also frequently found themselves billeting grenadiers. Woe to those forced to take in hussars or dragoons, with their horses and their attitudes. This sort of personal contact with soldiers did nothing to enhance the army's image. In fact, the level of hostility led to innumerable assaults and more than a few deaths among the *garnisaires* themselves. The fiscal and military crisis of 1799 provoked a veritable panic in Paris and a wave of billeting in the provinces that only subsided in 1801.[51] In this way, among others, the army earned the victories of the Consulate, both inside and outside of France.

Domestic deployment of the army did not come as a complete scourge on the country, however, and offered a range of more socially approved policing activities. Despite frequent nastiness, the army could also be a useful, even welcome, presence, and not just for national defense. Every military district had its own special assignments. Hundreds of soldiers provided security for the annual exploitation of the salt marshes at Aiguemortes; hussars patrolled the Swiss border to prevent smuggling; and cavalry were stationed at intervals along the entire Mediterranean coast to prevent Barbary corsairs from bringing plague and "ravaging the shores of the Republic."[52] The army also played a vital role in protecting the markets around France. Beaucaire, the site of a famous international fair each year, was kept safe by 300 infantry and 150 cavalry. Troops served to safeguard smaller markets as well, usually by providing crowd control, as was the case when religious antagonisms rocked Sommières (Gard).[53] Less common, but more dangerous, was the use of troops to quell subsistence riots, a particularly delicate matter due to the moral implications of enforcing starvation prices. But the republic did not suffer from serious subsistence crises between the winter of year IV and the generalized hardship of year X; any troubles in between were strictly local.

In all of these situations, success depended on intelligent leadership and disciplined troops. No amount of civilian oversight or loyalty to the republic could instill these attributes; they were strictly the product of experience and professionalism. The troubles that led to "taxation populaire" at Toulouse in March 1800 illustrate the delicacy of military policing. A misunderstanding of municipal orders resulted in cannons being brought out the second day. The crowd, using a shower of rocks to repel the cavalry escort, seized the cannons and returned them to the town hall. The cavalry, rather than charge the crowd, serried its ranks to prevent the trampling of women and children and remained on the edge of the market. With matters on the verge of a massacre, General Commes withdrew all his troops. He then appeared without an escort and on foot, together with several city officials, and walked among the people, haranguing them to go home. Commes' bravery, the city's willingness to lower market prices, and, above all, the discipline of the troops prevented a catastrophe.[54] Though only a single incident, it reflects the steady gains made in establishing "internal measure" in the use of armed force during the period, especially as the government chose officers more carefully and the rank and file acquired the discipline of grizzled veterans.

The army's most challenging police function at the time was to combat brigandage. Many aspects of the war on brigandage are covered elsewhere in this study; therefore, it is simply the ambiguity of the army's role in the struggle that will be noted here. Thwarting brigandage meant, among other matters, protecting public transportation. France's once-impressive network of highways and bridges was in shambles by 1795. Disrepair and a disastrous economy had sharply reduced traffic. The fewer people on the roads, the more dangerous they became. Many of the key arteries in the country were infested with highwaymen and brigands. The most dangerous routes were between Lyon and Strasbourg, Paris and Rennes, Toulouse and Montpellier, and, the absolute nadir, between Marseille and Lyon. So common was the danger that every time bank funds were transported between cities, a fee of 1.5 percent was added to cover the risk of robbery.[55] Constant peril required constant policing, but a lack of gendarmes often required soldiers to fill in. Every year the army provided thousands of escorts for stagecoaches, mail carriers, and treasury wagons throughout the country. Nonetheless, companies regularly complained about the slower pace their vehicles had to keep when under military escort, especially when on foot! We hear less complaining from passengers, however; there were simply too many holdups. Here it was not the citizenry who resented the omnipresence of soldiers but the soldiers themselves. Interior commanders frequently moaned about the heavy burden that providing escorts placed on their overstretched resources, especially in the west and south, but the issue was national and continual.[56]

The actual pursuit of brigands was another matter. Certainly few complained about the army hunting down *chauffeurs* and others of their ilk. Less satisfactory were the special expeditions sent after rebels and antirepublican outlaws. Most of these forays were into isolated areas where locals met outsiders with preemptive hostility. Armed youths and defiant notables opposed the state simply out of ancestral tradition. Brigands of this sort found a natural refuge in the entire region around Mount Aigoual in the Cévennes, especially in the magnificently treacherous Gorges du Tarn where the Aveyron, Lozère, and Gard come together. The army rarely had much success in such regions. A sweep through the area in June 1796 not only failed to capture any brigands, but column commanders "gave themselves over to abuses and pillage," thereby stoking fury against the republic.

Matters in the Lozère did not calm down until the swaggering Squadron Commander Rutteau was replaced by a more prudent commander who did not "spend time creating chouans and counter-revolutionaries in order to make himself valuable in appearing to fight them."[57] Across the highlands of the south, from the Ariège to the Ardèche, from the Basses-Pyrénées to the Basses-Alpes, the army confronted resistance from mountain villages, which, in the language of the republic, "teemed with brigands." The culture of guns in hill country posed a special problem. In the Ariège, the mountain people "were almost all armed with service muskets" and fully prepared to repel any expedition sent against them that did not consist of overwhelming force. But rarely did the republic have enough troops for the job. As a result, a desultory effort to take the struggle against brigandage to its topographical sources only inflamed passions. Almost insupportable fatigues on route to capture a rebel priest, an uprising of four hundred armed peasants, several gunshot casualties, and a return to base empty-handed did not make soldiers well disposed toward mountain villagers. "Abuses and pillaging" were predictable, either on the way home or the next time out. These were men who, after weeks of arduous excursions, might get a "bonus" of new shoes, and only if their commander were especially solicitous on their behalf.[58] Thus, an overstretched and undersupplied army, called upon to repress brigandage, that catch-all term for the most egregious lawlessness, had a strong tendency to behave badly. This could only lead to a loss of "internal measure" and corrosion of the army as a tool of domestic security. More will be said elsewhere on the military response to brigandage, but for now it provides the best example of the untenable ambiguity of the army's role in policing. As long as it had unstable leadership, inadequate resources, and served to coerce social change, the army would remain as much an instrument of domestic state violence as of legitimate force.

## Military Justice for Civilians

In addition to providing extensive police services, the army offered alternative forms of justice. Initially, these were exceptional measures and therefore were not well integrated into the broader system of criminal justice. In the years 1792–95, military justice perpetrated some of the worst excesses of the Revolution. Thereafter, the Thermidorian republic gradually refined its use of military justice to deal with violent threats to the regime. This helped to give military justice greater "internal measure" and thereby reduced the moral taint associated with applying truncated procedures to civilians. Many of these changes arose out of the army's own needs for more effective forms of punishment, not the demands of liberal lawmakers. Moreover, even these refinements left much to the arbitrariness and discretion of individual military courts called upon to judge civilians.

From its earliest days, the Convention had systematically resorted to exceptional forms of military justice to punish resistance. This began in October 1792, when military commissions composed of five officers and devoid of any jurisprudence were charged with judging and executing émigrés within twenty-four hours. The Vendée uprising and Federalist Revolts of 1793 vastly expanded the practice as a firestorm of revolutionary revenge burned down judicial obstacles to repression.[59] Even when operating "révolutionnairement" (mainly without juries), criminal courts and military tribunals alike tended to balk at merely expediting executions. Hence, representatives on mission created veritable killing machines. Some of these were known as *commissions révolutionnaires* or *commissions populaires,* but most were simply *commissions militaires.* Despite historians' focus on revolutionary tribunals, military commissions actually carried out much of the repression of year II.[60] Whereas the guillotine quickly became the symbolic face of revolutionary justice, it was the military firing squad that executed most judicial victims of the Revolutionary Government. How many images even exist of victims being shot while kneeling, blindfolded, in front of a small detachment of grenadiers, as was the practice of the day? And yet the uncontrolled killing perpetrated by military commissions actually prompted an executive order to suppress them across the country in the spring of 1794, just as the "Great Terror" was beginning in Paris.[61]

Despite the Thermidorians' claim to have ended the Terror and replaced it with justice, they continued to find military commissions useful. The general relaxation of repression in the winter of year III, as well as the pacification treaties of La Jaunaye and La Mabilais in the west, seemed to presage the end of military commissions, but the crises in the summer of 1795 revived them with a vengeance. The Paris uprising of 1–2 prairial (20–21 June 1795), the Toulon insurrection of 17–18 floréal (6–7 May 1795), and the Quiberon landings of mid-messidor III (July 1795) all led to the summary justice of military commissions.[62] Though not as bloody as those of year II, the military commissions of year III were just as numerous and just as devoid of basic due process. As the transition to constitutional government approached, the Convention sought to wind down these instruments of revolutionary exceptionalism.[63]

In the meantime, the regular form of military justice created in 1793—*tribunaux criminels militaires*—had proved utterly utopian.[64] Laudable in theory, they were lamentable in practice. The exigencies of war forced the Thermidorians to revert to more militarized forms of military justice. The law of 2 jour complémentaire III (18 September 1795) abolished the jury-based and quasi-civilian system of military justice and replaced it with *conseils militaires*. The new military courts lacked features of due process. They operated without juries, excluded anyone with legal training, and had no regulations governing the interrogation of the accused, the confrontation of witnesses, or the process of deliberating on verdicts. Finally, there were no appeals, and so verdicts were executed "immediately." The only safeguards provided to the accused came in cases subject to the death penalty: murder, rape, arson, and robbery committed either by more than two people, with violence, or with effraction. First, convictions in capital cases required six votes, rather than the usual five. Second, in these cases, the commanding general appointed twice the usual number of members, and the accused nullified half of them. This reinforced the impression, already created by the low rank of most of those appointed to a *conseil militaire* and the fact that they were supposed to serve only for a single case, that verdicts were being rendered by a panel of soldier-jurors rather than military judges.[65] In sum, *conseils militaires* resembled the Convention's military commissions more than any other form of military justice adopted during the Revolution. In fact, journalists and legislators alike often referred to them as *commissions militaires*,[66] which is how the public perceived them as well.

Despite the Thermidorians' recidivism regarding actual military commissions, they made some effort to regulate the judicial response to rebellion. Rightfully skeptical of the royalists' intentions in the west and confronted with continued chouan activity, the Convention passed the law of 30 prairial III (18 June 1795). Though conceived as a purely circumstantial measure, this law provided the basis for using regular military justice against rebels throughout the remainder of the First Republic, into the Empire, and well beyond. According to the new law, rebels who took up arms after the pacification agreements would be tried by regular *tribunaux militaires*. Leaders, captains, and instigators of rebellion, as well as those who recruited for the rebels, were to be condemned to death and executed by a firing squad. So too were deserters and rebels captured armed and outside their native departments. On the other hand, ordinary rebels captured in armed gatherings would only be subject to between two and four months in prison and fined half their annual income, provided they were not convicted of participating in murderous assaults. The mechanics of this legislation made its purpose clear: to separate sheep from shepherds and still punish wolves in sheep's clothing.

When the Convention dramatically transformed military justice by replacing permanent *tribunaux militaires* equipped with juries and legal experts with temporary *conseils militaires* composed of nine soldiers, it did not move to protect civilians from the new system. So attached were the Thermidorians to the new system for trying chouans that whenever legal or constitutional obstacles appeared to jeopardize it, they stepped in explicitly to ensure its survival.[67] Thus, participants in the Vendémiaire uprising were tried by *conseils militaires* applying the law of 30 prairial III. Such practices clearly violated the Thermidorians' ostensible commitment to ground the republic on the rule of law. There has been no study of how *tribunaux militaires* dealt with chouans in the last six months of the Convention, but it is clear that they worked extremely slowly and so left hundreds of accused rebels in prison for months on end.[68] The abandonment on the eve of the Directory of this extraordinarily liberal form of military justice in favor of juryless and purely military courts may have been necessary in the army, but it also severely eroded the protections afforded to civilians, especially those accused of guerrilla activities. And yet the Directorial government hoped to prevent *conseils militaires* from judging known rebels captured at any time other than in the act of rebellion, just as the law of 30 prairial III specified.[69] As Minister of Justice Merlin de Douai scornfully explained, trying rebels captured in flagrante delicto made it easy for the army to recognize those who were truly guilty. Less obvious cases would be tried by regular criminal courts.[70]

The actual practice of using *conseils militaires* to judge chouans did not merit the minister's confidence. He operated under a false assumption: it was not only rebels captured in the very act of rebellion who were justiciable by military courts; so too were rebels arrested outside armed gatherings but suspected of participating in deadly assaults.[71] Furthermore, the pattern of judicial pursuits against those tried for "chouannisme" in the Sarthe suggests that drawing a clear line between those who deserved civilian justice and those who merited military justice was easier done in the offices of a Paris ministry than in the chaotic conditions of a lingering guerrilla war. Even though the Criminal Court of the Sarthe tried a limited number of cases of *chouannerie,* even some of these should have gone to military courts where the vast bulk of such cases was heard.[72]

The nature of *conseils militaires* as temporary courts and the consequent loss of most of their records make it impossible to determine how many supposed rebels had the direct experience of a court-martial. Nonetheless, three surviving registers from the Sarthe indicate a massive use of military justice to prosecute civilians even after the shift to constitutional government.[73] *Conseils militaires* were empowered to try civilians during a period of about nine months.[74] During that time, 151 individuals, or almost half of those tried by the *conseils militaires* at Le Mans and La Flèche, were civilians. Almost all of these cases involved charges of *chouannerie* or counterrevolution and so led to twenty-three executions by firing squad.[75] Most of these men had been captured red-handed, either transporting munitions for the chouans or actually fighting with them. In cases where the accused had not been arrested in the act of rebellion, the *conseils militaires* heard convincing evidence of direct involvement in killing. Such was the case of the locksmith Pierre Meiche, a sedentary rebel who never joined an armed gathering; however, because he repaired guns for the chouans and personally mounted guard against the Blues in his native village of Ivré-le-Pôlin, the death of two soldiers in a shoot-out there led directly to his own death by firing squad.[76] The number of executions ordered by *conseils militaires* in the Sarthe contrasts with their overall leniency.[77] Not only did they acquit 56 percent of the civilians they tried, but half of those found guilty received punishments of only four months in prison or less.

The overall leniency of *conseils militaires* reflects the clumsy contrasts built into the law of 30 prairial III. Because it contained no provision for penalties anywhere between death by firing squad and a few months in prison, the law tended to punish rebels either as cold-blooded murderers or petty delinquents. Such absurdity led to creative solutions. Young men subject to the *levée en masse* and yet caught in chouan gatherings were supposed to be executed, but these facts alone did not lead to death sentences. Instead, in a customary practice as old as the Romans, these youths were simply enrolled in the army and sent directly to the front. *Conseils militaires* found other ways to avoid the death penalty as well. Rather than being condemned to death for trafficking in munitions, Ferdinand Bras-d'Or and André Leloup (*noms de guerres*?) received sentences of fifteen years in irons. The court admitted that they acted with criminal intent but considered "the sincere repentance" they showed once arrested and their practice of defrauding chouans by shorting their bags of gunpowder to be sufficient mitigating factors.[78] This was strictly illegal, and yet the punishment fit the crime. Nor was there any legal basis for the courts' repeated recourse to "imprisonment until peace." This represented a form of preventive detention similar to the *plus amplement informé* of the *ancien régime* or the "law of suspects" of 1793 in that the accused were clearly chouans who had violated the pacification agreement of year III but whose criminal intent or violent acts were insufficiently documented. In other cases, indefinite imprisonment offered a way of showing leniency. For example, Jacques Pioger had been arrested in possession of papers that proved that he was the leader of a group of chouans, and yet he was without arms, "had always prevented pillaging and theft and had saved several republicans from death while he stayed with the rebels."[79] Being jailed until peace both saved Pioger's life and kept him from rejoining his band. Such flexible sentencing provoked a noisy controversy,[80] and in mid–year IV, the Councils responded by introducing a new form of judicial oversight called *conseils de révision*.[81] This put an end to lengthy terms in the *bagne* or indefinite imprisonment until peace and thereby fostered the existing tendency toward leniency.[82]

The law of 30 prairial III and the speedy proceedings of *conseils militaires* proved an irresistible temptation for the repression of counter-revolutionary violence and even simple brigandage well beyond the civil war zones of western France. Internal commanders made credible arguments for using *conseils militaires* for repression in other areas of civil unrest. For example, the Cévennes Mountains all the way from the Haute-Loire to the Hérault were racked by attacks on republican purchasers of national land, violent incursions into villages and towns, and repeated clashes with the army. General Châteauneuf-Randon, commander of the Ninth and Tenth Military Districts and well-known in the region for his repression of the Charrier uprising in 1793, had no hesitation sending captured rebels before *conseils militaires* three years later.[83] Less legally credible were the various efforts to include ordinary brigandage under this rubric. Lejeune, court commissioner of the Eure, used the concept of "brigands chouans" to get the minister of justice to agree to have François Robillard and his notorious band of robbers judged by a *conseil militaire*. These were men with a history of serious crime extending back to the 1780s, and there was no indication that their latest attack, the violent robbery of a farmer at Préaux, had any connection to organized political insurgency. It may have looked like *chouannerie* from a distance, but it did not smell like it close up, and Lejeune was close enough to know the difference. Nonetheless, using a *conseil militaire* ensured two executions within hours of the trial.[84]

In contrast, there was nothing legally dubious about using *conseils militaires* to prosecute deserters for joining the chouans or engaging in brigandage. Many rebels and bandits, whether they operated in Maine, Languedoc, or Picardy, had first been conscripted into the armies of the republic. Once they deserted, all of their crimes, not just that of desertion, became justiciable by courts-martial. Furthermore, any civilian accomplices of crimes committed by deserters also faced military justice, an extension of a principle that had applied to soldiers throughout the Revolution.[85] These provisions cast the net of military justice wider than the law of 30 prairial III alone would imply. In fact, when this law appeared insufficiently broad, the Ministry of Justice encouraged *conseils militaires* to prosecute all draft dodgers and deserters caught in armed gatherings as authors of "attacks on public security," as the law of 1 vendémiaire IV (23 September 1795) specified. The Penal Code had made this a capital offense, and the use of military justice ensured numerous executions. The *conseils militaires* at Le Mans alone condemned nine deserters to death (two in absentia) for joining the chouans.[86] After all, this was "desertion in the face of the enemy" and thus the ultimate betrayal of their brothers in arms. *Conseils militaires* meted out similar penalties around the country. The extensive scope of military justice meant that at Castres four deserters and two civilians were judged by a *conseil militaire* on charges of "armed robbery with violence in the countryside at night and on public roads in the day … saying that their activities were the result of the revolution." Three of the deserters were executed the next day.[87] In general then, some interior commanders found the law of 30 prairial III insufficiently rigorous, whereas others, especially civilian officials, found it a useful way to extend the scope of military justice to ordinary bandits. The various provisions of the law, therefore, as well as the ability to envelop civilians who committed crimes alongside military personnel, including thousands of deserters, made *conseils militaires* a potential threat to a far larger number of rebels than Merlin de Douai had initially imagined.

Whatever the utility of *conseils militaires* in the repression of counterinsurgency, they proved woefully inadequate to restore discipline in the army. This was as true on the Loire and the Garonne as it was on the Rhine and the Meuse. The fault lay primarily with the deplorable conditions at the start of the Directory. Conscripts without a specified term of service, pressed into a war of conquest, and so badly provisioned that they could survive only by pillaging, simply could not be controlled by the new system. In these circumstances, the fact that the majority of judges on a *conseil militaire* had to be either ordinary soldiers or NCOs severely impeded any return to army discipline. Soldiers had little fear of being punished for looting. Their judges were too often guilty of the same thing.[88] Matters were especially bad during the brutal subsistence crisis of year IV. It is not surprising, therefore, that army discipline reached its nadir that year. This prompted a chorus of demands from senior officers for a more effective form of military justice.[89]

Legislators responded to these demands by creating yet another form of military court, only this time, the reform endured: the *conseils de guerre* created by the law of 13 brumaire V (3 November 1796) remained the basis of French military justice until well after World War I. The new courts were both more authoritarian and more carefully regulated than *conseils militaires*. *Conseils de guerre* were permanent standing courts designed to strengthen the authority of senior officers. Six of the seven judges, as well as the investigator/prosecutor (*capitaine-rapporteur*) and court commissioner (*commissaire du Pouvoir exécutif*) were required to be officers. Most held the rank of captain or higher; all were appointed by the commanding general. The procedures of *conseils de guerre* also served to concentrate authority in the hands of officers. In the trial, the prosecutor read the various pieces of evidence to the seven judges before the accused appeared in court.[90] Once the defendant was led in "free and without irons," he identified himself for the record and heard the formal charges (but not the evidence) against him. The court president then interrogated him. The president was always the highest-ranking officer and therefore at least a *chef de brigade* (colonel). He cut an imposing figure and left the defendant in no doubt about who was in charge. The other judges could also pose questions. A small audience, limited to three times the number of judges, then heard the witnesses for and against the accused. Once the military prosecutor presented his "conclusions" and the accused or his legal advisor summarized the defense, the accused was returned to his cell and the courtroom cleared of spectators. The seven judges remained to deliberate their judgment, three votes being needed for an acquittal.[91] The defendant was not brought back into court to hear the verdict but had it read to him later in prison and in front of assembled troops, which made sure that he could neither insult the judges nor receive outbursts of empathy from the public. The whole dramaturgy of the trial, with the judges always present and everyone else being admitted or excluded on cue, emphasized military authority and hierarchy. The frequent reliance on written evidence, including interrogations and depositions, the failure to delineate the precise form and order of questions that the court had to decide, and the simple majority needed for a conviction all contrasted starkly with the jurisprudence governing the criminal courts of the day. Furthermore, division generals not only initiated cases, they also could indict defendants even before they had even arrested or interrogated. Under these conditions, it is not surprising that one deputy called the new form of military justice "un despotisme régularisé."[92]

Hard on the heels of the new *conseils de guerre* came a more comprehensive penal code for the army. It specified death sentences for looting, destruction, arson, and recruiting for the enemy, as well as for the classic cases of murder, treason, and desertion under fire. Loss of rank was reinstated for any sentence over six months in prison. Such severity highlighted the wartime context and the desperate need to curtail marauding. It also had important implications for the army's role in domestic repression. Earlier forms of military justice had been limited to crimes committed by soldiers against soldiers and thus left crimes committed by soldiers against civilians to the regular system of criminal justice (except, of course, on foreign soil). The outbreak of war in 1792 extended the jurisdiction of military justice to include anyone attached to the army, its supply services, garrisons, or field camps.[93] This expansion of military justice to include a range of civilians provoked some loud controversies. Even the military penal code of 21 brumaire V (11 November 1796) did not clear up all of the ambiguities. It included "soldiers, individuals attached to the army and in its train, enemy recruiters, spies, and inhabitants of enemy territory occupied by armies of the Republic for crimes justiciable by *conseils de guerre*." Did "soldiers" include draft dodgers or officers on leave? Would "crimes justiciable by *conseils de guerre*" be determined strictly *ratione personae*? Did it make a difference whether crimes were committed inside the republic? All of these questions were eventually answered in the most expansive manner possible; that is, not only did civilians accused of spying or recruiting for the enemy fall under military justice, so too did draft dodgers who had never entered the army, officers who had temporarily left the army, and soldiers who committed any sort of crime against civilians at home or abroad. The results largely reversed the early revolutionaries' basic principles of military justice.

The vast extension of military justice into civil society did not stop with matters related to the army or its immediate servitors. In the wake of the Fructidor coup, the Second Directory sought to expand the law of 30 prairial III to include bandits and highwaymen. As we shall see, lawmakers decided instead to craft an entirely new set of criteria extending military justice into areas ordinarily covered by the regular system of criminal justice (law of 29 nivôse VI [18 January 1798]). In taking this route, the Councils made it clear that they had concerns about the imprecision and rude aspects of the military justice being used in counter-insurgency. *Conseils de guerre* improved considerably on both the military commissions of 1792–95 and the *conseils militaires* of 1795–96. In that sense, the new military courts constituted an important enhancement of both "internal" and "external" measure and, therefore, a reduction in the perceived violence associated with the army as a tool of domestic repression. And yet, as was the Directory's hallmark, progress toward more controlled repression was soon offset by the regime's political weakness. Just as the system of regular military justice had been sorted out, the Fructidor coup resurrected the summary justice of military commissions. As important as the army had become in domestic security during the early Directory, its role would only grow after Fructidor.

# 6 Refining Terror and Justice after Fructidor

What more could the most ferocious and bloody tyrant do than the five
Directors? Robespierre reigned by terror. They have reigned by terror.
Robespierre mutilated the Convention; they have mutilated the Legislative Body. Robespierre created revolutionary tribunals; they have created
military commissions. Robespierre had émigrés guillotined. They have had
them shot. Thus has reopened without obstacle and in another form, the
appalling butchery of men that the death of Robespierre seemed to have
irrevocably closed.
—Jean-Pierre Gallois, *Dix-huit fuctidor; ses causes et ses effets*
(Hamburg, 1799)

AT DAYBREAK ON 4 September 1797, a single cannon shot rang out in the
deserted streets of Paris. Thirty-six hours later, with eighteen thousand
troops around the capital and the walls plastered with shocking evidence
of a royalist conspiracy, a cowed legislature proscribed two Directors, fifty-
three deputies, three convicted royalist conspirators, two generals, and five
other assorted suspects. Rather than besmirch the recently renamed Place
de la Concorde with a lot of beheadings, however, the proscribed were ordered deported to Guyana. Seventeen were actually arrested and deported,
and eight of these died there, giving rise to the sobriquet "dry guillotine."
The legislature also annulled the elections of that spring in fully half the departments of France. This removed another 122 deputies, as well as scores
of departmental administrators, judges, and public prosecutors. The Directory added yet more dismissals over the next few weeks, as well as a massive
purge of government commissioners.[1]

Fructidor was the greatest coup d'état of the period. Not only was it
greater in political scope and immediate impact than the Brumaire coup
d'état two years later, it depended on a national deployment of military

force. The Directorial Triumvirate ordered a total of thirteen thousand troops sent to Dijon, Lyon, Marseille, Bordeaux, and the vicinity of Paris in order to consolidate the Fructidor coup. No serious resistance developed in these places, and most of the troops were sent back to the armies even before they reached their destinations.[2] It was surprising that the capital had remained completely calm despite the gathering of dozens of counter-revolutionary leaders there. But not every town acquiesced in the sudden destruction of the parliamentary opposition. The greatest resistance emerged in the Midi. Montauban erupted into "full counter-revolution," and General Pierre Sol had to respond by marching against the town with all the available troops and artillery from Toulouse.[3] In certain southern localities, military commanders actually encouraged resistance. This was especially the case in Provence, where reactionary commanders chosen by General Willot dotted the countryside. In response, General Lannes, in charge of a column sent from the Army of Italy, launched a chilling proclamation in which he threatened to wreak patriotic vengeance on the royalists of the region.[4] Though not needed in most parts of France, his mailed fist and chiliastic bombast befitted the events of Fructidor.

## The Republican Narrative

The coup d'état of Fructidor was a dramatic response to a genuine royalist conspiracy with international connections, but the measures that accompanied the coup went well beyond preempting a plot. These measures have been called the "Fructidorian Terror" and were characterized primarily by a renewed assault on refractory priests and émigrés. In addition to annulling elections and proscribing deputies, the law of 19 fructidor V (5 September 1797) required all electors, public officials, and clergy to swear hatred of royalty and anarchy, reimposed the recently revoked laws of 1792 and 1793 against refractory priests, gave the Directory the power to order individual deportations of clerical agitators, again barred the relatives of émigrés from holding public office, and sought to purge the republic of returned émigrés. Those already in custody would be deported, and those who did not leave or who returned later would be put to death. In order to make good this last threat, the law resurrected the military commissions first used in 1792. These had a single task: to decide if the person sent before them was the same person included on an official list of émigrés. If so, the accused was to be executed within twenty-four hours. Any dubious cases went to civilian authorities, who would investigate the individual's identity and then either release him or send him before a military commission again. Although military commissions were supposed to be established for a single case and the judges changed for each new case, many became quasi-permanent.[5] According to our contemporary critic, these new procedures reopened "the appalling butchery of men that the death of Robespierre seemed to have irrevocably closed." Thus, the Second Directory's military commissions became the sine qua non of the Fructidorian Terror.

The concept of the Fructidorian or Directorial Terror appears in all modern histories of the Directory;[6] and yet, this wave of politicized repression has not been the subject of sustained analysis since Victor Pierre's documentary diatribes of a hundred years ago.[7] Historians have simply accepted his conclusions about the work of the military commissions created by the law of 19 fructidor. These were: (1) that they convicted almost two-thirds of the time, (2) that even acquittals were of dubious legality, (3) that three-quarters of convictions went to clerics and former nobles, and (4) that the great majority of their victims "could only be blamed for having returned to France or for not having left in time." In other words, this was a brutal and clumsy persecution aimed overwhelmingly at clerics and nobles.[8] In this sense, the "Fructidorian Terror" was an echo of the Terror of 1793–94. Tocqueville even claimed that some of the Directory's laws were more barbarous than those of the Revolutionary Government.[9] However, such statements of similarity with a difference are made with little sustained analysis of the motives for returning to such extreme measures. It is inadequate simply to blame a Jacobin resurgence. Rather, as we shall see, the origins of the Fructidorian Terror lay in the mounting lawlessness of the summer of 1797 that enabled a republican narrative of the Revolution developed during the Thermidorian period to triumph over competing alternatives. Thereafter, the actual operation of military commissions produced waves of repression. The first wave was poorly regulated, whereas later ones became both less intense and more focused. This reduction in the range of targets made the Fructidorian Terror part of the Directory's broader use of military means of repression to restore order and ensconce the republic throughout the country. Although the terrorist trope of attacking nobles and priests did not disappear, the new evidence on the victims of military commissions reveals the government's intentions to judge and execute only those émigré notables whose presence in France posed an imminent danger to the republic.

The Triumvirate may have operated the Fructidor coup as a preemptive strike against a perceived legislative conspiracy to restore the monarchy, but the draconian measures that followed were harder to justify. By September 1797, the Vendée had been pacified and France was on the verge of peace with victory; the Directory was plainly not facing the kind of war crisis that had done so much to stimulate and justify the Terror in 1793. In these circumstances, renewing the heavy-handed and often arbitrary persecution of priests and émigrés further eroded the regime's legitimacy as a constitutional republic built on the rule of law. More important, however, Directorial republicanism needs to be understood as a set of discursive practices and reflex responses developed not so much in the Enlightenment, or on the basis of classical republicanism, as in the midst of violence, repression, and war. By the autumn of 1795, mainstream republicanism had repudiated the demagoguery of populist democracy, restricted power to the hands of property owners, put up a constitutional fence between political power and individual freedom, and asserted an even-handed application of the law as the key to personal security. It had also excluded refractory priests, émigrés, and the relatives of émigrés from the body politic, accepted military expansion as an essential source of legitimacy, and promoted the use of state power to transform social mores. Political debate under the Directory often brought out strains of democratic liberalism—even though arguments in defense of the constitution, freedom of the press, citizenship, and voting rights were motivated as much by factional advantage as political principles—and yet most republicans were too conditioned by their revolutionary past to renounce authoritarian responses to real or perceived threats to the fledgling regime. Thus, the harrowing years between 1792 and 1797 forged a strong, yet inflexible republicanism that was more the product of revolutionary praxis than the detritus of revolutionary ideology.[10]

In the year following the overthrow of Robespierre, republicans of all sorts were forced to confront fundamental issues about their revolutionary experience in order first to find their way out of the Terror and then to plot a path out of the Revolution itself. Such tasks could not be accomplished without developing an interpretation of their revolutionary experience thus far. During the Thermidorian Convention, therefore, a variety of competing narratives developed to explain the trajectory from 1789 to 1794.[11] The Fructidorian Terror should be understood as largely the fruit of one of these narratives. That is, the renewed persecution was greatly encouraged by a republican myth, a particular form of narrative developed to explain past massacres. The legacies of the Couvent des Carmes and the Fort Saint-Jean, of Machecoul and Quiberon, prevented the republic from mastering

Fig. 7. Entre deux chaises: le cul par terre. Eau-forte by Lemonnier, 1797. Prorevolutionary allegory of the Directory falling "between the two chairs" of monarchy and republic. (Courtesy of the Département des estampes et photographies, Bibliothéque nationale de France)

its past within the framework of a liberal constitution. The narrative of the Revolution propagated by most Directorial republicans did not admit that the Revolution had skidded off course in 1792. The dominant narrative continued to stress the multitude of threats to the republic and the need for constant vigilance and armed repression. Most republicans believed that the Revolutionary Government of 1793–94 had been a necessary response to an unprecedented coalition of internal and external enemies. In their view, the excesses of the Terror were the product of personal ambition and ideological fanaticism alone and were certainly not inherent in the revolutionary project itself. Furthermore, they believed that a failure to understand the difference between these two had produced the political inanition of year III, when the republic almost perished. This narrative stressed that the republic was founded more on collective security than personal liberty. Furthermore, it denied that genuine republicans, not just isolated *buveurs de sang, septembriseurs,* and *anthropophages,* might have provoked much of the resistance to the republic by adopting a Manichean view of politics. This account of revolutionary events exonerated republicans of responsibility for the injustices of year II but in doing so prevented them from developing more flexible responses to the problems of year V. In other words, here was a peculiarly powerful form of narrative that explained—and largely excused—the revolutionary past and yet in so doing constrained the republican present.

Narratives that purport to recount past events can be usefully divided into three types—legend, history, and myth. Legends are those that lack enough persuasive power to gain credibility. History is a narrative account based on sufficient evidence to become credible and gain general acceptance. Beyond history lies the rarefied category of myth, a narrative possessing both credibility and authority. A myth is a narrative that begins with credible claims about the past but has the power to transcend these and achieve the status of paradigmatic truth about the present. The authority of myth makes it both descriptive and normative. In other words, a myth encodes important, but selective, information about society and its past and in so doing helps people to mold society on that basis.[12] This concept is similar to Georges Duby's analysis of the tripartite conception of feudal society as a "collective imaginary"[13] but differs by stressing a narrative rather than structural understanding of the society in which the myth operates. This concept of myth is also similar to the notion of ideology, except that a myth is sociohistorically specific and therefore, unlike an ideology, lays no claim to explain or shape other societies. A myth does not even present a vision of the future for its own society but rather uses a widely believed, though tendentious, version of the past to meet challenges facing the contemporary social order.

This kind of myth cannot simply be fabricated; it must emerge from the course of events and only gains power when crucial elements of the narrative are supported by evidence and appear to be confirmed by subsequent developments. This happened late in the Revolution. During the Directory's first two years, political debate was shaped by the competing discourses of rigid constitutionalism and revolutionary exceptionalism. The most contentious subject in this debate was the law of 3 brumaire IV (25 October 1795), which revived the anticlerical laws of 1792–93 and excluded the immediate relatives of émigrés from holding public office. Naturally, conservatives saw refractory priests and the relatives of émigrés as potential allies and so used the language of civil liberty to discredit the regime's politics of exclusion. Staunch republicans defended the law as a vital prophylactic against the restoration of monarchy and managed to keep it largely intact until the right wing triumphed in the elections of 1797. Within three weeks, the new legislative majority annulled the law of 3 brumaire IV.[14] Supporters represented this measure as a return to the political liberalism of the early Revolution; in contrast, opponents considered it a royalist effort to sap the foundations of the republic. As the political winds blew against the exclusionary policies of the Convention, thousands of refractory priests and émigrés began returning from exile or emerging from forest shacks and farmhouse hideaways. Their reappearance brought the sale of national lands to a grinding halt. Crime and disorder spread rapidly, especially across the south, where antirepublican violence mounted throughout the summer. The trend included such headline affairs as the ambush and murder of Groussac, mayor of Toulouse in year II; the siege and massacre of members of the Constitutional Circle of Clermont-Ferrand; and repeated clashes between the "ganses blanches" and "ganses jaunes" around Castres. In each case, local magistrates showed little inclination to prosecute.[15] From the perspective of Paris, it appeared that the regime's authority was rapidly running into the sands of wait and see.[16]

Events in the spring and summer of 1797 confirmed republican fears about the sources and strength of antirepublican sentiment. This experience added sufficient authority to the republican narrative of the Revolution to elevate it from the status of a partisan history to that of transcendent myth. At the same time, these developments reduced the competing liberal democratic narrative of the Revolution from history to legend. Constitutional monarchists and moderate republicans—men who believed that the Revolution could be consolidated through political tolerance, strict constitutionalism, and the rule of law, such as Boissy d'Anglas, Thibaudeau, and Carnot—rapidly lost their purchase on national politics. Legislative committees, all now dominated by the right wing, introduced one bill after another designed to cripple executive power and especially the Directory's means of repression. The Triumvirate responded by sacking the three conservative ministers in charge of the security forces and replacing them with staunch republicans. The choice of General Hoche as minister of war raised a furor, however, for he was in double violation of the constitution. Not only was he too young to be a minister, but he had marched parts of his army too close to Paris. Both his appointment and his soldiers were withdrawn. Nonetheless, a new force was entering national politics. The Triumvirate stimulated a flurry of illegal addresses from the more republican units in the army. These excoriated "villainous émigrés," "religious fanatics," "rebels against the law," and "the great politicians of Clichy." They ominously exhorted the Directory to protect the republic and its oppressed supporters. "Speak, citizen Directors, and promptly the villains who stain the soil of liberty will cease to exist. Their lives are in our hands and their pardon at the point of our bayonets," wrote the Army of Italy under Bonaparte.[17]

Thanks to the army, Fructidor marked the triumph of the republican narrative at the national level. The defeat of liberal politics and the triumph of the republican narrative are particularly clear in the speeches made supporting the exclusion of former nobles from the rights of citizenship in the wake of Fructidor. The deputy Thomas Rousseau provided a condensed version of the entire Jacobin narrative of the Revolution: priests inspired ignorant peasants of the Vendée to revolt; counter-revolutionary nobles provoked the Terror elsewhere, later co-opted the reaction against it, and finally duped the electors of years IV and V into voting for royalists. His colleague Gay-Vernon went so far as to blame nobles for all the foreign and civil wars of French history—"were the massacres not the work of their ambitions?"—and Deputy Guchan brought the narrative up to date by including the *compagnies de Jésus et du Soleil,* murder gangs active in the Midi since 1795, as well as the electoral reaction of 1797 and the recent revolt at Castres.[18] In this context, the law of 19 fructidor V became a natural, even inevitable product of the republican narrative of the Revolution elevated to the level of paradigmatic myth.

The Fructidor coup enabled the Second Directory to respond to the resurgence of popular Catholicism and antirepublican violence by reimposing censorship, enforcing republican symbols, and reviving the politics of exclusion. The Directory closed forty-two newspapers, imposed a heavy stamp tax on political journalism, and banned the use of private delivery systems favored by right-wing publishers.[19] In place of the nefarious influence of opposition journalists, the Directory sought to revive flagging republican spirit by reinvigorating revolutionary festivals.[20] However, this "surfeit of festivals risked the evil of banality"[21] and failed to transfer sacrality to the republic. Worse, by emphasizing such polarizing events as the execution of Louis XVI on one hand and the overthrow of Robespierre on another, the new calendar of festivals fostered more social anomie than it overcame. Like Orangist marches in Northern Ireland, such events repeatedly became the scene of bloody clashes.[22] Furthermore, the law of 9 frimaire VI (29 November 1797) extended the politics of exclusion from the relatives of émigrés to all former nobles unless they could provide proof of active service to the revolutionary cause. Patrice Higonnet considers this the height of antinobilism during the French Revolution because it combined with the persecution of émigrés by the military commissions created on 19 fructidor V. Such an analysis presumes a return to the "émigré = noble" formula of 1791–92 and views antinobilism as symptomatic of the cull-de-sac of bourgeois revolutionary ideology.[23]

There is no doubt that the Directory had an antinoble bias and that the military commissions reflected it. Nevertheless, portraying these commissions in purely ideological terms overlooks their roots in the myth of republican self-defense and ignores the crying need to restore order in regions wracked by violence. In contrast, paying attention to the prevailing economy of violence reveals the extent to which the persecution of returned émigrés was part of a system of repression established to combat both political and criminal fomenters of disorder. The records of these commissions reveal that the government systematically narrowed their scope in an effort to make them finely tuned instruments of intimidation and extermination directed as precisely as possible against those whom the regime considered its most implacable opponents. It was the republican narrative of the Revolution developed during the Thermidorian Convention, not a universalist ideology concocted in 1789–91, that determined which émigrés would be exempted. In other words, recent political developments led the Directory to focus not on members of a *ci-devant* caste, but on individuals who had committed the politically charged act of leaving revolutionary France. Even then, however, it did not treat all émigrés as enemies. Rather, the government sought to define a subset of émigrés that included only those who threatened the republic's domestic stability. The Directorial government used military commissions to persecute returned émigré *notables*, not nobles or priests per se, and not even all émigrés as such.

## Exemptions

Concern over the damage the law of 19 fructidor V did to the regime's constitutional legitimacy led the government to modify the law's application in practice. Attenuating the law made it less ideological and more part of an authoritarian restoration of order. This was essentially a bureaucratic means of tempering some of the demands that the triumph of the republican narrative was making on the regime. The military commissions began as crude instruments of terror designed to eliminate all returned émigrés from the country. As a result, their victims inevitably included individuals who did little more than flout emigration laws. Did the republic's survival really depend on executing three widows by firing squads at Toulon and Marseille? What level of insecurity made it necessary to shoot a seventy-one-year-old peasant farmer at Avignon and a seventy-six-year-old priest at Marseille, or deport a fourteen-year-old boy from Mézières?[24] Although these cases were exceptional, they caused the government to worry about arbitrary choices and gross injustices perpetrated by zealots who had lost sight of the larger goal.

Such "excesses" could only damage the regime's reputation. The Directorialist newspaper *L'Ami des lois* made this point clearly: "It is not by multiplying victims that we will make the event of 18 fructidor benefit the republic. Emigrés in rebellion against the law must no doubt be punished; it is the means to purge France of this wicked race, always dreaming of proscriptions and massacres; it is the means to intimidate the stragglers and to restore peace in the departments. But it would be unfortunate if we found a lot of guilty; it would be dangerous to present the people with frequent tragic spectacles of firing squads, which would familiarize them with blood and lead them to cruelty. Let us be just and severe; but let us not be bloody."[25] In order to reduce the number of "excesses" and bloody spectacles, as well as to focus the commissions on true enemies of the republic, the Directory devised categories of exemption. These exemptions were created by administrative fiat and without fanfare or explanation. Together they had a substantial effect in reducing the scope and impact of the Fructidorian military commissions.

The Directory's first exemption was applied to the canonized enemies of the republic—priests. When the Councils annulled the laws against refractory priests shortly before the coup d'état, they reversed a policy that had been central to republicanism from the very start. The law of 19 fructidor V inevitably restored the discrimination. At first, this meant that refractory priests were once again assimilated to émigrés and subject to the death penalty,[26] only now, instead of benefiting from the de facto immunity provided by civilian justice, they faced the rigor of military commissions. However, the government quickly restored distinctions dating from 1792 and thereby restricted the repression.[27] All elderly or infirm refractories, regardless of their peregrinations, were to be interned under administrative surveillance, and original deportees were simply to be "re-deported." Only those who had "voluntarily" gone into exile were subject to firing squads. Nonetheless, refractory priests under sixty years of age and well enough to travel once again faced the death penalty if arrested, whether they had actually left France or just kept their heads down for the past five years. But even this was attenuated in practice. After a few months, the military commission at Besançon refused to define exiled priests as émigrés, and the one at Bayonne, justifiably concerned about sloppy and inaccurate lists of émigrés, handed all its priests back to civilian authorities.[28]

The second type of exemption applied to returned émigrés was based on the political timing of emigration. This intersected with the social status of the accused. Four months after the law of 19 fructidor, the Directory exempted workers and peasants who had left France after the Montagnards' seizure of power in 1793 and registered their return in 1795.[29] This reflected a version of the Terror invented during Thermidorian debates on emigration laws. Moderate deputies argued at the time that many émigrés should be redefined as refugees. The difference was that émigrés had deserted the fatherland in its time of regeneration, whereas refugees had simply fled terrorist reprisals.[30] Thus, the Second Directory exempted those of the laboring classes who had left France after 31 May 1793, especially the Alsatians and Toulonnais who fled the impending repression of representatives on mission.[31] On the other hand, those who left France before 31 May 1793 were given no special consideration. Someone in this category was, as deputy Riou put it, "a true émigré, that is, the most dangerous and irreconcilable enemy of the Republic."[32]

The Directory eventually recognized one category of exemption even for these "true émigrés," that of sex. After four women had been condemned to death (three were executed and one reprieved due to pregnancy), the

minister of police ordered that all further sentences against women be suspended and referred to the government.[33] Although military commissions
had already exiled sixteen women, the minister's directive virtually ended
prosecution of women. The few who later appeared before military commissions were either acquitted or exempted.[34]

The fourth type of exemption applied to émigrés was based on social
class. In July 1798, the government extended its politically defined exemption for the laboring classes to cover all workers, artisans, and peasants
even if they had not fulfilled the conditions of Thermidorian legislation.[35]
This accomplished by ministerial writ what had been narrowly defeated
in acrimonious legislative debate a year earlier. As always, the government
refused to exempt merchants (*négociants* and *commerçants*),[36] which put
them in the same category as former nobles and priests, as well as anyone
who lived from his property or profession. Conservatives had previously
excoriated such class-based exemptions. During the debate on refugees in
late year III, Tronson-Ducoudray cogently argued that such laws flouted the
concept of individual responsibility because they implied that "a citizen is
innocent because he belongs to a certain group; [that] he is guilty because
he belongs to a certain other one. Thus the landowner, merchant, man of
letters, lawyer, and investor (*rentier*) are criminals. . . . There is [a] privileged
caste for the scaffold."[37] He went on to argue that even those who handed
Toulon over to the English had been driven to this desperate measure by
the logic of mounting repression after 2 June 1793. This interpretation effectively absolved the perpetrators of individual responsibility for collective
treason against the fledgling republic. This was a powerful argument, but
it did little good, either for the émigrés of 1793 or for Tronson-Ducoudray,
who later died in Guyana, himself a victim of the Fructidorian Terror.

Within a few months of Fructidor, therefore, the government had exempted the majority of émigrés from the rigors of a military commission.
Herein lies the key to understanding the Fructidorian Terror and the work
of military commissions in particular. The categories of exemption—or,
viewed from the opposite side, the commissions' true target group—
emerged from the republican myth. The target group was first defined by
the defiance, if not fierce resistance, that members of the prerevolutionary elite had generally shown toward the republic. This concept of target
groups was then refined in terms of the Directory's crisis of public lassitude
and lawlessness in 1797. That is, after initially being instruments of terror
aimed at driving all returned émigrés from France, the military commis-

sions quickly became instruments of repression used against men whose social status gave them influence and who flouted the emigration laws expressly to foment opposition to the republic, or so the Directory justifiably believed. In the government's eyes, these people were as threatening to social and political stability as highway robbers. Simply put, although the republican myth served to justify the military commissions as an instrument of terror, it also made the work of military commissions part of a package of exceptional measures adopted to restore order and consolidate a democratic republic. This point needs to be emphasized: the military commissions created after Fructidor were instruments of both political terror *and* internal pacification. By treating these commissions solely as part of the "Fructidorian Terror," an inherently political concept, historians have neglected their place in the whole panoply of authoritarian and militarized responses to civil strife.

We can see the extent to which issues of public order and political stability combined in the Second Directory by looking at the types of people tried by military commissions. It comes as something of a surprise, given the prevailing image created by Victor Pierre, to learn that refractory priests and former nobles made up less than one-quarter of those arraigned before military commissions. This is particularly remarkable considering the massive exemption accorded émigrés from the laboring classes. Although the political prejudices of the period draw historians' attention to these categories, such individuals were generally condemned for their personal actions, not simply for being former nobles or priests. Each of them had chosen to join an outlaw group: that of émigrés who returned to France despite a constitutional ban on doing so. The republic treated all persons who violated that ban as traitors. In this way, the combined acts of leaving France during the Revolution and then returning illegally—whatever the real motives for either—were assigned a single motive: being an enemy of the republic come back to destroy it. Military commissions implemented a dubious and deadly form of political justice, but contrary to earlier claims they did not practice random acts of terror against individuals singled out solely on the basis of their social identity.

The Directory mistrusted all priests, but it concentrated on vigorous, mobile, refractory priests because it held them responsible for popular hostility to the regime. Above all, the republican narrative of the Revolution explained rural insurgency as the result of the influence fanatical priests had on a gullible laity. By September 1797, they saw such subversion spreading like a cancer through the countryside. Though dangerously simplistic, this explanation did not lack evidence. For example, Joseph Poirot, a refractory priest from the Vosges who returned from exile in November 1796, was arrested for distributing incendiary pamphlets against the Directory and was quickly condemned to death and shot by the military commission at Nancy.[38] This was also the golden age of brigand priests. Ex-*curé* Jean-Baptiste Robert, the leader of a brigand band in the Lozère, managed to escape from the citadel at Nîmes two hours before he faced a firing squad only to be recaptured a year later and finally shot at Montpellier.[39] *Vicaire* Jean-Joseph Glatier was dispatched more easily. Arrested while armed, in possession of goods stolen in a highway robbery, and accompanied by three chouans, Glatier freely admitted preaching the restoration of monarchy at clandestine masses and was duly condemned and executed by the military commission at Tours. His demise sent shock waves through the region.[40] But such ordained guerrillas as Robert and Glatier stood out from the garden variety of refractory priests, many of whom received surprising leniency from individual military commissions, especially considering the commissions' deadly purpose and bloody reputation. All the same, the republicans' abiding belief in Catholic conspiracy ensured that forty-eight clerics were sentenced to death and duly shot. Although another twenty-two were sentenced to deportation, only six were actually deported. The remainder were simply expelled from France or kept in local jails, essentially assimilated to the ten priests condemned to confinement (*réclusion*) due to their age or poor health. The Directory's draconian response to clerical activism meant that "Catholicism may have suffered as much from the prolonged disorganization between year V and year IX as from the crisis of year II."[41]

The Directory also mistrusted nobles and made sure that nobles were not eligible for any exemptions from the law of 19 fructidor. This discrimination arose from the republican perspective spelled out during the postcoup debates about excluding nobles from civic rights. At the time, Crassous seemed to clinch the case for political ostracism in the Council of Five Hundred, where he argued that nobles had proved their disloyalty by abusing their political rights (that is, supporting conservatives and royalists), and, therefore, these rights should be temporarily suspended in order to "preserve the social pact."[42] The Directorialist deputy Creuzé-Latouche took a broader view. He argued that revolutionary experience thus far proved that the republic had more to fear from "the class of wealth" than from nobles alone. In fact, he argued, the only nobility the republic should take precautions against—but not oppress—was that of wealth.[43] Though fellow deputies howled in protest, his attitude mirrored the government's policies toward émigrés.

## Executions

As the various categories of exemption indicate, the Directory was especially concerned about émigrés with status and influence, not just nobles and priests, as a purely ideological explanation would suggest. The work of military commissions strongly confirms this. The military commissions sentenced to death at least 289 individuals, all but fifty of whom can be identified by occupation. Nobles made up the same proportion of those condemned to death as clerics (17 percent each); however, nonclerical and non-noble notables were equally well represented (17 percent) among the dead. These figures make it clear that the Directory saw the broader range of émigré notables as the main targets of the military commissions. Only when merchants, bourgeois, investors, surgeons, lawyers, artists, and non-noble officers are included with the priests and nobles, do we arrive at half of the people executed by military commissions. The other half belonged to the laboring classes.[44] This wide range of victims indicates that individual responsibility played a greater part in the fate of both those with and those without significant social status than Ducoudray-Tronson anticipated or historians have realized.

These data also make it clear that military commissions dealt severely with men who posed a serious threat to the collective security of republicans. The records abound with one case after another of notables who left France only to take up arms against the republic. The military commission at Nice executed three locals for serving as officers in the Sardinian Army.[45] Those condemned to death for serving in Condé's army included Victor Cazeneuve, a rentier from Paris; Jean-Pierre Guy de Villeneuve, a former cavalry officer from Belfort; and Philibert, chevalier de la Bussière, a seigneur from Vienne.[46] The most famous victim of the Fructidorian military commissions, Louis-Fortuné Guyon, comte de Rochecotte, had also distinguished himself in the prince's army before becoming commander of the "Catholic and Royalist Army of Maine." His extraordinary maneuvers had enabled him to rescue Sir Sidney Smith, an important English spy, from the Temple in Paris.[47] Another aristocratic victim, Joseph-Étienne, marquis de Surville, was one of the Pretender's principal agents in the Midi organizing royalist operations funded by stagecoach robberies and counterfeiting.[48] These

TABLE 1

Location and verdicts of military commissions created by the law of 19 fructidor V

| Location | Verdicts | Death | Exile[a] | Prison[b] |
|---|---|---|---|---|
| Aix | 1 | | | |
| Angers | 1 | 1 | | |
| Avignon | 18 | 10 | 2 | |
| Bastia | 14 | 7 | | 5[c] |
| Bayonne | 4 | | 3 | 1 |
| Besançon | 30 | 13 | 8 | |
| Bordeaux | 4 | 2 | | |
| Brest | 1 | | | |
| Brussels | 3 | 2 | | |
| Caen | 23 | 14 | 1 | |
| Clermont-Ferrand | 5 | 4 | | |
| Colmar | 1 | 1 | | |
| Dieppe | 3 | | 1 | |
| Dijon | 26 | 4 | | |
| Douai | 26 | 8 | 1 | |
| Ghent | 3 | 3 | | |
| Grenoble | 29 | 11 | | |
| Huningue | 3 | 3 | | |
| Koblenz | 5 | | | |
| Laval | 1 | | | |
| Liège | 11 | 6 | 1 | |
| Lyon | 10 | 5 | | |
| Mainz | 9 | | 2 | |
| Mannheim | 3 | 2 | | |
| Le Mans | 1 | 1 | | |
| Marseille | 130 | 31 | 11 | |
| Metz | 12 | 3 | 1 | |
| Mézières | 8 | | 1 | 4[d] |
| Milan | 1 | | 1 | |
| Montbrison | 1 | | | |
| Montpellier | 42 | 6 | | |
| Nancy | 36 | 7 | 2 | 2 |
| Nantes | 12 | 6 | 2 | |
| Nice | 8 | 6 | | |
| Nîmes | 33 | 3 | | 5 |
| Paris | 65 | 29 | | |
| Périgueux | 17 | 4 | 1 | |
| Perpignan | 59 | 9 | 1 | |
| Poitiers | 7 | 1 | 1 | |

TABLE 1 (*continued*)

| Location | Verdicts | Death | Exile[a] | Prison[b] |
|---|---|---|---|---|
| Le Puy | 2 | 2 | | |
| Quimper | 2 | 1 | 1 | |
| Rennes | 2 | 1 | 1 | |
| La Rochelle | 3 | | 1 | 1 |
| Rouen | 1 | | | |
| Saint-Brieuc | 7 | 3 | 3 | |
| Saint-Lô | 1 | 1 | | |
| Strasbourg | 118 | 6 | 48 | 2[e] |
| Tarascon | 1 | 1 | | |
| Toulon | 215 | 66 | 25 | 1 |
| Toulouse | 2 | 2 | | |
| Tours | 11 | 4 | | |
| Valence | 1 | | | |
| Verdun | 1 | | | 1[d] |
| Total | 1033 | 289 | 119 | 22 |

[a]Deportation, banishment, reemigration.
[b]*Réclusion* and imprisonment.
[c]Accomplices sentenced to four years in irons.
[d]Escaped Austrian POWs sentenced to 6 years in irons.
[e]Émigrés who left France before 1789 sentenced to prison until peace.

were not isolated cases of guerrilla operations or organized crime directed by émigrés. It was returned émigrés who gave the counter-revolution the semblance of a national organization. For example, Etienne-Martial, baron de Mandat, was originally from Champagne but served as a regional chouan commander in the west. His capture near Bayeux and execution at Caen in 1798 "was the greatest loss that the royalists of Lower Normandy sustained before the death of M. de Frotté" in 1800.[49] In fact, forty-seven officers in the Catholic and Royalist Army of Normandy were returned émigrés.[50]

Military commissions also killed émigrés regardless of social status if they had earlier committed crimes against the republic. For example, the military commissions at Toulon, Marseille, and Montpellier, the busiest of them all (see table 1), ignored the amnesty of 4 brumaire IV (26 October 1795) for acts connected to the Revolution, and applied defunct laws from 1795 to distinguish between Toulonnais refugees and émigrés who had collaborated with the English. As a consequence, dozens of people who had fled France in the summer and autumn of 1793 were spared anything worse than reporting to their local municipalities. In contrast, at least a score of people who might otherwise have been exempted were executed, some for providing supplies, others for serving as gendarmes, one for helping to set the French fleet on fire, and another for having sat on a court-martial whose proceedings were dated "the first year of the reign of Louis 17."[51] Similarly, émigré brigands whose social status ranged from the chevalier Gérard de Saint-Elme to the farmhand Antoine Laquerre (nom de guerre: Intrepid) and the professionless Pierre-Charles Yvon all ended their days before military commissions.[52] These individual case histories make it clear that many of those executed by military commissions were men who at one time or another seriously threatened the republic's stability. The Directory expressed few regrets about applying a draconian law to such persons and was perfectly willing to accept the consequences.

The "Fructidorian Terror" involved more than military commissions. The law of 19 fructidor not only subjected deputies and royalist conspirators to the "dry guillotine," it also authorized the Directory to issue directives deporting individual priests without so much as a hearing. The Directory grossly abused this power and allowed department administrators to do the same. Purely administrative orders resulted in the deportation of almost 1,400 priests, 187 of whom died within two years.[53] As a result, three times as many priests died of deportation than were executed by firing squads.

Although military commissions also sentenced ninety-three people to "deportation," the total number of actual deportees was small—only five were sent to Guyana (three of whom died)[54] and thirteen to the islands of Ré and Oléron. Most of the rest were simply expelled from France, including forty-six people tried at Strasbourg who, in this respect, suffered the same fate as the twenty-six people sentenced to "re-emigration" by the commissions at Marseille and Toulon.[55] Military commissions resorted to expulsion in cases where people were deemed unable to obey the law of 19 fructidor, either due to imprisonment, illness, or infirmities (including insanity and old age), and when émigrés had been arrested on territory overrun by the French army. A number of émigrés were also expelled illegally. These expulsions could be either more harsh or more lenient than the law required.[56] Apparent clemency provoked a rash of denunciations from hard-line departmental authorities, which led the Directory to annul two dozen acquittals or lenient sentences on the grounds that individual military commissions had exceeded their authority.[57] Inscriptions on the list of émigrés, attestations of residency, and certificates of ill health were all the subject of a considerable traffic in money and influence. It took constant government vigilance to ensure that only departmental officials, and not military commissions, judged the authenticity of such documents. The dependence of military commissions on civilian authorities is reflected in the fact that one-third of the time military commissions neither acquitted nor convicted but simply referred the case to departmental administrators or the Ministry of Police.

The Directory's efforts both to narrow the focus of military commissions to those émigrés who posed a threat to republicans and to keep the commissions from exceeding their authority gradually reduced their impact over time. This decline in the activity of military commissions was not smooth or regular. In fact, sentencing patterns reveal distinct phases. These resulted as much from government efforts to restore order as from the influence of radical republicanism during the final two years of the Directory.

The initial phase extended from the antiroyalist coup of 18 fructidor V to the anti-Jacobin electoral machinations known as the coup d'état of 22 floréal VI (11 May 1798). Half of all the cases heard by military commissions were judged during these nine months (see figure 8). During this period, the activity of military commissions passed from considerable arbitrariness to increasingly well-regulated operations. At first, the law of 19 fructidor V inspired a mass exodus of returned émigrés, especially from the federalist cities of the Midi.[58] Large-scale roundups began almost immediately wherever emigration had been heavy in 1793. After two months of arrests, a hundred people were in prison at Strasbourg and two hundred in the Fort Jean at Marseille, all awaiting trial by military commissions.[59] Such early zeal was typical of the Jacobin resurgence that followed the Fructidor coup. Some of these cases clearly involved settling old scores. Déon Modeste of La Valette (Var) was stabbed nine times on the way to his appearance before a military commission at Toulon. This was a revenge assault for his part in the recent murder of Aubert, also from La Vallette, and now the commissioner for the correctional court at Toulon. One of Modeste's accomplices, André Geoffroy alias Le Chevalier, was later executed as an émigré, but the government quickly intervened to have several other political "cutthroats" transferred to regular criminal courts.[60] Such exploitation of military commissions for partisan ends only discredited the Directorial regime.

A relative lull in prosecutions during the three months following the elections of 1798 soon gave way to a renewed wave of trials and executions that summer. This sudden recrudescence was part of a broader effort to crack down on all forms of serious crime and resistance to the regime. In

**Fig. 8   Trials by Fructidorian military commissions**

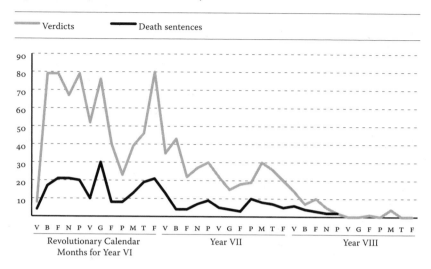

July 1798, lawmakers authorized the Directory to order and conduct house searches throughout the country in order to arrest English spies, returned émigrés, priests subject to deportation, *égorgeurs,* brigands, and chouan leaders. This yielded a second harvest of émigrés to send before military commissions. A final wave of trials, albeit smaller and less deadly than the previous two, occurred during "the Jacobin Hundred Days"[61] of mid-1799. Contrary to Victor Pierre's claim, the military commissions did not disappear after the legislature's "counter-coup" of 30 prairial VII (18 June 1799) that ended the so-called Second Directory. In fact, a handful of executions took place after 18 brumaire VIII (8 November 1799), and the last trials took place eight months later — at Koblenz, no less.[62] All the same, the Consulate quickly repudiated the policies of the Fructidorian Terror once the republican narrative of the Revolution lost its status as myth.

Adding another eight hundred cases to the two hundred previously discovered forces us to reconsider the claims that contemporaries and historians alike have made about the judicial massacres committed after Fructidor. Whereas earlier work emphasized the cruelties perpetrated in the name of the republic, the new evidence highlights the difficulty of separating political subversion from criminal disorder. Fructidor suggests that the Directorial regime's republican narrative made it congenitally incapable of establishing mechanisms for pacification and reconciliation on the way to ending the French Revolution. Whereas the Terror of year II had been conducted largely by local authorities imbued with extraordinary powers, the repression that followed Fructidor was generally a well-focused governmental operation. Military commissions were initially poorly regulated and truly terrifying, but the Directory's efforts to keep them from exceeding their authority and to sharpen their focus gradually reduced their impact. Although the trope of attacking nobles and priests continued to color the regime's efforts at pacification, the new evidence on the victims of military commissions reveals an effort to concentrate more on men of social status who had actively sought to bring down the republic. Military commissions, the sine qua non of the "Fructidorian Terror," can be understood only within the wider context of growing government repression. Both the resurrection of military commissions and their selective treatment of émigrés are best explained as the product of an exculpatory narrative of the Revolution that was elevated to the level of a paradigmatic myth on the basis of the rampant lawlessness and virtual collapse of government authority in the summer of 1797. This republican myth based on past massacres combined with the Directory's determination to restore order in the countryside through increasingly authoritarian means. Thus, more mundane matters of restoring public order—both shaped and distorted by the republican myth—provide a better explanation for political repression under the Second Directory than simple ideological prejudice. The result was a major shift in the regime's source of legitimacy. Fructidor moved the Directory from trying to end the French Revolution through constitutionalism and the rule of law (albeit with certain serious compromises), to trying to end it by restoring order in authoritarian terms (albeit within some important legalistic limits).

## More Republican Justice

The crisis of 1797 also encouraged the Directorial regime to intervene more directly in the operations of the regular civilian courts. Though not a feature of the "Fructidorian Terror" strictly speaking, increased government involvement in the exercise of criminal justice assuredly put defense of the republic ahead of defense of the constitution. The great exceptionalisms of the coup d'état were followed by other, less apparent transgressions that markedly increased the repressive capacity of the machinery of justice. As we have already seen, the system of criminal justice in place during the Directory did more to punish crime than is generally claimed, and a substantial increase in repression followed the Fructidor coup d'état.

The dramatic increase in executive authority and the resurgence in republicanism that flowed from Fructidor helped to make the criminal justice
system notably more responsive to the government's demands. Even before
the coup, the Directory had acquired more power to shape the judiciary
than intended by the Constitution of Year III. Early in the Directory, the law
of 22 frimaire IV (13 December 1795) authorized the government to fill judicial vacancies resulting from incomplete elections or subsequent depar-
tures. These appointments lasted until the elections of 1797. The disgruntled
mood of the electorate that spring ensured that their elected replacements
made the magistracy even more conservative, if not reactionary, than it
already was. Six months later, however, the law of 19 fructidor V covered
judicial elections as well and thereby eliminated scores of judges elected
to replace the government's appointees. This allowed the Directory to appoint replacements, only now the new men would serve the full five-year
term specified in the constitution rather than simply serving until the next
election.[63] The government predictably took the opportunity to appoint numerous staunch republicans, some of whom had no judicial experience at
all. For example, the four judges appointed by the Directory to the court at
Vesoul (Billard, Loys, Bouverey, and Garnier) were accused of "exaggerated
principles" and "hatred of wise and moderate republicans." It did not help
that Bouverey had no judicial experience, having only been an army officer
in the west before suddenly being appointed a judge.[64]

The Directory's influence on the choice of judicial personnel grew further in 1798. First, the law of 21 nivôse VI (10 January 1798) sacked all court
presidents and public prosecutors elected at the start of the Directory. This
opened all of these posts for election that spring. It also allowed the Directory to make temporary replacements at a time when the government
was putting great energy into influencing the electoral outcome. Despite
the use of so-called "road inspectors" sent out to find suitable candidates
and spread money around, the elections went badly, and the government
responded with the "coup" of 22 floréal VI (11 May 1798). In some ways this
postelection triage was a greater affront to democracy than the armed coup
of Fructidor. The elected officials eliminated by it certainly represented
less of an overt threat to the survival of the republic. The perverse Floréal
operation strengthened the "Directorialist" element in the judiciary. The
many splits in departmental electoral assemblies, most of them planned
and provoked by supporters of the government, enabled the regime to prefer one set of choices for court president and public prosecutor over a rival
set elected elsewhere in the same town at the same time. The choosing of

one slate of judges or another occurred in seventeen departments, most of them previously unaffected by the nullifications of 19 fructidor V. The law of 22 floréal went beyond settling disputed results and included a purge of undesirables. All judicial elections in a dozen departments, whether or not there had been a split, were nullified, even though few had experienced either violence or serious electoral fraud. In yet another dozen departments, the law targeted only specific individuals.

The Directory had paved the way for this travesty of democracy with a message to lawmakers about the election returns. It read, in part, "one sees men who would like to reopen the bloody chapter of revolutionary tribunals, the students of Fouquier-Tinville, reappearing in the position of public prosecutor." Such claims were not fictional bombast. The unrepentant Montagnard Joseph Fayau, an extremist in the Vendée and outspoken defender of the notorious Carrier, had been elected public prosecutor in the Seine-et-Marne; the "anarchist" mother assembly in the Allier chose Sadet as its public prosecutor and Gabriel Perrotin as its court president; both had been members of the infamous *Commission temporaire* at Lyon.[65] Such men were naturally eliminated along with many others, including a few royalists. In fact, the law of 22 floréal VI removed almost one-third of magistrates elected that year, a higher proportion than any other category of elected official.[66] The consequences were commensurately serious for the judiciary. It was one thing to leave fifty-three seats in the councils vacant; it was quite another not to complete the judiciary. Criminal justice would grind to a halt without replacements. Therefore, lawmakers once again authorized the Directory to fill vacancies.[67] These included twenty-one court presidents and sixteen public prosecutors.[68] And yet granting this renewed authority to the government did not always lead to new men. Louis-Nicolas Juteau-Duhoux, "a patriot of '89," was simply reappointed as public prosecutor of the Sarthe, for example.

Even counting the number of vacancies the Directory had to fill after Floréal understates the role the Second Directory played that year in the selection of key judicial personnel. In truth, the elections of year VI magnified the effect of executive influence by ensuring that many of the court presidents and public prosecutors appointed in the wake of Fructidor or on the eve of the elections received a form of rubber-stamp legitimacy from the assemblies of year VI. For example, when the law of 22 floréal VI accepted the choices of the electoral assembly in the Hérault, it was merely confirming the electors' choice of the Directory's own post-Fructidor appointees: Barthélemy Jouvent as public prosecutor and Joseph Fournier as court president. At the same time, two new judges elected by the same assembly were removed for being Jacobins.[69] This combination of selectively nullifying election results and determining key judicial appointments enabled the Directory to begin reversing the antirepublican tendencies of the country's least effective courts, especially those in the southeast and the annexed departments.

The Directory also intervened in judicial appointments by using its constitutional powers to prosecute individual magistrates for negligence or corruption. The extent of this practice is difficult to determine, especially if only individual magistrates were involved. Such was the case in the Haute-Saône, where the Directory ordered the criminal prosecution of Lécurel, jury director at Gray, after a refractory priest was arrested in his house at nearby Rigny.[70] At times, however, the prosecution of magistrates became something of a national cause célèbre. In April 1798, for example, the Directory issued arrest orders for three members of the notoriously reactionary Criminal Court of the Gard: Vigier-Sarrasin, the president; Blanc-Pascal, the public prosecutor; and Labaume, the jury director at Uzès at the time. They were quickly indicted and sent before the Criminal Court of the Drôme, which ultimately acquitted them all in year VII. This was typical. Judges did not like to try other judges, even if their politics were diametrically opposed.[71] Thus, whether it was through replacing the relatives of émigrés in year IV, sacking officials after Fructidor V, filling vacancies created by Floréal VI, or having magistrates prosecuted in year VII, the Directory took an increasingly active part in determining who would hold the key posts of court president and public prosecutor throughout the country. Though the government had less influence on the selection of ordinary judges, these too felt the strong hand of the executive from time to time.[72]

## Repressive Results

The Directory's increased role in choosing judicial personnel gave criminal justice a more republican aspect. But, as we have seen, the attitudes of ordinary jurors remained critical to the repressive capacity of criminal courts. Though jury directors and public prosecutors significantly shaped the caseloads of criminal courts, it remained up to jurors to decide the fate of the accused brought before them. Officials often complained about the composition of jury lists, especially those prepared after the elections of 1797. The administrators of the Haute-Saône appointed in the wake of Fructidor, for example, believed that many of those on the jury list that they inherited were either relatives of émigrés or electors that spring. Therefore, in order "to prevent the sort of persecution under legal forms meditated by royalism against friends of the Republic," they drew up "a new list composed of upstanding republicans." Their initiative got strong support from Minister of Justice Lambrechts, who pushed for a speedy revision of jury lists across the country.[73] No historian has yet risen to the daunting challenge of comparing the social and political composition of different jury lists during the Directory. Nonetheless, it is safe to assume that post-Fructidorian officials would find it easy to cull out some of the most obvious opponents of the republican order and to replace them with men of a more sympathetic stripe. It is less clear how matters unfolded in the confused climate after Floréal, but it is unlikely that royalists returned to the lists in any great numbers. It is equally unlikely that jury lists anywhere were made up of compliant citizens eager to enforce the Directory's harsh policies.

By mid-1798, there were signs that the substantial changes made within the magistracy and among jurors were yielding better results for the republic. The commissioner of the Doubs had no doubts: "the regeneration of juries has terrified villains," he reported after only a single trimester.[74] The deputy Poultier, editor of the centrist *L'Ami des lois,* was certainly convinced that criminal courts had become considerably more effective: "the operations of criminal courts are becoming so rapid and firm that soon the soil of France will be entirely purged of all the brigands who have desolated it for so long." However, more news from the provinces led Poultier to temper his enthusiasm, "True, there are *some* criminal courts where *certain crimes* find either *mercy* or *indulgence,* but let us hope that the government's resolve as well as cold impartiality from the Court of Cassation[75] will succeed in regularizing the operations of those courts that still adhere to dead practices (*le système des revenants*)."[76] Was Poultier's optimism warranted? Was criminal justice in years VI and VII significantly more effective than in years IV and V? What sorts of crimes continued to receive either mercy or indulgence? The best way to assess the impact of interventions in judicial personnel after Fructidor is to move beyond journalistic impressions and undertake statistical assessment. In order to ensure that all data are gathered and analyzed in a uniform manner, it is best to return to the verdicts rendered by the four criminal courts of the Haute-Garonne, Hérault, Haute-Saône, and Sarthe. These data will be treated cumulatively in order to discern national trends. They will also be broken down by department and by various categories of crime to determine regional differences.

It is natural to begin with rates of general repression as measured by acquittal rates and sentencing results. The Second Directory saw a clear decrease in rates of acquittal. Overall this decrease was modest, going from 43 percent for the years IV and V to 39 percent for the years VI and VII.[77] This decrease was not common in all departments or for all types of crime. In fact, the overall trend was contradicted by an increase in the acquittal rates in the Haute-Saône. This local anomaly was due mainly to a rise in the number of fraud cases, which were always hard to prove. On the other hand, the Sarthe and Haute-Garonne both saw their acquittal rates, which had been over 50 percent during the First Directory, fall sharply after Fructidor. This brought them more into line with other departments. Nonetheless, major differences remained.[78] In addition to declining rates of acquittal, the activity of the criminal courts climbed noticeably after Fructidor (see appendix A.1).[79] Together a decrease in acquittal rates and an increase in the number of people who appeared in criminal courts meant that the total number of persons convicted of felonies increased by almost one-fifth from the first half to the second half of the Directory. This translated into marked growth in sentences of lengthy terms in irons (that is, hard labor). The number of persons actually present in court who were sentenced to ten or more years in irons grew rapidly from 118 persons in four departments during years IV and V to 174 persons in years VI and VII, an increase of almost 50 percent. Even more remarkable was the sharp rise in the number of death sentences. These went from twenty-seven in the Directory's first two years to sixty-eight in its last two (up 150 percent). More than half of this increase in death sentences was due to the antibrigandage laws of 26 floréal V (15 May 1797) and 29 nivôse VI (18 January 1798) (see chapter 9),[80] which highlights the importance of armed robbery in the overall totals. Appendix A.4 clearly shows the prevalence of brigands and highwaymen among defendants convicted by the criminal courts. In addition to the increase in death sentences, the number of deportation verdicts grew from three during the First Directory to twenty-four during the Second. Most of these deportations were the result of the law of 22 germinal II (11 April 1794) against harboring refractory priests, but ten of the deportation verdicts were based on the law of 27 germinal IV (16 April 1796), which prescribed deportation for joining a seditious mob. This manifold jump in deportations during the Second Directory reflected a newfound ability to clamp down on civil unrest directed against the regime.

In order to understand the impact of these general trends on the Directory's chances for survival, it is useful to isolate the response of criminal courts to crimes that posed special problems for restoring order. These can be grouped into two types: interpersonal violence (including armed robbery) and overt opposition to the republic and its officials. To get a better sense of the repressive impact of the courts, the focus will be on cases in which defendants were present at trial. This reveals the increasingly repressive role of criminal courts during the Second Directory.

First, the number of persons prosecuted for interpersonal violence doubled in the two years after Fructidor.[81] This was a broad-based increase, both across departments and across types of crime. In general, France experienced an increase in prosecutions for every type of violence from infanticide and rape to homicide and highway robbery. This reflects both a higher rate of solipsistic violence and a greater determination to prosecute. It would be an abuse of evidence to claim a good correlation between the number of persons tried on charges of rape or assault and the actual frequency of these crimes. The changing attitudes of both society and the state toward these acts of violence made as much difference to criminal court statistics, if not more, as the actual incidence of such crimes. After all, this was a period when the prosecution of a gang rape by drunken sailors brought only a single sentence of six years in irons for the instigator, or when the fully attested rape of a ten-year-old shepherdess led merely to charges of "attempted rape" in order to protect the girl's future prospects for marriage. Outcomes such as these fit the pattern of contemporary social and judicial attitudes, not the pattern of actual crime.[82] And yet we need not abstain from drawing conclusions about the incidence of all types of violent crime. Prosecutions for highway robbery, for example, naturally correlate to their geographical incidence. Although many of the brigands and highwaymen tried in the criminal courts of the Haute-Garonne, Hérault, and Sarthe came from neighboring departments, it is not surprising to find these courts dealing with many more such cases than did that of the Haute-Saône. Plenty of other sources confirm that southern and western France had many more incidents of brigandage and highway robbery than eastern France.[83] Similarly, loose temporal correlations are worth noting. It was no accident that the greatest overall increase in prosecutions for acts of violence came in year VI. This surge in prosecutions directly reflects a surge in threats to public order in the second half of year V, combined with the normal delay in bringing such cases to trial, and a dramatic redrawing of the political landscape after Fructidor. The nature and implications of this republican redress merit closer examination.

As we have seen, trial juries had a strong tendency to acquit defendants charged with political crimes or resistance to public authority. These acquittals often went against the evidence and therefore constituted "jury nullification." Though relatively high rates prevailed throughout the constitutional republic, years VI and VII witnessed a dramatic drop in the acquittal rate for such crimes. By combining into a single category verdicts from such offenses as harboring a priest, freeing prisoners from the gendarmerie, striking local officials, calling for the return of royalty or the constitution of 1793, rioting against the republic, and other such offenses, we are able to see clearly the improved ability of the criminal justice system to uphold the republican regime. In the two years that preceded Fructidor, the acquittal rate for these sorts of crimes stood at 73 percent. In the two years following Fructidor, this rate dropped to 58 percent.[84] This decline was largely the result of more overtly republican jurors. The new jurors clearly had less hesitation in defending the new republican and state-based concept of order against village mores and popular resistance. On the other hand, the role of a more republican magistracy in the prosecution of such crimes is revealed by the massive increase in the number of individuals brought to court for these offenses. Whereas jury directors and public prosecutors brought 137 individuals to court for crimes against the republic and its agents in the years IV and V, their replacements had 219 individuals tried for the same sorts of crime in the years VI and VII, an increase of 60 percent.

Such a dramatic increase becomes even more remarkable when the two northern departments of our study are contrasted with the two southern departments. Making such a comparison quickly reveals that the southern departments were responsible for the entire increase. In fact, both of the northern departments saw a decline in the number of individuals prosecuted for opposing republican authorities. The decline was slight in the Haute-Saône, a department characterized by strong tensions over Catholic worship and a timeless hostility to forest watchmen, but one with little intracommunal violence based on revolutionary politics. In contrast, the number of persons prosecuted for political offenses in the Sarthe dropped by over half. Here the explanation lies in the amnesty that accompanied the "pacification" of western departments in year IV. If chouans violated the amnesty, they were no longer treated as political opponents but rather as common criminals and, therefore, were subject to laws against brigandage and highway robbery. This decrease in the Sarthe was matched by a commensurate increase in prosecutions in the Haute-Garonne. There the replacement of the former federalist Janole as public prosecutor in April 1798 opened the door for a number of prosecutions arising out of the wave of political violence that swept the south in the summer of 1797. However, the bulk of the overall increase in prosecutions for resistance to the republic or its officials came in the Hérault. The department's electoral assembly of year IV had produced a group of deputies and local officials who leaned to the right. The assembly of 1797 pushed this tendency further and included among its choice of deputies both the public prosecutor (Rouch) and the court president (Thourel). The assembly then elected two royalists (Auberet and Rech) to replace them. The result was a runaway antirepublican reaction. The election results in the Hérault were nullified at Fructidor, of course, and the entire department administration replaced.[85] This sudden replacement of royalists with staunch republicans led to the prosecution of numerous political offenses, most of which derived from riots and seditious speech during the reaction of year V.[86] This was a typical judicial response wherever the political complexion of department officials changed dramatically as a result of the Fructidor coup. In that sense, the mix of departments included in this study appears highly representative of the country in general. The most obvious changes came in the form of lower acquittal rates, harsher punishments, and increased prosecutions for resisting the regime.

In other words, there was an unmistakable movement toward both a more republican and a more repressive system of criminal justice. This development has been lost from view in the dark shadow cast back on the Directory by the judicial reforms of 1800. Historians have made little effort to analyze the effectiveness of the criminal justice system prior to these reforms and simply accept the criticisms that served to justify them. In this light, it is important to note that the system of juries survived the Consulate's reforms for more than ideological reasons. Once jury lists had been vetted for political undesirables, juries proved perfectly capable of defending both the republic and its new state-based concept of order. Furthermore, the vast majority of judges appointed during the Consulate had already been elected, appointed, or both during the Directory and so reflected greater continuity during the late First Republic than is generally acknowledged.[87] In fact, it was the Fructidor coup that constituted the most important turning point in the construction of authoritarian responses to the problems of public order. To appreciate the full significance of this moment for its contribution to ending the French Revolution, historians must move beyond the ideologically constructed notion of a "Fructidorian Terror." It was the regime's manner of asserting republican salvation over constitutional legitimacy, both through military commissions and greater executive control of the judiciary, that set the course for the future.

# 7 Strong-Arm Policing

> Ten years of experience has fully shown that the National Guard in
> constant service is a powerless means for maintaining order and even for
> preserving public liberties.
> —Deputy Duquesnoy, 7 July 1800

WHEN REVOLUTIONARIES REPUDIATED the social inequalities and corporative ethos that underpinned French absolutism, they inevitably changed
the nature of policing. The integrity and autonomy of individual communities, especially rural communities, dominated notions of collective identity well into the nineteenth century. The construction of revolutionary
patriotism and national identity, however, based as they were in individual
rights ostensibly granted to all Frenchmen, challenged and complicated
these established mores. The resulting clash of values sharply increased the
tension between the two "concepts of order," that based in the community
and that based in the state. Scholars have focused much attention on "the
republic in the village" and the power of "modernization" to turn "peasants
into Frenchmen."[1] Rather oddly, the contribution to this process made by
policing has been given short shrift. Scholars tend to think of the police as
an epiphenomenon of larger social changes—not as cause, just effect. As
was the case with jury duty, however, the actual practices of policing were
critical to how villages were absorbed into the nation. Before this happened,
collective autonomies needed to be accommodated as much as confronted.
The revolutionary institution of the National Guard made this possible.
And yet the National Guard proved notoriously unable to preserve order
and was often the source of disorder. Therefore, wherever the republic engaged in a protracted struggle to impose its concept of order on recalcitrant
communities, it turned to strong-arm policing. This involved making the
Gendarmerie Nationale into a truly national, truly professional police force.

In cases of extreme unrest, it also came to mean turning all local police functions over to the army by declaring a commune under "state of siege." Together these responses greatly accelerated the long-term shift from community policing to policing communities.

## National Guard

The National Guard, like liberty trees, popular societies, and festivals of federation, played a major part in the burgeoning political culture of the early Revolution. In many ways, however, the presence of the National Guard meant an absence of the state. At the very least, the National Guard embodied local autonomy and politicized policing. As Duquesnoy's remark in this chapter's epigraph illustrates, by 1800 maintaining order and preserving public liberties could no longer be entrusted to such a revolutionary institution. The corollary of such a claim was that only institutions of the state could safeguard the citizenry. One reason the Revolution did not end until well into the Consulate is that it took successive republican regimes more than a decade to replace the National Guard with a more thorough monopoly of armed force.

Though famous for its contribution to the war effort in 1792, the National Guard began as an instrument of local autonomy and something of an amateur police force. The National Assembly quickly legalized the activity of the new bourgeois militias that sprang up in 1789, but it took another two years before the organic law of 29 September/14 October 1791 standardized the organization of the National Guard throughout the country. In the meantime, various laws restricted admission to "active citizens" and required it to be requisitioned for duty by local magistrates. The annual election of officers often proved a popular affair and made the National Guard another training ground for democratic practices. Early decrees specified that National Guard units were to "restore order and maintain obedience to the laws," "to disperse all popular riots and seditious gatherings," and to seize and turn over to justice "those guilty of beatings and violence captured in the act."[2] Apart from routine service and daily patrols, commanders had no authority to act independently of civilian officials. Lawmakers did not want the National Guard to become an independent force in politics. This is evident from the term limits on officers, the ban on deliberating once assembled, and the regulations guaranteeing civilian ascendancy. In order to avoid making the National Guard a career option and to prevent ossifying elitism, an officer's term was limited to one year, and he could only be reelected after serving another year in the ranks. Moreover, any use of guardsmen required a written order from elected local officials. Such terms made the National Guard a community-based militia expressly designed to offset the state-controlled constabulary and line army.

After years of improvised chaos and political controversy during the early republic, the Thermidorian Convention overhauled the National Guard with the law of 28 prairial III (16 June 1795). Part of the purpose was to restore its bourgeois character.[3] Equally important, officers could now be reelected for successive terms, which made the National Guard a greater force in local politics, particularly in urban settings. The new service conditions made it possible for politically active notables to remain in control of an essentially bourgeois, though not exclusively elitist, local force. Unfortunately, little is known about the elections for the National Guard after 1795, partly because many never took place. Neglect in organizing the National Guard in the early Directory had much to do with the new system of local administration. Each of the nascent cantons grouped together a handful of villages, often embittered by local rivalry, and required them to cooperate in the election of officers. Thus, the National Guard no longer embodied communal autonomy, except in urban centers of five thousand inhabitants or more. Where elections for officers of the National Guard did take place, it was at the same time as the annual spring elections, and the results naturally reflected the political shading of other officials elected at that time. An important exception arose in the autumn of 1797, when new officers needed to be elected once the Fructidor coup nullified elections in half the departments of France.[4]

The government's primary interest in the National Guard lay in having a force available for local officials to mobilize at times of pressing need. This could mean escorting convoys of grain at times of dearth, providing security for a controversial trial, or arresting a returned émigré. Tasks of this sort rarely required mobilizing a canton's entire National Guard. And yet allowing officials to designate those who would perform special duties could be so invidious and lead to such bickering that it would cripple any efforts at policing. In order to have an armed force available at all times and in all places, on 17 floréal IV (6 May 1796) the Directory ordered every canton to form one-sixth of its national guardsmen into a "mobile column." Each mobile column constituted a volunteer police force on call for six months and ready to respond to threats to public order the minute local officials called upon them. Some viewed this as a sign of desperation and predicted a quick restoration of monarchy.[5] They were mistaken. By insisting that every canton have an active armed force, the Directory was creating a means to tip the balance in the republic's favor. The Constitution of Year III made guard duty a requirement of active citizenship; anyone who wished to vote had first to be a confirmed member of his local National Guard. During their time in the mobile column, guardsmen would assemble "only in exceptional circumstances" and only when formally called upon by local civilian officials.[6] These same officials determined the entire composition of the column, which included appointing the officers as long as they served at the rank to which they had originally been elected. Department officials and commissioners could both annul part or all of a cantonal column. This risked provoking partisan wrangling, however, and so rarely happened until after a column had performed badly. In practical terms, therefore, local officials had the ability to create and use an armed force favorable to their own opinions.

As one might expect, the effort to create mobile columns raised the political temperature almost everywhere. The willingness to organize them became a litmus test of commitment to the republic. Whether or not a canton formed a mobile column in 1796 was a good barometer of republican sentiment among leading inhabitants. Even staunch republicans, however, found it difficult to form a mobile column. Activating the National Guard had generally been used either as the basis for another military levy or to pursue refractory priests, émigrés, deserters, and draft dodgers. After all, the National Guard had served to impose the radical Revolution on the countryside and had been the basis of the "volunteer battalions" of 1791–92. The Ministry of Police tried to allay concerns that mobile columns would serve as a conveyor belt to the army by pointing out that mobile columns had rotating membership and so could not be used in military campaigns. The ministry made no effort to alleviate concerns about having to carry out dangerous or despicable police duties, however, for this was precisely why the Directory insisted on the formation of mobile columns in the first place. As the government commissioner of the Doubs reported, "Municipal officials generally say that they are threatened and that they fear for their families and their properties if they organize the mobile column."[7] Herein lay the causes of the protracted struggle to revive an institution that began as a spontaneous attempt to provide community-based policing.

Making the National Guard an effective force was special cause for concern in any place already torn by factionalism. Opponents of the Jacobins at Toulouse feared the political purposes to which the Guard would be put.

The *agents militaires* Fouché and Ferry did nothing to alleviate these fears by instructing department administrators to provide arms only to guardsmen whose "civisme" had been attested.[8] This veritable return to *certificats de civisme* led opponents to decry another *armée révolutionnaire* in the making. Such fears were neither uncommon nor unwarranted.[9] The Jacobins of Toulouse did, in fact, use the 2,000-man mobile column to dominate the city and impose "republican order" on surrounding communes. Several days of street fighting in January 1797 prompted the government to intervene by purging the senior command. According to Minister of Police Cochon de Lapparent, the majority of officers were republicans, but the four brigade chiefs were all "terrorists," and the rank and file drew heavily on the former *compagnie de Marat*.[10] In Montpellier, on the other hand, it was the conservatives who gained control of the mobile column. The young dandies heading the force provoked some nasty street brawls in early year V. Brigade General Frégeville, commander of the Hérault and an elector at Montpellier that year, blamed the royalist results of the local elections on a mobile column swollen with delinquent recruits. His pique brought the whole affair to national attention.[11] Politicization of the local mobile column was no less common in smaller centers. The very existence of mobile columns incited greater factionalism. "As for the mobile column," wrote Prefect Brun of the Ariège, "I have already had the sad experience in the Hérault that this selection from the National Guard is good only to antagonize citizens against one another and exclusively to arm one party and oppress the other."[12] As a result, mobile columns were "too often composed of men who see nothing but persons and parties where they ought only to see the Republic and order."[13] The men who controlled the mobile column controlled the canton. The power that had once come from social standing and networks of clientage increasingly passed to those who could muster the official armed force. These may have been the same people, but often they were not, especially after Fructidor. For example, contentious elections for the National Guard at Faucogney (Haute-Saône) in 1798 led to heavy state intervention in the form of troop billeting and criminal prosecution, a sure sign that traditional notables were no longer in control.[14]

The politicization of the National Guard also hampered its effectiveness away from home. Like the biblical demons who, when cast out of one man, entered a herd of swine and ran it into the sea, the Revolution's unclean spirit of partisan hatred took hold of hundreds of National Guard columns whenever they tromped off to a neighboring canton. Legion indeed are reports of national guardsmen who kicked down doors, smashed open chests, ransacked farms, stole cheese, shot chickens, slapped wives, and beat servants, all without making an arrest. These problems were worst under the Second Directory, when guardsmen were increasingly pressed into service to assist in "grand sweeps" intended to arrest all manner of outlaws. Such elaborately planned excursions, often involving dozens of communes from two or more departments,[15] risked inciting more resistance than they quelled. In such cases, success was purely relative. Officials could rejoice at the scores of conscripts flushed out of farmhouses and mountain villages, but the price was ever more antipathy between the republic and the populace. In fact, the approach of guardsmen at Mont-sur-Monnet in the Jura was cause to ring the tocsin and rally the village to resist the armed invasion.[16]

Already it is clear that the National Guard was not "destined to become a lifeless corps" under the Directory, as its only serious historian has written.[17] True, the innumerable circulars stirring guardsmen to action suggest widespread complacency and lassitude. Furthermore, early images of national guardsmen resplendent in colorful uniforms, all armed with muskets and drawn up in serried ranks, especially common during Lafayette's ascendancy in Paris, had little in common with the later experience of most guardsmen. So ragtag were many guardsmen that observers often mistook a mobile column for a hunting party or a band of brigands. Special armbands or tricolor cockades might be the only signs of belonging. Not even weapons set them apart. Many mobile columns formed in rural communities lacked a full complement of guns and had to equip themselves with swords, pikes, and even simple clubs.[18] Regulations required municipalities to keep weapons for the National Guard safely stored in the town hall of the cantonal seat. Once taken out and distributed, however, they could be difficult to retrieve. A lot of guns fell into the wrong hands. Even passing them out to guardsmen could mean arming a mob. A mobile column was rarely in person what it was on paper. Usually it was an irregular and unreliable force, such as the "compagnie des républicains" assembled to track down brigands in the Puy-de-Dôme.[19] Even when it was an actual mobile column requisitioned for duty, it usually had stand-ins, hired replacements from the lower social orders or the right political persuasion.[20] These were men willing to accept dangerous duty for twice a worker's daily pay. Unlike regular soldiers, they did not have to be away from home for long. Replacements were fully legal and formed what was called the "paid guard." Citizens did not find their own replacements but simply paid the municipality the going rate. Those without the means to pay, or the good luck to be ill, could be reluctant policemen indeed. Alongside them were replacements, that is, mercenaries. As such these men had less interest in local defense than in obtaining easy money, ready loot, or a thug's adventure. Thus requisitioning a mobile column could amount to nothing more than gathering a paid posse, supplying it with the community's stock of weapons, and giving it a license to kill.

Although the actual conditions of service in the National Guard did not match the ideals of the early 1790s, the National Guard did make a major contribution to the survival of the First Republic. Defense of the republic started at home. The presence of an organized mobile column could help communities, especially towns, retain their autonomy. The ability to supplement the gendarmerie with a few National Guardsmen had the potential to preserve such places from suddenly having a detachment of regular troops stationed there. Furthermore, the availability of a well-organized column—not a general experience, it must be admitted—also enabled communities to defend themselves against rebel incursions. Where the spontaneous organization of a mobile column was not primarily an extension of factional struggles within a community, it was a critical bulwark against a hostile environment. The durability of republicanism in western France in particular depended greatly on active National Guards, and not just in terms of political culture. Here uniforms were essential, so much so that they became the disguise of choice for chouans. Furthermore, in areas of *chouannerie*, a mobile column of guardsmen simply did not form unless it had service muskets and ample cartridges—anything less was suicidal. Generals always preferred the experience and discipline of regular troops over the partisan ardor of national guardsmen, and yet guardsmen often performed heroic feats in defending their native towns.

The security potential offered by the National Guard made it an irresistible temptation for the Directory. As the years passed, therefore, the government increasingly integrated local mobile columns into a larger strategy of republican self-defense. National guardsmen had always been available as a temporary stopgap when there were insufficient regular troops available; in some places guardsmen became a permanent substitute for troops.[21] A major turning point in this respect came in early 1798, when the Directory empowered municipal officials in communes of more than ten thousand inhabitants and department officials for all other communes to requisition mobile columns for continuous duty wherever and whenever they saw fit. This gave department officials the means to create their own defense forces for use anywhere in the department and, when the district commander asked, even in neighboring departments. Some officials made extensive use of this new opportunity. Officials of the Lozère, for example, ordered cantons along the border with the Ardèche to be activated in order to destroy all forest shacks in the region. But Minister of War Schérer considered this a misuse of guardsmen and ordered them all to return home.[22] A year later, the Directory gave departments even greater encouragement to activate their mobile columns by regulating ordinary and extraordinary service.[23] Though extraordinary services had always been an option, they were now fully militarized. As a result, mobile columns in department capitals and republican strongholds were activated throughout the country. They were called upon to press conscription, collect back taxes, disarm communes, and suppress resistance. This could well mean turning guardsmen into dreaded billets.[24] This aggressive repression operated by guardsmen—that is, by patriots and mercenaries who were armed and dangerous—explains much of the anti-Jacobin reaction of late 1799.

Once this power had been granted to departments, the state itself tapped into the resources made available, which was now done in closer conjunction with the army. The regime had quickly learned that activating mobile columns for service beyond their own commune was ineffective unless accompanied by gendarmes or regular troops. Members of mobile columns feared compromising themselves with friends and neighbors if they proved too helpful in enforcing unpopular laws. The addition of a few line troops, therefore, helped to stabilize and even stimulate a detachment on assignment. The pervasive culture of male honor meant that most guardsmen did not want to appear less committed or less brave than the accompanying soldiers when faced with equal danger. Combining forces in this way would create harmony and unity between citizen-soldiers and soldier-citizens, as one commander put it.[25] The Directory also insisted that where possible the citizen-soldiers—that is, requisitioned guardsmen—be chosen from "the prosperous class, whenever patriotism is found paired with wealth," because this made it easier for them to perform their duties and ensured a commitment to protect property.[26] The War of the Second Coalition massively expanded these joint operations. The military crisis of 1799 forced the Directory to transfer tens of thousands of soldiers from the interior to the frontiers and thereby left the gendarmerie, conscripts in ill-equipped reserve units ("auxiliary battalions"), and mobilized national guardsmen as the main sources of armed force to combat a resurgence in lawlessness.[27] Month after month national guardsmen stepped in to fill the shoes of regular soldiers. Although not trusted on night patrols, still inclined to partisanship, and prone to desertion when hunting brigands in difficult terrain, these mixed detachments proved valuable in manning military installations, guarding the coasts, patrolling roads, escorting stagecoaches, and responding to outbreaks of regional insurgency.[28] Using national guardsmen in neighboring departments had serious risks: "the chosen men will massacre, if only out of fear," wrote General Dutry about the men chosen from the mobile columns of the Loiret for use against *chouannerie*.[29] Nonetheless, they played an especially vital role in retaking towns and villages captured by rebels that summer and autumn.[30]

The crisis of 1799 reinvigorated the National Guard, but less as a source of communal self-defense than as a branch of the increasingly militarized state. When activated for more than two days at a time, guardsmen (or their paid replacements) essentially became soldiers controlled and directed by district and department commanders. Though they generally remained in their native departments, they were not always based at home. The departments of the Ninth Military District activated them in response to a rising tide of brigandage, and guardsmen formed a substantial portion of the forces sent against *chouannerie* in the Twenty-second Military District. In the Sixth Military District, they were mobilized explicitly for the purpose of defending the frontier, whereas in the Tenth Military District, guardsmen provided much of the armed force needed to press conscription. In fact, in many places, the efforts of national guardsmen were essential to form the "auxiliary battalions" that took shape in the autumn of 1799. Though of temporary use for domestic policing, these reserve units were soon called to the front, leaving national guardsmen once again as the main stopgap.[31] Therefore, despite being unreliable and often dangerous, scores of mobile columns and other temporary units remained in service well into the Consulate, especially in areas of prolonged turmoil.[32] The departments of western France formed a variety of units known as *compagnies franches, gardes territoriales,* or *légions françaises,* most of which remained active throughout the winter of year IX. Only after the Peace of Lunéville permitted a large number of troops to return in the spring of 1801 did the Consulate finally order the dissolution of all mobile columns on active duty. Even then many prefects, as well as Minister of Police Fouché, were reluctant to give up the irregular units created from the National Guard.[33] By 1801, however, the Consulate was committed to another major expansion of the gendarmerie, which further reduced the need for national guardsmen.

Some obvious lessons had been learned. The inability of the regular forces of order to cope with continued revolutionary upheaval had led to the transformation of the National Guard from its origins in community policing in 1789–90 into yet another instrument for policing communities a decade later. Despite claims to the contrary, the National Guard did not become moribund under the Directory; it simply became more an arm of the state than of the community. As soon as it became possible, the Consulate turned this task over to the gendarmerie, France's real police force.

## Gendarmerie Nationale

The Directory turned the gendarmerie into a modern, professionalized police force. This was not created ex nihilo. There were obvious continuities between the *maréchaussée* under the *ancien régime* and the Gendarmerie Nationale that served as the rural constabulary of nineteenth-century France. All the same, a Tocquevillian perspective obscures at least as much as it reveals. Reforms in the *maréchaussée* undertaken in the 1770s helped to improve the quality of service, but they did not make it a national police force. Besides, the progress toward central control and professionalization made in the early years of the Revolution was wiped out by the wrenching upheaval and abuses inflicted under the Convention. This left the Directory with a force riven by politics, practically unfunded, and bereft of service standards. In these circumstances, any efforts to restore law and order required completely rebuilding the force.

Alexis de Tocqueville famously claimed that even before the Revolution the monarchy's steady progress toward administrative centralization had led Frenchmen to depend almost entirely on the state to sustain the "social machine." Although his broadly sociological and structural analysis escaped many of the limitations inherent in a narrative approach, Tocqueville's analysis projected much of the strength and coherence of the Napoleonic state back to the *ancien régime*. This teleological flaw becomes especially apparent in a study of rural policing.[34] Robert Schwartz's otherwise fine study of the role of the *maréchaussée* in conducting the "great internment" of the poor and deracinated described the corps as the most extensive police of its day, "in many ways a modern national police force."[35] However, even a cursory look at the actual strength, activities, and composition of the force belies the claims of both Tocqueville and Schwartz.

The prerevolutionary *maréchaussée* simply lacked sufficient numerical strength to provide policing in the modern sense. The province of Brittany had fewer than 190 members of the *maréchaussée* to police a population of 2.2 million; in Languedoc, 204 cavaliers tried to keep law and order amongst a population of 1.7 million contentious Frenchmen. As a whole, France averaged only one rural policeman for every seven or eight thousand inhabitants.[36] Furthermore, no matter the size of territory and population for which they had nominal responsibility, the *maréchaussée* rarely brought malefactors into direct contact with the machinery of justice. In the Soissonais, the average cavalier made only about three arrests a year, one of which would be a simple vagabond. Even their role in investigating crime was small, being charged with following up no more than two or three thefts each per annum.[37] Their presence on the roads may have decreased the general sense of insecurity, but they certainly did not embody social order in rural communities. At worst, they were a provocative intrusion; at best, a last resort. Finally, the reforms of the 1770s aimed only at reducing some of the *maréchaussée*'s basic flaws. These ranged from personal failings, such as rampant drunkenness and physical decrepitude, to professional inadequacies, including lack of military service and inability to read or write. Despite signs of increased regularity in patrols and improved discipline, these all remained persistent problems down to the Revolution.[38] Such a deficient constabulary made a meaningful contribution to preserving public order only because so little was required in the largely self-regulating society of eighteenth-century France. When we consider the meager forces of the *maréchaussée*, and that by the 1780s it was burdened with "almost total disciplinary control of the marginal population in the countryside,"[39] it comes as no surprise that the monarchy failed to cope with the widespread disturbances of 1789.

The early Revolution did not substantially alter the nature of the rural constabulary; most changes awaited the republic. The *cahiers de doléances* sent to the Estates General in 1789 had consistently called for more effective policing. Two years later the Constituent Assembly almost doubled the size of the force to 7,250 men, some on foot for the first time, and renamed it the Gendarmerie Nationale. The appointment of officers and men alike devolved to the new departmental authorities. New recruits needed three years of military service, and the choice of senior officers was limited to men already in the *maréchaussée*. Otherwise, almost all of the criteria and conditions of service remained the same. The cavaliers still had to buy their own horses, which excluded the average peasant or artisan, and the vast majority continued to be stationed in their native regions.[40] The Legislative Assembly did little other than add 300 more brigades, which brought total strength up to 8,784 men in April 1792.

The war utterly transformed the corps. From the summer of 1792 on, the gendarmerie expanded at a dizzying pace in order to meet growing demands for both military manpower and domestic repression. By the end of 1795, the gendarmerie numbered over 21,000 men, only half of whom served as rural policemen.[41] Such pell-mell expansion had degraded the force. It was now gangrenous with incompetence, illiteracy, and inexperience. Although fighting units suffered most, the problems were ubiquitous. Besides basic issues of professional competency, brigades stationed in areas of political extremism had suffered repeated purges. Jacobin clubs and representatives on mission made it a point to replace "moderates" and "suspects" with political favorites regardless of their credentials. Matters were worst in the Midi. There the grain merchant Pierre Jourdan, known as Coupe-Tête for his part in the "Glacière massacre" at Avignon, became a squadron commander in charge of several departments. The Thermidorian Reaction inevitably brought wholesale purges and another confusing array of appointments made outside the chain of command.[42]

By the start of the Directory, everyone agreed that the gendarmerie needed immediate reorganization. "Nothing is more urgent," wrote the minister of police; "the gendarmerie must be severely purged, everywhere its current composition reveals insouciance, laxness, and even the desire, frequently realized, to favor all crimes, banditry, murder, and desertion."[43] The gendarmerie lacked even the most basic equipment, including horses and weapons, and so found it difficult to make their rounds or disperse fractious gatherings. In the Marne, five-man brigades had only a horse or two each. In the Haute-Garonne, they lacked sabers as well as pistols. But even being properly mounted and armed did not guarantee reliability. In many places, such as the Jura, gendarmes openly refused to arrest refractory priests. Elsewhere, they took sides in local quarrels. Lieutenant Liger's superiors wanted him tried by a court-martial for personally stirring up hatred and revenge in the Lozère.[44] The sheer monotony of complaints makes it easy to believe what critics said about the laziness and cowardice of most gendarmes. After all, why would men hampered by ill-shod horses, bad lodging, and delayed pay repeatedly risk their lives defending a widely detested regime? Who could expect them to reject bribes from families sheltering draft dodgers or track down bandits more numerous and better armed than themselves? Why did so many prisoners, whether priests, deserters, or bandits, manage to escape en route to prison? Who would believe the brigadier who claimed that his unit had been overcome by eighty men, every one of them masked and armed with double-barreled muskets?

At Castres, officials blamed not the officers but the ordinary constables, who were described as "undisciplined, given to debauchery, unconcerned about their duties, susceptible to seduction, unable to keep the secrecy needed for the success of their operations, and, in fact, poltroons."[45] The Directory had little hope of restoring order until the gendarmerie itself had been restored to order.

The Directorial regime effected the most dramatic changes in the history of rural policing in France. The nature of these changes merits close attention. Despite the urgency of reform, partisanship among lawmakers delayed reorganization until 1797. Meanwhile, desperately short of funds and unimpressed by their lackluster performance on the battlefield, the Ministry of War dissolved most of the units serving in the cavalry. This, together with attrition due to deaths, retirements, and resignations, reduced the gendarmerie to 16,500 men by the end of 1796. A bureaucratic study determined that this was still twice the size the country needed and—of greater importance—could afford.[46] Finally, on 25 pluviôse V (13 February 1797), the Councils undertook an organic reorganization. This laid the basis for the modern Gendarmerie Nationale. The new law began by eliminating all existing units and appointments. The new corps would consist of a reorganized command structure giving direction to a force of 8,475 men divided into 1,500 brigades and 100 department companies. In order to implement this reorganization, the central bureaucracy undertook a massive effort to compile service records and performance assessments on every officer and constable. A national inquiry asked deputies, department administrators, and district commanders to evaluate officers and make recommendations. The inquiry whipped up a blizzard of paper swirling between patrons and protégés, between Paris and the departments, between the Ministry of War and the Directory's military bureaus. Although massively oversized, the corps had a shortage of senior officers. Furthermore, a case-by-case analysis persuaded the Ministry of War that a quarter of those on active duty lacked the necessary experience, morality, or talent to continue in their posts. On the other hand, there were three times as many junior officers as the new law permitted. Paring the officer corps down to the mandated number required hundreds of forced retirements, suspensions from active duty, and outright dismissals. It took five months of laborious screening before the government could finally name all of the corps' officers: 25 division chiefs with the rank of brigade general and in command of four or five departments each; 50 squadron commanders or two per division; 110 company captains (one for each department plus a few for large cities); and 200 lieutenants, each in charge of seven or eight five-man brigades.[47]

All of this restructuring took place in a climate of rising antirepublicanism confirmed and encouraged by the elections in the spring of 1797. This made the choice of officers highly contentious. The government was internally divided, with Directors and ministers increasingly polarized into opposing camps. Director Carnot, Minister of War Pétiet, and their respective staffs, all moderate republicans at best, did most of the work on officer appointments. Nonetheless, right-wing deputies believed that many republican officers drawn from the army had been given posts formerly held by officers of the old *maréchaussée* with more conservative opinions. Therefore, the Council of Five Hundred tried to limit the Directory's "arbitrary" powers to appoint senior officers and again to give departmental committees the power to appoint junior officers. The Council of Elders wisely rejected this bridling of executive action. Shortly thereafter matters swung to the opposite pole, and the Directory gained even more independence. After the Fructidor coup d'état, the Councils authorized the Directory to "rectify" officer appointments made in the summer of 1797. The government immediately culled senior officers who "did not merit its confidence." It also made some astute reassignments: Squadron Commander Virveins, for example, demonstrated that he was not "assertive enough" (*assez prononcé*) for southern departments and was duly transferred north to quiescent Chaumont.[48]

Meanwhile the reorganization proceeded at the department level. Once the new officers had taken their posts and had a few weeks to assess the NCOs and constables under their command, departmental review committees (*juries d'examen*) met to purge the brigades. These review committees reflected the many constituencies interested in the quality of the local police.[49] Their actions mimicked those of the government, only on a smaller scale. The law required a cut in active personnel by at least a third. Although some received retirement benefits, redundancy pay, or transfer to the army, the bulk of those not included in the reorganization were abruptly dismissed. The politics of factionalism, patronage, personal rivalries, and squabbles over where the remaining brigades would be stationed dragged out the work of review committees for up to three weeks. Then, just as most committees were concluding their work, the Fructidor coup disrupted their plans.

The purged Councils not only allowed the Directory to revise officer appointments, they ordered new departmental committees (*juries de révision*) to revise the work of the review committees. Although the ex officio composition of these revision committees remained the same, a huge turnover in official personnel in some departments due to the nullification of elections produced a very different set of opinions around the table. The government believed that review committees had dismissed many gendarmes whose "attachment to the Republic was the most pronounced" while preserving those with "notorious and sustained *incivisme*." In order to retain experienced and dedicated men, the revision committees were allowed to relax professional standards. One gendarme in each brigade could be exempted from the literacy requirement and redundant junior officers and NCOs could be considered for vacancies in lower ranks. It was hoped that after this final purification, the gendarmerie would consist of men "entirely devoted to the Republic, strongly attached to the laws of military discipline, combining zeal, morality, bravery and intelligence."[50]

The extent of turnover in personnel in 1797, and the impact of the Fructidor coup in particular, can best be appreciated by examining the process at the departmental level. Here we see that, in contrast to government expectations, the revision committees did not significantly alter the work of their predecessors. Applying the law of 25 pluviôse V (13 February 1797) had required the corps to be cut by 44 percent in the Haute-Garonne and by 39 percent in the Sarthe.[51] These departments had not been dominated by openly reactionary leaders before the coup, and so changes made by the revision committees were minor: no gendarmes were sacked, and only a few older men were recommended for retirement. On the other hand, in the Hérault, the political pendulum had swung far between the spring and autumn, and so the revision committee differed substantially from the original review committee. All the same, revisions were not massive. The first committee had reduced the Hérault's contingent by 29 percent to ninety-one men by removing six officers and thirty-one brigadiers. After the coup, the second committee went over existing notes and reinstated a dozen men, half of whom had failed to meet the literacy requirement and half of whom had been rejected on the basis of suspicion, hearsay, and "vague remarks [now] contradicted by certificates worthy of credibility."[52] The Haute-Saône had a similar experience. There the revision committee had to do the entire reorganization man by man because the Fructidor coup broke up the first committee before it could finish its work. In this department, political motives mingled with professional ones in the dismissal of fifteen men. One was "suspected of *incivisme*," another "drunk and insubordinate," and yet another "lacked the height." However, "the obligation to suppress five brigades forced the jury to dismiss subjects who have favorable records," and they were marked as the first to fill future vacancies.[53] Thus, although political factors clearly had an influence on choices in the Hérault and Haute-

Saône, both before and after the coup, this influence was less damaging to the corps' professionalism than any of the other changes made since 1792. In fact, as the evidence from four departments indicates, the careers of the vast majority of gendarmes were not determined by political factors; where politics did matter was at the level of officers. As a safeguard against unprofessional and inadequate gendarmes, the Councils had ordered department-level reviews to take place immediately after spring elections each year. Despite the tumultuous elections of 1798, with their numerous split assemblies and falling out among republicans, the new review committees made few changes in the composition of the gendarmerie. At last, after a decade of vertiginous expansion and contraction, the corps achieved a certain stability. It had also made the biggest step toward professionalizing personnel in the history of the rural constabulary.

No sooner had the second review committees finished their work than the Councils issued a new law substantially augmenting the number of brigades. Cutting the corps to 1,500 brigades in 1797 may have left it twice the size of the old *maréchaussée,* but this was manifestly too few to cope with the myriad challenges to law and order under the Directory. Therefore, the law of 28 germinal VI (17 April 1798) created five hundred new brigades, thus raising the corps' strength to 10,557 gendarmes stationed throughout the expanded hexagon. The men for the new brigades were again selected by departmental review committees. Factional politics had little influence on who was admitted to the new brigades.[54] In fact, many of them had been the last men reluctantly eliminated in the drastic downsizing of 1797. In the end, although it had provoked a lot of arm twisting, lobbying, and heated debate throughout the country, the multistage reform of personnel in 1797 and 1798 generated a rough consensus in each department. After this intensive screening process, the men who held positions either as gendarmes, NCOs, or officers had solid professional credentials. Charges of political bias, negligence, and even gross incompetence still appeared, especially when magistrates needed to explain failures, but total complaints dropped sharply. Standards had risen dramatically, and future recriminations tended to be based on higher expectations than ever before.

The law of 28 germinal VI (17 April 1798) also provided a definitive statement on the gendarmerie's duties and responsibilities. This veritable constitution of rural policing described the gendarmerie's mission as "to maintain order and enforce the law" as well as to exercise a "continuous and repressive surveillance." More specifically, gendarmes were expressly responsible for dispersing rebellious crowds; patrolling roads, markets, and fairs; reporting any incidents that might affect public order; and collecting information about malefactors. In addition, the gendarmerie had the burden of maintaining order at elections, executions, and whenever requested by department or municipal officials. Public prosecutors and jury directors could also require them to perform the functions of judicial police. This meant assisting in investigations, executing arrest warrants, and escorting prisoners. In other words, they were at last thoroughly integrated into the civilian apparatus of control and repression. Professional admission standards were also refined. Entrants had to be between ages twenty-five and forty, stand at least 5 feet, 7 inches tall, and be able to read and write. Since only mounted units remained, all gendarmes needed to have served four years in the cavalry and have participated in three campaigns of the revolutionary wars. This would keep out shirkers and cowards. Candidates also had to present certificates attesting to their bravery, good conduct, upright morals, and loyalty to the republic. This general increase in professional standards was accompanied by a rise in pay and the assurance of a retirement pension at age sixty. Wage deductions were used to constitute a company chest for replacing horses, uniforms, weapons, and equipment. This removed the burden of being individually responsible for outfitting oneself. Finally, although the Directory chose all of the officers in the initial reorganization, thereafter a percentage of each grade, including NCOs, would be reserved for promotion by seniority.[55] This helped to build careerism and dedication to the service.

The massive personnel changes in 1797–98 and the organic law of 28 germinal VI completed the transformation of the gendarmerie into a modern police force established on a truly national footing. The tight control departments had exercised in the years after 1791, usually to the detriment of the local company, gave way to a balanced system. At the national level, the War Ministry managed appointments, promotions, discipline, and equipment; the Police Ministry made sure the brigades did their part to maintain order; and the Justice Ministry supervised their interaction with public prosecutors, jury directors, and justices of the peace. At the local level, departmental and cantonal officials could requisition brigades for special assignments, but once the assignment had been given, gendarmes executed it free of civilian interference. Finally, officers of the gendarmerie were empowered to requisition national guardsmen to assist in carrying out police functions.

Here we see a clear line between community policing and policing communities. Municipal officials had a heavy hand in determining the composition of the local mobile column. They also tended to determine when and how it would be deployed, which resulted in a parochial force motivated by local concerns. For the most part, guardsmen served when their community needed them and, therefore, proved notoriously unreliable for other assignments. In contrast, brigades of the gendarmerie belonged to a military corps. They were not antithetical to civilian law enforcement, however, but a professional extension of it. Only a dozen, or perhaps a score, of communities in each department had units of the gendarmerie stationed in their midst. Furthermore, brigadiers rarely came from the region where they served. Their assignment was implicitly to defeat villagers' resistance to the penetration of state authority. In that sense, gendarmes policed communities and the autonomy they sought to preserve as much as they policed individuals and the crimes they committed.

Despite all the obstacles to effective policing during the late First Republic, the gendarmerie acquired a genuine esprit de corps and a remarkably strong sense of duty in just a few years. The reforms of 1797–98 helped immensely, but more was needed than purges and organizational regularity. Even numerical expansion was not enough. True, size did matter. In the spring of 1800, the Consulate added 2,040 pedestrian gendarmes to fifteen departments in western France. In the summer of 1801, the gendarmerie expanded yet again, bringing it to a total of 15,689 men (11,179 mounted and 4,510 on foot). This was almost four times the size of the prerevolutionary *maréchaussée.* But quality mattered too. In each expansion, the government sought "elite men, fearless and above reproach." As we have seen, every candidate received careful and repeated screening. As a result, contemporary assessments indicated a rapid improvement in the quality of policing. Officials in the Haute-Saône, for example, unanimously agreed on the "zeal and exactitude" of the gendarmes in their department. The company of the Sarthe had "excellent officers, sharply turned out and widely respected." Though there was still room for improvement, notably in Brittany, Languedoc, and Provence, the overall force bore little resemblance to its shambolic state in 1795. By 1801, it had emerged as a thoroughly professional force with a daunting reputation for toughness.[56]

The demands of the service in the late First Republic discouraged the feckless and cowardly from joining. Life in the rural constabulary was never more dangerous than during the years of reform. It is no surprise that sustained police pressure often provoked a backlash from the local populace. Police reports about such incidents tended to exaggerate the danger gendarmes faced, and for a reason. The size of crowds, the number of men in gangs, or the ferocity of resistance excused their failures. But what rings most true about these reports is the utter isolation of the gendarmes when they found themselves under attack, especially when it came to enforcing the republic's most hated innovation: conscription. If local people intervened at all, it was on the side of the conscripts. This cast the gendarme as an enemy of the community. "For the *gendarmerie* the arrest and escort of conscripts was not only a dangerous and unpopular assignment, it was an activity that lost them much of the local good will on which even the most basic policing was dependent."[57] As a result, the aggressive repression used to impose the republican order provoked thousands of violent encounters and deadly gun battles around the country. By the end of the century, several gendarmes were being killed every week! In these cases, there was little need to exaggerate—the facts were gruesome enough. Witness the report filed in March 1800 by three gendarmes from Viarouge in the Aveyron who, having handed off six deserters to the brigade from Millau, had just taken charge of escorting the tax receipts from Rodez when they were ambushed by three groups of men, one from each side of the road and one from behind.

> They kept up a line of fire which forced us to fall back in order to try to take them from behind. It was in executing this maneuver, ordered by citizen Bessière, brigadier, that this brave commander received eleven gunshots from the squad that was crossing the road from the right side, to wit: a ball in the middle of the neck that came out his mouth, another a little lower that pierced his collar and jaw, three in the sides, three in the lower back, two in the shoulder and one in the left hand that pierced it. At this discharge citizen Bessière fell stone-dead from his horse. Gendarme Nouls received five gunshots at the same time, one breaking his right hand, another taking off his index finger, one in his horse's eye. Another gendarme, Solanet, received six shots, which ripped up his coat without injuring him, but four balls killed his horse instantly; the other gendarme, Record, received three shots in his coat, but was not hurt; his horse got three as well, which put it out of service.[58]

Such violence against gendarmes was especially intense in the Midi and Massif Central, but similar events occurred in many parts of France. In a single week, these ranged from the Indre to the Sarre, and from the Tarn to the Seine-et-Oise. As late as June 1801, the gendarmerie was still experiencing an average of two "events" a day in which gendarmes were killed or wounded and forced to abandon their prisoners.[59] That the gendarmerie did not crumble in the face of this onslaught is testimony to how much rural policing had changed since 1789.

Those who oversaw the gendarmerie attributed the rural "spirit of rebellion" to pusillanimous mayors and insouciant juries. In other words, gendarmes were being left to fend for themselves. It was essential that the gendarmerie be backed by sufficient force to preserve its integrity; otherwise, successful resistance would become a galloping contagion. Under these conditions, only external support could enable the gendarmerie to cohere. Therefore, when local resistance became especially fierce, the government responded with overwhelming force. At times this could lead to a virtual war on the populace. The Escalquens affair of 1799 illustrates the range of measures the republic was willing to deploy in defense of its gendarmes. When the brigade from Castanet (Gers) arrested a draft dodger at nearby Escalquens, a crowd formed to demand his release. The gendarmes refused and started back to their headquarters only to be fired on from a distance. Not one to be intimidated, Lieutenant Daure assembled a detachment of three brigades and returned to Escalquens to disperse the armed gathering. There he found the road blocked by a passel of gun-toting youths. Suddenly another swarm of men armed with everything from pitchforks to carbines enveloped the sixteen gendarmes. Attempting to beat a hasty retreat only brought a hail of lead that killed the lieutenant and wounded four gendarmes and several horses. General Augereau, commander of the Tenth Military District, responded with awesome force. A column of 350 men and two cannons under Squadron Commander Regnard marched on Escalquens. There they encountered several hundred men gathered on the heights and using self-propelled explosives ("fusés volantes") to defend their position. A sustained assault dispersed the rebels. Several days later, a department administrator came to Escalquens, and in a calculated affront to the entire community, publicly stripped the *agent* and his deputy of their offices. A detachment of sixty troops was then charged with helping to round up conscripts and disarm the populace of five villages. To prove the organized nature of the revolt, Augereau had a detailed map of the original ambush drawn by a military engineer and presented to the Civil Court of the Haute-Garonne. This persuaded the court to order the citizens of Escalquens to pay maximum damages: 15,000 francs to Lieutenant Daure's widow; 1,000 francs to each of the four wounded gendarmes; 200 francs to each of the other twelve gendarmes; and matching sums to the republic. This made a staggering total fine of 42,800 francs. Later, when this fine went unpaid, soldiers were sent to collect it by force.[60] A response of this ferocity was possible only because the army provided the force necessary to sustain the gendarmerie. The ultimate recourse, and a measure not actually used at Escalquens, was to turn local policing entirely over to the army. This was done through a state of siege.

## State of Siege

The Directory's campaign to restore order in areas of endemic civil unrest was further militarized by declaring individual communes in a "state of siege." The absolutist monarchy had long used the state of siege to quell various forms of resistance ranging from a wine-growers' riot in Dijon in March 1630 to the widespread "Flour War" of May 1775, when the whole area around Paris was put under a state of siege.[61] The collapse of the royal army's repressive role in 1789 and the emergence of the National Guard across the country, and especially in Paris, encouraged the National Assembly to formulate an alternative to the *ancien régime's* "state of siege." Once the torrent of urban and rural violence of 1789 had made possible a radical break with the prevailing order, the National Assembly created a new form of martial law on 21 October 1789. This decree authorized municipal officials to requisition the instruments of armed force, including the National Guard, *maréchaussée,* and regular troops, in order to crush mob violence. This was a modified form of the British Riot Act of 1715. In both cases, a "riot" was officially at least twelve individuals who, having been read an official order to disperse by a civilian magistrate, refused to do so. They then became guilty of a capital felony and could be dispersed by armed force.[62] The new law temporarily gave civilians complete control of local police and military power. As elected officials, municipal leaders derived their authority from the people, the new repository of sovereignty. As long as elected officials decided when to invoke martial law, the equivalent of acting in self-defense, there was little juridical basis for dictatorship. Jacobins and Cordeliers fiercely opposed martial law, however, especially after its deployment in the massacre on the Champs de Mars in 1791.[63] Their ascent to power was based on popular violence, and their exercise of power was legitimized by forms of political representation radically different from democratic election. Therefore, when martial law became a useful instrument for so-called federalist authorities, the Montagnard-dominated Convention promptly abolished the law (23 June 1793). Thereafter, state centralization took over, first as the Convention's Revolutionary Government, then as the Executive Directory.

Martial law as an instrument of local government was not revived despite the transition to constitutional rule. It was replaced instead by the state of siege. The differences between them were critical. The state of siege had been created by the law of 8 July 1791 as a purely military matter. It authorized a town's army commander to take direct control of everything pertaining to policing and public order inside the town at any time that it was besieged by an enemy. The original law described the wartime circumstances that created a state of siege and listed 218 fortified towns susceptible to it. This made military sense and kept the royal army from playing a role in domestic repression. Events soon erased these clear distinctions, however. During the Federalist Revolts of 1793, the National Convention used the regular army, now much modified by the desertion of noble officers and the incorporation of national guardsmen, to lay siege to Lyon, Marseille, Bordeaux, and Toulon. In a bit of twisted logic, representatives on mission sent to supervise the siege of these cities declared them under a "state of siege" only *after* they had fallen to the forces of the Revolutionary Government. This legal maneuver gave army commanders extra powers to mop up resistance and punish rebels. It also created a precedent for greater distortions of the state of siege.

Despite its rhetoric of constitutionality, the Directory completed the transformation of the state of siege from a defensive measure during times of war to a tool of domestic repression. Although not intended for use in internal repression, the state of siege was well suited for it. Declaring a state of siege transferred to the local fortress commander (*commandant de la place*) all the powers invested in civilian authorities for the maintenance of order and internal policing. This empowered the local commander to order arrests, expel people from town, control the prisons, and take whatever measures he deemed necessary to preserve order. It also enabled him to employ his troops without waiting for local civilian authorities to request them. In fact, municipal officials were not permitted to undertake any police action or introduce any security measures that had not first been authorized by the local commander.[64] Thus, more than a simple recourse to armed force to quell internal resistance, the Directory's use of the state of siege severely eroded municipal authority.

The Directory first made wide use of the state of siege in response to the civil war in the west. The secret instructions issued to General Lazare Hoche on 7 nivôse IV (28 December 1795) authorized him to declare all the large towns of the insurgent departments under state of siege, which was taken to mean all towns over three thousand inhabitants. This effectively militarized the administration of the entire civil war zone. Although this practice

conformed to the spirit if not the intent of the original legislation, local republican officials and even a few deputies bitterly opposed the measure, especially those from the Vendée. Officials at Les Sables-d'Olonne considered
themselves too far from the fighting to warrant such action, and those at
Fontenay-le-Peuple deemed it blatantly unconstitutional. Therefore, once
Hoche eliminated the royalist leaders Stofflet and Charette in March 1796,
he lifted the state of siege from all towns in the *Vendée militaire* except
for Angers, Nantes, and Noirmoutier. Thereafter, it was progressively lifted
from the towns of Brittany, Normandy, and Maine according to the pace of
pacification. Finally, in July 1796, the Directory completed the process by
lifting the state of siege wherever it still existed in western France, thereby
allowing the constitution to take effect.[65]

If putting towns under state of siege in the west skirted the fringes of
constitutionality, its use in the Midi during the First Directory was clearly a
travesty. Terror and counter-Terror in the Rhône Valley and along the Mediterranean coast had created a region of ferocious intracommunal violence.
Much of this radiated out from the major urban centers of the region. Lyon,
Marseille, and Toulon, therefore, remained under a state of siege long after
the Federalist Revolts had been crushed. This situation went largely unchal-
lenged until the advent of constitutional government in 1795. Even then,
Stanislas Fréron, on a controversial mission to end the bloody reaction in
the Midi, asked that the state of siege be maintained at Marseille, Toulon,
and elsewhere, in order to keep rival factions from tearing each other apart.
But Fréron had a partisan perspective. Many of his appointees were notorious Jacobins whose very lives depended on the sustained presence of
troops. After Fréron's belated departure in April 1796, the commanders of
the Eighth and Ninth Military Districts took it upon themselves to apply
the state of siege to various smaller towns.[66] As General Puget-Barbantane
put it to the minister of war, "This extraordinary measure is requested by
republicans; this proves their faith in the troops and in departing from the
principles of liberty that subordinate military authority to civilian authority;
[this measure] is necessary for the triumph of this same liberty in a region
where a disastrous reaction has so cruelly attacked it."[67] In other words, as
long as the army had the support of local republicans, it could supplant
elected officials. But the government officially discouraged such measures.
In accordance with its commitment to a constitutional rule of law, the Directory sought to restrict the use of the state of siege in the south, especially
after lifting it from the towns of western France. Nonetheless, the Directory
came to accept the state of siege as a necessary evil and condoned its use

in select towns and cities where political polarization prevented the legal machinery from functioning properly.[68]

Once allowed to apply the state of siege to southern towns, generals inevitably turned this measure into a personal instrument. Whether he sympathized with the right or the left, the local general used the tools at his disposal to hamstring his political opponents in the region. Thus, when the Directory replaced the staunchly republican Puget-Barbantane with the reactionary Amédée Willot in September 1796, Willot began lifting the state of siege from a number of towns where republicans had been persecuted. But this was not a return to constitutionalism. Willot considered Jacobins the greatest threat to stability in the region and so quickly applied the state of siege to towns supposedly subjugated by local "anarchists." This change in commanders rapidly politicized the state of siege as an instrument of repression. Once Marseillais republicans no longer had the army's support, they sent a petition with eight thousand signatures calling on lawmakers to lift the state of siege from Marseille and thus allow their city to enjoy the benefits of the constitution just as Vendéan rebels could now do. With their man Willot in charge, the reactionary deputies of the Bouches-du-Rhône opposed a return to civilian rule and backed their demand with another petition, equally signed by eight thousand Marseillais.[69] *Chef de brigade* Liégard, commander of Marseille, wrote a letter to the Council of Elders defending the Directory's domestic use of the state of siege. He stated: "The ill-intentioned keep saying that a town under state of siege is, so to speak, outside the constitution; but the constitution would be meaningless if . . . police powers were in the hands of men who have successively taken turns being the oppressors and the oppressed. The commander of a town under state of siege will uphold the government's views and preserve peace." He also argued that using the state of siege to maintain order in large cities like Marseille would prevent the constitution from being smothered in its cradle.[70] Caught between factions and inclined toward this form of law-and-order logic, the Directory let Willot decide what was best. Not surprisingly, he happily preserved the state of siege in Marseille, as well as at Toulon, Avignon, Aix, Tarascon, Arles, and several smaller towns.[71] Later, general ferment and a resurgence of political violence in the spring of 1797 prompted Willot to extend this measure to a half-dozen towns around Marseille.[72] The benefits of this policy soon paid off in personal terms: the Bouches-du-Rhône elected Willot to the Council of Five Hundred.

The triumph of conservative candidates in the elections of 1797 increased parliamentary pressure for a strict application of the constitution. Such an approach limited both the discretionary power of the government and of its subordinates in the field. Successive ministers of war largely agreed with the new parliamentary majority. Pétiet certainly believed that using the July 1791 law for internal repression was unconstitutional and twice ordered Willot to lift the state of siege from all the towns under his jurisdiction. Even Pétiet's more republican successor, General Barthélemy Schérer, did not like to see generals resorting to this measure. He wanted all future uses expressly approved by the Directory.[73] As a consequence, the number of towns under state of siege steadily dropped. Nonetheless, military commanders were reluctant to give up such a powerful tool of repression.[74] Despite the Directory's self-restraint, its use of the state of siege to restore order became a matter of heated debate during the summer of 1797, especially when Lyon, a crossroads of royalism and organized crime, was threatened with this measure.[75] The conservative-dominated legislature moved to eliminate the Directory's use of the state of siege on constitutional grounds. A special legislative commission reported that the state of siege had been vital to repressing rebellion in the west and south and had generally been used wisely, but that it now posed too many dangers and should be severely restricted. Told that the state of siege equaled military dictatorship, the Council of Elders passed a law requiring the Councils to approve every future application.[76] Here was a blatant attempt to usurp executive authority. Days later, however, the Fructidor coup restored the Directory's power to put towns under a state of siege without needing legislative approval.

Having removed the "constitutional opposition" to the state of siege and determined to stabilize the regime through force, the Directory made increasing use of this measure to assert its authority over rebellious communes. Although the War Ministry continued to advise limited use and strict control of the state of siege,[77] it seemed vital to consolidating the coup, especially in the Midi, where a wave of disturbances lent credibility to the government's claim of having nipped a royalist conspiracy in the bud. Therefore, when the Directory named General Pille overall commander of the Seventh, Eighth, Ninth, Tenth, and Twentieth Military Districts (a vast area taking in twenty-seven departments), it authorized him to proclaim a state of siege in any commune under his command.[78] Pille used this measure often. To the principal cities of Marseille and Toulon, already long under state of siege, Pille added Aix, Montauban, Montpellier, Béziers, and Castres, as well as at least twenty smaller towns. Lyon too fell under a state of siege.[79]

This extensive use of the state of siege in the Midi following the Fructi-

dor coup does not mean that the Second Directory used this measure in-
discriminately; indeed, the government continued to pay attention to legal
forms even when acting in an authoritarian manner. Parisian officials saw
the dangers of resorting to the state of siege—people at Montauban thought
it was intended to prepare a return to the Terror and the Maximum[80]—and
usually insisted that generals who applied such a measure have it confirmed
by an executive order. The government also blamed local authorities for
requesting the state of siege before they had made full use of the police
powers at their disposal.[81] In particular, the government wanted local authorities to apply the harsh law of 10 vendémiaire IV (2 October 1795),
which required communities to compensate victims of property damage
and violence committed on their territory by any sort of group, whether a
crowd of protestors or a gang of bandits. This could have been one of the
most effective ways to maintain order in areas of widespread brigandage,
but department authorities rarely asked courts to apply it, and when they
did, local judges often refused.

The government's wish to avoid abusing the state of siege and the reluctance of local authorities to apply the law of 10 vendémiaire IV reflect one
of the Directory's fundamental difficulties in trying to stabilize the regime.
How could the republic turn the force of communal solidarity to its advantage, and if this proved impossible, how could such solidarity be overcome? The Revolution had provoked massive opposition simply by creating a new state apparatus that intruded in the day-to-day activities of local
communities previously independent of most government authority. When
the republic demanded men and resources for its war effort, many people
put up a stubborn resistance. Community leaders who had sided with the
republic then had to call upon outside forces to overcome the opposition of
their neighbors. This violated the social code that gave village communities
their moral unity and turned local leaders into "outsiders" if they cooperated with the revolutionary republic. The law of 10 vendémiaire IV sought
to turn community solidarity against banditry and antirepublican violence
through collective responsibility. The government admitted that it would be
difficult for ordinary citizens to prevent antirepublican crimes committed
secretly by lone assailants, but it held communes collectively responsible
if they allowed groups of people to assault republican officials or destroy
national property. This resuscitated the absolute monarchy's notion of a fiscal *contrainte solidaire* and applied it to a vigorous defense of the republic,
thereby flagrantly contravening the revolutionary spirit of individualism.
Such a contradictory and punitive response was defended by casuistical ref-

erences to the constitution, which specified that every citizen had a duty to defend society against its enemies and made no distinction between foreign attackers and fomenters of domestic disorder.[82] The Second Directory was so convinced that this approach would bear fruit that it extended the law of 10 vendémiaire IV to cover stagecoach holdups as well.[83]

Relying on collective responsibility to turn community solidarity to the republic's advantage still required the intervention of outside authority whenever it failed, which was distressingly often.[84] Department officials would then have to intervene to prompt the civil court to impose penalties. Rather than run the personal and political risks of acting decisively, however, department authorities frequently asked that military authorities do their dirty work. Prompted by the government, military commanders began systematically to petition courts to apply the law of 10 vendémiaire IV to those communities that did nothing to prevent attacks on agents of the state, from tax collectors to gendarmes. Army commanders sometimes took charge of collecting these fines as well. Even if they recovered a derisory portion of the original fine, they took whatever they could and so ruined whole villages. For example, after the attack on the gendarmerie at Escalquens described earlier, an armed force dispossessed local residents of cash, wheat, millet, and wool, but the total came to only 1,023 francs of the preposterously huge fine of 42,800 francs.[85]

In theory, enforcing collective responsibility was distinct from imposing a state of siege, which was not intended to be a punitive measure per se, despite the massive intrusion of outside force.[86] In practice, however, putting a commune under a state of siege was usually accompanied by billeting troops or levying fines in order to punish entire communities, not just local officials who had failed to keep the peace. This sometimes meant proclaiming a state of siege and adding an application of the 10 vendémiaire IV law in order to compensate victims. This was the case in January 1799 at St-Jean-sur-Erve (Mayenne), where the inhabitants were forced to pay an indemnity to the widow Michelet for not preventing the murder of her husband, a gendarme there.[87] More often, reinforcing collective responsibility for preserving public order included requiring inhabitants to provide lodging and provisions for troops. These could be aggravated by heavy financial levies. Both of these measures accompanied the proclamation of a state of siege at Bouère (Mayenne), where a band of chouans had attacked a detachment of republican troops, killing the commanding officer and several grenadiers. The villagers of Bouère not only failed to take up arms against the band, as their neighbors in the commune of Ballée had done, but they provided a haven for "several ferocious brigands." In fact, eighteen members of the band lived at Bouère. For their collective failure to defend the republic, the villagers of Bouère were forced to billet the troops sent to implement the state of siege as well as being required to pay 10,000 francs to the army treasury (see figure 9). General Simon's orders emphasized that "using the state of siege was, in fact, an extreme measure, but the result

Fig. 9. Poster announcing the state of siege and fine imposed on Bouère (Mayenne) on 12 ventôse VII (2 March 1799) for a deadly attack on republican troops there. (Author's collection)

should be to correct not to irritate or provoke hostility from the communes where it is applied."[88] Whereas the army's intent may have been corrective, residents needed cool heads indeed not to be provoked by a military take-over of their bourg.

As the Directory became increasingly determined to establish its authority, it extended its use of the state of siege to do more than just restore order. The state of siege became an instrument of political influence, if not outright electoral domination. In the spring of 1798, it was applied to major centers such as Nîmes, Avignon, and Luxembourg in order to prevent violence during the elections and to ensure "a satisfactory result for the republican government."[89] Even primary assemblies could be the site of bloody clashes and so drew added attention from the army. Prompted by the departmental administrators of the Hérault, General Petit-Guillaume put Pézenas under a state of siege because "the election period imperiously solicits this rigorous measure."[90] Here was but one way in which armed force intervened to help shape the republican, not to say Jacobin, outcome of the elections of year VI.

The Directory also used the state of siege to facilitate a range of more routine security measures. In 1798, the minister of war ordered Le Puy and Yssengeaux to be put under a state of siege for a few weeks during the trial of "several major royalist cutthroats." This included Dominique Allier, a leader in the attack on Pont-St-Esprit in September 1797, whose supporters were organizing a massive prison breakout. Here a veritable siege was in fact quite possible. On the other hand, this measure sometimes followed relatively minor incidents, such as the rescue of a refractory priest from the gendarmerie or a mêlée provoked by a farandole celebrating the anniversary of the king's execution. Some people claimed that the Directory even put towns under a state of siege for failing to pay taxes. Though not strictly true, a state of siege could provide a good opportunity to clear arrears. Applying the state of siege was more commonly provoked by widespread resistance to the so-called Fructidorian Terror. In fact, the canton of Canourgue in the Lozère fell under a state of siege for failing to deport priests, arrest émigrés, prosecute brigands, or enforce the revolutionary calendar. Such sins of omission were tantamount to counter-revolution and drew a tough response.[91]

The late Directory made extensive use of the state of siege to defeat even more threatening forms of resistance and criminal violence. Areas of widespread banditry were usually areas of counter-revolution, although clearly not all banditry was inspired by counter-revolution.[92] All the same, similar measures could combat both. As recourse to army policing increased, a general rule of thumb emerged: a detachment of one hundred regular troops was to be stationed in every commune under a state of siege in order to impose order on the residents and the surrounding countryside alike.[93] This occasionally limited the number of places that could be subjected to this measure due to a shortage of troops in the district.[94] It also tended to transform the state of siege from a defensive measure to a basis for offensive operations. Moreover, such assumptions marked how the Directory's frequent recourse to this once-exceptional measure had come to standardize it.

During the crisis of 1799, when the republic again faced a powerful foreign coalition and a major recrudescence of banditry and counter-revolution, the Directory responded with a widespread application of the state of siege. Several district commanders received carte blanche to impose this measure whenever they deemed it necessary. The commander-in-chief of the *Armée d'Angleterre* was authorized to apply the state of siege to any commune in the four military districts under his command—a vast territory extending from the Charente-Inférieure to the Calvados. General Hédouville, overall commander of six departments in northern France (First, Fifteenth, and Sixteenth Military Districts), as well as Generals Colaud and Rey, commanders of the annexed departments of Belgium and the Rhineland (Twenty-fourth, Twenty-fifth, and Twenty-sixth Military Districts) all received the same power. Each of these authorizations was motivated by the need to extinguish renewed civil war and extensive brigandage.[95] Such blanket authorizations meant that by the coup d'état of 18 brumaire VIII, 40 percent of the country was under the jurisdiction of generals able to impose a state of siege on any town or village that openly opposed the republic. As a result of this new attitude, more than 220 communes saw the police powers of civilian officials pass to army commanders during the Second Directory. Most of these were towns, bourgs, and even villages in the Midi and the west. But the measure was not confined to these regions, nor was it applied only to small centers, for the list of places put under state of siege included France's second- and third-largest cities (Lyon, Marseille); its two principal naval ports (Toulon, Brest); several important annexed cities (Nice, Geneva, Antwerp, Ghent); and more than a dozen department capitals (see figure 10).

The Consulate did nothing to change this policy. In fact, the state of siege reached its apogee in the last months of 1799. The insurrection that erupted around Toulouse in August that year led to two dozen cantons in the Haute-Garonne, Gers, and Ariège being put directly under army rule, a state in which they remained many months after the rebellion ended.[96] The widespread revolt in western France swept away any concern about constitutional niceties, and whole departments were officially proclaimed under state of siege. At first this was something of a complement to the infamous law of hostages, which allowed the legislature to declare areas "in a state of civil strife." Although the Consulate quickly abrogated this law, it resorted to the state of siege instead. By December 1799, the army exercised police powers over the entire Maine-et-Loire, Mayenne, Sarthe, Vendée, and Côtes-du-Nord.

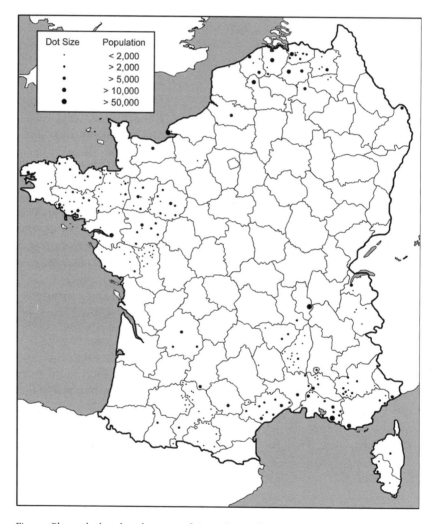

| Dot Size | Population |
|----------|-----------|
| · | < 2,000 |
| · | > 2,000 |
| • | > 5,000 |
| ● | > 10,000 |
| ⬤ | > 50,000 |

Fig. 10. Places declared under state of siege, September 1797–December 1799.

Such an extensive use of the state of siege contradicted the new Constitution of Year VIII as much as it had the Constitution of Year III. Therefore, the Consulate simply declared the departments of Brittany "outside the constitution." Matters did not change much elsewhere, either. Scores of cities and towns remained under an official state of siege well into year IX. In the meantime, however, complaints multiplied. The measure could be especially problematic when imposed on smaller communes because this left junior officers, who rarely had sufficient political skills, vulnerable to local passions. In larger towns, leaving police powers in the hands of army officers prevented the new Consular authorities from assuming their proper responsibilities.[97] Thus, by early 1801, widespread use of the state of siege had begun to prick consciences in Paris. The War and Police Ministries both began to compile lengthy lists of cities and towns under state of siege.[98] One such list reached the First Consul and prompted him to order an inquiry into the practice. According to the response, this measure had been overused and thus resulted in degradation of civilian officials and oppression of citizens. It may have served a useful purpose when authority was excessively divided, a functionary wrote, but the power of prefects now made it unnecessary. Therefore, the official advocated lifting it from all but a dozen places, most of which were naval ports or frontier cities. Such a proposal meant, in effect, restricting the state of siege to its original purpose as a tool of national defense against foreign enemies. The inquiry led to a steady stream of orders lifting the state of siege around the country. The last of these came in June 1802.[99] Nonetheless, the state of siege remained a specialized weapon in the Napoleonic arsenal of repression. In fact, it featured prominently in waves of domestic state violence throughout the nineteenth century. By the time of the Life Consulate, however, it was no longer a common response to localized lawlessness.

The persistent strife of the late First Republic fostered strong-arm policing. The chaotic state of the gendarmerie in the early Directory forced both the National Guard and the line army to play a greater role in domestic security than the Thermidorians had envisioned. Frequent requisitioning of mobile columns and extensive use of the state of siege were essential to impose the republican order on fractious communities. As long as republicans insisted on persecuting the Church and prosecuting the war, they would be unable to restore order without recourse to these exceptional measures. By late 1801, however, neither the National Guard nor the state of siege featured prominently among the tools of repression, having largely fulfilled their function of facilitating a return to order. By year X, the gendarmerie was in a position to handle most of France's security needs. The corps had been thoroughly professionalized, greatly expanded, and given a centralized command structure. It was, in the words of Napoleon, "a distinct organization that exists in no other country in Europe [and] the most effective means of preserving the peace."[100] Whereas the basis of the National Guard was community policing, the basis of the Gendarmerie Nationale was policing communities. These were never reconciled under the First Republic. By year IX, the idealized citizens' militia had become an obstacle to the state-based security forces.

# 8 Liberty versus Security in the War on Brigandage

> The unbridled temerity of brigandage supports the plans of external and internal enemies: the way to abort the hopes of one and the other at the same time is promptly to crush the murderous bands that infest the roads. A law should be passed that prescribes that any brigand seized while attacking travelers be immediately shot like a wild beast and without any form of trial, because we do not believe that society owes recourse in law to the monsters who are in open revolt against it.
> —*L'Ami des lois,* 10 brumaire VII (31 October 1798)

Here was truly a sign of the times: a mainstream newspaper whose title suggested a scrupulous devotion to legality advocating the instant execution of highwaymen with no regard for due process. But was public opinion ready to accept impromptu firing squads? Perhaps this should be dismissed as yet another example of the rhetorical excesses of the period. And yet, the licentious journalism of Marat and Hébert was not unrelated to the great bloodletting of the Terror. A look at the press in the late 1790s provides evidence of a rapid hardening of public opinion on matters of public order. The timing of these harsher views corresponded with the Directory's shift from strict constitutionalism to an imposition of republican order as its principal source of domestic legitimacy. This shift had a marked impact on the operations of the criminal justice system. Furthermore, the scourge of brigandage led lawmakers to authorize regular military courts to judge civilians. Taken together, the evidence from lawmakers and journalists suggests a widespread willingness to accept the erosion of liberty in the name of security. The actual work of military courts illustrates the nature of these compromises.

## Special Laws against Brigandage

A year after taking office, the Directory decided to respond more forcefully to the unprecedented level of criminal violence. As we have seen, the hallmark of year IV was the rapid degeneration of ritualized communicative violence into the solipsistic criminality of grain raiders, bandits, and murder gangs. Every day the government received a litany of reports containing lurid details of intercepted couriers, stagecoach holdups, assaults on government officials, and the intimidation of witnesses. The horrifying spread of *chauffeurs de pieds* in particular led lawmakers to adopt harsh penalties against this threat to the regime's social base. The law of 26 floréal V (15 May 1797) ordered the death penalty for robberies committed using arms, whether committed on a public thoroughfare or in a private home, as well as for robberies in which victims suffered bodily injuries. By making these into capital crimes, legislators intended to deter attacks on persons in the course of attacks on their property. Lawmakers also considered it better to use the courts to repress brigandage than to increase the use of armed force and thereby risk the excesses of the Vendée.[1] However, the minister of war had already sent a circular to all interior military commanders instructing them to treat armed bands as enemy formations to be pursued and destroyed in detail.[2] Under these conditions, the law passed easily. After six months of application, ministerial reports concluded that the new law had helped to reduce the number of *chauffeurs*, but that an increase in highway robberies had more than made up the difference. In light of this evidence, the government proposed even more draconian measures.[3]

The Directory's proposed response to brigandage went well beyond harsh penalties to include greatly strengthening the machinery of repression. The Directory wanted to expand the gendarmerie and be empowered to dismiss negligent officers. It also asked that department administrators, rather than civil courts, set monetary damages for acts of violence or robbery and that police agents (officers of the gendarmerie, municipal officials, and police commissioners) be able to issue imprisonment warrants (*mandats d'arrêt*) rather than simply to issue arrest warrants (*mandats d'ammener*). This would have given the police considerable influence over the judiciary and enabled them to force jury directors to seek indictments from a grand jury. Even more important, the government suggested that highwaymen and housebreakers be declared rebels so that they could then be tried in military courts.[4] These various proposed encroachments on the criminal justice system gave lawmakers pause. At first, a special commission of the Council of Five Hundred focused on extending the powers of arrest and broadening the anti-chouan law of 30 prairial III to permit highwaymen to be sent before military courts,[5] but this received a hostile response. Deputies opposed extending powers of arrest and worried about giving the army more judicial power. "Let us respect our constitution: punish without eroding liberty," expostulated Bontoux. He did not believe it was necessary to "strip away the protective rights that juries provide" and heartily opposed putting "the blade and scales of Themis into the hands of a soldier." This rhetorical challenge encouraged the Five Hundred to send the proposal back for repeated revision. The resulting modifications limited the powers of imprisonment, restricted the independence of military prosecutors, and narrowed the focus to crimes committed by at least three people, all clear efforts to protect liberty while strengthening security.

Throughout these weeks, the government fostered a sense of emergency and lobbied lawmakers to overcome their squeamishness about sidestepping juries and extending the writ of military courts. J.-P.-M. Sotin, the new minister of police, sent an alarming circular to all local officials: "The brigands' audacity has reached its limit; they gather in large, organized troops and no longer deign to cover themselves with the veil of night." He called upon all citizens to fulfill their constitutional duty and protect their communities from the onslaught of crime by enrolling in the National Guard. Finally, under further pressure from the Directory, the Five Hundred overcame its legal sensibilities and passed a resolution. After all, as deputy Ludot put it, "In extraordinary circumstances, when disorder is at its worst, extraordinary measures are required."[6] When the resolution reached the Council of Elders, Girot-Pouzol delivered a terrifying statement of support: "The brigands—assassins who infest the highways, break into homes, hold up coaches, rob public transport, and publish state secrets—are in a state of war against society. . . . Current laws are powerless to parry these brigandages that threaten the social order with dissolution. In order to avoid anarchy, it is necessary that the dictatorship of the law be established over brigands; this is the surest means of preventing them from establishing the dictatorship of their crimes over society."[7] With the matter put in these terms, the upper house had no qualms about voting the bill into law.

The law of 29 nivôse VI (18 January 1798) proved to be one of the most important pieces of repressive legislation in the period and had implications for both civilian and criminal courts. It required regular criminal courts to apply the death penalty for either highway robbery or housebreaking. Thus, certain offenses against property once again qualified as capital crimes, something the National Assembly had abolished as barbaric. If these crimes were committed by groups of more than two people, the accused, their accomplices, and those who encouraged them were all to be tried by a military court. This deliberate extension of military justice to cover civilian criminality marks an important change in the Directory's attitude toward law and order. The constitutionalism and rule of law so vaunted early in the Directory had been submerged by a mounting crime wave. On one hand, the Fructidor coup gravely undercut the Directory's constitutional legitimacy as well as making it considerably more unpopular. On the other hand, there is little evidence that ordinary Frenchmen thought the law of 29 nivôse VI seriously tarnished the regime, even though it violated the constitution by depriving civilian defendants of a jury trial (art. 237). If anything, the fact that the Second Directory was clearly determined to use military justice to restore order before relying on civilian justice to maintain it actually earned the regime support. Enlightenment thinkers such as Beccaria and Voltaire had inspired a humanitarian element in revolutionary reforms, and yet few Frenchmen thought brigands deserved to live. They had routinely seen them broken on the wheel during the *ancien régime,* especially in such major judicial centers as Toulouse. It is not surprising, therefore, that Toulousains blanched with fury in 1796 when they saw three highwaymen clapping their hands and rejoicing after being sentenced to twenty-four years in irons, the maximum accorded by the Penal Code.[8] Multiplying capital penalties and resorting to military justice apparently responded to the public mood.

## Public Opinion on Public Order

The Directory's more aggressive policies toward public order fit with public opinion. Public opinion is essentially the product of discourses circulating among the educated populace, or more tangibly, readers who took a serious interest in the issues of the day.[9] During the Directory, this meant the sort of men who were eligible (not in a constitutional sense, but in a practical sense) for election to local office. Such people had the basic skills of literacy, owned property, and constituted the political class, broadly defined. Their various discourses can be found in administrative correspondence, pamphlets, and newspapers. Newspapers are particularly useful for studying public opinion because they reduce the myriad of parochial interests to broad themes without homogenizing all regional or political differences. In paying special attention to newspapers, we see how influential they were in creating a national climate of insecurity. Even if the eighteenth-century monarchy had experienced a similar level of crime, and there is no evidence that it did, without the proliferation of newspapers that followed 1789, it would not have had the same impact on public perceptions of the regime's viability. In that sense, the Directory's need to be tough on crime reflected the emergence of a more modern political culture.

Although the press faced a range of difficulties during the Directory, it remained relatively vibrant until neutralized by Bonaparte after the Brumaire coup. Before this, Parisian presses generated between 75,000 and 150,000 newspapers a day, depending on the level of government censorship; 60 percent of these were distributed outside of the capital.[10] In addition, a dozen provincial centers sustained at least two papers each in the Directory's early years.[11] Thus, one can reasonably estimate that total circulation in France exceeded 200,000 copies a day in 1797. Reading rooms, cafés, political gatherings, and family settings allowed a single copy to reach an average audience of ten people.[12] Therefore, up to two million French adults encountered newspapers on a regular basis. Most readers lived in towns and cities, but virtually anyone who could have been elected to local office in the countryside would have been directly exposed to newspapers, even if not subscribers themselves. In other words, members of the political class, rural and urban alike, read about national political issues from partisan sources once or twice a week, at least.[13]

Historians who treated the newspapers of the period as an object of study and not merely as a source of information have invariably focused on their editorial content but have had little to say about the reporting of events, that is, about the news itself. It is time for a proper genre study that gets beyond the Terror. There is a good case to be made that in the late 1790s simply reporting crime on an unprecedented scale and with unprecedented frequency did more to influence public opinion about public order than anything else. Almost every issue of every paper carried brief reports on criminal acts of violence. Take, for example, the *Bulletin de l'Europe*, a large-circulation Parisian daily, chosen entirely at random.[14] During the month of pluviôse VII (January-February 1799), the *Bulletin* carried notices on the following events: a large peasant rebellion near Brussels; four incidents in which crowds used armed force to rescue priests; deserters or criminals from the gendarmerie; three prison breakouts; three stagecoach holdups (one in Lyon itself); two murders of government officials (one a former legislator serving as a *commissaire du Directoire*); the kidnap and ransoming of another *commissaire du Directoire;* and the disarming of several communes in the Mayenne by chouans. But the score was not entirely one-sided: the *Bulletin* recorded successes for the forces of order as well: the trial of 49 brigands by the Criminal Court at Rouen, including testimony from 279 witnesses; death sentences passed by military commissions against three émigrés and the capture of another bearing a commission from the Pretender, Louis XVIII; the sentencing of seven brigands by the Criminal Court of the Calvados; one commune declared under "state of siege" for rioting; and the organization of nightly patrols throughout the department of the Rhône. This was one ordinary month, and such a level of crime reporting was typical of the period. Indeed, the list would be considerably longer had it come from a newspaper published in one of the areas of serious unrest. Sometimes exaggerated statistics enhanced this impression: one Paris paper, *L'Ami de la Patrie,* claimed that the government had proof of 23,000 "murderous assaults" (*assassinats*) in the Midi.[15] This ubiquitous reporting of crime helped to create a national climate of fear. Readers did not have to be the victims of crime, or even know those who were, to feel personally vulnerable or to believe in galloping chaos.

Even in the octavo format of the 1790s, publishing all the news that fit the print did not restrict newspapers to reporting the facts; they freely exercised their editorial prerogative both in reporting crime and in commenting on matters of public order. Incidents of violence tended to be reported with a strong political bias, especially before the Fructidor coup. Thus the reactionary *Courrier républicain* reported a holdup of the stagecoach from Paris to Senlis as the work of seventeen "échappés des comités révolutionnaires."[16] Similarly, the *Observateur républicain* of Toulouse used a wide range of epithets when describing perpetrators of violence, adding "royalicoassassins" and "républicide" to the standard repertoire of "égorgeurs," "brigands royaux," "hordes chouaniques," and "compagnies de Jésus."[17] Such revolutionary rhetoric had the effect of politicizing common-law criminals. This process also worked in reverse. Newspapers made extensive use of the term "brigand" to criminalize political opponents: for example, the royalist *Journal du départment de l'Hérault* referred to government leaders as the pupils of "le brigand honteux Sieyès,"[18] and the republican *Bulletin du département de l'Eure* claimed that royalists were as likely to be army deserters, brigands, and criminals as to be members of the former privileged orders.[19] This process of simultaneously politicizing crime and criminalizing politics did not bode well for the future of liberal democracy in France. Jacobin papers naturally exulted when the government seemed finally to heed their call to defend patriots against the royalist onslaught rather than merely glorifying the republic as a regime based on the rule of law.[20] However, those papers that advocated a salutary use of violence in primary assemblies were quickly banned.[21] Some commentators saw political stability as the key to public order. The *Courrier patriotique* believed that the new harmony between executive and legislature would steadily increase security and called upon moderates, federalists, Thermidorians, and Fructidorians to unite against extremists on both ends of the political spectrum.[22] In contrast, other editors believed that political stability depended on first providing public security. "You want a republic? In good time. As for me, I want the rogues removed, the bandits defeated, the thieves hanged, and the assassins punished; after that we'll talk of a republic," wrote Joseph Lavallée, editor of the *Semaines critiques*.[23]

The circulation of news was as important as the circulation of individual newspapers. The timeless tendency for readers to subscribe to newspapers that fit their political prejudices no doubt prevailed during the Directory. Certainly the police believed that subscribing to Babeuf's *Tribun du peuple* was evidence enough of "anarchist" tendencies. Yet there is evidence that select papers attracted a more eclectic audience. These papers usually had better sources and therefore more accurate information. Such was the case with *L'Ami des lois,* a Parisian daily with a national circulation. Its progovernment slant together with an assiduous cultivation of ministerial contacts often gave it a reporting edge over other papers. This served to broaden its readership as well as to make it the source of the freshest news for other papers.[24] Therefore, its practice of providing details on the disastrous state of law and order in the Vaucluse or its habit of publishing the verdicts of every military commission held in Paris brought these matters to a truly national audience. Regardless of its editorial line, a paper such as *L'Ami des lois* both directly and indirectly focused public attention on the struggle to restore order. Furthermore, many provincial papers not only mixed local events with national news but often had special contacts in particular areas of unrest. The Jacobin-leaning *Chronique de la Sarthe,* for example, provided an amazing level of coverage on the tumult in the Midi. Such reporting helped to put local events in a broader context. It also provided an opportunity to offset bad news nearby with good news from elsewhere. For example, a story of the department's own central commissioner being stabbed to death in the streets of Le Mans was followed in the next issue with an item about sixteen "égorgeurs" from Marseille being arrested after a battle with troops near Lambesc. A week later, the *Chronique* reported the murder of the central commissioner of neighboring Calvados and immediately followed it with a report on three hundred finely worked knives collected from a distant battle site in Provence where "égorgeurs" had been soundly trounced. This can only be explained as a strategy of psychological reassurance practiced by the editor, Ragomier Bazin. His strategy both magnified the danger to republicans and provided reassuring news that the republic was getting the upper hand. In this vein, *La Trompette*, published at Besançon, reassured its readers that unrest in the Doubs, even when at its worst before Fructidor, was nothing like that in the Midi or along the Loire. This same paper supplemented this perspective by running a number of reports on the efficiency of the local gendarmerie throughout the tempestuous summer of 1799.[25] All of this indicates that even when massaged for partisan purposes, the coverage newspapers gave to provincial violence ensured that it was a national issue and, therefore, of importance even in areas of relative calm.

The belief in mounting violence logically led to support for increased security measures, regardless of the cost in terms of individual liberty. Obviously, political stability and personal security were closely linked. Equally obviously, both could be better assured by strengthening the executive. Throughout the Directorial period, right-wing papers ridiculed the government for its weakness while republican papers reiterated their support for a firm hand. Both attitudes encouraged the Directory to act in a more authoritarian manner. However, matters became ominous when republican papers shifted from defending liberal democratic principles to calling for vigorous measures "capable of sowing terror in the hearts of these villains and making them renounce their careers as brigands"[26] or warned the government that if it did not use enough force to combat this evil, patriots would be driven to protect themselves.[27] Such threats of vigilantism had the unmistakable ring of social chaos and implied the need for more vigorous repression.

It is difficult to tell the extent to which newspapers helped to shape public opinion in contrast to merely reflecting it. Perhaps it is safer to conclude that the massive spread of news about crime and the editorial amalgam of crime and political extremism both generated support for repressive policies that ran roughshod over personal liberties and community solidarities alike. Although large parts of the country had escaped the kind of endemic violence that plagued departments in the west and southeast, brigandage was a near-universal scourge—so much so that press coverage of criminal violence resonated everywhere.

## Breaking the Back of Brigandage

The support of public opinion for a more aggressive approach to public order puts the antibrigandage law of 29 nivôse VI in a different light. Historians of the period have largely ignored the law, despite its erosion of liberty in the interest of security, and its implementation is known only in anecdotal terms.[28] This ignorance is remarkable given that military courts tried several thousand civilians, many of whom were not engaged in brigandage at all. In fact, during a period of two and one-half years from the spring of 1798 to the autumn of 1800, regular military courts became a prominent feature of the judicial landscape in France and not just in areas of rampant lawlessness. Though this further eroded the regime's liberal credentials, it would be misleading to ignore the extent to which military courts both satisfied public opinion and fulfilled their new mission within the spirit of the law. Clémenceau is supposed to have remarked that "military justice is to justice as military music is to music."[29] This aptly describes the experience of civilians who faced the military courts of the late Directory and early Consulate. The music was martial all right, but it was still melodic, which was better than the cacophony of revolutionary tribunals or the dissonance of Quiberon.

Liberal instincts make it tempting simply to deplore the Directory's recourse to military justice, but such an approach would fail to appreciate the difficulties the republic faced in both protecting liberty and providing security. As we have seen, the law of 29 nivôse VI did not abandon all concern for the legal rights of civilians facing military justice. Furthermore, individuals who were sent before military courts under this law were better protected from miscarriages of justice than they would have been a year earlier. The creation of new courts and a new penal code gave military justice a more elaborate set of procedures. The new courts (*conseils de guerre*) were permanent, standing courts whose personnel, including the prosecutor (*capitaine-rapporteur*), were appointed by the district commander. Although a general could rotate personnel for the good of military operations, he could not do this in preparation for a particular trial. After their initial interrogations, defendants either hired a defense lawyer or had one appointed by the court.[30] Trial confrontations between witnesses and the accused took the same form as in civilian courts. Military trials were also public. Although the law limited the number of audience members to twenty-one (three times the number of judges), this regulation was frequently ignored. A year after adopting the new system, legislators added a three-judge review court to each military district to ensure that procedures were properly followed.[31] Finally, the sheer volume of cases handled by military courts in the army and across the country—over six hundred individuals a month (one-third of whom were actually present at trial) during the first nine months of the new system—helped to regularize procedures and create a more consistent jurisprudence. Problems remained, of course, but these were not all negative. The new courts had an illegal tendency to commute sentences or acquit on the grounds of intent.[32] Nonetheless, it is clear that the system of military justice had already improved substantially by the time lawmakers adopted the law of 29 nivôse VI.

It should not be forgotten, however, that civilians tried as counterrevolutionary rebels, rather than as brigands, could still find military justice rather nasty, brutish, and short. The law of 30 prairial III continued in effect despite the radical changes in military justice.[33] The nature of this law, focused as it was on rebels captured in armed gatherings, ensured that trials proceeded quickly, appeals followed promptly, and executions happened swiftly. As General Vimeux remarked about three chouans condemned to death by a military court, they will appeal, "but since military justice goes a bit faster than that of criminal courts, it will only prolong their lives by three or four days at most."[34] Just as the number of civilians tried under the law of 30 prairial III began to decline in the west, it increased in the southeast. Prior to Fructidor, military courts in Provence had rarely prosecuted civilians. Thereafter, however, military justice became an important tool of political redress against the reactionaries who had dominated the region since 1795. For example, in the early months of year VI, the military court at Marseille sentenced to death thirteen royalist *égorgeurs* charged with prison massacres and antirepublican murders.[35] They may not have been rebels captured with arms in hand, but any exactitudes attached to exceptional legislation meant little in such cases. The local criminal courts had done nothing to punish these men, and the chance finally to strike a judicial blow against the "compagnies du Soleil" was seized with relish.

On the other hand, civilians tried as brigands under the law of 29 nivôse VI had more procedural protections than those tried as rebels under the law of 30 prairial III. The regime sought to avoid too many travesties of justice—as well as judicial failures—by insisting that a civilian jury director, and not a district commander or military prosecutor, determine whether an accused was liable to appear before a military court. Thus, preliminary investigation was subject to all the strictures of the *Code des délits et des peines.* The accused were not handed over to a military court until after a jury director had interrogated them, taken witness depositions, and concluded that the circumstances of the crime clearly made it subject to military justice. In this respect, the new system for prosecuting brigands resembled the provostial courts of the *ancien régime.*[36] Once again, the overriding intention was "to be fair to the innocent and utterly merciless to the guilty."[37]

A look at the ways in which military courts applied the law of 29 nivôse VI exposes the dynamic tension between ensuring greater protection for civilians tried by courts martial and the continued rigor military justice provided. After all, there would have been no point resorting to military courts if they did not short-circuit aspects of the criminal justice system that were deemed obstacles to "prompt and just punishment" for bandits and brigands. It should first be noted that quite a few bandits who could have been sent before military courts were in fact tried under the ordinary system of criminal justice. Three of the most notorious brigand bands of the period, the *bande d'Orgères,* the *bande Salembier,* and the *bande Chandelier,* were all tried in regular criminal courts. Many of the crimes committed by these bands made them liable to appear before military courts. However, in order both to envelop as many accomplices as possible and to include crimes that predated the law of 29 nivôse, the Court of Cassation decided in all three cases that the accused (a staggering total of 118 from the *bande d'Orgères,* 83 from the *bande Chandelier,* and 41 from the *bande Salembier*) should be prosecuted in civilian courts.[38] These bands resembled the classic criminal gangs at work under the *ancien régime.* Their internal structure based on a nucleus of especially intrepid criminals, their extreme violence, and their unusual geographical range all made them especially terrifying. In these instances, the government could trust juries to get tough with bandits who lacked roots in the rural community or a royalist cause to justify their depredations.

Herein lay the single greatest advantage for the government in the law of 29 nivôse VI. It made it possible to clamp down on the sort of criminals who had enough local support or terrifying influence to paralyze juries, especially grand juries close to the scene of events. Thus, most jury directors took advantage of the new law to avoid both types of juries and instead send culprits before military courts whenever possible. Extending the writ of military courts to cover acts of brigandage put common criminals on much the same footing as chouans. Notorious bandits who terrorized the countryside, men known as "The Dragon," "Beat-to-Death," and "The Little Butcher," now faced the same military courts as "Little King" and "Smash-the-Nation," avowed counter-revolutionaries who raided farmhouses and pillaged stagecoaches in the name of God and king. The new law ensured that smugglers who ambushed customs agents in the Pyrenees, peasants who rescued priests from a military escort in the Franche-Comté, and burglars who stole a bolt of cloth in the Cévennes all faced military courts.[39] These could be frighteningly rigorous, even for ordinary thieves. When a military court convicted two Parisian couples in their twenties on two counts of almost routine housebreaking, the men were shot and the women sentenced to twenty-four years in prison.[40] Similarly, the fact that three masons, and not two, burgled a farmhouse at Abecour (Doubs) got them all condemned to death by a military court.[41] Though the penalties were extremely harsh, each of these cases fell within the spirit of the law of 29 nivôse VI. The vast crime wave of the mid-1790s had convinced lawmakers that preserving the republic required draconian treatment of ordinary criminals as well as counter-revolutionary guerrillas.

And yet many crimes tried by military courts under the law of 29 nivôse VI had little or nothing to do with banditry or armed robbery. In fact, interpreting the law in literal terms led to a wide variety of cases being sent before military courts. The letter of the law often eclipsed its spirit. So it was with seven young men charged with breaking into the widow Savoy's house, dragging her outside, cutting her hair off, and then using a rope repeatedly to plunge her into the Gers river. They admitted doing this "in order to scare her." The additional charge of stealing 63 francs saw them sent to the military court at Perpignan, where the prosecutor took the law literally and called for death sentences. His fellow judges, however, refused to hand down the supreme penalty for events that were more a matter of ritualized humiliation and intimidation than of gang robbery and so acquitted them all.[42] This was one of many occasions when military courts proved reluctant to apply the law in all its deadly terms. As is so often the case with such legislation, the very harshness of the law of 29 nivôse VI played a role in mitigating its application.

Especially zealous jury directors often played an egregious part in sending marginal cases before military courts. A decade of economic and social dislocation, of wigmakers thrown out of work, hospices closed, and sharecroppers evicted, had created a vast underclass of increasingly rootless peasants, artisans, and day laborers. Magistrates inured to sympathy by class hostility hoped that severe penalties would help to control the rising tide of property crime. Thus, with scant regard for the pettiness of their offense, a jury director in the Calvados sent three vagabond women before a military court for stealing nine *sous* and a few scraps of linen (they had dislodged the door of a woodcutter's shack and thereby technically violated the new law). The military court wisely acquitted them all and sent them back to the jails whence they came to be tried by civilian courts on other charges of theft.[43] The national expropriation of church property and émigré estates also proved a common source of personal hostilities and open conflict. This naturally led to a certain number of trials before military courts. Clearly some jury directors believed that in order to protect revolutionary changes in property holding, the best defense was an aggressive offense. This became especially apparent in areas of endemic and often politicized violence. Thanks to the jury director at Florac (Lozère), Jacques Guet, *cultivateur* at St-Germain-de-Calberte, and his two sons spent six months in jail before facing a military court charged with assault on a public road at night by an armed group. This sounds exactly like the sort of crime the law of 29 nivôse VI had been designed to repress. However, the facts in the case could hardly have been more mundane and less in need of military justice. Infuriated at having their lease bought up by their prosperous neighbor Théron, the three Guets avenged their loss by laying in wait for him on his way home and then knocking him off his horse with a well-aimed rock to the face. Théron may have lost a few teeth in the incident, but it was a cheap price to pay for the opportunity to expropriate the Guets entirely. While the three men sat in jail awaiting their court-martial, Théron bought the rest of the contracts and debts they had with the former comte de Dubarre and expelled the entire family from the mas du Chausse. Deeming their troubles punishment enough for a rash act of violence, a military court at Montpellier acquitted them all but sent one son to the army as a conscript.[44]

As these cases illustrate, the law of 29 nivôse VI could pose a considerable danger to many civilians. Although some jury directors magnified this danger by taking advantage of the new law, military courts were not as easily manipulated as some wished. In contrast to the usual stereotypes about courts-martial, military prosecutors frequently balked at taking on civilian cases.[45] Using force to extort six francs from a fellow customer in a tavern, being part of a post-wedding *charivari* that turned nasty, or committing a street robbery with a friend and then having a spouse hide the goods were the sort of cases military courts refused to decide and simply sent back to civilian magistrates.[46] This was done by declaring themselves "not competent" to judge a case. A decision of this nature invariably depended on the investigation conducted by the military prosecutor. Verdicts of noncompetence were fairly common. They usually derived from shoddy investigation by civilian magistrates[47] but could also be the result of cases tainted by politics or personalities. Persuasive persons occasionally duped jury directors into sending a dubious case before the most terrifying tribunal available in order to exact revenge on local rivals, even when convictions were highly unlikely. Such was the case for a long list of royalist agitators in the Ariège whose crimes had all taken place during the reaction of year V, and thus well before the law of 29 nivôse VI. The resulting verdicts of noncompetence were predictable and inevitable.[48]

Military courts were not the passive instruments of either the pushy or the powerful. The minister of justice insisted that military courts could not reject civilian cases on jurisdictional grounds before they came to trial, no matter how blatantly a jury director abused the law of 29 nivôse VI, or what the military prosecutor learned in the course of his investigation, but military courts had other ways of limiting misapplication of the law.[49] One military prosecutor felt obliged to conclude a case of supposed highway assault by saying, "in this affair, it seems, citizen judges, that I play the role of public defender rather than prosecutor, but since my duty requires me to present you with the truth, I believe my task is fulfilled by presenting the facts to you as they happened."[50] This led to acquittals, as intended. Army officers certainly gained no glory, and probably little respect, for condemning to death anyone other than a serious bandit. Civilian magistrates were the ones who expected them "to do their duty," and they did not always oblige. In fact, the comrades-in-arms of Captain Pavie, prosecutor for the First Military Court at Montpellier, mockingly nicknamed him "la fille," which the local court commissioner explained was due to his "wise and prudent conduct, the mildness of his character, and his good morals."[51] These were hardly the values most vaunted by eighteenth-century officers, nor do they fit preconceptions about the key member of a court-martial in the 1790s.

Even when military prosecutors or military courts went along with malicious or inappropriate prosecutions, the accused could always appeal to a military review court. Although this review focused on procedures and sentences, it frequently led to new trials.[52] Annulments and retrials by another military court could result from any number of procedural errors. These ranged from serious faults in judicial process such as failing to interrogate witnesses to quibbling items of document transcription.[53] In the majority of cases, an annulment by a military review court did not change the ultimate verdict. Nonetheless, from time to time, an annulment and retrial did save lives.[54] In other words, having the crimes investigated by justices of the peace and jury directors operating under the *Code des délits et des peines* and then investigated yet again by a military prosecutor, many of whom acquired a lot of experience in this role, greatly reduced the number of weak cases brought to trial. Furthermore, having permanent military courts functioning under a new procedural code for military justice, and a review court in each military district, all helped to ensure that the vast majority of those convicted under the law of 29 nivôse VI were the sort of criminals that legislators had in mind when they first adopted this measure. Let no mistake be made, however; even when applied with the utmost scrupulousness, the law itself remained draconian, a clear return to judicial practices abolished with such fanfare in 1790–91.

The last article of the original law limited its application to a single year. As the expiration date approached, however, the Directory asked lawmakers to prolong it for another year. The government argued that it had restored tranquility to a number of departments previously afflicted by brigandage, but that it had not been successful everywhere, notably in the annexed departments. Renewal of the law was indispensable until "the reduction in the number of criminals will allow them to be treated with less rigor." With the prospect of renewed war and in the midst of an interminable debate about restricting the rights of émigrés and their relatives, both councils endorsed the extension.[55] Nothing could have been more predictable in late 1798. As the letterhead for one *conseil de guerre* illustrates (see figure 11), military courts were seen to be slaying the hydra of anarchy, but without completely losing their grip on the scales of justice.

Mounting tension did more than encourage renewing the law of 29 nivôse VI. The political and military crisis of 1799 pushed the Directory to extend yet further its use of military courts for domestic repression. As disorder became rife in western France, the Directory ordered all brigands seized with weapons in hand to be sent directly to military courts as chouan accomplices. This directive repealed one of the most important safeguards earlier added by legislators: that a civilian jury director determine the appropriate jurisdiction for all civilians accused of brigandage.[56] With a stroke of the executive pen, common criminals became enemies of the state! Even this seemed inadequate by the summer of 1799, when large areas of the Midi, the west, and the annexed territories burst into open rebellion. This inspired a law permitting the creation of an additional military court for

any department declared "in a state of civil strife." The Directory had repeatedly asked the Councils to avoid delays caused by overworked military
courts by authorizing the creation of military commissions to judge those
accused of rebellion, assault, and banditry when caught in flagrante delicto.
Although willing to pass the "law of hostages," the Councils refused to resurrect military commissions; instead, they resorted to this proliferation of
regular military courts in areas of rampant rebellion.[57] It is not clear how

Fig. 11. République française: Conseil de guerre. Letterhead engraved by Roosing,
1798. (Courtesy of the Département des estampes et photographies, Bibliothèque
nationale de France)

widely this was applied, but it is certainly clear that the regime considered military courts effective instruments of repression.

Indeed, the republic's use of military courts to crack down on the most serious crimes of violence produced dramatic results. A study of military courts in a variety of districts reveals the importance of this new means of repression. In the Eighth Military District (headquarters at Marseille), seventy-five civilians went before military courts charged with various acts of brigandage and armed resistance in the two years from April 1798 to April 1800; fifty-six of them were condemned to death. To this total should be added the twenty deserters also condemned to death for banditry, armed robbery, and murderous assault.[58] The departments of the Basses-Alpes, Bouches-du-Rhône, Var, and Vaucluse had long been wracked by an ugly mélange of political hotheads, hardened bandits, and cold-blooded killers. The spate of military executions left no doubt about the republic's increased determination to end the bloody factionalism and professional thuggery.

Military justice featured prominently in a similar wave of aggressive repression in western France. Over a three-year period, the two courts of the Twenty-second Military District (headquarters at Tours) condemned to death 63 of 150 civilians who appeared before them.[59] These were a blurry mix of rebels and bandits. The troubled departments of the Mayenne, Maine-et-Loire, and Sarthe supplied the military courts with a large number of chouans. These included numerous die-hards who had violated their amnesty oaths[60] as well as a smattering of new recruits attracted by a joining bonus of 300 *livres* and regular pay of 30 *sols* a day.[61] Yet others, especially those from the Eure-et-Loir and Loir-et-Cher, were old-fashioned highwaymen trying, rather unsuccessfully, to hide behind the mask of royalism.[62] By also applying the law of 25 brumaire V (15 November 1796), which prescribed military justice and the death penalty for anyone who recruited for rebels, the military courts of western France could reach beyond the violent perpetrators and punish some of their influential accomplices in the local community. Where accomplices constituted a sizable share of defendants, however, military courts produced a higher acquittal rate. In the Thirteenth Military District (headquarters at Rennes), military courts tried at least 225 civilians as rebels, brigands, or their accomplices, 69 of whom were condemned to death. The large number of cases and considerable death toll naturally resulted from the persistence of *chouannerie* and the return of civil war in the autumn of 1799. Besides applying the usual short prison sentences for rebels not actually caught in armed gatherings, the military courts active in Brittany acquitted all but a handful of accomplices. This happened even when the courts relocated to places such as Port-Brieuc and Lorient in order to make it easier to obtain witness testimony.[63]

Few other regions matched the political violence and incessant brigandage of Provence or the desultory civil war in Brittany, Anjou, and Maine. Nevertheless, military justice played a major role in combating crime wherever the republic was plagued by continued resistance and endemic banditry. In the Ninth Military District (headquarters at Nîmes, then Montpellier), military courts held over fifty trials involving some two hundred civilians associated with various acts of brigandage over a period of two and a half years. This led to 51 death sentences (29 in absentia), 35 sentences of between three and twenty years in irons (eight in absentia), and eleven persons receiving misdemeanor convictions. Another 86 persons were acquitted and 25 sent to civilian courts.[64] This notably low rate of capital sentences compared to courts elsewhere[65] suggests less ruthless military judges. These courts frequently sentenced outlaws to prison or the *bagne* rather than apply the death penalty as prescribed by the law of 29 nivôse VI. This was a more calibrated response to crime and may have reflected a regional cultural of tolerance for banditry. Furthermore, most of the crimes were committed by residents of isolated Catholic villages along the southern Cévennes, where republicanism was largely confined to Protestant centers and witnesses were especially vulnerable to reprisals. Even military courts proved reluctant to convict without adequate witness testimony.

In the western half of Languedoc, the military courts of the Tenth Military District (headquarters at Perpignan, then Toulouse) proved more orthodox. They issued no less than seventy death sentences, although over half of these (thirty-nine) were in absentia. The insurrection in the Midi Toulousain in the summer of 1799 added scores of rebels to the ordinary bandits and brutal young men tried by these courts.[66] All the same, 60 percent of the death sentences were for aggravated forms of robbery.[67] The fact that this military district covered two-thirds of the Pyrenees, where smuggling was ubiquitous, contributed significantly to the number of civilian cases subjected to military justice.[68] The military courts at Perpignan also dealt with numerous individuals charged under the antibrigandage law for, in fact, pulling down houses under construction, an anomaly that can only be explained by a clash of cultures between revolutionary concepts of property and the Pyrenean tradition of exercising collective control over the number of dwellings in a community.[69]

The results of military justice were necessarily less dramatic in less tumultuous areas. The military courts at Besançon, headquarters of the Sixth

Military District, dealt almost exclusively with soldiers. When they did prosecute civilians, the outcome was rarely harsh: only two were actually executed.[70] And yet the military courts at Besançon were not inactive: though archival sources are incomplete, there are verdicts for twelve cases involving eighty-six civilians. Three of these cases arose out of planned attacks on the gendarmerie to rescue refractory priests and together account for more than forty defendants. Each of these cases involved prolonged and extensive judicial efforts, and yet not one person was convicted.[71] Furthermore, the military courts at Besançon acquitted thirteen individuals in cases of armed robbery and pronounced themselves incompetent to judge another two robberies involving nine civilians.[72] We should not interpret this as a failure on the part of the military courts of the Sixth Military District to provide any added law enforcement or deterrence against serious crime. The men who faced these courts first passed long months in the frigid cells of the Vauban fortress at Besançon, where they surely spent more time worrying about death by firing squad than they did admiring the view of the Jura Mountains and the winding Doubs below. Even if most of them ended up back in their own beds, their experience deterred others from taking similar risks.

The impact of military justice on quiescent areas such as the Franche-Comté stood in stark contrast to the prominent role it played in the annexed departments to the northeast. The Directory made unprecedented and unparalleled use of military courts in the aftermath of the so-called "peasant war" that erupted in the Belgian departments in early year VII. Over the following two and one-half years, the four military courts at Brussels and Liège, headquarters for the Twenty-fourth and Twenty-fifth Military Districts respectively, heard cases pertaining to an astonishing 1,771 insurgents. In the process, these four courts pronounced roughly 280 death sentences, 400 sentences of four months in prison, and 970 acquittals.[73] Most of these trials took place within a year of the rebellion, a time when the minister of war was demanding a purge of the military courts because they were known to have acquitted rebels captured with arms in hand.[74] It may be some time before historians compile complete statistics on the judicial repression that followed the "Belgian Vendée."[75] In the meantime, these new figures indicate a truly massive judicial repression pursued largely through the application of the law of 30 prairial III by military courts. The number of death sentences pronounced at Brussels alone would have meant holding a firing squad two or three times a week for months on end. One can only wonder how such a steady parade of victims affected residents of this new regional capital of the "Grande Nation."[76]

Thus, from 1798 to 1800, military justice became a crucial instrument of repression. By the time the councils prolonged the law of 29 nivôse VI for a second year, it had become an integral part of the judicial landscape. Not only had civilian magistrates developed the habit of construing all sorts of crimes to fit the law, the military courts themselves, especially those at Montpellier, began issuing sentences that conformed to the Penal Code of 1791 rather applying the harsher laws that brought civilians before them in the first place. Local military review courts were powerless to stop this practice because defendants were aware of their good fortune and declined to appeal the verdicts. The ineluctable intermeshing of civilian and military justice also meant that the Court of Cassation began to render judgments on appeals from civilians who had been condemned by military courts. This practice contradicted the whole ethos of military justice, based as it was on prompt execution of sentences, and threatened to paralyze trials of civilians.[77] Nonetheless, regular military courts rid the countryside of scores of dangerous royalist subversives such as the three chouans convicted and shot after months of systematic kidnapping, extortion, and armed robbery in the Mayenne.[78] Perhaps equally important for the survival of the republic was the capture, trial, and execution of six men who had roamed the departments of the Indre-et-Loire and Maine-et-Loire wearing the *cocarde blanche,* crying "Vive le roi," cutting down liberty trees, and taking pot-shots at republican troops sent to arrest them.[79] Although not convicted of specific acts of robbery or assault, these men faced summary justice for flouting the authority of the republic in a civil war zone. No less significant in consolidating the regime's authority was meting out exemplary punishment for common highway robbery. Hence the use of a military court to convict and execute four men and two women involved in the armed robbery of a lace merchant near the Provençal scrubland known as the Taillades forest.[80] The ferocity of these sentences and the wide publicity they received—most convictions resulted in hundreds of posters—should have gone a long way toward restoring order in provincial France. A sudden recrudescence of antirepublican insurgency in the summer of 1799, however, badly tarnished the Directory's image and made its collapse appear inevitable in retrospect.

In fact, the widespread lawlessness of late 1799 extended well into 1800 and beyond. It resulted mainly from redoubled conscription, financial and material levies, and the reluctant transfer of troops from the interior to the frontiers. Under these conditions, it is surprising that the Consular regime did not renew the law of 29 nivôse VI for a third year. The fact that brigandage was as bad in the autumn of 1799 as it had been when the law was first debated two years earlier could be interpreted either as evidence that the law had failed or as evidence that it needed to be renewed. Minister of Justice Cambacérès drew attention to some of the law's unfortunate features. It had produced an "excessive rigor" because the death penalty was applied both to housebreaking without violence and to accomplices who had merely received stolen goods. Although he recommended that the law be amended in certain particulars, he also reluctantly advocated its renewal. The three Consuls were less ambivalent and called on the temporary legislative commissions to prolong the law. But the rump of Brumairian lawmakers, apparently hoping to break with the discredited policies of the Directory, rejected this request and allowed the law to lapse.[81] Under these circumstances, the new minister of justice, André-Joseph Abrial, sought to hasten the return to regular justice by deciding that the sort of crimes covered by the law of 29 nivôse VI and committed while the law was in effect would no longer be tried by military courts but would be handled by regular criminal courts instead.[82] After all, the Consulate was in the midst of a wholesale reorganization of the criminal justice system, one purpose of which was to strengthen its ability to deal with serious crime.

Despite Abrial's directive, cases that fit the law of 29 nivôse VI continued to be tried well after the law expired. In fact, military courts were almost as busy trying civilians under this law in year VIII as they had been in year VII. The bulk of these cases had already been passed to military courts before the ministerial change of heart. Moreover, a few military courts continued to apply the law as much as a year or two later.[83] Thus, although the law of 29 nivôse VI was a quintessential product of the Directorial regime, and even though the law was not renewed in year VIII, it remained an important feature of judicial repression during the early Consulate. Even when the law lapsed and faded, widespread banditry and armed rebellion did not. Before long the new regime responded to continued violence by crafting its own judicial compromises, ones that had their own way of eroding liberty in the interest of security.

# PART III
## Liberal Authoritarianism

THAT THE FRENCH REVOLUTION did not end in 1799 is made abundantly clear by the high levels of civil strife that continued well thereafter, especially in the west and south. Though not typical of the country as a whole, the endemic violence of these regions did have national ramifications. In order to understand the interaction between local and national forces, therefore, it is essential to undertake two regional studies. The first looks at the persistence of civil strife in the west from the so-called pacification of 1796 to the recrudescence of *chouannerie* in 1799 and the relative return to order in 1801. Here special attention is paid to the lived experience of guerrilla warfare and the corrosive effects of counter-insurgency that produced a republican "dirty war." In the end, the conditions that made it so difficult for the republic to stamp out *chouannerie* gravely affected the authoritarian outcome of the French Revolution. In the south, our study of a prolonged cycle of violence around Lodève exposes the critical importance of purely local factors, such as the power of personalities, the influence of topography, and the force of cultural norms. It also questions the chronology of revolutionary violence, for here the Terror was mild and the Consulate was murderous. The chronologies and conclusions of these two cycles of violence serve to caution against overstating either the importance of the Terror in shaping subsequent violence or the coup of Brumaire in bringing a hasty return to order.

The coup d'état of 18 brumaire VIII did not end the French Revolution. Nor for that matter did the Constitution of Year VIII, despite the government proclamation claiming that it did. This has always been clear to astute observers of the many contingencies of high politics during the early Consulate.[1] But even those who avoid the teleological insouciance that makes the Empire inevitable have paid insufficient attention to the deep roots the Napoleonic dictatorship had in the political culture of the republic. The impatient politicians who planned the Brumaire coup wished to strengthen the power of the executive, not to create one-man rule. The purpose was to save the republic by ending the instability caused by annual elections. Moreover, Brumaire did not suddenly replace democratic republicanism with authoritarian reaction. The central problem of the entire republic—that of saving the Revolution while violating many of the principles it was intended to embody—had already proved too much for the Thermidorians to master. It was the Fructidor coup d'état that had brought about a decisive shift from seeking legitimacy through constitutionalism and the rule of law to seeking legitimacy through restoring order on republican terms, though without abandoning constitutionalism altogether. This produced a militarized authoritarianism whose very real achievements were obscured by the turmoil of the Jacobin Hundred Days and the renewed politicization of exceptional measures.

The paradox of Brumaire is that it was a liberal as well as antidemocratic response to the misuses of authoritarianism. Before long, however, the more liberal elements among the Brumairians succumbed to the force of Bonaparte's ambition and the logic of ruthless repression. The Consular Terror of 1801, with its purge of political opponents in Paris and proliferation of military commissions in the west and south, illustrated the potential for military dictatorship. It is in this context that the creation of "special tribunals" to deal with brigandage, while a stinging defeat of the liberal opposition to Napoleon, also constituted something of a return to legality. This "liberal authoritarianism" provided the basis for the Napoleonic security state that finally ended the French Revolution in 1802.

# 9 Guerrilla War and Counter-insurgency

Their first operations were to paralyze local authorities, to destroy their moral force, to discredit republican institutions. . . . Local hatreds took root, the National Guard was armed one against the other, one canton marched against a neighboring one, citizens from the same place took turns disarming one another. A countryside embittered by revolutionary rigors provided a favorable theater for the "discontents."

—"Chouannerie" in *L'Ami des lois,* 14 nivôse VIII (4 January 1800)

*CHOUANNERIE* WAS TO the Directory as the Vendée was to the Convention, both unique and emblematic.[1] It was unique in being an insurgency that was at the same time widely supported, clearly counter-revolutionary, and openly linked to foreign conspiracy; it was emblematic as the problem of order in which revolutionary expedients repeatedly triumphed over liberal principles. More than any other problem, *chouannerie* strained the republic's ability to undertake pacification without persecution and to transform coercion into reconciliation. As one would expect from a guerrilla struggle, *chouannerie* was highly fragmented and is best studied in a limited area. The Twenty-second Military District, and the department of the Sarthe in particular, compose an ideal area in which to uncover the nature of the movement and the counter-insurgency it provoked. Even from this vantage point, it is clear that the struggle against *chouannerie* was critical to the larger fate of the First Republic. The inability to achieve genuine pacification in western France contributed disproportionately to the Revolution's authoritarian outcome.

## The Nature of *Chouannerie*

The guerrilla war of *chouannerie* began in 1792 and reached its apogee in the first six months of the Directory. By then it engulfed the region south of the Loire known as the *Vendée militaire,* as well as Upper Brittany, Lower Normandy, Anjou, and Maine—the better part of ten departments in all. But *chouannerie* was a local phenomenon—the proverbial potatoes in a sack that form a sack of potatoes. Maps of *chouannerie* all show spotty implantations, the actual distribution of which resists easy explanation.[2] Topography mattered as much to the movement as anything. The thick hedgerows, enclosures, and hollowed-out roads of the *bocage* helped to preserve an insular rural world. They also allowed rebels to execute ambushes and hasty getaways while simultaneously preventing republican forces from using artillery or maneuvering en masse. Yet the *bocage* east of Le Mans was largely patriot country, and the Amoricain plateau of Brittany was far from uniformly rebellious.[3] Not only was *chouannerie* rather patchy, it also mobilized only a small proportion of the populace in the areas where it thrived. The men who actually became chouans never comprised more than one in fifty inhabitants of any parish.[4] Moreover, individual villages could suddenly change sides. Political loyalties of whole parishes often depended on whether the leading patriots fled or a company of soldiers arrived. And yet *chouannerie* proved painfully hard to extirpate, partly because it battened on a peasantry rich in grievances and partly because the regime lacked the state apparatus necessary to contain it.

Despite much debate, historians now generally agree that western insurgency had three main sources: defense of traditional religion, opposition to conscription, and hostility toward bourgeois beneficiaries of the Revolution. First, the dispersed nature of habitation in western France made religious rituals an especially important source of community. Parish priests in the west also generally enjoyed greater prosperity and social status than elsewhere in the country. Together these factors made the revolutionaries' attack on the church a source of especially intense hostility. Second, the refusal of military service determined who actually joined the chouans as much as opposition to the republic's religious policies determined which areas supported them. Military recruitment had always been bitterly opposed in the west, and most chouans were young men of conscription age. Third, the peasants of western France nurtured a profound hatred of prosperous town dwellers. Burghers were at the same time avatars of a more demanding market-economy, agents of a more intrusive state, and proprietors who felt fewer social obligations toward rural communities.[5]

It has been cogently argued that all of these traditions and motives were manifestations of a single phenomenon: the defense of an idealized rural community repeatedly aggressed by the revolutionary state. This explanation recognizes that these rustic rebels defended a community that was more ideal than real. A great many of the chouans' victims were as much a part of the actual rural community as the chouans themselves. District and departmental officials were loathed the most, but they were less vulnerable than their allies in the countryside, who became the principal victims. Constitutional priests in particular were treated as intruders in the village, even if they had ministered there for years, and a number were brutally murdered.[6] More often, chouans chose prosperous peasants, estate managers, mill owners, and other rural notables as their targets. In other words, the perpetrators often justified their violence with notions of community, but they did so while attacking neighbors who had lived beside them for decades, whose families had been part of the social landscape for generations.[7] At times, therefore, the insurgents' ideal of rural community was as much a conceptual fabrication as the revolutionaries' hated notion of nation. The compelling difference was the novelty and exorbitance of the sacrifices demanded in the name of the revolutionary republic.

The search for deeper social causes tends to obscure personal elements in chouan motivation, especially the powerful forces of resentment and revenge. Many chouans were inspired by sheer misery born of economic crisis and social dislocation—so much so that republican denunciations of chouans as both beggars and brigands bore a kernel of truth, above all in later years. Greater hardship bred greater hatred, especially of those who had benefited from the Revolution. Moreover, divergences between the social positions of chouans and their victims does not account for the many young men who joined the "cause" primarily to satisfy a desire for glory, a thirst for adventure, a taste for violence, or a lust for loot, all clichés brought to life by the opportunities of civil conflict. Among these many motives, only one was sufficiently compelling to knit together individual motives into a broader movement. If what chouans said about themselves or acted out in their raids is taken seriously, the most pervasive motive for chouan violence was the desire for vengeance, either personal or collective, for the violence committed by republican forces.[8]

Chouans did not wage war; they sowed terror. Any common pattern in their activities had little to do with a planned strategy and much to do with

simply barring the republic from the countryside. This meant terrifying local patriots through extortion, arson, and murder, and attacking the republic by ambushing army patrols and blockading urban centers. Purchasers of
"nationalized properties" came in for special ill-treatment, as did "patriot"
refugees who returned to their villages in the baggage train of the army.
Regardless of other aims, retribution provided moral cover for numerous
atrocities.[9] Both sides covered their misdeeds with exaggerated rhetoric
and the cloak of ideology. Chouan leaders spoke of "holy war"; republicans
rallied to the "sacred *patrie.*" But all the rhetoric could not mask the fact
that some of the violence was merely a matter of settling scores. So confused were the motives and methods, so devoid of ritual and so obviously
solipsistic were the signifiers, that it was hard to tell the purpose of some
assaults. As an administrator of the Ille-et-Vilaine reported: "one Plassais
from the commune of Vern was hacked up with an ax between the bourg
of Vern and the Grandchamp woods. People do not know if it was done by
chouans or by personal enemies who threatened him in the bourg itself."[10]
Such similarity between *chouannerie* and personal vendetta eroded any
sense of a broader movement or a higher cause.

Efforts to make *chouannerie* serve the cause of Bourbon restoration certainly boosted chouan activity. And yet only the leaders of *chouannerie* espoused clear royalist ideals. Nobles who refused to accept their loss of status
and the economic advantages of the seigneurie saw a restored monarchy as
their only hope. The military heritage of many *gentilhommes* also gave them
a chivalric attachment to the cause of the crown, and their atavistic code
of noble valor provided inspiration for sustained counter-revolution. In the
winter of year IV, such royalist nobles helped *chouannerie* metastasize from
a gangly, uncoordinated, and sporadic armed resistance to an increasingly
militarized guerrilla movement. But this transformation was never complete. Royalist grand strategy and *chouannerie* went together like oil and
vinegar. When thoroughly mixed, they spread effectively over western departments, adding a rich savor to otherwise common forms of resistance.
Also, like oil and vinegar, royalist planning and chouan action had a natural tendency to separate. Royalist leaders, whose authority derived from
the court in exile, appointed numerous émigré nobles as chouan officers
despite their being greenhorns unfamiliar with the territories assigned to
them. Peasant *chefs* seasoned by years of "la petite guerre" took offense, and
many of the new leaders had to be imposed. Mutual disappointment on the
part of émigrés and the chouan bands they were supposed to lead left them
unwilling to continue the fight against a rising tide of republican troops.[11]

Whatever strategic vision existed in London or Blankenburg, it could never be realized in the villages of western France.

## The Pacification of 1796

There is a republican version of the pacification of 1796 that runs like this. The brilliant young general Lazare Hoche succeeded where his predecessors had failed by combining a military dictatorship and conciliatory policies. The massive number of troops at his disposal made it possible to conduct a relentless pursuit of rebel bands, conduct a general disarmament, and use the military to administer the region, all at the same time. Where resistance abated, churches reopened. Draft dodgers were amnestied; deserters enrolled in local defense militias. Where villages failed to turn over the prescribed number of guns, the army seized livestock and imprisoned notables. The vigorous offensive was made more effective by a sustained effort to reduce military disorder and pillage. Furthermore, Hoche insisted that the return to Catholic worship be sincerely respected by officers and administrators alike. Although the intransigence of certain local officials and the duplicity of various subordinate officers presented serious obstacles to pacification, Hoche's skillful balance of firmness and tolerance, and insistence on always acting in good faith and from a position of strength, avoided prolonged use of exceptional measures. As a result, on 12 thermidor IV (30 July 1796), the Directory brought an official end to the civil war by extending "the benefits of the Constitution to the previously insurgent departments subjected to military government."[12]

Though none of this is wrong, it is incomplete. Above all, the republican account largely ignores the perspective of local inhabitants, those caught in the crossfire. Depredations and reprisals, extortion and coercion, refugees and revenge: these were the essence of the conflict for most inhabitants of the region. Ordinary residents in the west grew both increasingly antagonistic toward the rebels and experienced the republican victory as more subjugation than pacification. Only by paying attention to these aspects of lived experience does it become possible to assess the possibilities of a return to order after the departure of Hoche and the withdrawal of troops.

After two years of intense fighting, *chouannerie* began to alienate the mass of rural inhabitants. The growing divergence between residents and rebels owed much to the melding of heterogeneous elements into a vocational group: that of semiprofessional thugs. By 1796, chouannerie "had become an alloy of the indigenous and outsiders, of conscripts and deserters, of honest folk and bandits: whoever was disgruntled became a chouan. . . . Add to this disparate horde the young men chouans sometimes dragged along, by desire or by force, either by kidnapping or the lure of pay or a bonus, for a major action."[13] The inclusion of malcontents and other dubious elements, as well as the recourse to mercenaries and press-ganging, all gravely eroded rural support. So too did the chouans' lack of discipline, ruffian tactics, and sense of just desserts when plundering farmhouses or extorting "contributions." Intimidation and humiliation often became more important than any larger strategy. The sheer bloody-mindedness of the leadership ensured that although peasant hostility to republicans continued to run high, commitment to the "cause" began to wane.[14] It was not only the chouans' often-gratuitous brutality that offended their compatriots; it was also the increasingly grave risks villagers faced in ordinary life. Even selling grain took on political meaning, and once wealthier peasants turned against the movement, it could not be sustained.[15]

On the republican side, a horrifying lack of military discipline may have

Fig. 12. Execution of Charette at Nantes on 9 germinal IV (29 March 1796) (detail) following his condemnation by a *conseil militaire. Collection complète des tableaux historiques de la Révolution française,* 3 vols. (Paris, 1804). (Courtesy of the Division of Rare and Manuscript Collections, Cornell University Library)

been the single greatest hindrance to genuine pacification. Above all, the regime's total inability to supply its troops bred a multitude of depreda- tions. Soldiers fed themselves at the point of a gun, burned furniture for heat, ransomed property holders for cash and jewels, and killed each other over spoils. The spate of raids and extortions committed by frantic soldiers more than matched the chouans' brutality. "Pillaging, theft and murder by the chouans, pillaging and thefts of all sorts by the troops that go out in detachments," wrote one municipality in the Sarthe, "there is no more sub- ordination, no more discipline; the officer no longer has power over the soldier who, having only two *sols* a day, cannot procure basic necessities."[16] An unbridled soldiery made little distinction between republican villages and rebel ones. As the *Patriote d'Avranche* described it: "Soldiers spread out to the houses of a village and leave nothing, neither lard, nor bread, nor linen, nor silver. The inhabitants are just happy not to be beaten. [The soldiers] even kill those who displease them, patriots or not. Anyone who doesn't allow himself to be pillaged without saying a word is a chouan."[17] In a circular to his officers, Brigade General François Watrin, commander of the Sarthe, frankly acknowledged the indiscriminate provocations that army regulars had caused: "Pillage and disorder have armed many inhabitants against us—people who would never have thought to take up arms if the soldier had left them tranquil in their homes."[18] Hunger's corrosive effects on army discipline were made even worse by the soldiers' cruel vindictive- ness toward the populace. Exaggerated talk from extremists and stubborn defiance from the peasantry stirred their blood-lust. Whatever the origins of insurgency, the experience of counter-insurgency gave it a longer life.

Hoche sent eloquent missives to his generals admonishing them to maintain discipline among the troops, but fine words were one thing and actions another. As late as the end of April 1796, General Dumas, a special emissary to the west, informed the Directory of the deplorable breakdown of order and morality. He decried

> the excesses committed by our troops all over these departments, pacified or
> not, those infested with chouans as well as those delivered from them. Espe-
> cially in the last three or four months, disorder has reached a truly appalling
> point of immorality and inhumanity. Without mentioning the soldiers'
> pillaging of every consumable item, they break, destroy, and burn everything
> that is not personally useful to them. They even rape and sodomize everyone
> they meet, without the least regard for early childhood or the most decrepit
> old age.[19]

Though enriched with hyperbole, this was not mere rhetoric.

Military court records provide abundant evidence of the anarchy and violence sown by soldiers while also underscoring the difficulty of imposing order on them. The registers of the *conseils militaires* that sat at Le Mans and La Flèche during year IV include trial judgments for 118 soldiers charged either with violence against civilians or theft from them. The violence ranged from black eyes and saber gashes to gang rape, kidnapping, manslaughter, and murder. Even theft usually meant violence as well. Yet *conseils militaires* proved a weak reed when attempting to restore military discipline. Only one out of five of these soldiers received sentences of a year in irons or more, whereas roughly two out of five were sent to prison for six months or less, and the rest were acquitted.[20] Many of these acquittals and light sentences were accompanied by the phrase "guilty, but excusable." Drunken brawls were "excusable," thefts of poultry and grain were "excusable," farmhouse raids were "excusable," even ransoming prisoners was "excusable." The inherent weakness of military justice extended to efforts to discipline rogue officers. An extensive inquiry into the behavior of Battalion Chief Jacques Labarrère, the commander at Sillé-le-Guillaume (Sarthe), revealed that he had threatened republican administrators with violence, accepted bribes to exempt farmers from requisitions and urbanites from guard duty, revealed troop movements to the chouans, and even released two rebels from prison. General Watrin responded by relieving Labarrère of his command and charging him with corruption. However, one *conseil militaire* declared itself incompetent due to a lack of senior officers, and another acquitted Labarrère on "lack of evidence."[21] Even if military justice failed them, generals still had the power to cashier subordinates, and Hoche frequently used it.[22] Nonetheless, the Augean stables of military disorder could never be properly cleaned. Though army discipline steadily improved, it remained a concern well into the summer. In fact, tighter controls on marauding came at the same time as pay and provisions were again falling woefully behind and led to a spate of riots and mutinies within weeks of the "pacification."[23]

Further evidence that the general populace experienced subjugation more than pacification comes from the punitive nature of military administration. The most effective measures in the arsenal of repression—rigorous tax collection and systematic disarmament—succeeded because they targeted whole communities. The Directory had authorized Hoche to collect taxes in kind in order to supply the army and authorized the seizure of grain, livestock, and even hostages in towns or villages that refused to turn over weapons. Any recalcitrance in paying back taxes or meeting the quota of usable guns brought punitive fines. These fines were demanded in specie and collected by force. The new system of legalized extortion turned soldiers into gendarmes and bailiffs, as well as herdsmen and wagoneers. In the Sarthe, Watrin issued each commune an individual order requiring the immediate surrender of all guns and specifying in precise quantities how many head of cattle or swine, or how many *quintaux* of grain, fodder, or wood had to be deposited on the basis of their tax delinquency. Defaults were to be made up in hard coin—*assignats* were ruthlessly refused—and the quota of guns was set at one for every two inhabitants. Substitutions were accepted when the products were useful to the army—leather, cloth, canvas—and delays accorded when necessary. Showing too much flexibility could prove counterproductive, however; better to take hostages or billet troops. Occasional use of such tactics proved an inspiration everywhere.[24]

Such tactics, first applied in the Vendée and then extended north of the Loire, had brought rapid capitulation of the main chouan leaders. True to their word, however, republican generals continued to hunt down leaders who refused to surrender. Dozens were captured and killed; others took to living in forest shacks and underground dugouts. Those who gave up their arms were treated with great lenience: émigrés received passports to leave the country, and local *chefs* returned home to reclaim their properties. As a result, Hoche was able to announce in mid-July that the west had been pacified.[25] In fact, however, much work needed to be done. Collective subjugation had to be turned into actual pacification.

## The Directory and "Dirty War," 1796–99

For the next three years, *chouannerie* presented the Directory with a constant challenge to its constitutionalism. National politics and regional rebellion danced a pas de deux throughout the period. Although the coups d'état of Fructidor and Brumaire are commonly understood as parts of the national struggle for power, they were both disproportionately shaped by events in western France. Grand conspiracies and persistent brigandage continued to mingle in confusing and alarming ways. The continued threat of counter-revolution in the region prevented the Directory from overcoming its political insecurities and relying on constitutionalism and the rule of law to build legitimacy. Instead, republican authorities responded with exceptional measures ranging from preventive detention to coup d'état. The result was a prolonged "dirty war." The Directory was clearly winning this

struggle until the crisis of 1799. By then, however, the War of the Second Coalition gave royalists the opportunity once again to try to overthrow the
regime.

As noted earlier, the drift of the Directorial regime toward an increasingly
conservative politics in the summer and autumn of 1796 coincided with the
royalist "Grand Plan" to overthrow the republic through elections rather
than by force of arms. Western departments were crucial to this strategy
and were expected to elect a large number of royalist deputies and department officials. The shift of tactics on the part of counter-revolutionary leaders and the more conservative attitude from the government dramatically
reduced chouan violence. It did not end, however, and any relaxation of
vigilance or reduction in troops brought increased guerrilla activity. Carnot and Pétiet had appointed anti-Jacobin generals throughout the country.
This trend posed a particular risk to republicans in the west. In fact, General Guidot du Repaire, commander of the Twenty-second Military District for most of year V, habitually blamed chouan violence on provocations
from "the extreme party." He accused "these terrorists" of "stirring up the
royalists" in order to achieve their own ends.[26] His obvious hostility toward
republican officials limited repressive action and thus favored the "Grand
Plan." His subordinate, General Vidalot-Dusirat, commander of the Mayenne and Maine-et-Loire, the most chouan-infested departments in the
district, took a dangerously similar attitude. He was considered not only a
partisan of Pichegru but was also accused of deliberately protecting royalists and émigrés.[27] Rural notables took the opportunity to build effective
cadres of opposition, thereby continuing the civil war by political means.
Although the pacification had forced most aristocratic commanders to quit
the west, several soon made their way back. This included Count Rochecotte, who established a web of correspondence between the masterminds
of the "Grand Plan" in the Agence de Paris and local men of influence in
the Sarthe.[28] As a result, the electoral assembly at Le Mans proved solidly
royalist and even elected Rochecotte's treasurer to the town board. Similar
results prevailed throughout the areas of *chouannerie*.

At the national level, the elections of 1797 were a triumph for constitutional royalists, who quickly hesitated to act illegally. It took Hoche's *coup
manqué* of early July before the men of action, most of them inclined to
a full restoration of absolutist monarchy, could make themselves heard.
Prince Louis de la Trémoille, commissioned by the Pretender to create a
new conspiratorial council, arrived in Paris at about the same time. He rapidly gathered a galaxy of chouan and Vendéan commanders around him,

including Frotté, Bourmont, Mesnard, Rochecotte, d'Andigné, Suzannet, d'Autichamp, and La Rochejaquelin. A rapprochement with General Willot, now a deputy in the Council of Five Hundred, led to an invitation for even more chouan *chefs* to rally at Paris. By the end of August, the capital was swarming with royalist warlords and their assorted lieutenants. But again lawmakers hesitated. The coup d'état of 18 fructidor V quashed their inchoate plans. Though the police seized dozens of supposed conspirators, including two dozen deputies, the rebel commanders all escaped.[29] The Triumvirate's focus on the deputies who gathered at Clichy, as well as the failure to capture the emissaries of violent counter-revolution, have almost totally obscured the danger posed by the presence in Paris of so many royalist leaders at such a critical time.[30] The Fructidor coup preempted a royalist coup, only its heart was not in the legislature, but in La Trémoille's *"conseil royal."*

The Fructidor coup left counter-revolution in the hands of regional warlords. In order to have any hope of success against the increasingly mighty republic, they needed a Bourbon willing to set foot in France. Fructidor ruled this out. The coup nullified elections in all ten of the departments affected by *chouannerie* (though not those in the four departments of the *Vendée militaire*). The appointment of scores of new officials across this western zone was followed by a wave of arrests designed to cripple the Catholic and royalist underground. Sporadic and localized resistance ensued, inciting general alarm among republicans.[31] And yet any serious challenge to the republic would require effective leadership. In December 1797, however, the Comte d'Artois dealt a crushing blow to the prospects of renewed civil war in the west. An audacious letter signed in London by the most important leaders of western rebellion tried to shame *Monsieur* into putting himself at the head of a new insurrection. But Artois would have none of it. His refusal even to authorize an insurrection, on the grounds that it would only provoke useless bloodshed, left the leaders of western counter-revolution in complete disarray.[32] Puisaye left for Canada, while most of the rest spent the next two years in Britain, scheming and talking tough, but out of touch with conditions in France.

The royal refusal to head a unified insurrection reduced *chouannerie* to its local roots in peasant grievances and antirepublican animosities. The subjugation of 1796 had brought western departments into the constitutional republic. As long as the authorities exempted the region from conscription and showed a reasonable tolerance for Catholic worship, royalists had little hope of inspiring another mass uprising. Yet tensions remained

high. Together die-hard chouans and outright bandits painted a Hierony-
mus Bosch portrait of mail-coach robberies, farmhouse raids, kidnaps for
ransom, revenge killings, and bad-weather ambushes. Most of these were
committed by isolated bands of a dozen members or less. All the same, they
sowed considerable fear and prompted officials to warn already-wary peasants not to open their homes to strangers. Despite efforts to protect the
moral justifications of *chouannerie,* it increasingly deteriorated into ordinary brigandage. Michel-François Quesne, for example, a tenant farmer at
St-George-Le-Gaultier (Sarthe), had repeatedly threatened and even beat
Jean Bailleul to dissuade him from taking over his lease. When this failed,
Louis Perdreau, Quesne's former chouan commander, helped him to plot
an elaborate farm invasion. Perdreau advised the hapless Quesne and his
companions "to kill and steal as much as they could so that people would
not attribute the crimes to chouans, but to robbers and murderers."[33] This is
only one in a salad of examples in which criminal conduct served to spread
alarm. Isolated women became favorite targets, women such as the Widow
Crain from near Lorient, who gave up her savings of 660 francs only after
having her feet so badly burned that she was crippled for seven weeks. The
perpetrators were five chouans wearing masks, a sure sign of their descent
into brigandage.[34]

Heinous acts of *chauffage* against private persons were supplemented by
attacks on agents of the republic. Reports from the Twenty-second Military
District during the summer of 1798 provide a catalogue of such events:

- At Chantenay, near Sablé, a municipal agent was assaulted in his house
  by 4 brigands who took his money and his watch, plus the guns of the
  soldiers lodging there.
- Five leagues from La Flèche, at Foulletourte, *Coeur d'Acier* and 5 chouans
  held up the stagecoach from Paris to Nantes, and searched the trunk to
  see if there was any of the Republic's money.
- The receipts of the tax collector at Bazouges were taken by 7 villains,
  most of them disguised as soldiers, [who], by an iniquitous imposture,
  spread the rumor that the plunder had been committed by the soldiers
  stationed at Vaiges and Saugé.
- A former adjutant-general, Choltière, hunting with three youths from Laval, was massacred at the entrance to a nearby forest.[35]

And the list went on, not enough to cause panic, but certainly enough to
sap the regime's credibility.

Such attacks were made possible, in part at least, by the reduced level of armed force in the region. In the wake of pacification, massive troop transfers to Italy and the Rhine and the formation of an expeditionary force for Ireland cut the forces of the Army of Ocean Coasts in half. This left about 54,000 men for the four military districts (Twelfth, Thirteenth, Fourteenth, and Twenty-second) that reemerged once the army was dissolved on 1 vendémiaire V (22 September 1796).[36] The demands of coastal defense meant that only fifteen to twenty thousand regular troops were available to maintain security in the interior. Their extensive police operations included defending towns, patrolling roads, checking passports, making arrests, escorting mail coaches, and, most taxing of all, searching the many walled farms and small châteaux that dotted the region.[37] And yet foreign war brought further troop withdrawals. By 1 germinal VI (21 March 1798), the forces in these same four districts had fallen to thirty-five thousand men, still mostly stationed along the coast. As a result, the Twenty-second Military District now had only six light infantry battalions, two artillery companies, and a company of veterans, or 5,351 troops in all, to cover five departments. The glaring lack of cavalry was typical—and just cause for concern. Though various units came and went, the available forces remained much the same for the next year.[38]

The chronic shortage of manpower made it imperative for commanders to maximize troop effectiveness. The army's role in policing the Twenty-second Military District increased sharply when General Louis-Antoine Vimeux took over in the summer of 1797. Vimeux, a grizzled veteran with forty-four years of service, half of them in the ranks, was well acquainted with counter-insurgency. He had been in the Vendée since August 1793 and replaced the infamous General Turreau in May 1794. Despite his age, Vimeux had lost none of his vigor and made regular tours of his district. His *roturier* background fostered an abiding hatred of aristocrats and priests, which combined with his disinterest in politics to make him an ideal servant of the Second Directory. Vimeux insisted on maximum activity from his men and had them constantly formed into mobile columns out scouring the countryside. As many as thirty small columns could be on the march at once. Each was equipped with detailed instructions to ensure that no village went unsearched while also being admonished not to alienate the populace: "only individuals notoriously known to be dangerous" were to be disturbed. No matter the care in preparation, these exhausting expeditions rarely yielded impressive results. In one case, fourteen detachments crisscrossed the *bocage* of the eastern Mayenne, "searching all the mills, small inns and taverns, as well as the different *métairies*." They traced their routes in both directions over five or six days. The results: one arrest and the kill-ing of "a lot of mad dogs and cattle."[39] Vimeux blamed the fruitlessness of such exercises on the aid rural inhabitants gave to outlaws, whether refrac-tory priests or highway robbers, and advocated using more subtle methods such as disguising soldiers and paying spies.[40]

False chouans were a marked feature of counter-insurgency. Deserters from units stationed in western France, even those from vastly different parts of the country, often joined the rebels, thus making it easy to disguise regular soldiers as false deserters in order to penetrate the networks of re-sistance. False chouans, however, faced the great peril of being vulnerable to both sides. The report of Pierre Dusac, a gendarme from Le Mans, and four carabineers from the detachment stationed there, offers a rare glimpse into one of these missions. Disguised as chouans, armed with a musket and two pistols each, and claiming to have deserted their units in Brittany, the five men went looking for the hideouts of "Coeur-d'Acier" (Pierre Gaultier) and "Monsieur Charles" (Claude-Augustin Tercier). Several days of passing from one farm to another, then being directed explicitly to a widow's farm-house and from there to an isolated château, yielded several good meals but no good information. After a great deal of walking, the five men stopped for wine only to be rudely refused by the innkeeper, who had the tocsin rung, which forced them to scatter into the woods. The next day, after a night of grand hospitality at the château of Bellefille, to no practical purpose, and a dangerous encounter with a score of soldiers, they decided to act more like real chouans. The five men stopped a passing horseman, put a pistol to his head and accused him of being a republican. To prove his true loyalties, the horseman led them to three chouans hiding in his barn where a shoot-out ensued. One chouan was killed, another escaped, and the third was arrested. The false chouans then carried on with their mission. Just when they finally obtained useful information, however, they were surrounded by a detachment of troops. Only a convincing effort to throw off their assumed identities saved the lives of the intrepid imposters. This time their cover was truly blown, and they came away no closer to finding Gaultier and Tercier than when they began.[41] These five days of adventure typify the climate of suspicion and insecurity that hung over the whole region of *chouannerie.*

Vimeux was not alone in using trickery and espionage to ferret out op-ponents of the regime. Wherever *chouannerie* remained active, officials supplemented their use of force with various ruses. As a result, the chouan bands faced an infestation of spies and informants, many of them women. Erstwhile rebels also took advantage of promising offers by denouncing comrades, hideouts, and munitions stores. Furthermore, the authorities paid patriots and draft dodgers to enlist in elite counter-chouan units or enroll in more defensive "territorial guards." Though often effective, such special units proved difficult to sustain.[42] The more these techniques of deception appeared in the toolkit of counter-insurgency, however, the harder it became to make them work and the more dangerous life became for everyone. Given the level of treachery and betrayal, it is not surprising that Prévost alias Laurent, one of the republicans' most successful spies in the Sarthe, turned out to be a double agent and was soon arrested by his employers. Two other spies, a police commissioner from Le Mans and a gendarme from Saint-Denis-d'Orgue, were discovered by the chouans and summarily shot. In 1798, Vimeux, who had long employed espionage and counter-chouans, became convinced that these were now "exhausted means . . . dangerous to use at this time."[43] And yet the practice continued. The infamous Branche d'Or was a case in point. Antoine Dubois, masquerading as Grignet d'Enguy, marquis de la Geslinière, had joined the chouans in 1796. After a court-martial and time in prison, his spy-master at Angers arranged for him to escape in February 1799. He promptly joined the chouans around Le Mans and enlisted as an agent of the department commissioner, Baudet-Dubourg. But years of intrigue went to Dubois' head. Under the name of Branche d'Or, he organized his own band and perpetrated a series of villainous assaults and kidnappings that discredited the chouans. Pursued by royalists and republicans alike, the double imposter was finally killed in November 1799 by rebels acting on orders from the chief royalist commander, Count Bourmont, who was honoring a request from the new minister of police, Fouché himself![44] Such treacherous conditions made it almost impossible for the Directory to reconcile inhabitants to the republic.

Nor did the various prosecutorial practices used against rebels do much to restore confidence or heal divisions. The punctilious code of police procedures was difficult enough to follow for ordinary crime; it was little more than embarrassing when dealing with simmering insurgency and constant brigandage. Hoche knew that counter-insurgency could not be run according to the legal niceties of the *Code des délits et des peines* and had no illusions about how to proceed after the pacification. He planned to keep a number of Vendéan leaders in prison and advised arresting others whose "suspicious behavior" warranted it. He thought such men ought either to be imprisoned until peace or deported; they should be tried only if necessary.[45] This logic persisted in the ensuing years, especially during the Second Directory.

The Fructidor coup brought a wave of arrests across the country. Authorities in western France used the opportunity to round up the usual suspects. Operations in the Sarthe are illustrative. Two months after the coup, lieutenants of Count Rochecotte stabbed to death the department commissioner, Antoine Maguin, in the streets of Le Mans. Republicans were stunned. The minister of police promptly doubled the funds to pay for spies and informants, and the department issued a spate of arrest warrants. The risk of keeping leading royalists in the often-porous jail at Le Mans, however, as well as a general concern about the vagaries of the justice system, saw fifteen of them transferred to Paris.[46] There they spent the next six months in the Force state prison without ever facing charges. In the meantime, the army assisted the gendarmerie in "arresting all the chouan leaders of note as a security measure." A few were imprisoned at Le Mans, and others were sent to Angers, where they could be prosecuted by military courts.[47] Many did not go on trial for months; others never were prosecuted and yet remained in prison all the same.

These were not local aberrations; the tension between administrative orders and judicial norms ran to the very top. When the Directory issued arrest warrants in May 1798 for a half-dozen notables presumed to be part of Rochecotte's royalist committee at Le Mans, the magistracy declined to prosecute them. "It is impossible to put them on trial due to a lack of proof," wrote the court commissioner; "they have always put the fanatics out front and remained behind the curtain." Therefore, the administrators of the Sarthe ordered them interned under police surveillance, a dubious move that was endorsed by the minister of police nonetheless.[48] Much the same thing happened before the elections of 1799. As it was explained to General Jacques-Léonard Muller, newly appointed to command the Twelfth Military District (headquarters in Nantes), in areas affected by the Vendée rebellion and *chouannerie*, the minister of police, in concert with department authorities and "as an extraordinary measure of general police"—that is, without the participation of the judiciary—had ordered the arrest of rebel leaders "violently suspected of wanting to renew the civil war."[49] It is clear, therefore, that the preference for preventive detention over actual trials became common practice in the west, and probably in the south,[50] well before its general use in Napoleonic France.

It is not surprising that the practices of counter-insurgency did not conform to the normal code of police and judicial conduct. Perhaps more surprising, especially given the experiences of modern times, is the absence of complaints about systematic torture while in custody. No doubt the Enlightenment critique of judicial torture had a dampening effect. And yet common sense tells us that the brutal realities of a prolonged guerrilla struggle surely involved the serious abuse of prisoners. Many must have believed that lives depended on it. Perhaps the best indication of such practices comes from reading between the lines of a counter-insurgency operation in the Mayenne. On 7 fructidor VI (24 August 1798), the gendarmerie arrested two of the four Barbier brothers, René and Daniel, both educated weavers living at Saint-Berthevin, west of Laval. A bit of digging in their earthen cellar turned up a box containing two muskets, one with a cross and heart made of nail heads on the stock; two white flags; the last letter from a priest about to be executed ("From my cell, 10 May 1796: Just a few more hours, my dear parishioners, and I shall exist no more . . ."); a notebook entitled "Collection of the rarest secrets of the magical arts"; various pieces of linen and silver stolen in a recent holdup of the stagecoach from Rennes to Paris; and a list of those who were to receive proceeds from the robbery. Such a mass of incriminating evidence made it easy to send them before a military court, but department authorities had bigger fish to catch and so turned René and Daniel into bait. The first big fish was another brother, Joseph Barbier, who belonged to an elusive chouan band that had plagued the area for years. In order to get Joseph's cooperation, civilian officials arranged to have his brothers' conditions improved in prison, which included removing their agonizing leg irons, and intervened with the local jury director to delay their trial, no doubt suggesting that they might never stand trial at all. After some hesitation, Joseph Barbier and an associate named Clément agreed to cooperate with authorities against their former comrades. Therefore, when the two informers returned to their native St-Berthevin, a noted haven for chouans, the informers were put under the protection of local troops, at least for a time. Using their new information, these same troops managed to capture six of the band members at nearby Loiron, all of whom were killed en route to the prison at Laval. According to the official report, one prisoner broke free, and then "the others revolted in such a manner that the commander was forced and constrained to fire on them in order to prevent their escape." Far from conducting an inquiry into how six bound and unarmed men could not be safely escorted by a detachment of troops, the department administrators rewarded these "brave republicans" with 600 francs to be shared among them.[51] Here was a sign of things to come.

Once officials had broken up the band, Joseph and Clément were accused of renewing their criminal associations and soon "rendered incapable of doing harm," that is, they "died resisting the forces of order." Having disposed of these awkward turncoats, the authorities no longer had promises to keep and so transferred René and Daniel Barbier to the jury director at Vitré (Ille-et-Vilaine), who sent them on to a military court at Rennes. "The Barbiers had influence in Saint-Berthevin," wrote a local official; "everybody feared them and their arrest produced a general joy; some showed it openly, while others didn't dare, for fear of soon seeing them reappear." The military court ended these concerns. It convicted René and Daniel Barbier of receiving stolen goods and had them shot. The civil court also condemned Saint-Berthevin to paying 3,000 francs in fines, and shortly thereafter authorities rounded up another dozen residents.[52] Saint-Berthevin had been broken as a center of chouan activity. The whole operation turned on the ability of officials to manipulate both the conditions of imprisonment and the possibility of prosecution in order to extort information from hardened chouans. Set alongside the killing of eight band members, six while in army custody and two while under army protection, the treatment of the Barbier brothers leaves no doubt that those who engaged in counter-insurgency experienced few limits on how they dealt with prisoners. Though not an explicit part of the documentary record (even in chouan memoirs), police methods surely included systematic abuses.

The aggressive conduct of gendarmes earned them special antipathy. Their persistent harassment of amnestied chouans, their part in directing false chouans operations, and their abuse of prisoners made them the most feared and the most loathed members of the state apparatus. The chouans' merciless treatment of captured gendarmes is itself evidence of the ferocity of the police.[53] Add to this the frequency with which chouans were shot while in custody, either shortly after capture or while being transferred between prisons,[54] and it quickly becomes apparent that the "security forces" used all means fair or foul in their "dirty war" in the west. Civilian authorities were fully complicit. Department administrators, often inspired by their respective government commissioners, endorsed and even promoted the use of exceptional measures, including collective sureties and paid assassinations.[55] When they had doubts about the elasticity of the constitution, they sought advice from the government and got inconsistent answers. One thing was clear, however, the Second Directory interpreted violent resistance to the republic as a license to use whatever means were necessary to root it out, as long as they were used discretely.

And the regime was winning. This did not mean that the "perfect tranquility" intermittently described in official reports actually pertained to large areas or long periods. Such claims were all relative. Sporadic assaults, extortions, kidnappings, and robberies continued to plague the west, especially north of the Loire. As we have seen, much of this activity amounted to little more than criminal banditry. The lack of coherence in *chouannerie* resulted mainly from successful operations against key leaders, especially in the western departments of the Twenty-second Military District. The most important of these was the enterprising Count Rochecotte, royalist commander of "les provinces du Maine, du Perche et du pays Chartrain." Betrayed by one of his lieutenants, whose infidelity was rumored to have been purchased for 50,000 francs, Rochecotte was condemned to death by a military commission at Paris and shot on the Champs du Mars on 20 thermidor VI (7 August 1798).[56] A few months later, his interim successor, Claude-Augustin Tercier, a courageous but ineffective leader, was also arrested in Paris. The police failed to learn his true identity, however, and before long he escaped from the Temple prison.[57] In the meantime, numerous lesser *chefs* and their die-hard followers were tracked down and either killed in shoot-outs or captured and sent before military courts. Reports from Vimeux to the government during the summer and autumn of 1798 are replete with details of these local successes. As a result, the balance of fear tipped in favor of the army. As one biweekly report put it, "The numerous arrests being made in the district due to the troops' activity, and the zeal of their leaders, have terrorized the enemies of the government in the formerly insurgent departments."[58] And yet *chouannerie* refused to die.

By the spring of 1799, the persistence of isolated ambushes and uncoordinated assaults had provoked the full panoply of military repression. As chouan activities intensified in the winter of year VII, which they always did in the agricultural off-season, the authorities applied the laws of 10 vendémiaire IV (on communal responsibility for attacks on their territory) and 29 nivôse VI (on military justice for brigands) with ever more frequency.[59] And yet regional commanders asked for more. This included proposing the essentials of the law of hostages and the resurrection of military commissions *à la Quiberon*. The Directory declined to go that far but did respond with added repression. The government brought the four western military districts (a total of sixteen departments) under the Army of England, ordered a "grand sweep" (*battue générale*) throughout the region, enabled military courts to judge all brigands arrested while armed, and authorized local commanders to impose the "state of siege" wherever they saw fit.[60] Together these measures constituted a formidable arsenal in the hands of General Auguste Moulin, the army's new commander-in-chief. Though he had the means to contain *chouannerie,* he lacked enough troops to crush it. The Directory, therefore, required nine western departments exempted from conscription, plus the three departments of Normandy, to mobilize national guardsmen. Moulin demanded between two and six hundred men from each department. The response was slow and fraught with difficulties, especially in providing weapons and equipment. Although only "proven republicans" were enrolled, guardsmen made poor substitutes for regular troops and were unreliable far from home.[61]

Problems of this sort point to the exceptional delicacy of applying exceptional measures. Opinions differed sharply, even among those in charge of repression. Not only did the various ministries have different perspectives on the problems of security, but a rapid turnover in ministers kept policy in constant flux.[62] Minister of Police Duval cautioned Moulin: "Placed between the necessity of using rigorous measures to prevent a new explosion and the fear of exciting it by generalizing them, you must use great circumspection." Moulin agreed and focused on defeating active bands and punishing the communities that supported them. Nonetheless, he found himself on the defensive against Duval's new colleague at the War Ministry. General Milet-Mureau, a model apparatchik, reproached Moulin for directing all of his efforts against "brigands who made themselves conspicuous" while doing nothing "to arrest the other hidden brigands." Moulin forcefully opposed the idea of rounding up former chouan leaders, rightly fearing that such action would be decried as a violation of the pacification treaty and used to persuade former chouans that the regime had again proscribed them all. This would be the pretext for retired rebels to join a new insurgency.[63]

Moulin's concerns notwithstanding, local officials undertook another wave of arbitrary arrests. The purpose was not so much to combat *chouannerie* as to hamstring political opponents. On the eve of the elections of 1799, the Sarthe's administrators ordered a score of well-known royalists to turn themselves in at Le Mans. The central commissioner also secretly authorized a few arrests in each of the principal towns of the department. Despite the scandal these actions caused, the government's overblown rhetoric of counter-insurgency made it impossible to disavow them.[64] Furthermore, several departments, including the Sarthe and Mayenne, had begun to arrest family members of known chouans and to imprison local notables as hostages following acts of violence. These experiences, as well as those in Belgium the year before, persuaded the Directory to authorize the arrest of known royalists or former chouans wherever a "hostile act of chouannerie, rebellion, murder, kidnapping, arson, or pillage" had been committed.[65] Such responses to the continued threat of *chouannerie* in the spring of 1799 reflected a growing confusion between exceptional measures needed for pacification and an extension of these measures to target purely political enemies of those in power. Here was the slippery slope to the "law of hostages."

The law of 24 messidor VII (12 July 1799) fused Jacobin ideological assumptions about the republic's enemies with inadequate mechanisms for government control. Though nominally a means to combat brigandage, the law of hostages made the relatives of émigrés and former nobles the main targets of repression. The families of known bandits or rebel leaders were included as possible hostages, but they were explicitly given lower priority. In the case of an attack on a public official, soldier, or purchaser of national property, the Directory could deport four hostages, starting with relatives of émigrés, followed by former nobles, and only then by members of rebel families. Supporters even described the law of 24 messidor VII as a supplement to the exclusionary laws of 3 brumaire IV, 19 fructidor V, and 9 frimaire VI aimed at nobles, émigrés, and their relatives.[66] Opponents doubted the efficacy of such an approach to counter-insurgency. Would brigands really care if anyone other than their immediate family were interned, subjected to punitive fines, or deported? Besides, nobles did not pose the greatest threat.[67] The law's ideological thrust and the arbitrary power it gave local officials made it a terrorist measure par excellence.

This infamous law earned the Directory great opprobrium in exchange for little effective counter-insurgency. The inherent dangers of the law struck anyone interested in genuine pacification. Even the new minister of police, Joseph Fouché, never squeamish about harsh measures per se, worried about its use: "The leading authorities must have an eye constantly open on the application of the law of 24 messidor in order that it never be used impetuously, that it not become an instrument of vengeance, hatred or private interest, and that it never touch the peaceful citizen who respects the law, but only the one who, by his past conduct, current relations, movements and discourse, is presumed to be an accomplice of our enemies."[68] Though presumptions are not a good basis for internment, the tone of Fouché's letter helps to explain why, having adopted the law, the Councils rarely approved requests for its application. In place of whole departments, lawmakers whittled down zones of applicability to a specified list of cantons or even just a few communes. This prevented overly zealous department officials from conducting wholesale roundups and thereby stirring up trouble in areas of relative peace. The Councils authorized the law only for the Haute-Garonne following the insurrection around Toulouse, four western departments (Côtes-du-Nord, Ille-et-Vilaine, Mayenne, Sarthe), and parts of four other departments in the northwest (Maine-et-Loire, Morbihan, Manche, Calvados). These western areas were all regions of *chouannerie*. On the other hand, lawmakers pointedly rejected the law of 24 messidor VII for the four departments of the former *Vendée militaire*.[69] And for good reason. As General Moulin had feared, targeting political opponents as much as active chouans helped to spread the rebellion. Notables who merely despised the regime now had reason to work to overthrow it. As the chouan leader Chappedelaine later wrote, "The law of hostages alone did more for the party in two weeks than all the initiatives we undertook in several months of touring the region."[70]

## Renewed Rebellion

Much of the sporadic violence experienced in the west in the three years following the "pacification" of 1796 was the inevitable detritus of civil war. All the same, the provocations on the part of republican zealots had kept the embers of resentment glowing. Of greatest importance was the regime's unwillingness to honor the level of tolerance for Catholic worship contained in the pacification agreements. Even more than elsewhere in the country, tensions between juring priests, nonjuring priests, and republican officials often degenerated into open conflict. The law of 19 fructidor V had enabled department authorities to respond to these incidents by sending refractory priests before military commissions or by ordering the deportation of constitutional priests who stirred up trouble. Western departments made extensive use of these provisions. Those departments of the Twenty-second Military District most affected by *chouannerie* saw the greatest religious persecution. In the two years after Fructidor, forty-five priests were arrested in the Sarthe. Nineteen of these were deported and one executed. In the Mayenne, eighty priests were arrested, twenty-one deported, and three executed. The arrest orders were even higher in the Maine-et-Loire, where 140 warrants were issued and two priests executed. Those priests fortunate enough merely to be imprisoned tended to be old or infirm. Numbers alone do not reveal the arbitrariness of department authorities. Their wide discretionary powers made it easy to single out almost any priest who caused offense. Even married priests could find themselves consigned to the fetid prison colony on the Ile de Ré. Selective enforcement of the ban on public expressions of piety also aroused animosity. In particular, imposing collective fines for funeral processions or sending soldiers to dismantle calvary sites was heavy-handed and impossible to do with even a shred of equity,[71] Whereas the recourse to "preventive detention" mostly offended notables, the harassment of priests and sporadic crackdown on Catholic practices fostered support for continued resistance among all groups. Together they became the seedbed of renewed rebellion.

The recrudescence of *chouannerie* in the summer and autumn of 1799 helped to give the end of the Directory an air of inevitability. And yet the insurgency was less a sign of domestic collapse than a symptom of the international effort to defeat the French republic. That the Directory mismanaged the spring campaign, mainly due to domestic politics, only invited trouble. The Directors foolishly ordered an offensive by three well-separated armies, each of which was badly outnumbered and soon in retreat. Their concern about the impact on spring elections then led the Directors to refuse to evacuate southern Italy as well as to delay another round of conscription despite the desperate need for troops.[72] The consequences proved decisive for western counter-revolution. News of Russian and Austrian victories infused chouan leaders with sudden hope. Their desultory efforts to organize resistance grew into a grandiose strategy to aid the allies in toppling the hated republic. With inspiration came opportunity. The republican defeats in Italy and Switzerland forced the Directory to transfer large numbers of troops from the interior to the frontiers. The first wave of transfers, totaling twenty infantry battalions and fourteen cavalry squadrons, followed the elections of April 1799. Fear of domestic unrest led the Directors to oppose more withdrawals until early June, when intense pressure from the War Ministry finally pried loose another nineteen battalions and two squadrons. Half of these units came from the Army of England. The increased risk of an English landing required most of its remaining units to be stationed along the coasts and thus left interior areas with too few forces to maintain order. In particular, the Twenty-second Military District was reduced to 2,833 men, or less than half its usual complement.[73] It was this drastic cut in forces that made the autumn insurgency possible.

The *chouannerie* of 1799 was as much a part of the allied war effort as it was a resurgence of peasant rebellion. A royalist proclamation to republican troops and mobile columns began: "the royal army of the departments of the West is going to act en masse, in concert with the coalition powers, to put an end to the calamities of our *patrie*."[74] As a consequence, the uprising had a more military aspect than ever before. The leaders, all regional warlords with commissions from the Pretender, had planned the insurrection while still in exile and decided details at the château of La Jonchère on 15 September. The strategy was simultaneously to seize a half-dozen key urban centers before spreading to envelop the entire northwest. The timing was set for mid-October, after the harvest. In the meantime, restless bands escalated their violence and pressed recruitment. As had been the case four years earlier, both coercion and pay inducements helped to swell the ranks.[75] Each rebel army had a general staff, complete with officer titles and flashy uniforms. That of the Twenty-second Military District typified this newly militarized *chouannerie*. Louis-Auguste-Victor, comte de Ghaisne de Bourmont, named to command the "Royal Army of Maine," was the young scion of an ancient military family and a *chevalier de Saint-Louis*. He naturally envisioned a very orderly insurrection. Bourmont arrived from England with handpicked officers, arms, powder, and money. His "army" consisted of fifteen "legions," most of which had experienced leaders, even if they had not been active for a while. Together they established order, discipline, and regular payments.[76] Thus, the *chouannerie* of late 1799 was both less popular in origin and more coherent in form than anything seen to date.

Leaders of the new *chouannerie* went to great lengths to generate popular support. They began by astutely calling themselves "l'armée des mécontents." "Discontented" suited just about anyone fed up with political instability and the demands of war, and yet the mass of peasants were not inclined to revolt. Royalist leaders sought to allay fears and win support by exercising greater control over the insurgent forces. They issued a code of military justice in order to maintain discipline and killed brigands who committed their crimes under the cover of *chouannerie*. Dead bodies made the best messengers. "Verdict rendered by the royalists' military court, which condemns to death François Alier, assailant of the *femme* Dahibot," read the placard on a corpse left near Contregud (Maine-et-Loire).[77] Royalist commanders also promised to kill any chouan who deserted his unit, any official who applied republican laws, and any villager who provided information to the regime. Moreover, anyone who "refused to give their all to aid the royalists" would be driven from the countryside and forced to take refuge in towns.[78] Like the Jacobins of 1793, the royalists of 1799 treated indifference to their cause as treason.

The chouan subjugation of Le Mans for three days in October 1799 illustrates the more militarized nature of the insurgency. Bourmont formed his forces into five columns and mounted a coordinated attacked at daybreak on 23 vendémiaire VIII (14 October 1799). The initial assault left General Simon, commander of the Sarthe, badly shot up and unable to direct the republican defense. Otherwise the presence of three hundred regular troops and sixty gendarmes, as well as more than a thousand national guardsmen, might have put up considerable resistance. As it was, two thousand chouans poured into Le Mans before the troops could even get organized.[79] The rebels, well-armed and led by at least two hundred cavalrymen, quickly pinned down the soldiers in their quarters at the St-Vincent Abby. After seven hours of heavy fire, the rebels dragged cannons from the arsenal and forced the soldiers to retreat through a breach in the garden wall. They had suffered thirty to forty casualties, or about ten times the chouans' losses. Bourmont practiced a severe discipline over his men during the ensuing occupation and had three of them shot for pillaging. The vengeful inhabitants of the lower town proved harder to control, but only a few houses were truly ransacked. The bulk of chouan forces evacuated Le Mans each evening and returned in the morning in order to avoid being besieged by republican troops. On the third day, the rebels gathered in the Place des Halles, where Bourmont conducted a full military review. The rebel columns then marched out of town bearing enormous booty: 50,000 francs in tax receipts, six cannons, five to six hundred muskets, ten thousand cartridges, five or six barrels of powder, two hundred horses, and a mass of other effects valued at close to a million francs.[80] All of this was distributed among the various commanders, whose units then scattered in different directions.

The capture of Le Mans, a town of nineteen thousand inhabitants, was the greatest single triumph in the history of *chouannerie*. Early reports grossly exaggerated the number of chouans and the extent of devastation. A wave of panic naturally swept local administrations, many of whom simply fled. Those who had shown little political commitment to date plumped for the "discontents." News from Le Mans also inspired the insurgency elsewhere. The chouans invaded Nantes and Saint-Brieuc in late October, but a shortage of manpower forced them to withdraw immediately. Furthermore, attacks on Fontenay-le-Peuple, Vannes, and Vire all failed miserably. Even Bourmont's subsequent assault on the small bourg of Ballée became a bloody fiasco.[81] Although the coordinated rebellion came at a precarious time for the republic, the success at Le Mans could not be matched.

As was the case with the foreign war, the Directory clearly turned the tide of western insurgency before the Brumaire coup d'état. General Vimeux marched against Le Mans at the head of 2,800 regular troops. They were the first of 6,400 hardened veterans who, having been taken prisoner in Italy and then returned on condition of serving elsewhere, arrived in the west in the autumn of 1799. The defeat of the Anglo-Russian invasion in Holland enabled the Directory to transfer another four demi-brigades to the west. Various regional forces also bolstered the forces of repression. Seven departments south and west of Le Mans received orders to send mobile columns of national guardsmen, and battalions of conscripts from another eight departments south of the troubled zone were ordered to join the Army of England.[82] Moreover, the conscription law of 14 messidor VII (2 July 1799) required western departments exempted from conscription to muster their conscripts into special "free corps" for regional use. This proved ill-advised in places and at times even dangerous: local conscripts did not trust the government and had no desire to fight the chouans. Willingness to serve in such units improved only after they were reformed into departmental "legions."[83] Despite difficulties, this was an impressive buildup of armed force for a regime generally condemned for ineptitude. It was certainly enough to stymie further threats to the republic. The thwarting of the grand offensive in so many areas, the news of repeated republican victories in Switzerland and Holland, and the rapid redeployment of troops to the west combined to break up many of the larger chouan bands. Others simply went home. Even before the overthrow of the Directory, many royalist leaders had come to realize that militarized *chouannerie* was unsustainable.[84]

Matters were less obvious in Paris. The coup d'état of 18–19 brumaire VIII (8–9 November 1799) derived its immediate legitimacy from the crisis of 1799. That this crisis involved a resurgence of extremism on both the right and left seemed to prove that the Constitution of Year III was incapable of ending the French Revolution. The solution, therefore, appeared to lie in new political institutions. But it was the course of international relations that had done the most damage. The great resurgence in domestic unrest did not result so much from failed institutions as from a failed foreign policy, for which General Bonaparte had a lot to answer. The insurgents certainly included "discontents," many of them created by religious intolerance and police harassment. And yet it took the absence of regular troops and the presence of atavistic warlords and British guineas to make the insurrection possible. The impression created in Paris was disproportionate: western insurgency again became the stuff of republican nightmares. Throughout the summer of 1799, Jacobins fed these fears by regaling the legislature with daily accounts of chouan atrocities surging up from a roiling sea of rural hostility. Such breathless panic would undermine the men in power and secure ever more exceptional measures; the result was a resurgence of political extremism and a discredited regime. In this respect, *chouannerie* had a disproportionate part in the Directory's demise. Even as western counter-revolution was on the verge of deteriorating once again into a *micro-guerrilla*, not so much natural to the region as residual to civil war, it served to justify another coup d'état.

## Pacification *Déjà vu*

The Brumaire coup had little impact on efforts to pacify the west. Rather, the republic continued its return to the methods employed by Hoche in 1796: increased manpower, military justice, and massive disarmament. The Directory had given General Gabriel-Joseph de Hédouville, its last appointee as commander of the Army of England, a streamlined version of the instructions it issued to Hoche four years earlier. Even with dictatorial powers and a steady increase in forces, however, Hédouville preferred to negotiate. He had been one of Hoche's closest collaborators in year IV, and yet Hédouville misunderstood the balance between concessions and coercion needed to end the conflict. Rather than energizing the repression, as both the old and new governments wanted him to do, Hédouville sought a gradual disengagement. Without consulting the new government, he pronounced an almost unilateral suspension of hostilities on 3 frimaire VIII (24 November 1799), which included ordering local commanders to end military justice and to release all prisoners held "as a security measure." Hédouville then spent weeks in negotiations, first over armistice terms, then over an actual peace treaty. These were the failed methods of year III.

Anxious about the plebiscite results, the First Consul waited until after the new constitution had been safely adopted before revealing his true strategy, a return to the methods of Hoche and the late Directory.[85] Bonaparte's proclamation on 7 nivôse VIII (28 December 1799) first disparaged the "unjust laws" and "arbitrary acts" that had "offended personal security and freedom of conscience" and then promised a new regime in which "every day is and will be marked by acts of justice." The Consulate also authorized a reopening of churches under the terms of 1795 (nothing more) and granted a "complete and total amnesty" for past events. In return, the insurgents were commanded to dissolve their bands and surrender their weapons.

Communes that continued to resist would be declared "outside the constitution and treated as enemies of the French people."[86] There was nothing
new here. Apart from a few rhetorical particulars, this is how pacification
had begun four years earlier. Once again it was a limited set of inducements
hitched to armed might and exceptional justice that defeated militarized
*chouannerie.*

When royalist leaders hesitated, Bonaparte lost patience. He decided
to cauterize this "open wound" with a hot iron. He authorized the armed
forces to "saber to death inhabitants taken arms in hand" and to shoot immediately "anyone preaching resistance to the army." At the same time, the
government instructed commanders to use military commissions to judge
"brigands." On 16 January 1800, it suspended the constitution throughout
Brittany. At the same time, the Vendée, Mayenne, Maine-et-Loire, and
Sarthe remained under state of siege.[87] Bonaparte instructed the Jacobin
General Guillaume Brune, the severe new commander of the Army of
the West (composed of forty thousand regular troops and ten thousand
national guardsmen), to make the insurgents "feel all the weight and hor-
rors of war." This meant supplying the army at local expense, using military
courts to judge rebels, and delivering rebellious communes to the army's
discretion. Bonaparte even advised Brune to "burn some *métairies* and
some large villages in the Morbihan" in order to terrorize "the inhabitants
to unite themselves against the brigands and realize finally that their apathy
is self-destructive."[88]

After tough talk came mixed action. General Brune summarized his
strategy, "I bring terror and respect, and General Hédouville attracts trust."
By continuing to negotiate long after his policy had been disavowed, Hédouville split the royalist camp. His generous peace terms persuaded half
the rebel leaders to surrender before the truce expired on 21 January 1800.
Aggressive pursuit and official treachery took care of the rest. Bourmont,
believing that he was about to conclude surrender terms, was instead
ambushed and roundly trounced at Meslay near Laval in one of the few
pitched battles of the insurrection. He immediately wrote to Hédouville
seeking peace and within two weeks had surrendered. Bourmont ordered
his legions to disband, and they largely did as they were told, partly because
they would no longer be paid and partly because the population showed
little enthusiasm for armed resistance. Meanwhile, more leaders abandoned the struggle. Faced with Brune's build-up of troops, even Georges
Cadoudal in Brittany and the comte de Frotté in Normandy sought to make
peace on Hédouville's terms. Cadoudal fled to England, but Frotté was in-

famously condemned by an impromptu military commission and executed along with six fellow officers, promises of safe conduct notwithstanding.[89] Bonaparte had his way of waging "dirty war" too.

The surrender or execution of émigré warlords ended coordinated counter-revolution in the west. This did not, however, extinguish the embers of *chouannerie*. A republication of the amnesty on 14 ventôse (5 March 1800) now insisted that all chouans, not just "masterless men," turn in their weapons in order to qualify, a flagrant violation of several terms of surrender negotiated by Hédouville. No matter. In accordance with the master's orders, Brune organized an aggressive and sometimes brutal campaign of disarmament. One of the columns assigned this task killed thirty people at Champé (Mayenne) when the village refused to disarm. Two months of this yielded more than twenty-five thousand guns from eight departments, and still more were being collected. At the same time, the army engaged in heavy-handed and often illegal tax collection, in part because it was allowed to keep half the receipts. Certain officials inevitably took the atmosphere of sustained repression as an invitation to renew their factional persecutions. Localized bands answered these various aggressions with classic hit-and-run tactics designed to punish patriots and keep the republic at bay. These latter-day chouans have often been dismissed as pure brigands, but they were just as often die-hard royalists out to fund their operations and settle scores regardless of popular opinion. As a result, chouan violence continued to agitate significant parts of the west, notably in Maine and Basse-Bretagne, well after the civil war ended.[90]

The Consulate extended constitutional rule to Brittany on 1 floréal VIII (21 April 1800), thereby officially ending the civil war—again. This gave the regime a propaganda coup on the eve of its offensive against Austria. It also facilitated the transition to prefects. It did not mean, however, that the west had been fully pacified or that exceptional measures had been abandoned. Royalist leaders continued to receive large infusions of cash; the English fleet cruised the coast looking for an opportunity to land; and assaults on public coaches and purchasers of national land remained alarmingly common. General Debelle, interim commander of the Army of the West, responded to the persistence of such bands by ordering subordinate officers "not to escort to prison" any band leaders caught arms in hand. Roadside executions multiplied, as intended. When General Bernadotte arrived to take command, he both refused to lift the state of siege covering scores of communes and insisted that all chouans captured in Brittany be judged by army officers according to the code of military justice.[91] Thus, the Consulate's promise that every day would be marked by acts of justice was matched instead by continued use of exceptional measures to quell resistance. Once again, the area infected by *chouannerie* was not so much pacified as subjugated.

Despite the role of *chouannerie* in the coups d'état of both Fructidor and Brumaire, the continuities of the guerrilla struggle between 1795 and 1801 persisted. As long as the republic, whatever its constitutional framework, could not act from a position of armed strength, it could not subdue the rebels. Concessions on conscription and Catholic worship in year III and again in year VIII helped to erode popular support, but the enduring infrastructure of resistance—built on resentment, revenge, and royalism—meant that pacification always equaled military subjugation. The republic's chronic shortage of troops, inability to apply policies consistently, and recourse to "dirty tricks" in counter-insurgency lasted as long as it took to build an apparatus of order. Only in 1802, with the Peace of Amiens and the Concordat, did the dangers of a desultory insurgency begin to subside. By then the administrative and police apparatus of the emergent "security state" (see chapter 12) had sufficient capacity to master the rancor of returned émigrés and the truculence of the "petite église" with its refractory clergy and die-hard parishioners.

# 10 A Cycle of Violence in the South

The brigands who have attacked and pillaged public funds several times
on the highway continue to perpetrate excesses and to stamp terror on the
hearts of the citizens of Gignac and Lodève. . . . Justice is paralyzed by a
lack of witnesses and by jury decisions. . . . Military commissions ought to
be charged with prosecuting the crimes these brigands may commit.
—Nogaret, prefect of the Hérault, to the minister of justice, 7 frimaire IX
(28 November 1800)

AS WITH POLITICS, all violence is local. Also as with politics, local violence becomes increasingly significant when it resonates with regional or
national trends. Figure 13 is an attempt to schematize the reflexive relationship that existed between national political issues and local experiences of
violence and disorder during the First Republic. This is a sort of Ezekiel's
vision replete with four winged beings, each moving wheels within wheels.
The outer circle represents the entire country; the intermediate-sized circles
stand for regions of greater or lesser importance; and the smallest circles
take the place of smaller locales, such as single departments, major cities,
or rural districts. The circles should be understood not as cogged gears but
as smooth rims that tend to make each other turn due to friction. Although
the four forces of royalism, Catholicism, war, and Jacobinism are shown
propelling only the national cycle of violence, they should be understood as
equally at work on the smaller circles. As the physics of such a model would
suggest, when one of the smaller "local" circles turns rapidly, it transmits
kinetic energy to an intermediate "regional" circle and from there to the
"national" circle. The mechanical metaphor suggested by this graphic also
has the virtue of suggesting the consequences of slowing down local and
regional "cycles of violence," which then act as drag on the national "cycle of
violence," reducing its speed of rotation. The spatial distribution of circles

in the graphic could be taken to correspond to specific regional dynamics in republican France (the circle in the upper left containing the Vendée and *chouannerie,* the one in the lower right being Provence, with Marseille on the bottom), but perhaps this risks an excess of figurative literalism. It is more important to underscore the two main points conveyed by this image. First, local and regional experiences of order and disorder were critical to the stability of the late republic, perhaps more so than during any other phase of the Revolution. Second, the four main political forces propelling the wheels of local and regional violence, while variable in their respective influence on different localities, were essentially the same basic forces destabilizing the polity throughout the country.

It is easier to schematize the great forces at work in the many cycles of violence across the republic than it is to understand their role in any one of these. As an antidote to generalization at the national level, it is helpful to pick apart the tangled forces at work inspiring and prolonging violence

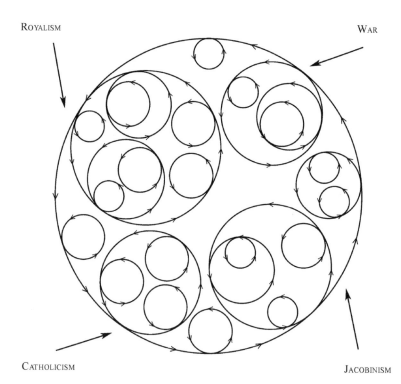

ROYALISM

WAR

CATHOLICISM

JACOBINISM

Fig. 13. Cycles of violence in France.

in a specific locality. This can reveal factors usually treated as background noise—the power of personalities, the influence of parochial issues, the effects of happenstance, etc.—and filtered out in a scholarly effort to draw broader, more meaningful conclusions. The methods of "microhistory" help to recover these elements of the past, but it is the quality and suitability of the case study that determines whether it has larger implications. When it comes to exploring the many factors at work in the local "cycles of violence" during the First Republic, one could hardly do better than the district of Lodève. Here politics and personality, local custom and national crisis, endemic brutality and systemic corruption all came together to create a sustained period of civil strife. This cycle of violence in the southern Cévennes has several larger implications: it belies the usual chronology of the French Revolution, it challenges long-standing claims about the nature of both "neo"-Jacobinism and Catholic royalism, and it highlights the power of regional culture to shape responses to national issues.

## The Setting for a Feud

A paroxysm of banditry and brutal repression rocked the region around Lodève from 1799 to 1801. An investigation into the background of events reveals, however, that more was involved than organized crime. The overlap between peasant resistance, common banditry, and overt counter-revolution is a commonplace of the period. Broad patterns have been widely asserted, but few efforts have been made to clarify the precise relationship in specific times and places. Historians interested in popular violence in Provence after Thermidor tend to see a waning of political factors from 1798 onwards.[1] This is not so clearly the case for Lower Languedoc (and probably not for the Massif Central either).[2] Rather, the forms of violence evolved in accordance with changes in the relationship between local factions and the instruments of state power at their disposal. In the months following the Fructidor coup, open opponents of the Revolution were systematically, and more or less permanently, excluded from serving as municipal agents, justices of the peace, or magistrates. This left them to choose between withdrawing from the contest for local power or becoming outlaws. Sometimes this choice depended on the extent to which the new officials used their authority to persecute past rivals. What is striking about the northern Hérault is how previous animosities inspired ever-greater violence just when it appeared that republicans had finally gained the upper hand. This is made most apparent by the experiences of Gignac, which, despite a fairly unremarkable trajectory through the Revolution, emerged in the late 1790s as one of the most troubled towns in the Hérault. Here violence did not peak during the Great Fear, the Terror, or the Thermidorian Reaction but spiraled out of control from 1797 to 1801.

As happened in so many places in France, Gignac refracted the Revolution through the prism of long-standing rivalries. Gignac was a bourg of 2,400 inhabitants dominated by agriculture (cereals, olives, viticulture) and spin-off manufacturing from the woolens industry at Lodève. A long-standing rivalry between White and Blue Penitents was quickly magnified by the early Revolution. The Hérault's brief flirtation with "federalism" in 1793 further heightened tensions, encouraging intrigue and abuse of authority. All the same, even when social upheaval and political uncertainty reached their apogee in 1794, the struggle to control the levers of power did not degenerate into open bloodletting. The local *comité révolutionnaire* imprisoned only a half-dozen suspects, none of whom perished on the scaffold.[3] There was little basis, therefore, for a violent reaction in 1795, and the transition to the Directory passed peacefully. Nonetheless, those who had been coerced and intimidated during the year II did not forgive easily. One family in particular remained sorely aggrieved.

The three Ponsy brothers, Joseph (thirty-seven), Barthélemy (thirty-three), and Jean (twenty-five) had more notoriety than was good for one family. They were all tall, handsome, blond-haired, blue-eyed, powerfully built, hard-drinking, foul-mouthed, quick-tempered, brutal, lazy, wagon-driving thugs. Their uncle Jean-Baptiste Ponsy (fifty) and his son François (c. twenty-five), also wagon drivers with a penchant for violence, added to the family's muscle-power. Although hardly members of the local elite, the Ponsys appeared in the vanguard of antirevolutionary resistance. They protected nonjuring priests and slaked their thirst for violence by selling their services to the lesser nobility of the area.[4] The eldest brother, Joseph Ponsy, developed a habit of responding to the revolutionary "ça ira" with a "ça n'ira pas" and a cudgel to back it up. As a result he spent the winter of year II in the citadel at Montpellier. Once released, the *comité révolutionnaire* at Gignac tried to have him rearrested, but he fought off the police, yelling, "Let me go, or I'll be guillotined!" and fled.[5] Joseph did not return to Gignac until the Jacobins had been removed from power. Even then, he and his kin did not favor peaceful coexistence. As long as local power remained contested, they were happy to lend a hand to the royalists and reactionaries of the region.

As was the case throughout the Midi, the First Directory lacked the necessary authority to repress the factionalism at Gignac. Although the town was spared serious trouble in the years 1795 and 1796, it continued to be deeply divided along pro- and antirepublican lines. This left it vulnerable to agitation from neighboring communities. For example, Martin Arnavielle of nearby Aniane often hosted gatherings of royalist agitators at his farm. These included his fellow villagers the Issert brothers, both tanners, and Tinte the school teacher, as well as other troublemakers from the region such as the two Peyrottes brothers, sons of the former seigneur of Soubès; the Rouch brothers, clothiers from Lodève; Antoine Causse alias Miquel, an émigré hiding out at St-Jean-de-Buèges; François Messier, hatmaker from Gignac; and, of course, the three Ponsy brothers, also from Gignac.[6] Here was a socially eclectic group of men who all had good reasons to detest the Revolution, whether it was due to a loss of privileges, confiscation of land, shake-ups in cloth manufacturing, or months in prison. Their common hostility to the Revolution papered over differences in social status. Their alliance was not a question of ties of vertical solidarity—they came from a variety of towns and villages—nor of shared class interests as their social origins could hardly have been more diverse, ranging from wagoneers and tanners to manufacturers and seigneurs. In fact, the group of agitators who gathered at Aniane represented the Revolution's democratic ideals paradoxically realized in the counter-revolution. This politically inspired social mixing fostered ties between antirepublican factions in different communities and thus promoted the growth of wider regional networks based on antagonism and fear. Such developments made it much more difficult to restore and maintain order than would have been the case during the *ancien régime*, when resistance to authority rarely reached beyond a single locality. In the case of the northern Hérault, the network created by the gatherings at Aniane managed to turn a family feud at Lodève into an escalating cycle of violence at Gignac.

The significance of the family feud at Lodève was magnified by the important political and economic changes experienced there during the Revolution. The immediate cause of the bitter dispute between Pierre Rouch, a merchant-manufacturer, and Barthélemy Teisserenc, a master tanner, was control of a precious water outlet. But matters ran deeper. Though recently attracted to woolens manufacture by the abolition of guilds and a boom in army contracts, Rouch really represented the traditional, *rentes*-based bourgeoisie of Lodève. He moved in the social circles where clericalism and royalism were inseparable.[7] On the other hand, Barthélemy Teisserenc belonged to one of the oldest and wealthiest clans in the business, an industry whose thousands of skilled workers had helped to make Lodève a republican stronghold. Thus as commercial rivals, as substantial employers, and as well-connected local notables, both men could mobilize considerable support. Furthermore, they each had two adult sons imbued with powerful notions of honor and machismo. Lodève was too big and too commercial to be dominated by a single family; therefore, the Rouches and Teisserencs needed the power of larger factions to pursue their rivalry. By taking opposing positions on the Revolution, both families gained opportunities to manipulate the instruments of justice and repression, thereby magnifying the significance of their feud and perverting the state's effort to secure a monopoly on legitimate force.

The feud flared up in the parching heat of August 1796. A potshot at Rouch père as he was closing his shutters one night lit the fuse. Municipal administrators anticipated more trouble and, in fact, were already discussing security measures for the town when news arrived that the Rouches and Teisserencs had "provoked each other with words, from words they came to blows, then to excesses and grave violence committed with a sword and a firearm." This lapidary formula captures neither the breathless description nor the gravity of events. Two days after the gunshot at Rouch père, his two sons, Pierre and Jean, confronted the two Teisserenc sons, Barthélemy and Olivier, in a bloody attempt to defend both their access to the water and their family honor. Threatening to use legal means to secure sole access to the water outlet led quickly to insults. Epithets flew: "Terrorists!" "Royalists!" "Anarchists!" "Cut-throats!" But feuds favored ritualized violence, and so the four men, all in their thirties, moved to settle matters in hand-to-hand combat on the sports pitch. First, those with pistols handed them to observers. Blows followed. Suddenly, the eldest Teisserenc pulled a knife and swiped at Pierre. The eldest Rouch reacted by grabbing a saber, slashing Barthélemy Teisserenc on the neck and then running him clean through. In the meantime, the youngest Rouch was succumbing to the youngest Teisserenc. Unable to stand by, Gabriel Connes, alias the Dragoon, took a shot at Teisserenc *cadet,* who wisely broke off the fight and fled for his life, leaving a companion to pull the sword from his agonizing brother. Blood soaked into the sand as a bystander rushed to the town hall.

Once the Teisserenc-Rouch rivalry degenerated into bloodshed and an open feud, it began to invest the instruments of law and order. Republicans had long dominated the municipal administration, which gave the Teisserencs an early advantage. Upon hearing of the battle at the sports pitch, town officials immediately ordered patrols by small detachments of national guardsmen. These consisted of ardent republicans, including one man wearing his usual "bonnet rouge à bordure noir," as well as members of the Teisserenc clan, Olivier first and foremost. Judging by the composition of the patrols and the proximity of events, there would have been a quick lynching had they caught their quarry. The preliminary investigation conducted by the justice of the peace, Jacques Teisserenc (!), compelled the jury director to issue arrest warrants for Gabriel Connes and Pierre and Jean Rouch. In a clear subversion of all principles of state control of coercive force, however, Teisserenc père obtained a copy of the arrest warrants and, together with his youngest son, led an expedition consisting of two bailiffs and thirty national guardsmen to seize the perpetrators. Rouch père described this as a descent on his house by thirty "bonnets rouges" who invaded his domicile and threatened his life. In contrast, Teisserenc père justified the size of the force as "imperiously commanded by the circumstances"—that is, "arresting three men armed to the teeth"—and claimed that everything passed in an orderly fashion.[8] He also claimed the right to head such an expedition because his sons were the plaintiffs and he was paying for it. When the jury director blocked any further fusion of police action and private vengeance, Teisserenc protested vehemently. He insisted that the arrest warrant was his property, that he should be given as many copies as he wanted so that he could send them to contacts, police officials, and gendarmes in other jurisdictions, and that the official searches conducted by the police did not preclude "those that the plaintiffs wanted to conduct at their own expense."[9] This belief in the plaintiff as not merely the instigator of judicial pursuit but its driving force and virtual proprietor had roots in the *ancien régime* and yet now threatened the credibility and independence of the new legal establishment. Here was a key reason for the prolonged cycle of violence in the area.

The Teisserencs' rush to revenge ironically helped to put some distance between their cause and the official prosecution of the Rouches and Connes for attempted murder. Unable to accept the jury director's lack of progress after three months on the case, the Teisserenc brothers and their friend Marie-Alexis Gastard mounted a second expedition. They went from Lodève to Gignac, where they gathered a few "patriots" into an "armed force" and headed to Aniane. On the way, the small troupe ran into the reactionary agitators who met regularly at Arnavielle's farm. The republican posse called out, "In the name of the law, drop your weapons!" Despite fierce resistance from the Ponsys and others, the republicans managed to seize the two Rouch brothers and escort them back to Lodève. The Rouches' ally, Joseph Ponsy, persuaded the new jury director Duran that this was "an offense against personal security," which was a grave violation of the constitution, and so obtained arrest warrants for both Olivier Teisserenc and Marie-Alexis Gastard. Before they could be arrested, however, Olivier Teisserenc took revenge on the combative Catherine Connes by shooting her in the shoulder with his carbine. The pellets were large enough that one passed clean through, and so a charge of attempted murder was added to his slate.[10] Each side was now employing both lethal private violence and the instruments of criminal justice to dispose of its enemies.

Once Olivier Teisserenc was arrested, the feud moved to the first of several judicial phases. A grand jury at Lodève indicted Pierre Rouch and Gabriel Connes for the attempted murder of Barthélemy Teisserenc but declined to indict either Jean Rouch or Olivier Teisserenc on similar charges. Apparently the jury believed that the two youngest brothers had simply been obeying the powerful code of family honor. Although Pierre Rouch and Gabriel Connes were sent to the criminal court at Montpellier, they were not easy to convict. A third of the witnesses for the prosecution, and undoubtedly the most important ones, were too afraid to testify at trial. In its confusion, the jury acquitted Rouch and Connes on the grounds that the stabbing and shooting were merely part of a brawl and therefore akin to self-defense.[11] The justice system had thus failed to do anything to quell the feud. With all the protagonists back on the streets of Lodève, the cycle of violence escalated.

National politics served as a mistral to spread the brush fire started at Lodève. Before any further trials took place, the elections of year V intervened to magnify the significance of the feud. The Rouches knew by bitter experience that the only way to triumph over the Teisserencs was to defeat the republicans at the electoral assembly. To this end, the reactionaries used a campaign of intimidation to gain control of the primary assembly at Lodève. As soon as the assembly elected a new anti-Jacobin town council, the Rouches moved against their enemies. The elections had brought most of the region's leading reactionaries to town, including all of those who gathered regularly at Aniane: the Ponsys from Gignac, the Peyrottes from Soubès, the Isserts from Aniane, and so on. On the night of 3 germinal (23 March), they fired a shot at Olivier Teisserenc as he entered his father's house. The following morning, one of them spotted Olivier Teisserenc and Marie-Alexis Gastard fleeing town. Both men were the subject of arrest warrants for having led a detachment of the National Guard that had shot a reactionary named Romignier the year before. The Rouches rallied their allies on the esplanade and promptly dubbed them the "forces of order." Rouch père harangued them: "If we can kill both of them, there will be peace in Lodève" and sent the men off in hot pursuit. Teisserenc and Gastard tried to outrun the posse, but Gastard began to flag and so ducked into a small hovel where he prepared to defend himself. The lead pursuer, the intrepid Joseph Ponsy, sneaked up on Gastard, grabbed the barrel of his protruding gun, and quickly disarmed him. Ponsy then ordered Gastard to his knees and shot him through the head. As soon as other members of the posse arrived, Ponsy forced each of them to fire a ball into Gastard's corpse, obviously believing that friends who slay together, stay together. People at work in nearby fields heard the shooting, ran toward the hovel, and arrived in time to see Gastard's clothes still smoking from powder burns.[12] In the meantime, Olivier Teisserenc got away. Back in Lodève, the tocsin was sounded and patrols organized. But the National Guard was now commanded by allies of the Rouches and so simply ignored the inn where the murderers were raucously bellowing the "Reveil du Peuple" and other reactionary songs.

Not content with his narrow escape, Olivier, armed with his usual two pistols and a musket, foolishly returned to Lodève the following day. He barricaded himself in his father's house and, unable to resist the opportunity, shot a passing national guardsmen from the window. Minutes later, Rouch père burst into the town hall shouting, "He's shot one of ours!" The new municipality acquiesced in a distribution of arms to his allies. The commanders of the National Guard and the gendarmerie even joined the Rouches' assault on the Teisserenc residence. The siege lasted well into the night. Having little success with mere firearms, Rouch père hired masons to sap the foundation. He then had a barrel of gunpowder inserted and blown up to breach the walls. As intrepid as any of the Ponsys, Olivier Teisserenc managed to shoot his way out of the burning house, through a storm of musket balls, and out of Lodève. But he did not escape. Hit several times in the breakout, he was easily pursued and killed not far from town. Although Teisserenc père and his wife were taken into custody to protect them from a lynching, they were badly beaten before finally being locked away. Some official connivance at the jail soon allowed them to escape and flee town.[13]

The deaths of Marie-Alexis Gastard and Olivier Teisserenc and the flight of Teisserenc père to Perpignan settled the feud in the Rouches' favor. Since their party had also won the elections, none of the new officials initiated an inquiry, let alone a prosecution. On the contrary, it was Barthélemy

Teisserenc who was arrested and put on trial for leading the "force armée" to Aniane to arrest the Rouch brothers six months earlier.[14] Following the elections of year V, "the 'auganasses' (in the regional patois this word meant the men of former times) were daily under arms; crowds of them turned up in different communes to help recover the possessions of deported priests returning from Italy."[15] The reaction was especially pronounced at Gignac and exceeded any violence the town had previously known. Joseph Ponsy, now called "the general," led the charge. He and a handful of fellow victims of the year II systematically targeted members of the former *comité révolutionnaire* and forced several to quit the town. This campaign of "murder, arson, beatings, and hatred of the republic" culminated in an assault on the Fulcrand family on the night of 14 thermidor V (1 August 1797). A gang led by five of the Ponsys used the pretext of disarming "terrorists" to invade the Fulcrand home. François escaped to the garden, where he hid for hours in a well. Guillaume was less fortunate. He suffered several saber wounds before finally escaping into a nearby copse, where neighboring villagers found him half-dead the next day.[16] Despite getting attention from the national press, none of the many incidents in this campaign of revenge and intimidation were the subject of prosecution. As long as reactionaries held power, the Ponsys enjoyed complete immunity.[17]

## Republican Riposte

Once again, national politics intervened. The Fructidor coup abruptly ended six months of reactionary license. The new department administrators appointed after the coup conducted a thorough purge of municipal officials throughout the Hérault. Gignac's town council swung from one extreme to the other. The new officials had all been members of the *comité révolutionnaire* in year II. Suddenly the oppressed became the oppressors. They armed their allies and disarmed their enemies.[18] This attempt to monopolize "legitimate force" did not go undisputed. The withdrawal of regular troops prompted a sinister remark from the feisty Elisabeth Montels, wife of Louis Ponsy: "Now that the brigands are gone, respectable folk can go out; the days are short, but the nights are long, and all cats are grey."[19] Blood soon flowed. On 23 frimaire VI (13 December 1797), opponents of the new republican order ambushed a guard patrol. Two members were wounded, and the commander, none other than Guillaume Fulcrand, was killed by a musket ball in the back fired by the redoubtable Joseph Ponsy.[20]

Though unable to arrest him or his allies, the local Jacobins were not going to let matters rest there. Most important, they needed to assure continued control of local power. To this end, they organized a "Constitutional Circle" and, thanks to their control of the "forces of order," easily dominated the elections in the spring of 1798.[21] The results gave the post-Fructidor appointees a veneer of democratic legitimacy. Armed with the sovereignty of the people, they pursued their opponents with renewed intensity.

The Jacobins of Gignac were led by the new justice of the peace, Auguste Laussel, a "hothead" prone to paranoia and equipped with "everything it took to make a faction leader."[22] Laussel's character and personal trajectory, no less than those of the Rouches, Teisserencs or Ponsys, served to perpetuate the cycle of violence in the region. Though raised at Gignac and educated at Montpellier, he had passed the early Revolution at Lyon, where he gained notoriety as an incendiary journalist. Elected constitutional priest of St-Bonnet-Le-Troncey (Rhône) in early 1792, Laussel was considered an *intrus* and rejected by his new parishioners. Undaunted, he cast aside his cassock and marched with the local *fédérés* to Paris, where he arrived in time to see the monarchy overthrown and get himself named a *commissaire du Pouvoir exécutif* during "la première terreur" of September 1792. Laussel soon returned to Lyon and quickly became city *procureur* during Châlier's stormy ascendancy there in 1792–93. Shortly before the insurrection of 30 May, the representatives on mission inadvertently saved his life by having him arrested on charges of fraud and sent to Paris. After six months in the Abbaye prison, he was tried and acquitted by the Revolutionary Tribunal on 8 frimaire II. Upon release, he returned to his native Gignac, where he married a former nun and became president of the local *comité révolutionnaire*.[23]

Having embraced the revolutionary dynamic with all his considerable fervor, Laussel was forced to keep a low profile during the years III, IV, and V. This was not easy for a man of his character, or his appearance; he could always be identified by his long ponytail, big nose, and flushed face when he talked, as well as the ever-present evidence of urinary incontinence on his clothes.[24] He reappeared after the Fructidor coup, appointed as Gignac's new justice of the peace. Despite his new title, Laussel was not the sort of man to bring peace to a southern bourg, especially not one recently subjected to a prolonged wave of ardent Catholicism and popular antirepublicanism. Dubbed the "Marat of Lyon," Laussel showed no signs of having become a "new" Jacobin. He was in the front lines of disarming the former administration and its supporters following the Fructidor coup and together with fellow *exclusifs* helped to organize the elections of 1798. Matters escalated after the elections. Once the scale of the republican victory in the Hérault became clear, the jury director at Lodève issued more than forty arrest warrants for the killers of Teisserenc and Gastard, all associated with the municipal administrators of Lodève sacked in the wake of Fructidor.[25] Laussel played his part in the new determination to prosecute by going after the participants from Gignac.

The Jacobins of Gignac were clearly a beleaguered minority. Counting no more than sixty families, their survival in power required the backing of both the department administration and the army. Overblowing a fracas in which Laussel's wife came to blows with the *femme* Pagès assured them of both.[26] On 20 prairial VI (8 June 1798), General Petit-Guillaume put Gignac under an official state of siege and bolstered the detachment of troops stationed there. Four days of intense crackdown ensued, all under the pretext of capturing the Ponsy brothers. Together the Jacobins and the army reigned over Gignac for the following year. Armed patrols and repeated house searches created an air of intimidation. Rey, government commissioner of the Hérault, complained that Laussel, "through his relations and intimacy with Pons, Marin, and Gibal, administrators of Gignac, furnished all the means to harass peaceful citizens that the law has given him for their protection." Matters degenerated to the point that the minister of police rebuked them all for arbitrariness and abuses of authority, remarking that "an exaggerated zeal always has the air of hatred and misplaced rigor looks too much like vengeance." Although not fond of their methods, department administrators protected the Jacobin officials at Gignac, arguing that there were no other republicans there to take their place.[27] This was a classic dilemma for the Directory. How many other towns around the country fell under the oppressive thumb of Jacobin zealots *faute de mieux* in the republican camp?

The Jacobin ascendancy at Gignac and Lodève had serious limitations. It relied too heavily on the army, offended the inhabitants' religious sensibilities, and failed to penetrate the countryside. Villages high on the Causse de Larzac north of Lodève—places such as Le Caylar, La Vacquerie, Sorbs, Le Cros, and St-Michel—provided safe havens for draft dodgers and reactionary vigilantes; hamlets on the edges of Mount Séranne stretching from Arboras to Brissac harbored returned émigrés; and farther east Argeliers, St-Martin-de-Londres, and Viols-le-Fort sheltered numerous refractory priests, including several considered to be the infamous *abbé* Solier called Sans-Peur. Amnestied chouans from the Aveyron and fugitives from justice like the Rouches, Ponsys, Peyrottes, and Isserts circulated with impunity throughout the region. A frustrated jury director from Lodève claimed that the gendarmerie "sees everything and says nothing." The audacity of the fugitives astonished him. On his way back from Gignac one day, the judge encountered "the too famous Ponsy *aîné*," who extended his arm, shook hands, asked about his health, and sarcastically bid him good day as they parted.[28] Although unable to clap irons on any of the main perpetrators, the magistracy proceeded with prosecution anyway. This led to several trials and a total of twenty-two death sentences pronounced contumaciously by the Criminal Court of the Hérault.[29]

Vexed by their inability to seize these men, the Jacobins once again resorted to an abuse of police powers, this time using democracy itself to ensnare their opponents. On the eve of the elections of spring 1799, Laussel issued thirty arrest warrants for leading members of the opposition. Sixteen of these men were actually arrested, some at the Festival of Popular Sovereignty and others the following day at the primary assembly itself. Few were charged with anything serious, and none were among the main killers of Gastard, Teisserenc, or Fulcrand.[30] Rough weather notwithstanding, they were immediately sent to Lodève under escort by a detachment of the National Guard while regular troops stayed in Gignac to control the elections. Laussel's maneuver split the primary assembly. The Jacobins' opponents registered an official protest and withdrew to the house of Michel Avellan, a supine moderate recently appointed commissioner of the canton.[31] Unable to make effective use of their police powers in normal times, the Jacobins at Gignac had decided that by the late Directory subverting the democratic process in the name of preserving the republic was one of the rules of the game in local politics.

The evolution of affairs at Gignac since the Fructidor coup reveals some of the reasons for continued cleavages within the republican camp, as well as the Second Directory's antipathy toward *exclusifs* like Laussel. The "scissionary assembly" was nullified by the legislature despite support from deputies Joubert and Curée. But the cause of the split—Laussel's strategically timed arrest warrants—led the Directory to order the JP's arrest on charges of "conspiracy against the sovereignty of the people," a capital offense. There could hardly have been a more devastating accusation for a self-proclaimed leader of the democratic avant-garde. By the time the order to arrest Laussel reached Gignac, however, he had gone into hiding. Meanwhile, his allies remained in charge of the municipality and took heart from the Jacobin resurgence at the national level.

As hard as some historians try to disassociate the Jacobins of the late Directory from those of year II, the ardent republicans of year VII were largely the same men with the same enemies and the same attitude to coercive methods. Back in 1793, before the Terror had become a matter of mass murder, the register of Gignac's *comité révolutionnaire* bore a crudely engraved liberty tree capped by a *bonnet rouge* and a skull and crossbones. Its caption read, "Republic one and indivisible or death; the shadow of this tree will be long and fatal and will end up giving death to tyrants." In 1799, when news of the parliamentary purge of the Directory on 30 prairial reached the Hérault, the republicans of Gignac, like scores of other such groups around the country, sent a petition to the Council of Five Hundred pushing for more extreme measures. Fully aware of the discursive resonances at work since the overthrow of Robespierre, the neo-clubists of Gignac nonetheless resorted to the language of year II. The self-styled "republicans of the canton of Gignac," almost ninety signatories in all, harangued the legislators: "Your work is imperfect.... Strike the guilty.... Our tyrants [that is, the government of the Second Directory] were not alien to the slaughter of our ministers at Rastatt.... Strike these eternal producers of conspiracies.... Issue severe laws that provoke fear in the hearts of the enemies of our independence." The emphasis here is not on democratic reform, freedom of speech, freedom of association, or social justice—the putative program of "neo-Jacobins"—rather, the entire document stresses severe measures to punish conspirators. This was the form of republicanism that Gignac experienced at least as strongly in years VI and VII as it did in year II. This was also the form of republicanism that provoked violent opposition.[32]

## Banditry and Bad Blood

Across Languedoc, the crisis of 1799 spawned resistance and civil strife. The military effort was a prime source of renewed conflict. The regime's resources in legitimacy and authority once again failed to meet the exigencies of the moment. Its exorbitant demands for men and money gave its enemies the motive, the means, and the opportunity for some spectacular crimes. Nothing was more hated than the demands of renewed war. Popular resistance to conscription supplied political outlaws with a mass of new recruits. At the same time, the need to transport large amounts of cash from the interior to the front also supplied them with new targets—truly golden opportunities to hit the republic where it hurt most.

On the drizzly morning of 22 messidor VII (12 July 1799), a dozen men with their white shirts untucked, either masked or with blackened faces, and armed with double-barreled muskets, held up a treasury pay wagon on its way from Rodez to the Army of Italy. They struck near a scrub-covered bluff known as the *taillade de Gignac* on the main road connecting Lodève and Montpellier. Overwhelmed by superior force, the paltry escort of two gendarmes could do nothing to prevent the robbery. The thieves drove the wagon into the woods, smashed open the wooden chests, and stuffed a staggering 59,000 francs in hard cash into their pockets and haversacks. They quickly dispersed, slipped through the woods north of the *taillade,* and headed for the hills. The use of disguises and facility with the topography left no doubt that this was the work of local men. Although the teen-aged wagon driver was promptly arrested as an accomplice, it soon became apparent that he had merely shot his mouth off about his wagon's contents back in Millau.[33] As for the actual bandits, what could be an easier and more rewarding way to support the cause of counter-revolution?

Embarrassed by the ease of this operation, the authorities paid more attention to providing convoys of cash with proper escorts. A brigade of gendarmes and thirty-five national guardsmen from Gignac accompanied the next large shipment of treasury receipts through the area. These precautions paid off. The bandits had again learned of the shipment well in advance and gathered near the *taillade* for a second attack. But seeing the size of the escort, and thinking patience the better part of valor, the masked men simply waited for the next shipment. This time they showed greater audacity. On 22 pluviôse VIII (11 February 1800), at least a score of well-armed bandits, once again disguised by charcoal-smudged faces and untucked shirts, attacked the fifteen-man escort accompanying a treasury destined for the naval base at Toulon. An intense gun battle felled the brigadier commanding the escort, wounded one national guardsman, and scattered the rest. Steady fire kept the other gendarmes at bay while a dozen bandits moved in and seized the 20,000 francs in cash. The robbers then beat a hasty retreat, unpursued by the shocked escort, whose commander, Guillaume Farouche, lay dying on the road.[34]

Two stunning successes in six months led to an even more daring heist a few weeks later. A treasury of 40,000 francs on its way from Rodez to Nice was escorted by ten gendarmes and twenty cannoneers—enough to destroy a hundred brigands, boasted the prefect of the Aveyron. Rather than test the escort's firepower, the bandits resorted to cunning. Having made it safely to Gignac on 8 floréal VIII (29 April 1800), the treasury was locked in a secure room on the second floor of the town hall and a dozen national guardsmen posted to protect it. That night over thirty well-armed bandits gathered at nearby Montpeyroux. At 2:00 a.m., they slipped into Gignac and quietly took up positions around town, paying special attention to the houses of republican stalwarts who might have tried to stop the robbery. Several bandits then surprised and disarmed the sentinels at the town hall. By threatening to kill the two men, the bandits convinced the other guards to cooperate, and they were quickly locked in the main-floor guardhouse. Meanwhile, at the back of the building other bandits arrived with a ladder and heavy rope. They broke into the second floor, smashed their way into the archives vault, and lowered the 500-pound chest out the window. Once they got it to the edge of town—no simple task, either—they chopped it open and bagged the impressive heap of coins.[35] The sheer audacity of this heist sent shock waves throughout the region.

Two months later, on 3 messidor VIII (22 June 1800), bandits tried yet another attack on a treasury wagon near Gignac. As had been the case with previous holdups, the robbers were well informed about the timing of the shipment and value of the cargo. Knowing there were almost 100,000 francs in the balance, the bandits mounted an all-out frontal assault despite the massive armed escort of 115 men. Although scores of national guardsmen quickly melted away, forty cannoneers and gendarmes succeeded in fending off the attack. The driver hastily turned his wagon around and sped back to Gignac. Sounding the tocsin at Gignac rallied over two hundred men—a rare response surely not unrelated to the fact that the citizenry had just been ordered to repay the 40,000 francs stolen from the town hall.[36] Though the volunteers did not risk their lives by going after the bandits, they did escort the treasury all the way to Montpellier. In the meantime, at least thirty bandits, some nursing gunshot wounds, paused for lunch at nearby Boissière before disappearing north into the *garrigues*.[37] This was a far cry from the claim of two hundred bandits given in initial reports. Nonetheless, it makes it clear that the leading robbers in the area had little to fear from local peasants. Draft dodgers, deserters, and even escaped Austrian prisoners of war added to the swelling pool of outlaws, which made it easy for leaders to round up scores of armed men for such a daring daylight raid.

The availability of criminal manpower and the lust for loot incited the bandits to extend their operations further afield. On 19 fructidor VIII (6 September 1800), more than two dozen heavily armed men overwhelmed a brigade of gendarmes escorting three deserters and a wagon full of cash on the road from Béziers to Montpellier. Once the gendarmes exhausted their ammunition, the bandits were able to free the deserters and seize the wagon. They promptly murdered the driver, smashed open the two chests, and made off with another huge pile of specie, this time a total of 43,369 francs. Walking north all day took them to Viols-le-Fort by nightfall, where they paused to divide up the treasury. Each bandit received 1,500 francs. In one day, admittedly a dangerous one, each bandit had gained the equivalent of several years of income for a farm laborer or woolens worker. In a rare show of solidarity, every man gave up part of his share to create a fund of 1,800 francs intended for three comrades imprisoned in the citadel at Montpellier.[38] Bandits with this kind of loyalty clearly had more in common than robbery. In fact, it was Joseph Ponsy, a multiple murderer, who insisted on the donations because the prisoners included his brothers Louis and Barthélemy.

A criminal network of this size, range, and apparent coherence gave republican authorities good reason for alarm. Matters were doubly worrisome in that most of the regular troops in the interior had been siphoned off for the war. Even those army units left in Lower Languedoc were tied up elsewhere, desperately trying to put down the wholesale insurgency in the Ardèche and the northern Gard. This absence of troops was an important factor in the vulnerability of treasury shipments. It also made anything more than half-measures difficult to undertake. To be successful, the police had to be blessed with luck and quality support from local national guardsmen, a rather rare phenomenon. Even then the judicial system often undid their work.

The first big treasury heist had prompted General Petit-Guillaume, commander of the Ninth Military District, and the department administrators of the Hérault, to undertake a massive manhunt. The plan involved deploying eight hundred national guardsmen and gendarmes to encircle the rugged hill country known as Mount Séranne that separted the Vis and Hérault rivers. This would cut off any escape routes to the Gard or the Aveyron while various detachments conducted a village-to-village search of the area. The arrests were few, but vital. One detachment surprised six men in an inn at St-Etienne-de-Gougas and captured one of them, Henry Peyrottes, the oldest son of the seigneur de Soubès. Although the bandits' firepower allowed five others to escape, one of them (Antoine Vergnettes) was badly wounded and could be easily seized the following morning. The authorities also recovered almost 5,000 francs in hard coin, equally divided among four haversacks, as well as two guns, five knives, and—ominously—a list of jurors. There was also a letter from Rouch to his father-in-law, Pascal, who owned the inn at Lodève where the reactionaries had gathered after killing Marie-Alexis Gastard. All this evidence made it clear that the murders in Lodève in 1797 and the treasury holdup at the *taillade de Gignac* in 1799 were intimately related. In fact, the bandits who shot their way out of the inn that night were Pierre and Jean Rouch, Gabriel Peyrottes, and Jean Maury, all previously condemned for murder.[39] The connection was confirmed two months later with the arrest of Pierre Gay, an innkeeper at Sorbs. He had recently met the elder Peyrottes, the Ponsy brothers, and a half-dozen other men who had come around asking about local caves that might serve as hideouts. Furthermore, the innkeeper said that these men considered the death sentences pronounced against them so many licenses to rob the republic, supposedly as repayment of what the republic owed them for confiscated property. These could only be the Rouches, Peyrottes, Ponsys, and their consorts. Now in possession of prisoners, hard evidence, and a witness willing to talk, the authorities both knew and could prove that the bandits were led by their political enemies from years past.

The connection between the murderous family feud at Lodève, the Catholic and royalist reaction of 1797, and the highway robberies of 1799–1800 made it easy for republican officials to justify cutting corners on legality. Despite the dubious election at Gignac, legislators ratified the results of the "mother" assembly there. Furthermore, the "Jacobin Hundred Days" purged numerous moderate republican commissioners (including the one at Gignac) and even allowed Laussel to return to his post as justice of the peace. Believing that he was making a virtuous habit of a recurring necessity, Laussel once again ignored the limits on his police powers. He mounted an extended investigation of the town hall robbery at Gignac and issued a mass of subpoenas and arrest warrants. Although most of these could not be enforced, they did lead to a few local arrests. The law required Laussel to turn suspects over to the jury director at Lodève within twenty-fours of their arrest. However, Laussel kept several people in custody for up to three weeks, including Elisabeth and Baptiste Ponsy. He later argued that the bandits controlled the road to Lodève and that he lacked sufficient force to have them escorted there. The JP also refused to relinquish control of the investigation to the jury director and gendarmerie at Lodève until he had completely exhausted his own police powers. Even Laussel's kinsman Gabriel-Nicolas Avellan, a former department judge and now court commissioner for the Hérault, described Laussel's behavior as "a veritable public scandal, presenting both a formal disobedience of the law and a disregard of government authority."[40] Only after sustained pressure from Avellan's replacement did Laussel finally transfer his prosecution to the jury director. on 18 thermidor VIII (6 August 1800), more than three months late. Even then he did not send everything, claiming that if he included six subpoenas, they would be converted into arrest warrants and delivered to homes of suspects, which would only delay their reappearance at Gignac.

Laussel acknowledged that his actions violated the law but defended himself saying, "the letter of the law kills, its spirit breathes life." The new minister of justice took a similar attitude: Laussel's "irregularities and delays in prosecution" would not be punished.[41] Priorities had clearly shifted since the early days of the Directory. The Consulate's legitimacy did not rest on its constitutionalism or a refined sense of the rule of law. Sustained civil strife had persuaded politicians that the vast majority of Frenchmen were more concerned about restoring order than about safeguarding individual liberties through a scrupulous devotion to the technicalities of police procedure prescribed by the code of brumaire IV. Auguste Laussel was pursuing murderers and highway robbers,. men who, whatever their initial personal and political motives for violence, had become irreconcilable enemies of the republic. Laussel may have had strident political views and a dangerous tendency to abuse his authority, but he was not alone in putting "law and order" ahead of the "rule of law." It became a hallmark of the Consulate and Empire.

Despite the anti-Jacobin rhetoric associated with the Brumaire coup, the early Consulate found it expedient to maintain Jacobins in office in those regions of the country where lawlessness and resistance had reached epidemic proportions. This had the advantage of ensuring an unstinting pursuit of criminals. It had the disadvantage of making it difficult to distinguish between common criminals and men who resorted to common crimes as an expression of their opposition to the antireligious and coercive policies of the republic. The greatest difficulty in trying to determine the role of counter-revolutionary politics in banditry was that most evidence came from the sort of republican officials who saw royalist conspiracies behind every bush. In the Cévennes, where the wars of religion had lasted into the eighteenth century, Protestant officials were especially prone to blame refractory priests for local hostility to the republic. Witness the treatment of *abbé* Jean-Louis Solier, better known as Sans-Peur, the most famous brigand-priest of the Midi. His reputation rests on the bigotry and paranoia of local officials under the Directory. They had reason to be suspicious of him, for he did have connections with enemies of the regime. As a refractory priest who had spent years on the run, he inevitably entered a vast underworld of criminals, draft dodgers, and overt counter-revolutionaries. During the reaction of year V, when a popular campaign of repossessing church property was underway, a number of unsavory characters visited Viols-le-Fort, where Solier had a semi-clandestine ministry. These included Martin Arnavielle from Aniane and the Ponsy brothers from Gignac. How much inspiration or actual direction he gave to these men, especially when brigandage became endemic two and three years later, is impossible to tell. Despite having compiled almost no worthwhile evidence against him, authorities remained convinced that he was the principal leader of bandits in the area.[42] Linking highway robbery to Catholic fanaticism and royalist conspiracy simply fit too well with republican prejudices to be challenged by other explanations.

## Failure in the Courts

As we have seen, however, the inspiration for this banditry lay just as much in the inability to make republican institutions operate effectively as it did in opposing ideologies or religious bigotry. This was especially true of the system of criminal justice based on elected magistrates and citizen jurors. The Rouch-Teisserenc feud combined a traditional system of blood vengeance with the pervasive factional politics of the French Revolution. The influence of factionalism badly eroded the system of sanctions and social control that was inherent in normal clan rivalries. Ordinarily, when a feud spread to engulf individuals and families who had ties of intermarriage and clientage with men and groups linked to the opposing family, the difficulty of choosing between competing loyalties inspired refusals to participate and mounting social pressure to limit the violence. Over the years, however, more and more people in the northern Hérault had been forced to take a position for or against the republic. This encouraged the spread of violence to groups normally isolated from a feud and made the reciprocal killing an "affaire de partie." Matters were further complicated by the fact that the apparatus of administrative and judicial authority remained somewhat inchoate. Annual elections and arbitrary dismissals led to repeated changes in personnel, which made it easy for rivals in an "affaire de partie" either to use the new instruments of local power to their own advantage or to flout them openly when in opposition. After Fructidor, however, republicans of one stripe or another tightened their grip on the levers of power. This permanently locked out the Rouches and their ilk. Once condemned to death in absentia by the Criminal Court of the Hérault, such men had few means of overcoming their rivals. Thus, to a certain extent, they were forced into banditry. They aimed their attacks at the fiscal-military state whose support was vital to keeping local republicans in office. This went beyond attacks on treasury pay wagons and included large operations to rescue conscripts being escorted to the front, multiple assaults on the customs barriers recently installed at Gignac and Lodève, and a series of brutal farm invasions.[43]

Although republicans had succeeded in excluding their enemies from local office, they could not make the machinery of justice function effectively against them. This failure did not stem from a groundswell of popular support for a guerrilla-style struggle against the republic. Certainly there was sympathy for antirepublicanism, especially in the southern Cévennes, where a string of Catholic villages formed the "Montagne Blanche" and contrasted with the Protestant-dominated areas to the north.[44] But the republicans of Lodève and Gignac were themselves Catholics. Besides, the effort to bring reactionaries to justice was not a matter of persecuting mere political rivals. As we have seen, the bandits were led by hardened killers. These men were thugs with a thirst for violence. In contrast to Colin Lucas's explanation for the intracommunal violence of Provence, they did not need to know their victims personally; nor were they acting out a "culture of retribution," as William Beik would have it, for urban revolts in the seventeenth century.[45] In fact, they sometimes behaved as hired assassins, attacking people they could not identify and perpetrating heinous assaults far from their local communities. For instance, just outside La Vacquerie, Ponsy ambushed two muleteers from Nant (Aveyron) and Sumène (Gard), shooting them both in the legs. He began battering one of them to death with his musket before suddenly realizing that he had the wrong men.[46] This sort of brutality cannot be explained as Ponsy protecting his family business in cartage—if so, why stop the beating?—and smacks of a hired assault gone awry. This supposition has other support. A turncoat highwayman from Bédarieux, badly shot up and hoping either to obtain medical aid or to clear his conscience, told judges that the bandits around Lodève were paid twenty sous a day from a fund set up by royalists in the region and that these men were regularly billeted in local châteaux. We might be tempted to dismiss this as a canard typical of the period except that police spies confirmed that some of the outlaws were regularly billeted in châteaux west of Lodève.[47] And if the Rouch brothers were motivated strictly by local concerns, why did they commit vicious robberies as far away as St-Affrique in the Aveyron?[48] This combination of gratuitous cruelty, mercenary vengeance, and wide-ranging robberies suggests that the principal aim was to destroy the credibility and viability of the republican regime. The escalating violence may have alienated potential supporters, but more important, it discredited the republic by generating a widespread sense of fear and insecurity.

Official justice failed to allay these fears. Despite several arrests shortly after the first big robbery in July 1799, a full year passed before anyone was put on trial. Other arrests expanded the number of accused, and hence the size of the trial, but failed to add much useful information. The delays in prosecution even provoked the prisoners to write the minister of justice to complain of their lengthy incarceration.[49] Finally, on 9 thermidor VIII (28 July 1800), the First Military Court of the Ninth Military District sitting at Montpellier found itself compelled to acquit eighteen men (twelve present and six absent) of the treasury heist at the *taillade de Gignac* the previous year. Although unhampered by weak-kneed jurors, the military court could not convict without adequate witness testimony. Therefore, it was only the shoot-out at St-Etienne-de-Gougas, well attested by gendarmes, that led the military court to condemn to death in absentia four of the accused— the Rouch and Peyrottes brothers—and to sentence one man—Antoine Vergnettes—to ten years in irons. All five of these men, as well as five others actually present at trial, but acquitted of armed robbery (Joseph and François Ponsy, Jean-Louis Reboul, Jean-Baptiste Issert, and François Messier), had previously been sentenced to death in absentia by the criminal court for the murders of Fulcrand, Gastard, and Teisserenc. Although the court-martial linked the series of treasury heists to the Rouch-Teisserenc feud, none of the acquitted was sent before the Criminal Court of the Hérault to purge his conviction.[50] This breathtaking failure was compounded two months later when a jury convicted Rouch père and Henry Peyrottes (called "monsieur le chevalier de Soubès" by locals), both actually present at trial, for the murder of Marie-Alexis Gastard two and a half years earlier, but the Court of Cassation nullified the whole prosecution on the grounds that Gastard's body had been exhumed by order of a JP from outside the canton where it was buried.[51] What can account for such catastrophic judicial failures?

As we have seen, the institutions of policing and local justice had been instruments of a deadly rivalry. This sometimes led to judicial nullification. More often, it deterred people who had not already taken sides from cooperating in any investigation or prosecution of crimes tainted by politics. The higher the personal and political stakes, the greater the aversion others had for getting involved. Partisanship bred uncertainty, and intense partisanship bred fear. Thus, the justice system's failure to deal effectively with antirepublican violence lay less in popular hostility to the regime and more in a combination of mistrust about the motives behind judicial action and fear of the consequences of getting involved. In the circumstances of 1800, fear was rational.

Guilty of serious crimes and permanently excluded from power, men like the Rouches, the Ponsys, the Peyrottes, and the rest of their kind relied on a frightening ruthlessness to survive. Systematic intimidation became their main defense. This extended from judges and gendarmes, to jurors, witnesses, and allies. Any magistrate who attempted to prosecute the bandits put his life at risk. Jury director Fontanier required a police escort every time he ventured into the highland villages north of Lodève.[52] Furthermore, successful police action often provoked a swift and deadly response. For example, a night patrol from Gignac surprised a group of outlaws playing boules by moonlight at Arboras. A fierce shootout ensued, leaving Barthélemy Ponsy badly wounded and under arrest. The next day, his comrades mounted an aggressive rescue effort. At dusk, a horde of men invaded Gignac and cleared the streets with gunfire. They killed the National Guard drummer as he beat out the call to arms. As soon as the new mayor, Antoine Laussel (Auguste's brother), lit his lamps, the bandits shot up his house. When the invaders realized that Ponsy *cadet* had already been transferred to Montpellier, they kidnapped Gabriel-Nicolas Avellan, a department judge. Avellan managed, however, to convince his captors that he had had nothing to do with Ponsy's arrest, and the leader released him. "Following their honorable custom," General Gouvion later ironized, "the inhabitants remained tranquilly at home and made no effort either to protect the patriots or to pursue the brigands." But what did he expect? It would have taken the courage of Daniel to challenge the bandits while the town was denuded of troops, all escorting the prisoner to Montpellier. As it was, one of the citizens put his life in serious jeopardy by informing authorities of a secret aqueduct that ran from the Ponsys' house in Gignac into the countryside. Thus, when the forces of order returned later that evening, they were able to arrest another Ponsy wriggling out the end in the dark.[53] Suddenly two elusive Ponsys were again in custody. And yet, as the recent court-martial had shown, arrests were one thing, convictions quite another.

The pervasive climate of mistrust and fear made it infuriatingly difficult to prosecute members of the Rouch-Ponsy gang. In the summer of year VIII, the jury director at Lodève finally charged dozens of men involved in blowing up the Teisserenc residence and killing Olivier as he fled. The act of indictment rested on more than two hundred depositions in which twenty-four of the accused were identified by at least five different witnesses each.[54] However, the grand jury assembled at Lodève failed to indict a single person. This calamity for the justice system can be explained only by political partisanship or the climate of fear in the region. Evidence suggests the latter. The bandits were known to have threatened neighbors with arson and fellow prisoners with death.[55] They were also well informed about prisoner transfers, so it was surely no secret that the police had found a list of jurors among the bandits' effects the year before. The same forces were at work in the failed effort to indict the Ponsy brothers and two others arrested for the town hall robbery at Gignac. All three dozen witnesses who appeared before the grand jury denied seeing the treasury being taken. Since all hearsay evidence was excluded, the hearing took only three hours. Predictably, the jurors refused to indict. Prefect Nogaret responded bitterly: "There isn't an individual in this department who doubts that Joseph Ponsy is one of the leaders of the gang that infests the area around Lodève and Gignac and yet I have every reason to fear that he will be acquitted again on other charges that are being brought against him."[56] The prefect had just cause to worry. Shortly thereafter, five men shot and nearly killed the Lodève merchant Jean Benoit, former president of the department. People agreed that this frightful attack was payback for his recent involvement in antibrigandage operations. A few days later, four men sitting together on the esplanade at Lodève were approached by a pair of thugs carrying guns. They led away Nicolas Boissière, an ordinary woolens worker, and shot him dead. The same thugs later confronted one of his companions, a baker named Corbière, dragged him into a tavern and threatened to kill him too if he dared to testify. This so terrified Corbière that he soon went mad, which rendered him useless as a witness.[57] Incidents such as these were the grizzly reality behind the wall of silence, too often dismissed as an excuse fabricated by negligent officials. As the minister of justice learned, "most of the many scandalous acquittals that have taken place, either by grand juries or trial juries . . . cannot be blamed on the personnel of the judiciary, but on the terror that brigands inspire in witnesses and jurors. . . . The brigands spread fear and dread everywhere to the point that everybody is deaf, blind, and dumb, and nobody dares to speak or bring a grievance."[58] As a result, by the end of 1800, despite repeated arrests, numerous prosecutions, long months in prison, and several actual trials, not a single individual had been judicially punished for the murders and robberies around Lodève and Gignac! In other words, the existing judicial establishment, including military courts, had done nothing to end the cycle of violence in the area. In fact, judicial impotence had exacerbated the situation, encouraging an abuse of police powers on the part of republicans and an enticing sense of impunity on the part of reactionaries.

## Militarized Repression

It is not necessary to trace the many twists and turns in the struggle to stamp out brigandage around Lodève and Gignac. Suffice it to say that the outcome was not a foregone conclusion. The investigation and pursuit of bandits were hindered by all the usual factors—abiding hostility to the republic on the part of Catholic villagers, rugged terrain riddled with caves and gorges, and a shortage of trained men able and willing to undertake dangerous missions in pursuit of die-hard killers. After living through ten years of revolutionary discourse, beleaguered republican officials who found themselves challenged by intrepid and elusive bandits simply could not see them as anything other than counter-revolutionaries against whom all force was permitted.

The inability of the "constituted authorities" to cope with brigandage forced the army to assume a greater role. Of course, the army had been involved in repression throughout the period. However, both its means and its methods had been severely restricted until late in the Directory. By this time, the foreign war had come to overwhelm all other considerations. Just as the polarization of national politics had exacerbated the factional strife at Lodève and Gignac from 1797 to 1799, the national war effort further escalated violence in the region from 1799 to 1801. As noted earlier, moving large amounts of cash from the interior to the armies created new targets of opportunity at the same time that widespread resistance to military service supplied the reactionaries with a growing pool of volunteers glad to join in lucrative holdups. But the republic's response to draft dodging also constituted a serious escalation of violence. Local republicans not only failed to bring brigands to justice, but national conscription policies risked making them into popular heroes defending a just cause. Whatever patriotic luster citizen-soldiers had once enjoyed largely evaporated by the late Directory. The euphemistic "volunteers" of the *levée en masse* were now unmistakably conscripts, and that meant forced recruitment.

*Grosso modo* the entire region from Nantes to Nice experienced severe problems. The republic responded by authorizing local commanders to billet the forces of order on those communities that failed to fill their quota of young men. One could hardly imagine a more coercive practice. Local authorities refused to pay for rations, the officers made exorbitant demands, and conscripts deserted as soon as billeted soldiers were withdrawn from private homes. All efforts to regularize the system failed—and yet it continued throughout year VIII. This earned the republic and its insatiable army unprecedented enmity. Gouvion provided a general overview of matters in the Hérault at the end of the year: "At Béziers, Pézénas, Montagnac, Villeneuve, Marseillans, etc, etc, and in almost all the communes, the mayors and their deputies create the greatest obstacles to the departure of young men; several have said that the government does not have the right to place *garnisaires* [and] justices of the peace refuse to require the payment of these soldiers, who are daily insulted and mistreated." He illustrated his summary with a recent incident at Cazouls-le-Béziers, where a detachment of thirty cannoneers and national guardsmen sent to escort 114 conscripts had been driven from the village. It required a reinforcement of another seventy national guardsmen before the troops could return. Even then the column managed to round up only thirteen recruits, the rest having fled to the mountains.[59] Prolonged resistance to conscription, sustained by dozens of confrontations like this, steadily reduced relations between the republic and many communities to a matter of armed coercion.

With the spate of murders and highway robberies continuing unabated throughout year VIII, the system of criminal justice utterly paralyzed by partisanship and fear, and conscription provoking massive resistance, the government turned to sheer force to end the cycle of violence. Consolidating power under the Consulate depended heavily on military means of repression. In contrast to two centuries of scholarship, it was less a matter of new men and new institutions and more a matter of force.[60] It was the army that consolidated the Consulate, both at home and abroad. This did not create a military dictatorship, but it did run roughshod over the rule of law.

Initial attempts to use armed force against the bandits had largely failed. Ignorance of the terrain, lack of cooperation from locals, and sheer ineptitude had repeatedly frustrated efforts to capture brigands, even those well known to authorities. Men unfamiliar with the many mule paths and upland passageways of the Cévennes inevitably had great trouble tracking their human quarry. Sometimes the pursuit of brigands became farcical. An expedition from Le Vigan, for example, got no support from the cavalry stationed there because the men lacked saddles, boots, and even shoes, leaving them to march in clogs. The dozen gendarmes who did ride out got lost in the dark on Mount Lespérou, barely found their way through the fog and rain the next day, and ended up surrounding three empty houses at La Mouliné.[61] Farce could also turn to tragedy. An expedition from Lodève just missed their prey at Sorbs, arriving in time to find a dinner for twelve and no one to eat it. Frustrated by the lack of cooperation they received and their wasted effort, the "forces of order" proceeded to pillage cheese and poultry from various farms on the way to Sauclières, where they harassed and threatened the local JP, François Sales de Costebelle, a former deputy in the Constituent Assembly. The resulting scandal echoed to Paris and back.[62] Such aggression sprang from undisciplined national guardsmen inflamed by political hatreds and contemptuous of country folk. But the general shortage of troops left local commanders with few options. The gendarmerie was too scattered to confront bands that sometimes swelled to thirty or forty men. And yet recent experiences convinced General Gouvion that the local National Guard was useless at best, and dangerous at worst, and that only regular troops could stop the brigandage.

The Consulate's determination to pursue an aggressive war effort, however, precluded sending reinforcements to the Ninth Military District. Once again it was forced to rely on local resources. The formation of auxiliary battalions in early year VIII provided a certain number of soldiers for the different towns under a "state of siege," including Gignac, but the spring campaign in Italy and Germany saw them all transferred out. The simple act of being sent to the front converted many of these young men from the forces of order to the sources of disorder. Indeed, the massive desertion of conscripts en route across Languedoc produced a crescendo of brigandage and criminality. General Gouvion, Prefect Nogaret, and even Minister of Police Fouché repeatedly asked the new minister of war for regular troops to restore order. Carnot responded by insisting that all available troops were needed on the frontiers. Therefore, not only did the Ninth Military District not receive more troops, but its main resource, the Tenth Regiment of Hussards, was ordered to depart for Italy. This left the division devoid of regular troops except for five companies of coast guard cannoneers.[63] Stripping the region of cavalry made it difficult to provide adequate escorts for treasury wagons and stagecoaches. It also stymied any sustained offensive against outlaws.

Aware of the appalling lawlessness in the region but unable to send troops, Carnot authorized each department in the Ninth Military District to mobilize two hundred national guardsmen for constant duty. In addition to pressing conscription across the department, the national guardsmen of the Hérault would be assigned to combat brigandage around Lodève. Recourse to national guardsmen was hardly new, and past experiences did not augur well. This time, however, the enterprise was given a more military aspect. To ensure obedience and effective service, the new mobile column and its various subunits would be commanded by reactivated army officers. Any serious lapses in discipline would be subject to court-martial. Furthermore, given delays and security leaks in the past, Prefect Nogaret, a brigadier general himself, authorized General Gouvion to dispense with having a civilian commissioner appointed for each mission.[64] As a result, soldiers and not civilians planned and led most operations. This greatly curtailed the partisan license that had so tainted the ragtag posses of previous years.

With diminished means on hand, the struggle to repress brigandage depended heavily on the bravery and cunning of the few trained men available, especially those in the gendarmerie. Conditions at the turn of the century made the work of the rural constabulary—difficult and poorly paid at the best of times—truly perilous. Nevertheless, the Directory's reorganizations of the gendarmerie and multiple screenings of its officers helped to ensure that their participation in the new mobile column gave it greater efficacy than past attempts to employ national guardsmen. Lieutenant Siran, commander of the gendarmerie at Lodève, acquired the reputation of a brilliant and dogged enemy of brigands. Having engaged them in several deadly gun battles, he had no illusions about the risks that national guardsmen would run if they came face to face with outlaws. The bandits were more numerous and better armed than the police and did not hesitate to challenge them on the roads.[65] It was especially alarming to learn that at Le Caylar, north of Lodève, as many as eighty young men, many masked and armed, had totally overwhelmed a brigade of gendarmes and a detachment of the mobile column assigned to escort two dozen conscripts to Montpellier. The "fusilade vigoureuse" unleashed by the rebels left one gendarme dead and two guardsmen wounded.[66] Such incidents rightly terrified the "forces of order" and inspired the government to adopt draconian measures.

The cycle of violence in the northern Hérault was finally settled by a ruthless deployment of military force. After countless pleas for more troops and baleful lamentations about the inadequacy of the judicial system, the government decided on a brief but ferocious period of repression. On 1 nivôse IX (22 December 1800), the Consulate issued a directive ordering General Gouvion to form a "flying column" (*corps d'éclaireurs*) composed of 180 infantry, 30 cavalry, and 30 mounted gendarmes, and accompanied by an "extraordinary military commission." The critical shortage of troops in the district, especially cavalry, delayed assembling the corps. Finally, on 13 January 1801, the column marched west out of Montpellier, fanned out to scour a dozen villages, and converged on Gignac. This was a symbolic place to begin. As General Gouvion remarked laconically, "a great example has become necessary" at Gignac.[67] Within forty-eight hours, the military commission had condemned and executed its first two brigands. These were local men who had deserted the army and taken up with the Ponsy boys. They had been caught in bed together with a third man, all dressed, armed, and resisting arrest.[68] The commission quickly passed to Lodève, where it tried and shot seven men, including Jean Rouch and Barthélemy Ponsy, for robbing the army treasury at the *taillade de Gignac,* the concept of double jeopardy notwithstanding.[69] These men did not last long once they faced the summary justice of the military commission rather than the loopholes, laxity, and concerns for due process shown by regular courts.

Rather than linger around Lodève trying to track down other members of the gang, the *corps d'éclaireurs* and its military commission moved to the Aveyron. It spent three weeks at Millau and Rodez, where it dealt mainly with members of three modest bands responsible for an amazing array of holdups and public assaults.[70] The family feud at Lodève had contributed greatly to a regional cycle of violence, and the work of repression in the Aveyron was critical to limiting the influence of the outlaws from the northern Hérault. "Deserters had perverted public spirit and fortified the brigands [and] in the arrondissement of St-Affrique deserters threatened to join the band leaders from Lodève," wrote the prefect.[71] In this climate, efforts to snap the pernicious link between brigands and local supporters led to some deliberately terrifying judgments. For example, no one had actually seen Pierre Baumel at a holdup, but twenty-five of his neighbors testified that he frequently provided food, shelter, and a meeting place for his brothers-in-law, the locally notorious Souldos alias Meillons, and their friends, and that he had been well compensated for it. How else could he, a simple weaver with seven children to feed, have built the finest house in the hamlet of Puech? One suspects that most of Baumel's neighbors stayed overnight in Millau to see him shot the following day; it would have been reassuring.[72] But the commission did not multiply such examples—that risked uniting the entire populace against it. In fact, the commission acquitted half the people it tried in the Aveyron, and even some accomplices were condemned to as little as two years in prison. The commission's discrimination encouraged those only marginally connected to brigands to prove their loyalty to the new regime by providing evidence against them. General Gouvion provided additional incentive by issuing exemptions from military service to draft dodgers who assisted in the capture of notable brigands. Fear gained added force when offset by leniency.

After dealing with this potpourri of small fry from the Aveyron, the military commission moved to Le Vigan in the western Gard. Here it tried and executed the *abbé* Jean-Louis Solier, nicknamed Sans-Peur. The commission's verdict described him as "one of the principal organizers of the system of brigandage in the departments of the Ninth Military District and one of the principal leaders of the bands which had committed the robberies of public funds, other thefts, and assaults . . . and of having himself murdered different individuals, military and civilian alike."[73] Despite the lack of evidence to support this claim, it was announced on hundreds of broadsheets plastered throughout the region and became the definitive historical version of the brigand priest Sans-Peur. Such a judgment has long obscured the true leaders, as well as the specific sources, of banditry in the region.

From Le Vigan, the military commission returned to Montpellier, where it dispatched more members of the Rouch-Ponsy gang. Word of the commission's activities in the Hérault and Aveyron began to loosen tongues, including those of accused criminals. Once in custody and facing sudden death, some bandits became rather garrulous with authorities. The deadly results lead one to suspect that promises of leniency were made but not honored. For example, Antoine Bascou, a farmhand from Gignac, confessed to the mayor that he had received an impressive 2,400 francs as his share from a robbery there. Despite giving a detailed description of the town hall heist and even naming a dozen of his fellow participants, Bascou was condemned to death and shot at Montpellier just like two other members of the band.[74] Though the commission soon moved into the Gard and the Ardèche, where it held over a hundred more sessions, it did not neglect the occasional judicial straggler from the band around Lodève. At Nîmes it condemned another two brigands involved in the armed robberies of year VIII, added a third at Alès, and finished up with Louis Ponsy at Privas. All of the ensuing executions took place back in the Hérault.[75] Posters could describe the army's success against brigands, but public executions brought the meaning home. This made it easier for citizens to judge for themselves who was more terrifying, the republic or its opponents.

The repression of early 1801 was not the work of the military commission alone but required relentless police activity. Though subprefects, mayors, and justices of the peace all made important contributions, the successful crackdown relied heavily on the gendarmerie and *corps d'éclaireurs*. Studying the individual cases sent before the military commission reveals the ability of continual patrols, roundups, and shake-downs to clean up inchoate criminal organizations.[76] The use of several companies of coast guard cannoneers proved especially critical to operations. Both better trained and more committed than other national guardsmen, the cannoneers provided extraordinary service. Together the companies of cannoneers and the gendarmerie gave detachments of the mobile column the backbone similar units had so often lacked in the past. Being used as local shock troops also meant that the cannoneers paid a high price. Tipped off that bandits were using a mill on the outskirts of Lodève as a refuge, the cannoneers surrounded it and then penetrated inside. Finding a trap door, the sergeant and three of his men climbed down into an underground moat. As they waded through the water, candles in one hand and muskets in the other, a waiting outlaw shot the sergeant dead. The other cannoneers quickly withdrew and resorted to smoking out their opponents. Despite the killing of their sergeant and taunts of "Come on down, filthy terrorists! We know we're lost, but others will die first," the cannoneers promised the two bandits safe conduct if they surrendered and then, surprisingly, kept their word. When the two men emerged, well-armed and wearing white cockades, they were delivered unharmed to the local prison.[77] This combination of daring and discipline was a truly precious asset. After years of pusillanimous policing and factionalized national guardsmen, the *corps d'éclaireurs* finally provided a reliable instrument of repression.

Courage and self-control were supplemented by spying and bribery. The Directory had sometimes provided small amounts of money for secret police work. Most of this was given to either executive commissioners or district commanders. The Consulate quickly turned this desultory practice into a regular system. Every six months, Prefect Nogaret received 1,000 francs for special police expenses, most of which were distributed by officers of the gendarmerie at Lodève and Montpellier. At one point, Lieutenant of the Gendarmerie Montels and Captain Stoos, commander of the First Company of Coast Guard Cannoneers, distributed a total of 362 francs "to various individuals who had participated in the pursuit and arrest of brigands" around Lodève. The relatively small amounts accorded certain individuals at Gignac give some sense of how far a few hundred francs in secret police funds could go in facilitating the war on brigandage. One Jean-Antoine Pelisse received twelve francs following the arrest of Bascou (who then proved very talkative himself); Catherine Peyronnet was paid 24 francs for "having cooperated in the arrest of Ponsy *cadet*"; and another 36 francs was distributed "to the spies who revealed the brigand [Joseph] Ponsy."[78] In other words, the government got an impressive return on its investment.

From time to time, the police would also try to infiltrate criminal networks. Though details are rare, and the subtleties of the process difficult to discern, some agents showed a particular aptitude for the job. Alexis Privat, a handkerchief maker from Montpellier, for example, repeatedly found ways to insinuate himself into groups of robbers, learn their plans, and then expose them to the authorities.[79] The most common subterfuge in penetrating brigand bands was for soldiers to pretend to be deserters. Although they often shed their uniforms, they always kept their guns. Toting guns, even a 1771-model musket made by the government arms factory at St.-Etienne, was generally taken more as a sign of hostility to the regime than as a threat to society. Furthermore, disguising soldiers as deserters served to cover differences in accent or colloquial expressions, ignorance about the immediate region, or an odd inquisitiveness about outlaw hideouts or the activities of local criminals. Even hardened cannoneers from the *colonne d'éclaireurs* found it easy to impersonate deserters and thereby penetrate the network of bandits around Lodève. In fact, all of these approaches were a major part of its operations.[80]

Though intended to help restore order, the systematic use of secret police funds to hire spies and reward informants, as well as the repeated use of false deserters to infiltrate brigand bands, also helped to unravel the fabric of community life by increasing the level of popular mistrust. Of course, more than a decade of revolutionary turmoil had already badly damaged the coherence of community life in the northern Hérault. This was especially true in places as deeply divided as Gignac or as large and diverse as Lodève. And yet paying ordinary citizens for information on the regime's opponents, even those increasingly prone to use fear and intimidation themselves, marked a significant stage in the erosion of an independent local politics. The populace of Paris had been subjected to secretive police spying for many decades before the Revolution,[81] but such practices were new to the countryside. Inevitably, the consequence was a similar growth in suspicion and alienation.

The *colonne d'éclaireurs* and its attendant military commission put an end to the cycle of violence in the northern Hérault. A number of loose ends remained, however. In fact, though the violence subsided, the most important members of the gang had yet to be brought to justice. Joseph Ponsy was not captured until June 1801, after yet another shoot-out with the gendarmerie. The transfer from St.-André to Montpellier and a lengthy interrogation by a judge on the newly formed Special Tribunal of the Hérault did not improve his chances of recovery. He died overnight in the citadel at Montpellier. More than a year later, the Peyrottes brothers were finally arrested in Barcelona, where they had continued their politics of revenge by robbing émigré aristocrats. In contrast, Pierre Rouch, who lost his father and brother to the Consular repression, somehow survived and returned to Lodève, where he lived the prosperous life of a local notable. He remained undisturbed by the justice system until 1812, when he was suddenly arrested and tried by the Assize Court for the murder of Olivier Teisserenc fifteen years earlier. Rouch sent a relative to plead with the Archichancelier Cambacérès (himself from the Hérault), but to little purpose, for jurors once again declined to convict.[82] This appears to have closed the book, at least far as the official record is concerned, on the cycle of violence in the district of Lodève during the First Republic.[83]

## Local Lessons

The spate of assaults, murders, arrests, robberies, trials, gun battles, and executions that made up the cycle of violence in the northern Hérault from 1796 to 1801 does not fit the usual explanations for sustained civil violence in the period. Profound social causes are missing. There were no significant differences in social status between the rival groups. In fact, both sides mobilized men from throughout the social hierarchy—manufacturers, seigneurs, ex-priests, teachers, farmhands, craftsmen, porters, and wagon drivers were sprinkled almost randomly throughout the conflict. Nor were the two factions constituted around clear poles of social, professional, or occupational patronage. The woolens industry had its ups and downs during the period, but this did not provoke craftsmen to band together against employers or take one side or the other in the factional dispute. Nor was this violence the product of rural resentment against urbanites expanding their reach into the countryside. The initial feud began as a rivalry between merchant-manufacturers at Lodève and simply mobilized existing tensions in neighboring bourgs such as Gignac and Aniane as well as upland communities along Mount Séranne. Furthermore, the long-standing animosity between Catholics and Protestants in the Cévennes contributed little or nothing to the troubles. Almost all of the towns and villages affected were Catholic. Nor were the robberies and assaults the work of royalist "companies," that is, paramilitary squads linked to grand conspiracies hatched beyond the frontiers. Moreover, though previous events in the Revolution had helped to sharpen differences and exacerbate long-standing rivalries, the region had been largely spared violence until the Directory. Unlike so many other parts of the Midi, the Federalist Revolts, with their ramifications in the Terror and Reaction, had not been bloody. Where there was resentment, it was over the loss of material and cultural advantages (the abolition of seigneurial rights, the sequestration and sale of émigré property, the confiscation of the local church) or comparatively minor mistreatment (being sacked from office or spending a few months in prison). Unlike in Provence, the deep reserves of bitterness and malice did not derive from the actual killing of friends and family members earlier in the Revolution.

With so many standard explanations counting for so little in this case, one can only conclude that the cycle of violence was produced by the interaction between peculiar, though not unique, local circumstances and the forces at work on a national level. The violence was local, but it was made possible by the inadequacies of the republican regime. Local government, criminal justice, national guardsmen and gendarmerie all failed miserably, allowing isolated rivalries to spin out of control. A family feud between the Rouches and the Teisserencs over a water supply at Lodève, and the long-standing rivalry between the White and Blue Penitents at Gignac, represented by the Ponsy and Laussel families respectively, triggered the first killings. But it was the national forces of royalism, Jacobinism, Catholicism, and war that turned these conflicts into regional strife. The elections of 1797 gave the royalists impunity to persecute their rivals. When the Fructidor coup put local Jacobins back in power, they took revenge. Their hard-line policies on religion, their disregard for legality, and their reliance on force to retain power prolonged the conflict. Once it became clear that the regime would not play by its own rules, that politics could not be "normalized" within the institutional framework of the republic, refractory priests like the *abbé* Solier and émigrés such Causse, Peyrottes, and Blachère had little choice but to associate with murderous outlaws like the Rouches and the Ponsys. The war added a ready supply of accomplices in the form of draft dodgers, deserters, and escaped prisoners of war, as well as creating the targets of criminal opportunity, large shipments of cash on their way to the front. However, it was not a removal of Jacobins from positions of power after Brumaire—which did not happen around Lodève—or the defeat of royalism elsewhere in France, notably in the west, nor even the Concordat or Peace of Amiens in 1802 that ended the cycle of violence in the northern Hérault; it was sustained, ruthless military repression.

# 11 Consular Crackdown

> Only by making the war terrible for them will the inhabitants themselves
> join together against the brigands and finally sense that their apathy is
> harmful to them.
> —First Consul Bonaparte to General Brune, 24 nivôse VIII
> (14 January 1800)

AFTER SIEYÈS AND BONAPARTE brought down the Directory, they sought
to break with its discredited policies, especially those with a Jacobin taint.
The Consulate gave the initial appearance of a return to regular justice and
an end to political persecution. It began by immediately revoking the law of
hostages, and Bonaparte appeared in person to release detainees from the
Temple prison. Although the government had no objection to using army
officers to judge civilians accused of brigandage, Brumairian lawmakers did
object and so let the law of 29 nivôse VI lapse. Prosecuting acts of brigandage and armed robbery would again fall on regular civilian courts. Finally,
the Council of State promptly ruled that the Constitution of Year VIII nullified previous laws of discrimination against relatives of émigrés and former nobles and thereby readmitted them to political participation. As L'Ami
des lois wrote in response to this series of measures: "If the government
perseveres in its principles and if all officials adopt them, we will be able
to say—and with such feelings of joy and gratitude!—that the Revolution
is over. Let us hope so!"[1] It was not so easy. Despite efforts to regularize the
new regime, the escalating level of violence made it obvious that people did
not like Bonaparte's republic any more than the Directory's. The supposed
return to legality would be no easier than it had been in 1795.

Excessive emphasis on the Brumaire coup as a watershed moment has
obscured the fact that the Consulate's first year was as strife-torn as the

Directory's last. Large bands of rebels and brigands swelled by hundreds of draft dodgers roved the countryside raiding treasury shipments, kidnapping and holding for ransom scores of wealthy property owners, and overwhelming local law enforcement. They preferred shooting gendarmes to disarming them. In numerous places in the west and south, they rode into towns in broad daylight to rob local tax collectors and burn administrative papers. Witnesses who dared to testify had their barns burned and their houses shot up. Others were murdered in cold blood. Whole departments again became gripped by fear. The Consulate and its officials responded to continued opposition with big dollops of postrevolutionary rhetoric backed by a ferocious determination to stamp out lawlessness and antirepublican violence. General Calvin, the new commander of the anarchic Vaucluse, reflected this attitude with his inaugural proclamation on 15 ventôse VIII (6 March 1800): "The reign of factions is over, that of order is beginning. The Government detests the wicked, and I declare in its name that I will make open war on the brigands who are devastating the countryside.... You have sacrificed so much for the fatherland! Soon it will no longer be necessary, and with the Revolution ended, all Frenchmen will enjoy, under a strong and just government, peace, liberty, and public security, without which there is no happiness."[2]

Such widespread lawlessness grew out of the Consulate's decision to continue pursuing the Directory's war aims while simultaneously undertaking a huge reorganization of the state's administrative and judicial apparatus. The victories at Zurich and Bergen-op-Zoom in late September 1799 had parried the threat of invasion weeks before the Brumaire coup, and just as the Directory's mobilization effort was reaching its peak. Department officials struggled desperately to provide boots, uniforms, muskets, and equipment for the new "auxiliary battalions." A levy of one in thirty horses had begun, and the forced loan continued to be collected, though under different terms. The war effort, and not speculations about the future of democracy, dominated local politics throughout the autumn and winter of year VIII. Thus, it was in the midst of mobilization that the Consulate undertook its massive shift from locally elected departmental, cantonal, and judicial officials to a highly centralized and tutelary system of appointed prefects, subprefects, mayors, and judges. The new institutions and procedures were not easy to establish. Many prominent citizens declined to participate, and the government had cause to regret a fair number of its initial choices.[3] The republic's survival, and thus the preservation of some basic revolutionary achievements, depended on a vigorous use of force in order to prosecute the war and establish the new institutions.

## Criminal Justice under the Consulate

The change of regimes from Directory to Consulate badly disrupted efforts to restore law and order. Not only did Brumairian lawmakers end the practice of sending brigands before military courts, but the activity of criminal courts plummeted in year VIII. Appendix A.1 shows the magnitude of this drop. Several factors produced the dramatic reduction in criminal prosecution, none of which had to do with a decline in criminal activity, which raged on ferociously. First, the Brumaire coup and the uncertainties of a new regime dampened enthusiasm for the pursuit of crime. Every official, whether elected or appointed, had reason to worry about the future of his position. The anti-Jacobin tenor of the coup gave special pause to the most ardent defenders of the republic—that is, to the very men who had helped to infuse the judiciary with added intensity after Fructidor. Second, the Consulate massively restructured the apparatus of rule. When new institutions were announced, old ones ground to a halt. Tens of thousands of local officials stopped performing their duties before replacements had been named, let alone agreed to serve. Senior officials raged about the great gashes such inaction tore in the net of law enforcement. Third, in its overhaul of the judicial system, the Consulate replaced all elected judges, public prosecutors, and court presidents with government appointees. This required making more than three thousand judicial appointments. The pool of candidates was large and well-stocked, which made it easier to exclude unworthy magistrates, and the new regime weighed political opinions much less than professional experience. Nonetheless, it took the government several months to make its choices; consequently, it was June 1800 before most courts were fully staffed.[4] Finally, the activity of criminal courts fell sharply in the Consulate because the law of 25 frimaire VIII (16 December 1799) recalibrated punishments for many types of crime. This included downgrading a range of thefts from felonies to misdemeanors.[5] The law's preamble indicates that reducing penalties for these crimes was actually intended to increase repression because a lack of proportion between crimes and punishments had too often been "a source of impunity and impunity is itself a source of crime."[6] But even if we exclude all "petty thefts" from the criminal court data for the Directory—which enables us to compare judicial activity directed against the most serious crimes—we see that less than half as many people were prosecuted for felonies in year VIII as in year VII. This leaves no doubt that the Brumaire coup was a source of impunity and, therefore, was itself a source of crime.

Any judicial redress effected by the Consulate was delayed until long after the Brumaire coup and even then did not come primarily from regular criminal courts (as we shall see later). In order to take the measure of criminal court activity in the early Consulate, we are better advised to use data from years IX and X. These teach us that although the judicial reforms of year VIII did not significantly alter the nature of criminal courts, these courts became decidedly less repressive than during the Directory. This decline in the level of "judicial repression" was experienced in a variety of ways. In the most general terms, the number of persons charged with felonies in the early years of the Consulate was well under half of what it had been during the last years of the Directory. This was due to a huge decrease in prosecutions in absentia. More significant was that remarkably fewer individuals were present at trial as well. Even though this number increased somewhat from its nadir in year VIII, criminal courts in years IX and X handled only 53 percent as many defendants charged with crimes greater than "petty theft" as the same courts had handled in years VI and VII (see appendix A.5). The steep decline in prosecutions in the Consulate was common to all four departments of our study, as well as three courts studied by others.[7] The level of "penal repression" handed out by regular criminal courts was also substantially lower after 1800 than it had been previously. The acquittal rate for persons present at trial increased 15 percent, and felony convictions decreased 9 percent between the Second Directory and the established Consulate.[8] Such a trend has no obvious explanation. It was certainly not the result of less carefully chosen jurors; the Consulate made the preparation of jury lists a key function of subprefects and prefects. Nor can the increase in the acquittal rate be attributed to a major shift in the type of crimes brought to trial. In fact, prosecutions for crimes that tended to benefit from "jury nullification," such as various forms of resistance to public authority or interpersonal violence, declined dramatically. The fact that such crimes continued to benefit from jurors' clemency makes it worth pausing briefly to consider the ways in which the criminal courts of the Consulate dealt with these sorts of crimes.

Persons charged with political crimes or resistance to public authority appeared before criminal courts far less frequently during the Consulate, dropping to 15 percent of the number of individuals prosecuted for similar crimes during the aggressive last two years of the Directory. Most of those charged with violence against public officials during the Consulate had opposed conscription or tax collection. Almost all were acquitted. Prosecutions of seditious speech became rare but did not disappear, although now a radical republican was as likely to be prosecuted as a royalist. For example, one nostalgic terrorist, a café owner from Frontignan (Hérault), was charged with "words against the government" for claiming that he and ten like him would have done a better job of assassinating "this villain, this usurper, this tyrant at Paris"; once they had succeeded, he is said to have claimed, the country would return to the Constitution of 1793, arrests would multiply, revolutionary committees would reappear, and guillotines would operate incessantly.[9] The trend toward punishing republican agitators was matched by the courts' lenient treatment of political cases against reactionaries. These cases were invariably the detritus of earlier trials and almost always led to acquittals. As a result, 1800 constituted a mass graveyard of political affairs.

One of the largest and longest-running trials of the period illustrates the Consulate's response to political prosecutions initiated under the Second Directory. In a desire to prove the merits of the Fructidor coup, the Directory had encouraged the prosecution of reactionaries in the Tarn on charges of conspiring to overthrow the republic. A jury director filed charges against 132 individuals, which a grand jury reduced to 92 (61 in absentia). These included three department administrators, five municipal administrators from Castres, and two National Guard commanders (those of Castres and Labruguière). In order to escape the Tarn's poisoned atmosphere, the Court of Cassation transferred the case to the Criminal Court of the Haute-Garonne.[10] A year later, on 1 germinal VII (21 March 1799), after six weeks of hearings and more than five hundred witnesses, republican jurors at Toulouse convicted fifteen of the nineteen defendants present at trial. Six were sentenced to deportation for conspiracy to restore monarchy, four were condemned to death for murder, and five were given short prison terms for acts of violence. None of these sentences was implemented, however. An appeal led the Consulate's Court of Cassation to nullify the original indictment and transfer the case to the jury director at Carcassonne. He excluded another forty of the original accused and prepared charges against thirteen individuals in custody and thirty-nine still at large. On 1 messidor VIII (19 June 1800), despite hearing testimony from ninety-nine witnesses, including one the judges and jurors had to visit in his sick bed, the grand jury at Carcassonne declined to indict anyone.[11] Thus, after defendants had spent almost three years in prison, after the criminal justice system had spent extraordinary time and money on prosecution, and after the credibility of the Directory had been sorely tested, the entire affair was quietly snuffed out. This granted judicial immunity to the perpetrators of several armed clashes and the brutal lynching of a republican farmer and his wife. The case had drawn national attention, and its pathetic denouement clearly signaled the Consulate's intention to abandon cases that arose out of the Directory's revolutionary politics. Here is an important reason for the significant drop in the caseload of criminal courts during the Consulate.

The Consulate also brought far fewer prosecutions for interpersonal violence. Though prosecutions did not decline to their previous level during the early years of the Directory, the total number of individuals who appeared in court charged with interpersonal violence of one sort or another (including armed robbery) did stand in stark contrast to the high level attained in years VI and VII.[12] The reduction by almost half that occurred in this interval should not, however, be taken as correlated to a similar drop in the actual incidence of crime. As previously noted, court data from the period reflect the rate of repression far more accurately than the rate of crime. All the same, the number of murders and assaults did decline perceptibly, if not by year IX, then certainly by year X. And yet various forms of armed robbery remained alarmingly common and not only in the west and south. As we shall see shortly, the national scourge of brigandage provoked yet another form of exceptional justice. All the same, in over two-thirds of departments in the country, regular criminal courts were left to cope on their own. Not surprisingly, their treatment of armed robbers proved at least as deadly as before. The Criminal Court of the Haute-Saône, for example, tried twenty-two individuals for robbery with violence in the years IX and X. This included ten men and four women assimilated into a gang and charged with several murders and armed robberies committed across three departments: five were guillotined at Vesoul, and six were sent to the *bagne* to do eighteen years of hard labor.[13] Their crime spree in a region otherwise generally free of criminal bands underscored the insecurity Frenchmen around the country continued to feel under the new regime.

Despite their harsh treatment of armed robbers, criminal courts meted out far less "penal repression" following the judicial reforms of 1800 than they had during the late Directory. This remains the case even when we alter Directorial data (for the purpose of making a more valid comparison) by excluding those defendants charged with the types of "petty thefts" that later passed to the Consulate's courts of first instance. Table 2 reveals that the overall level of penal repression fell below even that of the early Directory. It also shows several striking trends. First, the disappearance of judicial sentences of deportation reflects the Consulate's shift away from prosecuting political crimes. Second, the amount of punishment meted out for ordinary crimes also saw a dramatic decline. The number of sentences to short, medium, and long terms of hard labor fell to well under half what it had been in the late Directory. In fact, it did not even reach two-thirds of the level experienced in the early Directory, a period during which criminal courts were widely disparaged for laxity. Third, death sentences, too, declined to less than half of the previous total. Thus, as the early Consulate's combination of fewer defendants and a higher acquittal rate would lead one to expect, the total amount of "penal repression" meted out by criminal courts was substantially lower after the judicial reforms of 1800 than it had been in the Second Directory.

The rare studies of departmental criminal courts during the First Republic have interpreted the downturn in criminal court activities during the early Consulate as uncomplicated evidence of a dramatic drop in crime. They naturally credit the wisdom and determination of Bonaparte and his collaborators with this apparent return to law and order. Such evidence helps to confirm the black legend of the Directory, as well as the view that the Brumaire coup constituted a break with previous practices. This is highly misleading. The diminished activity of criminal courts under the Consulate needs to be understood in a broader context. On one hand, the decline in criminal court activity in departments that did not suffer from endemic unrest, such as the Haute-Saône, Marne, and Côte-d'Or, is evidence that the Second Directory's intervention in the realm of criminal justice had significantly improved law and order, even when imposed in stridently re-

TABLE 2

Total felony punishments meted out by four criminal courts to defendants present at trial (excluding "petty thefts" for years IV to VII)

| Two-year period | IV + V | VI + VII | IX + X |
|---|---|---|---|
| 2 to 9 years of hard labor | 137 | 119 | 46 |
| 10 to 18 years of hard labor | 64 | 115 | 65 |
| 20 or more years of hard labor | 54 | 59 | 28 |
| Deportation | 3 | 24 | 0 |
| Death | 27 | 68 | 29 |

publican terms. This appears to be true for at least three-quarters of the departments of France. Had it not been for the disruptions of year VIII, crime in these areas would undoubtedly have declined even sooner. On the other hand, following the trajectory of criminal court activity alone is misleading for regions afflicted with endemic brigandage or continued civil strife. Everything we have just learned about the activities of regular criminal courts during the Consulate needs to be seen in light of the regime's recourse to exceptional justice. The creation of military commissions for about a fifth of the country and the later introduction of special tribunals in a quarter of the departments of France together greatly increased the total "penal repression" meted out by the Consulate. This is evidence that the Consulate made even greater use of exceptional justice than did the Directory. This came in the context of renewed civil war in the west and rampant brigandage in the Midi.

## Military Measures for the Midi

The continued unrest of 1800 made it hard for the new regime to operate without using military justice to try civilians, especially when the entire apparatus of criminal justice was being reconfigured. Rather than seek a new law on military justice, however, the First Consul decided to handle matters his own way. In zones where violence had been especially intractable, with criminal and political elements inextricably tied together, Bonaparte reached for military commissions to cut the Gordian knot. In the spring of 1800, he ordered the creation of one military commission to fight brigandage in the upland areas of the Rhône Valley and Provence, another to combat *barbets* in the foothills north of Nice, and a third to deal with chouans in Brittany.[14] Each commission consisted of seven army officers unrestrained by either jurisprudence or appeal procedures. Although the three commissions lacked the considerable juridical restraints built into the expired law of 29 nivôse VI, they were tightly limited in geographic scope. The most important of these commissions sat at Avignon. Its role in confronting the intractable violence of the region greatly influenced later developments and merits a closer look.

On 22 ventôse VIII (13 March 1800), First Consul Bonaparte gave the implacable General P.-M.-B. Férino "extraordinary powers" to restore order in the departments of the Drôme, Ardèche, Vaucluse, and Basses-Alpes. This meant combining national guardsmen with regular troops to form flying columns and authorizing them to execute any brigands caught armed. Accomplices and those caught unarmed were to be sent before a military commission at Avignon.[15] Such drastic measures resulted from the striking failure of previous attempts to restore order, the collapse of state authority in the winter of year VIII, and the overt challenge posed to the army by swelling bands of outlaws.

The protracted violence of the Midi was more complicated than in western France. Relatively dense urbanization, southern sociability, and quick tempers had helped to breed intense and often violent revolutionary politics in the *garrigues* and low-lying regions of the Rhône Valley and Mediterranean coast. The Federalist Revolts and Thermidorian Reaction had urban epicenters whose shock waves reverberated throughout the lowlands. As one moved upland, the predominantly intracommunal violence gave way to a more atavistic resistance to external authority. In the rocky hills and isolated valleys of the Cévennes, Rouergue, Gévaudan, Vivarais, Dauphiné, and Haute-Provence, villagers generally accepted and often supported an almost anarchic mix of banditry, resistance to conscription, and counter-revolutionary conspiracy.[16] The proximity of Lyon, a wellspring of royalist machinations, irrigated the spirit of revolt in the region. According to Fouché, the frequency and ferocity of brigand assaults in the Basses-Alpes passed "all stretches of the imagination."[17] Matters were at least as bad in the Ardèche and Vaucluse. Even the less turbulent Drôme saw brigandage reach its apogee in year VIII. By this time, outlaw bands had become increasingly well organized, each with designated leaders, some of whom bore commissions from the Pretender. These "officers" were distinguished from their rustic followers by a crude uniform with epaulettes, as well as quality horses and excellent French. The smaller bands had between twenty and sixty men; the larger ones, such as that led by Blanc-Tristan, numbered over a hundred. The leaders referred to the mix of bandits, draft dodgers, and malcontents who served under them as "chasseurs de Louis XVIII," which they proudly proclaimed whenever they invaded a town to pillage the tax collector, set fire to houses, or kill the mayor. Many of these royalist leaders acted on instructions from the émigré court in England. As in western France, they planned a coordinated assault on urban centers timed to follow the harvest of 1799.[18] But the crescendo of violence in year VIII was not primarily the product of royalist conspiracy. Rather, it was the infusion of royalist leaders into an already chaotic mix of endemic lawlessness and long-standing local hatreds that made the violence of that year so spectacular.

This solvent of eunomia can be better understood by observing events in the southern Ardèche. Civil strife there went back to the earliest days of the Revolution. The massive mobilization of Catholics at Jalès in 1790 and 1791, the Saillans conspiracy of 1792, the mass attack on the military garrison at Barjac in April 1796, and Saint-Christol's seizure of Pont-Saint-Esprit in October 1797 all originated from the southern Ardèche. Each of these brief rebellions was roundly repressed. Furthermore, years of dogged police work eliminated the leading royalist commanders of the region, men like Dominique Allier, the chevalier de Lamothe, and the marquis de Surville. And yet their successive deaths in 1798 did not end political violence. Though most inhabitants refused to join a royalist insurgency, they were so alienated by anticlericalism, national land sales, and conscription that they happily sheltered the rebels among them. Over the next two years, the struggle between the republic and local outlaws proved as fierce as anywhere in France. Tough and cunning men like Guillaume Fontanieu (aka Jambe-de-Bois) and Marc Blaye led small bands of the disaffected in executing scores of assaults, incursions, holdups, extortions, midnight raids, pillages, and assassinations. The region drifted into chaos and guerrilla war, and public authority came to depend increasingly on the army.[19] Fifteen cantons of the southern Ardèche, including the entire Tanargue region, were put under a state of siege in the autumn of 1798. Only a lack of troops prevented the government from extending this to even more places.[20]

Jacobins won back power in the elections of April 1799, in part by having the army break up the alternative assembly at Privas. Their immediate response to resistance was to escalate repression. Some effective lobbying in Paris got the ruthless Adjutant-General Nivet appointed as department commander. He and the department administrators promptly organized six flying columns of national guardsmen. In the summer and autumn of 1799, the new columns conducted a series of "grand sweeps" in which up to five hundred men marched across the region for a week or two at a time. These aggressive expeditions rounded up numerous conscripts, a score of rebels, and few refractory priests. Though urban areas sometimes paid the price during the absence of armed force, such sustained activity disrupted the rebel companies enough to prevent their planned offensive. This momentary success was marred by unprecedented brutality. The columns of guardsmen, led by redundant officers and swollen with refractory conscripts, lacked all discipline. They treated the hill country as enemy soil, burning shacks, ransacking *oustas,* and living at the expense of local farmers. Their commanders, men such as Enjolras, the intrepid JP of Coucouron, and Captain Montchaussé, Nivet's fierce subordinate, took to threatening captured rebels with immediate execution unless they revealed their companions' whereabouts. Such threats were far from empty: Nivet and his men showed no more legal scruples than those who operated the "dirty war" against *chouannerie*. Encouraged by the Jacobin central commissioner, Robert, the security forces began arbitrarily arresting scores of people, including relatives of émigrés, supposed rebel sympathizers, and even whole families. Although these arrests were blatantly illegal, the torment and murder caused by the mobile columns "so terrified the region that the inhabitants did not dare to file a complaint."[21]

The republican columns badly discredited the republic. Their sustained harassment, arbitrary arrests, and political reprisals helped to justify the rebels' violence in the eyes of the populace. In order to escape the rapine of the mobile columns, peasants went from practicing a benevolent neutrality toward the rebels, to taking their side, calling on their assistance, and even actively joining their cause. Here was a cycle of violence typical of Provence. Unlike the flare-up of banditry around Gignac and Lodève in 1799–1800, the violence of the southern Ardèche was the culmination of a decade of regional hostilities that had repeatedly mobilized the forces of reaction against the Revolution. As a result, the violence there was more spectacular and a great deal more deadly than that of the Hérault. The remaining republicans lived as if in foreign territory, beleaguered and besieged. By the time of the Brumaire coup, larger, better organized, and more coordinated bands, both criminal and political, had but one obstacle to overcome: the army.

Months of intense repression provoked a stunning assassination. On 1 pluviôse VIII (21 Janurary 1800), three men carrying army muskets shot Captain Montchaussé through the head just after he left Nivet's lodgings in Aubenas. Needless to say, nobody recognized the killers.[22] Montchaussé's murder in a major town under an official state of siege revealed more than the rebels' audacity or the dangers of counter-insurgency: it highlighted the provocative nature of the repression deployed by Nivet and the Jacobin authorities. General Petit-Guillaume, newly reappointed commander of the Ninth Military District, recognized the need to restore the army's credibility in the Ardèche and so made a personal trip to Aubenas. Disturbed by what he learned there, he replaced Nivet with a more moderate commander, Brigade General Ruby, and instructed him to disarm and disband the reckless mobile columns so beloved by department officials. News that three newly enrolled national guardsmen had been stabbed to death at Chames, however, made it hard to find respectable men willing to form new units. This left barely a hundred regular troops to protect the "patriots," whereas the department needed at least a thousand in order to restore order. A spate of robberies, incursions, and assaults ensued. Republicans began to flee southern cantons in such numbers that it risked becoming a full-scale panic; the central commissioner even abandoned Privas for a time.[23] In a few weeks, residents had passed from one terror to another, from republican ruthlessness to rebel revenge.

The torment of the Ardèche was mirrored in the other departments subject to Férino's special assignment. By early 1800, rebel forces felt strong enough to take on the army command itself. Montchaussé was only one of several officers killed in the region. Outlaw bands across the river in the Drôme killed two other army captains, one at Colonzelle and the other at Mirabel.[24] The most spectacular assault on army officers took place at nearby Valréas, an enclave of the Vaucluse in the Drôme. This was a strife-torn town where four years earlier the populace had lynched the Jacobin commissioner, Victor Juge, when he ordered the arrest of former town officials. Valréas's reputation as a refuge for bandits and counter-revolutionaries only grew over time and peaked with the "Saint-Mathias Day massacre." On 5 ventôse VIII (24 February 1800), the local commander, Chef de Brigade Perrin, and fifteen of his men arrested a band leader named Armand during the local fair. Armand's comrades in crime quickly gathered in front of the town hall and demanded his release. When Perrin refused, they shot him and three officers to death in front of the crowd. The outlaws then dragged the bleeding bodies through the streets in imitation of ritual shaming practices. They smashed bottles on their heads, stripped them naked, and stuffed their mouths with dirt, all to cheers of "Vive le roi!" Some forty men danced a traditional farandole singing the "Reveil du peuple." Once the rebels had publicly flaunted their power, they ordered all the inhabitants off the streets, telling them, "We're not after you or the soldiers, just their officers."[25] The rebels finally quit Valréas the next morning when a column of troops approached. The town was put under a state of siege and a detachment of fifty soldiers posted there.

A fledgling regime whose credibility rested increasingly on the army and its ability to bring peace responded with ferocity to the murder and humiliation of its officers—whence the special powers assigned to General Férino. A few weeks at Avignon convinced him that brigandage persisted in the region due to (1) revolting partiality from local officials, (2) inept and corrupt magistrates, (3) the brigands' ability to terrorize "the friends of order," and (4) mobile columns composed of "all that was most impure."[26] The Consulate's appointment of a new slate of administrative and judicial officials would help to redress the first two problems. Their success would depend on the military commission at Avignon and more disciplined mobile columns. Férino planned a draconian response. His first proclamation, issued on 9 germinal VIII (30 March 1800), announced that troops would immediately shoot anyone caught in an armed gathering, anyone traveling armed without a passport or a gun permit, and anyone convicted of housebreaking in a group. Individuals who sheltered, supplied, guided, or transported brigands would face the military commission. Moreover, officials convicted of failing to prosecute brigands would be condemned to death and shot. Finally, any soldier convicted by the commission of armed robbery or violence against civilians would also be shot. In short, Férino's response to outlaw impunity, popular complicity, official duplicity, and militia brutality was about the same: executions and more executions.

The early months of Férino's mission saw an all-out war by both sides. In the Ardèche, a band of 150 to 200 rebels invaded the town of Les Vans. They disarmed the citizens, looted the town coffers, burnt the municipal records, chopped down the liberty tree, and killed the one citizen who tried to stop them. Their theft of five hundred muskets was especially worrisome. A similar incursion took place three months later at Joyeuse, the district seat and residence of forty soldiers. In between came a storm of lesser assaults and robberies known as the "Vendée cévenole."[27] These months included cold-blooded killings by both soldiers and brigands. Minister of War Carnot was furious to learn that a detachment of troops had summarily executed eight prisoners captured in an inn at Jaujac. He ordered Férino to stay within the law and to prevent it from happening again. But Carnot had just become minister and was unaware of the new order of things. Férino informed him that not only had more prisoners been shot since then, but that he was authorized to carry on doing so.[28] And carry on he did. In two months, his men killed twenty-three brigands, either in skirmishes or after capture, and arrested sixty-four others, thirteen of whom were condemned to death by the military commission at Avignon. These were unprecedented results. But they were also offset by forty-one murders or attempted murders, sixteen housebreakings, seven highway robberies, five town incursions, and five stolen treasuries in the same period.[29] The tide would not turn quickly or easily.

Despite his "extraordinary powers," Férino lacked sufficient means to overcome the complex of violence in the region. He found his troops in a pitiable state and never received the funding or reinforcements needed to fulfill his mission.[30] Férino also realized that force alone could never defeat southern brigandage; it was too much a product of overlapping forms of crime, politics, and resistance. At least three types of outlaws dominated the Rhône Valley: habitual robbers who made a life of crime, natural enemies of the Revolution such as émigrés and refractory priests, and a host of artisans and peasants who had participated in the reaction of 1795–97 and now served royalist elites because they needed their protection. This mix was complicated by two other, more numerous groups: deserters and draft dodgers who joined with outlaw bands in order to survive and preserve their impunity; and political refugees during the Terror who had returned to their towns and villages but were still on various lists of émigrés or subject to arrest warrants. Furthermore, the friends and families of these last two groups had a natural tendency to assist anyone who kept the republic at bay, whatever their methods or motives.[31]

In order to separate hardened outlaws and die-hard rebels from other, more tractable, forms of resistance, Férino proposed an amnesty. At the very least, an amnesty would help to dampen the ferocious political hatreds that infected the local magistracy. The amnesty of brumaire IV had never been fully applied, and those who were eventually released from prison "became tyrants in order to avoid prosecution by corrupt courts."[32] Therefore, with the approval of various prefects and ministers, Férino issued a detailed proclamation to his four departments on 15 thermidor VIII (3 August 1800). This included an amnesty for all men who had taken part in armed gatherings, all men whose "criminal errors and offenses" were the result of "the successive upheavals of the Revolution," and all draft dodgers and deserters who immediately departed for the army. The amnesty did not, however, apply to highway robbers or other "villains covered with crime." As this last phrase indicates, Férino kept the definition of those excluded from the amnesty rather loose and left it up to each prefect to decide on an individual basis just who qualified.[33]

The strategy of offering a broad but vague amnesty generated mixed results. Senior commanders of the gendarmerie condemned such leniency and claimed that it only encouraged the criminal element to persevere. Squadron Chief Gentile called it "complete lunacy."[34] On the other hand, the new authorities in the Ardèche had no doubts about its effectiveness. Prefect Charles Caffarelli described brigands "depositing their weapons and gaily submitting," while General Ruby boasted of record turnout at the recruitment depot.[35] The divergence of opinion arose mainly from differences of place and personnel. The amnesty had the greatest impact in the Ardèche and the least in the Vaucluse. A government emissary later estimated that at least a quarter of the four hundred beneficiaries in the Vaucluse returned to a life of crime.[36]

The variable success of the amnesty proved that it could succeed only when accompanied by effective judicial repression. Férino's forces continued to deliver a steady flow of prisoners to the military commission at Avignon, which took its judicial mission seriously. A quarter of the individuals who appeared before it were sent back to prison in order to allow for further investigation. Only one in ten was convicted when they appeared before the judges a second time. This suggests a certain conscientiousness on the part of the commission. Nonetheless, it generated a death toll that far surpassed regular military courts. During its nine months of operation, the military commission at Avignon judged about 160 people, half of whom were condemned to death.[37] It condemned to death soldiers as well as bandits, stealthy poisoners as well as brazen rebels, accomplices as well as killers, fences as well as robbers, arsonists as well as rapists, and women as well as men. Despite this eclectic range of defendants, over half of its death sentences were handed out to men either captured with arms in hand or proven to have participated in specific armed attacks. Whether these were royalist rebels or professional bandits is often unclear; the difference did not matter to the judges.[38]

In addition to the amnesty and military commission, Férino continued the aggressive pursuit of outlaws in the field. He later reported that "159 brigands had ceased living" during his mission. Half of these never appeared before the military commission. Many were killed either in skirmishes or while resisting arrest. Six died of their wounds in hospital. A sizable number of prisoners also continued to be summarily dispatched without trial. General Férino had no qualms about reporting all of this to the government.[39] After all, the new regime depended less on constitutionalism than on rising above factions and imposing order. A ministerial investigation concluded that accusations against the military commission for extortion and excessive severity were credible but inspired by partisanship and so simply blamed Férino for keeping the commission at Avignon "where all the passionate hatreds are organized." Fouché even inclined to cynicism: "In the departments in question, passions are so exalted and fiery that they soon discredit the men and the means used to calm them."[40]

The new government felt much the same way about operations against the *barbets* in the Alpes-Maritimes. General Pierre-Dominique Garnier's tenure there during the Directory had been marked by numerous outrages. These included bringing the corpse of a notorious *barbet* down from the hills on a donkey and parading it "like a wild beast" around the streets of Nice.[41] Nonetheless, when the French recaptured Nice on 9 prairial VIII (29 May 1800), the First Consul put Garnier back in command of the department and authorized him to form another military commission there. The new commission proved notably merciless. It condemned to death sixty-five of the seventy people brought before it, the highest execution rate (93 percent) of any judicial body since the Terror. Garnier's own papers indicate that a total of 136 *barbets* were shot during his second tenure. Although complaints from Prefect Florens brought the commission to an end, the pursuit of *barbets* by flying columns remained ferocious and highly partisan, hitting local notables as well as armed outlaws. No matter what Paris learned about the brutality of his operations, Garnier remained in charge of the department for a full year.[42] This should not be surprising, given Bonaparte's own nasty experience with *barbets* back in 1796. More important, however, it reflected a growing willingness to use whatever means were necessary to crush opposition to the regime.

## The Consular Terror

The survival of Bonaparte and the Consulate depended on an aggressive use of military might. This was true domestically as well as internationally. Bonaparte's victory at Marengo on 14 June 1800 did not consolidate the Consulate; it only consolidated his place within it. Moreau's victory at Hohenlinden on 3 December 1800 ensured the survival of the Consulate as a regime. That the regime took root in regions of unrest, however, depended on a wave of repression unleashed three weeks later. This was an echo of the Terror. Though fainter than the Directorial Terror that followed Fructidor, or the Jacobin Hundred Days of 1799, the Consular Terror of 1801 had the same key features. Bonaparte's wave of repression mixed an arbitrary political purge, a disregard for regular justice, and the use of military means to end violent resistance to the republic. It was the conjuncture of defeating Austria and nearly being blown up that propelled Bonaparte toward terrorist solutions.

As is well known, the First Consul blamed radical republicans for the "machine infernale." He rejected justice and demanded blood. But he was not alone. A spontaneous groundswell of opinion called for immediate reprisals against the "anarchists," those who attacked the nation in the person of its leader. Since this "handful of madmen" could now wreak national disaster with a single act of murder, vengeance had to be swift and severe.[43] Bonaparte did not hesitate to follow the Directory in ordering deportations without trial. Fouché knew the assassination attempt was the work of royalists but did as he was told. His list of 130 deportees eviscerated the Parisian left. (Of the 104 men actually deported, over half died in exile, far more than after Fructidor.) Nine other Jacobins already in custody were hastily tried and executed. An extensive round-up of republican radicals also took place in the provinces. This led to lengthy detentions but few trials.[44] Fouché quickly had proof that the attack had been the work of chouans, yet this did nothing to stop the arrests, executions, and deportations; it merely extended the repression. Two royalists were soon tried and guillotined, and over a hundred others were quietly arrested and interned without trial.[45]

Just as significant as this human toll was the echo of terror it brought to the Consulate, again in the name of "salut public." In order to implicate the entire regime in this act of political terror, the deportation order was issued by the Senate. The government could not link the deportees to the assassination or any other crime in particular, so they were simply described as "hommes de sang" and a continual source of hidden terror for peaceful citizens. Furthermore, the Senate's order cynically described the deportations as a "mesure conservatrice de la constitution." Councillor of State Berlier was almost alone in expressing concern to the First Consul about the damage the proscription would do to the regime's reputation. Here was a man who had coauthored the Constitution of Year III and who, four years later, had argued in favor of the "law of hostages" by saying, "How could it be unconstitutional to save the Republic (certainly anterior to the constitution which is only its auxiliary) by a measure directed against that rebellious part of society?"[46] His protest in 1801 indicates how slow many republicans were to realize that it was now Bonaparte who came first and for whom the constitution was only an auxiliary. Too late. Their own mix of political exclusions and military repression had paved the road.

Bonaparte's response to the assassination attempt is less startling when put in the context of other repressive measures he had already endorsed. The struggle against brigandage in the Rhône Valley and *chouannerie* in Brittany convinced Bonaparte that the new state apparatus would only take root in areas of endemic unrest after the government had tipped the balance of fear in its favor. Thus, far from condemning the repressive tactics of

Generals Férino, Garnier, and Bernadotte, he decided to extend them.[47] A few days before the "machine infernale," the First Consul expanded the use of military commissions by ordering the formation of four *corps d'éclaireurs* in the Midi—two for Basse-Provence, one for Bas-Languedoc, and one for the Drôme—and later added three more in Brittany.[48] Each of these seven flying columns received its own mobile military commission charged with trying brigands in twenty-four hours (that is, the actual trial could not last more than a day). Bonaparte insisted that numerous patrols, intelligently and aggressively conducted, combined with no tolerance for local sympathizers and some terrifying examples, would quickly eradicate brigandage in even the most violent regions of France.[49] Such an exhortation implicitly reduced relations between the new regime and communities where brigands found refuge to two factors: force and fear. The Consulate's answer to endemic violence was to apply enough repressive force to make local inhabitants more afraid of the security forces than they were of those who resisted them.

These flying columns and military commissions carried the Consular Terror to the provinces. The initial group created for the Midi amounted to a massive expansion of Férino's special mission. Because of the scope of this repression (and the historical confusion surrounding it), we need to clarify its various elements.[50] The government forced Férino to hand over all counter-insurgency operations in the Drôme to Adjutant-Commandant Henri Boyer. His rules of engagement were those originally set by Férino the previous year. Boyer's "flying column" consisted of 210 men and an extraordinary military commission, which met at Montélimar from 8 ventôse to 11 floréal (27 February–1 May 1801). During those two months, it judged a mere twenty individuals.[51] After the military commission at Avignon ended operations, the Ardèche came under the jurisdiction of the extraordinary military commission of the Ninth Military District. General Gouvion, the district commander, formed a "flying column" of 240 men commanded by Brigade General Tisson. Its accompanying commission held hearings in the Hérault, Aveyron, Gard, and Ardèche between 26 nivôse and 9 floréal (16 January–29 April 1801). During these fifteen weeks, it judged an impressive total of 179 individuals.[52] Across the Rhône in Provence, where brigandage was notably worse, the Consulate ordered the commander of the Eighth Military District, General Pouget, to create not one, but two extraordinary military commissions. Each commission would be attached to a much larger "flying column" composed of 420 men. The column in the Var was commanded by Brigade General Guillot and its military commission pronounced verdicts on ninety-three defendants between 19 nivôse and 19 floréal (9 January–9 May 1801).[53] The other flying column under Brigade General Garreau and its attendant commission operated mainly in the Bouches-du-Rhône but covered the Vaucluse and Basses-Alpes as well. Between 19 nivôse and 7 messidor (9 January–26 June 1801), at least 115 individuals came before this second commission.[54] In order to deal directly with the varieties of violence in the southeast, each of these extraordinary military commissions relocated from time to time. They held hearings in coastal cities (Montpellier, Nîmes, Marseille, Toulon), more remote *chefs-lieux* (Rodez, Privas, Digne), and isolated hill towns (Millau, Le Vigan, Alès, Montélimar). Such mobility ensured that their presence was felt throughout the region.

Several other aspects of repression changed following the end of Férino's mission. On one hand, the immediate shooting of brigands captured while armed was officially discontinued. Once again, all deaths in the field occurred, for reporting purposes at least, while brigands were resisting arrest or attempting to escape.[55] On the other hand, General Pouget, commander of the Eighth Military District, took Bonaparte's instructions to "be inflexible toward communities which harbor brigands" as the basis for his own version of the law of hostages. He ordered the "flying columns" to march directly to any commune where an attack occurred and to arrest and detain ten leading inhabitants until the culprits had been handed over to the army. In addition, he offered a large reward of 500 francs to members of the "flying columns" for every outlaw they killed or captured.[56] Such incentives, accompanied by twelve companies of regular troops (at sixty men each), two companies of cavalry (at thirty men each), and sixty mounted gendarmes all devoted exclusively to hunting down outlaws, ensured an unprecedented crackdown in the Eighth Military District. One wonders how the history of the region would have been altered had such measures been applied five years earlier. But then both constitutional constraints and political partisanship had long militated against such methods.

The four extraordinary military commissions created and operated in southern France in the early months of 1801 pronounced verdicts on at least 407 persons.[57] As table 3 indicates, half of these (203) were condemned to death and less than one-fifth (81) were acquitted and released. A certain number were acquitted of brigandage, either explicitly or implicitly, but sent to other courts to be tried for desertion or ordinary crimes. Each of the commissions developed distinctive sentencing alternatives, another sign that they lacked clear jurisprudence. The military commissions of the

TABLE 3

Verdicts of the extraordinary military commissions of 1801

| Jurisdiction | B-R | Var | Drôme | 9<sup>th</sup> Mil. Dis. | Total |
|---|---|---|---|---|---|
| Condemned to death | 52 | 46 | 13 | 98 | 203 |
| 5 to 20 years in irons | | | | 16 | 16 |
| 2 years in prison | | | | 3 | 3 |
| Acquitted (freed) | 63(26) | 47 (21) | 7 (3) | 62 (31) | 179 (81) |
| Sent to criminal justice | 3 | 2 | | 3 | 8 |
| Sent to military justice | 8 | 10 | | 10 | 28 |
| Sent to dis. commander | 12 | 13 | 1 | 17 | 26 |
| Sent to military depot | 3 | 1 | 1 | | 5 |
| Further investigation | | | 1 | 2 | 3 |
| Totals | 115 | 93 | 20 | 179 | 407 |

Eighth Military District were reluctant to release many of the acquitted back into society. Therefore, many of them were labeled "violently suspect" and sent to the district commander, who held them indefinitely. In contrast, the military commission of the Ninth Military District either sent them to the district commander to be incorporated into the army (regardless of age) or sentenced them to various terms in the *bagne* or prison. Such sentences fit various degrees of complicity and amounted to a moderating influence.

In procedure, this same commission acted much like a regular military court. Its records indicate that in many cases the commission's president and prosecutor interrogated an impressive number of witnesses and put substantial evidence before the commission. But this was not typical. These commissions embodied summary justice. They showed no regard for the judicial concept of "double jeopardy," often failed to call crucial witnesses, and routinely used written evidence alone to convict.[58] Defendants could rarely obtain a lawyer in time, but then the sheer vagueness of the charges often negated whatever assistance a lawyer may have provided.

More than merely dispatching a large number of brigands, the extraordinary military commissions provided various means of propaganda. Above all, in contrast to roadside shootings, military commissions offered at least a veneer of judicial process. While at Nîmes, for example, one commission sought to establish its credibility by using the locale of the regular criminal court as well as by opening its proceedings to the public. "An immense crowd of people filled the chamber and court area awaiting the outcome of the session," wrote the commission's president.[59] Military commissions also publicized their verdicts via broadsheets—up to eight hundred copies of each—plastered throughout the jurisdiction. These provided an education in the legal basis for their work. Each broadsheet cited the directives from the Consulate and commanding generals that empowered the commissions and legitimized the verdicts. Though legally redundant, references to the law of 30 prairial III also abounded (an old law being better than a new directive). Finally, broadsheets could be used to paint opponents in purely criminal colors. Rather vague charges gained credence when accompanied by lurid descriptions of wickedness: one Etienne Joseph was found guilty of "belonging to the murderous bands that desolate the region with iron and fire."[60]

The majority of the men, and occasionally women, condemned to death by these commissions were executed in the cities and towns where the commissions met. But even itinerant courts could not be on the move all the time or be expected to hold hearings in small bourgs and isolated villages. In order to deliver their message of intimidation closer to home, therefore, the commissions frequently had individuals shot in their native communities. This meant staging powerfully symbolic executions in villages and hamlets where most people had openly sided with counter-revolution or in areas where kidnapping and extortion, robbery and arson had become acceptable ways to resist an intrusive republic. Thus, while sitting at Protestant and prorevolutionary Nîmes and Alès, the military commission of the Ninth Military District condemned to death twenty-nine men for a bloody campaign of extortion and pillage directed against purchasers of "nationalized properties" in the northern Gard. These men were then shot by firing squads in nineteen Catholic communities stretching in a broad arc from Alès to Pont-Saint-Esprit. Holding these executions in small bourgs helped to intimidate the mayors, *adjoints,* and other leading citizens who had signed attestations of good conduct for men such as André Ode (alias "The Marshal") and Louis Plagnol, brutal extortionists who were subsequently convicted and executed in their midst. Similarly, a dozen highway robbers faced firing squads in the main towns along the route between Pont-du-Gard and Pont-Saint-Esprit, where the mail coach had been attacked so often the company threatened to suspend services.[61] Not since the wars of religion—and certainly not during the Terror—had so many people been put to death publicly in so many different places in the south.

Many of these executions carried a heavy load of symbolic value. The military commission at Avignon, which stayed put throughout its tenure, was the first to order executions elsewhere. These were intended to announce the army's terrifying supremacy, a point already being made in the field. When a detachment of light infantry captured three outlaws, including "the noteworthy Armand, murderer of the *chef de brigade* of the 92nd," it brought them back to Valréas and shot them on the square "that had served as the theater of this assassination." We can be sure that a large audience attended the spectacle. A successful show meant that when the military commission convicted other men of the same crime, they too were taken to Valréas for execution.[62] An equally important act of symbolic propaganda was carried out in the Ardèche. While at Privas, a military commission tried Pierre Auriol and Jean Paulin, two deserters who had joined the ragtag "Catholic and Royal Army of the Midi." Instead of executing them at Les Vans, where they had participated in a famous incursion, the firing squad set up on the impressive bridge at Maison-Neuve. Not only was it in the middle of the plain where hordes of Catholic peasants had gathered for the various counter-revolutionary *camps de Jalès* in the early 1790s, this was where brigands had recently butchered and thrown over five soldiers despite the screams and prayers of local women.[63] Holding the firing squad on the bridge at Maison-Neuve served to reclaim an important *lieu de mémoire* in the bloody struggle between the army and the rebels of the region. Sprinkling such symbolic executions across areas of prolonged resistance was the Consulate's way of saying that not only was the Revolution over, but the counter-revolution was too.

Holding firing squads in numerous towns and villages also served to terrify the outlaws' many accomplices. It was best to target people involved in obvious criminal activities. Military commissions sought to avoid unduly alienating the populace by condemning to death accomplices whose activities had already been rejected by the community. Shooting individuals who sheltered highway robbers, kept their horses, or fenced their stolen goods sowed exemplary fear with less risk of provoking widespread hostility. Even so, the use of firing squads for ordinary accomplices was often considered excessive. The military commission at Avignon, for example, condemned to death four petty shopkeepers from L'Isle (Vaucluse) for buying lace stolen in a highway holdup. A republican notable took particular offense at the execution of these people in his town: "Arnavon left six children; *femme* Brunel left seven. She was nursing; milk and blood flowed from her corpse. All of L'Isle closed its doors and moaning was heard throughout the town."[64] Reactions like this did not stop the practice of shooting accomplices. Though military commissions acquitted most of those who provided support to outlaws or, in the case of the Ninth Military District, sentenced them to years in irons, holding the occasional firing squad for a well-known brigand associate or a bandit host left no doubt about the Consulate's determination to isolate them from the rest of society.[65]

Despite often ameliorating verdicts for accomplices, female ones in particular, great severity remained the order of the day. During their four months in operation, the extraordinary military commissions of early 1801 held hearings an average of one day in three. The more than two hundred death sentences they pronounced amounted to more than one per day of hearings. The commissions had a combined acquittal rate of 44 percent, although only 24 percent were actually released (and many of them were put under administrative surveillance). Half of the rest were conscripts or draft dodgers and were treated accordingly. This left scores of individuals acquitted by the military commissions who were kept in jail pending authorization to deport them. In addition to this summary justice, the "flying columns" of 1801 killed at least fifty other men in skirmishes or resisting arrest.[66] Here was state-sponsored killing that rivaled many local experiences of the Terror. In fact, in dozens of southern communities, the violence of the early Consulate far surpassed anything they had previously experienced during the Revolution.

Areas of continued *chouannerie* in western France saw an equally ferocious crackdown. The work of the different extraordinary military commissions there has yet to be studied. Nonetheless, there is considerable evidence of impatient ruthlessness. Most of the major towns remained under state of siege, and regular military courts were working at full capacity. Ernest Daudet states that between September 1800 and February 1801, 1,200 chouans were arrested, 250 were condemned to death, and 150 were killed "while resisting arrest."[67] The addition of flying columns and military commissions sustained this regional terror throughout the spring of 1801.[68] This did not equal the death and destruction wrought from 1793 to 1796, but it certainly had a familiar ring. It exposes the extent to which the Consulate resorted to brute force and bloody intimidation to establish its authority in areas of endemic unrest.

The military commissions of 1801 killed more people in four months than the Fructidorian military commissions killed in two years. Because they were more focused in time, place, and purpose, however, they were far less controversial (hence their complete absence from survey histories). Unlike the military commissions after Fructidor, the military commissions after Brumaire did not target former aristocrats, priests, and other social notables and did not have them shot in the principal cities and towns of France. Instead, the victims of military commissions under the Consulate were almost all common folk with little social standing and a proclivity for crime. Their execution by firing squad in remote provincial locations made an impact locally, but not nationally. This regional specificity helped to make the military commissions of the Consulate especially efficacious. In western France, "numerous executions [were] assuring tranquility in the region," and General Bernadotte explicitly attributed his success in pacifying Brittany to three such commissions.[69] The south saw similar results. Not a single highway robbery took place in the Gard in four months, and the Basses-Alpes went a full six months without any incidents of brigandage. Army commanders began to boast that whole areas previously terrorized by brigands had been perfectly pacified.[70] This may have been overstated, perhaps due to the euphoria officials felt at finally gaining the upper hand. All the same, the scale of military repression in 1801, executed—literally and symbolically—at the village level, broke the back of brigandage in the south and *chouannerie* in the west. The brutal effectiveness of this "booted justice" has received almost no attention from historians more inclined to credit Bonaparte's military victories, amnesties, religious liberalism, and political ecumenism for his success in consolidating the Consulate.

But brigandage had not been completely stamped out by the summer of 1801, either in the south or the west. For this reason, the government continued to advocate harsh measures. These were based on its dictum that "in regions where the terror we want to inspire in brigands is less than that they inspire themselves, wherever their protection is surer than that of the law, and their vengeance feared more than justice, brigandage can not be destroyed."[71] This was an apology for terrorism as *raison d'état*. But flying columns and military commissions could not be used long without discrediting the regime. They lacked measure. Having such dreadful means at their disposal incited army commanders to reckless terror. General Férino caused a scandal by threatening to burn any village in the Rhône Valley that gave aid or comfort to brigands, and the flying columns operating under General Garnier in the Basses-Alpes had become a byword for brutality. Reports of systematic pillage and extortion in Provence got back to Paris and inspired the Consulate to seek more restrained alternatives.[72] Its new forms of exceptionalism would have more form and be less exceptional.

# 12 Security State and Dictatorship

> The Police of a free people no doubt must clothe itself in the many forms
> of Justice; but Justice itself must sanction and adopt the rapidity of the Po-
> lice when it acts against brigands who make war on this people's freedom.
> —Minister of Police Fouché, October 1800

THE FRENCH REVOLUTION ended in a personal dictatorship, that much
is clear. That the dictatorship did not begin at Brumaire and that it was not
largely the work of Bonaparte is less clear. The authoritarian regime constructed under his aegis was the product of widespread consensus among
Frenchmen. They did not despise the Directory because it failed to permit
the full exercise of democracy or to adhere to liberal notions of the rule
of law; they despised it for having failed to rise above factional politics
and restore order. But to end *la politique* was not to end *le politique;*[1] political contestation gave way to political domination. Drawing the poison of
politics required an astute exercise of power that concentrated authority in
the apparatus of rule even more than in the person of the ruler. Although
the emergence of such an apparatus was hastened by the First Consul, especially after the failed attempt on his life, the apparatus itself was shaped
above all by the need to end prolonged social disorder and the exceptional
measures it served to justify. Thus, liberty was sacrificed not to glory but to
security; only then was France presented with the myth of a savior.

When the Consular Terror erupted in the winter of year IX, the Consular
government was pursuing several major reforms to the system of criminal
justice. In most accounts of the period, these changes are eclipsed by the
high drama of the season. Between Moreau's victory at Hohenlinden and
the attempt to assassinate Bonaparte in the rue Nicaise, the government
submitted three bills designed to strengthen the apparatus of repression.
Liberal lawmakers protested this authoritarian drift, and so the bills were

withdrawn. Then came the "machine infernale" and the Consular Terror. These events created a favorable climate to cut back on liberty and enhance security. Deputies now found it easier to approve a drastic cut in the number of elected justices of the peace as well as to transfer their role in investigating and prosecuting crime to new "security magistrates" appointed by the government. Lawmakers found the government's third bill less palatable, however. It proposed to resurrect key features of the *ancien régime*'s provostial courts in the form of "special criminal tribunals." Liberals in the Tribunate such as Pierre Daunou, Marie-Joseph Chénier, and Benjamin Constant opposed the new courts as a grave erosion of civil liberties and corrosive of the constitution. The newfound outrage at curtailing the rights of the accused also had much to do with assembling a viable opposition to the Consulate's growing authoritarianism. As one supporter of the bill noted, lawmakers had expressed fewer such concerns when the Directorial councils created military commissions or passed the law of 29 nivôse VI. Cambacérès dismissed opponents as "malcontents" determined to weaken the government; Bonaparte even took the debate as a personal insult. After relatively close votes, the bill became law on 19 pluviôse IX (8 February 1801).[2] The liberals' eloquent stand in favor of due process and the rule of law was too little, too late. Their defeat marked the end of effective parliamentary independence.

## Special Tribunals

Liberal lawmakers took particular exception to special tribunals judging serious crimes without the safeguard of juries. This eliminated the most important feature of the Revolution's criminal justice system. Despite their genuine efficacy in much of the country, juries had proved weak reeds in areas of chronic antirepublican violence. As was the case around Lodève, where outlaws carried jury lists, shot witnesses, and kidnapped magistrates with impunity, grand juries rarely indicted, and if they did, trial juries usually acquitted. Advocates of the new law cogently argued that without special tribunals to deal with the greatest threats to public order, juries would fail to protect the population from serious crime and, therefore, would soon disappear. Thus, deputies paradoxically approved the creation of special tribunals, a form of exceptional justice largely borrowed from the *ancien régime*, in order to preserve the jury system, that revolutionary "palladium of liberty," for the rest of the criminal justice system.[3]

Though the debate surrounding their creation painted them as a travesty of due process and a fair trial, special tribunals ironically were a marked improvement over other forms of exceptional justice used during the period. True, the prosecuting judge on special tribunals did not need to inform defendants of evidence against them, as was the case with regular criminal courts, and could present written evidence at trial, as was the case with regular military courts. Unlike the provostial courts of the *ancien régime*, however, special tribunals held their trials in public, provided the accused with a defense lawyer, permitted oral debate, and relied on moral proof for conviction. These were all basic features of the revolutionary system of criminal justice. Although special tribunals combined military and civilian judges, their actual composition gave civilian magistrates a preponderance of influence.[4] Furthermore, although special tribunals judged without appeal, the Court of Cassation had to approve their jurisdictional competence on a case-by-case basis before sentences could be applied. Finally, the rebels, bandits, and robbers condemned to death by special tribunals were guillotined by the public executioner in departmental *chefs-lieux* like regular criminals, not forced to kneel blindfolded and shot to death by a handful of soldiers on a remote bridge or in an isolated village square. Thus, despite their manifest curtailment of judicial protections for the accused, the new courts constituted a substantial improvement over previous forms of military justice used to try civilians.

The operating procedures of the new courts made them *pièces de circonstances*, a hybrid of provostial justice and revolutionary experience. As such, they were the culmination of a long process of refining expedited justice during the First Republic. Deputies who had suffered through twelve years of upheaval now saw merit in absolutism's use of tightly regulated exceptional justice to complement the ordinary criminal courts. Only now, both embodied important revolutionary reforms. Like the provostial courts of the *ancien régime*, the jurisdiction of special tribunals depended on the status of the accused as well as the nature of the crime. Vagabonds, recidivists, and counterfeiters all fell under the new courts. Aggravated theft in various forms, namely armed robbery and housebreaking by more than two people, constituted the largest category of offenses heard by special tribunals. These were followed by a host of other threats to public order in the countryside: arson and threats of arson, attacks on purchasers of "national property," assaults committed by an armed group, seditious gatherings confronted in flagrante delicto, trying to recruit soldiers or refractories for rebellion, complicity in prison escapes, and even premeditated murder if accompanied by aggravating circumstances. Many of these crimes had little in common except their association with *chouannerie* and southern brigandage. In that sense, the jurisdiction of special tribunals was carefully tailored to fit the circumstances of 1801.

The Consulate created special tribunals in twenty-seven departments in the west and south in year IX and added nine more by year XI (thereby covering more than one-third of all departments). The new courts largely put an end to extraordinary military commissions. As soon as each new tribunal went into operation, all cases pending before the local military commission were transferred to it. Most tribunals began to render verdicts by June 1801, and they quickly became a major part of the machinery of justice. In their first four months, special tribunals pronounced verdicts in 724 trials encompassing 1,200 people.[5] Evidence from the special tribunals created in the Sarthe, Hérault, and Haute-Garonne indicates that two-thirds of the crimes they prosecuted up to the end of year X qualified as serious threats to public order, such as housebreakings or armed robberies committed by several people and with violence—in a word, brigandage.[6] Whether politically motivated or not, brigandage continued to ravage the Sarthe. As a result, the special tribunal at Le Mans proved especially severe with brigands of all stripes, even while being scrupulously fair, even generous, about chouan amnesties. Special tribunals in other western departments were equally severe. Pacifying the west involved more than accommodating religious sentiment, restraining patriots, and tolerating the return of émigrés; it meant imposing law and order, and special tribunals played a major part.

Special tribunals in the south were less harsh than those in the west, even when dealing with crimes of brigandage. Combined acquittal rates for the special tribunals of the Haute-Garonne and Hérault were double that of the Sarthe, and the two southern tribunals together meted out less total penal repression than the single northern tribunal. The general level of rural insecurity was not high in the Hérault and even lower in the Haute-Garonne. Some of the highway robbers tried by the special tribunal at Montpellier had pulled big heists, such as those involved in the spectacular banditry around Lodève, but many of the trials were for relatively minor acts of armed robbery and so brought modest sentences. The special tribunal at Toulouse was even less severe than the one at Montpellier. In fact, it is doubtful that the Haute-Garonne needed a special tribunal. Although brigandage and political violence had taken a higher toll elsewhere in the Midi, especially in Provence, special tribunals there also meted out less repression than anticipated. In fact, the special tribunals of the Vaucluse and the Drôme acquitted fully two-thirds of defendants, and that of the Alpes-Maritimes dealt less harshly with *barbets* then with ordinary criminals. As a result, special tribunals in Provence drew considerable criticism for being insufficiently repressive.[7] Such leniency was due to the attention judges paid to both legal forms and local factionalism.

Special tribunals may have been criticized for leniency in the tumultuous circumstances of 1801, but, in fact, they provided a major share of the Consulate's penal repression. Special tribunals immediately assumed a substantial caseload. During their first sixteen months in operation, that is, until the end of year X, the special tribunals of the Haute-Garonne, Hérault, and Sarthe handled almost as many verdicts as the regular criminal courts of these departments during the same period. Special tribunals also meted out a lot of punishment, as one might expect given the crimes they prosecuted. These three special tribunals pronounced 82 percent of the death penalties handed out between 1 prairial IX and the end of year X (21 May 1801–22 September 1802) as well as 59 percent of the lengthy terms in irons (fourteen to twenty-four years) in their departments. Thus, where they existed, special tribunals fully compensated for the decline in activity of regular criminal courts experienced during the Consulate. Although the change of regimes from the Directory to Consulate cut the prosecution of crime in half, the installation of special tribunals in mid-1801 soon raised the level of repression in areas of unrest above that seen in the late 1790s.

Data from three regular criminal courts in departments without special tribunals, together with the data from our three departments that had both types of courts, enable us to approximate the level of penal repression across all of France at the time. The expanded France of years IX and X saw about 800 death sentences and about 3,000 terms of hard labor (four to twenty-four years) emerge from the chambers of justice each year.[8] A report by Grand-Judge Régnier confirms the ferocity of a criminal justice system equipped with numerous special tribunals. In years XI and XII, 3,838 individuals were judged "spécialement" as compared to 7,619 judged either with juries or in courts of first instance.[9] In other words, fully one-third of all defendants charged with felonies faced neither a grand jury for indictment nor a trial jury for final judgment and did not have the right of appeal. We also find that in year XI, at a time when the Consulate had reached its maximum number of special tribunals and was busy subjugating six new Piedmontese departments, there were 882 death sentences and 3,202 felony sentences to hard labor or prison. The totals for year XII were lower but still staggering: 701 death sentences and 2,886 felony sentences to hard labor or prison. Steady progress toward the restoration of order brought significant declines in the early years of the Empire. All the same, the incorporation of a form of exceptional justice based on the reviled provostial courts of the *ancien régime,* one initially approved only as an expedient until the war ended, had taken permanent hold in the Napoleonic system of criminal justice.

Criminal courts and special tribunals were not the only forms of judicial repression during the years of Consular consolidation. The unsatisfactory results of southern tribunals spawned additional forms of repression. A few months after the installation of special tribunals in Provence, a spate of attacks there prompted the Consulate to authorize the resurrection of three "flying columns" and extraordinary military commissions. At the same time, three such commissions continued to operate in Brittany despite the creation of special tribunals in every department. Unlike their predecessors, all of these military commissions were restricted to judging men captured while armed. Many brigands knew this, as well as the value of legal protections (even limited ones), and tossed aside their guns before capture in order to be judged by a special tribunal instead of a military commission.[10] Not only did military commissions and special tribunals operate simultaneously in a half-dozen departments, but elsewhere regular military courts continued to apply the law of 30 prairial III (18 June 1795) to rebels captured while armed. This was of greatest significance in western France, as well as in the annexed departments of the northeast. My work suggests that military justice alone sentenced to death over 600 civilians in year IX and at least 100 in year X. Combining this with the figures above leads to the conclusion that the Consular regime executed a total of 1,400 to 1,500 civilians in year IX and 900 to 1,000 civilians in year X. This amounted to a staggering fivefold increase (at least) over the annual number of executions carried out in the 1780s, when the *ancien régime* was at the height of its repressive powers. Moreover, whenever special tribunals, military courts, and military commissions proved insufficiently repressive, the Consulate opted for administrative judgments. These allowed district commanders to force acquitted defendants to join the army and prefects to prolong detention or even deport "suspects." Such extrajudicial solutions were commonplace and fully endorsed by the government.[11] In other words, an extraordinary level of quotidian repression lay at the heart of the Consulate's return to law and order.

## Popular Attitudes to Public Order

The astonishing level of repression in the late Directory and early Consulate was not controversial, at least among the notables who set public opinion, and therefore is invariably missing from historical narratives of the period. How different interpretations would be had the Consulate accepted even the patchy press freedoms that did so much to erode the Directory's credibility. The disappearance of most of the truly partisan journalism in 1800 eliminated the constant reporting on the struggles to restore order in provincial France. As a result, contemporaries (and thus historians) remained largely ignorant of the brutal repression that accompanied Bonaparte's efforts to end the French Revolution. The news brownout and the reduced scope of legislative debate under the Consulate meant that civil strife gradually returned to being a local and at worst regional concern. Of course, it had always been intensely local, even when projected onto a national screen, as we saw with the cycle of violence around Gignac and Lodève. But the proliferation of newspapers in the 1790s had helped to spread fear about crime to a wider public as well as to encourage authoritarian responses to it. These newspapers tended to reflect public opinion while not really capturing popular attitudes. Therefore, it is worth asking whether support for increased repression and authoritarian policies spread beyond the educated, wealthy, political class. Did ordinary citizens firmly attached to their small parcels of land and the integrity of their communities have the same attitudes to problems of public order as the more urbanized social superiors who dominated regional and national politics? It is reasonable to assume that both news and editorial opinions spread from the reading public to the broader population and that both the authors and readers of newspapers were not completely out of touch with attitudes among the wider populace. But we can do better than simply to assume; we can address these questions by looking at the participation of ordinary Frenchmen in the struggle against brigandage.

The day after the murder and mutilation of four army officers at Valréas, 419 inhabitants signed a statement describing these events and naming twenty-five perpetrators, most of whom were from Valréas itself.[12] This unprecedented willingness to cooperate with the "forces of order" in a town famous for its opposition to the republic has at least two explanations. Either the majority of residents feared the wholesale destruction of the town (as had happened to nearby Bollène in 1794) and hoped that full cooperation would ward off such a disaster, or they viewed the arrival of troops and the state of siege as protection more than repression, at least as long as outlaws remained a powerful presence in the area. Support for the first explanation comes from Férino's threat "to burn and reduce to cinders" any town, village, hamlet, or rural abode that received brigands without resisting them, as well as evidence that the threat had inspired several communes "to rise up en masse" and arrest brigands.[13] On the other hand, the citizens of Valréas may well have deemed Armand and his fellow outlaws a blight on their bourg. Not only had they attracted the army to their town years earlier, the brigands' struggle for survival had led to escalating reprisals against those with the temerity to assist in bringing them to justice. What might at first appear to be a simple imposition of military rule at Valréas, therefore, may also have been the moment at which citizens finally decided to cooperate with agents of the state in order to purge their community of outlaws who, under the guise of fending off an intrusive state, had subjected inhabitants to ever greater violence. This second explanation is not incompatible with the first and is supported by evidence that the peasantry was neither as complicit nor as complacent as authorities often claimed. In this sense, events at Valréas in early 1801 encapsulate a set of forces at work in many other strife-torn communities during the later years of the First Republic.

During this period, magistrates and other local officials wrote a myriad of lamentations about the difficulty of getting witnesses to testify against bandits or jurors to convict them. Such statements make eminently quotable diatribes that fall into the lap of anyone who consults the archives.[14] Rarely does one find praise for the part ordinary villagers played in policing and criminal justice. Letters of this sort would be tantamount to officials informing the government that their jobs were easy. A more balanced perspective on popular attitudes, therefore, can only come from a careful reading of judicial dossiers. It is here that one uncovers numerous examples of ordinary men and women repeatedly telling authorities all they needed to know in order to bring dangerous criminals to justice.

The mix of obstacles and incentives in cooperating with judicial authorities is evident in the largest case brought before the Criminal Court of the Haute-Saône during the First Republic. Years of sporadic assaults and robberies along the back roads north of Combeaufontaine finally led to the arrest of five men. They included three sons of Barthélemy Hérard, a tenant farmer at Semmadon, and two of his employees. The local JP hoped that these arrests would make witnesses "less timid and more sincere in their future declarations." However, the fear the accused inspired in witnesses, even after months in custody, remained "the padlock that keeps all mouths closed." Only further arrests—notably of Barthélemy Hérard; his wife, Anne Beuveret; and a relative named Nicolas Proye (caught hiding on a roof in Paris)—enabled magistrates to develop their case. Yet by the time the actual trial opened a year later, one key witness had admitted being paid to lie and another had fled town for good. Furthermore, the JP at nearby Augicourt supported Barthélemy Hérard's claim that he was the victim of a plot to oust him from his lease. The unreliability of certain witnesses and the involvement of local notables only clouded an already complicated affair. Nine defendants were charged with a total of fourteen crimes ranging from collective assault on the driver of a wagonload of hay to the murder of two unidentified cadavers found "covered in moss and leaves at the thickest part of the forest" fifty paces from the Hérard farmhouse. Two weeks of testimony by two hundred witnesses led to 649 questions for the jurors. Despite many contradictions, the seventy-five witnesses called by the prosecution proved sufficiently courageous and convincing to inspire the jury to convict six people. Five of the men were then guillotined on 6 messidor VI (24 June 1798), the bloodiest day in Vesoul during the entire Revolution.[15] Even then the case was not over. The criminal court later tried six of the defense witnesses for felony perjury (a rare event at the time) because their testimony had led to three acquittals. The public prosecutor also used the testimony of one witness, an army officer, to indict him for taking part in one of the armed assaults.[16] These subsequent trials further exacerbated the already prolonged tension in the villages of Semmadon, Arbecey, Lambrey, Augicourt, and Gevigney. In other words, bringing a single family of thugs to justice had disrupted an entire *pays* for two years and no doubt more. The fact that the attacks had been largely directed against community outsiders such as the forest watchman from Lambrey or two bourgeois from Fort-de-Plânes in the Jura made villagers less inclined to get involved. And yet enough people braved the threats of the Hérards and the hostility of neighbors to testify, and testify repeatedly. Here is a good sign that peasants were not as complacent about problems of public order as officials often claimed.

In fact, events in the area the following year fully vindicated the inhabitants in the eyes of the nation. On 21 messidor VII (9 July 1799), a score of men from the villages around Jussey attacked four gendarmes on the road to Combeaufontaine in order to rescue two refractory priests and a protector they were conducting to Vesoul. Three of the gendarmes suffered gunshot wounds, and the prisoners and their rescuers disappeared into the *bois de Charmes,* the very woods made infamous two years earlier by the Hérards. The gendarmes raised the alarm and met an impressive response. No fewer than 450 national guardsmen and ordinary residents turned out from Combeaufontaine, Cornot, Arbecey, Semmadon, Lambrey, Augicourt and Jussey. "The devotion was so great on this occasion that women . . .

rivaled men in their temerity and courage in searching the woods to seize and arrest the culprits." This quick and massive response ensured that all three prisoners were recaptured along with fourteen of their rescuers. The fact that the two priests faced death or deportation and that the rescuers were led by notables from neighboring villages made this event all the more significant. So pleased was the government by this display of dedication to the republican order that a lengthy précis was inserted in the semi-official *Rédacteur.*[17] Thus, an otherwise inconsequential neck of the eastern woods had come to national attention twice in two years. And the two events were surely not unrelated. How better to redeem a reputation based on heinous crimes and contentious trials than to provide a bright example of commitment to law and order?

Popular attitudes to public order obviously varied widely by region and locality. Peasants living in the Franche-Comté, such as those around the *bois de Charmes,* made some of the greatest gains from the French Revolution. The lifting of the tithe burden, possibly the heaviest in France, the destruction of a still-vigorous seigneurialism, and the concomitant elimination of the last real vestiges of serfdom in the realm were bound to engender greater support for the republican regime than might have been the case elsewhere.[18] In addition, a low incidence of highway robbery, in fact a low crime rate in general, and a good record on conscription made the region subject to fewer problems of public order.[19] These factors alone made it more likely that peasants would support the authorities in the prosecution of violent crime.

Matters were more complicated elsewhere. Areas of endemic brigandage were also areas where peasants balked more often at assisting in the prevention or prosecution of serious crimes. This tendency has served as the basis for a vast literature on "social banditry." After a generation of criticism from fellow historians, however, Eric Hobsbawm, the greatest proponent of this interpretation, has come to accept that his original idea of "social bandits" paid insufficient attention to their political context. He recently concluded that "banditry as a mass phenomenon . . . occurred only where power was unstable, absent, or had broken down."[20] In general terms, this characterized all of France in the late 1790s, but some areas obviously suffered more than others. It is in these regions that popular attitudes to public order are hardest to assess. The easy answer is to assume, as Hobsbawm once did, that there existed general sympathy, if not broad support, for forms of violence that mainly targeted prosperous outsiders and agents of the state wherever such violence proved difficult to eradicate. Such facile assumptions fail to acknowledge the power of bandits to coerce consent. This usually required some exemplary intimidation. Take the experience of Jean-Paul Crose, *agent municipal* of Mercuer in the volatile southern Ardèche. One night, several bandits from nearby Aubenas shot him in the chest and chin while he cried for help from an upper window of his farmhouse at Farge. Although the bandits had disguised their faces with flour, Crose's wife denounced some of them by name to the local JP. Rather than go into hiding, these men soon paid her a visit, this time undisguised, and insisted she look at their faces. She refused but took their point. These men clearly had criminal associates fully prepared to carry out the threats their comrades had made against the Crose household. She later retracted her denunciation at trial, and all four were acquitted.[21] It is this sort of retraction that lent credence to claims that the fear of brigands reigned throughout the Ardèche and that authorities could do little about it.[22]

As common as such claims were, they need to be balanced with cases in which ordinary folk found the courage to testify against the bandits in their midst. Unlike the Croses, victims of serious crime could generally be counted upon to provide the basic testimony to build a case. If assorted other countryfolk, even shepherd boys or aged beggars, could tell about seeing a group of armed men hurrying down the road, or if guests at a tavern were willing to divulge arrival times, snippets of conversation, or the color of jackets worn by a trio of strangers, or if farmhands would confirm seeing a donkey laden with supplies or a woodpile left unguarded, then the victims' story could be sufficiently corroborated to turn arrests into convictions, and possibly executions. These witnesses did not testify as an act of solidarity within the propertied classes—many had little or no property to defend. Nor did they necessarily sympathize with the republican regime or even changes wrought by the Revolution. In fact, it is especially significant when third-party witnesses shatter stereotypes about peasant indifference or cowardice in areas of enduring hostility to the republic. Indeed, in these places it took considerable fortitude to cooperate with the instruments of repression.

The mountainous Tanargue region in the Ardèche was such a place. This had long been a haven for outlaws and deserters, a veritable museum of retarded development and atavistic antistatism. Even the flare-up of antiseigneurial violence in the early Revolution degenerated into an almost indiscriminate brigandage. After 1792, the inhabitants displayed a deep loathing of republican Aubenas, the nearest administrative center, and repeatedly defeated patrols of troops sent to discipline the populace.[23] And yet even here, in a zone of "social banditry" par excellence, individuals with little to gain and a life to lose provided key testimony that sealed the fate of local scofflaws. When Jacques Rouvière (alias Cinq-Francs) scaled a garden wall and knocked on the door of an isolated farmhouse near Prunet, he and his four companions received shelter from the rain but nothing more, even though the owner was a relative, Cinq-Francs had just escaped custody, and one of his companions was badly hurt (a blunderbuss having exploded in his face). This refusal to provide material aid to outlaws saved the residents of the farmhouse from many years in the *bagne*.[24] Pierre Guérin, who leased a small *fabrique* on the neighboring farm, was less fortunate. He had supplied the injured man with a mule and so became the subject of an intense police investigation. Rose Bernard, a domestic servant, said that she had regularly seen small groups of men, sometimes armed, at the *fabrique*, including the night the tax receipts from Joyeuse were stolen on the road to Aubenas. She even provided names. Although officials questioned numerous silk workers and tailors in the area, none admitted to having seen bandits hanging around Guérin's *fabrique*. Eventually, however, a few other witnesses gave depositions against Guérin. These not only confirmed Rose Bernard's account but added that Guérin had been recruiting for a planned rescue of two brigands imprisoned at Le Puy and that he had bragged of helping other outlaws sneak muskets out of Aubenas.[25] This testimony came from a handful of individuals with no connection to one another or the perpetrators. Revenge was certainly not the motive for testifying, for these men had not troubled local folks. Rather, a domestic servant, a carpenter, a conscript, and a small-scale farmer, all of whom lived somewhere nearby, deemed it worth cooperating with authorities in the prosecution of a neighbor simply for quietly sheltering outlaws. Though we can never be sure of all the factors at work, prima facie evidence suggests that these willing witnesses had no sympathy for "social banditry" and were quite prepared to see it ruthlessly punished. As a result of their testimony, a military court at Montpellier sentenced Guérin to twenty years in irons.[26] If such a result could be obtained in one of the most unruly parts of France, then surely the application of severe judicial repression to the problem of brigandage would resonate with popular attitudes in less dangerous parts of the country. Unless local officials were directly engaged in resisting the republic, a few ordinary citizens could usually be found to cooperate in bringing bandits to justice.

Many people assisted in the prosecution of serious crime, despite the risks involved, for reasons of either personal or collective honor. Honor constituted a form of "psychic property"[27] and like physical property, required specific claims and careful protection. Men who easily succumbed to intimidation were abandoning some of their "psychic property." Discretion may have been the better part of valor, but it was the lesser part of honor. Much the same was true of communities that neither supported nor resisted brigands. In such cases, force and fear defeated both individual and collective honor. If brigands were the principal threat to this psychic property, then assisting the police and army lost its stigma and became a means to defend and protect honor. This was especially clear in direct confrontations with brigands. When sixteen outlaws from the Ardèche attacked the mail coach from Marseille to Lyon, one of the cavaliers escorting the coach galloped into nearby Gaujac (Gard) to get help. Eight men armed with muskets agreed to join a posse and go after the brigands. The slowest of the bandits was overtaken by the two leading citizens, Pical and Guigne. Guigne called out: "Stop rogue! Let's see if you shoot better than I do." At this, Joseph Theraube turned to confront his pursuers. Guigne fired twice, but Theraube, although hit, remained standing. Rather than waiting for the rest of the posse, Guigne stayed where he was, turned sideways, and said, "Now it's your turn, shoot!" Theraube fired once and missed; a second attempt did not go off. Only then did Pical join Guigne in arresting the wounded Theraube.[28] This single incident is richly suggestive. First, there were good reasons why the men of Gaujac should have stayed home: the event happened at the height of the "Vendée cévénole," when it was far from clear that the republic would ultimately triumph; this was a highway robbery, not an incursion into their town; and the bandits outnumbered the posse. Therefore, that a posse formed at all indicates a willingness to avenge Gaujac's honor. Brigands from the Ardèche would not be allowed to exploit the local ravine, known as the *combe de Gaujac,* and stain the town's image in the process. Furthermore, by turning the confrontation with Theraube into an impromptu duel, at real peril to himself, Guigne put masculine bravado ahead of self-defense. His act was proof that his stock of personal honor was greater than merely joining the "forces of order" to capture a brigand. As with many individuals and communities, a cultural defense of honor had brought the men of Gaujac onto the side of the republic.[29]

It is this sort of response that lay behind the belated willingness of southern communities to reclaim their territories from the domination of outlaws. Such efforts were generally too dangerous to undertake until the republic's forces of repression had been fully deployed. The presence of a significant number of troops, especially in the form of "flying columns," and the assurance of punishment offered by military commissions provided the catalyst communities needed before finally acting in concert. Though it required considerable state support, there should be no mistaking the fact that ordinary citizens themselves banded together in order to defeat highwaymen, cutthroats, bandits, and rebels.[30] Such an attitude appears to have swept the south. "The spirit of the region has totally changed; today the inhabitants are willing to hunt down brigands who dare to sully the soil of their communes," wrote General Ruby, commander of the Ardèche.[31] The prefect of the strife-torn Var captured the new attitude when he triumphantly reported in June 1801 that seventy-four communes "had armed themselves in defense of public security and were in a state of insurrection against the brigands."[32] Citizens of the south were finally joining the state in defense of their communes.

## Security State

Viewed in this light, vastly expanding the use of military means of repression not only contributed significantly to restoring order in provincial France, it also served to win support for the regime.[33] In the process, stamping out insurgency and banditry helped to transform the relationship between state and society. The interplay between traditional community particularism, an encroaching legal universalism associated with the nation, and state intervention to assert the regime's authority produced new attitudes to public order. As both judicial records and administrative correspondence reveal, by the late 1790s, many communities were eager to cooperate with agents of repression in ways that the *ancien régime* had never expected. Of course, numerous cases reveal strong bonds of familial and communal solidarity with those waging open war on the republic. Despite some ferocious legislation, scorching rhetoric, and brutal examples, however, military justice tended to treat ordinary accomplices with clemency. Many of the people tried as brigand or chouan accomplices were women, most of whom were acquitted or given lenient sentences. Even though in one case a chouan's mother was condemned to death for recruiting young men for her son's band, the other eight women and three men charged as rebel accomplices in this case were dealt with lightly.[34] Similarly, the willingness to treat thousands of rebels as either coerced or misled, notably after the insurrection around Toulouse, and simply to release them shows a concern to disrupt the nexus between political extremism and the defense of community. Furthermore, it took a long time to see significant changes in popular attitudes to the judicial system in areas where rebels and outlaws could inspire a conspiracy of silence through intimidation. Of course, the murder of witnesses en route to a trial tended to make convictions difficult. Only by dramatically increasing the machinery of repression and meting out hundreds of executions was the republic able to obtain the assistance of terrified villagers against brigands whose solipsistic violence had gone far beyond the limits of community tolerance. When this form of cooperation took place, a more modern polity emerged: what had been an organic society became a security state.[35]

This transition took place in several ways according to specific local circumstances. A rich variety of factors as diverse as forms of sociability, clan rivalries, the presence of nonjuring priests, market integration, and geography all shaped these circumstances. So too did the interaction between local particularities and the major forces at work across the country, namely Jacobinism, royalism, Catholicism, and war. With such a myriad of influences to take into account, it is hazardous to propose any rigid typology of responses. Nonetheless, it is helpful to outline and illustrate four broad types of community response to state repression.

First, substantial parts of France adapted to the Directorial regime and then the Consulate without much need for exceptional coercive force. The Directory's penchant for suddenly replacing many of its commissioners for each department, canton, municipality, and court as well as dismissing elected officials—whether department administrators, municipal agents, public prosecutors, or civilian judges—overcame much passive resistance and strengthened the state's control of society. There is no doubt that this came at a cost to the regime's constitutional legitimacy—its opponents made sure that it did. Nonetheless, heavy-handed tampering with election results and often poorly informed interference in local politics were believably justified as temporary expedients needed to preserve the republic. It was really the absurd pettiness of the political purges in year VII that could no longer be justified. By then, electoral turnout was so low and political involvement so limited that there was no need to fix the results later. And yet two waves of turnover in administrative personnel followed. The first wave "regenerated" authorities across the country, often by reappointing Jacobin-style officials sacked on the eve of the spring elections. The second wave replaced many of these *exclusifs* with conservative republicans favored by Sieyès and the revisionists.[36] Such antics made the Consulate's transition to appointed officials far less of a break with democracy than is usually suggested. Furthermore, the steady shift from community policing to policing communities helped to overcome some of the negligence and partisan abuses that had infected so many local incarnations of the National Guard. The reforms made in the gendarmerie between 1797 and 1801 greatly enhanced its professionalism, tightened the government's control over the corps, and increased its numerical strength to four times that of the *maréchaussée* in 1789.[37] Thus, a shift to administrative appointments and improved policing was all that was needed in most parts of France. Apathy and mistrust remained high, and recourse to the lower courts could be a source of increased rancor as much as of pacification,[38] but most property owners were willing to accept such changes provided the roads remained safe and the economy buoyant.

Second, the late republic made this transition by providing protection for republican communities that had been repeatedly attacked by enemies of the regime. Protestant villages in the Gard, for example, took up the revolutionary cause from the start and came to rely on the republic, regardless of its iniquities and ineptitude, as a bulwark against the surrounding Catholic countryside. Such communities might have complained about the Directory's authoritarianism or the Consulate's rejection of democracy, but they needed the government's protection in the form of Protestant local officials and garrison troops.[39] Likewise, beleaguered republican towns in the west had too long been forced to defend themselves to protest their loss of political autonomy. These towns needed troops and begged incessantly for them. Having taken up arms against chouans from Bouère, the bourg of Ballée (Mayenne) was rewarded with a small detachment of troops. These few soldiers, plus Mme. Nicolas's threat to blow out the brains of any coward who talked of surrender, enabled Ballée to withstand a five-hour siege by the Comte de Bourmont and two thousand chouans armed with cannons.[40] Such centers positively welcomed the advent of a security state.

Third, in some communities, internal struggles for power between extremist factions could be ended and stability restored only by calling upon the army to protect the interests of the moderate majority, even if it was not sympathetic to the republic. Such was the case at Valréas in the Vaucluse (see above). The majority of residents undoubtedly viewed this more as protection than repression, at least in the short term. Though loath to have the state ensconce itself in their midst, temporary acceptance of it led to just that. Such intervention in 1797–1801 became permanent once the Consular regime took root.

Finally, this transition was all too often made by increasing the level of repression through military means and exemplary punishment until the balance of fear in communities dominated by opponents of the regime tipped from villagers' concerns about reprisals or social exclusion to concerns about the cost of not cooperating with the forces of order against brigands and neighbors who sheltered them. A response of this sort was generally confined to the most turbulent or remote areas such as the canton of Montsalvy (Cantal), where a band of brigands "had terrorized the inhabitants to the point that they stopped cultivating parts of their land because they dared not go out before sunrise or after sundown."[41] Likewise, after the full panoply of repression had been deployed in the Drôme, the department commander described four communes that had taken heroic action against brigands after having long been too afraid to act. The protection the citizens of St-Etienne-de-Lugdarès (Ardèche) accorded their tax collector when a band of twenty armed men attacked him was especially noteworthy. "The fear of having to pay has gripped these communes and, I assure you, they will show spirit," General Ruby told his superior.[42] Publicizing such actions gradually became a leitmotif of administrative correspondence in 1801–2.

The conclusions of this study do not depend on developing a map to chart these four types of responses across the country, as interesting as that might be. It is sufficient to know that the level of lawlessness rose high enough to persuade important elements of society to accept undemocratic and illiberal—and sometimes quite draconian—methods of repression in order to defeat outlaws, bring order to communities, and improve safety on the roads. National leaders came to believe that preserving liberties first required providing security and so violated the Constitution of Year III. But republican institutions could not take root until local notables put public order before communal autonomy. When and where this happened, the regime's ability to provide security made its extension of authority acceptable. The Consulate also overcame much hostility by gradually reopening churches, ending requisitions, and finally achieving peace with victory. The importance of these palliatives does not change the fact that the Consulate employed even harsher means of repression than used by the Directory in order to impose order in the most turbulent parts of France. As Frenchmen came to accept this approach, the liberal democratic polity that had dislocated the organic society of the *ancien régime* became the authoritarian security state of the Consulate and beyond.

The late republic's transition to a security state did not end resistance, nor did it constitute a complete loss of communal autonomy; it merely confirmed the hierarchy of state institutions connecting each of the 16,206 communes to Paris.[43] The quickest and most effective way to do this was through administrative and judicial institutions that enabled communities to keep internal tensions or outside intrusions from threatening public safety and, at the same time, provided the government with the means to overcome open hostility to taxation, conscription, regulation, and exploitation. The Consulate tried to do this by appointing mayors and justices of the peace who could both manage the internal tensions of their communities and preserve their collective stock of honor, thus earning a modicum of support from their fellow citizens, but who would also conform to the government's most pressing demands. Such men were hard to find, especially when mayors received no pay and justices of the peace had their jurisdictions greatly enlarged. It took major reforms in policing and criminal justice to preserve these offices and thereby reify the new relationship between the state and local communities. The improved and greatly expanded gendarmerie combined with a steady return of troops in the spring of 1801 to provide a more effective police presence across France. At the same time, it became apparent that the state of siege was no longer needed in so many places. The creation of commissioners-general of police in ten of France's principal cities provided a more flexible means of removing police powers from municipal officials steeped in partisan animosities.

The early Consulate also strengthened the criminal justice system. The reforms of 1800 replaced ostensibly elected judges with ones appointed by the government. By giving them tenure for life, the new regime hoped to isolate judges and public prosecutors from both national politics and local factionalism. This made them judicial functionaries rather than aspiring politicians. In 1801, the regime substantially enhanced the power of public prosecution. In order to make indictments easier, the law of 7 pluviôse IX (27 January 1801) eliminated both the need to hold interrogations in the presence of the accused and any oral testimony from grand jury hearings, which meant returning to the prerevolutionary practices of conducting closed investigations and basing judicial verdicts on written depositions. This same law further strengthened the hand of prosecution during the indictment phase by attaching "security magistrates" to each court of first instance. Officially entitled "substitutes of the court commissioner," these government-appointed agents took over many of the investigative and prosecutorial functions of jury directors. Security magistrates supervised the police work of gendarmes and justices of the peace, issued warrants of arrest and detention, and helped to write the indictments presented to the grand jury.[44] Such changes were all intended to insulate the justice system from factionalism and to overcome obstacles to the prosecution of crime. All the same, jurors continued to thwart the wishes of central authority by rendering verdicts based on community mores rather than the law, acquitting known murderers, for example, on grounds that they had acted in self-defense against witchcraft, or refusing to treat resistance to the gendarmerie as rebellion.[45] These verdicts tempered the state's ability to impose the law in universalist terms, but they posed no threat to the viability of successive regimes. Such threats were more likely to come from political opponents for whom the Consulate had other solutions.

Napoleonic France is often called a police state, and with some justification. Though their effectiveness has often been exaggerated, the minister of police and his network of agents provided an important prophylaxis against political opposition. They helped to prepare two lengthy proscription lists of prominent Jacobins (November 1799 and January 1801), arbitrarily deported the unconvicted detritus of brigand bands, and locked up hundreds of political opponents in special state prisons without trial. Napoleon's regimes also perfected a system of administrative surveillance akin to internal exile. Whereas the Directory had employed preventive detentions in areas of civil strife, the Napoleonic system of putting suspects under surveillance spread across the country. This purely administrative measure had no basis in law and yet forced several thousand men and women to live away from their preferred residences and to report regularly to local officials. These arbitrary and often illegal practices were so acceptable to Napoleonic lawmakers that the Senatorial Commission on Personal Liberties, which considered more than 550 cases of dubious detention from 1804 to 1814, never openly opposed police decisions and only rarely even questioned them. Many historians take these measures as evidence that Napoleon turned France into a police state.[46]

Describing Napoleonic France as a "police state" has some justification, but it is better termed a "security state." The semantic change does not reflect a difference of moral judgment but more fully captures the nature of the new regime. "Security state" emphasizes the importance of surveillance and regulatory control to maintain public order rather than simply using coercive force to restore it. The term "security state" has the additional advantage of reflecting the social justification, and therefore the main source of political legitimacy, for the new tutelary administrative and judicial apparatus that supplanted the democratic institutions of the Revolution.[47] The Consulate not only eliminated representative democracy and fortified criminal justice, it helped to construct a security state by undertaking a vast administrative investigation of society. At first motivated by political concerns, this investigation quickly became a wide-ranging and increasingly fine-grained social and economic analysis of France.[48] This gave the government an unprecedented ability to chart societal change and thereby respond to perceived threats to public order more with regulatory control than overt force. Thus local communities became inescapably enmeshed in the security state, at first through repression and then through supervision. The Empire went on to devise a harsher penal code, streamline criminal procedures, and revise the system of courts. But these only confirmed the authoritarian character of Napoleonic rule;[49] they did not change the fundamental nature of the security state. While delivering the security that many had good reason to want, the Consulate produced a state that few would have chosen.

## Dictatorial Denouement

Bonaparte won many admirers for the political acumen he showed in adopting solutions that appeared impossible only a few years earlier. It is vital to note, however, that these solutions became possible only after years of building up the republic's capacity for controlled repression. The Consulate's answer to the problem of émigrés, a source of controversy and conflict throughout the republic, illustrates the changed situation. In March 1800, the Consulate closed the list of émigrés, which stood at well over 100,000, and established a large commission in the Ministry of Justice to screen applications for removal from the list. The commission judged every case on an individual basis, which meant that fame, fortune, and favorable influence played the leading roles in being readmitted to the "Grande Nation." Six months later, a partial amnesty for émigrés extended the irenic process. The directive of 28 vendémiaire IX (20 October 1800) created numerous categories to distinguish between émigrés granted automatic readmission and those who still needed to be screened on an individual basis.[50] The terms of these categories left wide discretion to Minister of Police Fouché, who had repeatedly instructed provincial authorities to enforce rigorously the laws against émigrés. Fouché's unraveling of the royalist conspiracy directed by the "agence anglaise" in the summer of 1800 proved the efficacy of the police apparatus in containing them and helped to persuade a reluctant Bonaparte that a partial amnesty was possible if swaddled in police controls. Here was the key to the amnesty: every émigré who wished to benefit from it, whether removed from the list by category or individually, had to register with a prefect or one of the new general commissioners of police who then forwarded his name to Paris. Such a provision allowed the government to refuse to admit any individual émigré or to prescribe special police surveillance for any returned émigré it deemed dangerous. So massive was this operation that it occupied one-third of the personnel in the Police Ministry. At the same time, Fouché did not hesitate to have scores of émigrés arrested and locked away in state prisons without trial. The victims included a number of former chouan commanders suspected of planning another uprising, men such as Bourmont, d'Andigné, and Suzannet.[51] The whole process violated the Constitution of Year VIII, which, like its Thermidorian predecessor, barred the return of émigrés to France. Nonetheless, the political success of combining an amnesty that offended republican sensibilities with police measures that contradicted all principles espoused by the early revolutionaries led to the almost total amnesty for émigrés endorsed by the Senate on 6 floréal X (26 April 1802). This dropped most of the discretionary categories but none of the police surveillance. Many returned émigrés had shown a haughtiness and insolence that shocked republican leaders and alarmed purchasers of "national properties." Some continued to conspire against the government. Under these conditions, Fouché instructed provincial officials to repress "with inflexible severity" any disobedience or usurpation of property.[52] Thus, the rigors that accompanied the magnanimity of the Consulate's progressive amnesty for émigrés would have been impossible—and had been unimaginable—without the security apparatus in place by year IX.

Much the same was true for the Consulate's handling of refractory clergy. The reopening of churches, release of deported priests from the islands of Ré and Oléron, and the simplified civic oath are all famous precursors to the Concordat. They were also a repetition of the Convention's strategy in the spring of 1795. In fact, the early Consulate retained the same Thermidorian restrictions on public worship imposed five years earlier. The great difference is that by 1800 the republic had enormously greater ability to police the conduct of priests and parishioners alike. Historians invariably note the new tolerance but pay less attention to the broad use of administrative surveillance, the numerous prohibitions on priests appearing in a former parish, and the repeated use of internal exile, all of which made the growing tolerance possible. Priests who refused the new oath qualified as refractories and could be pursued accordingly. A few were even deported. Thus, the life of a refractory priest remained precarious under the early Consulate. Exemplary acts of rigor, all the more effective for being neither utterly arbitrary nor truly equitable, encouraged caution. Intransigent refractories caused plenty of trouble and thereby helped to legitimize the police measures directed against them.[53] Seen in this light, the Consulate's apparently impossible solutions to the problem of émigrés and refractory priests became possible only in the context of a burgeoning security apparatus.

The French Revolution ended with the Life Consulate of August 1802. This came rather suddenly—it has even been called a coup d'état—and yet depended on longer-term trends. The revolutionary forces so central to the economy of violence in the previous decade—royalism, Jacobinism, war, and Catholicism—were not suddenly eliminated; rather, they were tamed by a long series of repressive responses. Counter-revolutionary royalism had been decisively defeated, though not destroyed, during the Directory. The pacification of the west in 1800–1801 and the undoing of two royalist conspiracies thereafter provided the necessary military and political mopping up. Although elusive armed bands continued to operate throughout the west, especially in the Morbihan, the forces of repression always had the upper hand.[54] Even in the pressing international circumstances of early 1813, the Empire was able to devote 1,200 troops for a full six months to the pursuit of a mere thirty-three chouans in the Sarthe.[55] Though less needed than before, the army remained crucial to ensuring the triumph of the Napoleonic regime over the royalist possibilities of regional resistance.

Jacobinism too ceased to pose a serious threat early in the Consulate, especially after its clubs and newspapers were banned in 1800. Any lingering doubts disappeared with the mass deportations following the rue Nicaise affair. Thereafter, the regime dealt severely with any violence inspired by keepers of the Jacobin flame. The taint of revolutionary politics always added to the regime's repression. *Sans-culottes*–minded artisans and laborers had made the Mediterranean port of Sète a bastion of republicanism. Two days of sporadic violence between soldiers and locals there in April 1802 gave the Consulate an opportunity to send a message to Jacobin officials throughout the Midi: they would be tolerated only as long as they unhesitatingly backed the government and its agents—drawing support from a politicized populace was totally unacceptable. Following the violence at Sète, in which no one died, the government ordered General Gouvion Saint-Cyr, commander of the Ninth Military District, to put Sète under a state of siege, to disarm the populace, and to set up an extraordinary military commission. Over two thousand national guardsmen, cavalry, and gendarmes—that is, more troops than were used against urban riots in Rennes, Grenoble, or Paris in 1788 and 1789—occupied the town. A month later, the military commission tried fifty-eight individuals, including a justice of the peace, a police commissioner, and two deputy-mayors! Though only one-third of the accused were present at trial, one of them was sentenced to death and another to deportation. The commission handed out seven death sentences and twenty-nine deportations in absentia. It also stripped the officials of their functions and banished them from town.[56] A regime willing to deploy repression of this magnitude against a single Jacobin town left no doubt that it would not tolerate the persistence of revolutionary politics.

Though the Directory had parried the threat of invasion, it took the Consulate to bring the war to a triumphant close. The treaties of Lunéville (February 1801) and Amiens (March 1802) did more than add to Bonaparte's glory, however. These peace treaties both freed troops for domestic policing and made it possible to avoid calling another cohort of conscripts in year IX. Authorities then had the time and means to cajole or coerce draft dodgers into the army without adding to their numbers. By late 1801, the Consulate was able to grant permanent release to an eighth of every unit, so long as the beneficiaries had served at least four campaigns.[57] The break from conscription and return of war heroes proved a vital balm for the countryside. Since nobody knew that it was only a temporary respite, the cessation of conscription gave the impression of a permanent relaxation of state demands and a return to order.

Finally, promulgating the Concordat and Organic Articles in April 1802 resolved the religious issue as a source of endemic instability. The Concordat offended a great many republicans, and it remains something of a mystery that it did not inspire more opposition on the left. A decade of fighting religious obscurantism and sacerdotal influence had crippled the church, and republicans saw no reason to let up, let alone to relinquish their gains. Nonetheless, Bonaparte considered this a price worth paying in order to separate Catholic commitment from royalist sentiment. Although the hardliners of the "petite église" proved endlessly irksome, they did not pose a serious threat to the new order.[58] A certain level of disorganization and agitation festered throughout the following year while the new hierarchy was being set up. Once in place, however, the Concordataire bishops became another buttress to the regime, Napoleon's "prefects in purple." It is remarkable that after years of the most bitter partisanship, the Consulate could engineer these solutions without losing all support among republicans or seeing the country drift into royalism. This is itself a measure of the unequivocal assertiveness of the new government and its capacity to make life miserable for individuals who opposed its policies.

It was inevitable that Bonaparte would receive most of the credit for addressing these problems, and so he used it to push through a radical transformation of the regime, one that ended the republic in all but name. Unsatisfied by the Senate's offer to add ten years to his term, Bonaparte had the Council of State adroitly preempt the plan by proposing a national plebiscite on making him first consul for life. The purge of the Tribunate in March 1802 had removed the most outspoken liberals from the Consular regime, and the few who remained had their objections overcome by Bonaparte's vague claim that he was the "best guarantee" for men of the Revolution. With political consciences on hold and courage in check, the plebiscite went forward. The results of the plebiscite of May 1802 were the least fiddled and therefore most accurate of the four Napoleonic plebiscites. The actual yes-vote (the only meaningful number) was twice as high as two years earlier and amounted to half the electorate. Although an enthusiastic effort from mayors and subprefects helped to bolster turnout, the results were legitimately interpreted as a popular endorsement of one-man rule.[59] The plebiscite gave Bonaparte all he needed to transform the regime into a full-blown dictatorship.

The *senatus consultum* of 16 thermidor X (3 August 1802) combined constitutionalism and exceptionalism in a highly formalized fashion. In addition to establishing the Life Consulate, this "Constitution of Year X" eliminated all but sham vestiges of democracy, representative government, and communal independence. The new Conseil Privé became the supreme organ of state and was empowered to write Senatorial decrees that amended the constitution and dissolved the legislatures. It also initiated suspension of the constitution in areas of trouble. This meant eliminating juries from criminal courts, extending the government's powers of arrest, and allowing trial verdicts to be annulled. Exceptional measures thus became less exceptional by embedding them in the constitutional prerogatives of government. Furthermore, the Constitution of Year X also gave the government a large influence in the composition of electoral colleges. Since membership was already restricted to the most heavily taxed members of each department and was for life, they became little more than a permanent pool of social dignitaries that the regime expected to influence local opinion and from which it could draw replacement legislators. As a final precaution against the vagaries of democracy and the expression of local independence, the regime reduced elections for justices of the peace to a selection of nominees.[60] With the National Guard now moribund, the gendarmerie more numerous and more responsive to the state than ever before, and security magistrates in charge of criminal investigation and prosecution, the appointment of JPs completed the transition from community policing to policing communities. Like every other official in the Napoleonic hierarchy, JPs became agents of the state as much as representatives of the countryside. We can wonder whether this is what Frenchmen wanted when they supported Bonaparte's lifetime rule, but we cannot doubt that most of them preferred it to their experiences of the First Republic thus far. To have presided over the return to order, even though achieved with bloody repression and the erosion of liberty, was the only credential Bonaparte needed. Military glory gave Bonaparte the edge over his Brumairian rivals, but the Napoleonic dictatorship was built on the foundations of the security state that they had all helped to construct.

Liberal democracy failed and the French Revolution came to an end only after prolonged violence had generated a public sentiment willing to accept exceptional justice and brutal repression as the price of restoring order. The Constitution of Year III did not equip the republic to cope with the shift from a pattern of communicative violence rooted in the rituals and limitations of traditional society to the solipsistic violence of subsistence raids, murder gangs, and endemic brigandage. Profound ambiguities in the forms of violence joined with official discourses to magnify the sources of fear. Crime was politicized and politics were criminalized. These trends were simply unimaginable under the *ancien régime*, with its many forms of indirect rule, and thereby cast the relationship between crime and the republic's legitimacy in an entirely new light. Authoritarian responses to public disorder became desired and demanded. Judicial and military repression were both far greater after the Terror than scholars have realized and provided the central continuity between the Directory and Consulate. The jury-based justice system not only provided much more judicial and penal repression than had the much decried courts of the *ancien régime*, but regular courts became an increasingly effective means of imposing "l'ordre républicain" in the years VI and VII. Moreover, a variety of exceptional measures brought military justice into the republican mission to impose order and a revolutionary settlement on the country.

The myth of Napoleon as the savior of France has largely been based on his ending the French Revolution by restoring order. The First Consul overcame much indifference and hostility to the republic by reopening churches, suspending conscription, and achieving peace with victory.

But these laudatory palliatives were also accompanied by a brutal repression that rarely appears in standard histories.[61] Although widely ignored by scholars, the noisy crescendo of military repression that began in 1797 reached a shuddering climax in the Consular Terror of spring 1801. In fact, in parts of France, the volleys of gunfire celebrating the Treaty of Lunéville could easily have been mistaken for the repeated crack of firing squads. The brutal effectiveness of this "booted justice" has received little attention from historians more inclined to credit Bonaparte's military victories, amnesties, religious liberalism, and political ecumenism for his success in consolidating the Consulate. Furthermore, the success of these measures depended on the extensive security apparatus built up in the late 1790s. Thus, it was armed coercion deployed as much at home as abroad that brought peace to France after more than a decade of revolution. That the French Revolution ended in dictatorship was not inevitable, but the trajectories of violence, justice, and repression made it probable.

## Conclusion

The revolutionaries of 1789 had hoped to create a liberal democracy in France but found that their precious new polity could not survive without violating the principles they sought to establish. A mix of determination and desperation, fear and resentment carried them into the Terror. The excesses committed in the republic's name tainted any subsequent effort republicans made to realize the revolutionary goal of constructing a liberal democracy. The very men whose political identity was based on ending the Terror repeatedly resorted to some of its key features—political purges, summary justice, and military repression—all in the name of saving liberty and the republic. In his pamphlet *Des effets de la Terreur* published in early 1797, Benjamin Constant argued that the Terror had not been a necessary stage in the French Revolution and that the Revolutionary Government had saved the republic despite the Terror. Thus, Constant conceded that coercive measures had been necessary to overcome resistance and public lassitude, but he did not define such measures as terror. He restricted the Terror to the arbitrary proscription of suspects and their condemnation without due process. This was essentially the argument made by Thermidorians when they claimed to be ending the "system of terror" while carrying on with revolutionary government. But how, in practice, could these distinctions be made? Like distinguishing terror from revolutionary government, the syndicate of Thermidorians who ran the Directorial regime could not separate the sort of exceptional measures used to impose the new order from the sort of exceptional measures needed to preserve it. In the process, failed, misdirected, or excessive repression helped to turn antirevolution into counter-revolution. The republic had such shallow roots and so few friends in 1795 that it had to be imposed by force. Many republicans treated this necessity as an opportunity. The need for exceptional measures to defend the republic became the chance to press the transformation of French society.

The First Directory was schizophrenic: it attempted a leap forward in constitutionalism, the rule of law, and due process at the same time that it amnestied "terrorists," reinstated the revolutionary persecution of priests and émigrés, and continued an expansionist war effort. Furthermore, the tension between the rule of law as the Directory's basic source of legitimacy and the need to restore order as its most pressing problem placed enormous importance on the fledgling system of criminal justice. My study of criminal courts indicates that the judicial system was much more effective than previously thought, except when it came to "political" crimes. Even this aspect improved markedly after Fructidor, when both jury lists and magistrates were more republican. However, the elections of 1797 had brought a collapse in government authority and a crescendo of politicized violence in the provinces. This served to confirm the exculpatory narrative republicans had generated about the drift toward terror in 1791–93—crisis circumstances created by the treachery of nobles and priests—and thereby to justify similar responses. The Fructidor coup and its attendant measures exploited the "royalist plot," which was real enough, though not located in the Councils, as justification for exceptional measures that would restore republican authority across the country. It is clear from the endemic violence and incessant brigandage that some exceptions to the rule of law were necessary.[62] The exceptional measures adopted in the wake of the coup, however, were largely shaped by the republican myth about the sources of opposition. These exceptional measures were poorly designed and poorly managed and so became discredited forms of transformative violence. Using such measures to continue the social and cultural revolution, and adding a lot of arbitrariness to boot, led directly to the failure of liberal democracy in France.

When Thermidorians and Brumairians believed that violent resistance threatened the republic, they resorted to repressive measures that clearly violated their constitutions and the rule of law in ways that echoed the Terror. The Directorial regime used responses to violent resistance as opportunities to accelerate the transformation of the social order by persecuting members of the former elite. The Fructidorian Terror of 1797 in particular drew on the same wellspring of fear and resentment that had fueled the worst excesses of the Revolutionary Tribunal and Popular Commission of Orange. Although nobles and priests remained privileged targets of discrimination throughout the Directory, individual actions, not mere group identity, came to assume greater significance, as our inquiry into the Fructidorian military commissions revealed. The "dirty war" against *chouannerie* prolonged these tensions, however, as doses of political persecution were added to the unpleasantries of counter-insurgency, especially at election time. Republicans had established a solid grip on the country by 1799. The elections of that year were free only insofar as the right-wing majority was excluded because its power base had been destroyed and exceptional measures were increasingly better focused on real threats to the regime. However, the renewal of war both increased demands on the populace and stripped the interior of troops. The Jacobin revival of 1799, like the Terror of 1793–94, turned the twin perils of foreign and civil war into an opportunity to reinvigorate the identity politics of the early republic. This is most evident in the discrimination against former nobles built into the law of hostages and forced loan, another disagreeable mix of necessary security measures and political persecution. The Consulate, too, found that exceptional measures adopted in defense of the republic provided an opportunity to persecute political opponents. The Consular crackdown of 1801 briefly revived the Revolutionary Government's response to enemies on both the left and the right, as well as reviving aspects of its ruthless repression of inchoate opposition, whether overtly political or simply disobedient, through flying columns and military commissions. In these circumstances, it was natural for contemporary observers of republican government to denigrate its various exceptional measures by drawing parallels with the Terror. Their criticisms point at a red thread of continuity: bloody state violence that trampled on the rule of law in the name of saving the republic and securing liberty. Yet there was a clear trajectory to these practices. Although arbitrary purges and political persecution accompanied each round of repression, their ramifications were felt in diminishing circles with each passing wave. Aspects of the Terror continued to echo, but less and less audibly over time.

Repression did not always mean persecution; exceptional measures could also be part of the process of pacification. The combination of high crime rates, constant exaggeration of threats due to the banditry psychosis and plot mentality of officials, and the massive reporting of crime by newspapers meant that any regime that successfully addressed these issues would win popular support almost regardless of its methods. Thus, when the republic deployed armed force and summary justice against rebels and brigands, it could more credibly claim to be using legitimate force even though the methods often violated its proclaimed principles. The greatest difficulty in these circumstances, however, was to ensure that the various means of repression did not lack measure. This usually required limiting the role local men played in managing the "forces of order." Repeatedly resorting to exceptional justice, military force, and strong-arm policing served to refine these practices into more precise instruments of coercion. It also took some of the means of defending the republic out of the hands of men steeped in local factionalism. As repression became increasingly regulated, it did not necessarily become less harsh or even less arbitrary; it simply became more controlled and therefore generated less terror in the wider populace. This culminated in the flying columns and military commissions of 1801. Once these had killed enough rebels and brigands to terrify refractory regions into submission, the Consulate turned the judicial fight against brigandage over to special tribunals. Unique among historians, Adolphe Thiers recognized this moment as a triumph of legality under the circumstances. Not only had 130 individuals just been proscribed without trial, and military commissions formed in several departments, all without public outcry, but Bonaparte had threatened members of the Senate who opposed the law with governing by dictate.[63] From this perspective, it becomes clear that passing the law of 19 pluviôse IX actually limited the tendency to military dictatorship, both in the provinces and in Paris. Though usually presented as a return to provostial justice, these new courts epitomized the growing compromise between the rule of law and exceptional measures that helped to end the cycles of violence generated by the interaction of revolution and resistance.

This book's analysis of this process has revealed several salient features. Above all, it is clear that the return to order in France was far more brutal than historians have realized. Recourse to the army to provide domestic policing and expedited justice became pronounced in year IV, increased massively in year VI, and came to a shuddering climax in year IX. In the process, the National Guard was transformed from an instrument of communal self-defense or factional domination to an increasingly important tool in the government's arsenal of repression. And yet its dual character as both useful and dangerous persisted down to 1801, especially in the west. At the same time, the gendarmerie was completely remade. It emerged as a modern police force, increasingly professionalized and responsive to state direction. Roederer wrote of the gendarme as the real face of the regime in the countryside, more even than Bonaparte himself. "The people are full of respect and trust for the gendarme. . . . Sometimes he is cursed for arresting a conscript at the home of his parents or his mistress, but he is considered the guardian of property and the enemy of thieves and brigands."[64] Despite the build-up of repressive capacity, rural resistance to the republican concept of order remained substantial throughout the period, as the continued practice of "jury nullification" for crimes of honor and resistance to authority made apparent. But such resistance did not preclude cooperation with the security forces. Many individuals and communities had good reasons to accept and even assist military means of repression in order to obtain security. In doing so, they helped to undermine both the community and the polity they sought to preserve. Thus, the republic's efforts to stamp out brigandage and violent resistance, together with communal responses to these efforts, were decisive in replacing an organic society with a security state. The emergence of this security state was essential to ending the French Revolution.

## Epilogue: Political Theory and the End of the French Revolution

Numerous scholars have emphasized the First Republic's part in inspiring totalitarianism.[65] Others have heralded its invention of democratic republicanism as the essence of a modern political culture.[66] But few have explored how its handling of emergency circumstances created longer-term problems for liberal democracy. A modern liberal state is defined in juridical terms; therefore, any exceptional measures are significant for their precise juridical nature. This is also true of dictatorship. Carl Schmitt, an opponent of the Weimar Republic, argued that liberals from the French Revolution onward had failed to devise a political system that could both remain true to liberal principles and cope with emergency circumstances. In other words, he argued, despite wishful thinking and claims to the contrary, dictatorship had always been a part of the liberal state.[67] Schmitt identified two types of modern dictatorship: "sovereign dictatorship"—a transitional regime established to create a new social and political order—and "commissarial dictatorship," a temporary suspension of the political norms and ideals of a liberal regime undertaken in order to save it. In the French Revolution, sovereign dictatorship was used to create and implement a liberal democratic constitution, that of 1795. Thereafter, sovereign dictatorship disappeared and commissarial dictatorship became possible.

Schmitt believed that the Constitution of Year III ended the French Revolution because it marked the end of "sovereign dictatorship." My research into the modalities of repression after 1795, however, indicates that persistent recourse to exceptional measures in the name of preserving the republic too often turned into transformative violence akin to that perpetrated under "sovereign dictatorship." Equally important, we have seen how the Directory and Consulate evolved various means to contain and focus the use of coercive force on genuine threats to the republic. This process planted the juridical seeds of commissarial dictatorship that later became a permanent feature of European liberal democracies. Schmitt's insight rested on the repeated use of the state of siege to repress insurrections in nineteenth-century France. But Schmitt lacked an adequate history of repression during the First Republic and therefore believed that the state of siege had rarely been used for domestic purposes until the July Monarchy.[68] He emphasized the law of 24 December 1811, which modified the state of siege to enable the local commander not only to exercise all police powers but to apply military justice to insurgents. This combination of extraordinary military policing and expedited military justice provided the modalities of repression following the insurgencies of 1832 and 1834, the bloody June Days of 1848, the coup d'état of 1851–52, and the Commune of 1871.[69]

It was not the July Monarchy, however, but the Directory that first made extensive use of the state of siege and military justice in the name of preserving a regime based on a liberal democratic constitution. As we have seen, the Montagnard Convention abolished martial law as a dangerous tool of local municipalities during the Federalist Revolts of 1793 and replaced it with the state of siege designed for frontier forts by the law of October 1791. This change in methods transferred police power from local officials elected by the people, the repository of sovereignty, to army officers appointed by the government. Thus, the state of siege entered the arsenal of political repression: a proclamation issued by a district commander no longer followed from an actual wartime siege and yet remained the juridical basis for exceptional measures. This turned the state of siege into a juridical fiction because it was no longer based on the well-defined criteria of the original law. The laws of September 1797 completed the process by making the proclamation of a state of siege entirely a government prerogative, which removed all obstacles to using this juridically fictive state of siege for the purpose of domestic repression. As we have seen, by the end of 1799 over 220 cities, towns, and villages were officially under state of siege, and widespread use of this measure only subsided in 1801.

The First Republic also evolved ways of using military justice outside its intended context. Military commissions had been responsible for much of the judicial bloodletting during the Terror. (If the sheer number of executions were the basis of symbolic representation, the firing squad would have pride of place over the guillotine.) The Thermidorians revived the use of military commissions in 1795 and then passed the law of 30 prairial III, which made rebels captured while armed justiciable by military courts. This law remained the basis for military justice as a tool of counter-insurgency well into the nineteenth century. The Second Directory's use of military commissions to judge returned émigrés and regular military courts to prosecute brigands and highwaymen were significant variations on the theme. When these forms of military justice ended in 1800, extraordinary military commissions attached to flying columns were created in the south and west to extirpate criminal and political brigandage. In each case, the laws were deemed exceptional: they were temporary measures that violated the constitution only in order to save it. There were other exceptional measures used for the same ostensible purpose. The republic repeatedly turned to election nullification, deportation, preventive detention, and administrative supervision. Yet none of these became codified and thus remained the juridical equivalent of little coups d'état. On the other hand, using the state of siege for domestic repression and using military justice to try civilians became permanent weapons in the state's arsenal. Though they were not fused until 1811, they functioned in tandem from 1797 to 1801 and therefore perfectly fit the notion of commissarial dictatorship.

The First Republic's use of the state of siege and military justice for domestic repression was a key moment in the history of the liberal state, for it constituted the epitome of dictatorship paradoxically fixed at the core of liberal democracy. Using these measures in a domestic situation obviously violated the norms of a liberal constitution. Nonetheless, they were deemed legitimate means of defending the constitution or, in other words, acts of self-defense in response to a grave threat to the polity. Even though these measures turned policing and justice over to the army, this was for limited duration and only in order to return to liberal norms. In this vein, legislation on exceptional measures developed before Bonaparte and refined after

him was carefully designed to permit the suspension of constitutional restrictions on state power without fostering Caesarism. And yet, the French
Revolution ended in 1802 because this "seed of dictatorship" could not be
contained within the republic's version of a liberal democracy.[70] The "state
of exception," to use Giorgio Agamben's preferred expression, was becoming quasi-permanent.

The Brumaire coup was yet another desperate attempt to save the republic. But for the ambitions of Bonaparte, the Consulate would have consolidated an undemocratic and yet largely liberal regime. Witness the rejection
of exceptional measures by the temporary commissions of 1799 and the
Tribunate's resistance to the creation of security magistrates and special
tribunals in 1801. But the passage of these bills indicated that exceptional
measures were becoming less exceptional and a more regular feature of
Napoleonic rule. The "seed of dictatorship" had destroyed democracy. This
was not due to inherent contradictions in parliamentary democracy itself,
as Schmitt would have it for the Weimar period. Rather, it was because Directorial republicans remained staunchly revolutionary. That is, the Directory made repeated, nay constant, use of exceptional measures and coercive
force to transform cultural mores, persecute traditional elites, and defeat
rival factions—all purposes that went well beyond defense of the constitution, pacification of rebellion, or restoration of order. This tendency turned
measures that would have been regrettable, and yet legitimacy-earning,
exceptions to the rule of law into domestic state violence, that is, into a discredited, delegitimizing use of force. The law of hostages—with its mix of
blatant revolutionary biases and carefully regulated repression—perfectly
embodied this dangerous duality. Under these circumstances, Frenchmen
became willing to see the arbitrary tyranny of exceptional measures replaced by Napoleonic Caesarism. As Hobbes had understood, endemic fears
about violence and personal security turn a state's use of force into political legitimacy even as it destroys personal liberty.

The Constitution of Year X not only consolidated a personal dictatorship, it marked the end of the French Revolution by ending the legal and
political indeterminacy that lay at the heart of exceptional measures. The
Napoleonic Senate's oversight of preventive detention, for example, made
little difference to police action. Whatever tensions arose, they were never
interpreted as a constitutional crisis or even a crisis in the regime's political
values. And yet the effort to instill the rule of law in France had an enduring legacy. After the experience of the Directory and early Consulate, even
exceptional measures adopted in response to emergency circumstances

came packaged in well-defined legal restraints. Large portions of the populace experienced republicans' use of force from 1795 to 1802 as aggression against them and their communities, rather than defense of the social order. As far as they were concerned, republican repression was domestic state violence. Successive incarnations of the republic, however, developed better ways to control the use of coercion and curtailed the revolutionary ambition to transform the social order. Both tendencies enhanced the republic's authority and legitimacy. Thus, the crackdown concentrated in the years 1797 to 1801 was a pivotal moment in the history of repression in France, not as bloody as the Terror but more significant in generating the pattern of "liberal authoritarianism" that confronted every social upheaval of the next century. Subsequent forms of political repression can be characterized as "liberal authoritarianism" due to two features. Above all, a liberal—that is, a rights-based and constitutionally defined—legal system placed clear limits on the powerful police apparatus. And yet, when successive nineteenth-century regimes responded to sociopolitical crises with heavy doses of armed force, liberals—that is, those who represented the *juste milieu*—generally supported these inherently authoritarian aspects of governance. Neither totalitarianism nor democratic republicanism was the most important outcome of the French Revolution. Rather, the Faustian pact citizens made with the instruments of repression sapped the foundations of an organic society and fostered the emergence of a modern security state, one whose legitimacy derived above all from restoring and then preserving order. The French Revolution ended with the triumph of Hobbes over Rousseau.

# Appendix A: *Criminal Court Verdicts*

## A.1  Verdicts rendered by four criminal courts
Includes defendants tried in absentia

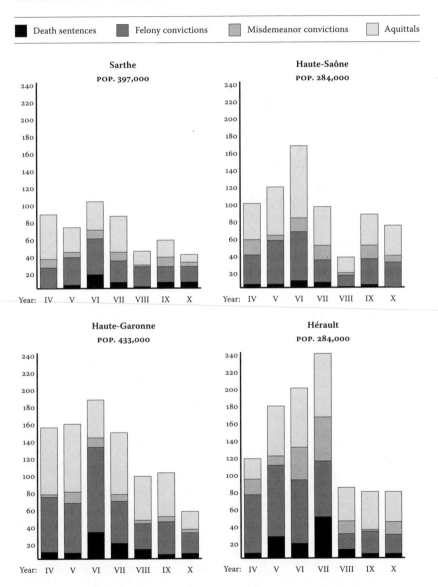

■ Death sentences    ■ Felony convictions    ▨ Misdemeanor convictions    ▢ Aquittals

Note: The population fiigures are the average population for each department during the period.

## A.2  Comparison of verdicts

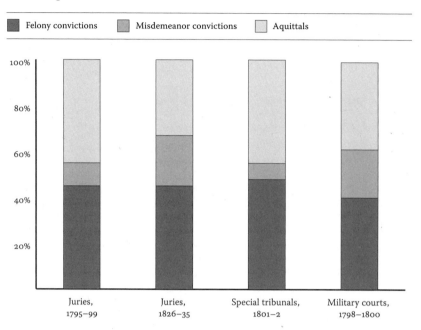

## A.3 Criminal court verdicts according to type of crime

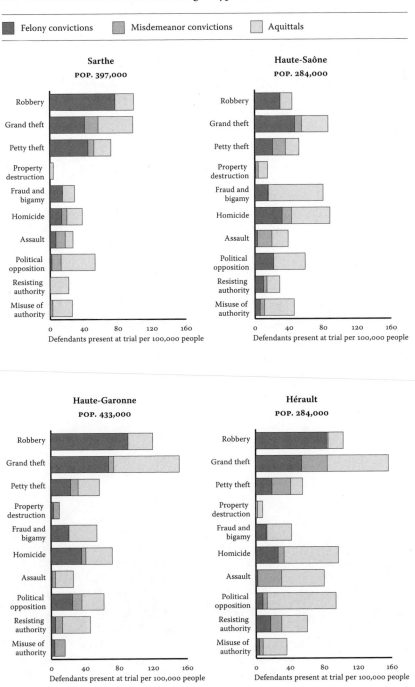

■ Felony convictions    ■ Misdemeanor convictions    □ Aquittals

**Sarthe**
POP. 397,000

Defendants present at trial per 100,000 people

**Haute-Saône**
POP. 284,000

Defendants present at trial per 100,000 people

**Haute-Garonne**
POP. 433,000

Defendants present at trial per 100,000 people

**Hérault**
POP. 284,000

Defendants present at trial per 100,000 people

## A.4 Verdicts rendered by four criminal courts
Defendants present at trial

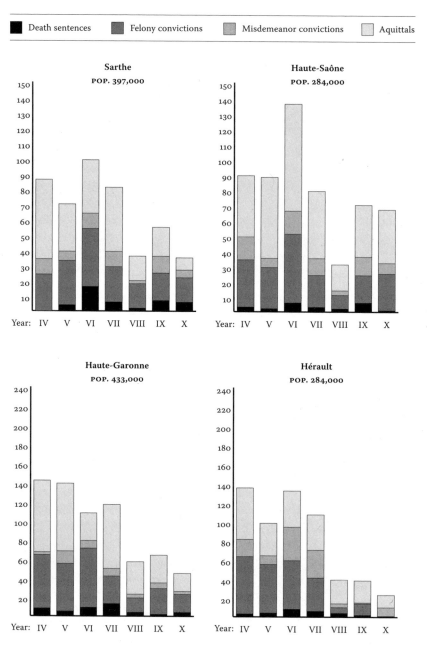

Note: The population figures are the average population for each department during the period.

**A.5  Verdicts (excluding cases of petty theft) rendered by four criminal courts**

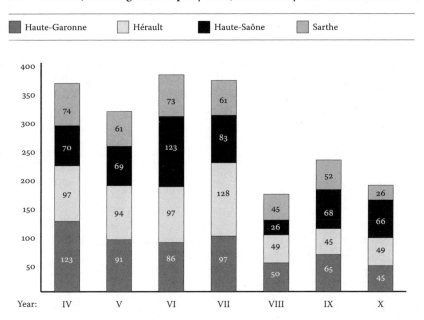

# Appendix B: *Crime and Punishment*

## B.1 Categories of crime

ROBBERY *(theft with violence, weapons, or other aggravating circumstances = 14 years in irons or more)*

Theft with violence = 10 years in irons (+ 4 years if on a highway, in a public square, or inside a house) or (+ 8 years if achieved by breaking, climbing, or duplicate keys, or if the perpetrator was a guest or worker in the residence) or (+ 4 years if committed at night, or by several people, or armed with a deadly weapon).

GRAND THEFT *(felonious thefts)*

Theft with breaking, climbing, duplicate keys, or if the perpetrator was a guest or worker in the residence = 8 years in irons (+ 2 years if committed by breaking, or climbing, or in a home, or at night, or by several people, or armed with a deadly weapon, or using duplicate keys); theft from a home by several unarmed people or one armed person = 6 years in irons; theft of public property = 4 years in irons.

PETTY THEFT *(felony thefts reclassified as misdemeanors by the law of 25 frimaire VIII, sometimes applied retroactively: see appendix b.2)*

Theft from taverns, inns, cafés, lodging houses, public baths = 8 years in irons before year VIII; from theaters, shops, public buildings, enclosed areas adjacent to homes, public places, and domestic thefts during the day, or by workers or coachmen entrusted with the property they stole = 4 years in irons before year VIII; from enclosed areas not adjacent to homes or from the public trust = 4 years in prison (+ 2 years if at night) before year VIII.

PROPERTY DESTRUCTION

Arson = death; threat of arson = 4 years in irons; vandalism = 6 years in irons (+ 3 years if by a group); if by someone entrusted with the property = loss of civic rights.

FRAUD *(felonious misrepresentation)*

Perjury in criminal case = 20 years in irons or death; making or distributing counterfeit currency = 15 years in irons; bigamy = 12 years in irons; destroying the record of civil identity = 12 years in irons; public document forgery = 8 years in irons; private document forgery = 4 years in irons; commercial document forgery = 6 years in irons; false bankruptcy = 6 years in irons.

HOMICIDE

Premeditated murder (*assassinat*), attempted murder, parricide, or infanticide = death; unpremeditated murder (*meurtre*) or abortion = 20 years in irons; manslaughter (*meurtre excusable*) = 10 years in solitary confinement; accidental death due to imprudence or brawling = misdemeanor penalty.

## ASSAULT *(not intended to kill)*

Castration = death; ambush, assault, and mutilation = death; mutilation of a parent = 20 years in irons; forcing a girl under age 14 into sex = 12 years in irons; rape = 6 years in irons (+ 6 years for girl under age 14, if committed with violence or with accomplices); assault causing injuries that prevent working for 40 days = 2 years in prison (+ 1 year for a broken limb or + 2 years for loss of an eye or limb or + 4 years for blindness or loss of two limbs and + 2 years if committed in a brawl).

## POLITICAL OPPOSITION *(combines attacks against the regime and explicit counter-revolution)*

Treason, espionage, attempting to overthrow the constitution or disband the legislature by force = death; using force against electoral assemblies = 15 years in solitary confinement; using force against administrative or judicial bodies = 3 years in prison (+ 3 years if armed); counter-revolutionary statements made in public = death (reduced to deportation for attenuating circumstances); attacking republican symbols = 4 years in prison; harboring a refractory priest = deportation.

## RESISTANCE TO AUTHORITY *(use of force against public officials)*

Resistance to enforcement of the law or striking a public official = 2 years in prison; using force to rescue a prisoner = 3 years in irons; armed resistance or resistance by 3–15 people = 4 years in irons; resistance to enforcement of the law by 16 or more people (*attroupement séditieux*) = 8 years in irons (+ 8 years if armed).

## MISUSE OF AUTHORITY

Misappropriation of public funds = 15 years in irons; facilitating a prisoner's escape = 15 years in irons; inciting resistance to the law = 6 years in solitary confinement; false arrest = 6 years in solitary confinement; malversation in tax collection = 6 years in irons; accepting a bribe = loss of civic rights.

## EXPLANATION OF CATEGORIES

The process of creating these eleven categories and sorting actual crimes into them raises important epistemological issues. As the categories *felonious misrepresentation,* and *robbery* illustrate, this classification scheme eschews the dichotomy between crimes against people and crimes against property that underpins quasi-Marxist analyses of criminal conduct in early modern Europe. During the late First Republic, the crime of armed robbery could have been perpetrated as much as an act of violence designed to terrorize republicans as an act of thievery to obtain material goods. How then can the violence be distinguished from the theft? Furthermore, the categories used here reflect a desire to analyze the institutions of repression and public responses to them, not the incidence of particular types of crime. Modern police statistics tell us about the incidence of reported crime, whereas eighteenth-century court records tell us about the incidence of prosecuted crime. Deducing the incidence of actual crime from the former is hazardous at best; deducing it from the latter is absurd, notwithstanding the legion of historians who have tried. Furthermore, the categories adopted in this study reflect concerns of special significance to the fledgling republic. For example, shortly after legislators elevated violent housebreaking and armed robbery to capital crimes, they sharply lowered the penalties for numerous other forms of theft. It is this differential response that provided the incentive to subdivide theft into three categories. The same rationale applies to categories of counter-revolution and resistance to public authority. With this in mind, theft has been subdivided into *robbery*, *grand theft*, and *petty theft* on the basis of penalties, themselves driven by aggravating circumstances rather than value of property, as in English law. Crimes of violence and counter-revolution are subdivided into categories on the same basis, namely, circumstances and possible penalty. In cases of attempted murder, *assault* has been distinguished from *homicide* less by the charges—prosecutors had a notorious tendency to exaggerate a perpetrator's intentions and described any serious blow to the head or buckshot wound as attempted murder—than by the apparent motives of the nonlethal violence. It is impossible to distinguish clearly between criminal and political violence, but it is possible to separate different forms of opposition to legitimate authorities at the national and local levels. The most serious crimes of opposition fit easily under the heading *violent counter-revolution*. These are high crimes against the state such as treason and espionage, as well as efforts to overturn the constitution, and using force against the legislature, electoral assemblies, or official bodies such as courts or municipal councils. In contrast, the category of *nonviolent counter-revolution* reflects the republic's "lois de circonstances" against harboring refractory priests, refusing to take a clerical oath, contravening political exile, making counter-revolutionary statements in public, and vandalizing republican symbols, especially liberty trees. This category shades into *resistance to public authority*. Although rescuing a priest from the gendarmerie would clearly have been deemed counter-revolutionary activity by the Directory, as would various instances of armed resistance or rioting if they had overtly political motives, their confrontational form rather than their motivational content make them suitable for inclusion with other crimes against authority such as rescuing draft dodgers, freeing prisoners, resisting law enforcement, and striking a public official. After all, much of this resistance would have occurred regardless of the political bent of the regime in power at Paris.

### B.2 Crimes and punishments reduced from felonies (*délits criminels*) to misdemeanors (*délits correctionnels*) by the law of 25 frimaire VIII

The following crimes were to be pursued "par voie de police correctionnelle": the prescribed punishments indicate new minimums and maximums as well as the former mandatory sentences according to the Penal Code of 1791. The abbreviations used are:

mp = months in prison; yp = years in prison; (*italics*) = former mandatory punishment.

- Theft in the daytime by a household inhabitant, regular visitor, or employee (excluding domestic servants), 1 yp–4 yp (*8 yp*)
- Theft from "rooming houses, inns, taverns, workmen's quarters, cafés, and public baths," 1 yp–4 yp (*8 yp*)
- Theft from "theaters, shops, public buildings," 6 mp–2 yp (*4 yp*)
- Theft by two or more people without aggravating circumstances, 6 mp–2 yp (*8 yp*)
- Theft of "effects entrusted to coaches, postal services, or other public transportation" by a driver or service employee, 6 mp–2 yp (*4 yp*)
- Theft of such effects by a passenger, 3 mp–1 yp (*4 yp*)
- Theft in the daytime from an enclosed plot of land attached to a house, 6 mp–2 yp (*4 yp*)
- Theft in the daytime from an enclosed plot of land *not* attached to a house, 3 mp–1 yp (*4 yp*)
- Theft at night from an enclosed plot of land *not* attached to a house, 6 mp–2 yp (*6 yp*)
- Theft of plows, agricultural implements, horses or other beasts of burden, cattle, beehives, merchandise, or effects exposed to public trust, either in the countryside or on roads, at wood auctions, fairs, markets, and other public places in the daytime = 3 mp–1 yp (*4 yp*), or at night = 6 mp–2 yp (*6 yp*)
- Misappropriation of goods or movable property, or titles or obligations on it, by those charged with delivering them, 1 yp–4 yp (*dégradation civique*)
- Threats of arson, 6 mp–2 yp (*4 yp*)

*Note:* Recidivism within three years of the previous offense would result in an increase in all of these crimes to the level of felonies.

TABLE C.1  Generals commanding military districts

| District | | *1 vent. IV* | *1 fruc. IV* | *1 vent. V* | *1 fruc. V* | *1 vent. VI* | *1 fruc. VI* | *1 vent. VII* |
|---|---|---|---|---|---|---|---|---|
| 1ST, 16TH | LILLE | Vialle | Liébert | Liébert | Liébert<br>*Desbruslys* | Bessières | Bessières | Pille |
| 2ND | CHÂLONS | Picot-Bazus | Thierry | Férino | Férino | Puget-Barbantane | Cervoni | Bonnard |
| 3RD | METZ | Bessières | Laprun | Laprun | Laprun | Morlot | Morlot | *Morlot* |
| 4TH | NANCY | Gilot | Gilot | Gilot | Gilot | Gilot | Gilot | *Colle* |
| 5TH | STRASBOURG | Lajolais | Moulin | Moulin | Moulin<br>*Pachtod* | Sainte-Suzanne | Châteauneuf-Randon | Chât.-Randon |
| 6TH | BESANÇON | Dufour | O'Keefe | Labarolière | Labarolière<br>*Clémencet* | Muller | Muller | Massol<br>Desnoyers |
| 7TH | GRENOBLE | Freytag | Freytag | Freytag | Kellermann | Massol<br>*LeDoyen* | Massol | Muller |
| 8TH | MARSEILLE | Puget-Barbant. | Willot | Willot | Sahuguet<br>*Bon* | Pille | Quantin | Quantin<br>*Grenier* |
| 9TH | NÎMES | Châteauneuf.-Randon | Châteauneuf.-Randon | Châteauneuf-Randon<br>*Merle* | Carteaux/Haquin | Dugua, *Garnier*, Petit-Guillaume<br>Quantin | Petit-Guillaume | Carteaux<br>Petit-Guillaume |
| 10TH | PERPIGNAN | Lamer (Chât.-Randon) | Lamer (Chât.-Randon) | Lamer | Lamer<br>Morlot | Augereau | Augereau | Augereau<br>*Duvignau,*<br>*Commes* |
| 11TH | BORDEAUX | Moncey | Moncey<br>*Mauco* | Moncey | Moncey<br>*Mauco* | Huet | Huet | *Mauco* |
| 12TH | LA ROCHELLE | Rey (Sud) | Grouchy (Sud) | Grouchy (Hédouville) | Grouchy | Grouchy<br>Victor-Perrin | L. Muller | Grigny<br>Rey |
| 13TH | RENNES | Labarolière (Ouest) | Labarolière (Ouest) | Hédouville | Menou | Michaud<br>*Roulland* | Michaud | Michaud |
| 14TH | CAEN | Dumesny (Est) | Dumesny (Est) | Dumesny (Héd.) | Dumesny | Dugua | Dufour | *Avril* |
| 15TH | ROUEN | Huet | Huet | Laubadère | Laubadère | Laubadère | Laubadère | Laubadère |
| 17TH | PARIS | Bonaparte | Hatry | Hatry | Augereau<br>Lemoine | Moulin<br>Carteaux | Gilot<br>Joubert | Marbot |
| 18TH | LE PUY | Pille | Pille | Pille | Pille<br>Desenfants, Parein | Dépaux | Chapsal | Meynier |
| 19TH | DIJON | Chapsal | Chapsal | Chapsal | Chapsal | Chapsal | Bessières | |
| 20TH | PÉRIGUEUX | Sahuguet | Chalbos | Chalbos | Chalbos | Chalbos | | |
| 21ST | POITIERS | Mouret | Mouret | Mouret | Mouret | Mouret | Mouret | |
| 22ND | TOURS | Dumesny (Est) | Vidalot-Dusirat | Guiot-Durepaire | Vimeux | Vimeux | Vimeux | Vimeux |
| 23RD | BASTIA | — | — | Vaubois | Vaubois | Mesnard | Ambert | Ambert |
| 24TH | BRUSSELS | Tilly | Souham | Souham | Souham | Bonnard | Bonnard | Cervoni |
| 25TH | LIÈGE | Micas | Micas | Micas | Micas | Micas<br>Colaud | Micas<br>Colaud | Beguinot<br>Cervoni |

*Note:* Italics = provisional commander; second line = other appointees between dates; (name) = superior commander of more than one district.

| | 1 fruc. VII | 1 vent. VIII | 1 fruc. VIII | 1 vent. IX | 1 fruc. IX | 1 vent. X | 1 fruc. X |
|---|---|---|---|---|---|---|---|
| 1ST, 16TH LILLE | Pille (Hédouville) | Pille | Pille | Pille | Pille | Vandamme | Vandamme |
| 2ND MÉZIÈRES | Beguinot | Beguinot | Beguinot | Beguinot | Beguinot | Beguinot | Dupont de L.f. |
| 3RD METZ | Morlot | Châteauneuf-Randon | Châteauneuf-Randon | Châteauneuf-Randon | Châteauneuf-Randon | Férino | Férino |
| 4TH NANCY | Gilot | Gilot | Gilot | Gilot | Gilot | Gilot | Gilot |
| 5TH STRASBOURG | Freytag | Freytag | Freytag | Leval | Leval | Leval | Leval |
| 6TH BESANÇON | Mengaud | Montigny | Montigny | Mesnard | Mesnard | Mesnard | Mesnard |
| 7TH GRENOBLE | *Pellapra* (Grenier) | Férino | Férino | Férino | Férino | Molitor | Molitor |
| 8TH MARSEILLE | Quantin (Grenier) | Saint-Hilaire | Saint-Hilaire | Cervoni | Cervoni | Cervoni | Cervoni |
| 9TH MONTPELLIER | Carteaux (Frégeville)<br>Petit-Guillaume Lannes (9th + 10th) | Gouvion | Gouvion | Gouvion | Gouvion<br>Frégeville (jr) | Gouvion | |
| 10TH TOULOUSE | Albignac (Frégeville)<br>Lannes (9th + 10th) | Commes | Servan | Servan | Gudin | Gudin | Gudin |
| 11TH BORDEAUX | Dembarrère | Dufour | Dufour | Dufour | Dufour | Dufour | Mathieu |
| 12TH NANTES | Desbureaux<br>Moncey | L. Muller | Chabot | Chabot | Chabot | Lapoype | Dumuy |
| 13TH RENNES | Michaud<br>Taponier | Labarolière | | Hédouville | Delaborde | Delaborde | Delaborde |
| 14TH CAEN | Rey<br>Dupont-Chaumont; Canclaux | Gardanne (Lefebvre) | Labarolière | Labarolière | Labarolière | Lagrange | Laroche |
| 15TH ROUEN | Verdière (Hédouville)<br>Hatry | Lefebvre | L. Muller (Mortier) | St-Hilaire (Mortier) | St-Hilaire | St-Hilaire | St-Hilaire |
| 17TH PARIS | Lefebvre | Lefebvre | Mortier | Mortier  1st | Mortier | Mortier | Mortier |
| 18TH DIJON | Meynier | Meynier | Meynier | Meynier | Meynier | Meynier | Meynier |
| 19TH LE PUY | Bessières | Moncey | Piston | Piston | Duhesme | Duhesme | Duhesme |
| 20TH PÉRIGUEUX | Chalbos | Servan | Mathieu | *Pierre de Viantaix* | Gardanne | Souham | |
| 21ST POITIERS (BOURGES, FRIMAIRE X) | Mouret | Mouret | Dumuy | Dumuy | Dumuy | Dumuy | Dufour |
| 22ND TOURS | Vimeux | Sahuguet | Liébert | Liébert | Liébert | Liébert | Liébert |
| 23RD BASTIA | Ambert | Ambert | Ambert | L. Muller | L. Muller | L. Muller | Marand |
| 24TH BRUSSELS | Bonnard (Tilly) | Bonnard | Bonnard | Tugnot | Bonnard | Belliard | Belliard |
| 25TH LIÈGE | Micas (Tilly) | Carteaux | Chalbos | Roget | Loison | Loison | |
| 26TH KOBLENZ | — | — | Laroche | Lorge | Lorge | Lorge | Lorge |

Note: Italics = provisional commander; second line = other appointees between dates; (name) = superior commander of more than one district

# Notes

*Note:* The archival source is the Archives Nationales unless otherwise noted. The place of publication for French sources is Paris unless otherwise noted. The name of a *département* in isolation means the *administration centrale du département*. Full bibliographic information is provided the first time a secondary source is cited in each of the three parts of this book. Furthermore, restraint has been exercised in multiplying references to secondary sources.

INTRODUCTION

1. Notwithstanding the remarkably creative treatment of "representative" aspects of the revolutionary project by works such as Sophia Rosenfeld, *A Revolution in Language: The Problem of Signs in Late Eighteenth-Century France* (Stanford, 2001) and Paul Friedland, *Political Actors: Representative Bodies and Theatricality in the Age of the French Revolution* (Ithaca, N.Y., 2002), the concept "representative democracy" is used in here in a strictly formal sense and assumes that legitimacy is enhanced by being elected to office.

2. On the importance of "illiberal democracy" in the emergence of modern polities, see Fareed Zakaria, *The Future of Freedom: Illiberal Democracy at Home and Abroad* (New York, 2003).

3. François Furet, *Interpreting the French Revolution*, trans. Elborg Forster (Cambridge, UK, 1981); Steven L. Kaplan, *Farewell Revolution: The Historians' Feud, 1789/1989* (Ithaca, N.Y., 1995); *French Historical Studies* (2000); Gary Kates, ed., introduction to *The French Revolution: Recent Debates and New Controversies* (New York, 1998).

4. Pierre Rosanvallon, *La démocratie inachevée: Histoire de la souveraineté du peuple en France* (2000), esp. 66. See also Andrew Jainchill and Samuel Moyn, "French Democracy between Totalitarianism and Solidarity: Pierre Rosanvallon and Revisionist Historiography," *Journal of Modern History* 76 (2004): 107–54.

5. For a sense of the historical silence on these issues, see Arno Mayer, *The Furies: Violence and Terror in the French and Russian Revolutions* (Princeton, 2000); Keith M. Baker, ed., *The French Revolution and Modern Political Culture*, vol. 4, *The Terror* (Oxford, 1994); and Patrice Gueniffey, *La politique de la Terreur: Essai sur la violence révolutionnaire* (2000).

6. Alphonse Aulard, *Histoire politique de la Révolution française*, 4 vols. (1901); Albert Mathiez, *Le Directoire du 11 brumaire an IV au 18 fructidor an V* (1934); Georges Lefebvre, *La France sous le Directoire, 1795–1799*, 2nd ed. presented by Jean-René Suratteau, (1984); Albert Soboul, *La 1ère République* (1968); Denis Woronoff, *La république bourgeoise de Thermidor à Brumaire 1794–1799* (1972); Jacques Godechot, *La vie quotidienne en France sous le Directoire* (1977).

7. Boissy d'Anglas on 5 mess. III, *Moniteur, réimp.*, 25:92.

8. At least 500,000 individuals, or 10 percent of all households, were involved in purchasing "nationalized properties," which constituted one-tenth of the land in France. "The bourgeoisie and urbanites clearly prevailed over the peasantry and country folk, not in number but in importance and in the value of acquisitions." Bernard Bodinier and Éric Teyssier, *L'événement le plus important de la Révolution: La vente des biens nationaux* (2000), 439.

9. This sort of interpretation has appeared in conservative, liberal, and social democratic forms: Albert Vandal, *L'avènement de Bonaparte*, 2 vols. (1902–7); Albert Meynier, *Les coups d'état du Directoire*, 3 vols. (1927–28); Michael J. Sydenham, *The First French Republic, 1792–1804* (Berkeley, 1973).

10. Isser Woloch, *Jacobin Legacy: The Democratic Movement under the Directory* (Princeton, 1970); Bernard Gainot, *1799, Un nouveau Jacobinism? La démocratie représentative, une alternative à brumaire* (2001).

11. Mona Ozouf, *La fête révolutionnaire, 1789–1799* (1976), 202.

12. Lynn Hunt, *Politics, Culture, and Class in the French Revolution* (Berkeley, 1984).

James Livesey, in *Making Democracy in the French Revolution* (Cambridge, Mass., 2002), also develops a strongly positive interpretation based on bringing together lofty debates on the political economy of liberalism and evidence of a growing democratic ethos in the countryside, but without considering the political realities or formal institutions of the Directory.

13. Clive C. Church, "In Search of the Directory," in *French Society and the Revolution,* ed. Douglas Johnson, 261–94 (Cambridge, UK, 1976), quote on 280.

14. Richard Cobb, *Reactions to the French Revolution* (London, 1972); Gwynne Lewis and Colin Lucas, eds., *Beyond the Terror: Essays in French Regional and Social History, 1794–1815* (Cambridge, UK, 1983); Marcel Marion, *Le brigandage pendant la Révolution* (1934).

15. Hobbes fled the English Civil Wars only to end up in France during the Fronde and wrote *Leviathan* to help resolve both conflicts. Richard Tuck, ed., *Leviathan,* 2nd ed. (Cambridge, UK, 1996), x-xii.

16. On these characteristics, see Simone Goyard-Fabre, *Le droit et la loi dans la philosophie de Thomas Hobbes* (1975), 135, and Lucien Jaume, *Hobbes et l'État représentatif moderne* (1986), 108, 226.

17. Hobbes has too often been caricatured as a theorist of absolutism and tyranny. Such an approach ignores the importance of individual rights and the elemental democracy inherent in his idea of a social contract: sovereignty derived from the consent of individuals who agreed to limit their rights in exchange for security. Even Carl Schmitt, generally suspect as an early apologist for Nazism, considered Hobbes the theoretical father of the strong liberal state. Carl Schmitt, *The Leviathan in the State Theory of Thomas Hobbes: Meaning and Failure of a Political Symbol,* ed. George Schwab (Westport, Conn., 1996). See also James B. Rule, *Theories of Civil Violence* (Berkeley, 1988), 18–26.

18. "Force" is the preferred translation of the term *Gewalt* (see H. H. Gerth and C. Wright Mills, eds., *From Max Weber: Essays in Sociology* [1991], 78), which can also mean power or violence. The frequently used phrase "legitimate violence" is an oxymoron in a moral sense; furthermore, Weber's idea loses all meaning when scholars define the state as a monopoly of violence tout court.

19. Hannah Arendt, *On Violence* (New York, 1970), 52. See also James B. Brady and Newton Garver, eds., *Justice, Law, and Violence* (Philadelphia, 1991), 9–12.

20. Sergio Cotta, *Why Violence? A Philosophical Interpretation,* trans. Giovanni Gullace (Gainesville, Fl., 1985). Cotta's effort to distinguish violence from force in terms of three "modalities of measure" adds much to Walter Benjamin's distinction between "lawmaking" and "law-defending" violence in "Critique of Violence," in *Walter Benjamin: Selected Writings,* ed. Marcus Buttock and Michael W. Jennings, 3 vols. (Cambridge, Mass., 1996), 3:236–52. See also Newton Garver, "Violence and the Social Order," in *Philosophy of Law, Politics, and Society: Proceedings of the Twelfth International Wittgenstein Symposium* (Vienna, 1988), 218–23, and Kenneth Baynes, "Violence and Communication: The Limits of Philosophical Explanations of Violence," in *Justice, Law, and Violence,* ed. Brady and Garver, 82–89.

21. For example, a highly bureaucratized gulag (internal measure) designed to defend a communist regime (purposive measure) remains characterized by extreme violence because many of its victims are "dissidents" and "subversive elements" as arbitrarily determined by the regime, not by well-defined or broadly accepted definitions (lack of external measure). Similarly, the phrase "police brutality" reflects a lack of internal measure in polities that enjoy a high degree of consensus and a commitment to the rule of law.

22. Some scholars might see a problem here: if the use of coercive force is well managed, sanctioned by law, and designed to uphold an exploitative and coercive socioeconomic order, then such a use of force would seem to lack legitimacy. If it lacks legitimacy, then it would appear to deserve to be called violence. However, this blurs means and ends as well as the distinction between contemporary moral judgements and those of the historian. As far as the historian is concerned, it is important to recognize that if a particular sociopolitical order used force exclusively within three modes of measure, calling it violence is not analytically helpful but rather a way of passing moral judgment on that sociopolitical order. Historians who feel that such a judgment is appropriate should critique the injustices of the sociopolitical order itself rather than the use of force to preserve it. This provides plenty of leeway to analyze the ways in which force is deployed, whether the specific polity is deemed oppressive or not, and to include moral judgments in such an analysis, preferably those of contemporaries.

23. Howard G. Brown, "Domestic State Violence: Repression from the Croquants to the Commune," *Historical Journal* 42 (1999): 597–622.

24. Geoffrey de Q. Walker, *The Rule of Law: Foundation of a Constitutional Democracy* (Melbourne, 1988), 5.

25. This is made clear by Jacques Godechot, *Les institutions de la France sous la Révolution et l'Empire*, 3rd ed. (1985), 476, and Jean-Pierre Royer, *Histoire de la justice en France* (1995), 400.

26. Carl Schmitt, *La Dictature*, trans. Mira Köller and Dominique Séglard (2000); Giorgio Agamben, *State of Exception*, trans. Kevin Attell (Chicago, 2005).

## 1. THE CRISIS OF REPUBLICAN LEGITIMACY

1. *Achevons la Révolution, par P.J. Audouin* (fructidor III), BL F. 785(7). It should be noted, however, that the Thermidorians did not view liberalism as an isolated set of political principles, which it later became, but as a republican achievement. In other words, they viewed the survival of the republic as a necessary precondition of liberty. This is echoed by numerous papers in Roger Dupuy and Marcel Morabito, eds., *1795: Pour une république sans révolution* (1996).

2. Marcus Ackroyd, in "Constitution and Revolution: Political Debate in France, 1795–1800" (D.Phil. thesis, Oxford University, 1995), provides a good introduction to the diversity of this discourse and casts a lifeline to the concept of "public opinion," which is understandably gasping for air in Jon Cowan's chapter, "From Thermidor to Brumaire," in *To Speak for the People: Public Opinion and the Problem of Legitimacy in the French Revolution* (New York, 2001). Recent scholarship on the Directorial constitution pays little attention to the issue of political legitimacy: Jean Bart, Jean-Jacques Clère, Claude Courvoisier, and Michel Verpeaux, eds., *La constitution de l'an III ou l'ordre républicain* (Dijon, 1998); Gérard Conac and Jean-Pierre Machelon, *La constitution de l'an III: Boissy d'Anglas et la naissance du libéralisme constitutionnel* (1999); Andrew Jainchill, "The Constitution of Year III and the Persistence of Classical Republicanism," *French Historical Studies* 26 (2003): 399–435.

3. François Furet wrote that the exceptional measures adopted on the eve of the Directory "destroyed what was at the heart of [the Convention's] project, the Republic founded on law." From this perspective, the Directory never really constituted a liberal democracy, not even a flawed experiment. In contrast, Colin Lucas discounts the exceptional measures of 1795 and argues that "the policy adopted by the First Directory to deal with its

inheritance of division and disorder was the rule of law." In this view, the Directory largely maintained its commitment to the constitution until the Fructidor coup d'état. Both views rightly focus on the importance of the rule of law in the Thermidorians' attempt to end the French Revolution, but neither captures the complexity of the Directory's dilemma in dealing with the problem of order. François Furet, *La révolution française 1770–1880: De Turgot à Jules Ferry* (1988), 174; Colin Lucas, "The First Directory and the Rule of Law," *French Historical Studies* 10 (1977): 231–60.

4. See Louvet's speech in the Council of Five Hundred on 22 fruc. IV, *Moniteur,* an IV.

5. See the Directory's address of 14 ger. IV: "Republicans of the Midi, your happiness is now in your hands. It is above all in a sincere forgetfulness of all hatreds, in a total and honest renunciation of all of these appalling plans for vengeance and reaction that an evil genius has nourished among you. . . . Irascible but good men, open up to the holy love of the *patrie,* to holy friendship . . . these wounded and hardened hearts, devoured by six years of anger and hatred!" *Moniteur, réimp.,* 28:165–66.

6. The law of 3 brum. IV (25 October 1795) prohibited all male relatives of émigrés (including nephews and brothers-in-law!) from holding office, as well as anyone who had signed a "seditious petition" during the recent elections. Furthermore, it revived the draconian laws of 1792–93 against émigrés and refractory priests, once again making them subject to the death penalty. This included priests who had never left the country but who qualified as "deportees" all the same.

7. A. Debidour, *Recueil des actes du Directoire exécutif,* 4 vols. (1910–17), 1:19–20.

8. J. Duval-Jouve, *Montpellier pendant la Révolution,* 2 vols. (Montpellier, 1881), 2:272, 279, 288–91; Malcolm Crook, *Elections in the French Revolution: An Apprenticeship in Democracy, 1789–1799* (Cambridge, UK, 1996), 136–38.

9. Meynier, *Coups d'état,* 1:12.

10. Cf. John Borneman, *Settling Accounts: Violence, Justice, and Accountability in Post-socialist States* (Princeton, 1997); A. James McAdams, ed., *Transitional Justice and the Rule of Law in New Democracies* (Notre Dame, Ind., 1997); Kees Koonings and Dirk Kruijt, eds., *Societies of Fear: The Legacy of Civil War, Violence, and Terror in Latin America* (London and New York, 1999).

11. The only detailed treatment of the amnesty is in Howard G. Brown, "Political Violence, Retributive Justice, and the Amnesty of 1795," presented at the conference "The Impossible Settlement: Problems of a New Order Post-Revolutionary France," Atlanta, November 1999. The Thermidorian context is well covered by Mona Ozouf, "Thermidor, ou le travail de l'oubli," in her *L'école de France* (1984), 91–108; Bronislaw Baczko, *Comment sortir de la Terreur. Thermidor et la Révolution* (1989), 191–245; and Sergio Luzzatto, *L'automne de la Révolution: Luttes et cultures politiques dans la France thermidorienne,* trans. S.C. Messina (2001).

12. Baudin and Quirot speaking on behalf of the Commission des Onze in the Convention on 2 and 4 brum. IV, respectively. *Moniteur, réimp.,* 26:301, 348

13. Camus in Council of Five Hundred on 15 flor., *Moniteur,* an IV, 919.

14. In fact, Chénier argued that the amnesty should be adopted precisely because it was not general. *Moniteur,* an IV, 174.

15. ADHS 368 L 11, 16 brum. IV.

16. The lynching of former "terrorists" in the Vaucluse was described to the Convention by a republican member of the department administration as "executions that only lack the seal of the law to make them acts of justice." Quoted in René Moulinas, "Le département de

Vaucluse en 1795: La contre-révolution en marche?" in *Le tournant de l'an III: Réaction et terreur blanche dans la France révolutionnaire,* ed. Michel Vovelle (1997), 529–38.

17. The Directory's messages to the Council of Five Hundred on 14 and 19 ger. IV, in Debidour, *Recueil,* 2:85, 113, together with supporting documents in C 495, d. 311.

18. Council of Five Hundred on 15 flor. and 22 fruc., *Moniteur,* an IV, 919, 1427–28, 1431–35.

19. Riou in Council of Five Hundred on 3 vend., *Moniteur,* an V, 25–28.

20. Council of Five Hundred on 30 vend., *Moniteur,* an V, 142–44, 146–47.

21. Council of Elders on 3 frim., *Moniteur,* an V, 263–75 passim.

22. Sergio Luzatto, "Comment entrer dans le Directoire? Le problème de l'amnistie," in *La république directoriale: Actes du colloque de Clermont-Ferrand (22–24 mai 1997),* eds. Philippe Bourdin and Bernard Gainot, 218–29 (Clermont-Ferrand, 1998); Richard Cobb, "Note sur la répression contre le personnel sans-culotte de 1795 à 1801," in his *Terreur et subsistances (1793–1795)* (1964), 179–219; Woloch, *Jacobin Legacy,* 48–49.

23. Fully half of the 217 priests who took the oath of submission to the laws of the republic at Toulouse had recently been released from prison, including 31 who had been deported, but who only got as far as the hulks at Rochefort. Jean-Claude Meyer, *La vie religieuse en Haute-Garonne sous la Révolution (1789–1801)* (Toulouse, 1982), 371.

24. Meyer, *Vie religieuse,* 390–91; Marcel Reinhard, *Le département de la Sarthe sous le régime du Directoire* (Saint-Brieuc, 1936), 123.

25. Between the law of 3 brum. IV (25 Oct. 1795) and the repeal of draconian measures against priests on 14 frim. V (4 Dec. 1796), the court systematically reduced sentences for deported priests arrested in France from the statutory death penalty to ten years in solitary confinement (seven cases), perpetual banishment (two cases), and deportation (one case) and simply acquitted priests who had retracted their oaths (four cases). ADHS 368 L 192 for Cornibert; 371 L 11 and 12 passim, for other priests; $F^7$ 3065, court commission of Haute-Saône to MP, pluv. IV; Jean Girardot, *Le département de la Haute-Saône pendant la Révolution,* 3 vols. (Vesoul, 1973), 3:284–85.

26. Girardot, *Haute-Saône,* 3:282; BB[18] 364, R 8223. For similar examples from around the country, see Pierre de la Gorce, *Histoire religieuse de la Révolution française,* 5 vols. (1921), 4:95–101.

27. Rita Hermon-Belot, *L'Abbé Grégoire: La politique et la vérité* (2000), 396; see also Colin Lucas, "L'église constitutionnelle dans la Loire après la Terreur," *Cahiers d'histoire* 30 (1985): 309–39.

28. ADHG 7L 202 U 138 and 201 U 2, 22 mess. IV.

29. Olwen Hufton, *Women and the Limits of Citizenship in the French Revolution* (Toronto, 1992), 90–130; Suzanne Desan, *Reclaiming the Sacred: Lay Religion and Popular Politics in Revolutionary France* (Ithaca, N.Y., 1990), 197–216.

30. Reprinted in full in Jean Leflon, *Histoire de l'église depuis les orgines jusqu'à nos jours,* vol. 20, *La crise révolutionnaire, 1789–1846* (1951), 143. See also Bernard Plongeron's penetrating discussion in Jean-Marie Mayeur et al., eds., *Histoire du christianisme: Des origines à nos jours,* vol. 10, *Les défis de la modernité (1750–1840)* (1990), 461–66.

31. *Moniteur,* an IV, 9 fruc.

32. La Gorce, *Histoire religieuse,* 4:118–33; Meyer, *Vie religieuse,* 416–21; Girardot, *Haute-Saône,* 3:287; Lefebvre, *France sous le Directoire,* 237–39.

33. The success of "grands vicaires" and "missionaires" inside France is especially indica-

tive: Charles Ledré, *Le culte caché sous la Révolution: Les missions de l'abbé Linsolas* (1949), 406–24; Yves Dreux, "Religion et Contre-Révolution: La mission laonnoise 1795–1802," *AHRF*, no. 297 (1994): 547–61; Robert Dartevelle, "Stratégie missionnaire et 'rechristianisation' pendant le Directoire: Unité ou diversité dans l'espace provençal et dauphinois," in *Religion, révolution, et contre-révolution dans le Midi, 1789–1799,* ed. Anne Marie Duport, 129–49 (Nîmes, 1990).

34. The only truly significant law was that of 7 fruc. V (24 Aug. 1797), which annulled laws against refractory priests who had been exiled, deported, or imprisoned.

35. Jacques Godechot, *Les commissaires aux armées sous le Directoire,* 2 vols. (1937–41), 1:passim.

36. Laws of 19 frim. and 15 pluv. IV, respectively.

37. François Crouzet, *La grande inflation: La monnaie en France de Louis XVI à Napoléon* (1993), 401–4; AD XVIII$^F$ 11, *Second rapport fait par le Ministre de la Guerre au Directoire Exécutif sur l'administration de son départment depuis pluviôse jusqu'au 28 messidor V* (an VI); AF III 183, d. 739, deputies of Eure to Directory, 21 flor. V, and MW to Directory, 22 flor. V.

38. For a list of *agents militaires,* see Howard G. Brown, *War, Revolution, and the Bureaucratic State: Politics and Army Administration in France, 1791–1799* (Oxford, 1995), 208–9, and for their methods, see letters from Fouché and Ferry in AG B$^{13}$ 41, 28, and 29 pluv. IV and B$^{13}$ 43, 14 ger. IV.

39. AG B$^{13}$ 41, Gen. Lamer to MW, 12 niv. IV, and Gen. Sol to Gen. Lamer, 24 niv. IV, and to Directory, 7 pluv. IV; B$^{13}$ 42, Lamer to MW, 13 pluv. IV; and *chef de bat.* Rey to *chef de brig.* Soyez, 15 pluv. IV; Jean Lacouture, *Le mouvement royaliste dans le sud-ouest (1797–1800)* (Toulouse, 1932), 16, 25. For general trends in this especially refractory region, see Louis Bergès, *Résister à la conscription 1798–1814: Le cas des départements aquitains* (2002).

40. Ledré, *Culte caché,* 237–47.

41. Alan Forrest, *Conscripts and Deserters: The Army and French Society during the Revolution and Empire* (Oxford, 1989), 150–62.

42. For example, Sydenham, *First French Republic.*

43. See the model study by Maurice Hutt, *Chouannerie and Counter-Revolution: Puisaye, the Princes, and the British Government in the 1790s,* 2 vols. (Cambridge, UK, 1983).

44. AG B$^{13}$ 44, Gen. Châteauneuf-Randon to MW, 23 and 30 ger., 2 flor. IV.

45. AG B$^{13}$ 45, Châteauneuf-Randon to MW, 21 ther. IV; Claude Petit, "Les brigands de Mandailles: De la contre-révolution au brigandage," in *Brigands en Rouergue, XIe-XIXe siècle* (Rodez, 1993), 167.

46. Harvey Mitchell, *The Underground War against Revolutionary France: The Missions of William Wickham 1794–1800* (Oxford, 1965); W. R. Fryer, *Republic or Restoration in France? 1794–1797: D'André and the Politics of French Royalism* (Manchester, 1965); Elizabeth Sparrow, *Secret Service: British Agents in France, 1792–1815* (Woodbridge, 1999), 38–128.

47. Both Fryer (*Republic or Restoration,* 143) and Mitchell (*Underground War,* 134) indicate that the strategy of violence had been temporarily abandoned by the summer of 1796, but they give no evidence of how the change of strategy was communicated to local leaders or how they responded. For such a message, see Claude Faure, "L'affaire Dominque Allier," *Bulletin de la société littéraire, historique et archéologique de Lyon,* 15 (1937–39): 117–39.

48. Fryer, *Republic or Restoration*, 194–95; Mitchell, *Underground War*, 103–4, 182–83; Meynier, *Coups d'état*, 1:186–89, 194–95.

49. This was unwittingly confirmed by the vacuous investigative reports on the extent of the royalist plot delivered to the Directory by the various ministers after the fateful event. AF III 44.

50. Saint-Christol later claimed that he had been inspired to act by public opinion, Pichegru's supposed willingness to lead a coup, and his correspondence with Job Aymé and Madier, two conspiratorial deputies in the Council of Five Hundred. *Précis des mémoires de M. le baron de Saint-Christol, adjoint à l'Agence royale de Souabe, depuis 1796 jusqu'en 1805* (Avignon, 1818). See also Gwynne Lewis, *The Second Vendée: The Continuity of Counter-revolution in the Department of the Gard, 1789–1815* (Oxford, 1978), 102–3.

51. Pierre Serna, *Antonelle: Aristocrate révolutionnaire* (1997), 243. Cf. *Journal de Toulouse*, 4 mess. IV, 6 and 20 vend. V. There are a number of important works on Jacobinism under the Directory, but they focus largely on forms of political sociability and pay little attention to the Jacobins' role in provoking unrest; in addition to Woloch, *Jacobin Legacy*, see Christine Peyrard, *Les Jacobins de l'Ouest: Sociabilité révolutionnaire et formes de politisation dans le Maine et la Basse-Normandie (1789–1799)* (1996), and especially Gainot, *Un nouveau jacobinisme?*

52. For example, Adj.-gen. D'Hallencourt at Château-Gontier (Mayenne) in year V.

53. Article entitled "Derniers adieux à la Terreur" published on 19 pluv. IV. See also the issue of 20 vend. V, where the editor denies that "terrorist" and "republican" are synonymous, as well as the 24 vent. VI issue of *La Chronique de la Sarthe*, which rejects the terms "Jacobin," "terrorist," and "anarchist" as appropriate for ardent republicans.

54. For an introduction, see Norbert Rouland, *Anthropologie juridique* (1988), and Sally Falk Moore, *Law as Process: An Anthropological Approach* (London, 1978).

55. La Révellière-Lépaux later regretted having chosen so many "anarchists" for these various positions (*Mémoires publiés par son fils*, 2 vols. [1895], 1:357–58), and Carnot, himself responsible for the appointment of numerous radicals, later felt the need to exclude "this crowd of immoral beings, incorrigibles who brought disorder, discontent, and terror to every part of the republic." Quoted in Ludovic Sciout, *Le Directoire*, 4 vols. (1895–97), 1:452.

56. ADHS 368 L 11, 12 vent. and 30 germ. IV; Girardot, *Haute-Saône*, 2:200–201, 3:82, 267.

57. R. B. Rose, *Gracchus Babeuf: The First Revolutionary Communist* (Stanford, 1978), 239–40; Robert Legrand, *Babeuf et ses compagnons de route* (1981), 219–27.

58. Martyn Lyons, *France under the Directory* (Cambridge, UK, 1975), 24–36; Woloch, *Jacobin Legacy*, 59–64.

59. Peter M. Jones, "*La République au village* in the Southern Massif-Central, 1789–1799," *Historical Journal* 23 (1980): 793–812, 812.

60. Marc Deleplace, "La notion d'anarchie pendant la Révolution française (1789–1801)," *AHRF*, no. 287 (1992): 17–45.

61. The newspaper *Le Préservatif de l'anarchie ou l'espion constitutionnel de la Sarthe* sent out a prospectus addressed "to the friends of order" that promised that the paper would oppose "the anarchic minority," "turn away its devastation, defend the Constitution, and restore morality." Peyrard, *Jacobins*, 326.

62. Yves Castan, *Honnêteté et relations sociales en Languedoc, 1715–1780* (1974), 1–60.

## 2. THE ECONOMY OF VIOLENCE

1. Michel Vovelle, *Ville et campagne au 18e siècle (Chartres et Beauce)* (1980), 277–304; Cobb, *Terreur et subsistances*, 307–81; Serge Bernin and Claude Langlois, eds., *Atlas de la Révolution française*, vol. 8, *Population*, ed. Bernard Lepetit and Maroula Sinarellis (1995), 36; Crouzet, *Grande inflation*, 338–99.

2. Philippe Grimoard, *Tableau historique de la guerre de la Révolution de France*, 2 vols. (1808), 1:403; Forrest, *Conscripts and Deserters*, 98–168.

3. Gordon Wright, *Between the Guillotine and Liberty: Two Centuries of the Crime Problem in France* (Oxford, 1983), 34.

4. For example, officials never explicitly used clues about grief or descriptions of funerals—the size of the procession, the social origins of the mourners, the presence of key figures, such as a refractory priest, present or former officials, etc.—to support their conclusions about the purpose and meaning of certain violent actions.

5. Brian Singer, "Violence in the French Revolution: Forms of Ingestion/Forms of Expulsion," in *The French Revolution and the Birth of Modernity*, ed. Ferenc Fehér, 150–73 (Berkeley, 1990); Colin Lucas, "The Crowd and Politics between *Ancien Régime* and Revolution in France," *Journal of Modern History* 61 (1989): 421–57; "La violence thermidorienne et société traditionnelle: L'exemple du Forez," *Cahiers d'histoire* 24 (1979): 3–43, quote on 41; Cobb, *Reactions*, 44.

6. As Colin Lucas puts it, "despite the recourse to fragments of symbolism, the supremacy of ritual had disappeared. Violence was paramount." "Themes in Southern Violence after 9 Thermidor," in *Beyond the Terror: Essays in French Social and Regional History, 1794–1815*, ed. Gwynne Lewis and Colin Lucas, 152–94 (Cambridge, 1983), quote on 177.

7. My thinking on this subject has been stimulated by Anton Blok, "The Enigma of Senseless Violence" in *Meanings of Violence: A Cross Cultural Perspective*, ed. Göran Aijmer and Jon Abbink, 23–28 (New York, 2000), and Kenneth Baynes, "Violence and Communication," in *Justice, Law, and Violence*, ed. James B. Brady and Kenneth Baynes, 82–89 (Philadelphia, 1991).

8. For the general situation in the Hérault at the time, see Robert Laurent and Geneviève Gavignaud, *La Révolution française dans le Languedoc méditerranéen (1789–1799)* (Toulouse, 1987), 250–51.

9. Three trials produced ten convictions. Although the law of 16 prai. III was designed specifically for this type of incident, none of the rioters was sentenced to death; instead, seven were sent to the *bagne* for between eight and sixteen years, and three to prison for a year or less. ADH L 6726*, 10 ger. and 23 ther. IV; L 6756*, 9 prai. IV; BB[18] 364, especially MJ letters of 4 vent. IV; Duval-Jouve, *Montpellier*, 2:286–88.

10. The literature on subsistence riots during the *ancien régime* is voluminous; for broad syntheses, see Charles Tilly, *The Contentious French* (Cambridge, Mass., 1986), and Jean Nicolas, *La Rébellion française: Mouvements populaires et conscience sociale (1661–1789)* (2002), esp. 221–89.

11. Vovelle, *Ville et campagne*, 227–76.

12. Cynthia Bouton, *The Flour War: Gender, Class, and Community in Late Ancien Régime Society* (State College, Penn., 1993).

13. Peyrard, *Jacobins de l'Ouest*, 302–5.

14. Only a few weeks earlier, the court had regretted that the Penal Code was not rig-

orous enough in dealing with people who stole grain from fields, a sentiment echoed throughout the country at the time. ADS L 1914*, 15 vend. IV; F⁷ 3065.

15. This paragraph is based on the following trials in particular: ADS L 1914*, 16 vend., 23 brum., 15 niv., 17 pluv., 16 vent. IV. Six months later, a joiner from Les Aulnaux was sentenced to twenty-two years in irons for his part in four group assaults on wagon drivers around Mamers. These may have been part of the chouans' campaign to cut off grain supplies to republican areas; if true, this only magnifies the uncertainty surrounding such incidents (ibid., 15 ther. IV).

16. Jean-Claude Gégot, "La violence au temps du Directoire dans l'Hérault," *Bulletin d'histoire économique et sociale de la Révolution française* (1977): 15–33, 23–24.

17. See the trials for highway robbery in ADH L 6728*, 23 brum. V, 6732*, 14 ger. and 7 prai. VI, which included holdups of, among others, the postal coach from Toulouse, an adjutant-general and his valet, and a professor from the School of Health.

18. AG B¹³ 44, Gen. Châteauneuf-Randon to Directory, 29 and 30 ger. IV; Charles Jolivet, *Les chouans du Vivarais. Essai sur l'agitation contre-révolutionnaire dans l'Ardèche sous le Directoire* (Lyon, 1930), 29–30. On royalist "companies," see Lewis, *Second Vendée,* 86–102.

19. Gwynne Lewis, "Political Brigandage and Popular Disaffection in the South-East of France, 1795–1804," in *"Beyond the Terror,* ed. Lewis and Lucas, 195–231.

20. Philippe Grandcoing, *La 'Bande à Burgout' et la société rurale de la Châtaigneraie limousine (1830–1839)* (Limoges, 1990), 167.

21. André Zysberg, "L'Affaire d'Orgères: Justice pénale et défense sociale (1790–1800)," in *La Révolution et l'ordre juridique privé: Rationalité ou scandale?* ed. Michel Vovelle, 2 vols., 2:639–51 (1988); Cobb, *Reactions,* 178–215. The indictment listed 118 individuals (Cobb, 186), but a staggering 64 individuals (out of more than 300 imprisoned at Chartres in connection with this case) died in prison before the trial (Zysberg, 645).

22. Richard Cobb, *Paris and Its Provinces, 1792–1802* (Oxford, 1975), 141–210; for an example of "banditry psychosis" in the south, see Ernest Delcambre, *La vie politique dans la Haute-Loire sous le Directoire,* 2 vols. (Rodez, 1943), 2:190–206.

23. F⁷ 4282, d. 12 (bande noire).

24. BB¹⁸ 733, DD 4521 (some of which was forwarded by the MJ to the MP and is therefore in the police file on the "bande noire").

25. ADS L 1914*, 18 fruc. IV, 20 flor. V.

26. C 403, d. 351, 11 frim. V. This message received a great deal of publicity, being quoted at length in subsequent reports in both chambers of the legislature, which meant extensive reporting in newspapers as well. See, in particular, *Rapport fait par J. E. Richard, au nom d'une commissions spéciale … sur la répression du brigandage,* Conseil des Cinq-Cents, séance du 26 pluviôse, an V (BN 8 Le⁴³ 740); and *Rapport fait par Rousseau au nom d'une commission nommée pour examinée une résolution du Conseil des Cinq-Cents, sur la répression du brigandage.* Conseil des Anciens, séance du 18 floréal, an V (BN 8 Le⁴⁵ 355).

27. This had been part of the description of banditry from early in the Directorial regime. As Minister of Police Merlin de Douai wrote in his circular of 24 February 1796: "The enemies of the fatherland … have conceived of a new system of crimes and social dissolution. They have said: 'We will spread desolation and death across the surface of the Republic. We will organize bands of brigands and assassins to murder energetic republicans, burn the homes of peaceful proprietors, devastate the fruits of farm labor, sterilize the fields that

feed this people we can't subjugate. We will intimidate public officials. We will render the laws impotent and the government without force. Soaked in blood and sated with crime, we will be able to rally to the flag of Louis XVIII and establish his throne on the ruins of the Republic and the corpses of its defenders.'" ADHG 1L 354.

28. A. Pons-Devier, "Le banditisme sous le Directoire," *Revue historique et archéologique du Béarn et du Pays basque* (1928): 27–34.

29. Richard Cobb, *A Second Identity: Essay on France and French History* (Oxford, 1969), 199–200.

30. D. M. G. Sutherland, *Murder in a Small Town: Aubagne* (forthcoming).

31. Lewis, *Second Vendée*, 100–101.

32. Lucas, "Themes in Southern Violence," 168.

33. For example, Bodinier and Teyssier, *L'événement le plus important*, 400.

34. After a generation of historical criticism, Eric Hobsbawm has come to accept that his idea of "social bandits" paid insufficient attention to their political context and has recently concluded that "banditry as a mass phenomenon . . . occurred only where power was unstable, absent, or had broken down." *Bandits* (New York, 2000), 16.

35. *Procès-verbal des séances du Conseil des Cinq-Cents, frimaire VI*, 251–52; also in C 426, d. 106.

## 3. CRIMINAL COURTS AND CONCEPTS OF ORDER

1. These terms are from Keith Wrightson, "Two Concepts of Order: Justices, Constables and Jurymen in Seventeenth-Century England," in *An Ungovernable People: The English and Their Law in the Seventeenth and Eighteenth Centuries*, ed. John Brewer and John Styles (New Brunswick, N.J., 1980), 21–46.

2. Pierre Lascoumes, Pierrette Poncela, Pierre Lenoël, *Au nom de l'ordre: Une histoire politique du code pénal* (1989), 65–87; Philippe Raynaud, "La Déclaration des droits de l'homme," in *The French Revolution and the Creation of Modern Political Culture*, ed. Keith M. Baker, vol. 2, *The Political Culture of the French Revolution*, ed. Colin Lucas (Oxford, 1989), 139–49.

3. There is a sizable literature on this: see especially T. J. A. Le Goff and D. M. G. Sutherland, "The Revolution and the Rural Community in Eighteenth-Century Brittany," *Past & Present* 62 (1974): 96–107; Olwen Hufton, "Le paysan et la loi en France au XVIIIᵉ siècle," *Annales: Économies, sociétés, civilisations* 38 (1983): 679–701; Nicole Castan, *Justice et répression en Languedoc à l'époque des Lumières* (1980), esp. 220–22; Jean-Pierre Gutton, *La sociabilité villageoise dans l'ancienne France* (1979), 141–51; Iain Cameron, *Crime and Repression in the Auvergne and the Guyenne, 1720–1790* (Cambridge, UK, 1983), 174–75; Robert M. Schwartz, *Policing the Poor in Eighteenth-Century France* (Chapel Hill, N.C., 1988); Clay Ramsay, *The Ideology of the Great Fear: The Soissonnais in 1789* (Baltimore, 1993), 159–69. Seigneurial justice played a role in this self-policing, usually as leverage to obtain an infrajudicial settlement, and only rarely acted as an arm of the state: Jeremy D. Hayhoe, "Neighbours before the Court: Crime, Village Communities and Seigneurial Justice in Northern Burgundy, 1750–1790," *French History* 17 (2003): 127–48.

4. Peter King, *Crime, Justice, and Discretion in England, 1740–1820* (Cambridge, UK, 2000), 231–333.

5. A village assembly could generate "unity of purpose," but this should not be mis-

taken for "unanimity of purpose" among all inhabitants of a geographically bounded unit in which lordship played the central role. Cf. Karl H. Wegert, *Popular Culture, Crime, and Social Control in Eighteenth-Century Württemberg* (Stuttgart, 1994), 28.

6. D. M. G. Sutherland, *France 1789–1815: Revolution and Counterrevolution* (London, 1985), 14. As Le Goff and Sutherland had put it earlier, "The consciousness of the rural community was reaffirmed as violent political opposition to a régime harsher and more demanding, and yet more arbitrary and lacking in moral force, than the monarchy of the old régime had ever been" ("Rural Community," 119).

7. Peter M. Jones, *Liberty and Locality in Revolutionary France: Six Villages Compared, 1760–1820* (Cambridge, UK, 2003); see also Georges Fournier, *Démocratie et vie municipale en Languedoc du milieu du XVIIIe au début du XIXe siècle*, 2 vols. (Toulouse, 1994), 1:338–39.

8. Each village (*commune*) elected a representative (*agent*) and his deputy (*adjoint*) to the *administration municipale;* the president was elected at the cantonal primary assembly, just like the justice of the peace. In this way, individual villages had no administrative identity beyond their *agent* and *adjoint*. For a fine introduction, see Isser Woloch, *The New Regime: Transformations of the French Civic Order, 1789–1820s* (New York, 1992), 112–27; however, his rosy interpretation should be balanced by Jean-Pierre Jessenne's summary of the latest work on local administration, "Entre local et national: Pratiques et liens politiques du Directoire au Consulat," in *La Révolution française: Idéaux, singularités, influences,* ed. Michel Vovelle, 345–58 (Grenoble, 2002).

9. F$^7$ 3820, responses to the MP circular of 4 niv. IV.

10. Woloch, *New Regime,* 350ff. For more detail and an even more positive assessment, based in part on an overly negative image of seigneurial justice, see Anthony Crubaugh, *Balancing the Scales of Justice: Local Courts and Rural Society in Southwest France, 1750–1800* (State College, Penn., 2001).

11. See the articles on JPs in northern departments by Jacques Logie, Sylvie Humbert-Convain, and Pascale Bréemersch in *Du Directoire au Consulat,* ed. Jacques Bernet, Jean-Pierre Jessenne, and Hervé Leuwers, vol. 1, *Le lien politique local dans la Grande Nation* (Lille, 1999). Unfortunately, these articles provide little insight into the role of JPs in prosecuting felons.

12. Following prerevolutionary traditions of alternating judicial posts, four department judges at a time served six-month terms on the criminal court; another three to six judges served six-month terms as the head of each district correctional court; and the remainder served in five-man sections on the civil court. Thus, at any one moment about half of the men elected as judges were serving criminal justice, either as judges on the department's criminal court or exercising the combined roles of correctional court presidents and jury directors. Typically, there were twenty to thirty times as many civil cases as criminal ones each year (P. Clémendot, *Le départment de la Meurthe à l'époque du Directoire* [Nancy, 1966], 328–31). For various introductions to the judicial system created in year III, see Jean Bourdon, *La réforme judiciaire de l'an VIII,* 2 vols. (Rodez, 1941), vol. 1, and Frédéric Chauvaud et Jean-Jacques Yvorel, *Le juge, le tribun et le comptable: Histoire de l'organisation judiciaire entre les pouvoirs, les savoirs et les discours (1789–1930)* (1995), 68–71; on the other hand, Jean-Pierre Royer, *Histoire de la justice en France* (1995), omits these reforms, and Godechot, *Institutions,* 476–82, is unreliable, notably on jury directors. The most detailed study of criminal justice in this period is Robert Allen's *Les tribunaux*

*criminels sous la Révolution et l'Empire, 1792–1811* (Rennes, 2005), which appeared after this book was written.

13. Despite the prohibition on keeping court transcripts, the role of a court president can be ascertained from the rare *Procès par le Tribunal criminel du département de la Seine, contre les nommés Saint-Réjant, Carbon, et autres, prévenus de conspiration contre la personne du permier Consul* (an IX).

14. "I have to exercise an active surveillance over almost 2,400 *officiers de police judiciaire,* the great majority of whom lack enlightenment and education," complained Janole, public prosecutor of Haute-Garonne. BB[18] 328, 5 vent. IV.

15. On the experience of jury directors, see Alfred Hiver de Beauvoir, *Histoire critique des institutions judiciaires de la France de 1789 à 1848* (1848), 406–18, and Amédée Combier, *La justice criminelle à Laon pendant la Révolution, 1789–1800,* 2 vols. (1882), 2:586–87.

16. "I must watch over and ensure the execution of laws and verdicts, but it is not up to me to interpret or explain them. On your side, you must apply yourself to knowing them and once known, you must seek with honesty and loyalty to understand them, and then to apply them," explained the court commissioner of Hérault to a jury director at Lodève. BB[18] 365, D4 372. See also James Donovan, "Magistrates and Juries in France, 1791–1952," *French Historical Studies* 22 (1999): 379–420.

17. For the context of the *Code des délits et des peines,* see Hervé Leuwers, *Un juriste en politique: Merlin de Douai (1754–1838)* (Arras, 1996), 267–76, and Jean-Louis Halperin, "Continuité et rupture dans l'évolution de la procédure pénale en France de 1795 à 1810," in *Révolutions et justice pénale en Europe: Modèles français et traditions nationales, 1780–1830,* ed. Xavier Rousseaux, Marie-Sylvie Dupont-Bouchat, and Claude Vael, 109–30 (1999). For the *Code* itself, see Jean-Baptiste Duvergier, *Collection complète des lois, décrets, ordonnances, règlements et avis du Conseil d'État,* 51 vols. (1824), 8:386–439.

18. David Cohen, *Law, Violence and Community in Classical Athens* (Cambridge, 1995); Daniel Lord Smail, *The Consumption of Justice: Emotions, Publicity, and Legal Culture in Marseille, 1264–1423* (Ithaca, N.Y., 2003).

19. See the discussion of the "justice gap" in the British government's white paper, *Criminal Justice: The Way Ahead* (London, 2001).

20. A. Esmein, *Histoire de la procédure criminelle en France* (1882), 442.

21. Unfortunately, the *Code* banned oral testimony from being systematically recorded and thereby made it impossible to analyze the various defense tactics commonly employed at trial.

22. See Walker, *Rule of Law,* esp. 18–19. The following summary captures the progress toward due process made by the *Code des délits et des peines:* "The general functions of prosecution, defined by the law of 16–29 September 1791, were maintained, but guarantees for the defense were protected by nullification *and multiplied almost to excess* (emphasis added)." André Laingui and Arlette Lebigre, *Histoire du droit pénal,* 2 vols. (n.d.), 2:140.

23. Jean-Louis Halperin, *Le Tribunal de Cassation et les pouvoirs sous la Révolution (1790–1799)* (1987), 15.

24. ADHG 7L 201 U 2, 19 mess. V.

25. ADH L 6757, 20 flor. VI.

26. The registers of the other two departments in this study do not provide sufficiently reliable data; however, the Court of Cassation annulled only 3.25 percent of verdicts from the Criminal Court of the Nord. See David Moyaux, "Heur et malheur de la justice crimi-

nelle dans le Nord sous le Directoire," in *Du Directoire au Consulat,* ed. Bernet et al., 1:249–62, 256.

27. These figures do not include those who benefited from amnesties or unexplained releases; nor does it include the many indictments for participation in the insurrection of August 1799, all of which were systematically nullified in 1800 as a form of tacit amnesty. The Criminal Court of the Nord pronounced many more nullifications: 126 in four years pertaining to 295 individuals (Moyaux, "Heur et malheur," 251). A. Combier, *La justice criminelle à Laon pendant la Révolution,* 2 vols. (1882), 2:443, also noted that the number of such annulments grew steadily in the late 1790s, an indication of higher standards of jurisprudence.

28. Despite a grand jury indictment, the magistrates in the Haute-Saône refused to put the Taulet boys, aged eight and ten, on trial for sedition (that is, calling out "vive le roi, vive la nation; vive la nation, vive le roi.") and sent them home to Chargey. ADHS 368 L 11, 30 prai. IV.

29. Jean Vercier, *La justice criminelle dans le département de l'Hérault pendant la Révolution, 1789–1800* (Montpellier, 1926), 209–10.

30. Reinhard, *Sarthe,* 210; Bourdon, *Réforme judiciaire,* 47.

31. Albert Mathiez, *Le Directoire* (1934), 13; Reinhard, *Sarthe,* 210.

32. Charles Doyle, "Internal Counter-Revolution: The Judicial Reaction in Southern France, 1794–1800," *Renaissance and Modern Studies,* 33 (1989): 106–24; Lucas, "First Directory," 231–60.

33. The basis for this account is Damien Garrigues, "Jean-Joseph Janole: Magistrat toulousain (1757–1839)," *Revue historique de Toulouse* 13 (1926): 129–51; 14 (1927): 81–95, 159–77; 15 (1928): 84–104; 16 (1929): 159–85; 17 (1930): 37–46, 76–91, 132–40.

34. Martyn Lyons, *Revolution in Toulouse: An Essay on Provincial Terrorism* (Berne, 1978), 46–50.

35. The High Court later acquitted Vadier of conspiracy charges, and yet, despite being a beneficiary of the amnesty of 4 brumaire IV, the Directory used a deportation decree of 12 germinal III to have him transferred to the Fort of Ile Pelée at Cherbourg, where he remained until amnestied by the Consulate in nivôse VIII. A. Kusckinski, *Dictionnaire des Conventionnels* (1916), 593–94.

36. *L'Anti-terroriste,* 17 fruc. IV, 22 brum., 8 frim. V; *Journal de Toulouse,* 12, 16, 24 ther., 12, 24 fruc. IV. The verdict also condemned Vadier fils to 5,000 francs in personal damages and ordered him to pay for publishing the verdict throughout the country.

37. ADHG 1L 363; 7L 201 U 2 and 5, 14 mess V; BB[18] 329, dd 1415.

38. ADHG 7L U 2, trial of Henemont Calmettes, 22 vend. VI; *Journal de Toulouse,* 24 vend. VI; BB[18] 329, report from MJ to Directory (c. mid-fruc. V) and "Des républicains de Toulouse au Ministre de la Justice," 8 frim. VI.

39. Garrigues, "Janole," 80; BB[18] 330, circular from Janole, 1 vend. VI, and draft report from the Ministry of Justice (with two paragraphs of rebuke for his past conduct struck out).

40. *Journal de Toulouse,* 28 vent. VI.

41. Georges Duruy, ed., *Mémoires de Barras,* 4 vols. (1895–96), 2:205.

42. The law of 24 fruc. IV settling this issue explicitly stated that the recent law of 22 mess. IV, which limited the jurisdiction of *conseils militaires* to members of the army and its supply services, did not abrogate any dispositions of the law of 30 prai. III created to deal with *chouannerie* (Duvergier, *Collection des lois,* 9:176). The law of 30 prai. III had already been used to prosecute the insurgents of Vendémiaire.

43. Raymonde Monnier, "Justice d'exception et justice militaire: L'exemple de la 'Commission militaire' du Temple, de fructidor an IV," in *La Révolution et l'ordre juridique privé: Rationalité ou scandale?* ed. Michel Vovelle, 2 vols. (1988), 2:707–20; Halperin, *Tribunal de Cassation,* 225–26.

44. *Débats du procès instruit par le conseil de guerre permanent de la XVIIe division militaire, séant à l'ancienne Maison commune de Paris, contre les prévenus Brottier, Berthelot-la-Villeurnoy, Dunan, Poly et autres* (n.d.), BL F. 1134; BL F. 1132, pamphlets 1–20, illustrate the scope of the controversy. For summaries, see Halperin, *Tribunal de Cassation,* 228–33, and Sciout, *Directoire,* 2:278–87.

45. This and the following paragraphs are based on Rose, *Gracchus Babeuf,* 287–328; Legrand, *Babeuf,* 217–72; R. M. Andrews, "Réflections sur la conjuration des Égaux," *Annales: Économies, sociétés, civilisations* (1974): 75–105.

46. Woloch, *Jacobin Legacy,* 56–63.

47. "Various public prosecutors have assured me that individuals accused of execrable deeds and fully convicted in the court of public opinion, nevertheless have been acquitted by criminal courts on the basis of three corrupted jurors," wrote Merlin de Douai to Pastoret, a member of the Committee on the Revision and Classification of Laws, on 18 mess. IV (6 July 1796). BB[18] 863.

48. Bernard Schnapper, "Les systèmes repressifs français de 1789 à 1815," in *Révolutions et justice,* ed. Rousseaux et al., 25.

49. No two departmental courts kept records on verdicts in the same way; therefore, it is worth identifying the precise sources used for this study. Data on verdicts in the Haute-Garonne are based on the cryptic "registre des jugements du tribunal criminel, 1792 à 1811" (10L 270 U 71) supplemented by two "registres du plumitif des audiences" (7L 201 U 2 and 3) and three "registres du procès-verbal des séances" (7L 201 U 4 to 6). Data on verdicts in the Hérault are based on fifteen "registres des jugements définitifs" (L 6725 to 6738 and 7 U² 3) completed by five "registres des ordonnances d'acquitements des accusés" (L 6756 to 6760) and one "registre des procès-verbaux du président du tribunal criminel" (L 6769). Verdicts in the Haute-Saône were all recorded in three voluminous "registres des jugements" (368 L 11 to 13), and the Sarthe resorted to two "tables chronologiques de jugements" (L 1914 and 1 U 952).

50. Sarthe (pop. 397,000) had 52 trials per annum; Haute-Saône (270,000) had 70; Haute-Garonne (433,000) had 78; Hérault (284,000) had 95. The population figures are an average of the projected figures for 1791 and 1801 given in *Atlas de la Révolution Française,* ed. Serge Bernin and Claude Langlois, vol. 8, *Population,* ed. Lepetit and Sinarellis (1995), 69–70. This figure of 74 trials per annum on average is consistent with findings from other criminal courts of the period. The Marne held 53 trials and the Meurthe 81 trials per annum in the years IV through VII. These calculations are based on René Demogue, "Un tribunal criminel sous la Révolution: Le tribunal criminel de la Marne," *Revue de Champagne* 18 (juillet–août 1911): 161–77; 19 (septembre–octobre 1911): 208–16; 20 (novembre–décembre 1911): 225–40; Hubert Thomas, *Le Tribunal criminel de la Meurthe sous la Révolution (1792–1799)* (Nancy, 1937). Allen, *Tribunaux criminels,* provides extensive data on verdicts from sixteen criminal courts based on the broader time span of 1792–1811.

51. Julius R. Ruff, *Crime, Justice, and Public Order in Old Regime France: The Sénéchaussées of Libourne and Bazas, 1696–1789* (London, 1984), 183; Steven G. Reinhardt, *Justice in the Sarladais, 1770–1790* (Baton Rouge, 1991), 96. These jurisdictions averaged about 100,000 inhabitants each, whereas the departments in question averaged somewhat

over 300,000 each. However, most of the crimes prosecuted in *sénéchaussées* did not rise to the level of the felonies (*délits criminels*) heard in department criminal courts.

52. Haute-Garonne: 126 defendants per annum at 1.61 per trial (or 29 persons—7 in absentia—per 100,000 per annum); Hérault: 135 defendants per annum at 1.43 per trial (48 persons—15 in absentia—per 100,000 per annum); Haute-Saône: 95 defendants per annum at 1.36 per trial (35 persons—6 in absentia—per 100,000 per annum); Sarthe: 68 defendants per annum at 1.31 defendants per trial (17 persons—1 in absentia—per 100,000 per annum).

53. Defendants tried in absentia: South = Haute-Garonne (211 of 883) + Hérault (395 of 947); North = Haute-Saône (104 of 664) + Sarthe (21 of 479). Ten percent of those recorded in the famous Inventaire 450 for the Parlement of Paris were contumacious, whereas 17 percent of the verdicts rendered by the Parlement of Burgundy in the 1770s and 1780s were contumacious. Jean Lecuir, "Criminalité et 'moralité': Montyon, statisticien du Parlement de Paris," *Revue d'histoire moderne et contemporaine* 21 (1974): 445–93, 455; D. Ulrich, "La répression en Bourgogne au XVIIIe siècle," *Revue historique du droit* (1972): 398–437, 406. The court commissioner in the Hérault complained about the high number of defendants absent at trial and blamed it partly on feckless JPs and gendarmes. BB[18] 364, letter to MJ, 9 frim. VII.

54. The southern courts, which were generally more prone to convict, produced a felony conviction rate of 62 percent for those tried in absentia compared to a rate of 73 percent in the otherwise more lenient courts of the north. In the Haute-Garonne, 211 of 883 defendants were tried in absentia (24 percent), but 135 (67 percent) of them were convicted of a felony; and in the Hérault, 395 of 947 defendants were absent from their trials (42 percent), and 242 (61 percent) of these were given felony convictions. On the other hand, in the Haute-Saône, 104 of 664 were tried in absentia (16 percent), with 72 (69 percent) receiving felony sentences; and, finally, in the Sarthe, only 21 of 479 defendants were absent during trial (4 percent), and yet fully 19 (90 percent) of these were convicted of felony offenses.

55. In general, the ferocity of punishments declined during the eighteenth century (though not when it came to murder, robbery, or banditry), while the number of criminal cases and conviction rates increased markedly. See Dominique Muller, "Magistrats français et la peine de mort au XVIIIe siècle," *Dix-huitième siècle* 4 (1972): 79–107, as well as the sources in the following paragraph, some of which I owe to the generosity of Al Hamscher and Julius Ruff.

The calculations for rates of punishment in the late *ancien régime* are based on the following sources and extrapolations. These are only intended to capture a general order of magnitude. The Parlement of Dijon pronounced an average of six executions per annum in the 1770s and 1780s for a Burgundian population of about one million people (Ulrich, "Répression en Bourgogne," 410); from 1780 to 1783, the Parlement of Rennes handed out an average of nine executions a year for a population of approximately two million people in Brittany (Louis-Bernard Mer, "Réflexions sur la jurisprudence criminelle du Parlement de Bretagne pour la seconde moitié du XVIIe siècle," in *Droit privé et institutions régionales: Études historiques offertes à Jean Yver* [1976], 505–30, esp. 513); during the same years, the Parlement of Paris ordered an average of at least 51 executions per annum, and possibly as many as 60, for a population of around 9.75 million inhabitants (Lecuir, "Montyon," 485), and the Parlement of Toulouse sentenced to death 25 people each year out of a population of 3.5 million Languedociens (Castan, *Justice et répression,* 280). This amounts to between 80 and 100 executions per annum for 16.25 million people (perhaps two-thirds of the population of France). It is not unreasonable to conclude, therefore, that between 120 and 150 executions were ordered by *parlements* each year throughout France during the late *ancien régime*. To this should be added another 70–75 death sentences meted out each year by provostial and presidial courts judging in the last resort. This yields a total annual number of executions of between 190 and 225 on average throughout the kingdom.

The figure for lower courts judging in the last resort is based on Nicole Castan, "Summary Justice," table 4.6, 130 (3rd period, 1776–86), which shows an average of 370 cases a year for provostial and presidial courts across France. Deducting 15 percent from this total in order to account for individuals judged in absentia (see 156, n. 65), and then using her percentage breakdowns for 1776–86 produces an average of 72 death sentences, 70 sentences to life in the galleys, and 144 sentences to specified terms in the galleys. Furthermore, working with data for 1748–90, Marc Vigié calculated that between 750 and 950 individuals were condemned to serve sentences of hard labor throughout France each year. "Justice et criminalité au XVIII⁰ siècle: Le cas de la peine des galères," *Histoire, Economie, et Société* 3 (1985): 345–68, 352.

56. All of these figures exclude sentences issued in absentia. Calculations are based on using the "corrected" population data from Lepetit and Sinarellis, *Population*, 69–70, together with sentencing data from nine departmental criminal courts: Drôme, Haute-Garonne, Hérault, Haute-Saône, Sarthe, Côte-d'Or, Marne, Meurthe, and Vienne.

57. This excludes the work of the Directory's military courts and commissions, themselves prolific killers. Their contribution will be examined later. In the meantime, it should be noted that a sentence to the *bagne* was often deadly. Mortality rates were three to four times the average for comparable age groups in regular society, and this did not depend on length of sentences; most deaths occurred in the first few years of a sentence. André Zysberg, "Politiques du bagne, 1820–1850," in *L'impossible prison: Recherches sur le système pénitentiaire au XIXe siècle*, ed. Michel Perrot (1980), 165–205, esp. 190–93.

## 4. TRIAL BY JURY

1. Furet, *Interpreting the French Revolution*. Hunt, *Politics, Culture, and Class*, and Baker, ed., *The French Revolution and Modern Political Culture*, provide a rich variety of perspectives on democratic political culture in the period. Despite low voter turnout and electoral manipulation, Patrice Gueniffey and Malcolm Crook conclude that the Directory was a vital period of apprenticeship in modern democracy, a view supported by James Livesey for noninstitutional settings. Patrice Gueniffey, *Le nombre et la raison: La Révolution française et les élections* (1993); Crook, *Elections*; Livesey, *Making Democracy*.

2. Gueniffey, *Nombre*, 100–105, puts the number of *éligibles* in 1795–99 at 600,000, whereas Crook, *Elections*, 118–19, simply claims "less than 1 million." Though Allen's *Tribunaux criminels* appeared after the following pages were written, it provides detailed supporting evidence for the conclusions drawn here; see esp. 155–88.

3. BB¹⁸ 865, MJ to public prosecutor of Tarn, 29 niv. VI; *Journal de Toulouse*, 2 vend. VI.

4. Robert Allen, "The Criminal Courts of the Côte-d'Or, 1792–1811" (Ph.D. diss., Columbia University, 1991).

5. François Fortunet, "Des droits et des devoirs," in *Constitution de l'an III*, ed. Bart et al., 17–28.

6. Magistrates had only a formal role to play in jury verdicts when at least ten jurors

voted for conviction. If the presiding judges disagreed with this conviction, they could add to the jury panel the three supernumerary jurors who had sat through the entire trial. The fifteen jurors would then deliberate together and hold a new vote. Reversing the original conviction required four votes for acquittal, which rarely happened because the overwhelming majority of verdicts were unanimous. Woloch, *New Regime,* 361–62.

7. The judicial system received no attention in the landmark collection *The French Revolution and the Creation of Modern Political Culture,* ed. Keith M. Baker, Colin Lucas, François Furet, and Mona Ozouf, 4 vols. (Oxford, 1987–92), nor does it appear in Livesey's *Making Democracy.* In contrast, Woloch, *New Regime,* 355–79, and Bernard Schnapper, "Le jury criminel" in *Une autre justice, 1789–1799,* ed. Robert Badinter, 149–70 (1989), are useful introductions to the revolutionary jury.

8. Data for sixteen criminal courts in the years 1792 to 1811 yield an average acquittal rate of 45 percent, a conviction rate for felonies of 43 percent, and a misdemeanor conviction rate of 12 percent. Allen, *Tribunaux criminels,* 59. However, Allen's conclusion that an acquittal rate of this level indicates the inadequacy of the revolutionary jury is based on misleading comparisons with English juries in the seventeenth century and American juries in the twentieth century.

9. See chapter 8. Military courts in general had an acquittal rate when defendants were present at trial of 52 percent, a misdemeanor rate of 27 percent, and a felony conviction rate of 21 percent. This calculation is based on the table of military court judgments between their creation and 1 vend. VII given in B.-L.-J. Schérer, *Compte rendu par le Ministre de la Guerre de son administration pendant l'an VI* (vent. VII), 36.

10. Although it appeared after this was written, Laura Mason, "The 'Bosom of Proof': Criminal Justice and the Renewal of Oral Culture during the French Revolution," *Journal of Modern History* 76 (2004): 29–61, interestingly argues that exclusive reliance on courtroom testimony constituted a revalorization of oral culture.

11. Thomas A. Green, *Verdict According to Conscience: Perspectives on the English Criminal Trial Jury, 1200–1800* (Chicago, 1985), 267–317; J.M. Beattie, *Crime and the Courts in England, 1660–1800* (Princeton, 1986), 410–13; J.S. Cockburn and Thomas A. Green, eds., *Twelve Good Men and True: The Criminal Trial Jury in England, 1200–1800* (Princeton, 1988), 391–99; King, *Crime, Justice, and Discretion,* 238–40.

12. Results for individual departments are in Appendix A.3. The different categories are described in detail in Appendix B.1. These categories were defined largely on the basis of the Penal Code and subsequent exceptional laws, as well as other considerations. For example, rather than include bigamy with crimes of violence as is the case in the Penal Code, it has been included under fraud (that is, felonious misrepresentation) in order to isolate violence from other crimes against the person. Similarly, false arrest has not been treated as a crime against the state but as a misuse of public authority like graft or malversation in office.

13. ADHS 368 L 14, 18 pluv. IX.

14. ADH L 6757, 14 ger. VI.

15. ADH L 6727*, 21 fruc. IV.

16. The *question intentionnelle* had been introduced on 14 vendémiaire III (5 October 1794) in order to protect legitimate self-defense and to specify the culpability of defendants.

17. This becomes blatant in crimes that had multiple trials, such as the "seditious gather-

ing" at Verdun on 5–6 ther. V (23–24 July 1797): compare verdicts at ADHG 7L 201 U 2, 28 prai. VI and 9 prai. IX.

18. A precise figure is not helpful because it could not distinguish between convictions on some charges but acquittal on others on the grounds that the crimes were not sufficiently proved.

19. ADH L 6756*, 28 pluv., 27 flor. V, L 6758*, 14 frim. VII.

20. ADHS 368 L 12, 22 flor. V.

21. ADH L 6758* and 6734*, 16 niv. VII.

22. ADHS 368 L 14, 18 niv. X.

23. ADS 1 U 952*, 15 vent. X.

24. ADH L 6760, 5 jr. co. X.

25. ADS 1 U 952*, 15 brum. IX.

26. ADHG 7L 201 U 2, 17 brum. VI.

27. ADHG 7L 201 U 2 and 5, 15 mess. V.

28. ADS L 1914*, 19 pluv. VI.

29. ADS L 1914*, 18 vent. VII; ADS 1 U 952*, 16 vend. IX.

30. Élisabeth Claverie, "De la difficulté de faire un citoyen: Les "acquittements scandaleux" du jury dans la France provinciale du début du XIX^e siècle," *Études rurales,* 95–96 (1984): 143–66, 149.

31. ADHS 368 L 14, 19 pluv. IX.

32. ADHS 368 L 12, 19 niv. VII; 368 L 13, 24 vend. IX; 368 L 14, 28 vent. X.

33. A series of incidents led to three trials, two involving a group of people going to various houses forcing people to sell grain to them, and the other related to "attroupements" practicing "taxation populaire" on the roads. ADS L 1914*, 15 niv., 17 pluv., 16 vent. IV.

34. ADH L 6760*, 20 pluv. X.

35. ADHG 7L 201 U 2 and 5, 22 prai. V.

36. ADHG 7L 201 U 2 and 5, 21 niv. IV.

37. On the elastic concept of "counter-revolution" and its instrumental uses, see Jean-Clément Martin, *Contre-Révolution, révolution, et nation en France, 1789–1799* (1998). However, Martin's schematic on page 304 fails to account for the bipolar language of "counter-revolution" deployed by the Directory in 1798.

38. ADHS 368 L 11, 20 mess. IV.

39. ADHS 368 L, 14 vent. VI, 28 frim. VII; ADH L 6731*, 14 vent. VI.

40. ADH L 6732*, 18 ger. VI; ADHG 7L 201 U 2, 15 ther. VI.

41. ADHG 7L 201 U 2, 21 fruc. VII, 7L 201 U 3, 23 frim. VIII.

42. ADHS 368 L, 5 frim. VI, 2 niv. VI.

43. ADH L 6760*, 22 brum. X.

44. BB[18] 733, D 563, Bordier, public prosecutor of Sarthe, to MJ, 4 frim. IV, as well as a number of petitions to MJ sprinkled throughout this box.

45. ADH L 6757*, 17 ger. VI, 20 flor. VI, 25 ther. VI, 6 fruc. VII; The following were exceptions: in the Frontignan trial, François Tenton was convicted of singing "Vive le comte d'Artois, vive le comte de Provence et leurs belles fleurs de Lyon" and ordered deported (6732*, 20 flor. VI); in the Béziers trials, Antoine Mainie was condemned to six months in prison and a fine of 500 francs for instigating a personal assault (6759*, 2 fruc. VII), and Pierre Roland Jr. was condemned to deportation for using the rallying cry "Amis pour le roi" (6737*, 28 brum. III).

46. Quoted in Leuwers, *Juriste en politique*, 272.

47. ADHG 7L 201 U 2, 1 ger. VII; BB[18] 684; ADA 10 L 1194, 10 mess. VIII.

48. Schnapper, "Jury criminel," 164.

49. BB[18] 866, court commissioner of Tarn to MJ, 9 frim. and 11 niv. IX.

50. Compare Robert Muchembled, *La violence au village (XV^e–XVII^e siécle)* (1985) and Frédéric Chauvaud, *Les passions villageoises au XIX^e siècle* (1995), esp. 254.

PART II: THE MILITARIZATION OF REPRESSION

1. See, for example, Jacques Godechot, *Les commissaires aux armées pendant le Directoire*, 2 vols. (1934), and Jean-Paul Bertaud, *La Révolution armée: Les soldats-citoyens et la Révolution française* (1979); for a contrasting emphasis on the political consequences of growing military professionalism, see Howard G. Brown, "Politics, Professionalism, and the Fate of Army Generals after Thermidor," *French Historical Studies* 19 (1995): 133–52, and Rafe Blaufarb, *The French Army, 1750–1820: Careers, Talent, Merit* (Manchester, 2002), 133–63.

5. THE ARMY AND DOMESTIC SECURITY

1. Alf Lüdtke, *Police and State in Prussia, 1815–1850* (Cambridge, UK, 1989), 182–98.

2. Constant's brochures are published in Philippe Renaud, ed., *Benjamin Constant* (1988).

3. Colin Lucas, "The First Directory and the Rule of Law," *French Historical Studies* 10 (1977): 231–60; Charles Doyle, "Internal Counter-Revolution: The Judicial Reaction in Southern France 1794–1800," *Renaissance and Modern Studies* 33 (1989): 106–24.

4. A.-C. Thibaudeau, *Mémoires sur la Convention et le Directoire*, 2 vols. (1824), 2:142.

5. Nicole Castan, *Justice et repression en Languedoc à l'époque des Lumières* (1978), 195–211; John Batt, "Royal Authority, the Army, and the Maintenance of Public Order in France at the End of the Ancien Régime" (Ph.D. thesis, University of Reading, 1985), 100–222. I am grateful to Tim Le Goff for introducing me to this valuable work. See also Cynthia Bouton, *The Flour War: Gender, Class, and Community in Late Ancien Régime French Society* (University Park, Penn., 1993), 99–103.

6. Ted Margadant, "Summary Justice and the Crisis of the Old Regime in 1789," *Historical Reflections* 29 (2003): 495–528.

7. John Markoff, "Violence, Emancipation, and Democracy: The Countryside and the French Revolution," *American Historical Review* 100 (1995): 360–86.

8. Samuel F. Scott, "Problems of Law and Order during 1790, the 'Peaceful' Year of the French Revolution," *American Historical Review* 80 (1975): 859–88, and Samuel F. Scott, *The Response of the Royal Army to the French Revolution: The Role and Development of the Line Army, 1787–93* (Oxford, 1978), esp. 135–36.

9. Colin Lucas, "Revolutionary Violence, the People, and the Terror," in *The French Revolution and the Creation of Modern Political Culture*, ed. Keith M. Baker, 4 vols., 4:57–79 (Oxford, 1988–94).

10. Richard Cobb, *The Police and the People: French Popular Protest, 1789–1820* (Oxford, 1970), 189.

11. Bertaud, *Révolution armée*; Howard G. Brown, *War, Revolution, and the Bureaucratic State: Politics and Army Administration in France, 1791–1799* (Oxford, 1995); John A. Lynn, *Bayonets of the Republic: Motivation and Tactics in the Army of Revolutionary France, 1791–94* (Champaign, Ill., 1984).

12. Gilbert Bodinier, "La Révolution et l'armée" in *Histoire militaire de la France*, ed. André Corvisier, 4 vols., 2:268 (1992–94).

13. Compare the following passages: "La justice sans la force est impuissante, la force sans la justice est tyrannique" (Blaise Pascal, *Pensées*, [reprinted 1963], fragment no. 103, 298); "Car l'authorité sans forces seroit méprisée, et presque inutile: et les forces sans l'authorité légitime, ne seroient qu'une tyrannie" (Jean Domat, *Le Droit public* [1697], Livre 1$^{er}$, Titre II, Section I, 8); "le ressort du gouvernement populaire en révolution est à la fois la vertu et la terreur: la vertu, sans laquelle la terreur est funeste; la terreur, sans laquelle la vertu est impuissante" (E. Esprez et al., eds., *Œuvres complètes de Maximilien Robespierre*, 10 vols. [1910–67], 10:357).

14. Georges Carrot, *Le maintien de l'ordre en France depuis la fin de l'ancien régime jusqu'à 1968*, 2 vols. (Toulouse, 1984), 1:196–98; Malcolm Crook, *Toulon in War and Revolution* (Manchester, 1991), 168–71.

15. The actual term *division militaire* is here translated as "military district" to avoid confusion with the army's divisional structure on campaign that is reflected in the rank of *général de division. Divisions militaires* originated as a combination of territorial and operational commands concentrated along the frontiers. Corvisier, *Histoire militaire*, 2:34–35.

16. Brown, "Politics, Professionalism," 150–52.

17. Compare the military bureaucracy's policy proposal at the end of "État des officiers généraux . . . actuellement employés dans les armées de la République" (c. mess. III) in AG X$^{EM}$ 33, which became the basis of the Directory's system, with the Committee of Public Safety's plan for a significantly lower number of generals in the interior in AG B$^{13}$ 41, year IV, no date.

18. In mid-1797, the War Ministry proposed that 25 division generals and 43 brigade generals be assigned to military districts in peacetime (there were a total of 80 division generals and 147 brigade generals active throughout the army at the time). In 1799, in the midst of the War of the Second Coalition, there were 26 division generals and 36 brigade generals assigned to military districts. AG B$^{13}$ 65, "État major général de l'armée," 30 mess. V; B$^{13}$ 109, "État des corps des troupes employés dans les divisions militaires à l'époque du 1$^{er}$ Vendémiaire an 8$^{e}$."

19. See Aubry Dumez and Pierre-Grégoire Chanlaire, *Atlas national de France contenant la topographie de tous les départemens qui composent la République française* (an II), map.

20. AG B$^{13}$ 41, MW to Gen. Haquin, 3 pluv. IV.

21. AG B$^{13}$ 44, MW to Directory and reply, 28 ger., 2 flor. IV.

22. Decrees of 21 Oct., 12 Dec. 1789; 26 Feb. 1790; 3 Aug. 1791; Carrot, *Maintien de l'ordre*, 1:20–21, 35–44, 85–87.

23. Although the legal bureau in the Ministry of Police claimed that district commanders could not withdraw troops from a department without the approval of department officials, this extreme position on civilian authority did not prevail. F$^7$ 3003, 18 frim. VI.

24. Department authorities often called upon national guardsmen to perform various special assignments beyond their own cantons. In such cases, guardsmen were supposed to receive the same rations and pay as regular soldiers, which proved a source of endless squabbling (for example, the exchange between the ministers of police and war in AG B$^{13}$ 58, 16 and 19 vent. V).

25. F$^7$ 4368, Directory dir., 7 pluv. IV; AG B$^{13}$ 52, Directory dir., 21 brum. V; for example, B$^{13}$ 70, MW to Haute-Garonne, Lot-et-Garonne, Gers, and Aveyron, 20 vend. VI; F$^7$ 4368, Directory dir., 14 vent. VII.

26. AG B¹³ 88, Directory dir., 8 frim. VII.

27. See Christopher Durston, *Cromwell's Major-Generals: Godly Government during the English Revolution* (Manchester, 2001).

28. F⁹ 39ᵃ, d. 1, 8 niv. IV.

29. Historians have made little use of this material, but for obvious reasons. The main repository is the series AG B¹³ ("correspondance militaire générale, du 14 décembre 1791 au mai 1804"), which is the product of an absurd reorganization and massive culling of documents in the nineteenth century. All case files and bundles, if deemed of significance for military history, were pulled apart and each document was placed in chronological, but otherwise random, order. The result is a highly irregular collection without a modern inventory, but one that is indispensable to a serious study of the problems of order from the years III through IX.

30. AG B¹³ 74, MP to Gen. Pille, 15 frim. VI.

31. AF III 187, d. 862.

32. These were: L.-A. Choin de Montgay de Montchoisy, who openly connived with émigrés while the commander of Lyon; F.-M.-F.-J. de Lajolais, rightly suspected of being part of the Pichegru conspiracy while commander of the Fifth District (headquarters at Strasbourg); and the equally treasonous, but slightly more deft, Jacques Ferrand, whom the British agent Wickham counted on to use his position as commander of the Sixth District (headquarters at Besançon) to launch a royalist revolt in the region. AF III 146, d. 689, MP to Directory, 18 niv. and 2 vent. IV; AF III 147, d. 692, MW to Directory, 6 vent. IV; AG B¹³ 72, Doubs to Gen. Labarollière, 19 brum. V; Debidour, *Recueil*, 1:447–48 (29 niv. IV), and 640–41 (2 vent. IV); Ernest Daudet, *La Conjuration de Pichegru et les complots royalistes du Midi et de l'Est, 1795–1797* (1901), 115–47.

33. The evidence, but not the conclusion, comes from Jonathan Devlin, "A Problem of Royalism: General Amédée Willot and the French Directory," *Renaissance and Modern Studies* 33 (1989): 125–43.

34. These included military district commanders Liébert (1st and 16th), Férino (2nd), Laprun (3rd), Labarollière (6th), Kellermann (7th), Moncey (11th), Grandjean (20th), Souham (21st), Vidalot du Sirat (22nd) and Micas (25th); military district subordinates Merle (8th—Vaucluse), Grandjean (10th—Pyrénées-Orientales and Aude), Perrin (13th—Saône-et-Loire), Baillot-Farrol (14th—Orne), Quesnel (14th—Manche), Canuel (19th—Rhône), Piston (19th—Haute-Loire), and Pierre de Viantaix, (20th—Lot); and fort commanders Saignes (Dunkerque), Vernier (Strasbourg), and Dumas (Valenciennes). Furthermore, several other generals dismissed as a result of Fructidor had recently held posts in the Eighth Military District: Liégard, Sahuguet, and Willot (député fructidorisé). This list is based on the series AF III and AG B¹³, and it includes those removed within three months of the coup for having favored "the faction crushed on 18 fructidor."

35. See Brown, *War, Revolution, and the Bureaucratic State*, 224–25.

36. AF III 177 to 181 contain dossiers on hundreds of suspect officers.

37. Comparison made between lists in AF III 183, d. 833 and d. 834.

38. See the microanalysis of officer appointments in Jonathan Devlin, "The Army, Politics and Public Order in Directorial Provence" (D.Phil. thesis, Oxford University, 1987).

39. AG B¹³ 79, 22 vent. VI; see also Jean-René Suratteau, *Les élections de l'an VI et le "coup d'état du 22 floréal" (11 mai 1798)* (1971), 186–87, 246.

40. Ibid., 270. The Floréal "coup" ensured that only five actually became deputies.

41. AG B¹³ 124, 3 prai. VIII; see also correspondence with Servan in B¹³ 122, 123, and 124.

42. The government's source was the influential and always well-informed *commissaire ordonnateur* C.-A. Alexandre. AF IV 1300[B], d. frim. IX.

43. AG B[13] 102, Gen. Augereau, deputy in the Five Hundred, to Directory, 13 mess. VII.

44. Gustave Cunéo d'Ornano, *Hoche: Sa vie, sa correspondance* (1892), 255–57.

45. Marcel Reinhard, *Le département de la Sarthe sous le régime directoriale* (Saint-Brieuc, 1936), 298–307; Isser Woloch, *Jacobin Legacy: The Democratic Movement under the Directory* (Princeton, 1970), 138–40; Christine Peyrard, *Les Jacobins de l'Ouest: Sociabilité révolutionnaire et formes de politisation dans le Maine et la Basse-Normandie (1789–1799)* (1996), 338–46.

46. *Journal de Toulouse*, 6 flor., 4 mess. IV; 8, 16 pluv. 18, 20 vent. V; 4 vent. VI.

47. Compare the similarly defensive letters sent by successive commanders of the Sixth Military District, the first a closet royalist and the second an ardent republican: AF III 148[a], d. 2696, Labarolière to MW, 17 mess. V; B[13] 83, F. Muller to MW, 2 mess. VI.

48. For example, after four years in the Loire, a battalion of the Twenty-sixth demi-brigade reached the point of "making common cause with the royalist cutthroats." AG B[13] 77, Loire to MP, 16 pluv. VI.

49. AG B[13] 85, MW to Muller, 2 fruc. VI; B[13] 66, Rhône to MW, 15 ther. V.

50. AG B[13] 77, reports on 25 and 26 pluv. VI.

51. AG B[13] 58, Mayenne to MF, 24 vent. V; B[13] 85, commissioner of Lozère to MW, 22 ther. VII (misfiled); ADH L 970, fruc. VII; F[7] 7714, d. 64, prai.-mess. VIII; BB[18] 866, subprefect of Lavaur (Tarn) to MJ, 28 niv. IX.

52. AG B[13] 75, 8 niv. VI; B[13] 95, MW to commanders of southern districts, 25 vent. VII

53. AG B[13] 82, Petit-Guillaume to MW, 8 prai., 13 ger. VI.

54. *Journal de Toulouse*, 22–26 vent. VIII.

55. AG B[13] 134, Guérard, banker, to his associate Gobert, 25 vent. IX. For other material in this paragraph, see B[13] 63, Administration des Postes et Messageries to MF, 23 prai. V, B[13] 85, contract with Dumorey Co. for treasury wagons, 1 fruc. VI.

56. For example, AG B[13] 58, Gen. Haquin (9th Mil. Dis.), Gen. Guiot-Durepaire (22nd Mil. Dis.), 15 vent. V, B[13] 82, Gen. Sionville, (2nd Mil. Dis.) to MW, 8 prai. VI.

57. AG B[13] 46, Châteaneuf-Randon to Directory, 12 mess. IV; B[13] 58, Haquin to MW, 18 vent. V.

58. AG B[13] 82, Adj.-gen. Noguès to Gen. Duvignau, 30 flor. VII; B[13] 81, MP to MW, 21 ger. VI; B[13] 70, Noguès to Gen. Morlot, 20 vend. VI.

59. The relevant laws are: 9 and 24 October 1792, 28 March, 26 April 1793 (pertaining to émigrés); 19 March, 26 April, 10 May, and 5 July 1793 (counter-revolutionary insurgents and their leaders); 16 June 1793 (spies); 3 September 1793 (traitors and deserters), and the decree of 29–30 vendémiaire III (clergymen linked to revolt or counter-revolution).

60. In 1793–94, almost sixty military commissions carried out over eight thousand executions, or more than half of the executions during the Terror based on "judicial" sentences. The legislation establishing the jurisprudence of military commissions proved little more than a fig leaf for the operation of such instruments of extermination as the Parein-Félix Commission at Angers and the Bignon Commission at Nantes, together responsible for over four thousand executions. Berriat-Saint-Prix, *La justice révolutionnaire* (1870); Donald Greer, *Incidence of the Terror during the French Revolution* (Cambridge, Mass., 1935).

61. Laws of 27 ger. and 19 flor. II.

62. G. Thomas de Closmadeuc, *Quiberon, 1795: Émigrés et chouans, commissions militaires: Interrogatoires et jugements* (1899).

63. Muddled legislation allowed two military commissions—one for *barbets* in the Alpes-Maritimes and another for chouans in Brittany—to continue to operate until mid-year V, even though legally they should not have existed. BB¹⁸ 114, MJ to MW, 29 vent. V.

64. On changes to military justice during the Revolution, though strictly in terms of its application to soldiers, see Georges Michon, "La justice militaire sous la Révolution," *Annales révolutionnaires* 14 (1922): 1–26, 99–130, 197–222; Bernard Schnapper, "Le droit pénal militaire sous la Révolution: Prophétisme ou utopie?" in *Travaux de l'Institut de sciences criminelles de Poitiers* 5 (1986): 1–13; and *L'Ami des lois*, 30 brum. and 12 frim. IV.

65. The law of 2 jr. co. III actually interchanged the terms *conseil de guerre* (the name of courts-martial in the *ancien régime*) and *conseil militaire* (the term used in all later correspondence). The method to determine the judges in a capital trial was much the same, in fact, as the method to determine the jurors in a *tribunal criminel militaire* (law of 12 May 1793).

66. *Moniteur*, Temple case of 3 jr. co. IV; laws of 21 fruc. IV and 13 frum. V; L.-J.-G. de Chénier, *Guide des tribunaux militaires, ou législation criminelle de l'armée, contenant, avec des notes et des commentaires explicatifs, le texte entier des lois, décrets, arrêtés, ordonnances, avis du conseil d'état, rendus depuis 1789 jusqu'à ce jour*, 2 vols. (1838), 1:189–91.

67. See the law of 1 vend. IV, the *Code des délits et des peines*, art. 598, laws of 22 mess. and 24 fruc. IV, and BB¹⁸ 114, MJ to commissioner of Alpes-Maritimes, 2 jr. co. IV.

68. BB¹⁸ 733 has several requests for prompt judgment from long-term detainees, including the Guibert sisters, who had spent nine months in prison accused of supporting *chouannerie*.

69. BB¹⁸ 297, 9 flor. IV.

70. BB¹⁸ 267, MJ to commissioner of Eure, 2 frim. V. The law specified that men accused of joining the rebels, but arrested outside an armed gathering, were to be indicted by the public prosecutor, thus bypassing a grand jury, and then tried in a regular criminal court.

71. Debates about the justiciability of civilians by military justice under the law of 30 prai. III (18 June 1795) rarely dealt adequately with this point, and it eventually became a major bone of contention in the late Directory. See Howard G. Brown, "Revolt and Repression in the Midi Toulousain, 1799," *French History* 19 (2005): 1–28.

72. During year IV, twenty-five people were tried by the Criminal Court of the Sarthe for participating in "chouannisme." This limited their sentences to a maximum of four months in prison. However, at least five of these men were charged with crimes justiciable by a *conseil militaire*—recruiting for the chouans or supplying munitions to them—and punishable by death (see ADS L 1914). The three surviving registers generated by *conseils militaires* in the Sarthe (which cover three courts at Le Mans and one at La Flèche) contain six times as many cases of "chouannisme" than the Criminal Court, and even this is an under-representation given evidence that other *conseils militaires* were also operating at Château-sur-Loir, Sillé, and Sablé (see ADS L 336). Furthermore, eleven of sixty-eight cases in the register of the *conseil de révision* at Le Mans come from these other courts, which suggests on the basis of extrapolation that *conseils militaires* in the Sarthe actually tried seven times as many people for *chouannerie* as the Criminal Court.

73. Although *conseils militaires* were supposed to be convened for a single case at a time, the first *conseil militaire* established at Le Mans sat continuously from 13 vend. to 7 flor. IV and issued verdicts in 141 cases. A second *conseil militaire* was constituted at Le Mans and, despite rotating judges, maintained a single register containing verdicts for eighty-four cases tried between 11 ger. IV and 7 frim. V. The third known register for a

*conseil militaire* in the Sarthe comes from La Flêche, where thirty-seven cases were heard between 30 vend. IV and 11 brum. V (ADS L 1743, 1744, AG J2 289). Disputes recorded in BB¹⁸ 733, D 6295 reveal that a lack of competent officers made it impossible to form a new set of judges for every case.

74. The law of 22 mess. IV (10 July 1796) limited the jurisdiction of *conseils militaires* to members of the army in order to protect supply contractors. When lawmakers realized, however, that this had inadvertently ended the practice of trying chouans with military courts, they explicitly revived the practice two months later (24 fruc. IV). See BB¹⁸ 733, D 8232, MJ to court commissioner of the Sarthe, 28 ther. IV and AG B⁵ 40, MJ to Gen. Dugua, 1 ther. IV.

75. Only six civilians were charged with crimes not directly related to *chouannerie*, three for receiving goods stolen from the army (all of which could serve the chouans), one for sheltering a priest, and two nonjuring priests who were sentenced to be interned in the *archevêché* at Le Mans. ADS L 1744, 8 flor. IV.

76. AG J2 289, 29 brum. IV.

77. AG J2 142 contains two other serial records for *conseils militaires* at work in areas of *chouannerie*. These are (1) an inventory of judgments rendered by *conseils militaires* at Vannes and registered with the Tenth Battalion of the Var between 22 vend. IV and 14 vend. V; and (2) a register containing the verdicts of the *conseil militaire* of the town of Vire for 6 brum. to 16 prai. IV. In eight months, these courts sentenced thirty-two individuals to death, six to short terms in irons, and five to a few months in prison for crimes related to *chouannerie*, which is the inverse of sentencing ratios in the Sarthe.

78. ADS L 1744, 29 prai. IV.

79. ADS L 1744, 12 prai. IV.

80. See BB¹⁸ 735, D 2960, *conseil militaire* at Le Mans to MJ, 18 pluv. IV; AG B⁵ 36, Devillers, *capitaine rapporteur*, to Hoche, 5 vent. IV and Hoche to Directory, 11 vent. IV.

81. *Conseils de révision* consisted of the three highest-ranking officers under the commanding general who formed the *conseil militaire*. These three-man panels were given twenty-four hours to review trial procedures and sentences before they were implemented.

82. See the cases judged by the Criminal Court on 17 vend. V and 18 niv. VII (ADS L 1914), and the *conseil militaire* at La Flêche on 23 pluv., 25 pluv., and 3 flor. IV (AG J2 289). On the law of 17 ger. IV, see AG B⁵ 37, MJ to Gen. Quesnel, no date (c. April 1796), where it was made clear that revisions could only reduce illegal sentences or nullify verdicts based on illegal procedures. See also the correspondence between MJ and Generals Hoche, Dugua, and Dumesnil (B⁵ 39, 18, 19, and 23 prai. IV), in which the generals persuaded the minister to accept that *conseils de révision* could consider acquittals as well as convictions.

83. AG B¹³ 44, Gen. Châteauneuf-Randon to Directory, 2 flor. IV; J2 3, *conseil militaire* at Rodez, 10 pluv. IV.

84. AG B⁵ 37, exchange between Lejeune and MJ, 17, 18, 21 ger., 21 flor. IV; BB¹⁸ 297.

85. Law of 4 brum. IV (26 October 1795).

86. These were in addition to the twenty-three civilians they had executed.

87. BB¹⁸ 735, D 2960, MJ to *conseil militaire* at Le Mans, 1 vent. IV; BB¹⁸ 863, MJ to *Chef de brig.* Glaujaud, commander at Castre, 15 flor. IV; ADS L 1743 and 1744; BB¹⁸ 863, *conseil militaire* at Castres, 13 flor. IV.

88. AG B⁵ 36, Gen. Hédouville to MW, 8, 11, and 23 ger. IV.

89. AF III 182, d. 837, MW to the Commission on Military Justice (Council of Five

Hundred), 18 mess. IV, and C 494, d. 294, "Les généraux de l'armée de Sambre-et-Meuse et le commissaire du gouvernement au Directoire exécutif," 25 fruc. IV (signed by C-in-C Jourdan and thirteen other generals).

90. As was the case with regular criminal courts, military courts did not record full trial proceedings. Nonetheless, one such record exists. It is from the high-profile trial of royalist conspirators in 1797: *Débats du procès instruit par le conseil de guerre permanent de la XVIIe division militaire, séant à l'ancienne Maison commune de contre les prévenus Brottier, Berthelot-la-Villeurnoy, Dunan, Poly et autres (recueillis par des sténographes)* (n.d.) BL F. 1134. This was a complicated affair in which it took ten hours, spread over several sessions, to read aloud all of the relevant documentation before the accused even appeared in court.

91. Legislators knew that they had placed "entre les mains du commandant en chef toute la puissance de la loi." *Moniteur,* an V, 196, Mathieu Dumas, rapporteur, séance du 13 brum. V.

92. Le Menuet la Jugannière, member of the Council of Elders quoted in Michon, "Justice militaire," 203.

93. Laws of both 16 May 1792 and 18 pluv. II expanded the definition of *délits militaires.*

### 6. REFINING TERROR AND JUSTICE AFTER FRUCTIDOR

1. Between 19 fruc. V (5 September 1797) and 13 brum. VI, 63 department administrations and 178 cantonal administrations were reconstituted, and 19 department commissioners and 462 cantonal commissioners replaced (*L'Ami des lois,* 16 brum. VI). For detailed accounts of the coup itself, as well as the general line of debate about its relationship to royalist conspiracy, see Albert Meynier, *Le dix-huit fructidor an V* (1927), 141–216, and Georges Lefebvre, *La France sous le Directoire, 1795–1799,* 2nd ed., presented by Jean-René Surratteau (1944, 1984), 418–33, 729–36.

2. AF III, 463, pl. 2803, 18 fruc. V; AG B¹³ 68, dirs. of 18, 21, 22, 26 fruc. V.

3. *Journal de Toulouse,* 2 jr. co. V, 14 vend. VI.

4. *Chronique de la Sarthe,* 2 brum. VI.

5. For a full description of how military commissions were intended to function, see AG J2 51, MJ to MW, 21 pluv. VI; on de facto permanence, see B¹³ 79, WM circular, 12 vent. VI. A later circular from the minister of police stated that "no administrative decision on the fact of emigration is valid unless it has been confirmed by the Directory." *L'Ami des lois,* 5 frim. VII.

6. Lefebvre, *France sous le Directoire;* Denis Woronoff, *La République bourgeoise de Thermidor à Brumaire, 1794–1799* (1972); Michael J. Sydenham, *The First French Republic, 1792–1804* (Berkeley, 1973); Martyn Lyons, *France under the Directory* (Cambridge, UK, 1975).

7. Victor Pierre, *La Terreur sous le Directoire: Histoire de la persécution politique et religieuse après le coup d'état du 18 fructidor* (1887); *18 Fructidor: Documents pour la plupart inédits recueillis et publiés pour la Société d'histoire contemporaine* (1893); *La déportation ecclésiastique sous le Directoire: Documents inédits recueillis et publiés pour la Société d'histoire contemporaine* (1896). His summary data and conclusions have been included in virtually all general histories and reference works on the period; however, Pierre's apparently

exhaustive search for documents on the Fructidorian military commissions yielded only two hundred individuals, whereas my own research is based on over a thousand trials.

8. For a discussion of sources, see Howard G. Brown, "Mythes et massacres: Reconsidérer la 'Terreur directoriale,'" *AHRF,* no. 325 (2001): 23–52.

9. Jean-Pierre Mayer, ed., *Œuvres, papiers, et correspondance d'Alexis de Tocqueville,* 18 vols., vol 2., partie 2 (3rd ed., 1953), 270.

10. Though the intellectual roots of Directorial republicanism merit analysis (see Raymonde Monnier, "Républicanisme et révolution française," and Andrew Jainchill, "The Constitution of Year III and the Persistence of Classical Republicanism," *French Historical Studies* 26 [2003]: 87–118 and 399–435), more needs to be done to relate these to political action.

11. Bronislaw Baczko, *Comment sortir de la Terreur: Thermidor et la Révolution* (1989).

12. The notion of myth used here is based on Bruce Lincoln's discussion of the relationship between fable, legend, history, and myth elaborated in *Discourse and the Construction of Society: Comparative Studies of Myth, Ritual, and Classification* (Oxford, 1989), esp. 15–26, and on Yves Barel, "Le mythe et le sens: Esquisse d'un mythe du mythe" in *Mythe et Révolutions,* ed. Yves Chalas, 45–99 (1990), where narrative, evidence, and action are stressed as crucial aspects of myth. J. G. A. Pocock arrived at a concept similar to my own but via a very different route, "[For the Florentine *ottimati*] Venice became a myth, a paradigm exercising compulsive force on the imagination." *The Machiavellian Moment: Florentine Political Thought and the Atlantic Republican Tradition* (Princeton, 1975), 102.

13. Georges Duby, *The Three Orders: Feudal Society Imagined,* trans. Arthur Goldhammer (Chicago, 1980).

14. The law of 14 frim. V had annulled article 10 of the law of 3 brum. IV against refractory priests but left their status unclear until the law of 7 fruct. V definitively repealed the laws of 1792–93. In the meantime, the law of 9 mess. V repealed the rest of the law of 3 brum. IV as well as that of 14 frim. V. This made it possible for the relatives of émigrés, *vendémiairistes,* and even *amnistiés* to hold public office.

15. Jean Adher, "La conspiration royaliste dans la Haute-Garonne en l'an IV et l'an V," *Révolution française* 41 (1901); Philippe Bourdin, "Les 'Jacobins' du bois de Cros (Clermont-Ferrand, an V): Chronique d'un massacre annoncé," *AHRF,* no. 226 (1997): 249–304; on Castres, BB[18] 684 and F[7] 7296.

16. François de Neufchâteau was especially eloquent on the rise in crime and decline in administrative zeal since the elections of year V. "Ministre de l'intérieur aux administrations centrales et aux administrations municipales, 15 fructidor an 5," in *Recueil des lettres, circulaires, instructions, programmes, discours, et autres actes publics, émanés du Citoyen François (de Neufchâteau), pendant ses deux exercices du Ministère de l'intérieur,* ed. Randonneau, 2 vols. (an VII), 1:liv-lix. Lefebvre, *France sous le Directoire,* 294–97, takes the Directorial point of view, saying that the provincial reaction "threatened republicans with extermination."

17. Bertaud, *Révolution armée,* 327–30.

18. *Opinion de Rousseau sur la résolution relative aux ci-devant nobles et anoblis,* Conseil des Anciens, séance du 7 frimaire an 6; *Motion d'ordre de Gay-Vernon, sur la discussion relative aux cidevant nobles,* Conseil des Cinq-Cents, séance du 25 vendémiaire an 6; *Opinion de P. Guchan, sur la résolution relative aux ci-devant nobles et anoblis,* Conseil des Anciens, séance du 9 frimaire an 6.

19. Hugh Gough, *The Newspaper Press in the French Revolution* (Chicago, 1988), 141–42.

20. Mona Ozouf, "De thermidor à brumaire: Le discours de la Révolution sur elle-même," *Revue historique* 243 (1970): 31–66.

21. Marcus Ackroyd, "Constitution and Revolution: Political Debate in France, 1795–1800" (D.Phil. thesis, Oxford University, 1995), 215.

22. For example, the commander of the local National Guard presided over a violent antiterrorist farandole at St-Jean-la-Blaquière (Hérault) on 9 ther. V during the anniversary celebration of the overthrow of Robespierre (ADH L 6737*, 9 ther. VII). Cf. James Livesey, *Making Democracy in the French Revolution* (Cambridge, Mass., 2001), 210–22.

23. Patrice Higonnet, *Class, Ideology, and the Rights of Nobles in the French Revolution* (Oxford, 1981), argues for the irreconcilable nature of universal individualism and bourgeois class interests.

24. AG J2 126, 9 ger. VI, Donnadieu; AG J2 16, 13 ger. VI, Cosnac.

25. *L'Ami des lois*, 27 vend. VI.

26. The law of 26 August 1792 had required all refractory priests to leave France or else be deported to Guyana. All priests who fell under this law were labeled "deportees" (including those who went into hiding) except those over age sixty or infirm, who were subject to internment. The law of 13 September 1793 assimilated all "deportees" to émigrés, and thus the anti-émigré law of 25 brumaire III increased the penalty against such priests from deportation to death.

27. MP circulars, 3 and 14 brum. VI. For these and other circulars mentioned below, see AG C$^{18}$ 4, généralités.

28. Jean Girardot, *Le département de la Haute-Saône pendant la Révolution*, 3 vols. (Vesoul, 1973), 3:314–16; AG J2 144.

29. That is, those covered by the laws of 22 niv., and 4 jr. co. III and who had fulfilled their terms and conditions.

30. This difference rested on arguments made earlier by Benjamin Constant, *Les réflexions de Marchéna sur les fugitifs* inserted in *Le Républicain français;* Pierre-Louis, comte de Roederer, *Des fugitifs français et des émigrés* (28 thermidor an III); and Jean-Jacques Leuliette, *Des émigrés français, ou réponse à M. De Lally-Tollendal* (1797). The distinction persisted throughout the debates on the resolution adopted by the Council of Five Hundred on 17 mess. V but ultimately defeated by the Elders on 12 fruc. V. See especially the report Harmand presented to the Elders on 7 fruc. V in *Moniteur, réimp.*, 28:784.

31. MP circular, 18 brum. VII.

32. Commission report to Council of Five Hundred on 3 vend. *Moniteur,* an V, 26.

33. MP circular of 2 flor. VI; BB$^{18}$ 880, (Toulon) 28 niv. and 13 pluv. VI; AG J2 126, (Marseille) 11 ger. VI and (Toulon) 19 ger. VI.

34. A total of 67 women were tried: 5 were sentenced to death, 14 were sentenced to re-emigration, 43 freed, and 5 sent to civil authorities (the practical equivalent of exemption).

35. The MP circular of 6 ther. VI authorized administrative surveillance rather than prosecution for émigrés whose occupational status would have qualified them for the exemption covered by the laws of 22 niv. and 4 jr. co. III. This encouraged even more leniency in the provinces: "Besides, the Executive Directory having subsequently shown a softer disposition toward them, the military commission thought it must adopt the same attitude by not following to the letter the rigors of the law." Bas-Rhin to MP, 23 pluv. VIII, quoted in Rodolph Reuss, *La grande fuite de décembre 1793 et la situation politique et religieuse du Bas-Rhin de 1794 à 1799* (Strasbourg, 1924), 303.

36. MP circulars of 12 niv. and 6 ther. VI.

37. *Rapport de Tronson-Ducoudray, au sujet de la résolution concernant les fugitifs de Toulon, séance du 23 thermidor an V,* BL F. 744(4).

38. AG J2 51, 12 niv. VI.

39. AG J2 132, 3 vend. VII.

40. AG J2 289, 3 ger. VI; Pierre, *Terreur,* 441–42.

41. Serge Bonin and Claude Langlois, eds., *Atlas de la Révolution française,* vol. 9, *Religion,* ed. Claude Langlois, Timothy Tackett, and Michel Vovelle, (1996), 62.

42. *Moniteur,* an VI, 129 (29 vend. VI).

43. *Moniteur,* an VI, 296 (26 brum. VI).

44. The actual numbers were 49 nobles, 48 clerics, 48 other notables, 50 artisans and shopkeepers, 32 peasants, and 11 servicemen. Few of the other 50 individuals were likely to have been notables because significant social status was usually recorded in order to add legitimacy to sentences. These figures, as well as the accompanying graphics, are slightly revised from Brown, "Mythes et massacres," which includes a nominative list of 267 individuals condemned to death (45–52); the revisions are based on additional cases found in *L'Ami des lois* and AF III 272.

45. AG J2 126, 21 ger. VI (Macagno), 1 fruc. VI (Truchi), 5 vend. VII (Barmando).

46. AG J2 112, (Grenoble) 13 niv. VI; Pierre, *18 Fructidor,* 388; AG C[18] 5, (Paris) 15 brum. VII; Schaedelin, *Emigration révolutionnaire,* 122; AG J2 285 (Poitiers) 6 pluv. VI.

47. AG C[18] 5, (Paris) 19 ther. VI; Alphonse de Beauchamp, *Mémoires du comte Fortuné Guyon de Rochecotte* (1818); Charles Girault, *Rochecotte et la chouannerie mancelle* (Laval, 1949).

48. Charles Jolivet, *Les chouans du Vivarais. Essai sur l'agitation contre-révolutionnaire dans l'Ardèche sous le Directoire* (Lyon, 1930), 29, 40–41, 59–64; Ernest Daudet, *Les conspirations de Pichegru et les complots royalistes du Midi et de l'Est, 1795–1797* (1901), 150–52, 294–316.

49. AG J2 200, 5 vend. VII; *Mémoires de Michelot Moulin sur la chouannerie normande,* 4 vols. (1893), 1:119.

50. Jean Vidalenc, *Les émigrés français, 1789–1815* (1963), 123–24.

51. These examples are from AG J2 132, (Montpellier) 6 vent. VI, Escoffier, 29 prai. VII, Mistral; AG J2 126, (Toulon) 6 frim. VI, Lion, 9 vend. VII, Fougue—*membre du tribunal martial;* (Marseille) 6 ger. VI, Delille, 11 ger. VI, Morin, 12 ger. VI, Etienne—*gendarme;* BB[18] 880 (Toulon), 11 brum. VI, Geoffroy; 7 frim.VI, Marquisant—*gendarme;* 18 frim. VI, Vidal—*huissier;* 19 niv. VI, Calze—*gendarme.*

52. AG C[18] 5, (Paris) 15 thermidor VI; AG J2 200, (Caen) 27 prai. VII.

53. Another 8,553 priests (including 7,847 from Belgium) were ordered deported but were not actually sent to Guyana or the islands of Ré and Oléron because the vast majority were never caught, and some who were simply remained in prisons around France. The total number of deaths includes those who died at Rochefort and on board ship: Pierre, *Terreur,* 423–61. Jean-Claude Vimot, *La prison politique en France: Genèse d'un mode d'incarcération spécifique XVIII<sup>e</sup>–XX<sup>e</sup> siècles* (1993), 57–58, presents the death toll for those sent to Guyana.

54. AG J2 212; Girardot, *Haute-Saône,* 3:314; Pierre, *18 Fructidor,* 260–61; Pierre, *Terreur,* 420–21, 425, 431.

55. AG J2 81, (Strasbourg); J2 126, (Marseille); J2 51 (Marseille) (misfiled); BB[18] 880 (Toulon).

56. See the contrasting cases handled by military commissions at Saint-Brieuc: AG J2 152, 6 frim. VI and 7 pluv. VI. Other commissions committed such irregularities as handing out a dozen prison sentences to émigrés' accomplices, escaped prisoners of war, and persons' who had emigrated well before the Revolution: J2 291, (Bastia) 8 brum. VII; J2 16, (Mézières) 3 frim. VIII, (Verdun) 15 frim. VIII; AG J2 81, (Strasbourg) 12 flor. VI and 29 mess. VI.

57. F⁷ 4374. See also BB¹⁸ 271, Gen. Montigny to Doubs, 5 jr. co. VI, 8 mess. VII, and 10 prai. VIII.

58. The new municipality at Marseille claimed that fifteen thousand people fled the city after the law was promulgated there. Antoine Bernard, "Le 18 fructidor à Marseille et dans les Bouches-du-Rhône," *La Révolution française 41* (juillet-septembre 1901), 200–201.

59. AG J2 81, adj.-gen. Croz to MW, 8 frim. VI; Ludovic Sciout, *Le Directoire*, 4 vols. (1895–97), 3:32.

60. BB¹⁸ 880, 4 and 7 brum., and 22 pluv. VI. For a detailed description of an émigré's part in the extended Thermidorian Reaction in Provence, see the case of Claude Ferrand, condemned to death at Montpellier, 23 vend. VIII. ADG 2R 1165.

61. Jean-Paul Bertaud, *Bonaparte prend le pouvoir* (Brussels, 1987), 109.

62. Lefebvre, *La Révolution française*, 3rd ed. (1963), 500, states that only one execution took place after March 1799, when in fact at least forty-five did, the last two in France the day after Christmas 1799: AG J2 126 (Toulon) 5 niv. VIII, and for those at Coblenz, AG J2 314, 28 flor. and 15 mess. VIII.

63. The law of 5 vent. V had filled a lacuna in the constitution by specifying that public prosecutors would be elected for five-year terms, but the law of 21 niv. VI reduced this to three years and set the term of court presidents at two years. As for political considerations, compare Poullain-Grandprey's scathing criticism of judges elected in 1795 and 1797 (Council of Five Hundred, 11 brum. VI) and Boulay de la Meurthe's defense of judicial independence (Council of Five Hundred, 1 frim. VI).

64. Jean Bourdon, *La réforme judiciaire de l'an VIII*, 2 vols. (Rodez, 1941), 2:353.

65. Jean-René Suratteau, *Les élections de l'an VI et le "coup d'état du 22 floréal" (11 mai 1798)* (1971), 382–87, where "Sadet" is spelled "Sayet"; Richard Cobb, "La commission temporaire de Commune-Affranchie (Brumaire-Germinal an II)," in his *Terreur et subsistances* (1964), 55–94.

66. Suratteau, *Coup d'état*, 437. The purge covered eighty-five duly elected judges.

67. Law of 29 prai. VI. The law of 30 ger. V had transferred the authority to make necessary replacements until the next election from the Directory to serving judges.

68. These figures are derived from the table in Suratteau, *Coup d'état*, 210–25. Sciout, *Directoire*, 3:472–73, substantially understates the total, whereas Suratteau's lists of "floréalisés," which contain thirty-seven court presidents and thirty-five public prosecutors, indirectly overstate it; these are misleading because they combine any type of nullification and fail to identify where appointments were needed to fill actual vacancies.

69. J. Duval-Jouve, *Montpellier pendant la Révolution*, 2 vols. (Montpellier, 1881), 2:372. Although the first elections to the magistracy in the nine annexed departments of Belgium took place in year V, not year IV, one suspects that the ratio of the magistrates elected that year who were still in place at the end of the Directory (61 percent) is not far from the overall turnover in the rest of France during the Second Directory (that is, 39 percent of magistrates). Jacques Logie, "Magistrature et organisation judiciaire d'un état en gestation: La Belgique de 1795 à 1830," in *Le pénal dans tous ses États: Justice, états, et sociétés en Europe (XIIe-XXe siècles)*, ed. Xavier Rousseaux and René Lévy (Brussels, 1997), 385–404.

70. BB[18] 711, Directory dir., 2 frim. VI.

71. Gwynne Lewis, *The Second Vendée: The Continuity of Counter-revolution in the Department of the Gard, 1789–1815* (Oxford, 1978), 124–25. The harshest punishment meted out to the many reactionary judges of the Midi was the loss of citizenship for twenty years imposed by the Criminal Court of the Isère, the most reliably republican court in the Rhône valley, on seven judges from the Bouches-du-Rhône, all charged with the capital crime of "conspiracy against the internal security of the state." Charles Doyle, "The Judicial Reaction in South-Eastern France, 1794–1800" (D.Phil. thesis, Oxford University, 1986), 233.

72. Unusually high turnover had resulted in the election of ten judges in the Côtes-du-Nord in 1797, all of whom were replaced by government appointees as a result of the law of 19 fruc. V. Hervé Pommeret, *L'esprit public dans le département des Côtes-du-Nord pendant la Révolution* (Saint-Brieuc, 1921), 386. On the difficulty of tracing the many changes in judicial personnel during the Directory, see A. Combier, *Justice criminelle à Laon pendant la Révolution, 1789–1800*, 2 vols. (1882), 2:291–93.

73. BB[18] 711, dd 6709, preamble to list of jurors, 11 vend. VI, and letters from MJ.

74. ADD L 243, "compte rendu . . . du département du Doubs," pluv. VI.

75. This is a subtle allusion to the perceived royalist bias of the Court of Cassation before Fructidor and its improvement after the law of 19 fruc. V, which enabled the Directory to appoint twenty-six of its fifty judges. Many of these appointments went to former ministers and ex-*Conventionnels* with Jacobin credentials. Jean-Louis Halperin, *Le Tribunal de Cassation et les pouvoirs sous la Révolution (1790–1799)* (1987), 237–39.

76. *L'Ami des lois,* 21 ther. VI. See also 30 vend., 1 and 23 brum. VII.

77. These figures are based on all verdicts combined, not on departmental averages. A focus on acquittal rates simplifies the statistics; convictions could be either on the original felony charge or on a lesser misdemeanor offense and therefore to combine the two would be misleading.

78. These differences were based as much as anything on the large number of individuals in absentia at the time of trial in southern departments. For example, the fact that the Criminal Court of the Hérault tried a massive number of individuals in absentia in year VI contributed significantly to reducing its acquittal rate to a mere 20 percent.

79. This accords with the tables in H.R.O. Maltby, "Crime and the Local Community in France, the Department of the Drôme, 1770–1820" (D.Phil. thesis, Oxford University, 1980), and Robert Allen, "The Criminal Courts of the Côte-d'Or, 1792–1811" (Ph.D. diss., Columbia University, 1991).

80. Together these accounted for 23 additional death sentences in three of the departments chosen for this study: 10 in the Haute-Garonne, 8 in the Sarthe, 5 in the Hérault. Although neither of these laws led to more death sentences in the Haute-Saône, either law could have been applied in the Hérards case. The Criminal Court of the Meurthe meted out an additional 14 executions in the years VI and VII due to the laws of 26 flor. V and 29 niv. VI: tabulated from Hubert Thomas, *Le Tribunal criminel de la Meurthe sous la Révolution (1792–1799)* (Nancy, 1937), trial synopses.

81. The totals were 154 present and 44 contumacious in years IV and V for a total of 198 persons, compared to 294 present and 144 contumacious in years VI and VII for a total of 438.

82. ADH L 6760*, 17 mess. IX, 15 ther. IX, 15 fruc. IX and 16 flor. X; ADS 1 U 952*, 17 fruc. VIII. The criminal courts of the First Republic confirm the findings of Georges Vigarello, *Histoire du viol, XVIe-XXe siècles* (1998), that child rape was more likely to be prosecuted in eighteenth-century France than any other form of sexual violence.

83. It is worth noting, however, that the Haute-Saône was not immune from this scourge and experienced a moderate spike in prosecutions for armed robbery in year IX.

84. This is for verdicts rendered when the accused were present at trial. The rate of acquittal drops even more sharply when verdicts rendered for persons absent from trial are included.

85. Suratteau, *Coup d'état,* 55–59; Jean-René Suratteau, "Les élections de l'an V aux Conseils du Directoire," *AHRF* (1958, no. 5): 21–63, 44–50; Duval-Jouve, *Montpellier,* 2:320–21.

86. This meant prosecuting batches of people from such centers of reaction as Bédarieux, Lunel, Pignan, Frontignan, and St-Jean-de-Fos.

87. Bourdon, *Réforme judiciaire,* 190ff.

## 7. STRONG-ARM POLICING

1. A vast literature responded to Eugen Weber's *Peasants into Frenchmen: The Modernization of Rural France, 1870–1914* (1977), but rarely took policing into account. For a representative sample of otherwise fine work, see Peter M. Jones, *Politics and Rural Society: The Southern Massif Central c. 1750–1880* (Cambridge, UK, 1985), and James Lehning, *Peasant and French: Cultural Contact in Rural France during the Nineteenth Century* (Cambridge, UK, 1995).

2. On the early National Guard, see Georges Carrot, *La Garde Nationale (1789–1871): Une force publique ambiguë* (Paris, 2001), 45–125; on enthusiasm in rural areas, see Peter M. Jones, *Liberty and Locality in Revolutionary France: Six Villages Compared, 1760–1820* (Cambridge, UK, 2003), 136–38.

3. On 2 ger. IV (22 March 1796), the Directory moved to reverse the tendency toward elitism and specialization by eliminating cannoneers, departmental cavalry, and elite units of grenadiers and chasseurs. Carrot, *Maintien de l'ordre,* 1:201–2, 225, 238–39.

4. P. Clémendot, *Le département de la Meurthe à l'époque du Directoire* (Nancy, 1966), 129; *Chronique de la Sarthe,* 16 brum. VI; F[7] 3618, Haute-Saône dir., 24 frim. VI.

5. AG B[13] 44, Châteauneuf-Randon on Ninth and Tenth Military Districts, 15 ger. IV.

6. Duvergier, *Collection,* 2nd ed., 9:95 (17 flor. IV).

7. ADD, L 593, MP circular to departments, 15 fruc. IV, and commissioner of Doubs to MP, 25 fruc. IV. At the time, only twenty-six of fifty-two cantons in the Doubs had organized their mobile columns. It took two more months of intense efforts, including the appointment of special commissioners to accelerate the formation of columns and the sacking of municipal officials who refused to cooperate, to raise this to forty cantons.

8. *Journal de Toulouse,* 9 vend., 6 vent. IV.

9. For example, ADD L 593, Besançon to Doubs, 15 prai. IV.

10. *Journal de Toulouse,* 8 ther. IV, 28 flor. V; ADHG 1L 363, MP to commissioner of Haute-Garonne, 19 vent. V.

11. AG B[13] 63, Hérault to MP, 8 mess. V.

12. F[7] 7724, d. 16.

13. AG B[13] 79, Petit-Guillaume to MW, 24 vent. VI.

14. BB[18] 711.

15. Reports on the "grand sweep" through the entire pays de Sault and surrounding areas (Ariège and Aude) in search of priests and draft dodgers provide a model of this genre. AG B[13] 96, Gen. Duvigneau to Augereau, 7 ger. VII and AG B[13] 97, Augereau to MW, 3 flor. VII.

16. F⁷ 7637, d. 91, commissioner of Jura to MP, 15 brum. VIII.

17. Carrot, *Garde nationale*, 154 (where facts are equally in error).

18. For example, F¹ᶜ III Haute-Saône 6, commissioner of Haute-Saône to MI, 11 vent. VI.

19. AG B¹³ 72, commissioner of Puy-de-Dôme to MP, 23 brum. VI; B¹³ 74, MP to MW, 12 frim. VI.

20. For example, after the Fructidor coup, the new administrators of the Hérault suspended several cantonal administrations and sent forces there to disarm the populace. This force consisted of a few regular troops and others "known for their morality and their love of republican government whom the municipal administration of Montpellier has had armed." F¹ᶜ III Hérault 9, commissioner of Hérault to MI, 11 vend. VI.

21. The Directory had permanently requisitioned 500 guardsmen for various assignments around the country on 18 niv. V (7 Jan. 1797), but this was small in comparison to later developments. Another 520 were requisitioned at Lille in the wake of Fructidor, and several permanent flying columns of guardsmen were organized in western departments (Loire-Inférieure, Ille-et-Vilaine, Mayenne, Maine-et-Loire). AG B¹³ 91, table of national guardsmen "requisitioned in order to provide military service in the interior," 18 niv. VII.

22. AG B¹³ 82, Lozère dir., 12 flor VI, and MW to Gen. Petit-Guillaume, 2 prai. VI.

23. If a mobile column had to perform "extraordinary service," it received military pay and rations, an expensive proposition given the inferior performance of most mobile columns.

24. AG B¹³ 99, Hérault dir., 7 prai. VII; AG B¹³ 102, Haute-Loire dir., 30 prai. VII.

25. AG B¹³ 42, MP to MW, 14 pluv. IV; ADS L 197, Gen. Simon to officers in the Sarthe, 11 flor. VII.

26. F⁷ 4374, Directory dir., 13 flor. VII.

27. AD XVIIIᶠ 7 provides this figure as a total for the ministry of Milet-Mureau (19 pluv.–29 mess. VII); a table of force distribution in the interior on 1 vend. VIII (AG B¹³ 109) shows a total of 55,000 men (excluding the Army of England, that is, the west), but only 33,600 of these were line units, and most of them were either in the northeast or at Paris. This left several interior military districts without any veteran troops at all (11th—battalion of *miquelets*; 18th, 20th, 21st, no troops whatsoever; 2nd, 4th, 5th, 6th, 7th, auxiliary battalions only).

28. AG B¹³ 100 to 110 passim indicate extensive use of national guardsmen around the country. For example, General Duvigneau, interim commander of the Tenth Military District, reported on guardsmen mobilized in the departments of Pyrénées-Orientales (659), Aude (216), and Ariège (539) for a total of 1,415 men in the district. This was on 15 mess. VII (3 July 1799), well before the outbreak of insurrection around Toulouse.

29. AG B¹³ 108, 27 fruc. VII.

30. See Brown, "Revolt and Repression," 1–28.

31. The law of 14 mess. VII ordered departments to create "auxiliary battalions" out of conscripts who had yet to leave for the frontiers, but the Consuls' directive of 4 pluv. VIII ordered them all incorporated into existing demi-brigades. On the results, see Gustave Vallée, *La conscription dans le département de la Charente (1798–1807)* (1937), 97–106.

32. For example, on 23 flor. VIII (13 May 1800), the MW ordered the Gard, Hérault, Aveyron, Lozère, and Ardèche each to mobilize two hundred national guardsmen, who then remained at the disposal of the district commander for the next ten months. AG B¹³ 124.

33. F$^7$ 7635, d. 10; AG B$^{13}$ 134, Consuls dir., 15 vent. IX; B$^{13}$ 135, MW to MP, 13 ger. IX.

34. On the specific question of policing, Tocqueville wrote, with characteristic hyperbole: "In the opinion of the great majority of people only the government was capable of maintaining public order. The populace had a respectful dread of the *maréchaussée;* for the landed proprietors it was the force worthy of some confidence. The cavalier of the *maréchaussée* was not merely the chief defender of order, he represented order itself." *L'Ancien régime et la Révolution* (1967 ed.), 106.

35. Robert M. Schwartz, *Policing the Poor in Eighteenth-Century France* (Chapel Hill, N.C., 1988), 41. See also, Thomas McStay Adams, *Bureaucrats and Beggars: French Social Policy in the Age of the Enlightenment* (Oxford and New York, 1990), Iain Cameron, *Crime and Repression in the Auvergne and Guyenne, 1720–1790* (Cambridge, UK, 1980), and the exhaustive Jacques Lorgnier, *Juges bottés,* 2 vols. (Lille, 1994).

36. Nicole Castan, "Summary Justice," in *Deviants and the Abandoned in French Society: Selections from the Annales,* ed. Robert Forster and Orest Ranum (Baltimore, 1978); Olwen Hufton, "Le Paysan et la loi en France au XVIII$^e$ siècle," *Annales: Économies, sociétés, civilisations,* 38 (1983): 679–701, 679.

37. Clive Emsley, *Gendarmes and the State in Nineteenth-Century Europe* (Oxford, 1999), 32–33.

38. Schwartz, *Policing the Poor,* 160–62; Clive Emsley, "La Maréchaussée à la fin de l'Ancien Régime: Note sur la composition du corps," *Revue d'histoire moderne et contemporaine,* 33 (1986): 622–44.

39. Castan, "Summary Justice," 132.

40. Emsley, *Gendarmes,* 41–43.

41. The Convention had drafted thousands of gendarmes into the regular cavalry; created special units to protect the legislature, to guard the prisons of Paris, and to serve provincial courts; and allowed *vainqueurs de la Bastille* and *hommes du 10 août* automatic admission to the corps. There were 10,663 stationed in the interior, 7,344 organized into army units, and 3,234 serving as military police. *Rapport fait par le Ministre de la Guerre au Directoire Exécutif sur l'administration de son département depuis l'organisation du gouvernement constitutionnel (4 brumaire an IV à pluviôse an V)* (germinal V).

42. Hubert C. Johnson, "The Decline and Rise of the National Gendarmerie as a Peace-Keeping Force in the Midi, 1794–1800," *Proceedings of the Western Society for French History* 25 (1998): 131–41.

43. AF III 146, d. 689, MP to Directory, 15 brum. V; cf. BB$^{18}$ 329, MP to MJ, 26 brum. V.

44. AG B$^{13}$ 63, Marne to MW, 23 prai. V; B$^{13}$ 45, MP to MW, 14 flor. IV; B$^{13}$ 44, Gen. Châteauneuf-Randon, "Rapport politique et militaire . . . ," 15 ger. IV.

45. BB$^{18}$ 863, Corbières, court commissioner of Tarn, to MJ, 10 ther. V.

46. AG B$^{13}$ 52, 11 brum. V, "Mémoire sur la gendarmerie nationale"; 138 AP 22*, register 1; Pétiet, *Rapport fait par le Ministre de la Guerre . . . 28 mess. V.*

47. On the delays, see AP 22*, r. 1; on the reorganization, see AF III 160$^a$, esp. d. 757, MW to Directory, 25 pluv. V, and the many draft lists in d. 758; AF III (457), Directory dirs., 22 prai., 15 mess. V; AG B$^{13}$ 65, WM to Directory, 30 mess. V; Pétiet, *Second Rapport fait par le Ministre de la Guerre au Directoire Exécutif sur l'administration de son département depuis pluviôse jusqu'au 28 messidor V.*

48. In accordance with the law of 21 fruc. V, the Directory finalized its revision of officer appointments in the gendarmerie with a directive issued on 5 vent. VII. Those eliminated

were to cease their functions before 10 ger. VII, that is, in time for the new officers to join departmental review committees when they met to screen NCOs and gendarmes, as laid down by the law of 18 vend. VI. B.-L.-J. Schérer, *Compte rendu par le ministre de la Guerre de son administration pendant l'an VI* (ventôse VII); AF III 160[b], MW report to Directory, 15 brum. VI; AF III 160[a], d. 758 contains all of the draft lists and comments, whereas AF III 493, d. 3089, has the final list of officers based on post-coup revisions.

49. Each committee combined officers of the gendarmerie (the squadron commander, department captain, and two lieutenants), elected officials (two department administrators and the public prosecutor), and executive agents (the commissioners attached to the department and the criminal court). The War Ministry instructed the committees to begin operations on 1 fruc. V.

50. AG B[13] 79, MW circular, 13 vent. VI.

51. The Haute-Garonne went from 174 men to 97. This was achieved by retiring 27 men (including four lieutenants), giving 3 lieutenants redundancy pay, transferring 10 gendarmes to the line army, and simply dismissing 37 others, most of whom had begun their military careers in the National Guard and joined the gendarmerie under the Convention. In the Sarthe, 8 officers and 38 regulars had to be removed from active duty, leaving a department contingent of 73. AG X[F] 71 and 77, procès-verbaux des séances des juries d'examen and various lists.

52. AG X[F] 72, procès-verbal des séances du jury, 23 frim. VI.

53. AG X[F] 76[bis], procès-verbal des séances du jury de révision.

54. There were exceptions, of course; for example, the government removed Captain Teyssier and Lieutenant Martel from the Haute-Garonne shortly after the elections. AG X[F] 71, Micas, capitaine commandant la gendermerie de la Haute-Garonne, to MW, 14 prai. VII.

55. These procedures were not implemented until a year after the law. AG B[13] 93, MW circular to *chefs des divisions de la gendarmerie*, 18 pluv. VII.

56. Duvergier, *Collection*, 12:120, 491–501, Consuls dir., 29 pluv. VIII, 12 ther. IX; BB[18] 712, public prosecutor of Haute-Saône to MJ, 22 mess. VII; commissioner of Haute-Saône to MI, 2 vend. VIII; F[7] 7520, d. 41 (arrest records); AF IV 1154, Gendarmerie Inspector Wirion to Councilor of State Bernadotte, 30 ther. VIII.

57. Alan Forrest, *Conscripts and Deserters: The Army and French Society during the Revolution and Empire* (Oxford and New York, 1989), 133.

58. AG B[13] 120, 23 vent. VIII.

59. AG B[13] 127, Gen. Radet, Inspector General of the Gendarmerie, to MW, 29 prai. IX; AF IV 1154, MW to First Consul, 7 mess. IX.

60. F[7] 7499, B[6] 2016; AG B[13] 87, esp. Adj.-gen. Campagnol to Augereau, 19 vend. VII, and commissioner of Haute-Garonne to MW, 1 brum. VII, which includes the verdict. Cf. B[13] 138, Gen. Gouvion to MW, 27 mess IX, where the damages for an attack on the gendarmerie at St. Laurent (Aveyron) were 9,000 francs: 1,000 francs for the widow and each of three children, 500 to a wounded gendarme, plus a matching sum for the republic.

61. Charles Tilly, *The Contentious French* (Cambridge, Mass., 1986), 14; Vladimir S. Ljublinski, *La Guerre des farines*, (1979), 143.

62. See Ian Gilmour, *Riot, Risings, and Revolution: Governance and Violence in Eighteenth-Century England* (London, 1992), 139–46.

63. The Convention also used martial law to suppress the *journées* of 1–2 prairial III.

64. F$^7$ 4321, "avis du Bureau des lois," 28 vent., 4 fruc. V; AG B$^{13}$ 119, MP to Adj.-gen. Nivet, 23 pluv. VIII.

65. A. Debidour, ed., *Recueil des actes du Directoire Exécutif,* 4 vols. (1910–17), 1:622, 639–40; Charles-Louis Chassin, *Les pacifications de l'Ouest, 1794–1801,* 3 vols. (1896–99), 2:280–88, 312, 348–50, 363, 403–442; AG B$^5$ 35, 27 pluv. IV and 10 vent. IV; and AF III 391, d. 2049, 12 ther. IV.

66. See Châteauneuf-Randon's letters in AG B$^{13}$ 45, 1 prai. IV, B$^{13}$ 49, 15 fruc. IV. He had used the state of siege at four places in the Hérault (Claret, Lauret, Montagnac, Florensac) as well as the canton of Bannes in the Ardèche.

67. AG B$^{13}$ 45, 18 flor. IV.

68. See the correspondence between Directory, MW, and Châteauneuf-Randon, commander of the Ninth and Tenth Mil. Dis., from May to August 1796 in AG B$^{13}$ 45 to 49.

69. AG B$^{13}$ 52, 26 brum. V, B$^{13}$ 53, 29 frim. V.

70. AF III 144$^a$, d. 679, 30 niv. V.

71. AG B$^{13}$ 52, Willot to Directory, 10 frim. V.

72. AGYB$^{13}$ 59, Willot to MP, 4 ger. V: St Chamas, Lambesc, Gardanne, Graveson, Trets, Éguilles.

73. AG B$^{13}$ 59, MW to Willot, 6 germ. V; AG B$^{13}$ 66, MW to Gen. Sahuguet, 18 ther. V; AG B$^{13}$ 68, WM report to Directory, 23 fruc. V.

74. AG B$^{13}$ 60 to 66 contain a steady stream of correspondence to this effect.

75. Conservatives reacted strongly to a government directive authorizing the local commander to put Lyon under a state of siege whenever he deemed it necessary. Although it was frequently threatened, Lyon was not put under a state of siege until 14 pluv. VI (2 Feb. 1798). AF III 455, d. 2714, 13 mess. V; AG B$^{13}$ 77; AD XVIII$^c$ 46, *Motion d'ordre de Mayeuvre, sur la faculté donnée par le Directoire au général commandant la force armée dans le dép. du Rhône de déclarer la commune de Lyon, en état de siège.* Conseil des 500, séance du 6 thermidor an V.

76. AD XVIII$^c$ 461, *Rapport fait par Jourdan (de la Haute-Vienne), au nom d'une commission chargée d'examiner si la mise en état de siège est une mesure qui puisse concorder avec l'esprit et les principes de la constitution.* Conseil des 500, séance du 21 thermidor an V; *Rapport fait par Chateauvieux au nom d'une commission chargée de l'examen de la résolution relative à la mise en état de siège des communes de la République.* Conseil des Anciens, séance du 10 fructidor an V; *Bulletin des lois, an V, deuxième semestre,* 15.

77. AG B$^{13}$ 68, WM report to Directory, 23 fruc. V.

78. AF III 466, d. 2838, directive of 4 jr. co. an V, naming Gen. Bernadotte, who then refused the post.

79. *Alpes Maritimes:* Grasse, Vence; *Basses-Alpes:* Manosque, Castellan, Entrevaux, Forcalquier, Greaux, Oraison, Riez, Sisteron, Les-Mée, Valensolles; *Bouches-du-Rhône:* Aix, Martigues, Tarascon, Lambesc, Trets, Gardanne, Auriol, Orgon; *Dordogne:* Sarlat; *Gard:* Roquemaure; *Hérault:* Montpellier, Béziers, Lunel; *Tarn:* Castres. This list has been constituted from a wide variety of sources, especially AF III and AG B$^{13}$.

80. AG B$^{13}$ 71, Gen. Chalbos to MW, 28 vend. VI.

81. AG MR 2015, niv. VII. As the Ministry of Police later reported, "local officials, far from appearing jealous of their rights, cast them off, and were the first to solicit a measure that seemed to shield them from responsibility." F$^7$ 7729, d. 91, MP report to Consuls, c. frim. IX.

82. F$^7$ 3003, "avis du Bureau des lois" on MF's draft message to the Councils, 21 vend. VI.

83. Directory dir. of 4 niv. VI. The department administrators of the Doubs were not typical in claiming that vigorous application of this measure had secured safety on the roads (ADD L 42, summary report to the Directory, 15 flor. VI).

84. MW to MP on 17 brum. VII: "I have just instructed General Garnier to provoke an application of the law of 10 vendémiaire IV to the commune on whose territory this attack was committed. . . . But I must not mislead you . . . ten events of similar significance, against which the authority of the law has been uselessly provoked, have been ignored by the courts responsible for its application." BB$^{18}$ 109, D3 4772.

85. F$^7$ 7499, bureau report to MP, vend. VII.

86. See F$^7$ 4323, "avis du bureau des lois," 18 brum. VII.

87. ADS L 197, Gens. Moulin and Vimeux to Sarthe, 3 and 10 pluv. VII, respectively.

88. ADS L 197; Chassin, *Pacifications*, 3:271.

89. AF III 509, d. 3223, WM report and Directory dir., 21 vent. VI; AG B$^{13}$ 80, Gen. Dugua to MW, 5 ger. VI; AG B$^{13}$ 77, Gen. Morand to MW, 14 pluv. VI.

90. AG B$^{13}$ 79, 18 vent. VI.

91. AF III 543, d.3605, WM report and Directory dir., 21 fruc. VI; AG B$^{13}$ 89, Gen. Petit-Guillaume to MW (Viols-le-Fort); AG B$^{13}$ 76, Hérault to MW, 5 pluv. VI (Mèze); F$^7$ 7540, d.53, MJ to com. du Dir., Haute-Saône, 16 pluv. VII; F$^9$ 44, ad. mun., Anvers (Deux-Nèthes) to MI, 12 pluv. VII; AF III 537, WM report and Directory dir., 13 vend. VII.

92. See especially, Gwynne Lewis, "Political Brigandage and Popular Disaffection in the South-east of France, 1795–1804," and Colin Lucas, "Themes in Southern Violence after 9 Thermidor," in *Beyond the Terror: Essays in French Regional and Social History, 1794–1815,* ed. Gwynne Lewis and Colin Lucas (Cambridge, 1983); Richard Cobb, *Reactions to the French Revolution* (London, 1972); Marcel Marion, *Le brigandage pendant la Révolution* (1934), chap 5.

93. AG C$^{18}$ 80, "Tableau des différentes communes en état de siège à l'époque du 7 frimaire an 9"; AF III 149, d. 701, MW to Directory, 13 mess. VI and Directory dir. of 18 mess. VI; AG B$^{13}$ 78, Gen. Garnier to MW, 3 vent. VI.

94. Such was the case with Corsica and the Ardèche. AF III 149, d. 701, MW to Directory, 13 mess. VI.

95. See the WM reports and Directory dir. in AF III 620, d.4379, 27 mess. VII; AF III 621, d. 4391, 26 ther. VII; and AF III 622, d. 4407, 4 fruc. VII.

96. AG B$^{13}$ 108, 7 and 29 fruc. VII; B$^{13}$ 110, 15 and 21 vend. VIII; for a list, see Brown, "Revolt and Repression," 26.

97. AG B$^{13}$ 122, prefect of Basses-Alpes to MP, 19 ger., 3 flor. VIII; B$^{13}$ 135, prefect of Léman to MP, 11 ger. IX.

98. AG B$^{13}$ 250; F$^7$ 7729, d. 69.

99. F$^7$ 7729, d. 69, MP report to Consuls, with list dated frim. IX. The following would remain under state of siege: Genêve, Toulon, Briançon, Nice, Fontenoy-le-Peuple, Brest, Port-Malo, Laval, Le Mans, Bastia, Ostende, Mayence. Some places lingered in this state for several more months at least (see lists in AG B$^{13}$ 132, 1 pluv. IX; B$^5$ 69, 1 ger. IX), and a score of towns in the Ille-et-Villaine did not have the state of siege lifted until a Consular directive on 4 mess. X (23 June 1802).

100. Quoted in Carrot, *Garde nationale*, 170.

8. LIBERTY VERSUS SECURITY IN THE WAR ON BRIGANDAGE

1. C 403, d. 351, Directory message to Council of Five Hundred, 11 frim. V; *Moniteur,* an V, 344–47; *Rapport fait par J. E. Richard, au nom d'une commission spéciale . . . sur la répression du brigandage.* Conseil des Cinq-Cents, séance du 26 pluviôse, an V (BN 8 Le[43] 740); *Rapport fait par Rousseau au nom d'une commission nommée pour examinée une résolution du Conseil des Cinq-Cents, sur la répression du brigandage.* Conseil des Anciens, séance du 18 floréal V (BN 8 Le[45] 355).

2. AF III 442, d. 2577, 18 ger. V.

3. Directory message to Council of Five Hundred, 13 frim. VI, in response to request of 7 frim. VI: *Procès-verbal des séances du Conseil des Cinq-cents, frimaire VI,* (séance du 16), 247–66.

4. *Moniteur,* an VI, 344–47.

5. *Projet de résolution présenté par Roemers au nom d'une commission spéciale, sur le message du Directoire exécutif en date du 13 frimaire an 6, concernant les brigandages qui s'exercent sur les grandes routes, contre les couriers de la malle, etc.* Conseil des Cinq-cents, nivôse an 6 (BN Le[49] 1638[bis]).

6. ADD, 1L 833, MP circular, 13 frim. VI; *Procès-verbal des séances du Conseil des Cinq-cents, nivôse VI,* 281–83 (Directory message of 16 niv. VI); *Moniteur,* an VI, 390, 427, 431–34, 442–44, 446, 456, 458 (Council of Five Hundred, 28 frim., 9, 11, 14, 15, 16, 17 niv. VI).

7. *Moniteur,* an VI, 507 (Council of Elders, 29 niv. VI).

8. BB[18] 329, court commissioner for the Haute-Garonne to MJ, 19 niv. V; *Journal de Toulouse,* 22 niv. V: "The Directory must not neglect any means in its power to stop similar outbursts, which tend to subvert social principles and the security that everyone has a right to expect."

9. Though not mutually exclusive, public opinion should be distinguished from popular attitudes because they arise in different milieux. Public opinion manifests itself most clearly in printed texts with wide circulation, whereas popular attitudes can be discerned only from indirect records such as judicial depositions (see chapter 12). For two attempts to expand the Habermasian idea of a bourgeois public sphere in ways that take account of social groups usually omitted from discussions of eighteenth-century opinion, see Arlette Farge, *Dire et mal dire: L'opinion publique au XVIIIe siècle* (1992), and Raymonde Monnier, *L'espace publique démocratique: Essai sur l'opinion à Paris de la Révolution au Directoire* (1994).

10. Hugh Gough, *The Newspaper Press in the French Revolution* (Chicago, 1988), 212, and 118–59 on the vicissitudes of the press during the Directory.

11. For another way to assess the vibrancy of newspaper production in this period, see Hugh Gough, "The Provincial Press in the French Revolution," in *Reshaping France: Town, Country, and Region during the French Revolution,* ed. Alan Forrest and Peter Jones, 193–205 (Manchester, 1991).

12. Jeremy D. Popkin, *Revolutionary News: The Press in France, 1789–1799* (Durham, N.C., 1990), 84–85.

13. For example, the government commissioner for the obscure municipality of Lezoux in the Puy-de-Dôme was aware of at least sixteen local newspaper subscriptions in year IV. Philippe Bourdin, *Des lieux, des mots, les révolutionnaires: Le Puy-de-Dôme entre 1789 et 1799* (Clermont-Ferrand, 1995), 344.

14. Jeremy D. Popkin, *The Right-Wing Press in France, 1792–1800* (Chapel Hill, N.C., 1980), 23.

15. *Chronique de la Sarthe,* 16 brum. VI.

16. *Courrier Républicain,* 26 mess. V.

17. *Journal de Toulouse, ou l'Observateur républican,* an V.

18. This article concluded, "Virtuous writers and readers, hasten to announce that in the end we prefer to massacre leaders of the Jacobins than to cut one anothers' throats" (13 mess V). Cited in Pierre Albret and Gilles Feyel, eds., *La Presse départementale en Révolution (1789–1799): Bibliographie, historique, et critique,* t. 1 (1992), 357.

19. Hugh Gough, "National Politics and the Provincial Jacobin Press during the Directory," *History of European Ideas* 10 (1989): 446.

20. Jeremy D. Popkin, "Les Journaux républicains, 1795–1799," *Revue d'histoire moderne et contemporaine* 31 (1984): 155.

21. Gough, "National Politics," 450.

22. *Courrier Patriotique des départements de l'Isère, des Alpes et du Mont-Blanc,* esp. 14 vend., 8 and 10 frim. VI.

23. *Semaines critiques, ou gestes de l'an cinq,* 19–20.

24. As one correspondent noted, despite the fact that Jean-de-la-Motte (Sarthe) had never had a republican spirit, "your paper is nevertheless generally received there, but it is in order to satisfy an anxious curiosity rather than to absorb the republican principles that it contains" (*L'Ami des lois,* 10 niv. VII). On its relationship to other papers, see the issue of 7 ger. VII.

25. *Chronique de la Sarthe,* 22 and 24 brum. VI; *La Trompette, ou Journal du département du Doubs,* 3 ther. VII to 8 vend. VIII.

26. *Journal de Toulouse,* 12 brum. V.

27. *Chronique de la Sarthe,* 14 vend. and 12 frim. VI.

28. In fact, even histories that ought to pay particular attention to this law pass over it in silence: Robert Charvin, *Justice et politique (évolution de leurs rapports)* (1968); Jean-Pierre Royer, *Histoire de la justice en France de la monarchie absolue à la République* (1995).

29. Quoted in William C. Fuller Jr., *Civil-Military Conflict in Imperial Russia, 1881–1914* (Princeton, 1985), 111.

30. Though it is difficult to judge, these lawyers appear to have done a credible job of upholding defendants' rights. Those unwilling to do so were unlikely to accept the role. Witness the attitude of one citizen D'Haucour, who retracted his agreement to serve as the defense lawyer of Mathurin Evano *dit* Mentor, a chouan captain in the Morbihan: "The more I think about the Montor case, the more I see no possibility of defending him, even of articulating the least thing in his favor. I am fully convinced (1) that he took up arms after the pacification, (2) that he took part in the murderous assault on the guard at Camord, (3) that he was in the front rank of the murderous assault on Pontaugau, (4) that he has been, at different times, part of armed gatherings. . . . The law surely did not intend for an honest man to betray his feelings in order to defend ferocious beings soaked in the blood of others." AG J2, 1e c.d.g. (Rennes), 8 mes. VII (letter of 6 mes.).

31. The laws of 13 and 21 brum. V created permanent *conseils de guerre* and a new military code, respectively. The law of 18 vend. VI created a *conseil de révision,* as well as a second *conseil de guerre* to handle retrials, for each military district, and the law of 27 fruc. VI later allowed both military courts in a military district to conduct first-time trials and retrials when the other court's judgment had been annulled by a *conseil de révision.*

32. The minister of war deplored the practice of commuting sentences and acquitting defendants on the "question of intent," neither of which had a place in military jurisprudence (AG B¹³ 79, MW to generals commanding armies and interior districts, 12 vent. VI). One source of the problem lay in the sentencing procedure of military courts. A two-vote majority from the seven judges was required in order to apply the harshest penalty opined by them. This need for a strong majority often led to the imposition of the more lenient sentence opined by a three-vote minority.

33. Uncertainty on this matter was quickly cleared up; see letters between Gen. Pille and MW in AG B¹³ 72, 14 brum. VI, and B¹³ 73, 5 frim. VI.

34. ADS L 196, 3 mess. VI.

35. Several cases focused specifically on the prison massacres at Aix. ADBR 2R 465*.

36. The chief difference was that a prisoner could challenge the competence of a provostial court by appealing to the local presidial court (Sylvain Soleil, *Le Siège royal de la sénéchaussée et du présidial d'Angers (1551–1790)* [1997], 125, 132–34), whereas it was not until year VIII that civilians could contest the competence of a *conseil de guerre* by appealing to the Court of Cassation. AG B¹³ 59, MJ to presidents of c.d.g., 29 vent. V.

37. Cameron, *Crime and Repression,* 173–74.

38. On the *bande d'Orgères*, see Cobb, *Reactions,* chap. 5, and André Zysberg, "L'affaire d'Orgères: Justice pénale et défense sociale (1790–1800)," in *La Révolution et l'ordre juridique privé: rationalité ou scandale?* ed. M. Pertué (1988): 639–51; on the *bande Chandelier,* see BB¹⁸ 299, and on the *bande Salembier,* see G. Sangnier, *Le brigandage dans le Pas-de-Calais de 1789 à 1815* (Blangermont, 1962), 125–203.

39. AG J2 86, 2ᵉ c.d.g. (Besançon) 3 mess. VII; J2 133 and ADHG L93 10, 1ᵉʳ c.d.g. (Toulouse) 19 fruc. VIII; ADG 2R 703, 2ᵉ c.d.g. (Montpellier) 23 prai. VII.

40. AG J2 102, 1ᵉʳ c.d.g. (Paris), 27 ther. VI, confirmed by the review court, 4 fruc. VI.

41. AG J2 86, 1ᵉʳ c.d.g. (Besançon), 23 vend. VII.

42. AG J2 137, 1ᵉʳ c.d.g. (Perpignan), 13 vent. VII; ADHG 93 L 5; see also the case of dunking a woman at Castelsarrasin (Haute-Garonne), ibid., 25 prai. VIII; ADHG 93 L 2.

43. AG J2 126, d. Le Goff; J2 128, 1ᵉʳ c.d.g. (Rennes), 18 flor. VII.

44. AG J2 112, 2ᵉ c.d.g., 28 frim. VII; ADG 750 and 755, d. 6.

45. This reluctance on the part of army officers to allow civilians to exploit military justice for ulterior ends is more common than generally presumed. For a comparative context, see Fuller, *Civil-Military Conflict,* 111–28.

46. AG J2 130, 2ᵉ c.d.g. (Montpellier), 9 vent. VII; J2 128, 1ᵉʳ c.d.g. (Montpellier), 7 vend. VIII; J2 133, 1ᵉʳ c.d.g. (Toulouse), 14 niv. VIII.

47. See the silly case of dual identities in AG J2 128, 1ᵉʳ c.d.g. (Montpellier), 19 niv. VIII.

48. AG J2 137, 1ᵉʳ c.d.g. 3 niv. VII, annulled by review court, 5 niv. VII; 2ᵉ c.d.g., 23 mess., 6 and 15 ther. VII; ADHG 94L 1, 166–203, esp., jury director at Pamiers to substitut du capitaine-rapporteur, 2ᵉ c.d.g., 28 niv VII; 94 L 5; BB¹⁸ 137, court commissioner, Ariège, to MJ, 22 flor. VII. For other egregious examples of politicized prosecution, see AG J2 133, 1ᵉʳ c.d.g. (Perpignan) 5 vend. VII, and ADG 2R 755, 2ᵉ c.d.g. (Nîmes), 28 ther. VII.

49. See letters from MJ and the public prosecutor of the Hautes-Pyrénées to commander of the Tenth Military District, 3 and 8 vent. VII, in ADHG 93L 6.

50. ADG 93L 6, "Conclusions" presented by *capitaine-rapporteur* Thirent to the 1ᵉʳ c.d.g. (Perpignan) 16 mess. VII. The *capitaine-rapporteur* was the prosecutor, and in this sense the adversary of the accused, but, unlike the plaintiff, he was not his personal adversary; rather, "he was the man of the law, of justice, and of society; it is his duty to make

known [*faire apercevoir*] that which militates in favor of the accused. . . . But *rapporteurs* are essentially different from *accusateurs publics* and are much closer to current *juges d'instructions.*" Chénier, *Guides des tribunaux militaires*, 1:310, 312.

51. BB¹⁸ 164, Avellan, court commissioner of the Hérault to MJ, 26 vent. VII.

52. A systematic study of decisions by military review courts is made difficult by the lack of registers dedicated to this purpose. ADBR 2 R 609* "registre du conseil de révision de Nice ouvert le 1 vendémiaire VIII" is a rare exception.

53. The trial of four notorious brigands from the Gard provides an exemplary list of technical pitfalls. The military review court of the Ninth Military District nullified four death sentences because: (1) the prosecution dossier (*instruction*) did not indicate that the written evidence had been read to the defendants; (2) one deposition was misdated (the clerk wrote year VII two days into year VIII); (3) almost all the judges had been changed between the day the military prosecutor received the case and the day the trial began; (4) various "complex questions" had been posed to the judges when they should have been broken down and posed separately; (5) the court heard the ninety-nine pieces of the procedure on one day but did not render its verdict until the following day. As scrupulous as this review was, it did not change the final outcome. All five defendants were infamous bandits known throughout the region for their daring and cruelty. Guillaume Fontanieu (alias Jambe-de-bois), Antoine Dalverny (alias Le Boiteux), Maurice Dalverny (alias Gely le Borgne), and Philippe Delbos (alias Le Petit Volage) were all condemned to death by the first military court and later executed. AG J2 130, 2ᵉ c.d.g., 3 frim. VIII, conseil de révision, 8 frim. VIII, 1ᵉʳ c.d.g., 28 niv. VIII.

54. The lengthy ordeal of supposed bandits from Lacoste (Haute-Saône) is instructive: ADHS 368 L 13, 30 prai. VII; AG J2 94, 28 brum. and 13 frim. VIII.

55. C 495, d. 205, Directory message to Council of Five Hundred, 16 brum. VII; *Procès-verbal des séances du Conseil des Cinq-cents, brumaire VII*, (séance du 18 brum. VII), 445–8; *Moniteur*, an VII (Council of Five Hundred, 28 brum. VII; Council of Elders, [4] niv. VII).

56. AF III 565, d. 3829, Directory dir., 5 niv. VII.

57. MW reports and Directory messages to the Councils in C 586, d. 173, 7 ther. VII; C 462, d. 35, 18 ther. VII; AF III 617, d. 4348, 7 ther. VII; AF III 624, d. 4429, law of 9 fruc. VII.

58. Four others were condemned to death in absentia. ADBR 2 R 465*, 466*, 467*, 468*, and AG J2 115, 116. Severe paper rot has made the military justice registers at Marseille unreadable beyond April 1800.

59. This is a minimum figure for the period from 1 prai. VI to 30 ther. IX. AG J2 287, 288, and 289 contain most of these judgments, but this collection is incomplete; for example, it does not include the important conviction and execution of Le Métayer (*alias* Rochambeau) and Leroux (*alias* Aimable) at Tours as reported in *L'Ami des lois*, 16 ther. VI.

60. Noms de guerre tell half the story: *Bon-sujet* (Pierre-Etienne Gilbert), *Brise-la-nation* (Pierre Préjean), *Mont-à-l'assault* (Jacques Plot), *Risque-à-tout* (Leroy), *L'ami-du-roi* (François Morillon and Pierre Aubry), *Brise-ville* (Gilles Moreau), *La Grenade* (Michel Hamon), *Passe-par-tout* (François Beauvais), *Mousqueton* (Guillaume Chéron), *Sabre-tout* (Alexandre Goyau), *Bivouac* (René Briand), *La Fosse* (Julien Adde). Of course, there were also less martial nicknames, such as *Matelot* (René Chevalier), *Painchaud* (Louis Lenoir), *Pigeon* (Louis Moreau), *Sans-chagrin* (Jacques Tribondeau), *Joli-coeur* (François Chaligné and Mathurin Guinoiseau), and *Grand-amour* (Noël Chaligné).

61. For example, the trials of Pierre Manceau (alias Martin) and René Freslon (2ᵉ c.d.g., 24 ther. VII and 21 vend. VIII).

62. For example, the trial on 13 flor. VIII by the 2^e c.d.g. (temporarily transferred to Vendôme) of nineteen men, led by a middle-aged mason named Jean-Pierre Chemineau, all charged with holding up the stagecoach on 15 and 26 ger. VIII. *L'Ami des lois*, 24 flor. VIII.

63. AG J2 154, 155, 156, 161.

64. AG J2, 127, 128, 129, 130, ADG 2R 703, 704, 705, 750, 751, 755.

65. The military courts of the 20th Mil. Dis. (headquarters at Périgueux) embodied the opposite extreme. In the year between 1 frim. VII and 1 frim. VIII, these two courts applied the law of 29 niv. VI in five cases, all of housebreaking, which led to fifteen death sentences (one in absentia), two terms in prison, and nine acquittals (one in absentia). AG J2 80.

66. See Brown, "Revolt and Repression," 19–25.

67. In addition to the 186 individuals tried (57 in absentia) for participating in the royalist rebellion of year VII, the military courts of the 10th Mil. Dis. issued verdicts pertaining to 169 individuals (64 in absentia). Of those present at trial, 19 were condemned to death, 2 to long terms in irons, 61 acquitted, and 47 sent to other courts. AG J2 133, 137, ADHG 93 L 1 to 17 (procédures du 1^er c.d.g.); 94L 1 to 10 (procédures du 2^e c.d.g.), *Journal de Toulouse*, F^7 7602.

68. ADHG 93L 1: "Conclusions" before 1^er c.d.g., 22 niv. VIII.

69. Christian Desplat, *La guerre oubliée: Guerres paysannes dans les pyrénées (XII^e–XX^e siècles)* (Biarritz, 1993), 61–68.

70. These courts sentenced fourteen men to death under the nivôse law, but six were condemned in absentia, three had their sentences quashed by a review court, and three were in fact soldiers on active duty. AG J2 86, 1^er c.d.g., 3 vend., 23 vend., 18 frim. VII, 2^e c.d.g., 29 vent. VII; AG J2 94, military review court, 13 frim. VIII; ADHS 368 L 13, 30 prai. VII.

71. AG J2 86, 1^er c.d.g., 21 flor. VII, for an armed attack that rescued four priests on the road from Belfort to Lure on 13 mess. VI (11 defendants, 169 "pièces de procédure"), 2^e c.d.g., 26 flor. VII for an armed attack that rescued two priests and left two civilians dead at Mercy on the road to Besançon on 6 pluv. VII (15 defendants), J2 94, 2^e c.d.g., 16 pluv. VIII, for an armed attack that rescued two priests and wounded four gendarmes at Semmadon on the road to Vesoul, 21 mess. VI (22 defendants, 172 "pièces de procédure"); ADD L 204, jury director at Baume to Doubs, 13 vent. VII; L 7105, correspondence register for 2^e c.d.g. (Besançon).

72. AG J2 86, 1^er c.d.g., 24 flor. VII; 2^e c.d.g., 5 pluv., 21 vent. VII; J2 87, 1^er c.d.g., 20 prai. VIII; J2 94, 2^e c.d.g., 19 prai., 8 ther. VIII.

73. Another 121 did not receive definitive sentences. These calculations are based on figures generated by D. Stevigny and reproduced as a table in Xavier Rousseaux, "Entre droit, état et liberé: La justice pénale dans les départements belges sous le Directoire," in *Du Directoire au Consulat*, ed. Jacques Bernet, Jean-Pierre Jessenne, and Hervé Leuwers, vol. 1, *Le lien politique local dans la grande nation* (Villeneuve d'Ascq, 1999), 263–87.

74. Several civilian courts also prosecuted rebels, many of whom were apparently acquitted on the question of criminal intent. Rousseaux, "Entre droit," 270.

75. At least 350 rebels were transferred to Lille, headquarters of the combined 16th and 1st Mil. Dis., but it is unclear whether they were tried by local military courts or sent back after processing (F^7 7520, d. 28). Furthermore, the military courts at Luxembourg (3rd Mil. Dis.) tried at least 85 individuals accused of participating in the "Klöppelkrieg" that erupted in the department of Forêts at the same time, and condemned 35 of them to death (5 in

absentia) (AG J2 309); the Criminal Court there also tried 78 insurgents and condemned 35 of them to death (G. Trausch cited in Dupont-Bouchat, "Les résistances," 135).

76. The Belgian experience contrasts sharply with the response to peasant insurgency in the southwest less than a year later. Despite almost 5,000 rebels being taken prisoner, the two military courts at Toulouse faced fewer than 150 individuals and condemned and executed only 15 of them (another 59 were judged in absentia). See Brown, "Revolt and Repression."

77. Appeals by certain leaders of the royalist insurrection around Toulouse in 1799 as well as that of Xavier Bertrand, the JP at Valgorge (Ardèche) condemned to death for orchestrating the murder the local cantonal commissioner, both snarled up the prosecution of civilians for months. See BB¹⁸ 473, especially the "Consultation" for the minister.

78. AG J2 31, 2ᵉ c.d.g. (Tours), 9 ger. VII.

79. AG J2 29.

80. ADBR 2R 467*, 29 fruc. VII.

81. C 470, d. 97, MJ to Consuls and Consuls to legislative commission of the Council of Five Hundred, both on 21 frim. VIII.

82. MJ dir., 4 vent. VIII, quoted in ADBR 2R 467*, review court (Marseille), 5 prai. VIII.

83. For example, a man first condemned in absentia was finally tried in person two and a half years after the law had expired. AG J2 283, 2ᵉ c.d.g. (Perigueux), 13 vent. and 10 mess. X.

## PART III: LIBERAL AUTHORITARIANISM

1. Thierry Lentz, *Le Grand Consulat 1799–1804* (1999), 114–15, states the case with brio: "The Constitution of Year VIII changed the rules of politics without modifying either the players or the particulars. That the regime veered toward authority and the concentration of all powers in the hands of the First Consul changes nothing about the matter: the Consulate was a period of the Revolution."

## 9. GUERRILLA WAR AND COUNTER-INSURGENCY

1. D. M. G. Sutherland, "Vendée: Unique or Emblematic?" in *The French Revolution and the Creation of Modern Political Culture*, ed. Keith M. Baker, vol. 4, *The Terror* (Oxford, 1994).

2. Marcel Reinhard, *Le département de la Sarthe sous le régime directoriale* (Saint-Brieuc, 1935), 28–29; Paul Blois, *Paysans de l'Ouest* (Le Mans, 1960), 376; D. M. G. Sutherland, *The Chouans: The Social Origins of Popular Counter-Counter-Revolution in Upper Brittany, 1770–1796* (Oxford, 1982), 52.

3. Blois, *Paysans*, 311–12.

4. Sutherland, *Chouans*, 12; Roger Dupuy, *Les Chouans* (1997), 186, claims 5 percent, but this is calculated on the basis of inflated figures given by boastful rebel leaders.

5. A brief summary cannot do justice to the rich sociological literature on western resistance. In addition to those already cited, key works include: Charles Tilly, *The Vendée* (Cambridge, Mass., 1964); T. J. A. Le Goff and D. M. G. Sutherland, "The Revolution and the Rural Community in Eighteenth-Century Brittany," *Past and Present* 62 (1974): 96–119, and "The Social Origins of Counter-Revolution in Western France," *Past & Present* 99 (1983):

65–87; Timothy Tackett, "The West in France in 1789: The Religious Factor and the Origins of the Counter-Revolution," *Journal of Modern History* 54 (1982): 715–45.

6. Louis de la Sicotière, *Louis de Frotté et les insurrections normandes, 1793–1832*, 2 vols. (1889), 1:427–28.

7. Le Goff and Sutherland, "Rural Community"; Sutherland, *Chouans*, passim, esp. 46–47, 168; Roger Dupuy, *De la Révolution à la chouannerie: Paysans en Bretagne, 1788–1794* (1988), 308–9.

8. See the declaration by chouan leaders in Pierre-Michel Gourlet, *Révolution, Vendée, Chouannerie: Mémoires inédits (1789–1924)*, ed. A. Racineux (Cholet, 1989), 20.

9. See examples of post-Quiberon retribution in AG B⁵ 29 and passim, and Jacques-Philippe Champagne, *Quiberon: La répression et la vengeance* (1989), 140–50; see also Guy-Marie Lenne, *Les réfugiés des guerres de Vendée de 1793 à 1796* (La Crèche, 2003), 82–87.

10. Quoted in Alain Racineux, *Brigands du Roi, 1793–1795: Chouannerie en Haute-Bretagne et Bas-Anjou* (Maulévrier, 1985), 200.

11. See the bitter remarks by the *chef* Gourlet in his *Mémoires*, 130, and the *Mémoires du comte Fortuné Guyon de Rochecotte, rédigés par Beauchamp, sur ses notes et sur les papiers de ses principaux officiers*, (1819), 69. For more on their social relations, see Sutherland, *Chouans*, 167–94.

12. See especially Gustave Cunéo d'Ornano, *Hoche: Sa vie, sa correspondance*, 2 vols. (1892); Louis Dubreuil, *Histoire des insurrections de l'Ouest*, 2 vols. (1929–30); Jean-Clément Martin, *La Vendée et la France* (1987), 276–84.

13. Dupuy, *Chouans*, 121; Charles Girault, *Rochecotte et la chouannerie mancelle* (Laval, 1949), 111.

14. For examples from both sides, see Jean Morvan, *Les chouans de la Mayenne, 1792–1796* (1900), 388; Sicotière, *Frotté*, 1:492.

15. E. Biré, ed., *Mémoires du général d'Andigné*, 2 vols. (1900), 1:333.

16. F⁷ 3065, Coulié to Sarthe, 4 vent. IV.

17. Quoted in Sicotière, *Frotté*, 1:596.

18. ADS L 195, 22 pluv. IV.

19. AG B⁵ 37, 11 flor. IV. See also letters from the commissioners of Mayenne (29 flor.) and Morbihan (11 prai.).

20. Three-quarters of these soldiers were charged with violence, extortion, or coercion. One soldier was condemned to death for rape, 3 received fifteen years in irons, 22 received between one and six years in irons, 45 received prison sentences of six months or less, and 47 were acquitted (ADS L 1743 and 1744).

21. ADS L 1744, 26 ther. IV; Girault, *Rochecotte*, 146–47.

22. Charles-Louis Chassin, *Les pacifications de l'Ouest, 1794–1801*, 3 vols. (1896–99), 2:241–43, 405–6.

23. AG B⁵ 39, 40, and 40ᵇⁱˢ, passim.

24. Chassin, *Pacifications*, 2:240–41; Dubreuil, *Histoire des Insurrections*, 201–2; Reinhard, *Sarthe*, 81–83.

25. Chassin, *Pacifications*, 2:469–580; Hutt, *Counter-Revolution*, 430–79.

26. AG B¹³ 61, Guiot-Durepaire to MW, 23 and 25 vent. V.

27. AG B¹³ 71, Moreau, commissioner of Maine-et-Loire, to MI, 30 vend. VI.

28. AG B¹³ 61, Sarthe to MW, 23 vent. V; Girault, *Rochecotte*, 198–216; *Moniteur, réimp.*, 28:805, declaration of Duverne-Dupresle.

29. Harvey Mitchell, *The Underground War against Revolutionary France* (Oxford,

1965), 205–11; Gustave Gautherot, *Un gentilhomme de grand chemin, le maréchal de Bourmont (1773–1846) d'après ses papiers inédits* (1926), 62–3; Elizabeth Sparrow, *Secret Service: British Agents in France, 1792–1815* (Woodbridge, UK, 1999), 131.

30. For example, this goes unmentioned in the famous debate between Georges Lefebvre and Albert Meynier over the reality of an "anglo-royalist plot." See Georges Lefebvre, *La France sous le Directoire*, 2nd ed., presented by Jean-René Suratteau (1984), 728–36.

31. See the reports and circulars printed by the *Chronique de la Sarthe* during frim. VI.

32. Sicotière, *Frotté*, 2:138–49.

33. ADS L 1914*, 22 frim. VII.

34. AG J2 164, 8 vend. VII; J2 161, d. Ledoze.

35. AG B⁵ 45, 21 and 22 ther., 6 fruc. VI.

36. The original order and the progressive lifting of the "state of siege" can be followed in AG B⁵ 40 and 40ᵇⁱˢ; troop numbers are from Ramsay Weston Phipps, *The Armies of the First French Republic and the Rise of the Marshals of Napoleon I*, 5 vols. (Oxford, 1926–39), 3:56; Chassin, *Pacifications*, 3:1.

37. ADS L 196, Adj.-gen. D'Hallancourt to Sarthe, 12 prai. VI; AG B¹³ 68, Gen. Vimeux to MW, 26 fruc. V; B¹³ 74, MW circular to 12th, 13th, 14th, 22nd Mil. Dis., 24 frim. VI.

38. AF III 148ᵃ d. 696, 1 ger. V; AG B¹³ 65, 1 ther. V; B¹³ 71, 1 brum. VI; AF III 149, d. 700, 1, 1 ger. VI.

39. Georges Six, *Dictionnaire des généraux et amiraux de la Révolution et l'Empire* (1934), 2:558; AG B⁵ 43, Vimeux to MW, 22 flor. VI; B⁵ 43, Baudet-Dubourg, commissioner of Sarthe to MW, 6 mess. VI; ADS L 196, Vimeux to Baudet-Dubourg, 14 and 29 prai, and Adj.-gen. D'Halancourt to Vimeux, 12, 21 and 29 prai. VI; AG B⁵ 44, *Chef de bat.* Chevillet to *Chef de brig.* Ferrey, 29 prai. VI.

40. AG B⁵ 44, Vimeux to MW, 24 prai. and 3 mess. VI.

41. AG B⁵ 45, procès-verbal du gendarme Ducros, 19 ther. VI. For more on the techniques and advantages of using false deserters, see the case of Captain Ballet and Marquis Levieux-Ville alias Henry in AG B⁵ 36, no date (March 1796).

42. On women as informants, see AG B⁵ 48, Vimeux to MW, 27 brum. VII; on the territorial guards, see Chassin, *Pacifications*, 1:54–55, on elite units, see E. Laurain, *Chouans et contre-chouans* (1928; repr., Laval, 1980), 148–92.

43. A. Belin, "Laurent-Prévost," *La Révolution dans la Maine* (1934); BB¹⁸ 734, D3 723; AG B⁵ 41, Vimeux to MW, 17 pluv. VI.

44. Jean Lepart, "Branch d'Or, le contre-chouan ou les exploits d'un agent secret du Directoire (1772–1799)," *Bulletin de la Société d'agriculture, sciences et arts de la Sarthe* 71 (1968): 464–506, and 72 (1970): 363–405.

45. Hoche to Directory, 25 mess. IV in full in Chassin, *Pacifications*, 2:570–74.

46. Reinhard, *Sarthe*, 294–6; AG B¹³ 74, Gen. Cambray to Vimeux, 14 frim. VI, and MP to MW, 15 frim. VI. On repeated escapes from the Évêché prison at Le Mans, see BB¹⁸ 733, DD 5117 and BB¹⁸ 734, D3 901.

47. AG B¹³ 74, Vimeux to MW, 25 frim. VI; B¹³ 75, Vimeux to MW, 8 niv. VI. See also Théodore Lemas, *Le district de Fougères pendant les Guerres de l'Ouest et de la Chouannerie, 1793–1800* (1894; repr., Rennes, 1994), 276–77.

48. BB¹⁸ 734, D3 1388.

49. AG B¹³ 84, MJ to Muller, 25 mess. VI; Chassin, *Pacifications*, 3:136–37, 182–85.

50. For example, F⁷ 7949 S5 781.

51. J2 161, d. Barbier; AG B⁵ 47, Vimeux to MW, 28 vend. VII; ADS L 197, Vimeux to

commissioner of Sarthe, 27 vend. VII, where the six men are described as "the too famous brigands Beissier, Sans-Pareil, Jamois dit Brin-d'Amour, La Marche, Bourny, and Lapin." In a sign of the times, *L'Ami des lois*, 3 brum. VII, reported the incident with cold detachment.

52. J2 161, d. Barbier; AG B[5] 48, "bulletin historique" of the 22nd Mil. Dis., 16–30 brum. VII.

53. C. de la Chanonie, ed., *Mémoires politiques et militaires du général Tercier (1770–1816)* (1891), 296, 330; Chassin, *Pacifications*, 3:166–8; AG B

54. For examples of each: AG J2 287, 2e c.d.g., Tours, 29 frim. VII and J2 161, 2e c.d.g., Rennes, 16 ther. VII.

55. Lemas, *Fougères*, 297–300.

56. Apart from his memoirs and the biography by Girault, see his trial in AG C[18] 5 and *L'Ami des lois*, 20, 21, 22 ther. VI.

57. Chanonie, *Mémoires*, 285–90.

58. AG B[5] 44 to 48 passim, quotation from the "bulletin historique" of the 22nd Mil. Dis., 16–30 brum. VII. "In the 22nd Mil. Dis. . . . mobile columns have arrested more than 150 individuals in the last while and notably principal leaders who played a famous role in the chouan war." AG B[13] 85, WM to Directory, 5 fruc. VII.

59. See chapter 7. In fact, army commanders were illegally extending these laws: for example, Moulin imposed a fine of 10,000 francs on Bouère and collected it "militairily" before asking the Civil Court of Mayenne to apply the law of 10 vend. IV. AF III 150[b], d. 705, 72–73.

60. AG B[5] 50, MW to commander, Army of England, 10 pluv. VII.

61. Chassin, *Pacifications*, 3:274–77; Reinhard, *Sarthe*, 578–79.

62. There were six ministers of police and four ministers of war in the two years between Fructidor and Brumaire.

63. Duval to Moulin, 1 vent. VII, quoted in Chassin, *Pacifications*, 3:272; AG B[5] 52, MW to Moulin, 23 vent. VII, and Moulin to MW, 27 vent. VII.

64. AG B[13] 96, MW to commanders of 12th, 13th, 14th, 22nd Mil. Dis., 27 vent. VII.

65. AG B[13] 99, bulletin de la police générale, 27 flor. VI; B[13] 103, MW to MP, 10 ther. VII (on Belgium as precedent); Reinhard, *Sarthe*, 591–95; Robert Anchel, "La répression de la chouannerie dans l'Eure en l'an VII et en l'an VIII," *La Révolution française* 41 (1901): 516–32.

66. *Opinion de Berlier, sur le projet de responsabilité à appliquer aux cas de troubles civils*, Conseil des Cinq-Cents, séance du 21 mess. an 7.

67. Officials in the southwest chafed under the law's hierarchy of enemies, arguing that most of the truly dangerous men and rebel leaders were "ci-devant roturiers" and not former nobles, who were "in general much less turbulent." AG B[13] 105, president and commissioner of Gers to MW, 28 ther. VII.

68. F[7] 3820, MP to Directory, 11 vend. VIII.

69. For details on applying the law of hostages, see Howard G. Brown, "Echoes of the Terror," *Historical Reflections/Réflexions Historiques* 29 (2003): 528–58, esp. 544–49.

70. Quoted in Eric-Marie Guyot, *Vendéens et chouans contre Bonaparte (1799–1814)* (1990), 11–12.

71. Victor Pierre, *La déportation ecclésiastique sous le Directoire* (1896), passim. Reinhard, *Sarthe*, 560–68; Gaugain, *Mayenne*, 4:438, 485–86.

72. Howard G. Brown, *War, Revolution, and the Bureaucratic State: Politics and Army Administration in France, 1791–99* (Oxford, 1995), 245–47.

73. The withdrawal of troops can be followed in AG B[12]* 37, 16 ger. to 14 mess. VII; B[13] 103, MW to Directory, 8 and 16 ther. VII; B[13] 103, Bureau du mouvement des troupes, 24 mess. VII.

74. AG B[5] 57, 1 fruc. VII.

75. F[7] 3820, bulletins décadaires de la police générale, fruc. VII; AG B[5] 61 passim. Courts-martial at Tours revealed that recruits received a sign-up bonus of 300 *livres* and regular pay of 30 *sols* a day. J2 288, trial of Pierre Manceau (alias Martin) (2ᵉ c.d.g., 24 ther. VII); J2 289, trial of René Freslon (2ᵉ c.d.g., 21 vend. VIII).

76. Lepart, "Branche d'Or," 363–75; Gautherot, *Bourmont*, 19, 79–93; Chanonie, *Mémoires de Tercier*, 315–16; *Conspiration Anglaise* (an IX), notes kept by Hyde de Neuville, indicate a payment of 16,000 pounds to Bourmont.

77. AG B[13] 134, "Historique de la troisième décade [niv. VII]," 14th Mil. Dis. (misfiled). See also, *Souvenirs de la Comtesse de la Bouëre: La guerre de la Vendée, 1793–1796, mémoires inédits*, 3rd ed. (1907), 233.

78. On the rebel code of military justice, see AG B[5] 69, "copies des pièces trouvées sur Maigniet, chef des brigands" sent by Gen. Tilly to MW, 9 vent. IX; the various proclamations are cited in Chassin, *Pacifications*, 3:352–55, 369–71.

79. Though most historians give the figure of 3,000 chouans, Bourmont wrote the night before that he had 2,180 ready for the attack, and the JP at Vendôme corrected contemporary exaggerations and set the figure at 1,800. Gautherot, *Bourmont*, 93; AG B[13] 111, bulletin de la police générale, 28 vend. VIII.

80. Robert Triger, *La prise du Mans par les chouans le 15 octobre 1799* (Mamers, 1899); Chanonie, *Mémoires de Tercier*, 328–37; "Relation historique de la prise du Mans par les Chouans le 15 octobre 1799 ou 23 vendémiaire an 8," mss. de la Crochardière, tome III. Bibliothèque du Mans, 21A; Chassin, *Pacifications*, 3:383–87; AG B[13] 111, bulletins de la police générale, 1 and 3 brum. VIII (on booty).

81. Reinhard, *Sarthe*, 618; Chassin, *Pacifications*, 3:388–429; Sicotière, *Frotté*, 2:344–58.

82. AG B[13] 111, MW to Directory, 28 vend. VIII; B[13] 113, MW to Consuls, 26 brum. VII.

83. AG X[k] 6, légions de l'ouest; Reinhard, *Sarthe*, 581–83; Louis Benaerts, *Le régime consulaire en Bretagne: Le département d'Ille-et-Vilaine durant le Consulat* (1914), 70–71.

84. Those in the former *Vendée militaire* were in favor of peace; those in areas of intense *chouannerie*, such as Maine, Lower Normandy, and the Morbihan, preferred to fight on.

85. Paul Robiquet, "Un sous-pacificateur de la Vendée: Le général d'Hédouville," *Revue historique* 78 (1902): 288–319, 298–99.

86. Sicotière, *Frotté*, 2:389–90.

87. The law of 26 niv. VIII (16 Jan. 1800) suspended the Constitution throughout the 12th, 13th, 14th, and 22nd Mil. Dis. (a total of sixteen departments), but a Consular directive limited the law to the 13th, that is, the four departments of Brittany (Duvergier, *Collection des lois*, 12:59–60). On the state of siege, see AG B[5] 69 passim.

88. These various directives are in Chassin, *Pacifications*, 3:512–13, 523–24, 545–47.

89. Robiquet, "Hédouville," 304–11; Sicotière, *Frotté*, 380–523; Dubreuil, *Histoire des insurrections*, 2:264–75; Benaerts, *Régime consulaire en Bretagne*, 84–94.

90. On the pacification from the republican perspective, see Chassin, *Pacifications*, 3:545–644, and from the rebel perspective, see Gautherot, *Bourmont*, 110–14, and Guyot, *Vendéens et Chouans*, 28–58.

91. AG B[5] 68–69 passim; J2 161; Chassin, *Pacifications*, 3:624–44.

10. A CYCLE OF VIOLENCE IN THE SOUTH

1. Colin Lucas, "Themes in Southern Violence after Thermidor," in *Beyond the Terror: Essays in French Regional and Social History, 1794–1815,* ed. Gwynne Lewis and Colin Lucas (Cambridge, UK, 1983), 155–56; Warren Wilson, "Les journées populaires et la violence collective dans le Vaucluse rural après Thermidor," *Canadian Journal of History* 28 (1993): 41–57, 56.

2. In his *Reactions to the French Revolution* (London, 1972), 62, Richard Cobb noted that his earlier *Police and the People: French Popular Protest, 1789–1820* (Oxford, 1970) had drawn too stark a contrast between the brigandage of the north and the political murders of the south.

3. Gignac had one of the more prominent Jacobin clubs in the Hérault, numbering over 250 in 1792, but it was at the limits of "political sociability" in the region: Jean-François Dubost, "Le réseau des sociétés politiques dans le département de l'Hérault pendant la Révolution française (1789–1795), *AHRF,* no. 278 (1989): 374–411. On the earlier absence of traumatic violence, see BB[18] 364, Avellan, court commissioner of the Hérault to MJ, 2 flor. VII, and Christopher Johnson, "Revolution, Enterprise, Survival," 56–57, an unpublished manuscript that he generously sent to me. On the woolens industry in late 1797, see also F[1c] III Hérault 9, commissioner of Hérault to MI, 11 vend. VI.

4. On the Ponsys, see ADH L 8777, Rochier, commissioner of Gignac to commissioner of the Hérault, 7 prai. and 27 ther. V, and ADH L 6374*, 12 pluv. VII.

5. ADH L 5706, registre du comité de surveillance de Gignac, 30 brum., 3 and 4 prai. II.

6. ADH 8777, exchange between commissioners of Hérault and Gignac, 2 and 7 prai. V.

7. Pierre Rouch had recently moved into the town's principal industry, the manufacture of woolens, thanks to the abolition of guilds and the surge in demand created by army contracts. These changes allowed both skilled artisans from inside the industry and respectable bourgeois from outside it to set up as small-scale producers. However, during the Directory, the least-efficient producers gradually folded when large military supply companies replaced the government as the principal source of contracts. Christopher H. Johnson, "Artisans vs. Fabricants: Urban Protoindustrialization and the Evolution of Work Culture in Lodève and Bédarieux, 1740–1830," *Mélanges de l'école française de Rome: Moyen Age-Temps Modernes* 99 (1987): 1047–84, esp. 1066–80.

8. The large expedition resulted from a previous excursion to Aniane by a half-dozen men armed with guns but no arrest warrant. This led to a shoot-out that injured Joseph Ponsy and landed Olivier Teisserenc and two companions from Montpellier in jail for a short time. Each side filed a formal complaint: ADH L 7240, 15 and 16 frim. V.

9. ADH L 6802, Rouch père and Teisserenc père to public prosecutor, 25 and 21 fruc. IV, respectively.

10. ADH L 6756*, 27 flor. V; ADH L 8129, interrogation of J. Ponsy, 6 mess. IX; ADH L 8130. Catherine, the sister of Gabriel Connes, had exchanged insults and rock blows with Barthélemy Teisserenc and then initiated a prosecution against him for assault. In a typical diagnosis that would keep the possible conviction for the gunshot to a misdemeanor, the local health officer reported that her wound would heal in thirty-eight days—more than forty days would have made it felony assault. ADH L 8131.

11. ADH L 7222, Duran, jury director at Lodève, to public prosecutor, 23 pluv. V; ADH L 6756*, 27 pluv. V.

12. Antoine Vergnettes, a former gendarme, was the first to arrive and the first to conform to Ponsy's demands; the others included François Messier, Pierre and Barthélemy Rouch, and Jean Ponsy. One witness later claimed that Joseph Ponsy bragged of putting his gun into Gastard's mouth before firing.

13. ADH L 8128 and 8129 hold depositions on the events of 4–5 ger. V from 199 witnesses.

14. He was acquitted of an "offense against personal security": ADH L 6756*, 27 flor. V.

15. BB¹⁸ 364, Avellan, court commissioner of Hérault, to MJ, 2 flor. VII.

16. F⁷ 7447, B⁵ 8421, "Tableau des délits et excès commis dans la commune de Gignac . . ." and Hérault to MP, 7 vend. VII; *L'Ami des lois*, 6 mess. VI.

17. When two of them, Barthélemy and a cousin known as Jeannot, were arrested for a stabbing at the market at Le Pouget, hundreds of people from Gignac rallied to mount a rescue. The rapid arrival of regular troops from Montpellier dispersed the crowd only to have the jury director at Lodève later release them. BB¹⁸ 364, Avellan to MJ, 2 flor. VII.

18. ADH L 5706 and 5707, registers of the *comité révolutionnaire*; ADH L 773, election results for year VI; ADH 8777, list of those disarmed, 1 brum. VI.

19. ADH L 7293, deposition by Joseph Pommier for the prosecution of Jean Ponsy on charges of trying to restore the monarchy.

20. ADG 2R 1176, JP at Gignac to president of the extraordinary military commission of the Ninth Mil. Dis., 5 pluv. IX. On 12 pluv. VI, the Criminal Court of the Hérault convicted Jeannot Ponsy and sentenced him to deportation for provoking the restoration of monarchy by leading farandoles through the streets of Gignac chanting, "Vive les royalistes! Vive le roi! Merde à la république! A bas les républicains!" He was deported on the *Bayonnaise* and died at Sinnamary, Guyana, on 27 November 1798. ADH L 6731*, 12 pluv. VI; L 7293; Victor Pierre, *La Terreur sous le Directoire* (1887), 432.

21. AF III 273, 181, "Adresse des républicains de la commune de Gignac réunis en Cercle constitutionnel," 5 pluv. an VI; F⁷ 7447, B⁵ 8421, Montels to MJ, 25 prai. VI.

22. F⁷ 7559, d. 36, commissioner of the Hérault to MP, 10 pluv. VIII.

23. In addition to the sources above, see W. D. Edmonds, *Jacobinism and the Revolt of Lyon, 1789–1793* (Oxford, 1990), 139–40, 171; Pierre Caron, *La Première Terreur (1792): Les missions du Conseil Exécutif Provisoire de la commune de Paris* (1950), 197; and Gérard Cholvy, *Le Languedoc et le Roussillon* (Montpellier, 1982), 406, who also notes that later, when mayor of Gignac, Laussel "s'élevera avec violence contre le Concordat."

24. ADH L 2473, Avellan, court commissioner of Hérault, to Rey, commissioner of Hérault, 28 ger. VII.

25. ADH L 7422.

26. ADH 8777, especially Hérault dir. of 23 prai. VI; F⁷ 7447, MP report to Directory, early ther. VI.

27. F⁷ 7559, d. 36, commissioner of Hérault to MP, 5 prai. VII; F⁷ 7521, d. 58, especially MP to Gignac, 17 pluv. VII. Despite this support, department officials later had to reprimand municipal officials at Gignac for turning an order to conduct weapons searches into an opportunity to billet troops on households simply suspected of concealing weapons. ADH L 969, Benoit, commandant de la place de Gignac, to Hérault, 4 vend. VIII, with marginalia.

28. ADH L 8130, Faur, jury director at Lodève, to public prosecutor, 19 vend. VII.

29. ADH L 6758*, 22 niv., 26 niv., and 12 pluv. VII.

30. Most of Laussel's warrants were for forming a seditious gathering intended to rescue two of the Ponsy brothers following their arrest at Le Pouget in early year VI.

31. BB$^{18}$ 364, Avellan, court commissioner of Hérault to MJ, 2 flor. VII; F$^7$ 7559, d. 36.

32. Cf. Bernard Gainot, *1799, un nouveau Jacobinisme?: La démocratie représentative, une alternative à brumaire* (2001), 308–17, where the "néo-Jacobins" of Gignac receive careful analysis, but their intolerance goes unmentioned.

33. AG B$^{13}$ 102, procès-verbal de la gendarmerie, 24 mess. VII; ADG 2 R 705.

34. ADH 2 U2 21, procès-verbal de la gendarmerie, 22 pluv. IX; 7 U2 1, 26 flor. X.

35. F$^7$ 7734, d.26, prefect of Aveyron to MP, 13 flor. VIII; procès-verbal des agents et adjoint municipal de Gignac, 10 flor. VIII; ADG 2R 1173, d. Goutes, who named himself, four Ponsys, Euzet (father and son), Querelles, Michel Hubac (alias le Comte d'Étain), Louis Vallard, Vernières, Benoit, and twenty others he did not know, including the leader.

36. AG B$^{13}$ 126, MF to MW, 22 mess. VIII, and B$^{13}$ 123, Gen. Gouvion to MW, 19 flor. VIII.

37. ADH 2 U2 21, procès-verbal de la gendarmerie and procès-verbal de la commune de Gignac, 3 mess. VIII; F$^7$ 7734, d. 26, prefect of Hérault to MP, 4 mess. VIII.

38. ADH 7 U$^2$ 1*, 26 flor. X.

39. F$^7$ 3678$^3$. The department's instructions of 3 ther. VII constitute a model of military precision; ADG 2R 705, procedures for the c.d.g.

40. BB$^{18}$ 364, court commissioner of Hérault to MJ, 18 vent. VIII. Note that this is Gabriel-Nicolas Avellan, not Michel Avellan, who was briefly commissioner at Gignac in year VII.

41. BB$^{18}$ 365, D4 4987, Belmond, court commissioner of Hérault, to MJ with reply, 8 brum. and 5 niv. IX, respectively.

42. Solier's reputation as a notorious brigand-priest and the interpretive tradition it has created are explored in Howard G. Brown, "An Unmasked Man in a *Milieu de Mémoire:* The Abbé Solier as Sans-Peur the Brigand-Priest," *Historical Reflections/Réflexions Historiques* 26 (2000): 1–30. This article apparently escaped the attention of Valérie Sottocasa, whose recent *Mémoires affrontées: Protestants et catholiques face à la Révolution dans les montagnes de Languedoc* (Rennes, 2004), 90–92, 181–87, replicates older views of Solier but has the merit of also situating him in the context of long-standing religious animosities in the Cévennes.

43. BB$^{18}$ 365 passim.

44. Philippe Sénart, "La Montagne blanche ou une Vendée cévenole," *Revue des deux mondes* (1979): 103–12, 306–19; Daniel Robert, *Les Églises réformés en France (1800–1830)* (1961), 519–20; André Encrevé, *Protestants français au milieu du XIX$^e$ siècle: Les réformés de 1848 à 1870* (Geneva, 1986), 416–17.

45. Cf. Lucas, "Themes in Southern Violence," and William Beik, *Urban Protest in Seventeenth-Century France: The Culture of Retribution* (Cambridge, UK, 1997).

46. ADH L 7431, deposition by Vernede, 29 fruc. VI.

47. ADH L 969, court commissioner to commissioner of Hérault, 4 jr. co. VII; see also F$^7$ 7979, Nogaret, prefect of Hérault, to MP, 27 pluv. X, who writes of "misérables" who had been enrolled in the brigand band "by force and in hope of a salary."

48. ADH 2 U$^2$ 21, interrogation of Pierre Correge by judge Clémont, 10 prai. IX.

49. BB$^{18}$ 365, fifteen prisoners at Montpellier to MJ, 22 pluv. VIII.

50. ADG 2R 705, 9 ther. VIII. The eldest Peyrottes escaped shortly after his capture and could be sentenced only in absentia (ADH L 970, commissioner of St-Jean-de-Fos to commissioner of Hérault, 5 brum. VIII). For the criminal court cases, see ADH L 6735* (22 and 26 niv. VII), L 6736* (21 ger. VII), L 6737* (3 brum. VIII). Despite witnesses clearly identify-

ing Reboul and Vergnettes—who was wearing his uniform and waving a sword—among those pursuing Gastard out of Lodève, both men were acquitted at this third trial, thereby purging their previous convictions in absentia.

51. ADH L 6759*, 3 brum. VIII; L 7504, judgment recommencing prosecution, 3 brum. IX.

52. ADH L 969, to president of Hérault, 4 fruc. VII.

53. AG B$^{13}$ 127, Gouvion to MW, 27 ther. VIII; F$^7$ 7734, d.26, Prefect Nogaret to MP, 26 ther. VIII, and Gouvion to MP, 27 ther. VIII.

54. The following list names the ten principal accused based on the number of witness depositions against each of them: Pierre Rouch père (35); Joseph Ponsy (29); Pierre Rouch fils (22); Rouch *cadet* (17); Louis Reboul (16); André Merle, former lieutenant in the gendarmerie (14); Nougaret (alias Lou Bastard), livestock trader (13); François Messier, hatmaker (13); Ponsy *cadet* (11); and Martin Arnavielle, landowner at Aniane (9). ADH L 8129, three deposition notebooks with summary statement.

55. ADG 2R 1176, procedure against Martin Arnavielle.

56. F$^7$ 7734, d.26, Prefect Nogaret to MP, 15 brum. IX

57. F$^7$ 7734, d.26, Prefect Nogaret to MP, 25 brum. IX; ADG 2R 1173, d. Pierre Rigal; BB$^{18}$ 366, D4 6044, Belmond, court commissioner of Hérault, to MJ, 3 frim. IX, and BB$^{18}$ 366, D4 9638, Astruc to MJ, 16 ther. IX. Even in prison, the names Rouch and Ponsy served to intimidate other malefactors. ADG 2 R 1176, statement by Jean Guigou, 1 vent. IX.

58. BB$^{18}$ 365, D4 4987, jury director at Lodève quoted by Belmond, court commissioner of Hérault, to MJ, 15 pluv. IX.

59. AG B$^{13}$ 128, Gouvion to MW, 3 jr. co. VIII.

60. The administrative and judicial reorganizations undertaken in 1800 provoked some turnover, but firm republicans remained in control of the local levers of power.

61. F$^7$ 7714, d. 97, Gentile, capt. of the gendarmerie, to commissioner of Gard, early VIII.

62. BB$^{18}$ 365 passim; ADH L 970.

63. AG B$^{13}$ 122, letters of 22, 29, and 30 ger. VIII. The shortage of troops even prevented Gouvion from putting Gignac under a state of siege in response to the spectacular robbery from the town hall. B$^{13}$ 123, 11 flor. VIII.

64. AG B$^{13}$ 124, MW dir., 23 flor. VIII; prefect of Hérault to MW, 26 flor. VIII; and Gouvion to MW, 5 prai. VIII.

65. Witness the confrontation between the gendarmerie and brigands at La Roque, F$^7$ 7812, d. 45, prefect of Hérault to MP, 28 brum. IX.

66. AG B$^{13}$ 128, procès-verbal de la gendarmerie, 28 fruc. VIII, and prefect of Aveyron to MW, 3 jr. co. VIII.

67. AG B$^{13}$ 131, Consuls dir., 1 niv. IX, and Gouvion to MW, 7 niv. IX.

68. AG J2 132, 26 niv. IX; ADG 2R 1173.

69. AG J2 132, verdicts of 1 to 9 pluv. IX.

70. ADG 2R 1172 and 2R 1173.

71. Quoted in Bruno Ginisty, "De la désertion au brigandage sous la Révolution et l'Empire," in *Brigands en Rouergue, XI$^e$–XX$^e$ siècle* (Rodez, 1993), 139.

72. ADG 2R 1176 d. Baumel; AG J2 132, 3 vent. IX. There was a continual fear of reprisals. Two days earlier, the military commission had condemned to death Louis Lacoste, a three-time deserter who threatened to murder anyone in his village who testified against him; even his own father feared for his life and implored the gendarmerie not to release his son. ADG 2R 1173.

73. AG J2 132, 19 vent. VII; ADG 2R 1176; Brown, "Unmasked Man."

74. It is worth noting, however, that he did not know the names of many other participants, including that of the main organizer. ADG 2R 1173, d. Goutes, "aveux fait le 30 nivôse an IX par Bascou au citoyens Gibal et Bouillon" and 2R 792, verdicts of 22 vent. and 1 ger. IX.

75. ADG 2R 792 and AG J2 132, verdicts of 1 and 2 ger., 22 ger., and 9 flor. IX. François Lapeyre, a saddler from Gignac, and Jean Pioch, a flax spinner from Lodève, were executed at Montpellier. AG B¹³ 135, "bulletin historique" of the 9th Mil. Dis., 1–15 ger. IX.

76. AG B¹³ 132, prefect of Aveyron to MW, 5 pluv. IX. Fouché insisted that everyone already arrested for brigandage, but not yet the subject of criminal prosecution, be sent before the commission. ADG 2R 1174, MP to Gouvion, 24 niv. IX.

77. F⁷ 7812, d. 45, esp. the procès-verbal de la gendarmerie, 26 vent. IX.

78. F⁷ 3251, secret police funds given the prefect of the Hérault, 8 flor. VIII–9 prai. X.

79. Courts-martial of 7 and 9 ther. VIII in ADG 2R 705.

80. Gen. Gouvion received 6,000 francs "to meet the expenses of espionage and bonuses accorded to soldiers who would arrest or kill bandits captured arms in hand." F⁷ 3251, Gouvion to MP, 25 niv. IX.

81. Arlette Farge, *Fragile Lives: Violence, Power, and Solidarity in Eighteenth-Century Paris*, trans. C. Shelton (Cambridge, Mass., 1993); David Garrioch, "The People of Paris and their Police in the Eighteenth Century: Reflections on the Introduction of a 'Modern Police Force,'" *European History Quarterly* 24 (1994): 511–35.

82. ADH 2 U2 269; F⁷ 7949, S5 660; BB²¹ 157.

83. Of course, this does not rule out possible links to later acts of violence. For a long-delayed flare-up, see Peter McPhee, *Revolution and Environment in Southern France, 1780–1830: Peasants, Lords, and Murder in the Corbières* (Oxford, 1999).

## 11. CONSULAR CRACKDOWN

1. BB¹⁸ 775, MJ to Consuls, n.d., and 20 flor. X (which includes a draft law to replace that of 29 niv. VI long after it expired and a year after the creation of Special Tribunals!); *L'Ami des lois*, 12 niv. VIII.

2. AG B¹³ 120, 16 vent. VIII.

3. See the many regional treatments of this issue in Jean-Pierre Jessenne, ed., *Du Directoire au Consulat*, vol. 3: *Brumaire dans l'histoire du lien politique et de l'état-nation* (Rouen, 2001).

4. Jean Bourdon, *La réforme judiciaire de l'an VIII*, 2 vols. (1941), 2:231, 382.

5. I have categorized these as "petty theft" in previous calculations.

6. Duvergier, *Collection des lois*, 12:32–34. At the same time as the penalties for some types of theft were downgraded, the penalties for other types of theft were increased. A dozen varieties of theft either by individuals who had been entrusted with goods or duties, or from lodging houses or enclosures attached to a dwelling, were henceforth all punished twice as harshly as in the Penal Code of 1791. But this did not change their status; they were already felonies.

7. During the First Directory, the criminal courts of Haute-Garonne, Hérault, Haute-Saône, and Sarthe had pronounced verdicts on 679 defendants present at trial and charged with more than "petty theft." The number jumped to 788 such defendants during the Second Directory, only to fall to 415 during years IX and X. See Robert Allen, "The Criminal

Courts of the Côte-d'Or, 1792–1811" (Ph.D. diss., Columbia University, 1991), 413–14; Roger Maltby, "Crime and the Local Community in France: The Department of the Drôme, 1770–1820" (D.Phil. thesis, Oxford University, 1980); and René Demogue, "Un tribunal criminel sous la Révolution: Le tribunal criminel de la Marne (1792-an IX)," *Revue de Champagne* 4, no. 18 (1911): 161–177; no. 19 (1911): 208–40; 5. no. 23 (1912): 321–36, esp. 236, 325–26. By including data from seven departments, we learn that there were about as many prosecutions before criminal courts in year X as in year IX.

8. Years

| Years | Acquittals (%) | Misdemeanor Penalties (%) | Felony Convictions (%) |
|---|---|---|---|
| IV + V | 43 | 7 | 50 |
| VI + VII | 39 | 13 | 48 |
| IX + X | 46 | 10 | 44 |

9. ADH L 6760*, 22 brum. X.

10. The Court of Cassation played an important role throughout the case, first by transferring prosecution from the jury director at Castres to the one at Gaillac (15 brum. VI), then by transferring the trial from the Tarn to the Haute-Garonne (16 mess. VI), later to the Aude (19 ther. VI) on the basis of an appeal from the accused, and yet later, after the Directory called for reconsideration, back to the Haute-Garonne (19 fruc. VI). In the meantime, twelve defendants had escaped from prison at Albi. BB[18] 684; F[7] 7296; ADHG 7L 201 U 2, 1 ger. VII.

11. These included two former members of the municipality of Castres and one former member of the department administration. Archives Départementales de l'Aude, 10 L 1194, 1 mess. VIII (material kindly sent to me by Director Sylvie Caucanas).

12. Persons prosecuted by four criminal courts for interpersonal violence: years IV and V—198 (154 present, 44 absent); years VI and VII—438 (294 present, 144 absent); years IX and X—231 (178 present, 53 absent).

13. ADHS 368 L 14, 1 ther. IX.

14. AG B[13] 120, First Consul dir., 22 vent. VIII. Brune created a military commission at Hennebont in the Morbihan on 6 flor. VIII (26 April 1800), and Bonaparte authorized General Garnier to create a military commission in the Alpes-Maritimes on 14 prai. VIII (3 June 1800). Émile Sageret, *Le Morbihan et la chouannerie morbihannaise sous le Consulat,* 4 vols. (1911–17), 2:53 Michel Iafélice, *Barbets! Les résistances à la domination française dans le pays niçois (1792–1814)* (Nice, 1996), 176, 190.

15. AG B[13] 120, First Consul dir. (not to be published).

16. On patterns of violence in Provence, see the articles by Colin Lucas and Gwynne Lewis in their collection *Beyond the Terror.*

17. AG B[13] 120, MP to MW, 16 vent. VIII. For details, see Abbé Joseph-Marie Maurel, *Le brigandage dans les Basses-Alpes, particulièrement depuis l'an VI jusque'à l'an X* (Marseille, 1899).

18. AG B[13] 109, MW to Directory, 8 vend. VIII; Roger Maltby, "Le brigandage dans la Drôme, 1795–1803," *Bulletin de la société d'archéologie et de statistique de la Drôme* 79 (1973): 116–34. The pockets of a noble killed in a skirmish near Largentière contained orders for the coordinated uprising. They were headed "throne and altar, 19 October 1799," and signed "Ducrot de Tauriers, captain of the 1st company of grenadiers of the coalition, commanding in the absence of senior leaders, the royal troops of the provinces of Languedoc, Cévennes, Haut and Bas Vivarais." The comte de Brison fils had also been designated as a regional commander of the insurrection. Tauriers and Brison had been the main military

leaders of first *Camp de Jalès* in 1790. AG B¹³ 112, Nivet to Gen. Carteaux, 4 brum. VIII; B¹³ 118, MP to MW, 15 pluv. VIII; Charles Jolivet, *Les Chouans du Vivarais: Essai sur l'agitation contre-révolutionnaire dans l'Ardèche sous le Directoire* (Lyon, 1930), 92–98.

19. Jolivet, *Chouans du Vivarais*, 80–90; M. Riou, "Les chouans du Tanargue: De la clandestinité à la guerre populaire (1795–1799)," *Revue du Vivarais*, special issue (1979), 191–224; AG B¹³ 88, Petit-Guillaume to MW, 17 brum. VII.

20. AG B¹³ 86, Directory dir., 4 vend. VII; B¹³ 87, Petit-Guillaume to MW, 16 vend. VII.

21. AG B¹³ 97, Malye to MW, 11 flor VII; B¹³ 110, Ardèche to MW, 22 vend. VIII; B¹³ 110, Ardèche to MP, 28 vend VIII; Nivet to Carteaux, 4 brum. VIII; B¹³ 119, Petit-Guillaume to MW, 25 pluv. VIII; B¹³ 91, JP report of 21 niv. VII.

22. AG B¹³ 117, Adj.-gen. Nivet to MW, 1 pluv. VIII.

23. Petit-Guillaume replaced Carteaux on 30 frim. VIII (21 Dec. 1799) (AG B¹³ 115, "bulletin historique" of 9th Mil. Dis., 15–30 frim. VIII); B¹³ 119, Petit-Guillaume to MW, 25 pluv. VIII, and Ardèche to MI, 5 vent. VIII; B¹³ 121, MI to MW, 6 ger., commissioner of Ardèche to Ardèche, 4 ger. VIII.

24. Maltby, "Brigandage dans la Drôme," 122–24.

25. AG B¹³ 120, Captain Déoux to Adj.-gen. Lecourt-Villière, 15 vent. VIII. The dead officers were a *chef de brigade, chef de bataillon,* captain, and commander of the National Guard.

26. AG B¹³ 121, Férino to MJ, 26 ger. VIII (misfiled together with his proclamation of 9 ger. VIII); B¹³ 122, Férino to MP, 17 ger. VIII.

27. On Les Vans (30 vent. VIII): AG B¹³ 121, Petit-Guillaume to MW, 5 ger., and Gouvion to MW 14 ger. VIII; on Joyeuse (3 ther. VIII): B¹³ 126, Gen. Ruby to Gouvion, 4 ther. VIII.

28. AG B¹³ 124, MW to MI and MW to Férino, 8 prai. VIII; B¹³ 125, Férino to MW, 25 prai. VIII

29. F⁷ 7724, d. 39, summary reports for prai. and mess. VIII.

30. As Férino noted, order could never be restored as long as residents faced the cruel alternative of being "either pillaged by brigands or scoured by troops"; therefore, he seized tax receipts and had prefects impose forced loans to sustain his operations (AG B¹³ 122, Férino to MW, 29 ger. VIII; F⁷ 7714, d. 98, Ardèche dir., 15 flor. VIII; B¹³ 126, Férino to MW (lui seul), 19 mess. VIII). AG B¹³ 127, Férino to MW, 10 fruc. VIII, gives the following troop distribution: Vaucluse—840, Drôme—229, Ardèche—657, Basses-Alpes—510, total—2,236; many of these were soon sent to Italy.

31. On brigandage in the Midi in 1800, see F⁷ 7724, prefect of Vaucluse to MI, 30 ger. VIII, and AG B¹³ 124, Gen. Milhaud to Férino, 4 prai. VIII.

32. Férino circular to jury directors, 10 mess. VIII, in Maurel, *Brigandage*, 180–81.

33. For the many preparatory discussions and a poster of the amnesty, see F⁹ 39ᵃ, d. "Opérations du Général Férino," and AG B¹³ 121–27 passim, especially Fouché's letters to Carnot on 17 mess. and 9 ther. VIII.

34. F⁷ 7499, B⁶ 2011.

35. AF IV 1154, prefect of Ardèche to MW, 16 ther. VII; AG B¹³ 139, prefect of Ardèche to MW, 26 ther. VIII (misfiled); B¹³ 140, Férino to MW, 15 fruc. VIII (misfiled).

36. Félix Rocquain, *L'état de la France au 18 Brumaire* (1874), 5–6.

37. Incomplete evidence rules out greater precision. Known verdicts run from 21 ger. VIII to 30 frim. IX, but the commission continued to operate for another month. F⁷ 7724, d. 39, has six monthly tables but is missing four monthly tables. AG J2 112 helps to fill lacunae with individual verdicts but contains none for niv. IX. Known verdicts pertain to 123 indi-

viduals: 63 sentenced to death, 46 acquitted, 4 sent to criminal courts, 10 "plus amplement informé" and not the subject of a definitive verdict (29 other individuals who received this same preliminary verdict have been tallied according to the final verdicts pronounced on them). The absence of data is confirmed by a report stating that the commission had pronounced 79 death sentences as of 16 niv. IX. AG B¹³ 132, Férino to MW.

38. Jean Vergier, a draft-aged wagoneer known as "Sapeur," epitomized the confusion of criminal categories at the heart of southern brigandage. He was a hired assassin who associated with numerous outlaws, both in prison and out, and served as a courier in the royalist conspiracy linking Lyon and Montpellier. Though willing to sell out a key royalist leader as well as any number of ordinary brigands in exchange for a reprieve, he was sentenced to death and shot in his native Avignon. AG B¹³ 122, Milhaud to Gouvion, 16 ger. VIII; J2 112, 6 mess. VIII.

39. AG B¹³ 133, Férino to MW, 30 pluv. IX; B¹³ 132, Férino to MW, 11 niv. IX; F⁷ 7724, d. 39; AF IV 1154, d. police militaire.

40. AG B¹³ 128, internal report to MW, 8 vend. IX; F⁷ 7724, d. 39, MP report to First Consul, 19 ther. VIII.

41. AG B¹³ 63, bureau report to MW, 5 mess. V, in response to outrage from the MJ.

42. Total for verdicts is from AG B¹³ 134, 5 ger. IX; on the brutality of Garnier's columns, see AG Xᵏ 46, d. 16, Monet, sous-inspecteur de la gendarmerie, to Malus, inspecteur général de la gendarmerie, 21 mess. VIII, B¹³ 134, MW to Consuls, 21 vend. IX, and Iafélice, *Barbets*, 172–90. Although Iafélice asserts that the commission rendered its last verdicts on 5 brum. IX, a verdict dated 25 vent. IX is mentioned in Jean-Michel Bacquer, "Le 'brigandage' dans les Alpes-Maritimes en l'an IX et en l'an X (d'après les procédures du tribunal criminel spécial)," *103ᵉ Congrès national des Sociétés savantes: Histoire Moderne*, 2 vols. (1980), 2:313–30.

43. Isser Woloch, *Napoleon and His Collaborators: The Making of a Dictatorship* (New York, 2001), 72–73.

44. In the Haute-Garonne, for example, twenty-six individuals with Jacobin credentials (including a former general, former JP, and constitutional priest) were prosecuted as part of the conspiracy. The total lack of credible evidence led a grand jury to refuse to indict but only after the accused had spent almost two years in prison. BB¹⁸ 335, D4 6696.

45. Michael J. Sydenham, "The Crime of 3 Nivôse," in *French Government and Society, 1500–1800*, John Bosher, ed. (London, 1972); Richard C. Cobb, "Note sur la répression contre le personnel sans-culotte de 1795 à 1801," in his *Terreur et Subsistances, 1793–1795* (1964), 202.

46. *Opinion de Berlier sur le project de responsabilité à appliquer aux cas de troubles civils.* Conseil des Cinq-Cents, séance du 21 messidor an 7.

47. Fouché personally pressed Bonaparte for additional military commissions. He cited prefects' repeated demands for them and forwarded a list of over two hundred brigands currently in prison awaiting trial. AF IV 1314–15, MP to First Consul, 18 frim. IX (in Fouché's hand).

48. AG B¹³ 131, Consuls dirs., 29 frim., 1 niv. IX; B⁵ 70, Consuls dirs., 21 niv., 13 flor. IX, MW to MJ, 15 flor. IX. Hédouville, commander of the 13th Mil. Dis. (Brittany) was reluctant to implement this measure and created only one commission until Bernadotte, commander of the Army of the West, returned from Paris with renewed instructions to create a "flying column" and military commission for each of the Morbihan, Côtes-du-Nord, and Finistère. Chassin, *Pacifications*, 3:682, 700.

49. AG B¹³ 132, First Consul Bonaparte to Gen. Cervoni, 8th Mil. Dis., no date.

50. The activities of these flying columns and military commissions are poorly known, largely because the sources are fragmentary. Existing work is afflicted with confusion, notably Stephen Clay, "Le brigandage en Provence du Directoire au Consulat (1795–1802)," in *Du Directoire au Consulat,* ed. Jean-Pierre Jessenne, vol. 3, *Brumaire dans l'histoire du lien politique et de l'état-nation,* 67–89 (Rouen, 2001). Clay errs by (1) cutting the term of the commission at Avignon to four months (a reduction of six months); (2) amalgamating five different military commissions in the 8th Mil. Dis. into one; and (3) claiming that his statistical data are based on the "totality of verdicts for it [*sic*]."

51. AG B¹³ 132, Boyer to MW, 13 pluv. IX; J2 126; Maltby, "Brigandage dans la Drôme," 133.

52. AG B¹³ 134–38 passim; ADG 2R 792, register of verdicts; 2R 1171 to 1176, "procédures"; J2 132, individual verdicts. On its itinerant operations, see chapter 11 of this volume and Howard G. Brown, "Bonaparte's 'Booted Justice' in Bas-Languedoc," *Proceedings of the Western Society of French History* 25 (1998): 120–30.

53. Maurice Agulhon, *Vie sociale en provence intérieure au lendemain de la Révolution,* 2 vols. (1970), 1:384–91, located ninety-three decisions. Eleven of these are postmortem verdicts that served to specify the crimes, determine the fate of the culprit's property, and distribute reward money. See examples in AG J2 126.

54. This is based on the summary list up to 30 flor. in BB²³ 1^{A-B} plus the individual judgment (pertaining to three men) at Avignon on 21 mess. IX in AG J2 126.

55. Whereas the decree of 4 vent. IX (23 Feb. 1801) ordered extraordinary military commissions to cease operations as soon as special tribunals had begun to function, it made an exception for the two commissions of the Var and Bouches-du-Rhône, which were to continue judging those brigands captured while armed. AG B¹³ 133.

56. AG B¹³ 131, Pouget to column commanders, 5 niv., and dir., 6 niv. IX.

57. Military commissions at Avignon and Nice had tried about another 230 individuals in 1800.

58. For a detailed example, see Brown, "An Unmasked Man." On the use of simple written evidence, see the case of Pierre Tassy, condemned to death at Aix. AG J2 126, 27 pluv. IX.

59. F⁷ 7805, d.121, Gentile to Gouvion, 7 ger. IX.

60. AG J2 126, verdicts of the extraordinary military commission of Bouches-du-Rhône, 22 niv., 4 vent. IX.

61. ADG 2R 792, 1171, 1172, 1176; AG J2 132.

62. F⁷ 7724, d. 39.

63. AG J2 132, 9 flor. IX; ADG 2R 1176; AG B¹³ 121, Petit-Guillaume to MW, 5 ger. VIII.

64. AG B¹³ 128, Ag. Nouveau to Gendarmerie Inspector Radet, 26 fruc. VIII.

65. This explains the inclusion of women among the defendants, even though they were rarely condemned to death; two had their lives spared due to pregnancy. Rocquain, *L'état de la France,* 69; AG J2 126, 4 vent. IX.

66. AG B¹³ 136, "bulletin historique" of 9th Mil. Dis., 1–15 flor. IX; AG J2 132; Rocquain, *L'état de la France,* 69; Maltby, "Brigandage dans la Drôme," 133.

67. Ernest Daudet, *La Police et les chouans sous le Consulat et l'Empire, 1800–1815* (1895), 23.

68. AG B⁵ 69, esp. Gen. Tilly to MW, 16 ger. IX, "Ordre générale de l'armée de l'Ouest,"15 flor. IX, and Gen. Bernadotte to MW, 6 prai. IX. There is evidence of ad hoc military commissions being created throughout the west on the basis of the Consuls' directive of 21

niv. IX: e.g., J2 209, 29 vent. IX (sixteen men and women tried at Rouen for a stagecoach holdup), B⁵ 69, "bulletin historique" of 22nd Mil. Dis., 20 vent., 30 vent. IX (verdicts at Le Mans).

69. AG B⁵ 69, "bulletin historique," Army of the West, 21–30 prai. IX; Chassin, *Pacifications*, 3:701.

70. AG J2 166, Gouvion to MW, 13 vent. IX; D.M.G. Sutherland, *France 1789–1815: Revolution and Counterrevolution* (1985), 351.

71. AG B¹³ 140, War Ministry report to the Consuls, 27 fruc. IX.

72. AG B¹³ 138, prefect of Ardèche to MW, 12 mess. IX; Maurel, *Brigandage,* 179; AG B¹³ 136, MP to Gen. Cervoni, 15 flor. IX.

## 12. SECURITY STATE AND DICTATORSHIP

1. See Steven Englund, *Napoleon: A Political Life* (New York, 2004), 198–200.

2. Laurence Chatel de Brancion, ed., *Cambacérès: Mémoires inédits,* vol. 1. *La Révolution et le Consulat* (1999), 548; Louis Madelin, *Histoire du Consulat et de l'Empire,* 16 vols. (1939), 4:69–71.

3. For the debate, see Adhémar Esmein, *Histoire de la procédure criminelle en France* (1882), 470–80, and Irene Collins, *Napoleon and His Parliaments 1800–1815* (1979), 42–44.

4. See Dominique Bouguet, "Une juridiction d'exception: Le tribunal spécial d'Indre-et-Loire (an IX—1811)," *Histoire de la Justice* 7 (1994): 89–116.

5. Marcel Marion, *Le brigandage pendant la Révolution* (1934), 223.

6. For sources and details, see Howard G. Brown, "The Napoleonic Security State: Special Tribunals" in *Napoleon and the Empire,* ed. Phillip Dwyer and Alan Forrest (New York, 2006).

7. See especially Bacquer, "'Brigandage' dans les Alpes-Maritimes," 329–30, and Agulhon, *Vie sociale,* 394.

8. For the basis of these calculations, see Brown, "Security State."

9. *Rapport sur le résultat des travaux des Cours de Justice criminelle pendant les années 1803, 1804, 1805, et 1806* (29 février 1808) BL 5403.a 2 (3).

10. AG B¹³ 140, Consuls' directive, 28 fructidor, and MP to Cervoni, 29 fructidor IX, created one of each for the Var, Bouches-du-Rhône, and Basses-Alpes; Bernadotte operated a "flying column" and military commission in each of the Morbihan, Côtes-du-Nord, and Finistère. Chassin, *Pacifications,* 3:700.

11. For example, F⁷ 4327 and 8075.

12. Louis Devès, *Les brigands: Épisodes inédits de la Réaction thermidorienne (1794 à 1804) dans le canton de Valréas et dans la ville de Bollène* (Avignon, 1885), 9–15, 24–32; AG B¹³ 120, Lecourt-Villière to MW, 15 vent. VIII.

13. AG B¹³ 126, Férino to MW, 13 mess. VIII. The prefect of Basses-Alpes responded to Férino on 22 mess. that his threat had served "to electrify the apathetic and conquer the self-interested."

14. For example, the bundle BB¹⁸ 764, D3 9738.

15. ADHS 368 L 11, 3 flor. VI; *L'Ami des lois,* 23 prai. VI. ADHS 368 L 405 contains the judicial file; quotations are from JP to jury director at Vesoul, 4 frim. and 21 vent. V. A fine map illustrates how the Hérard's farm served to ambush travelers in the *bois de Charmes.*

16. ADHS 368 L 11, 16, 17 and 25 prai. VI; 368 L 424.

17. BB¹⁸ 712, commissioner of Haute-Saône to MI, 23 mess. VII (for quotation), and Vi-

vein, *chef du 39ᵉ escadron de gendarmerie* to MJ, 26 mess. VII; *Redacteur*, ther. VII; ADD L 710⁵; AG J2 94, 2ᵉ c.d.g. (Besançon), 16 pluv. VIII. The rescuers came from Blondefontaine, Cemboing, Raincourt, and Buffignécourt.

18. Peter M. Jones, *The Peasantry in the French Revolution* (Cambridge, UK, 1988), 94–97.

19. This was true except along the highways between Lyon and Strasbourg and between Paris and Belfort, both of which served as main arteries for troop movements.

20. Eric Hobsbawm, *Bandits* (New York, 2000), 16.

21. ADG 2R 703 and 704; AG J2 128, 1ᵉʳ c.d.g. (Montpellier), 19 niv. VIII.

22. AG B¹³ 88, Gen. Petit-Guillaume to MW, 17 brum. VII.

23. Peter M. Jones, *Politics and Rural Society: The Southern Massif Central c. 1750–1880* (Cambridge, UK, 1985), 173, 176–77.

24. Instead, the municipality of Largentière issued a certificate attesting the good conduct of Claude Rouvière, his son Jean-Louis and his brother Jacques, "detained for several months in the jail at Largentière for a case in which they unfortunately found themselves implicated." ADG 703, 15 mess. VII.

25. These were the famous marquis de Surville and Dominque Allier, imprisoned at Le Puy since 15 fruc. VI (1 Sept. 1798). Ernest Daudet, *La conjuration de Pichegru et les complots royalistes du Midi et de l'Est, 1795–1797* (1901), 300–304.

26. ADG 703 contains the entire case; AG J2 127, c.d.g., 9th Mil. Dis., 15 mess. VII, is the final verdict, which included ten years in irons for the two draft dodgers, and five years in irons for a gun-toting neighbor arrested that night at the local inn.

27. The phrase is from Malcolm Greenshields, *An Economy of Violence in Early Modern France: Crime and Justice in the Haute Auvergne, 1587–1664* (State College, Penn., 1994).

28. F⁷ 7714, court commissioner at Uzès to MJ, 14 pluv. VIII.

29. Note the description of events at St-André-de-Cruzière (Ardèche): "Citizen Délibre, mayor of the commune, . . . convoked the leading inhabitants in order to get them to see the dangers that surrounded them; that it was time to rise above this panic terror that until then had prevented the inhabitants from showing their zeal to repress brigandage; that honor, property, and the life of every citizen was involved. At this invitation, a general cry went up and all the inhabitants demonstrated their desire to exterminate the brigands. . . . The result was the arrest of seven brigands, the scourge of this area." AG B¹³ 131, Gen. Ruby to Gen. Férino, 9 niv. IX.

30. For example, an attack on a purchaser of "national property" near Neuvillalais (Sarthe) led to a sounding of the tocsin, which quickly drew a large number of men from nearby communes. Several mayors led them in capturing three of the armed assailants, all of whom went before a military court. AG B⁵ 68, Gen. Tilly to MW, 1 niv. IX, and Gen. Liébert to MW, 4 niv. IX.

31. AG B¹³ 131, 8 niv. IX. See similar remarks from the prefect of Gard and subprefect of Lodève. B¹³ 132, 11 niv. IX; B¹³ 133, 22 pluv. IX.

32. Quoted in Agulhon, *Vie sociale*, 390.

33. As Fouché put it in late 1800, "Les magistrats chargés d'une autorité qui se déploie et se manifeste dans tout son éclat, attirent souvent la reconnaissance publique par leur sévérité même." AF IV 1043, "Compte rendu . . ."

34. AG J2 127, 1ᵉʳ c.d.g., 13th Mil. Dis., 9 ther. VII.

35. Howard G. Brown, "From Organic Society to Security State: The War on Brigandage in France, 1797–1802," *Journal of Modern History* 69 (1997): 661–95.

36. These administrative purges have been studied in admirable detail in Gainot, *1799, Un nouveau Jacobinisme?* 39–40, 392–400. About one-quarter of departments were repeatedly purged and half received partial regeneration; only a quarter remained largely unscathed.

37. Pierre Miquel, *Les Gendarmes* (1990), 79–81.

38. Frédéric Chauvaud, *Les Passions villageoises au XIX^e siècle: Les émotions rurales dans les pays de Beauce, du Hurepoix et du Mantois* (1995), 192–202.

39. AG B^13 108, Gen. Servan to MW, 25 fruc. VII, writes that the conscription law was executed throughout the 9th Mil. Dis. wherever the majority of inhabitants was Protestant.

40. ADS L 197; Chassin, *Pacifications,* 3:389–92.

41. BB^18 215, court commissioner of Cantal to MJ, 1 mess. X.

42. AG B^13 140, Gen. Ruby to Gen. Férino, 1 jr. co. VIII (misfiled).

43. Pierre-Louis du Couëdic de Villeneuve, *La Nouvelle géographie de la France, d'après la division actuelle de son territoire en 102 départements,* 2 vols. (1802), 1:48.

44. Esmein, *Procédure criminelle,* 451–61; Jacques Godechot, *Les Institutions de la France sous la Révolution et l'Empire,* 3rd ed. (1985), 616–30; Jean Bourdon, *La réforme judiciaire de l'an VIII* (Rodez, 1941), 1:311–95.

45. Élisabeth Claverie, "De la difficulté de faire un citoyen: Les 'acquittements scandaleux' du jury dans la France provinciale du début du XIX^e siècle," *Études rurales,* 95 (1984): 143–66.

46. Michael Sibalis is the leading proponent of this view and has developed much evidence to support it. See his "Napoleonic Police State," in *Napoleon and Europe,* ed. Philip Dwyer, 79–94 (2001); "Arbitrary Detention, Human Rights, and the Napoleonic Senate" in *Taking Liberties: Problems of a New Order from the French Revolution to Napoleon,* ed. Howard G. Brown and Judith A. Miller, 166–84 (Manchester, 2002); "Prisoners by *mesure de Haute Police* under Napoleon I: Reviving the *lettres de cachet,*" and "Internal Exiles in Napoleonic France, 1800–1815," in *Proceedings of the Annual Meeting of the Western Society for French History* 18 (1991): 205–13, and 20 (1993): 189–98; "La Côte-d'Or, Terre d'exile," *Annales de bourgogne* 64 (1992): 39–51. Cf. J.-C. Vimont, *La Prison politique en France* (1993).

47. My formulation of the concept "security state" derives from Michel Foucault's lectures on "governmentality," a neologism he used to capture the continuities between the *Polizeistaat,* or well-ordered police state, of enlightened absolutism and the liberal democratic polities of western Europe in the nineteenth century. In part, "governmentality . . . is a complex form of power, which has as its target population, as its principal form of knowledge political economy, and as its essential technical means apparatuses of security." Graham Burchell, Colin Gordon, and Peter Miller, eds., *The Foucault Effect: Studies in Governmentality* (Chicago, 1991), 102. See also the articles by Laura Englestein, Rudy Koshar, and Jan Goldstein in the forum "Foucault, Russia, and the Liberal State," *American Historical Review* (1993): 338–81.

48. See Marie-Noëlle Bourguet, *Déchiffrer la France: La statistique départementale à l'époque napoléonienne* (1988), 64–82, and Jean-Claude Perrot, *L'âge d'or de la statistique régionale française (an IV—1804)* (1977), 28–41.

49. In addition to Godechot, *Institutions,* 627–38, see Bernard Schnapper, "Compression et répression sous le Consulat et l'Empire," *Revue historique du droit français et étranger* 69 (1991): 17–40.

50. The amnesty confirmed all previous removals from the list, including provisional ones made by local authorities except if made during the two periods of aggressive political reaction (1 ger. III to 1 brum. IV and 1 prai. V to 1 vend. VI). It also automatically amnestied all those who had come to be excluded from the writ of the Fructidorian military commissions, that is, most women, artisans, laborers, etc., and in this sense was a continuation of a Directorial initiative.

51. Guyot, *Vendéens et chouans,* 75.

52. Louis Madelin, *Fouché, 1759–1820,* 2 vols., 2nd ed. (1903), 1:327–49; Jean Vidalenc, *Les émigrés français, 1789–1825* (1963), 52–55; Louis Madelin, *Histoire du Consulat et de l'Empire,* 16 vols. (1939), 4:23–25.

53. For example, after the authorities broke up the services of a refractory priest, a placard was nailed to the church door at Lucé (Sarthe): "To arms, royalists. The republic is done for *(foutue).* The last hour of republicans has tolled. To arms, the faith *(la religion)* commands you." AG B⁵ 68, Gen. Liébert to MW, 14 niv. IX. See also F⁷ 7979, Pierre de la Gorce, *Histoire religieuse de la Révolution française,* 5 vols. (1923), 5:139–53; Nigel Aston, *Religion and Revolution in France, 1780–1804* (Washington, D.C., 2000), 318–20.

54. The correspondence in AG B⁵ 68–70 shows the army coping with the remnants of *chouannerie* even before troops returned from the front and the gendarmerie expanded.

55. After six months, the troops had killed or arrested only six band members; another six had been captured by mobile columns or local inhabitants, and nine gave themselves up. A dozen remained at large, however, including the leaders. AF IV 1314–5, MP to Emperor, August 1813.

56. Town officials ended the violence on 22 ger. but did not arrest or prosecute anyone. After the Consulate insisted that the Court of Cassation reject sending the case before the Special Tribunal of the Hérault, the commission proceded and rendered its verdict on 30 flor. X. ADH 7 U¹ 1; AF IV 1154, MW to First Consul, 9 prai. X.

57. Louis Bergès, *Résister à la conscription 1798–1814: Le cas des départements aquitains* (2002), 58–59; Jean Morvan, *Le soldat impérial (1800–1814),* 2 vols. (1904), 1:130.

58. There were only about 250 to 300 priests in this camp, although at least half of them were concentrated in western departments. Serge Bonin and Clause Langlois, eds., *Atlas de la Révolution française,* vol. 9: *Religion,* ed. Claude Langlois, Timothy Tacket, and Michel Vovelle (1996), 70.

59. Malcolm Crook, "Confidence from Below? Collaboration and Resistance in the Napoleonic Plebiscites," in *Collaboration and Resistance in Napoleonic Europe: State-Formation in an Age of Upheaval, c. 1800–1815,* ed. Michael Rowe, 19–36 (Basingstoke, 2003); Woloch, *Napoleon and His Collaborators,* 91–96.

60. Godechot, *Institutions,* 570–77, is the best introduction to the changes of year X. See also Jean-Yves Coppolani, *Les élections en France à l'époque napoléonienne* (1980), 56–128; Geoffrey Ellis, "Rhine and Loire: Napoleonic Elites and Social Order," in *Beyond the Terror,* ed. Lewis and Lucas, 232–67.

61. Compare Vandal, *L'avènement de Bonaparte;* Georges Lefebvre, *Napoléon* (1965); Louis Bergeron, *L'épisode napoléonien. Aspects intérieurs (1799–1815)* (1972); Michael J. Sydenham, *The First French Republic 1792–1804* (Berkeley, 1973); Jean Tulard, *Napoléon ou le mythe du sauveur* (1977); Martyn Lyons, *Napoleon Bonaparte and the Legacy of the French Revolution* (New York, 1994); and Lentz, *Grand Consulat,* none of which goes much beyond the pacification of *chouannerie.* In contrast, D. M. G. Sutherland, *France, 1789–1815,* and *The French Revolution and Empire: The Quest for Civic Order* (Oxford, 2003), are the

only survey histories to pay serious attention to repressing resistance in the early Consulate.

62. This is not to go as far as either Madame de Staël or Georges Lefebvre, who both believed that the liberal democracy installed in 1795 had been premature. She believed that republicans needed to assure their long-term grip on power; he believed that failure to choose a Jacobin-style dictatorship inevitably led to one based on the army. Madame de Staël, *Des circonstances actuelles qui peuvent terminer la Révolution et des principes qui doivent fonder la République en France (1798)*, ed., Lucia Omacini (1979), 129–30; Lefebvre, *France sous le Directoire*, 727.

63. Adolphe Thiers, *Histoire du Consulat et de l'Empire*, 20 vols. (1845–62), 2:341–42.

64. Cited in Vandal, *L'avènement de Bonaparte*, 2:499.

65. For example, Jacob Talmon, *The Origins of Totalitarian Democracy* (New York, 1960); François Furet, *Interpreting the French Revolution*, trans. Elborg Forster (Cambridge, UK, 1981); Ferenc Fehér, *The Frozen Republic: An Essay on Jacobinism* (Cambridge, UK, 1987); Patrice Gueniffey, *La politique de la Terreur: Essaie sur la violence révolutionnaire* (1999).

66. For example, Lynn Hunt, *Politics, Culture, and Class in the French Revolution* (Berkeley, 1986); Isser Woloch, *Jacobin Legacy: The Democratic Movement under the Directory* (Princeton, 1970); James Livesey, *Making Democracy in the French Revolution* (Cambridge, Mass., 2001); Gainot, *1799, Un nouveau Jacobinisme?*

67. Carl Schmitt, *La Dictature*, trans. Mira Köller and Dominique Séglard (2000). See also William E. Scheuerman, *Carl Schmitt: The End of Law* (New York, 1999).

68. AG MR 1998.

69. See Howard G. Brown, "Domestic State Violence: Repression from the Croquants to the Commune," *Historical Journal* 42 (1999): 597–622.

70. Giorgio Agamben, *State of Exception*, trans. Kevin Attell (Chicago, 2005). In later writings, Schmitt's political prejudices led him to fold "commissarial" and "sovereign" forms of dictatorship into a modern Caesarism. John P. McCormick, "From Constitutional Technique to Caesarist Ploy: Carl Schmitt on Dictatorship, Liberalism, and Emergency Powers," *Dictatorship in History and Theory. Bonapartism, Caesarism, and Totalitarianism*, ed. Peter Baehr and Melvin Richter, 197–219 (Cambridge, UK, 2004).

# Bibliography of Primary Sources

ARCHIVES NATIONALES

*AF III  Directoire Exécutif*

| | |
|---|---|
| 44 | Ministry of Justice reports to Directory |
| 46–47 | Ministry of Police reports to Directory |
| 147–151$^B$ | Ministry of War reports to Directory |
| 160$^A$–160$^B$ | reorganization of gendarmerie |
| 188$^C$ | (Cambray) |
| 268–280 | "affaires particulières" (alphabetical by person or place) |

*AF IV  Consulat et Empire*

| | |
|---|---|
| 1042–1043 | Ministry of Police reports |
| 1092 | Ministry of War reports |
| 1154 | officiers de la gendarmerie |
| 1300$^B$ | bureau militaire, officer appointments |
| 1314–15 | Ministry of Police reports |

*Archives Privées*

| | |
|---|---|
| 138 AP 22 | Papiers Daru |

*C  Assemblées Nationales*

390, 403, 426, 470, 483, 495, 500, 546, 685

*BB³  Ministère de la Justice (criminal affairs)*

| | |
|---|---|
| 7 | jugements des commissions militaires extraordinaires, 8$^e$ div. mil., an IX |

*BB⁵  Ministère de la Justice (court personnel)*

| | |
|---|---|
| 75 | tribunaux criminels, ans VIII–XIII |
| 349 | tribunaux spéciaux, 7$^e$, 8$^e$, 9$^e$ div. mil., ans IX–X |

*BB¹⁸  Ministère de la Justice (criminal affairs by department)*

| | |
|---|---|
| 109 | Basses-Alpes |
| 114 | Alpes-Maritimes |
| 137 | Ariège |
| 164–165 | Aveyron |
| 215–216 | Cantal |
| 267–271 | Doubs |
| 297–299 | Eure |
| 328–335 | Haute-Garonne |
| 364–366 | Hérault |
| 471–473 | Lozère |

| 640–641 | Puy-de-Dôme |
|---|---|
| 710–713 | Haute-Saône |
| 733–735 | Sarthe |
| 760, 764, 775 | Seine |
| 863–865 | Tarn |
| 880 | Var |

$BB^{21}$–$BB^{23}$ *Ministère de la Justice (pardons)*

| $BB^{21}$ 157 | affaire Rouch |
|---|---|
| $BB^{23}$ 1$^{A\text{-}B}$ | commissions militaires extraordinaires, 8$^e$ div. mil. |

$F^{1c}$ III *Ministère de l'Intérieur*

| Haute-Garonne 8 | comptes rendus administratifs |
|---|---|
| Hérault 9 | comptes rendus administratifs |
| Haute-Saône 6 | comptes rendus administratifs |

$F^7$ *Ministère de la Police générale*

| 3003 | avis du bureau des lois |
|---|---|
| 3065 | esprit public, circular of 19 nivôse IV |
| 3243 | dépenses pour la police secrète, Ardêche |
| 3264$^3$ | dépenses pour la police secrète, Sarthe |
| 3251 | dépense pour la police secrète, Hérault |
| 3678$^3$ | police générale, Hérault, ans V–VII |
| 3687$^2$ | police générale, Haute-Saône, 1792–an VIII |
| 3693$^2$ | commission militaire extraordinaire du Var, an IX |
| 3693 | bulletins de la police générale, ans VII–IX |
| 3820 | bulletins décadaires sur la situation des départements, ans VII–VIII |
| 3902 | rapports de la gendarmerie par département, ans V–X |
| 4374 | commissions militaires du 19 fruc. |
| 4282 | "bande noire," an V |
| 4321–4322 | avis du bureau des loix |
| 6229–6230 | chouannerie, ans VIII–X |
| 6238 | situation du Midi, an VIII |
| 6612 | affaires politiques, Seine-et-Oise—Yonne |
| 7296 | troubles du Tarn, ans V–VII |
| 7367$^b$ | procédure contre les ex-administrateurs du Tarn, an VI |
| 7398 | commissions militaires du 19 fruc. V |
| 7447 | situation politique de Gignac, ans VI–VII |
| 7458 | commissions militaires du 19 fruc.; état de siège (Ardêche) |
| 7499 | Sans-Peur, Escalquens, etc. |
| 7521 | Hérault |
| 7540–7548 | miscellaneous, an VII |
| 7585 | Hérault |
| 7602 | troubles de la Haute-Garonne, ans VII–VIII |

| 7724 | Férino, commission militaire, Avignon, ans VIII–IX |
| 7729 | Rouch, Ponsy, Soubès |
| 7741 | Haute-Garonne |
| 7767 | affaire Laussel, ans VII–VIII |
| 7812 | affaire Pioch, an VIII |
| 7949, 7979 | émigrés, ans IX–X |

*F⁹ Ministère de l'Intérieur*

| 39ᴬ | mission du général Férino, ans VIII–IX |
| 45 | affaires du Midi, ans VI–VII |

SERVICE HISTORIQUE DE L'ARMÉE DE TERRE

*B⁵ Correspondance des armées de l'ouest*

| 35–40ᵇⁱˢ | Armée des Côtes de l'Océan, an IV |
| 41–48 | Armée d'Angleterre, ans VI–VIII |
| 68–70 | Armée de l'Ouest, ans VIII–IX |

*B¹³ Correspondance militaire générale*

| 37–40 | 1 Aug.–31 Dec. 1795 | 14 ther. III–10 niv. IV |
| 41–53 | 1796 | 11 niv. IV–11 niv. V |
| 54–75 | 1797 | 12 niv. V–11 niv. VI |
| 76–90 | 1798 | 12 niv. VI–11 niv. VII |
| 91–115 | 1799 | 12 niv. VII–10 niv. VIII |
| 116–131 | 1800 | 11 niv. VIII–10 niv. IX |
| 132–141 | 1801 | 11 niv. IX–10 niv. X |
| 166 | colonnes mobiles dans l'Ouest, ans VII–IX |

*C¹⁸ Justice militaire*

| 1–3 | bande de chauffeurs, VI–VIII (procédure) |
| 4–5 | commission militaire de la 17ᵉ div. mil., ans VI–VII (procédures) |
| 66–68 | conseil de guerre, 5ᵉ div. mil., VII–1806 (procédures) |
| 78–86 | désertion, lois, prisons, etc. |

*J2 Justice militaire*

CONSEILS MILITAIRES

| 3–4 | divers, an IV |
| 192 | Vire, an IV |
| 231 | Paris, an IV |
| 287 | Le Mans, an IV |

CONSEILS DE GUERRE

| 84–87, 94 | 6ᵉ div. mil. |

114–116     8ᵉ div. mil.
127–130     9ᵉ div. mil.
133, 137, 139   10ᵉ div. mil.
152–165     13ᵉ div. mil.
196     14ᵉ div. mil.
231, 239–243    17ᵉ div. mil.
283     20ᵉ div. mil.
287–289     22ᵉ div. mil.

*COMMISSIONS MILITAIRES CRÉES PAR LA LOI DU 19 FRUCTIDOR V*

16     Mézières
41     Metz
51     Nancy
81     Strasbourg
85     Besançon
112     Grenoble, Valence
126     Marseille, Toulon, Nice, Avignon, Tarascon, Aix
132     Montpellier, Nîmes
139     Toulouse, Perpignan
144     Bayonne
145     Nantes, La Rochelle
160     Saint-Brieuc, Rennes, Brest, Vannes
200     Caen
209     Dieppe, Rouen, Amiens, Fécamps, Le Havre
212     Douai
263     Dijon, Marseille (misfiled)
270     Lyon, Clermont, Le Puy, Montbrison
283     Périgueux
285     Poitiers
288     Le Mans
289     Tours, Angers
291     Ajaccio, Bastia
308     Liège
314     Koblentz
339     Mainz
352     Lucerne
354     Manheim, Mainz

*COMMISSIONS MILITAIRES EXTRAORDINAIRES*

112     7ᵉ div. mil. Avignon, ans VIII–IX
126     8ᵉ div. mil. Marseille, Nice, Toulon, Antibes, Aix, Tarascon, Avignon, Brignoles, Montélimar, St. Maximim, an IX
132     9ᵉ div. mil. Montpellier, Nîmes, Lodève, Alais, Rodez, Millau, Privas, Le Vigan, Gignac, an IX

160             13ᵉ div. mil. Vannes, Morlaix, Lorient, Brest, Guingamp, an IX
                Vannes, Pontivy, Moncontour, St. Brieuc, an X
177             13ᵉ div. mil. Rennes, an X
200             14ᵉ div. mil. Alençon, an IX

Xᴬ  *Etat-major*
45ᵇⁱˢ           officiers de la gendarmerie

Xᶠ  *Gendarmerie Nationale*
9               laws and circulars
71, 72, 76ᵇⁱˢ, 77  departmental reorganisations, ans V–VII

MR  *Mémoires et reconnaissances*
1951            justice militaire, 19ᵉ siècle
1998            état de siège
2000            état de siège


ARCHIVES DÉPARTEMENTALES DES BOUCHES-DU-RHÔNE

2 R 464*–469* registres des jugements du 1ᵉʳ conseil de guerre, 8ᵉ div. mil., 10
                vent. V–18 frim. IX
2 R 470*        registre des procédures du 2ᵉ conseil de guerre, 8ᵉ div. mil., 24
                fruc. VII–2 flor. VIII


ARCHIVES DÉPARTEMENTALES DU DOUBS

L 42            comptes rendus au Directoire
L 204           police générale, ans VI–VIII
L 215           désordres, an VI
L 243           tableaux généraux de la situation du département, ans IV–VII
L 593           gardes nationales, colonnes mobiles, ans IV–VII
L 710²–710⁴     registres des interrogatoires du conseil de guerre permanent de
                la 6ᵉ div. mil., 11 frim. V–14 ger. VII
L 710⁵          registre de la correspondance du 2ᵉ conseil de guerre, 6ᵉ div. mil.,
                26 vent. VI–26 niv. IX


ARCHIVES DÉPARTEMENTALES DE LA HAUTE-GARONNE

1L 354          sureté publique, généralités, an IV
1L 359          agitation politique, an IV
1L 363          menées jacobines, ans IV–V
1L 364          menées royalistes, ans IV–V
1L 444–509      insurrection royaliste de l'an VII
1L 912          correspondance militaire

7L 201 U 1–3    registres du plumitif des audiences du tribunal criminel, 1 fév. 1792–19 avril 1811

7L 201 U 4–6    registres du procès-verbal des séances du tribunal criminel, 1 fév. 1792–19 avril 1811

7L 201 U 7      registre des ordonnances du tribunal criminel, 1 fév. 1792–an VII

7L 202 U 156    affaire Gotty-Roquebrune

7L 202 U 164    affaire Cahuzac

7L 202 U 167    affaire Duchein

10L 270 U 77    registre des jugements du tribunal criminel, 2 jan. 1792–18 mai 1811

93L 1–17        procédures du 1ᵉʳ conseil de guerre de la 10e division militaire, an VII

94L 1–10        procédures du 2ᵉ conseil de guerre de la 10e division militaire, an VII


ARCHIVES DÉPARTEMENTALES DE LA GIRONDE

2R 695–706      registres des procédures et des jugements du 1ᵉʳ conseil de guerre, 9ᵉ div. mil., 23 pluv. V–11 vend. IX

2R 750–751      registres des procédures du 2ᵉ conseil de guerre, 9ᵉ div. mil., 29 niv VI–24 frim. VIII

2R 755          registre des jugements du 2ᵉ conseil de guerre, 9ᵉ div. mil., 10 niv. VI–18 brum. VIII

2R 1144         correspondance sur les poursuites contre les émigrés, ans III–VII

2R 1149         procédures de la commission militaire, an VI

2R 1172–1176    procédures pour brigandage jugées par la commission militaire extraordinaire, 9ᵉ div. mil., an IX


ARCHIVES DÉPARTEMENTALES DE L'HÉRAULT

L 773           district of Lodève, elections an VI

L 833           MP circulars

L 880           jugements du tribunal civil pour infraction à la loi du 10 vend. IV

L 968–970       police générale, ans IV–VII

L 2573          affaire Laussel, an VII

L 5706*         registre du comité de surveillance, Gignac, 18 vend.–7 flor. II

L 5707          sociétés populaires de Gignac, Aniane, etc., an II

L 5720–5721     individual dossiers from comité de surveillance, Lodève, year II

L 6708*–6709*   registres de transcriptions des délibérations et arrêtés du tribunal et des jugements du tribunal de cassation

L 6713*   registre de jugements préparatoires du tribunal criminel, 2 brum.–2 ther. IV

L 6725*–6738*   registres des jugements définitifs du tribunal criminel, 15 prai. III–22 frim. X

L 6756*–6758*   registres des ordonnances d'acquittements du tribunal criminel, 21 flor. IV–9 ger. VII

L 6769*   registre des procès-verbaux du président du tribunal criminel, an IV

L 6708, 6802, 6807, 7222, 7240, 7260, 7293, 7310, 7311, 7339, 7422, 7431, 7549, 7553, 8128, 8129, 8130   procédures du tribunal criminel, ans IV–VIII

L 8608   police générale, ans IV–VIII

L 8777   canton de Gignac, police générale, ans IV–VIII

L 8890   canton de Lodève, police générale, ans IV–VIII

1 M 829   esprit public, Lodève, an X

7 U² 1*   registre des jugements définitifs du tribunal criminel spécial, 1 prai. IX–8 pluv. XI

7 U² 3*   registre des jugements définitifs du tribunal criminel, 23 frim. X–17 frim. XI

7 U² 8*   registre des jugements de compétence du tribunal criminel spécial, 27 flor. IX–18 brum. XI

7 U² 10–16   procédures du tribunal criminel spécial, ans IX–X

7 U² 111   correspondence avec le commissaire du gouvernement auprès le tribunal criminel, ans VIII–X

7 U² 369   affaire Rouch, 1812

ARCHIVES DÉPARTEMENTALES DE L'ISÈRE

1R 2   conseil de guerre permanent et conseil de révision, 7ᵉ div. mil., 23 brum–8 niv. VI

1R 3   1ᵉʳ conseil de guerre, 7ᵉʳ div. mil., 2 fruc. VI–15 niv. VII

1R 4   1ᵉʳ conseil de guerre, 7ᵉ div. mil., 18 flor. VI–16 vent. VIII

1R 5   conseil de révision, 7ᵉ div. mil., 11 niv. VI–6 ther. XII

1R 6–7   registres du 1ᵉʳ conseil de guerre, 7ᵉ div. mil., 29 brum. VI–26 vent. VIII

1R 8   2ᵉ conseil de guerre, 7ᵉ div. mil., 19 brum.–29 ther. VIII

*La Vedette des Alpes ou Journal Patriotique de Grenoble*

ARCHIVES DÉPARTEMENTALES DU JURA

L 493–495      police générale, ans V–VII

ARCHIVES DÉPARTEMENTALES DE LA HAUTE-SAÔNE

368 L 11–13      registre des jugements du tribunal criminel, 21 vent. III–27 pluv. XI

368 L 318      affaire Duhaut

368 L 377      affaire de la colonne mobile de Colombier

368 L 378      affaire Gravier

368 L 405      affaire Proye

368 L 405      affaire de résistance à la gendarmerie

368 L 424      affaire Barizien

ARCHIVES DÉPARTEMENTALES DE LA SARTHE

L 195–98      correspondance des généraux employés contre les armées royales de l'Ouest, ans II–VIII

L 320–21      registres des conseils militaires séants au Mans

L 332      tableaux de l'emplacement des troupes, 1793–an VIII

L 336      procès des conseils militaires, ans III–IV

L 1743–44      jugements des conseils militaires séants à La Flèche, au Mans, au Château-du-Loir

L 1914*      table chronologique des jugements du tribunal criminel, 1792–22 flor. VIII

1 U 734      registre des arrêts de compétence du tribunal criminel spécial, 15 flor. IX–6 niv. XI

1 U 736–37      registres des arrêts définitifs du tribunal criminel spécial, 1 prai. IX–19 fruc. XIII

1 U 952      répertoire des condamnations, an VII–1811

BIBLIOTHÈQUE NATIONALE DE FRANCE

*Newspapers*
*L'Ami des lois*
*Chronique de la Sarthe*
*Journal des Hautes-Pyrénées*
*Journal des Hommes Libres*
*Le Moniteur universel*

BIBLIOTHÈQUE MUNICIPALE DE BESANÇON

*La Trompette ou Journal du département du Doubs,* 3 ther. VII–29 mess. VIII

BIBLIOTHÈQUE MUNICIPALE DE CHAUMONT

*Journal de Toulouse,* ans IV–V

BIBLIOTHÈQUE MUNICIPALE DE TOULOUSE

*Journal de Toulouse,* ans VI, VII, VIII

BRITISH LIBRARY

*Achevons la Révolution, par P. J. Audouin* (fructidor III).
*Débats du procès instruit par le conseil de guerre permanent de la XVII<sup>e</sup> division militaire, séant à l'ancienne Maison commune de Paris, contre les prévenus Brottier, Berthelot-la-Villeurnoy, Dunan, Poly et autres* (n.d.).
*Rapport de Tronson-Ducoudray, au sujet de la résolution concernant les fugitifs de Toulon, séance du 23 thermidor an V* (1797).
*Rapport sur le résultat des travaux des Cours de Justice criminelle pendant les années 1803, 1804, 1805, et 1806* (29 février, 1808).

KROCH LIBRARY RARE BOOKS AND MANUSCRIPTS COLLECTION,
CORNELL UNIVERSITY

*Newspapers*
  *Bulletin de l'Europe*
  *Courrier Républicain*
  *Le Moniteur universel, ou la Gazette nationale*
  *Le Nécessaire*
  *Semaines critiques, ou gestes de l'an cinq*
  *La Quotidienne, ou Feuille du Jour*

*Printed Collections*
  *Procès-verbaux des séances du Conseil des Anciens* (1796–1800).
  *Procès-verbaux des séances du Conseil des Cinq-Cents* (1796–1800).
  Debidour, A. *Recueil des actes du Directoire exécutif,* 4 vols. (1910–17).
  Duvergier, J.-B. *Collection complète des lois, décrets, ordonnances, règlements et avis du Conseil d'État,* 51 vols. (1824).
  *Rémpression de l'ancien Moniteur,* 31 vols. (1847–54).

# Index

Italicized page numbers refer to illustrations

## Winners of the Walker Cowen Memorial Prize

Elizabeth Wanning Harries
*The Unfinished Manner: Essays on the Fragment in the Later Eighteenth Century*

Catherine Cusset
*No Tomorrow: The Ethics of Pleasure in the French Enlightenment*

Lisa Jane Graham
*If the King Only Knew: Seditious Speech in the Reign of Louis XV*

Suvir Kaul
*Poems of Nation, Anthems of Empire: English Verse in the Long Eighteenth Century*

Richard Nash
*Wild Enlightenment: The Borders of Human Identity in the Eighteenth Century*

Howard G. Brown
*Ending the French Revolution: Violence, Justice, and Repression from the Terror to Napoleon*